Confederate Reckoning

Confederate Reckoning

Power and Politics in the Civil War South

Stephanie McCurry

Harvard University Press
Cambridge, Massachusetts · London, England

For Declan and Saoirse

Publication of this book has been supported through the generous provisions of the Maurice and Lula Bradley Smith Memorial Fund.

Printed in the United States of America

First Harvard University Press paperback edition, 2012

Library of Congress Cataloging-in-Publication Data

McCurry, Stephanie.
Confederate reckoning : power and politics in the Civil War South / Stephanie McCurry.
p. cm.
Includes bibliographical references and index.
ISBN 978-0-674-04589-7 (cloth : alk. paper)
ISBN 978-0-674-06421-8 (pbk.)
1. Confederate States of America—Politics and government. 2. Confederate States of America—Social conditions. 3. United States—History—Civil War, 1861–1865—Social aspects. 4. Women—Southern States—Social conditions—19th century. 5. United States—History—Civil War, 1861–1865—Women. 6. African Americans—Southern States—Social conditions—19th century. 7. United States—History—Civil War, 1861–1865—African Americans. 8. Slavery—Political aspects—Southern States—History—19th century. 9. Slavery—Social aspects—Southern States—History—19th century. I. Title.
E487.M18 2010
973.7′1 dc22 2009051647

Contents

PROLOGUE

The Confederate Project

SOMETHING STUNNING—EPIC EVEN—transpired in the American South between 1860 and 1865. Then, in a gamble of world historical proportions, a class of slaveholders, flush with power, set out to build an independent proslavery nation but instead brought down the single most powerful slave regime in the Western world and propelled the emergence of a new American republic that redefined the very possibilities of democracy at home and abroad. In the process, too, they provoked precisely the transformation of their own political culture they had hoped to avoid by secession, bringing into the making of history those people—the South's massive unfranchised population of white women and slaves—whose political dispossession they intended to render permanent. The story of the Confederacy is a story of intentions, reversals, undoing, and unlikely characters that form an arc of history rarely matched for dramatic interest and historical justice.

The short-lived Confederate States of America was a signal event in the history of the Western world. What secessionists set out to build was something entirely new in the history of nations: a modern proslavery and antidemocratic state, dedicated to the proposition that all men were not created equal. Confederates were fully caught up in the turbulent currents of history that roiled the hemisphere in the age of emancipation; their proslavery experiment was part of a far larger struggle then being waged over slavery, democracy, and the powers of nation-states. Theirs was a nation founded in defiance of the spirit of the age. Emboldened by the "failure" of emancipation in other parts of the hemisphere, convinced that the American vision of "the people" had been terribly betrayed, Southern slaveholders sought the kind of future for human slavery and republican government no longer possible within the original Union. Theirs was to be a republic perfectly suited to them as a slaveholding people, a republic of white men, defined by slavery and the political exclusion of the mass of the Southern people.[1]

It was a risky undertaking, to say the least. Even in the absence of war—a distinctly looming possibility—the political demands of independence were daunting. The South was a particular, some would have said peculiar, place—a territory of nine hundred thousand square miles and fifteen separate slaveholding states. It would be no mean feat to unite it behind secession and independence. Of its twelve million people, four million were enslaved and disfranchised, and another four million, free white women, were formally citizens but possessed of none of the political rights or privileges of their male compatriots. Secessionists worried openly about the nonslaveholders, about how to secure the support of the region's white male population of voters and citizens who owned no slaves. And well they might have. The campaign to get the South out of the Union would offer a painfully public demonstration of how difficult it was to unify even white men behind the Confederate project. But what of the eight million other Southerners who were never consulted about the wisdom of secession, national independence, or war? Would they remain nullities in the momentous events unfolding in the American South? Still, this was the Confederate project: to build a nation, perhaps in war, while winning the support of the majority of white Southerners who were not slaveholders, nullifying the individual and collective agency of women, and holding much of the population in slavery.

It is hard to exaggerate the drama of what unfolded in the Confederacy when its founders were free to pursue this reactionary dream. One of the most compelling parts of that story was the trial of its national vision by its own people in the war. Confederates' proslavery and antidemocratic experiment was tested at every point, not just by the enemy armies arrayed against them but by the very people the founders had so definitively counted out. For, as it turned out, the vision of "the people" so passionately pursued proved utterly inadequate to the nation-building project Confederate architects undertook. The crisis of legitimacy unleashed in Southern life was not confined to matters of culture and ideology but played out decisively in the arena of politics and policy as the chrysalis state confronted, and attempted to surmount, the structural problems inevitably faced by a slave regime at war.[2]

Within months of secession the fledgling C.S.A. was at war. In attempting to escape history, Confederates had lowered themselves into its most dangerous currents. War immeasurably upped the ante in the new white man's republic and subjected its body politic to the kind of test few modern slave regimes willingly hazarded. As the new government turned to its white citizens to support and defend the bid for national independence, it faced the necessity of building support too among those whose consent for secession, nationhood, and war it had never solicited. Then began a relentless process in which government officials and military men all the way up the chain of command scrambled to execute policies designed to build a state and wage war, while preserving slavery and feeding and protecting a civilian population of women increasingly denied the support of their men. Then the slaveholders got a hard lesson in the political powers of the Confederate unfranchised. There would be far more of the people to contend with in the making of history in the Civil War South than the founders ever bargained on.

The struggle with the nonslaveholders was expected and it exacted its price. But nobody expected to have to contend with the women. White women, although citizens, were not a population that figured in anybody's political calculations. Women had never been of much interest to state officials. As a matter of law and custom they were regarded, like Antigone, as outside politics and war, members of the household, under the governance of husbands and fathers. But war had barely begun when officials on both sides were thrown into a series of confrontations with women engaged in what could only be called political acts, forcing fundamental recalculations about loyalty, treason, and political clout.

As war exacted its toll and old assumptions crumbled, politicians and military men in the Civil War South ended up contending with the women—even, some charged, making war on women. In the occupied South, Union forces struggled to limit the damage done by Confederate women and were eventually forced to recognize them as enemies in war. Women would be required to take oaths of allegiance, subjected to Union court-martial, and clapped in prison. In the heart of their own national territory the mass of white Southern women emerged as formidable adversaries of their government in the long struggle over the military policies of the C.S.A. Pushed into a newly intimate relationship to state authorities, and embracing a new identity as soldiers' wives, they forged a politics of subsistence by which to claim entitlement and demand justice. By insisting that the state live up to its promises to protect and support them, even taking up arms to do so, the women—poor white rural women with no previous history of political participation—defied notions about their incapacity and irrelevance to step decisively into the making of history. If the new political assertiveness of Southern women did not bring down the Confederacy, it did represent a powerful challenge to the Confederate vision of "the people" and the republic, and speaks to the particular pressures and ruptures of war in slave society. Any state that took their men would ultimately have to answer to them.

More critical still was the way the problem of slaves' political allegiance—a problem that had troubled Thomas Jefferson from the birth of the republic—reared up decisively in the face of Confederate politicians, policy makers, and military men, forcing them into a constant confrontation with slaves' own political objectives in the war.[3] The idea that a republic could be built in war without contending with the political desires of four million slaves strikes moderns as fantastic. But Confederates' hubris on this account is stunning, especially given the troubling hemispheric history in which they operated. For the relationship between war and emancipation weighed heavily on every slave power in the nineteenth century. Since the late eighteenth century, slave regimes at war and chronically short of men had been forced into negotiations with their own slaves, usually to recruit them as soldiers, often on condition of emancipation. In that hemispheric history Saint-Domingue, or Haiti, was the critical case. Confederates were haunted by the history of that island. Indeed, many Southerners embraced secession precisely to avoid the fate of whites in that (to them) dystopian post-emancipation society. But it wasn't just white Confederates who looked to Saint-Domingue. Confederate slaves did too, drawing the opposite lesson that in the maelstrom of war, slaves had been able to fight for their own emancipation and the wholesale destruction of the institution of slavery. Confederate slaves were entirely alert to the meaning of national and international developments. Would the C.S.A. manage to escape the fate of other slave regimes at war? The two remaining slave regimes in the hemisphere, Cuba and Brazil, attended carefully to the answer.[4]

The idea that Southern slaves shaped the history of the American Civil War is now a foundational part of the national narrative. But that new story—about how slaves transformed a war for the Union into a war for emancipation—is really a story about the Union side in the war.[5] It traces out a particular historical dynamic of slaves' flight to Union lines, labor for the Union military, and eventual enlistment in the armed forces of the United States. Developments in the C.S.A. are of little significance in the drama of emancipation it plots. Yet the slaves' war started in Confederate territory, was first waged against their own masters on their own plantations, and, in ways we have never really appreciated, forced constant revision not just in Union but in Confederate politics and policy. As every enslaved man, woman, and child knew, the destruction of slavery required the destruction of the slaveholders' state, with all of its horrifying national ambitions. The revolt slaves unleashed thwarted every administration attempt to make them an element of strength in war, and fundamentally shaped Confederate military labor policies. Indeed, one of the most dramatic elements of the Civil War story is how slaves compelled Confederates into a competition for the political loyalty, labor, and military service of slave men that implied the recognition of exactly the human and political personhood the proslavery republic had tried to deny. In the end, the proslavery C.S.A. would be forced down its own path to slave enlistment and partial emancipation, recapitulating elements of a struggle that had unfolded across the hemisphere since the American and French revolutions. The C.S.A. was transformed by war, and the Confederate political project was undone by those who had been taken for ciphers in it.

This is a book about politics and power in the Civil War South, about the bloody trial of the Confederacy's national vision, and about the significance of the disfranchised in it. In that sense it engages a critical methodological question about how we write political history and whose political history it is we write. If Confederate founders routinely discounted the salience of slaves and white women in laying their political plans, it was not a posture they could sustain once the nation-building project got under way. A history focused on the original "men of the community," as Jefferson Davis put it—a conventional political history of voters and politicians—would hardly grapple with what was fundamentally at stake in the history of the Confederacy or take its full historical measure.[6]

The story told here thus strikes out in new directions. It asks not why the South lost the war, the usual approach, but why Southerners seceded when they did, what happened when they did, and what it meant that they failed. It focuses more on processes than outcomes, putting the emphasis not on defeat but on the profound and unpredictable transformation into which the Confederacy was propelled by war. It looks at the interplay of political and military forces in ways that bring a whole new cast of characters into the making of history, including poor white rural women. And it takes an international perspective on the history of the C.S.A., which both brings to light a gendered history of war and emancipation otherwise obscured, and firmly establishes the centrality of developments in the C.S.A. to the history of the Civil War and emancipation as it is now told.

It is no exaggeration to say that the literature on the Confederacy has long been characterized—and limited—by a preöccupation with the matter of military defeat and related questions about the strength or weakness of Confederate nationalism. The question of why the South lost the Civil War is hardly a minor one.[7] But the preoccupation with defeat has made it difficult to ask other questions about the slaveholders' war and the profound changes it propelled in Southern and American political history. Even the rare scholar who emphasizes the revolutionary nature of the Confederate experience has cast it as an aberrant episode in the long continuity of Southern history, a discrete and self-contained experiment entirely comprehensible within the history of the region and of significance primarily to itself.[8]

From my perspective, the social and political transformations into which the nation was propelled, including the enlistment of slave men, are best understood in an international context. In terms of causes, dynamic, and consequences the entire history of the C.S.A. was part of a far larger set of historical struggles over the future of slave and servile systems, the political survival of slave states, the terms of emancipation, and the democratic imperatives of male citizenship in societies at war that erupted across the Western world in the age of emancipation. Far from working within national boundaries, what happened in the C.S.A. really only makes sense in light of related developments in other times and places. As a result, I adopt a broad set of coordinates for the history of the Confederacy and draw on an abundance of literature on comparative slavery and emancipation, state formation, agrarian and subaltern studies, and women's and gender history to write it.

This book is also a political history of the unfranchised. This approach, it seems to me, is virtually mandated by the particular proslavery and antidemocratic objectives of the Confederate political project. For if "policing the interior frontiers of a national community"—fencing off those disqualified from membership—is a key function of political systems everywhere, it was the very raison d'être of the C.S.A.[9] The relationship between state actors and the nation's vast population of free women and slaves thus necessarily emerges as a central focus of the analysis and in that the broad perspective was crucial. These were people, after all, in a formally democratic society, excluded from the official domains of political life, with no rights by which to levy claims but possessed of other means by which to engage in the act of making history. To write that story I have borrowed liberally from historical and theoretical literatures on other times and places.

To write about Confederate women I have drawn on feminist theories and histories, but I have also looked to agrarian and subaltern studies to illuminate the political strategies of rural poor people.[10] Planter women are not the key characters in this story. It was yeoman and poor white women who moved decisively into the practice of politics in the Civil War South, reshaping labor and welfare policy in their own image. Theirs is not a political history easily assimilated to the usual frameworks of nationalism or citizenship, with the expectation of claims made in terms of political rights. Poor white women did not usually speak of themselves as members of the nation or as citizens. Their political strategies were those common to rural people everywhere excluded from official political life. It is to the politics of the governed in most of the world and not to the liberal frameworks of American political history that I look to write the history of the female unfranchised in the American Civil War.[11]

The international perspective also lends new significance to the struggle over slavery waged on Confederate plantations and to the particular dynamic of war and emancipation that played out so dramatically in the short-lived C.S.A. For if the heroic story of black Union soldiers' struggle for freedom and citizenship is one central dynamic of war and emancipation in the American Civil War, it is hardly the only one.[12] It is surely worth remembering that only about 150,000 slaves served in the Union army and navy, that military service was a route to emancipation open only to men, and that while as many as 500,000 slaves may have made it to Union lines over the course of the war, the rest—as many as three million more—remained on plantations and farms in the Confederate South in a state of presumptive slavery. The vast majority of slaves, in other words, ended the war precisely where they began it, locked in Confederate territory, consigned to waging their war against slavery and the slaveholders' state exactly where they lived.[13] If the enlistment of black soldiers in the Union army "made strikingly clear the monumental changes wrought by the war," as a group of prominent historians have rightly insisted, then what did the decision to enlist slave men in the Confederate army mean for the history of the Confederacy, the American Civil War, and the comparative history of slavery and emancipation?[14] The Davis administration's decision to enlist slave men is no indication that it chose independence over slavery, as so many continue to insist; it is, rather, a profound indication of the structural problems faced by that and every other slave regime at war since the French Revolution.[15] And it is the ultimate measure of what slaves wrought in Confederate political life.

The focus on the Confederacy is a critical reminder that the struggle for emancipation proceeded on many fronts in the American Civil War. It was advanced by people and processes only partly aligned with the Union state's emancipation policy, and it cannot be reduced to a history that follows a route through war to emancipation taken by some (but not most) men and no women. In that sense it reanimates a vital part of the national narrative. But it does something else as well: it illuminates a new history of gender and emancipation. The history of slave women in the struggle for emancipation—their political history—fits no state narrative, Union or Confederate. The recent focus on black soldiers makes that much clear. But the emphasis here on the actions of slaves in a war against slavery that started on Confederate farms and plantations, in developments not captured by federal agencies or their statist agenda, highlights the messy, uneven, and protracted process by which slaves fought for and won their freedom. Indeed, Union emancipation policy emerges from this analysis in sharper focus as a specifically *military* policy that opened up entirely different possibilities for men and women. In Confederate and Union territory alike, enslaved men and women were forced to take different paths through war to emancipation. For the most part, as in Saint-Domingue and other slave regimes at war, men (when they could) took the martial route and women (when they could) took the marital route. Indeed, one of the things this perspective unexpectedly reveals is the common recourse of military powers to the institution of marriage in their attempts to manage populations of enslaved women and children en route to freedom. Gender, as the Confederate experience reminds us, was a fundamental, not incidental, feature of emancipation wherever it transpired.[16]

The Confederate experiment in nation building and war transformed the United States, and the American South and the people in it. Vital political change did not arrive in the South only with defeat, wasn't all imposed on the region by a victorious army and a powerful Republican Party state. The four-year juggernaut of state building in war, the Southern people's unprecedented experience of a radically activist state, and the unprecedented mobilization of the unfranchised were all part of a brief but searing national history. The C.S.A. was defeated, but the Southern people's experience of the Confederate war lived on.

The road to the postwar South ran through the bloody struggles waged on Confederate ground. The people, male and female, black and white, Southern and Northern, who confronted each other in 1865, and engaged anew in paramilitary struggle over the terms of social and political life, were not the same people they had been in 1860. They had been through the fire, and it had remade them all and the governments under which they lived. The lessons of that war, and of the Confederate experience, registered in the region, the nation, and in the hemisphere.

The Confederate war involved a profound reckoning. Before Confederates were defeated, their political project had failed. The new nation Confederates set out to build had fallen victim not just to enemy armies but to the manifest poverty of its reactionary vision of the republic, and the determined resistance of the Confederate people to it. Their story tells us something surely worth remembering: That power counts in politics, is often exercised brutally, and almost always wins, but that once in a very long while—as in the Civil War South—history opens up, resistance prevails, and the usually powerless manage against all imaginable odds to change the world.

CHAPTER 1

Who Are the People?

THE CIVIL WAR BEGAN with a political campaign as complicated as any in American history. For as long as a year and a half and in some cases much longer, a group of Southern politicians conspired, schemed, and colluded to maneuver their states out of the Union. From the Southerners' perspective, secession represented both an end and a beginning: an end to the frustration and stagnation of sectional conflict; a beginning of the great work of making a new nation. The brute fact of Confederate defeat in the American Civil War and the short-livedness of the Confederacy's national career has made it difficult to grasp what they attempted. But the singularity of their political project and its significance as an event in the history of the United States and the nineteenth-century Western world means that we should try.

The architects of the Confederacy had a powerful vision born out of the struggles and endemic tensions of the nineteenth century. They sought nothing less than to build the first independent slaveholders' republic in the Western Hemisphere and to launch it into a leading role in the game of nations. "We have all the essentials of a high national career," as Alexander Stephens, Georgia politician and just-named vice president of the breakaway state put it early on. What they had in mind was an explicitly proslavery and antidemocratic nation-state, one that would put slavery on a permanent footing and provide a resolution to the problems of labor, capital, and democracy which beset other Western states in the nineteenth century.[1]

Confederates had an expansive vision of their political future; they traded in big ideas. The original American Union, Stephens explained in March 1861, "rested upon the assumption of the equality of races." "Our new government is founded upon exactly the opposite ideas: its foundations are laid, its cornerstone rests, upon the great truth that the negro is not equal to the white man; that slavery is his natural and moral condition. This, our new government, is the first, in the history of the world, based upon this great . . . truth." What Stephens and others imagined, in other words, was the first nation-state erected on the modern scientific "truth" of negro inferiority. The Confederate States of America was to be a tribune of racial truth throughout the world.[2]

Peculiar as it now sounds, that vision marks the Confederacy as part of a broad reactionary movement among regional agrarian and slaveholding elites that formed a steady counterpoint to the age of revolution and emancipation in Europe and the Americas. But it also marks the Confederacy's anomalous status among those elites. For alone among them, Southern secessionists and proto-Confederates attempted to found an independent nation. Confederates, that is, present the only case of a proslavery ruling class confident enough to launch its own state-building project and the only example of proslavery nationalism to arise in the Western Hemisphere.

Secessionists saw a bright future for slavery if they could set its destiny in a new republic. To them slavery was no worn-out vestige of the past but a social system uniquely adapted to the conditions of the modern world. "Slavery—our institution of it at least, is scarcely a half century old. It is just beginning its career," the South Carolinian politician and historian William Henry Trescott offered in 1859. Amid what Southerners saw as the heap of failed experiments in slave emancipation—Haiti, Jamaica, and the rest of the French and British West Indies—the Confederate States of America would stand for a different future for slavery in the hemisphere. Like the Alabama politician Jabez Lamar Curry, many secessionists would point to the West Indies as "a conclusive refutation of antislavery theories." Escaping the fate of slaveholders in Haiti, the British

West Indies, and other failed post-emancipation societies, they chose secession from the United States and a risky national independence. "We will not consent to become another Jamaica or San Domingo," as the Georgian Henry Benning put it. Against the perversion of the United States Constitution by a Northern antislavery party and ideology, they would preserve slavery and with it the liberty of the people unimpaired into the next generation. The Confederate States of America would represent a new birth of liberty: theirs was to be a proslavery nation and a white man's republic.[3]

But if secessionists' experiment in proslavery nationalism was hemispheric in scope and ambition, it was also uniquely American in origin and design. The political system white Southerners proposed to export was simply, as many claimed, the original republic of the United States redeemed and perfected. Secessionists' political project represented a reckoning with the republican form of government at home as well as in the eyes of the world. In March of 1861 Alexander Stephens charged the Union with the original sin of racial equality. But that was a late political conversion. He had been an avowed Unionist all his life and had embraced secession only after his state went out.[4] Devotion to the Union ran deep even among secessionists, and it was the desire to redeem and perfect it that drove so many to the dangerous experiment of independence.

Certainly that was the case with Jefferson Davis, longtime congressman, U.S. senator from Mississippi, and, starting in February 1861, the first and only president of the slaveholders' new republic. Davis was a reluctant secessionist. In him, love of the original republic and its perfect Constitution provided the only reason sufficient to destroy the Union. He had long struggled against the necessity. But when, on January 21, 1861, Davis received notice that his state had voted itself out of the Union, he rose on the floor of the Senate to explain why that had to be. Mississippi, he said bluntly, had no choice but to secede because "we are to be deprived in the Union of rights which our fathers bequeathed to us." And that, he observed bitterly, proceeded from an elemental and irresolvable conflict over the very nature of the political community. At issue in secession, according to Davis, was nothing less than the American conception of "the people."[5]

Jefferson Davis's views of the people and the republic were revealing and historically consequential, for, as it turned out, they had to carry the burden not just of secession but of nation making and war. Davis's personal political history, his tortured course through secession, national independence, and war, serves as a touchstone of the Confederate experience registering the impress of many of its key moments and developments. In Davis, foundational Confederate principles found both their fullest expression and most profound trial. Davis laid out his views fully and clearly in the course of the secession crisis and the precarious opening months of the new Confederate States of America. They tell a good deal about what politically moderate white Southerners like him valued so dearly they would risk all to secure it.

Jefferson Davis's views were well known from public speeches over his many years as a congressman, then as a senator. Although to our ear they may sound cryptic and euphemistic, his construction of the people and their rights would have been instantly discernible to his colleagues on the Senate floor and to the men and women who packed the galleries to hear his farewell speech. The rights in question were, of course, property in slaves, and "the people" were those whose rights to such property the Constitution was bound to protect. In January 1861, in the midst of the secession crisis, Davis's strict constructionism was plainly on display. "Mississippi," he said disdainfully, "has heard proclaimed the theory that all men are created free and equal, and this made the basis of an attack upon her social institutions." But that, he declared, was a deliberate perversion of the Declaration of Independence. When they wrote the Declaration, he insisted, "the people of those communities were asserting that . . . men were created equal—meaning the men of the political community; that there was no divine right to rule; that no man inherited the right to govern; that there were no classes by which power and place descended to families, but that all stations were equally within the grasp of each member of the body politic. These were the great principles they announced . . . They have no reference to the slave."[6]

For Davis there was no mistaking the point. Politically speaking, slaves were property, not persons. They were not "put upon a footing of equality with white men." And they were not, and never could be, members of the political community. "The condition of slavery is with us nothing but a form of civil government for a class of people not fit to govern themselves."[7] Slaves, as he once put it, were part of a separate polity; slavery was the slaves' state, masters the authority to which they owed allegiance. Against the fanatically innovative ideas of Black Republicans and Abraham Lincoln, their president-elect, Senator Davis, Mississippi, and yet-unknown numbers of the slaveholding states would stand even unto civil war.[8] Secession for them was nothing less than an attempt to reconstitute the original American notion of "the people," and of the republic, in a new proslavery state. That he had to repudiate the Declaration of Independence confirms that far from embracing a proslavery view of the people and the government that had been uncontroversial among the founders, Davis was in fact choosing sides in a political fight that had raged since the origins of the republic itself.

Senator Davis did not just speak for himself; he spoke for his state and his section. His views were mainstream and commonplace in early 1861. They were widely shared by other Confederate founders, and they took firm constitutional ground. Indeed, they bore striking resemblance to the definition of citizenship Chief Justice Roger Taney had offered in his decision in the critical Supreme Court case, *Dred Scott v. Sandford,* just three years before, which stood as the definitive ruling on the subject in the late antebellum period. Taney held firm to the view that people of African descent "formed no part of the people who framed" the Declaration of Independence; that citizenship was a status reserved for those men of the political community—white men—who had always possessed the right to vote and the obligation to bear arms. "The words 'people of the United States' and 'citizens' are synonymous terms," he ruled in *Dred Scott.* More so even than aliens, he declared, negroes are "rejected from the duties and obligations of citizenship." This was the eminently useful formulation Davis and other Southern politicians claimed simply to uphold through secession.[9]

Chief Justice Taney's decision was embraced by white Southerners as a final answer to the increasingly troubling question, "Who are the people?" And indeed, as a legally binding Supreme Court decision and the new law of the land, Taney's decision can be taken, as Southerners claimed, as the definitive statement of the status quo antebellum with respect to rights of property in slaves and American citizenship.

This notwithstanding the two dissents written by other justices in the case, and the storm of public outrage and declarations of resistance with which it was met in the North. Even Abraham Lincoln agreed to abide by it.

But like Davis's stated opinions in defense of secession, Taney's decision in *Dred Scott* raised a host of important historical questions—about race and citizenship certainly, but also about American citizenship more broadly in the divisive late antebellum moment. For Taney cut a wide swath through contemporary fights over representation and suffrage waged between abolitionists and their woman's rights allies and proslavery forces, North and South. On black citizens Taney was definitively negative. Whether slaves or free blacks, they were excluded. But what about white women? Were they citizens by his definition? Were they part of the people? A married woman "has no political relation to the state any more than an alien," a Massachusetts lawyer had argued before the state supreme court in 1805. Nor was that position entirely obsolete by the outbreak of the Civil War, feminist encroachments notwithstanding. On white women Taney's view as expressed in *Dred Scott* was ambiguous, simultaneously indicating membership and exclusion. A person, he acknowledged, may be a citizen but exercise no share of the political power. "Women and minors . . . form a part of the political family" although they "cannot vote." But if Taney recognized white women's citizenship, the terms of membership he used (in the political family) suggests the importance he attached to their exclusion. When he cited the 1792 United States Militia Law—which specified membership only of "free able-bodied white male citizens"—as prima facie evidence of the exclusion of "the African race" from American citizenship, he explained that "the word 'white' is evidently used to exclude the African race, and the word 'citizen' to exclude unnaturalized foreigners." Who the word "male" sought to exclude apparently went without saying, so obvious and unquestioned was women's exclusion from the political rights or privileges of citizens.[10]

For Chief Justice Taney as for U.S. Senator Jefferson Davis, citizenship was synonymous with the political rights possessed by white men and not by slaves or women. Such views of slaves' and white women's political incapacity, although lately under challenge, had long undergirded the defense of slavery and conservative resistance to the expansion of democracy in the United States. By 1860 they were being put in the service of secession. As writer of the majority opinion, Chief Justice Roger Taney had put Southern politicians, including Jefferson Davis, on firm ground in the secession crisis. Secessionists claimed his highly restrictive view of "the people" as the constitutionally orthodox one through secession and new nationhood.

But that vision of the people had to do more than justify secession and take the South out of the Union. It also had to do much of the challenging work of nation building as well. On February 9, 1861, about a month after he left the U.S. Senate, Jefferson Davis was in his garden at Brierfield, his plantation on the Mississippi River, when he received notice that he had been nominated as president-elect of the new Confederate States of America. In the long secession winter of 1861, Davis struggled to give constitutional form and emotional substance to the idea of a Confederate people. The new president did not embrace that task with the joyous optimism of some Confederate founders. He was a realist. He never could convince himself, as many more-eager fire-eaters did, that there would be no war. But as he made his slow way from home to the new Confederate capital in Montgomery, Alabama, Jefferson Davis began the task of converting the constitutional arguments of past sectional struggle and the still-raging secession crisis into a powerful image of the new nation.

Who were the Confederate people Davis called into being? Would they provide a strong foundation for the making of a new republic? In his inaugural address as provisional president of the new Confederate States of America in Montgomery in February, Davis celebrated the Confederacy as a living illustration of the "American idea that governments rest upon the consent of the governed." As before, he left no doubt about whose consent mattered; it was white men who had the right to alter or abolish governments. The people were still those white men who had used the vote to exercise their constitutional right to secession. But now Davis moved to infused that cold category with a new living, breathing identity. Standing on the balcony of the Exchange Hotel a few nights before, he had spoken emotionally to the crowd of men and women below, evoking a strong sense of national feeling. "Fellow Citizens and brethren of the Confederate States of America," he addressed them, "for now we are brethren, not in name merely but in fact, men of one flesh, one bone,

one interest, one purpose, and of identity of domestic institutions." In 1861 when the Confederate president envisioned the people, it was the brothers he saw—the voters and the soldiers—not the great Southern majority, the white women and enslaved men and women removed from public vision and political relevance by the South's domestic institutions.[11] Jefferson Davis's view of the body politic was strictly fraternal and patrilineal. Liberty was the Southern freeman's patrimony, passed from fathers to sons in strict succession. "They have labored," he said of the Southern people, "to preserve the Government of our fathers in its spirit," to preserve "the richest inheritance that ever fell to man," and to transmit it, as he once put it, "untarnished to our children." The Confederate president had no doubt about what history was and who made it. "When the time and occasion serve," he would say a few months later, "we shall smite the smiter with manly arms, as did our fathers before us and as becomes their sons . . . We will drench [the battlefields of Virginia] with blood . . . We will make a history for ourselves."[12] Like politics, history was a martial affair, its chapters were war, and in it the defense of the state, like that of liberty, was entrusted only to citizen-soldiers. Jefferson Davis's view of the Confederate nation and people at the outset of the American Civil War was as brethren, a band of brothers, dedicated to the proposition that all men were not created equal.

Jefferson Davis's fraternal conception of the nation was hardly unique to the Confederacy. It had often served as a myth of national origin. But if its ordinariness is not really in question, its meaning certainly is.[13] Far from simply describing the natural landscape of nineteenth-century American politics, Davis's fraternal vision mustered powerful affective and potentially coercive ties of race, gender, and generation to give shape to a new Confederate nation facing war. It did so, in part, by staking out a particularly conservative position in a rapidly escalating conflict over the nature of citizenship and democracy, sustaining a reactionary vision of a republican polity defined by a perfect "homogeneity" of white men's persons, interests, rights, and duties. In 1860 free black men could vote in only four New England states (and that in small numbers), women of any race in none. But slavery as the normative status for four million African

American men and women was under relentless assault, and traditional grounds of civil and political exclusion were being challenged by activists of various abolitionist and woman's rights stripes in the Northern states in the late antebellum moment.[14] So while it is true that all native-born white men could vote in the North and the South by 1860, in the South slavery rendered the white man's franchise more exclusive by effectively excluding the region's working class. Secessionists made much of the fact that slavery constituted white men as a privileged class in the South; that it made them members of a political elite and turned the franchise into a particularly valuable possession and mark of manhood and whiteness. This was the centerpiece of their campaign strategy. Thus to naturalize Davis's fraternal notion of the people, as political historians typically do, is to miss something that was essential (and not incidental) to Southern political culture both before and after secession.

If Alexander Stephens, Jefferson Davis, and other Southern politicians thought secession settled the question of political membership, they were terribly wrong. Fundamental questions about the composition of the body politic not only took secessionists out of the Union but plagued the racial and patriarchal state they set out to build. Jefferson Davis's delimited notion of the people might have been adequate to the imagined new nation, but it would prove utterly inadequate in the struggle that lay ahead. The political history of the Confederate States of America was one long bloody trial of their foundational principles and stated objective: to build, once and for all time, the perfected republic of white men.

When Alexander Stephens spoke in late March 1861 about the grand future envisioned for the new Confederate nation, he referred confidently to the "late United States." But from the point of view of many Southerners still in the Union, that obituary was a little premature. The problem, of course, was that to take part in the game of nations they first had to bring theirs into existence. Dislike it as they might—and many did—secessionists could proceed only by electoral means. First they had to win the consent of the people, and then they had to have it confirmed at the ballot box. As of March only seven of fifteen slave states had seceded from the Union, and that after hard-fought and always downright dirty election campaigns that raised questions about democratic legitimacy. Given the great American principle Jefferson Davis identified, that all legitimate government rests on the consent of the governed, the act of nation making had to be done in the name of the people.[15]

A more vivid portrait of "the people" was rarely offered by an American political campaign than the one that emerged on the ground in the last moment of peace before the outbreak of war. It was a prelapsarian view, innocent in its assumptions about political life, about whose consent mattered in the fate of the nation heading into war and whose did not.

In the winter and spring of 1861, Southern politicians of every stripe, from fire-eating secessionists to ironclad Unionists, fanned out to the most remote points of their districts to make their case for Union, for secession, or for a wait-and-see moderatism. Hardly anyone escaped their net. In the long secession season, the battle to don the mantle of the people constituted the form and substance of the political fight. It could hardly have been otherwise. For much as the movements for secession in every Southern state were orchestrated by cadres of elite politicians and resisted by others, ultimately only the people could confer legitimacy on each state's decision to secede from or stay in the Union. So all looked to the people. Every politician, everywhere, claimed to speak as and for them, and the sheer volume of appeals is striking still. But it was a highly conventional identification of "the people," notwithstanding the momentousness of the decision for the nation and the entire Southern population who would have to share its fate. It gives a very useful account of whose consent was solicited and of the ambit of citizenship in the first days of the C.S.A. against which future developments could be charted.

Politicians were pretty explicit about whom they meant by the people. The secession crisis was an orgy of speechifying, and every speech began and ended with a direct appeal to those whose support was courted. There was not much variation between the imagined audiences of the Unionist and secessionist parties, or among politicians of different stature. Thus when the moderate Unionist, Virginia governor John Letcher, addressed the General Assembly, he urged legislators to live up to their sacred trust "to the people, our common constituents." He then proceeded to identify the people as the citizens who owe allegiance to Virginia and who are bound "every man . . . to risk himself" to restore peace to the nation and to protect Virginia, "the land of our birth, the burial place of our fathers, and the peaceful homes of our wives and daughters." Similarly, the secessionist governor of Alabama, A. B. Moore, wanting to know the "minds of the people," looked forward to the decision of "each voter of the state . . . He must decide the great and vital question of submission to an Abolition Administrator or of secession from the Union." "Fellow Citizens," the secessionist Henry Benning of Georgia began one of his speeches, cutting right to the chase. The immediate association of the people with the citizens and the voters was a commonplace of political speech. And although hardly surprising it is nonetheless meaningful, for it communicated, then and now, something essential about the understanding of consent and political obligation that obtained in the crisis of the Union, and something important about the sense of national belonging in that precarious nation-making moment.[16]

Yet predictable as it might seem, that restricted definition of the people was controversial on numerous counts. For there was little about the identity of the citizen and the voter that could be taken for granted in 1860. Just who were the citizens and who were the voters in the American republic? That was a key national question in the election of 1860 and in the secession crisis. Virtually everyone in the South put the racial threat to white men's exclusive citizenship front and center in the campaign. From state and local meetings all over the South a chorus of charges erupted that Lincoln had been elected by black men's votes and that the Republican Party was advancing a radical agenda of abolition and racial equality. All believed that slavery, the bulwark of the white man's republic, was under direct assault. Against the humanitarianism of the Black Republicans and the horrific future that awaited a post-emancipation South—"Our lovely land an American Congo," as one put it—Southern politicians worked to secure slavery and the permanent exclusion of black men from citizenship and the political community.[17]

That much was clear in the great debate over secession staged in Milledgeville, Georgia, during the third week of November 1860, shortly after Lincoln's election to the presidency. As the state legislature deliberated on the necessity of calling a state secession convention, in the evenings the state's leading orators rehearsed all the arguments pro and anti before capacity audiences of citizens, subjects, and legislators. Alexander

Stephens, not yet vice president of the Confederate States nor a secessionist, spoke powerfully for the Union camp, insisting that slavery was safest in the Union. He abhorred precisely the kind of rash experiment in government for which he later became a spokesman. But while Stephens fetishized "the people," filling his speech with obsequious references to their sovereignty and majesty, it was the spokesman for secession, state legislator Thomas R. R. Cobb, who mastered the populist appeal. Cobb headed straight for the bottom line: "This Constitution was made for white men—citizens of the United States," he bellowed to the crowded hall. "This Union was formed by white men, and for the protection and happiness of their race." The right "of suffrage should be given to none but citizens of the U.S," he insisted, and it slandered the "memory of our fathers" when free negroes were declared to be citizens of this nation, allowed to vote and "to select rulers for you and me."[18] Cobb's point was clear: the citizen was, and had to remain, white. Secession—in the name of slavery and white supremacy—was the only remedy.

Cobb was a fire-eater, meaning that he supported immediate separate state secession and was given to extreme formulations of the Black Republican threat. But outraged statements about the way black men were being introduced to citizenship and political equality arose surprisingly often from public meetings of citizens out in the rural counties of Georgia in mid-November 1860. Nor was the complaint restricted to secessionists. From a meeting in Merriwether County came demands that the North admit that "negroes shall not vote [and] are not citizens under the Constitution of the U.S." Security in the Union, not necessarily out of it, was their early aim. Men in Spalding County, Georgia, sounding exactly the note Jefferson Davis would in exiting the U.S. Senate two months later, proclaimed that in 1787 the people of Georgia entered into "solemn constitutional compact with the white people of other states to 'form a more perfect union'" and that "this Government is and ought to be, the Government of the WHITE PEOPLE . . . Made by and for the citizens—men capable and worthy to be free citizens." Citizens in still-Unionist Habersham County complained that the Black Republicans and Lincoln had elevated to the "right of suffrage, citizenship and equality a race of beings never contemplated as citizens by the Constitution" and charged that it was black men's votes that had elected Lincoln. "These sovereign states of Union were composed solely of white men, and formed governments only for white men," the people of Bibb County insisted in a rough restatement of Cobb's view.[19]

The racially exclusive character of citizenship was no arid constitutional principle but a volatile touchstone of popular politics in the late antebellum South. Ideologically speaking, it was not far from the county meetings to Alexander Stephens's cornerstone speech about the Confederacy as the white man's perfected republic. Accusations that Lincoln had been elected by black votes epitomized the challenge to foundational Southern beliefs about the character of the people in their republic. Talk of white supremacy was increasingly overt. One representative to the Alabama secession convention put it: "We are sent to protect, not so much property, as white supremacy" against the danger of abolition rule.[20]

In defining the people and the citizens as white, politicians not only proscribed black men from the body politic; they also dispensed with white women. In moving seamlessly between citizens and voters, they elided white women entirely and arrived at a radically delimited definition of the people. Adult white women were citizens in a constitutional sense although the obligations of citizenship had been defined by gender throughout the nation's history. In the North and South, women's standing as citizens had always been refracted through their normative adult status as wives, and by the state's equal or greater commitment to upholding marriage and the law of coverture. That law put women under their husbands' legal power in the interests of marital unity. The transformation of woman into wife made "citizenship—a public identity as a participant in public life—something close to a contradiction in terms for a married woman." The terms of female citizenship had always been set by the perceived necessities of marriage and its gender asymmetries between man and woman, husband and wife. In the North by 1860, agitation for the woman citizen's natural right of suffrage had, in conjunction with antislavery, already made serious political inroads. Increasingly women's continued exclusion had to be dignified by an argument. But nowhere in the nineteenth-century United States did any women's rights, not to mention demands for the vote, emerge outside of the context of antislavery politics. So in the South, where a proslavery agenda set the tone in politics and where politicians regularly dragooned marriage into the work of legitimizing slavery (as just another desirable form of domestic dependence suitable to the weak), women's status as citizens hardly mattered.[21] There, politicians were habituated to thinking of women as existing at a remove from the body politic, as part of the family or the household, and not of the people and the citizens.

The gender of the people, unlike the race, was communicated largely by thoughtlessness and indirection and often simply by the saturation of male pronouns. Georgia governor Joseph Brown could hardly have been clearer when he elaborated citizens' obligations in his special message to the state legislature in November 1860. "The state," he said, "has the right to require from each citizen, prompt obedience to her [Georgia's] laws; to command his services in the field of battle against her enemies, whenever, in her judgment, it may be necessary to her protection or the vindication of her honor; and to tax him to any extent which her necessities may at any time require." Georgia can make these demands on all her citizens. In return, the citizen "is entitled to demand and receive . . . full and ample protection of his life, his liberty, his family, his reputation and his property of every description."[22] The effect is cumulative and inescapable: the state is female and the citizen is male.

Certainly this was nothing new or unusual. It reiterates precisely what John Adams had laid out at the dawn of the republic as the grounds of women's mandatory exclusion from political life: unfitted by nature for the businesses of life or hardy enterprises of war, they had nothing of value to offer the state. That was what Governor Brown said: A woman cannot meet the primary obligation of the citizen in military service; having no personal property, she cannot be taxed to support the state; she has no rights that can be plundered or that are worth defending; she is part of the citizen's "family" but is not the citizen whose family it is; she requires protection but cannot offer it. Brown's view effectively proscribed women from the identity of citizen. Women were homebound: part of the family or the household government. They were not part of the public deliberative life of the community by which the people make their will known to their representatives. In that most important sense they were not part of the people. When the battle comes in earnest, one anguished West Virginia Unionist would warn late in that state's secession debate, it will be women's battle too.[23] New Confederates would have plenty of time to learn that lesson. But in 1860 and 1861 women citizens' consent for secession and new nationhood was neither solicited nor secured.

What is significant is not the fact of white women's political exclusion but the meaning of it in time and place. The drawing and maintaining of boundaries around membership—setting "the 'interior frontiers' of national communities"—was an elemental task of every political system. In marking the body politic as the exclusive preserve of white men, Southern politicians and voters maintained the central principle of Southern political life, one so fundamental it was never the subject of partisan politics.[24]

But if women were absent from serious deliberation in political life, they were ever-present in another role, as objects of protection symbolic and real. Governor Brown did not just imagine the citizen as male; he also imagined the state as female. And that strict division constituted a case for the political obligation of white men to the state as a woman, and to their own wives and daughters. In a very real sense, it was women's absence from the deliberative domain of politics that made them available as symbols in the political culture. In convincing white men of the immediate vulnerability of the state and their households to Black Republican invasion, in demonstrating the necessity of defense, either in the Union or out of it, and, especially, in framing the kind of appeal that would bridge the looming social divide between slaveholders and nonslaveholders, we begin to see the real significance of gender in the secession crisis. In the so-called Black Republican threat to womanhood, politicians attempted to render abstract fears about the republic and the political and civil equality of black men concrete, immediate, and emotionally compelling.

Images of the state as woman proliferated in Southern political discourse and iconography. True, there were antecedents. Ireland's tragic Dark Rosaleen, France's martial Marianne, and the United States' regal Columbia all evidence the same symbolic structure. The individual Southern states in question were not yet nations (and never would be in their original form), but they were invoked as homelands, beloved birthplaces, and thus as states in an affective and not just administrative sense. In that respect, the Southern partakes of the more general case and problem of the fusion of the national and feminine in literature, politics, and history.[25]

In the late antebellum Southern states, the female figure of the state took many forms—genius of liberty, old lady in hoop skirts—but none more commonly than mother, the better, presumably, to summon the loyalty of her sons. If the Black Republicans trampled on Virginia, Henry Wise said, even the Unionists would "rush to some Sister Commonwealth and beg her to come and help me save my mother." Thomas Cobb rallied the people to the secessionists' cause "as brothers, as friends, as Georgia's sons[.] [L]let us come and take counsel together, how we shall avenge her wrongs, promote her prosperity and preserve her honor." Images of the political mother proliferated in secessionist discourse in the upper and lower South states, feeding into a larger theme of politics as filial piety, and rooting the political and martial duties of male citizens, not in the abstraction of the state but the intimate body of the mother, "the soil which gave him birth," as one put it. We must be "united at home as a band of brothers ready to defend the honor of an insulted mother," a South Carolinian warned in late 1859.[26] Images of mother and sons gave powerful form to the gender and generational character of the people and, in some wishful sense, to the nation they were trying to make.

But symbolic representation could go only so far. Politicians anxious about their ability to draw the people behind them reached for more immediate and emotionally laden ways to present the threat the Republican Party posed to Southern men. Women figured centrally, indeed ubiquitously, as embodied symbols of the property and rights at risk in the crisis: not just as the abstract Mother state but as real, vulnerable wives and daughters. In Georgia, the populist governor Joseph Brown offered women as the fundamental basis of man's property and manhood rights and as what distinguished poor white men from slaves. What interests do "the large class of nonslaveholders and poor white laborers" have in maintaining the rights of wealthy slaveholders, Brown asked, bearding the lion in its den. "If our rights of property are assailed by a common enemy shall we not help each other? Or if I have a wife and children and a house, and another has neither wife nor children nor house. Will he therefore stand by and see my house burned and my wife butchered because he has none? . . . We all poor and rich have a common interest, a common destiny . . . a common enemy."[27] Images of women as objects of protection were reached for most readily in nervous briefs about nonslaveholders' loyalty to the planters' regime.

Unionists used the strategy, too, although to opposite political ends. In Alabama the spirited resistance of Unionists to the straight-outs (as the radicals were called there) turned on the image of Eden destroyed, "our lovely state . . . converted into a kind of American congo," as one North Alabama man put it. In averting that future he pleaded ostensibly on behalf of "our mothers and our sisters—of helpless humanity throughout the borders of our state," for the radicals to concede something to these brothers of North Alabama. Virginia Unionists pointed to the dangers that awaited a separate South and to the necessity of saving "wife and children . . . from the red and reeking hand, from the midnight torch, from the danger of the assassin, and from ruined, ruined property."[28] Clearly Unionists could play the scare game too, and by late February 1861 the stakes in that political struggle had been considerably ratcheted up.

The specter of rape loomed larger in appeals to the people as secessionists became more desperate. Vague insinuations about pollution and dishonor had long been a part of the political discourse. The idea that so-called Black Republicans would rape the South itself was sometimes ventured. "Is there a son of her [Virginia's] classic soil who would not blush to see her clinging to those free states who would degrade and dishonor her," one Virginia secessionist reportedly put it at a public meeting in Richmond. John Townsend, the South Carolina moderate turned propagandist for secession, used a less genteel version when he asked a public audience in October 1860 whether they were prepared "to drag out a dishonored existence under Black Republican rule." A few short weeks will bring us "under subjection to that ravening [Black Republican] majority," he warned ominously, and then they could expect the "sort of leniency shown by a conqueror over a subjugated and craven people." "Will the South remain a passive victim" facing destruction after "a few years of besotted indulgence," or will she mount "timely and manly resistance." Townsend's conception of power and powerlessness was relentlessly sexual.[29] The rape of the South was imminent, and where the people were all male, it could seem at times as if it were men's bodies that would be violated.

More commonly white women's bodies were the ones allegedly at risk. Beginning around the time of Harper's Ferry and escalating up to the moment of Lincoln's inauguration, politicians and propagandists pointedly insisted that political action was necessary to protect white women from imminent rape at the hands of Black Republicans and their (male) slave allies. The tactic was most commonly secessionist, most pronounced in the Deep South campaigns, and most in evidence when the loyalty of nonslaveholders was most in doubt. By the time of Lincoln's election the tone often verged on the hysterical, with secessionists routinely using images of rape to cast the protection of women and the family as the unassailable values at stake in the fight.[30]

Thomas Cobb, the Georgia secessionist, used the image of rape prominently in his bid to unify that state's white men around immediate secession during the great debate in November 1860. He offered a graphic vision of violation that purposefully conflated state and household, "black" Republicans and the black men (slaves) they aroused to their foul work. "I think I see in the future a gory head rise above our horizon," he began. "Its name is Civil War. Already I can see the prints of his bloody fingers upon our lintels and doorposts." Only secession could avert the scourge. Reminding his listeners that, as he spoke, slaves on a plantation a mere seven miles away had "revolted from their labor, declaring themselves free by virtue of Lincoln's election," he said. "I cannot say but that your home or your family may be the first to greet your returning footsteps in ashes or in death." The woman who needed protection was no longer just Georgia. "Remember the trembling hand of a loved wife," he said, "as she whispered her fears from the incendiary and the assassin. Recall the look of indefinable dread with which the little daughter inquired when your returning footsteps should be heard—And if there be manhood in you, tell me if this is the domestic tranquility which the 'Glorious Union' has achieved." In pointing to the household, the family, and vulnerable wives and daughters, and identifying the ultimate violation, Cobb cast the Black Republicans as a threat to every white man's property and honor. "What then is our remedy," he railed that night in Milledgeville. "Shall it be the boy's redress of recrimination? The bully's redress of braggadocio. Or the manly freeman's redress of independence?"[31] The freeman was, presumably, everyman.

Fire-eaters' political work was crudely done. At one level, it was racial fear mongering. In all of the speeches and appeals, the truly inflammatory pair presented was white women and black men. The threat of violence

Black Republicans posed was always directed not at the white race in general but at white women in particular, and the threat itself was posed not by "black" Republicans (who were mostly white men) but by black and usually slave men incited to rape and pillage. The racial and gender threats were invariably a linked pair. And they were linked in pursuit of the nonslaveholders' vote.

On the eve of the presidential elections in 1860, a propaganda association was formed in Charleston, South Carolina. Called, appropriately enough, the 1860 Association, one of its avowed aims was to prepare, print, and distribute tracts and pamphlets. The publications committee made good on its promise, ultimately distributing more than 166,000 pamphlets. None had a bigger circulation than John Townsend's two incendiary contributions, "The South Alone Shall Govern the South" and "The Doom of Slavery in the Union." Both directly considered the effects of Black Republican government, which Townsend construed to include slave emancipation, on "the nonslaveholding portion of our citizens." Both insisted that the poor white man's racial superiority was bolstered only by slavery and would disappear with it, and both insisted that submission to Black Republican rule would touch off a race war between poor white and black men. "The midnight glare of the incendiaries' torch will illuminate the country from one end to another," Townsend railed in one of the pamphlets, "while pillage, violence, murder, poison, and rape will fill the air with the demonic revelry of all the bad passions of an ignorant, semi-barbarous race, urged to madness by the licentious teachings of our northern brethren."[32] If they did not secede, Southern freemen would live to see their women seized as booty of war or, worse, raped by bestial and now emancipated black men. In Townsend's apocalyptic scenario the gender and racial threat to white men's rights are inextricably linked, their common property identified as white women, beloved objects men were pledged to protect. All over the South, but particularly in the Deep South, politicians eager to unite voting men—the people—behind their plans envisioned the defense of the state as the defense of white men's wives from rape and murder.

The fusion of the national and the feminine in Southern pleas has been repeated ever since along with the images and rhetoric of 1860 and 1861 in the argument that Southern men went to war to protect their womenfolk. In treating those images as truisms, as unproblematic and transparent articulations of men's beliefs, historians and others continue to deploy women as objects and symbols in a history made exclusively by men, just as Jefferson Davis had said. Where the nation became a woman, the woman took on a national posture.[33] But the women offered to us in fire-eaters' and Unionists' narratives in 1860 and 1861 were not real. Like the virgin emblazoned on one side of the Virginia flag (who matched the shield on the other), or the female form adorning the hilt of a sword, they were figurative versions edited and simplified to serve as signs. They never spoke for themselves, never offered up their complicated and divisive perspective on events, their perceived truths about the dangers and the necessities in the historical moment. They were timeless forms, outside history. The challenge is to make women subjects of, as well as images in, the history we write.[34]

The exclusion of women and slaves from the body of the people was not a part of the natural landscape of late antebellum Southern political culture but its most telling man-made feature. Historians pass over it at their own peril, for the most significant lines drawn in any political culture are the ones that mark the boundary between inside and out, between trusted members and persons held under sufficient suspicion that they had to be kept out. Any practice of political history focused exclusively on the enfranchised thus misses this essential dimension of the system. In the slave South, as in many other political societies known as democracies, lines were drawn so as to admit some and keep many more out of the privileges of membership. The condition of exclusion and disfranchisement cast both white women and slaves as referents for white men's status as citizens and voters; it established the men as freemen, as their contemporaries would have put it, and grounded their claims to manhood and whiteness. A freeman was neither a woman nor a slave, as Townsend put it, unwilling either to accept a submissive position within the Union or to wear the "federal collar."[35]

More so even than white women, enslaved men and women were unable to speak for themselves in the political crisis. As slaves they were, by definition, subjects for whom masters spoke. And indeed, it is startling to fathom the extent to which Southern whites (including nonslaveholders) internalized an instrumentalist view of slaves, regarding them as tools for use by them or their enemies. That slaves had no politics of their own—no strategic interests to pursue in the crisis—went without saying. It was the rare Unionist who suggested otherwise. As a result, during the secession crisis in the South, slaves were routinely figured in one of two ways: as bestial murderers and rapists, violent instruments of Black Republican rule; or as an element of strength, productive resources in an independent Southern nation. Either way, slaves' exclusion was central to the Confederate political project.

It is immensely difficult to understand just how completely white Southerners wrote off slaves in their political calculations. How, we ask, could they contemplate war without worrying about the possibilities it opened up to four million enslaved people? But so irrelevant were slaves to their thinking that William Yancey, the influential Alabama fire-eater, could recommend secession as a resolution of all the old struggles. It would augur, he said, a future with "no irrepressible conflict and no domestic enemy to incite our vigilance." Black Republicans—that is to say, white Northern men and not slaves—were the domestic enemy Yancey had in mind.[36]

Southerners of all political persuasions worried publicly and to good effect about the way abolitionists incited slaves to violence. One can readily discern the heavy weight of racial thinking about people of African descent. It was hard for white Southerners to think of slaves as "the enemy within." More than thirty years of proslavery training had mostly dissuaded them from that view. But the fear lurked just below the surface, and a benevolent paternalism always confronted a deeper antagonistic view. One can hear their conflicting emotions when white Southerners learned of John Brown's attempt to raise slave support in his raid on Harper's Ferry. One contributor to the *Charleston Mercury* opened with a brave denial that planters had anything to worry about at all—"they would as soon suspect their children of conspiring against their lives"—but descended quickly into a tortured consideration of circumstances in which slaves might indeed pose a threat. When "constantly tampered with," the writer fretted, faith in the Africans' good nature could prove a flimsy defense. "Our negroes are constantly tempted to cut our throats or pink us" with rifles. It was well to be prepared for the worst. Those "foot peddlers" from New York trolling the neighborhoods could "put the devil in the negros' heads," and could have been down there already "for all we know, arming the troops." The conflicted view of slaves' nature was palpable but controlled. Slaves were said to be, by nature, good, childlike, and loyal servants to their masters; they posed a danger only when white outsiders attempted to "rouse an ignorant people [by appealing] to their superstition and lust." Thus when secession dispensed with the Black Republicans, as Yancey promised, slaves would no longer represent a force of any sort.[37]

That slaves were incapable of independent action, devoid of political subjectivity, was an article of faith, communicated usually (as with white women) by grammatical default. Slaves had to be "incited" to violence by Yankees—this was Southern orthodoxy. But in November 1860, Joseph Brown, the Georgia governor, offered a rare consideration of slaves' capacity for political action. His ostensible purpose was to dispute the northern claim that in the event of secession the Southern people "would be in great danger from their slaves." He admitted that Northern spies might be able to incite small numbers to murder innocent women and children, but those would be rare. To prove the point, Brown listed slaves' considerable political disabilities in the South: "They have no means of communication with each other at a distance" as they could not read, write, travel on the railroads, or use the mail; "they have not been accustomed to claim or exercise political rights," and "few of them have any ambition beyond their present comfort and enjoyment." In the event of a plot, some would "immediately communicate it to their masters." Slaves lacked not only the means but the capacity for independent political action. For the more important (and comforting) fact, as Brown explained it, one "well known in Southern society, is that nine-tenths of them are truly and devotedly attached to their masters and mistresses, and would shed in their defence, their last drop of their blood." Like many others, then, Brown attributed to slaves a subjectivity constructed entirely from racial characteristics generated out of proslavery ideology. They "feel and recognize their inferiority as a race, and their dependence upon their owners for their protection and support." Racial thinking, ingrained by years of proslavery schooling, provided the only political analysis required.[38]

Slaves were resolutely racial subjects, not political ones, in the late antebellum South. The racialized slaves whom white Southerners conjured for themselves in the secession crisis were available to do whatever work white men required. Unionists, warning that "secession would be no holiday work," predicted war and even emancipation, and thus worried openly about slaves as ready tools of Black Republican armies. Jonathan Worth, a bitter North Carolina Unionist, thought secession insane if the preservation of slavery was the object. The first thing the Northern masses will do, he said, is "proclaim freedom to the slaves and arm them against us." In Unionist discourse, slaves often appeared in their old eighteenth-century guise as the enemy within.[39]

But secessionists saw it differently when their strategic intention was to maneuver their states out of the Union. They spoke in glowing terms of the resources to which the South would lay claim in its new career as a separate nation, among which they counted slaves prominently. And while they denied that secession would mean war, they talked gleefully about slaves as an element of strength in the unlikely event that war should come. "Both our wars with England and the whole history of the world, demonstrate that a slave population is an element of strength in war, and not of weakness and insecurity," the editor of the *Richmond Dispatch* declared confidently a few weeks before South Carolina troops fired on Sumter, the federal fort in Charleston Harbor. "Give us 4 millions of slaves under the management and discipline of Southern planters and southern men," a Virginia secessionist similarly boasted, "and they will give you more sinews of war, than ten millions of free men, agitated with the cares of families and the harassments of military duty." Slaves, with no commitments or interests except those of their masters, "would produce the means of subsistence" and strengthen Confederate military operations.[40]

African slaves in New World societies underwent a process of instrumentalization rather than simple suppression or exclusion. White Southerners were so deeply implicated in that process that they had great difficulty shaking an instrumentalist view of African American people even when confronted with evidence to the contrary. Rare, indeed, was the commonsense observation like that of Waitman Willey, a western Virginia Unionist, who, disparaging the secessionists' argument that slavery would be safer out of the Union, asked bluntly what the consequences of destroying the Union would be: "What then. The common national obligation [to return fugitive slaves] is destroyed. Will not the negro find out? The motives to flee across the line would be increased, because he would know that whenever he crosses that line he will be free." What Willey predicted was precisely what most white Southerners denied: that slaves had motives and interests entirely their own, channels of communication that kept them apprised of relevant developments, and allies whose help they knew to seek.[41] It would take Confederates a long time to learn those lessons.

When Southerners made the decision for secession or for Union in 1860 and 1861, they did so in the name of the people. But who were the people? In every utterance that question was posed and answered, by direction and indirection, express and customary proscription, and the endless reiteration of terms of address and inclusion. Identifying the people was the fundamental undertaking of the political culture in the crisis, recovering it a key task in writing its political history. What had emerged from the pivotal secession campaign in the American South was nothing less than a collective portrait of the people as a band of brothers. In June 1861, the Rubicon crossed, the governor of Virginia attempted to forestall treason to the new Confederate States of America by urging Unionists in the northwest of the state to abide by the sovereign people's decision for secession. Secession, he wrote, was a "right which no person should ever relinquish." Then, correcting himself, he crossed out "person" and in his own hand wrote "freeman." "The troops are posted at Huttonsville," he rallied the Union men. "Come with your own good weapons and meet them as brothers."[42]

The idea of the people and the nation as a band of brothers had a long provenance in Southern and American history. The original Union had been perceived as such. Robert M. T. Hunter, a Virginian and an ambivalent secessionist, fantasized about the restoration of the original Union, purified by a brief separation, as "united once more, brothers in war, and brothers in peace, ready to dominate the game of nations where the prizes are power and empire." Protagonists in the long political struggle that preceded the war, they saw the sections as brothers contending for power and distinction within the national family. One Southerner likened the North and the South to Spenser's *The Faerie Queene,* a poem featuring "two brothers, one of whom saw the soil of his inheritance daily wasting away and added to that of his rival, without the power of maintaining or restoring the original unity." The freemen were always a band of bothers —in the Union, in resistance to it, in the new nation secessionists imagined making. "Let us unite as a band of brothers in the now holy cause of PROMPT RESISTANCE," a Virginia secessionist urged his fellow voters before that state's election of delegates to the secession convention.[43] The fraternal conception of the nation significantly predated "the Brothers' War."

There was a mythic element to the idea of national origins and belonging as brotherhood. Schoolchildren learn the tale of brothers Romulus and Remus founding Rome, but the list goes on into modern times. Beyond its classical and early modern antecedents, the generational identity of the brothers—and the horizontal ties of membership it invoked—had special utility in a republican polity like that the secessionists attempted to build. Generationally speaking, the brothers were the sons, free white men newly arrived at manhood and looking to secure their claim to its privileges. In every version, Unionist and secessionist, that threshold of race, gender, and generation was pivotal to the political message. Southern Unionists leaned heavily on the model of filial piety, urging the sons to protect the heritage of liberty secured by revolutionary fathers. Secessionists had their version, urging young men to prove themselves "worthy sons of worthy sires" by securing the substance of the original constitutional liberty in a new national compact. But secessionists also plied more dangerous waters, making bellicose claims that a new generation of men was upon the stage, ready to oust the too-cautious fathers. The oedipal charge was intentional. "It is time for you to stand forth the *men* you claim to be," one editorial in the radical *Charleston Mercury* taunted, "to be known not by words but by deeds." Urging action as the proof of manhood, the writer powerfully evoked the sensitive coordinates of that gender and racial identity in the late antebellum slaveholding South. "We are young men," he prodded them. "We are ignorant, unwise, impolitic, devoid of judgment. We are told that we are 'boys' in these particulars. But *I* tell you that you *are* men."[44]

The brothers had something to prove and a new stage on which to prove it. Suggestions that the young were particularly prone to radicalism were made with regularity in time and place and have lingered on ever since. Both Henry Wise and Robert Hunter, Virginia political leaders, were gripped by old men's fears about the propriety of secession. Not so their sons, who stole the march on the fathers by taking extralegal action to break the political impasse in the state. Jokes abounded about young men "who are full of fight and . . . will never be satisfied until they get to fighting with somebody"; "elder citizens" occasionally wrote public thanks "to the young men . . . [who] are preparing to defend the rights and honor of Virginia."[45] Gender, race, and generation were not just described by the fraternal image of the nation; in the right historical moment they contributed to making a new nation.

The fraternal conception of the people resonated powerfully in the quickened political life of the South in the secession crisis because the voter and the man armed in defense of the state were, and always had been, one and the same. Freedom, Christopher Memminger, the secession commissioner from South Carolina, reminded the Virginia Assembly, was not a beautiful young girl but a bearded and scarred warrior. That image collapsed the figure of liberty into the soldier charged with its defense, merging politics and war in an entirely conventional way.[46] In nineteenth-century America, North and South alike, the voter had to have the attributes of the soldier. In that sense, the brothers were always poised to become the band of brothers.

The politics of secession in the American South, like so many other dramas of revolution and nation making, unfolded as a family romance, deploying metaphors of family relations to imagine political order, prescribe obligation, and evoke belonging. The story of the band of brothers animated the "affective charge implicit in the notion of fraternity" and tried to harness it alternately for secession, for union, and, potentially for war. In the end it posited a theory of politics and history as the transmission of liberty across generations in an exclusively male lineage. History was the story, one South Carolinian said, "of great heroes . . . martyrdom . . . triumph . . . the wise and the good, the gallant and the noble," which together represented the "monumental summits of the nation."[47]

In the American South in 1860 and 1861, as in many other places and times, people reached for images of brotherhood to represent the ideal political and national community. In the commonplace idea of the people as the band of brothers white Southerners set the terms of national belonging as they imagined them before the war. Secession, war, and nation making were to be the work of freemen, a band of brothers creating a white man's republic, dedicated to the proposition that all persons were not created equal. Secession was not the most difficult test of Confederates' political vision, but it was the first. It is surely worth noting that the vision of fraternal unity summoned was prescriptive, the unity itself ever illusive.

CHAPTER 2

The Brothers' War

THE SOUTHERN MOVEMENT for secession constituted the opening and critical first campaign of the American Civil War. It was also the first public trial of the Confederate founders' view of the political community that would constitute the slaveholders' republic. In secession the idea of the people as a band of brothers was put to the test and its limits sounded. For far from demonstrating the homogeneity of a white republic, the movement triggered a profound crisis of democratic legitimacy. War would test the Confederate republic and the people in ways unimaginable in the political crisis of 1860 to 1861. Still, it was a political drama arguably unparalleled in the whole history of the United States and every bit as compelling as the war that ensued. On its outcome hung the future of the slaveholders' new republic and, of course, the United States itself.

"Politics now is our epic poem," the South Carolinian Lawrence Keitt wrote as the crisis of the Union arrived.[1] Braggart though he was, he had a point. Few, then or now, would be tempted to dispute the enormity of the Southern undertaking or the difficulties of accomplishing it. To take fifteen slaveholding states out of the American Union and forge them into a new proslavery nation was indeed an epic task. Yet Keitt's elevated rhetoric hardly did justice to the low-down tactics of the movement. With outcomes bitterly contested in most states, secession campaigns involved a process of popular mobilization on a scale even Jacksonian democracy had not anticipated. The stakes were high; no mere majority would do. Nothing short of the unity of the people could legitimize separation from the United States of America. As a result, each state campaign was a struggle by politicians to win—or appear to win—the unanimous consent of the people. The battle to claim the mantle of the people was the essence of the political fight. "Unity" and "harmony" were the watchwords of politicians everywhere.[2]

The idea of the consent of the governed is one of those foundational beliefs of American political life, the kind more subscribed to than understood. As a historical proposition it is at once massive (embracing the story of American democracy) and elusive (Who are the governed? What constitutes legitimacy?). Confederate founders were deeply committed to it and faced the necessity of making it real: real enough, that is, to justify treason, to ground a claim to national independence, and maybe, if they were unlucky, to support a war. As a political project it was daunting.

It is difficult to exaggerate the amount and kind of politicking that went into the secession campaigns across the length and breadth of the slave states. No contemporary political machine, even with its army of pollsters and operatives, could have done more. Then, as now, party leaders and operatives pressed to get out the vote on their side and suppress it on the other. As one Unionist put it, politics required that he submit to his "master—democracy."[3] Politicians all over the South, but especially secessionists in the Lower South, attempted to cheat the master—by limiting the decisions and choices that went to the people, by the liberal use of executive power, and the muscular, even paramilitary, management of the candidates, ballots, and polls. But submit to these processes in the end they did—to the nerve-wracking necessity of turning the decision over to the voters and abiding by their decision. There was an irreducible contingency to the politics of secession. Campaigns were incredibly hard fought, and the results, virtually everywhere, far too close for comfort. In the end, secession in the American South was neither a popular democratic movement nor the accomplishment of a small slaveholding political elite. It was instead a hybrid thing, evincing at once the character of an administrative coup and of an open-fisted democratic brawl.[4] The consent of the governed, as it turned out, was not so much a shining ideal as a prize to be wrested from the enemy in a down-and-dirty political fight.

It all began in South Carolina, precisely as the proslavery advocates of Southern nationalism had long planned. South Carolina seceded from the United States of America on December 20, 1860. It was the first state to do so. It seceded in grand style, passing a resolution dissolving the Union by lunchtime on the first day of the state convention—unanimously and without debate. The roll recorded 159 Yeas and 0 Nays. Three days later the official ordinance of secession was reported out of committee, voted up unanimously again, this time to an even heftier 169 to 0. Five minutes later, copies of the ordinance were out on the Charleston streets, published as an extra by the leading city daily, the *Charleston Mercury,* and the state's delegation to Congress had been telegraphed; by dinnertime that day the men in Washington had resigned. New flags were run up the flagpoles in Charleston and immediately the *Mercury* began to report on proceedings in Washington under the heading "Foreign News." By 7 p.m. on the evening of December 20, before a public assembly of three thousand people, the ordinance of secession was signed and sealed and South Carolina was officially declared "an Independent Commonwealth." "We are out alone," as the diarist and senator's wife, Mary Chesnut, put it.[5]

Predictably the leaders of the state campaign preened, about their historical accomplishment in general and the degree of popular unity in particular. "Virtually an unanimous resolution . . . carried us out high and dry," the delegate John S. Palmer rejoiced to his wife from the convention two days after the initial resolution was voted up. "Today it is hoped we shall get the old Lady South Carolina out of the crowd without damaging her hoops or tearing her dress." The politicians credited the people. "The people have with unexampled unanimity resolved to secede and to dare any consequences that might follow their act," John Berkley Grimball, another planter delegate wrote in his diary. "It is a complete landsturm, a general rising of the people," the novelist and nationalist William Gilmore Simms crowed.[6] It was indeed a remarkable accomplishment.

South Carolina was the secessionists' dream scenario. But not only was the South Carolina script not easily replicated, the secession campaign there was far more interesting than the vote would suggest—and more telling of the stresses felt in every state that attempted to do the same thing. South Carolina did present uniquely suitable conditions for a popular secession movement. In the state where the ideological and political defense of slavery had been assiduously nurtured since the origin of the republic, fire-eaters really did hold sway by the fall of 1860. Slaveholding and plantation agriculture covered every corner of the state except for a small mountain region; there was a complete absence of two-party competition; planters were systematically overrepresented; and the legislature and its caucuses arrogated political power to themselves.[7]

But even under such ideal conditions, a deep worry about the loyalty of "the people" or "the democracy" drove secessionists' strategy. Planters were blunt about their intentions in secession. "All are united now with *few* exceptions in the belief that now a stand must be made for African slavery or it's forever lost," the planter William Grimball wrote to his sister just before the convention. But to unite the planter class behind secession as a means to perpetuate slavery was not enough. Even in South Carolina it had to be sold to yeoman and poor white voters who were, after all, the majority of the electorate. Like their counterparts everywhere, fire-eaters worried about what might happen when the people and especially the nonslaveholders were allowed to vote. Even that eminently powerful political elite had to have an electoral strategy, and so there, as elsewhere, they schemed: about how to delimit the popular vote, and how to win it.[8] South Carolina was the exception that proved the rule.

In South Carolina as elsewhere, one of the main tasks facing Southern nationalists was to manage the challenge issuing from nonslaveholding voters. Carolina's planter politicians had long faced the necessity of courting the people and found it distasteful. "Bumpkin after . . . Bumpkin on my hands as usual," whined U.S. Senator James Henry Hammond while at home at Redcliffe in 1858. His correspondent and colleague, Congressman William Porcher Miles, had to be reminded not to neglect his constituents even when he was up for reelection: "I know that you despise all this sort of thing—any attempt at . . . seeking popular favor," one of his backers told him, "but we can't have things just the way we want them . . . in this out of joint world." By the late antebellum period, the antidemocratic principles of slavery were in full flower, and concern about the tyranny of the majority was politics as usual in John C. Calhoun's home state. Planters routinely denounced the general suffrage of white men as "mob-oc-racy." Washington bequeathed us a republic, and "Mr. Jefferson swap'd it off for a 'Democracy,'" one David Gavin railed in 1858. Like more than a few secessionists, he wished for a new Southern nation and "no general suffrage." Politicians might rage about having to court the support of the people. But that didn't change the necessity. David Gavin put it in his inimitable style: "The politicians must humbug the democracy or the people."[9] They did their level best.

Worry about nonslaveholders' loyalty to the planters' regime was a steady theme in South Carolina politics since at least the 1830s. It had long undergirded the resistance with which low-country planter politicians (the "chivalry," they were called) met their upcountry peers' demands for a more equitable system of representation. Unlike other Southern states, South Carolina apportioned representation under the federal three-fifths formula and not the "white basis" system that just counted white population. The counting of property and white population inflated the power of the low-country districts where slaves were most numerous. It was this "Carolina system" that "made us the conservative people that we are." A "system of rotten boroughs and aristocratic incubi," Hammond called it not uncritically.[10] The issue was alive and well in 1860.

As fire-eaters readied for the big campaign of 1859 and 1860, concern about nonslaveholders hit new heights. To prevail they had to eliminate all sources of division: among political elites still divided over a national versus a separatist strategy to defend slavery; between the slaveholders and the people whose resentment of the planter stranglehold on power bubbled steadily below the surface in electoral politics. In tight races, even planter candidates would play the class card, bidding for votes by saying they stood for the "the right of the people" to elect members of the state's electoral college, a privilege the legislature retained in South Carolina. Even fire-eaters, as radical secessionists were called, could recklessly stir up class antagonism, as a zealous minority did in 1860 when they moved to reopen the African slave trade. They presented it as a democratizing measure (more white men could buy slaves) and talked ominously about slaveholders as "an aristocracy of possession" and the dangers to the institution posed by the "twenty to one" who owned no slaves. All of these tactics were bids for the nonslaveholders' vote. But nothing caused more of a popular uproar than the law passed in 1857 to toughen penalties for white men caught trading (illegally) with slaves, making a second conviction punishable by whipping. "This is all the people seem to care about," one worried observer wrote, that white men not be whipped like slaves. The radical elite were apoplectic about the damage to the cause, worrying openly about how all such issues were "calculated to widen the breach between the slaveholder and non-slaveholder and do no practical good."[11]

It was precisely those kind of dangerous divisions that fire-eaters, like their counterparts elsewhere, had to contend with in the elections of 1860. As fire-eaters formulated their strategy for the secession campaigns, the state's nonslaveholding majority were a powerful spectral presence. Daniel Hamilton, the U.S. marshal for Charleston, put the matter bluntly in private correspondence to Congressman William Porcher Miles. "Mark what I tell you," he wrote Miles, "when the battle comes in earnest, when talking is at an end and we find ourselves fairly embarked on a contest which will shake the world, you will find an element of great weakness in our own non-slaveholding population." It was a grave mistake to have brought the contest "upon the question of slavery" to a government controlled by a popular majority. "Think you that 360,000 slaveholders, will dictate terms for 3,000,000 of non-slaveholders at the South.—I fear not, I mistrust our own people more than I fear all the efforts of the abolitionists." Hamilton's fear that secession had been staked out on the wrong ground found powerful echo in the Upper South, a place he clearly—unlike most of his peers—already had in mind. In North Carolina, C. B. Harrison, fretting about how to carry the masses, declared that "secession in favor of slavery alone won't do." In December 1860 he eerily predicted that secessionists would prevail only when the doctrine of federal force was introduced and the issue changed from slavery "to popular liberty."[12] Such anxiety about the plain folk was not often openly acknowledged in South Carolina, but Hamilton's view of nonslaveholders as the weakest link figured centrally in fire-eaters' aggressive propaganda campaign and electoral strategy in the critical fall of 1860.

Nowhere in the South had secession been pursued as long or as purposefully as in South Carolina. Fire-eaters had made their first attempt in 1851, failing to unite even their own state and suffering a sound defeat in the yeoman-majority upcountry. That failure certainly suggested a wariness about radical action among the great mass of citizens that loomed large on the second try.[13] In 1860, reluctant to risk isolation again, they tried to get Virginia to take the lead, calculating that the alarm raised by radical abolitionist John Brown's raid on Harper's Ferry in October 1859 made it a safe bet; then they tried to talk some other Lower South state into it.[14] When those tactics failed they prepared themselves for another try, this time making a fetish of unity within their own state.

A large part of the fire-eaters' strategy in 1860 involved the destruction of the national Democratic Party—and its powerful contingent of moderates in the state—as a viable vehicle for protecting slavery in the Union. When the party collapsed, finally (and fittingly) in Charleston at the 1860 national convention, the last institutional alternative to a secessionist and Southern nationalist political party was eliminated. "So far, so good," Robert Barnwell Rhett telegraphed William Porcher Miles from the convention. By the summer of 1860, the vast majority of the state's planter politicians, including the powerful leader of the National Democratic faction, James L. Orr, were on board for secession, and together the old moderates and the longtime "ultras" turned to the last task—to bring "the people" up to the mark.[15]

At the center of their strategy was a highly orchestrated effort to appeal directly to nonslaveholders by casting the decision over secession as one in which their future (and not just that of the planters) was at stake. To that end, old moderates-turned-fire-eaters built their own propaganda machine, an organization called the "1860 Association," formed in September 1860 by the Charleston merchant, Robert Gourdin, and a handful of men from the wealthiest planter families in the low country. They were a propaganda group functioning as a revolutionary club. The purpose, they boldly announced, was to prepare the South in the event of the "accession of Mr Lincoln and the Republican Party to power," and, specifically, to prepare, print, and distribute tracts and pamphlets "designed to awaken" the people of the slave states to a conviction of their danger and to urge the necessity of resisting Northern and federal aggression. The 1860 Association aimed, that is, to unify the public opinion of the state and the South behind secession as the proper response to the election of a "Black Republican" president.[16] By the fall of 1860 every newspaper in the state, including the traditionally moderate *Charleston Courier* had fallen in line. The Association published and distributed all over the South some 166,000 pamphlets, all within the few months surrounding the presidential election. Tellingly enough, they specifically commissioned a pamphlet on the problem of the nonslaveholding voter.

Tract No. 5, James D. B. DeBow's *The Interest in Slavery of the Southern Nonslaveholder,* met the challenge head-on, offering an aggressive argument about how nonslaveholders "were even more deeply interested than any other in the maintenance of our institutions and in the success of the movement now inaugurated . . . [for] the political independence of the South." The value and dignity of white men's labor in a slave society formed the crux of DeBow's appeal: "No white man at the South serves another as a body servant, to clean his boots, wait on his table, and perform the menial services of his household. His blood revolts against this and his necessities would never drive him to it." But just for good measure he finished with a threat, offering a dystopian image of the post-emancipation South as a scene of sexual and racial degradation that the rich white man would escape by emigration, but that nonslaveholders and their families would have to endure. DeBow's pamphlet was a virtual handbook for politicians and editors crafting the populist appeal, and it was recycled heavily through the fall of 1860 in local newspapers and speeches.[17]

In South Carolina there were two critical elections, the first in October for state legislators (the men who would decide whether to hold a secession convention) and the second in December for the election of delegates to the secession convention. In the days immediately preceding both, appeals to nonslaveholders were ratcheted up. Planter politicians, driven out to make the case to yeoman farmers and poor white men at muster fields, on courthouse steps, and in local country stores, addressed them ostentatiously as "freemen," stressed the "deep and vital interests" of every man, nonslaveholder as well as slaveholder, urged them to fight for self-protection and invariably called out some version of the question: "Are you afraid? Will you adopt the posture of submission?" In a speech to the Edisto Island Vigilant Association in October 1860, John

Townsend, a very wealthy Colleton planter and one of the converted National Democrats, pointedly asked his audience, "Where are the white nonslaveholders of Hayti?" before proceeding to conjure the poor whites' future of racial war, murder, poison, rape, and ultimately "extermination . . . or amalgamation" under a Black Republican regime.[18]

If it sounds sexual, it was. Here, as in so many other cases before and after, the political impulse was to use the violation of women and the home to drum up support for war. Secessionists had their own form of atrocity propaganda, and it included the same emphasis on the brutality of the enemy and the safety of women and the family advanced by modern liberal regimes like Britain in justifying war against Germany in World War One by reference to the rape of Belgium. In the majority-black districts of the South Carolina low country, the potent and linked racial and sexual threat posed to yeoman households by Lincoln's election was routinely advanced as sufficient cause for secession. It was in this context that propagandists like DeBow and Townsend strategically evoked the rape and murder of vulnerable women at the hands of black and Black Republican beasts. The only question, according to planter politicians, was: "Whether we should live as slaves or as freemen." For that reason Townsend declared that there were no people in the South who "abhor Abolitionists more than the non-slaveholders or who are more ready to resist their machinations." They "[are] one in sympathy, interest and feelings. They have equal rights, and privileges—one fate."[19] In the end, it was not the slaveholders' regime but the freemen's that secessionists declared at risk of invasion. Declarations of nonslaveholders' loyalty were a dead giveaway that politicians couldn't count on it in the fall of 1860.

The unity of the body politic to which fire-eaters aspired was pursued through strategies that combined popular political mobilization and tight (some said "oligarchic") control of the electoral process. The former, of course, was necessary to get out the vote. In that effort South Carolina's radical clique proved themselves adept, innovative, and entirely unscrupulous. The centerpiece of the strategy was a highly centralized campaign to draw yeoman and poor white voters into their networks through paramilitary organizations created for the purpose. Onto the established military system of beat districts, which organized all male citizens into state militia units and slave patrols, they grafted a network of explicitly secessionist vigilant and Minute Men associations, armed organizations of local "freemen." It was tactically brilliant. Militia districts had long provided the structure of local politics in South Carolina—muster fields were every rural man's political hall—and militia units had nurtured many of the personal loyalties and associations on which candidates counted. But along with providing immediate access to every yeoman farmer and poor white voter in the state, the new associations meant planter politicians approached them in their identity as citizen-soldiers, astutely harnessing white men's common privilege as arms-bearing citizens (in a world of slaves) to their own secessionist ends.[20] So even as Southern congressmen packed pistols inside their coats on the floor of the U.S. Senate and walked the halls of Congress in imminent anticipation of gunplay, ordinary citizens at home prepared for the confrontation over Lincoln's election by turning their neighborhoods into armed camps.[21]

Violence was politics as usual in 1860, the fire-eaters' electoral strategy a paramilitary one. Vigilant committees, like the one John Townsend addressed in Edisto, were organized at public meetings called by the local elite. The initial justification was the alarm raised by Brown's raid on Harper's Ferry. But by the spring of 1860, vigilant committees and Minute Men associations could be found in every parish and district in the state. Founded ostensibly to "guard and protect the safety of our homes," they elected committees of vigilantes to police the community, punishing not just slaves and strangers but, as one association's bylaws put it, "persons not strangers or now residents." Like the other groups of men empowered to accuse, harass, brutally beat, whip, shave, tar and feather, run out of town on a rail, and lynch, these forces contributed greatly to the state of imminent danger they were ostensibly formed to allay. Vigilantes in their very existence dramatized the dangers of invasion about which poor white and yeoman voters had been warned. "I am for trusting no one here on earth but ourselves," "Vigilance" proclaimed in the *Charleston Mercury* in November 1859. So fearsome were the committees throughout the countryside that some elites (including those who initiated them) tried to shut them down, fearing that too much control had gone to the lesser sorts. "We are under a reign of terror and the public mind exists in a panic," the planter William Campbell Preston admitted. Not for nothing did the leading abolitionist publisher William Lloyd Garrison write about "The New Reign of Terror in the Slaveholding States."[22]

But the political utility of the vigilant committees was indisputable precisely because of their success in drawing the state's yeoman farmers and poor whites into participation in the fire-eaters' campaign. When the "citizens" of St. Peter's Parish in the rural low country near Beaufort responded to the call for a meeting at a country store in January 1860 to form a committee, two local leaders, a minister and a militia captain, gave the speeches, but more than half of the "gentlemen" elected to the committee were yeoman farmers. And when they rode out to discipline their unreliable or heterodox neighbors, it was yeoman farmers who led.[23]

Using the traditional form of the militia beat company, fire-eaters managed to build a massive political network. The Minute Men companies represented, if anything, a more overt bid for the nonslaveholders' vote than vigilant associations. They formed, tellingly enough, on October 3, the very eve of legislative elections in the state. Their political purpose was acknowledged in the original Constitution drawn up in Columbia by Robert Barnwell Rhett and James Hopkins Adams. In it, every district in the state was called on to prepare for immediate resistance to the election of a Black Republican president by forming volunteer infantry and cavalry companies. A blue cockade would signify membership; activities would include drilling and parading day and night. In the critical last few months of 1860, companies of Minute Men shadowed political events large and small. When the newly elected state legislature met in Charleston in November to decide whether to call a secession convention, armed companies of Minute Men drilled outside the hall, issuing threatening resolutions and demanding decisive action when legislators hesitated. They also exerted a muscular presence at public meetings in the countryside to nominate delegates to the state convention in December, insisting, as in Charleston, that they would vote only for those who favored immediate separate state secession.[24] Their armed presence made it pretty clear that secession and consent were a lot less hazardous to the health than opposition and Unionism of any sort in the fall of 1860.

Popular mobilization was clearly not the only purpose of the various paramilitary political associations. Indeed, the paramilitary organizations worked in two ways simultaneously: as outreach, mobilizing yeoman and poor white voters to make the fire-eaters' cause their own; and as suppression, threatening physical violence and exile to those still disposed to dissent. The newspapers were filled with accounts of the committees' bloody discipline of white men, although charges of voter intimidation surfaced only later, when it was safe to report. Four or five years before the secession elections, "men could speak their sentiments . . . freely and fought about it," one low-country resident recalled after the war. But by 1860 a man "with a public reputation for unionism . . . would not have been allowed to live here." "We had to be very quiet," Joseph Brandt, one of those Unionists, would recall. "We were too few in numbers and the secessionists were too overbearing." Slaves knew the few Union men in their area who could be trusted, but the white men and women oftentimes did not know one another. So frightening was the surveillance that men claimed they were afraid not to vote: the "feeling ran so high," one Beaufort farmer remembered, that he "could not abstain from voting." Because there was no Union ticket, he put a blank vote in the box. Lawrence McKenzie left his neighborhood on election day "to keep from voting," he said, "and from being annoyed by those who would vote for it and would be after [me] to do the same." "Well, Lawrence," his neighbors said when he returned, "we have today voted South Carolina out of the Union and you did not help us."[25]

In October and December 1860, South Carolina voters went to the polls in a climate of political terror, surrounded by armed companies of men and hordes of citizens all wearing the blue cockade. The harmony of the body politic about which fire-eaters boasted was the product, in part, of that black shirt campaign. But it was as much administrative coup as open-fisted brawl. It was quite true, as more than one farmer would later charge, that voters simply "could not vote for the union" in South Carolina, that there was "no opposition ticket in this section."[26] The management (and constraint) of popular democracy was a matter of pride among the political elite and was key to planter politicians' insistence on restricting the number of offices put to popular election in the state. Unlike their counterparts elsewhere, South Carolina voters did not choose their governor, United States senators, state senators, many local officeholders, or, crucially, the members of the state's electoral college. In South Carolina the General Assembly arrogated that prerogative to itself.

South Carolina voters thus did not cast votes in the presidential election of 1860, and left no indication, as in other states, of pockets of dissent in blocs of votes for the Democrat Stephen Douglas, Constitutional Unionist John Bell, or as in Virginia, for Lincoln. That would have been impossible. There was no Douglas campaign organization in South Carolina, not to mention Bell or Lincoln organizations, and thus no opposition parties or opposition tickets onto which a Unionist party or faction could graft itself. The state legislators all cast their vote for Breckinridge, the extreme  Southern rights candidate, as expected. The key election at which "the people's" views would become known was not the presidential election but the October 8 election of delegates to the state legislature (charged to decide about calling a secession convention), and the December 6 election of delegates to the state secession convention thereby authorized.[27]

For fire-eaters these elections were "the great agony." Secessionists did everything in their power to limit the unpredictability of developments at the polls, to circumvent the democratic process by tight control of the ballot itself. Ideally they wanted to eliminate not just party contests—they had long ago done that—but opposition itself. A week or so before the October election the editor of the *Beaufort Enterprise* laid out the strategy, warning local leaders to shut down the kind of populist sideshows witnessed in recent races in the district. It was critical, he said, that gentlemen in the heat of the contest not be tempted to kowtow to the nonslaveholders and open up dangerous divisions of opinion. The key was for the districts to "call public meetings, and select such men to represent them as will render all opposition vain," that is, to run only one candidate. South Carolina "never had impending so important an election," he emphasized. Nonslaveholders were a problem. The solution was to not consult them. The voters must not be given any choice.[28]

In the legislative elections in October and again in December, secessionists adopted a strategy of nominating candidates at mass public meetings where political leaders urged single "fusion" tickets to present a united front. Sometimes they failed and districts had more than one ticket or slate of candidates, thus offering a choice between those pledged to immediate secession upon Lincoln's election and those with a stated preference to move only in cooperation with other Lower South states. Even the fire-eaters could not control the process entirely. But the number of uncontested elections was high, more than half by some estimates. "This thing of walking around the track alone is rather dull," one old politician wrote William Porcher Miles. Dull, but effective. The legislature returned by the October elections was "tremendously out and out secession." And the convention delegates elected on December 10 were almost all publicly on record as supporting immediate and separate secession. As in other Lower South states (except Texas), fire-eaters made sure that the ordinance of secession was not submitted to the vote of the people. There might, indeed, have been some sentiment left for the Union. But there was no public advocacy for it, no party that represented it, and no way for ordinary voters to register dissent.[29] In South Carolina the vaunted harmony of the body politic registered the circumvention or preemption of the democratic process as much as, or more than, the consent of the people to secession.

Even the openly secessionist governor used his executive authority to preempt the democratic process. William Gist had been in league with the most rabid separate-state secessionists since at least August 1860. And although the formal power in his hands hardly matched that of the legislative oligarchy, he played a crucial role in one regard. By clandestine communication with other Southern governors, Gist offered assurances, as early as October, that his state would secede immediately upon Lincoln's election and solicited their commitment to follow. More than a month before Lincoln was elected, before even his own state's election of legislators tested the temperature of the people or the legislature called a convention to deliberate on secession, Governor Gist presented secession in South Carolina as a fait accompli. Operating without any mandate from "the people," Democratic governors thus colluded on secession to make it happen. Such executive assumption was critical in all of the Deep South states (or those, unlike Texas, with Democratic Party governors) but especially in South Carolina, where the only resistance that remained to out-and-out secession was offered by men who called themselves cooperationists. With the requisite assurances from governors of Mississippi, Florida, Alabama, and Georgia in hand, Gist met the incoming legislature with the message that "the long awaited cooperation was near at hand."

Adeptly undercutting the forces of opposition and delay in the legislature, he recast a risky decision for separate state secession as the much safer cooperative venture the moderates sought.[30]

But even in South Carolina, even after all the violence, collusion, and suppression of public debate, unity eluded the fire-eaters. When the first vote was taken in the legislature on the question of holding a secession convention at the earliest possible date (with elections scheduled for December 6)—meaning that the state would make its decision before any other Southern state—fourteen upcountry legislators balked. Not a powerful opposition, to be sure, but it took guts nonetheless. Failing even in South Carolina to achieve perfect unity, secessionists turned to fabricating it instead, insisting on a revote to get the unanimous decision for a secession convention that went down in the books: 117 Yeas and 0 Nays.[31] Not for the last time in the secession crisis was "harmony" on display as a method of enforcing internal discipline. In the clandestine use of his executive power, Governor Gist vanquished what was left of the moderates within the state's political leadership, leaving the fire-eaters' in full command of the field.

"The Tea has been thrown overboard, the revolution of 1860 has been initiated," the *Charleston Mercury* roared in delight when news of Lincoln's election reached South Carolina on November 5. As the voters went to the polls in December to elect their delegates to the secession convention, there was really very little left to decide, and even less to sustain opposition to the juggernaut of separate state secession. By that point, as the planter William Grimball put it, the "cooperation party is *extinct*. It has no leaders it has no voters." With Governor Gist calling for a public day of fasting, prayer, and humiliation to give the state "one heart and one mind" in its hour of difficulty, and citizens besieged on all sides by calls for unity and assurances that other states would quickly follow their lead, white men, although in strikingly small numbers, went to the polls once again on December 6. They voted up a convention full of men, once moderate, but now virtually unified around the immediate secession of South Carolina from the Union.[32]

Secession was a brilliant campaign, designed and executed to produce the consent of the governed to the degree required for the democratic legitimacy of the new Palmetto Republic. In South Carolina the unity of the people, which is to say the voters, around secession from the Union had been accomplished. The yeomen and poor white men who cast the majority of the votes had, apparently, been convinced. It had been a major undertaking. And it took every trick in the political book to pull it off.

After South Carolina went out, the secession movement advanced rapidly. Six more Lower South states voted themselves out of the Union by February 1. But then it stalled. For five long months, from December 1860 to mid-April 1861, the remaining eight slaveholding states of the Upper South either refused secession outright or were locked in paralytic political struggle over it. Four of them—Kentucky, Missouri, Maryland, and Delaware—would never secede. Four more—Virginia, North Carolina, Tennessee, and Arkansas—would, but only after Abraham Lincoln called for troops to put down the rebellion in the Deep South.[33] War won the argument there. In the Upper South unity was entirely elusive.

The contrast between the course of events in the Upper and Lower South is certainly striking, and it has made secession in the Lower South seem a foregone conclusion.[34] But the question of consent and popular support was not entirely an Upper South affair. In some of the Lower South states, too, immediate state secessionists, though ultimately successful, faced considerable difficulty in accomplishing solid majorities, never mind the desired unanimity. In some, things went pretty smoothly and secessionists racked up respectable delegate majorities in the state secession conventions and in the critical votes on the ordinances of secession, the legal instruments that dissolved the ties to the government of the United States. But in a number of other states the battle over the will of the people was open, direct, and violent, the divisions and fraudulent attempts to conceal them so apparent that in the end nothing resembling democratic legitimacy could be claimed.

In Mississippi, Florida, and to a lesser extent Louisiana, things did go smoothly. All three were safely in the hands of Democratic and openly secessionist governors, and although Louisiana had divided seriously in the presidential election in November, by January all three states assembled conventions with comfortable majorities pledged to immediate and separate state secession: 66 percent of Mississippi counties returned immediatist delegates, and in Florida and Louisiana immediatists held about 60 percent and 64 percent of the seats, respectively. There was opposition to the radical straight-out position in the conventions, coming in Mississippi, for example, from Whiggish planters in the very rich delta counties, from hill country yeomen, and from town and city merchants worried about access to Northern credit. A loose coalition of opposition forces—the "do nothings," as they were dubbed in Mississippi (in contrast to the secessionist "do somethings")—collected under the moderate banner of "cooperation," and held out for action in conjunction with other Southern states. In all three states cooperationists tried the same delaying tactics of proposing that Southern conventions seek security for slavery in the Union and secession only in conjunction with other Southern states, and, especially, demanding that the convention's decision be referred back to the people for ratification.[35]

But in all three states they were easily pushed aside and the states quickly propelled into secession, precisely as the moderates charged. If we wait for a specific act of Republican aggression against slavery as cooperationists advised, Governor Perry of Florida said, "our fate will be that of the whites in Santo Domingo." Delay was the one thing immediatists would not brook. Secession assumed an onrushing quality. James Lusk Alcorn, a leading Mississippi moderate, reached for an equestrian metaphor: "The epithet of coward and submissionist will be everywhere applied to us" if they persisted in opposing the move, he wrote of the convention in Jackson. "I and others agreeing with me determined to seize the wild and maddened steed by the mane and run with him *for a time.* We voted for secession and signed the ordinance."[36]

To be sure, the usual circumstances of radical victory were in evidence: the martial mobilization, intimidation of voters, and a climate of political repression created by vigilant and Minute Men organizations everywhere; the demagogic racial and sexual appeals to nonslaveholders; tight control of the electoral apparatus; and, probably critical, state governors' clandestine use of executive power to usurp the democratic process. Governor Pettus of Mississippi was tireless in his efforts: lining up the state's congressional delegation behind a binding commitment to immediate secession; communicating with other radical governors to secure guarantees of common action and then advertising them; using his position as executive to suspend specie payments on the state banks and as commander in chief to appropriate funds for military hardware, begin troop buildup, and generate a sense of the imminence of invasion. As early as December 1860, working on Pettus's orders, Jefferson Davis, the U.S. senator from Mississippi, was scouring Washington, D.C., for arms, buying up every Maynard Rifle (about five hundred) to be found in the city.[37]

Louisiana governor T. O. Moore was even more proactive. On January 3, 1861, he ordered the seizure of federal forts on the lower Mississippi River, the barracks and arsenals at Baton Rouge and Fort Pike on the Rigolets—all of this weeks before the state's secession convention assembled, before even the election of delegates. Like Gist, Moore forecast the outcome of a democratic process not yet unfolded.[38] A preemptive use of executive power over the military—something of a coup—his actions significantly changed the political situation on the ground.

Nowhere in the Lower South outside of South Carolina were ordinances of secession passed unanimously. But in Mississippi, Florida, and Louisiana, after a series of votes that demonstrated the weakness of the opposition, significant proportions of cooperationists jumped on the tear-away steed, and convention delegates voted decisively for secession: 84 to 15 in Mississippi; 62 to 7 in Florida; 113 to 17 in Louisiana. In Texas, where things played out differently because of Governor Sam Houston's unmovable opposition to secession and because the convention vote had to be ratified directly by the people, the vote for secession was still 166 to 8.[39] To the extent that the conventions represented the will of the people, their consent in those states had been solicited and secured for secession.

It could not have been more different in Georgia. So deep were the divisions of voters there, so inconclusive the democratic process, that the governor suppressed the electoral results in total violation of state law. Three months later, with the state safely out of the Union, probably thinking no one would notice, Governor Brown cooked the numbers, retroactively claiming a slim 54 percent majority for secession. Until the 1970s those were the numbers historians used. But the likely result was far, far closer.[40] It is an interesting story about what legitimacy requires—or what will do in a pinch. All through the autumn and into January 1861 when the Georgia secession convention met, electoral processes, far from settling questions about the course the state should steer, seemed only to raise more. In the presidential election in November after a bitter campaign, Breckinridge Democrats managed to win only 48 percent of the popular vote, while the Bell Constitutional Unionists took 40 percent; even Stephen Douglas's regular National Democrats took a good 10 percent. It was a troubling political index, to be sure, especially for those who wanted to take the state straight out. Little wonder, then, that Governor Brown hedged his bets in early November. With Lincoln's election mere hours from official confirmation, he equivocated, sending a special message to the state house of representatives offering outrage at Northern acts, demagogic appeals to "the free white population," but no recommendation for secession without the cooperation of all fifteen slave states. Brown would come around by December, but before he did the citizens of that state (and everyone else) would have a full-throated airing of views. In Georgia, that included not just immediate secessionists and cooperationists but a core group of prominent conditional Unionists and a handful of unconditional ones as well.[41]

In Georgia the decision to secede was highly contested every step of the way, and unity was not the upshot. The decision to call for a state convention was made by the legislature, but only after two weeks of vigorous debate in the legislature itself and in a virtuoso debate between political leaders of all stripes in the hall of representatives in Milledgeville, the state capital. Here the parties were evenly matched. Indeed, some think the Unionists gained the upper hand. In their speeches, Alexander Stephens (still a Unionist), Hershel Johnson, and Benjamin Hill expressed an ebullient faith in the people: in their ability to discern the benefits of Union and dangers of war. "Secession is no holiday work," as the Unionist Benjamin Hill famously said.[42]

The secessionists' uneasiness in going before the people was palpable by contrast. Thomas R. R. Cobb begged the legislature to enact secession by legislative fiat because he was afraid to face the decision of the people in convention elections: "Wait not till the grog shops and cross roads shall send up a discordant voice from a divided people," he begged the legislators, telling them to make the decision themselves. "I am afraid of

Conventions," the radical Robert Toombs yelled out in the middle of Alexander Stephens's oration. It was quite a spectacle. As Unionists struck a reasonable note of wait and see, celebrating the "majesty of the people" at every turn, secessionists delivered a couple of the most inflammatory appeals to the people of the entire Lower South campaign. Worrying openly about divisions among the people—"Suppose we are equally divided. A small majority will decide the question?" Cobb asked—Tom Cobb and Governor Joseph Brown responded by trying to bully voters, and especially nonslaveholding ones, into manly resistance with images of political submission, servile insurrection, rape, sodomy, murder, gory heads, and bloody fingers on mountain yeomen's lintel posts.[43] When, on November 20, the Georgia legislature finally did call for a state convention to deliberate on secession and for election of delegates on January 2, secessionists burst out of Milledgeville onto the campaign trail, to seek out and conquer the opposition.

They had reason to worry. A raft of resolutions written by citizens in public meetings in mid-November and sent to their representatives to be read in the legislature suggest that the matter was still wide open. Virtually every possible position was argued, from Greene County's angry Unionist denunciation of the war "madness" of radical secessionist politicians to Fayette County's immediate secessionist demand to "recognize Georgia as our country" and resume the powers delegated to the federal government. In between there were many like the citizens of Habersham County who, denouncing Lincoln's election by "Negro" votes, wanted a convention of Southern states to defend constitutional citizenship "in the Union or in independence out of it." Secessionists out on the hustings sent panicked reports to their compatriots about the state of public opinion. "By all means come directly to Athens," Tom Cobb wrote his brother Howell, who had just resigned from President Buchanan's cabinet to work for the secession campaign. "We have trouble above here and no one but yourself can quell it." When Howell Cobb arrived in the upcountry in late December on a speaking tour, he was worried too: "I found the union or *submission* sentiment *overwhelming*," he wrote his wife.[44] When voters went to the polls on January 2, Cobb and his radical friends could only hold their breath.

They would wait a long time for the result. On January 16, when delegates elected to the state convention hoofed it into Milledgeville for the first meeting, they still didn't know the outcome and could only guess the distribution of forces in the delegation gathering. On the third day of the convention, one cooperationist delegate tried to pass a resolution requiring the governor to release the election data as the law required. He was put off. The delegate persisted. The next day he repeated the resolution, this time meeting the firm resistance of secessionists, who voted for an indefinite postponement of the issue. Not until mid-April would Governor Brown release the election results. By that time it was moot, and cooperationists of all stripes were left to judge the strength of their numbers by a variety of test votes in the convention itself. One critical vote came on the third day, when cooperationists united against a proposed ordinance of secession. that showed them to be a major, but not majority, presence in the convention: their proposal to confederate with other Southern states to "secure our rights in the Union if possible, or to protect them, out of the Union if necessary" went down to defeat 133 to 164. Secessionists had a critical edge. The first test vote on secession they proposed passed by 166 to 130, and the final one, after secessionists' dominance had been amply demonstrated, passed 208 to 89. But clearly opposition to immediate secession in Georgia was considerable—even with four other states already out of the Union and cooperation already at hand. Judging by the votes, cooperationists had about 45 percent of the delegates, making claims of unity of any sort a joke. Even at the bitter end, when they knew they couldn't win, 30 percent of the delegates refused to bend to secession, far higher resistance than was offered in any other but one Lower South state.[45]

But even that does not tell the whole story of Georgia's "paralyzing indecision" in the critical secession elections of 1861. For one month later, when he did finally release the election results, Governor Brown claimed that at the convention election delegates pledged to immediate secession had taken a comfortable 57 percent lead at the polls. The people, in other words, had given secessionists a mandate. But it turns out that Brown cooked the numbers. One careful recount now accepted as definitive confirms that Brown counted in the secession camp men who had been elected on cooperationist tickets. Using contemporary newspaper reports of poll results and political affiliations derived from convention voting lists, the most accurate estimate indicates that cooperationists had won just over 50 percent of the votes.[46] The votes cast on January 2 suggest that the people had rejected the secessionist solution by a tiny majority. In Georgia, there was no mandate for secession.

There was one final part to the Georgia drama. Embarrassed to go on the historical record with their evidence of division so clear for all to see, secessionists managed to push through a resolution binding all convention delegates to sign the ordinance of secession, explicitly "including those who voted against" it. Presented, threateningly, as "a pledge of the unanimous determination of this Convention to sustain and defend the State, in this her chosen remedy," the resolution abrogated the opposition's last right to refuse consent—coerced unity, so to speak. The implied threat became explicit six days later when, as one of its first legal acts, the newly independent republic of Georgia wrote and passed a new treason statute that defined treason as, among other things, enduring allegiance to the Union. It carried the death penalty.[47] By January 26, 1861, political dissent was a capital offense in Georgia. By suppression, fraud, and coercion the secessionist politicians had fabricated a majority for secession where the democratic process had failed to produce it.

Questions about secession's legitimacy persisted in Georgia. They were never entirely dispelled. Throughout the spring of 1861, watchdogs, particularly from "upper Georgia," would write Governor Brown alerting him to pockets of treason in their neighborhoods. Many in his section were finding fault with the establishment of the Southern government, J. R. Earle wrote Brown in late February, still justifying the North and blaming the crisis on "Our big Men." All but inviting charges under the new treason statute—"there are those in Upper Georgia who would give aid and comfort to the enemy"—he wanted to police and disfranchise political dissenters. Another alerted Brown to persistent Unionism in his neighborhood and charged that it had metamorphosed, in the heat of the secession campaign, from antisecession and antiplanter sentiment into "anti-nigger slavery." One detailed the pointed refusal of a group of justices of the peace in Morgantown, all of whom had run on the Union ticket, to take and administer the new oath of office required by the republic of Georgia renouncing allegiance to the United States of America.[48]

In Georgia, it's fair to say, a significant question remains about whether the people—meaning the majority of the white male voters—ever gave their consent to secession and new nationhood. In Alabama, by contrast, questions about democratic legitimacy were directly and repeatedly engaged from the outset and, in fact, constituted the central theme of the fierce struggle waged over the immediate and separate secession of the state. From the time in late September 1860 when the governor, A. B. Moore, sought a $200,000 military appropriations bill, through December when he seized the federal forts and arsenals and suspended state banks' specie payment, and right into the secession convention in Montgomery in early January 1861, a combined opposition of cooperationists and Unionists fought him and his "straight-out" allies every step of the way. From the opening bell of the state convention they came out swinging, resisting the straight-outs' claim to represent the popular will of the state, charging them with "usurpation of power," and repeatedly and doggedly denying the legitimacy of any decision of the convention not returned to the people for ratification by a direct vote.[49] In every possible way they denied the legitimacy of the secessionists' claim to the mantle of the people.

Cooperationists' ferocity in Alabama was a function in part of their numbers. From at least early December, the rabidly secessionist governor had been declaring to all who would listen that secession was a foregone conclusion in his state, and in his arrogance he effectively declared war with the United States. So while paying extravagant obeisance to the right of the people to decide "the great and vital question of submission to an Abolition Administration or of secession from the Union," he simultaneously cast the outcome as inevitable and moved to make it so through clearly illegitimate uses of executive power, especially in his capacity as commander in chief. For at every juncture at which they were consulted, the voters of Alabama registered profoundly divided and regionally fractured opinions about the state's proper response to the crisis. In November's presidential elections they had divided between Breckinridge (who won 54 percent of the popular vote), Bell (who earned 31 percent), and Douglas (15 percent).[50]

Moore and his cronies could not have known that many northern Alabama voters who had supported Breckinridge like good Democratic Party stalwarts in November would cut out on their own in the January elections for delegates to the state convention. It was hardly the rousing mandate Moore had forecast, and this after the usual election shenanigans. Cooperationist strength held strong at about 46 percent of delegates from the time the election results were posted until the delegates were finished voting in the secession convention. Even when it was clear that the ordinance of secession would pass and that dissent was pointless, opposition never dropped below 39 percent. This is a very high percentage, given the historical reputation of the Lower South for out-and-out secession.[51]

More striking than the numbers was the fight the dissenters put up. The concentration of opposition in northern Alabama and the presence of powerful leaders from that section set the stage for a full-out brawl in the secession convention. On the first day, the cooperationists came out swinging. Fighting a resolution of resistance clearly intended to flush out those "opposed to all resistance," cooperationists resisted the attempt to dub them "submissionists." One cooperationist leader played political hardball, pointedly reminding the author of the straight-out resolution that if he insisted on pressing his insulting test, he would only succeed in publicizing the fact that almost half of the members of the convention were in favor of submitting to the rule of a Black Republican. He also pointedly reminded his opponents that they would soon have a need for harmony, because, as he said, there would be war. "I am no believer in peaceable secession," Jeremiah Clemens said. "I know it to be impossible. No liquid but blood has ever filled the baptismal fount of nations." No nation was every christened at any altar but "that of the God of battles."[52] There was no harmony of the body politic in Alabama and nobody pretended otherwise.

In Alabama the matter of the unity of the people passed beyond discourse and bombast to become a remarkable debate about the very legitimacy of the democratic process itself. As cooperationists mounted a rearguard action to resist secessionists' many attempts to hurry the state out of the Union, they challenged straight-outs' claims to the mantle of the people and contested the legitimacy of any measure of such significance not ratified by the direct vote of the people themselves. The issues came to a head in an exchange between William R. Smith, a cooperationist delegate from Tuscaloosa, and William Yancey, the famously intemperate leader of the straight-out faction, over an aggressive resolution to pledge Alabama's (presumably military) aid to already seceded states. To cooperationists it was a declaration of war and act of treason because the state had not yet dissolved its ties to the United States. It was classic precipitation of the fire-eater stripe. Outraged, Smith urged respect for cooperationists' objections on the grounds that they, "the minority here were really the representatives of the majority of the sovereigns of this State," citing population statistics to buttress the claim.[53] The Yanceyites, he said, did not speak for the people of Alabama.

Yancey launched into a tirade, the substance of which confirmed the charges levied against his party. He didn't deny the opposition's popularity or his faction's slim majority. To the contrary, he seemed to revel in it, as if worshipping raw power itself. "It is useless," he said, "to disguise the fact that in some portions of the state there is disapprobation towards our action," but "when that Ordinance shall be passed, even if it be by the meagre majority of one, it will represent the fullness, and the power, and the majesty of the sovereign people of Alabama." And after it passed, he warned, there would be no more minority or majority: the state "will expect and demand, and secure unlimited and unquestioned obedience to that Ordinance." For Yancey, unanimity was not a measure of democratic legitimacy but the effective result of winning the crucial vote. Those who opposed the "expressed will of the people . . . [are] the Enemies of the people of Alabama." Like his counterparts in Georgia, he could hardly wait to pass the ordinance of secession so as to dispense with the problem of political opposition. "There is a law of Treason, defining treason against the state," he warned, and those who dare oppose secession "will become traitors—rebels against its [the state's] authority and will be dealt with as such."[54] In this exchange Yancey, like so many other Lower South secessionists, showed himself to be less interested in winning the consent of the people than in coercing conformity.

Cooperationists would lose the next day when the ordinance of secession went up for the vote. But in Alabama they fought to the bitter end. Yancey's enraged attack served their point. Did he intend to go into "those [disloyal] sections of the State and hang all who are opposed to Secession?" one Unionist pointedly inquired. "Will he hang them by families, by neighborhoods, by towns, by counties, by Congressional

Districts? Who, sir, will give the bloody order? Who will be your executioner? Is this . . . the first fruits of a Southern Republic?" "Does the Convention represent the popular will of the State?" The question was posed directly and unflinchingly in Alabama by a cooperationist faction not strong enough to win but strong enough to fight.

In Alabama, cooperationists never ceased agitating the question of ratification of the ordinance of secession by the people. They raised it more than three times in the debates, once after the ordinance had passed, and again in March when the same convention was asked to ratify the new Confederate Constitution. Secessionists would never—could never—concede. They feared any new attempt at debate or dissent as an opportunity for the reconstruction of the Union. But they could never get the high ground on the issue either. The matter could be settled by a referendum—or by other means, cooperationists threatened. As one put it, should Yancey try the coercion promised, "We will meet him at the foot of our mountains, and there with his own selected weapons, hand to hand, face to face, settle the question of the sovereignty of the people."[55] Was this not, too, a band of brothers? In Alabama, secession was pushed through amid a bare-knuckle fight over the legitimacy of the process and the result.

By the end of January 1861, eight slave states remained in the Union, more yet than had left it. North Carolina, Virginia, Maryland, tiny Delaware, Arkansas, Missouri, Kentucky, and Tennessee all balanced precariously between North and South, republic of free labor and republic of slavery, Union and protean Confederacy. Choices were becoming narrowed and stark, politics dangerous like a force of nature. One North Carolina Unionist evoked the mood: "We are swallowed up and hurried along by the rushing tides of time." Metaphors of danger roiled anxious minds, particularly those still harboring dimming hopes of Union. "The sky is dark, politically—dark as midnight," the Tennessee congressman and Unionist Robert Hatton wrote his wife on New Years Day, 1861.[56]

In the effort to stem the secessionist tide, Upper South Unionists drew strength and firepower from the inglorious chapter in the history of democracy just played out in the slave states directly below them. "This movement [secession] from its inception to the present hour, had its origin in, has been carried on in contempt of the people," Virginia Unionists charged again and again. "In what State that has passed an ordinance seceding from the Union, have the people spoken or been heard from?" "Alabama went out of the Union with a popular majority against her action," another offered. "The same may be said of Mississippi; and it is recently ascertained that Louisiana did the same thing." Secession did not have legitimacy in their eyes, nor did the new government of the Confederate States of America as it took shape in February 1861: "erected by an aristocracy, in violation of every Republican principle," as one Virginia Unionist put it. As Deep South secession sunk in, Upper South Unionists refined the critique of a democracy sold out. North Carolina should hold a convention to consider the state's course in the crisis, the western politician Zebulon Vance insisted; changes so extraordinary and fundamental in her national condition must be "committed directly to the people, in whom all political power is vested." Clear now that the Union was ruptured, glimpsing war on the horizon, the character of "the people" took on a sharpened aspect. "Though some of our southern sisters have contemptuously refused to consult the wishes of 180,000 fighting men, over whose dead bodies an invading host treading through the ashes of their homes must reach them," Vance scathingly wrote, "yet there are others who anxiously seek general and fraternal counsel." In the Upper South the band of brothers was gathering, still conceived as a democratic conclave. Together they would consult, and then—and not before, as in the Lower South—would determine the people's choice for Union or for secession.[57]

And indeed the Upper South would do what the Deep South did not: engage in a process of substantive consultation with the people. From January to May 1861 the Upper South states hosted a virtual festival of democracy, nineteenth-century Southern style at least. The people there not only had the opportunity to vote for presidential candidates with all four candidates on the ballot in all of the states, they operated in a political culture with still vibrant opposition parties determined not to let secessionists "precipitate" the people out of the Union. "They fear lest the people shall think," Zeb Vance wrote of the radicals' strategy, "hence the hasty action of South Carolina, Georgia and the other states in calling conventions and giving so short a time for the election of delegates."[58] So, contra haste, delay was the Unionists' strategy. In three states (Maryland, Delaware, and Kentucky), Unionists managed to defeat the movement to call secession conventions, effectively shutting down the entire disunion process. In the other states, they grasped for the advantage of the sober second thought by insisting that the question of convention or no convention be put to the vote of the people at election, demanding long canvassing periods for the delegates' election and putting off the meeting dates: none met before February. In two states—Tennessee and North Carolina—when it was put to a vote, the voters rejected outright the idea of convention, although by a bare majority in North Carolina. In the end, only two Upper South states—Virginia and (briefly) Arkansas—even held conventions, and in both cases Unionists imposed the final requirement that the people ratify any decisions by a direct vote at the polls. More checks on the secessionists' ability to precipitate the people out of the Union meant more chances for the people to have their say. Many leaders expected, as the secessionist governor of North Carolina put it, that "the will of the people once expressed, will be a law of action with all, and secure that unanimity so necessary in an emergency like the present."[59]

But unanimity turned out to be the one impossible thing. For the fuller and more substantive the consultation, the greater the political yield of division, impasse, and, in critical Virginia, a virtually paralytic struggle between the forces of Union and secession. In this instance the Upper South presented a textbook case of the difficulties of the principle of the consent of the governed. For in none of the states but Delaware was any firm resolution of the people's divisions produced out of the regular workings of the democratic process.

At one level it was very clear. Secessionists lost. Of the eight Upper South states, not one left the Union between February and April 15, when Lincoln's call for troops to suppress the rebellion fundamentally redefined the question. Prior to that, secessionists were defeated everywhere in the Upper South. As early as December 1860 one North Carolinian, C. B. Harrison, had astutely predicted the pattern. "You cannot unite *the masses* of any southern state much less those of North Carolina against the Union and in favor of slavery alone," he observed. But let Lincoln go for "the doctrine of coercion," let him add "love of liberty to the *avarice of Negro Slaveocracy,*" and then, he predicted, "North Carolina cannot be held in the Union."[60] Harrison might as well have written the Upper South script. Between November 1860 and April 1861 secessionists struggled and failed to win the people over to their view of the crisis.

Things had not looked good for the secessionists in the Upper South from the outset. In November, returns in the presidential election signaled a preference for compromise. John Breckinridge, the candidate of the radical Southern-rights Democrats, took four states (North Carolina by a hair and Arkansas, Maryland, and Delaware), but the rest, including critical Virginia, returned majorities for Bell or a resolutely moderate Bell/Douglas combination. Indeed, the elections of February 1861 amounted to a massive realignment in class politics in the slave South and signaled the emergence of a "union party constituency [that] came closer to being non-planter if not yet anti-planter" than any that had yet held power in a slave state. "I think the people, mind you *the people* are in favor of the Union for a while yet," one correspondent assured Zebulon Vance about the climate in his home district in western North Carolina in late January or early February. By March 1861—even with seven Deep South states out, Republican president Abraham Lincoln inaugurated, and the Confederate States of America formally defying federal authority—no Upper South state chose secession. As late as April 4, Virginia, whose convention had been sitting through the entire tense secession spring, voted it down. Secessionists simply could not win the consent of the people. "The nonslaveholder says not now," wrote William H. Holden, the North Carolina Unionist.[61]

But although the Unionists had the upper hand in the Upper South, their hold was tenuous and highly contingent. The hodgepodge alliance of men joined by a common opposition to immediate secession (and thus including the men who in the Lower South were called cooperationists and were counted with the secessionists) included a majority whose Unionism was predicated on securing constitutional protection for slavery. What they wanted was the Crittenden Compromise, the set of terms offered by Senator John Crittenden of Kentucky, which included the critical provision of a constitutional amendment giving positive protection to slave property in the territories south of the old 36°30′ Missouri Compromise line.

Radical Southern rights men had been willing to split the Democratic Party over that provision in May 1860 when Stephen Douglas refused to accept it in the party platform. But it was not just the Deep South or the radicals who had that as their bottom line. Many so-called Unionists did too. "Less than [this] she could not accept," one North Carolina Unionist put it. Will the Free States accept those terms, one wrote his congressman in early February, nerves taut. "Why do they hesitate longer? Will they wickedly persist in straining the Conservative element, until its cords are snap't asunder—I hope not!" But hope, it turned out, was insufficient. By March 4, Crittenden had been voted down five different times in Congress and the Upper South's Unionist congressmen and delegations trudged home from Washington to deliver the bad news. "Everything showed the spirit of the Republican," the North Carolina congressman George Davis raged at a public address on his return from the failed peace conference in Washington. "No arrangement had been made—none would be made. The division must be on the line of slavery." He had gone to Washington a Unionist and returned a secessionist. He and North Carolina, he said, had better go with the South.[62]

Upper South Unionism was contingent on a strategy that many of its advocates regarded as certain to fail and, more importantly, over which they exercised no control. With Crittenden, Unionists demanded precisely the terms the new Republican administration would never concede and not only because the Republican party was explicitly committed to the nonextension of slavery in the territories. After all, President-elect Abraham Lincoln was a man of the territories himself, with a concern for the dignity of human labor—not excluding black people's labor—that had been nurtured there and that deeply moored his position on slavery. Lincoln's position was no secret; to the contrary, it was well known by the time he came into office. There were other high-ranking Republicans, William Seward among them, who would have been willing to cut a deal. But Lincoln was not. Pushed and pressed from all directions before and after his inauguration, he remained unmovable on the matter of slavery in the territories. On that, the party platform and the man were one. "On the territorial question," he wrote a Southerner, "I am inflexible." Upper South Unionists were powerful enough to hold their states back from the precipice of secession, but they had no power to deliver the compromise necessary to keep them there. The fate of Upper South Unionism lay in other hands. In the Upper South, Unionists tried to hold the middle ground, but in terms of politics and ethics, it was quicksand.[63]

That much was clear as hopes for compromise and peace came crashing down. By early March, though still in control in their own states Unionists had become entirely irrelevant to developments in the nation. Even before South Carolina opened fire on federal troops in Charleston Harbor on April 12, the middle ground had moved out from under them as one politician after another returned from Washington to report failure. "I fear that at last the ground upon which the Union men of the South have been standing is to be taken from us," John Gallagher wrote despairingly to Governor Letcher of Virginia on April 6. "Authorized to proclaim a peace policy, we are to have bloodshed." Upper South Unionists had long agreed that federal coercion would be "the death knell of the Union." In January 1861 Governor Letcher of Virginia had drawn the Unionists' line in the sand: "I will regard any attempt to pass federal troops across the territory of Virginia for the purpose of coercing a Southern seceding state as an act of invasion which should be met and repelled"; the Tennessee General Assembly had passed a resolution to the same effect. It was a thoroughly popular position, too. "I am a Union man," one North Carolina voter wrote in January, "but when they send men South it will change my notions. I can do nothing against my own people." As Lincoln's intention to reclaim federal property became known, as his inaugural address was read as a declaration of war, as it became increasingly clear that the middle ground was no longer there to hold, still most Unionists insisted, implausibly, on standing "just where [we have] always stood—in the Union."[64] In the end, it wasn't the Unionists who moved; it was the Republicans—pressed by Confederate provocateurs—who crossed the line.

On April 12 but not before, the Upper South impasse—between Unionists and unreconciled secessionists, between United States and Confederate States—was finally broken. Then South Carolina troops in Charleston Harbor opened fire on U.S. troops still stationed in the federal fort, Fort Sumter. The Rubicon was crossed. President Lincoln called on Southern governors to provide their quota of the seventy-five thousand troops to suppress the rebellion against what was still their country. Lincoln is "the most efficient auxilliary of the secessionists," railed Jonathan Worth, the North Carolina Unionist. "Lincoln has made us a unit to resist until we repel our invaders or die."[65] Worth, like so many other Unionist leaders, followed the people of his state into secession.

Was that consent? Upper South Unionists had worked on the assumption that if democracy was observed it would produce a vote for the Union and unify the people behind it. But in the Upper South, democracy had yielded not a clear choice for Union or for secession, but division, irresolution, inaction, impasse. In the Upper South it was the "Force Bill" (as Lincoln's call for troops was known) and civil war that finally forced the choice between Union and secession. What is really striking about the extended struggle between secessionists and Unionists in the Upper South is how materially profound were the divisions mapped by partisan positions. In the complex political economy of the eight Upper South states on the eve of the Civil War, political resolution was impossible precisely because the differences among the people—by section, by class—went to bedrock. Division was not a creation of political conflict and partisan effect but a mirror of political conditions on the ground.[66]

The political struggles waged in Virginia in the spring of 1861 were a telling indication of the nature of the contest in the Upper South as a whole. All eyes were on Virginia.[67] At every stage of the conflict there, the political difference between Unionists and secessionists was clear: in elections to the state convention, in convention debate, in the vote on the ordinance of secession and its aftermath. Virginia was not "a homogenous people," the *Richmond Whig* acknowledged matter-of-factly; it was two societies, one with slavery "almost universal" and another where it barely existed. There were fundamental divisions in the political economy of Virginia by 1861, and they registered fully in the state's debate over secession.[68]

The rough topography of the political terrain was apparent as early as January in the contrasting positions staked out by Robert M. T. Hunter and John Letcher, conditional secessionist (or cooperationist) and conditional Unionist, respectively. Hunter, although advising against immediate secession and seeking a means to preserve the Union, nonetheless made it clear that if "guarantees" were refused and Virginians forced to choose to which "division of the Union . . . they would attach themselves," they would have to lean South to the slave states whose "interests" were identical to theirs. Unable to imagine a world without slavery, Hunter fatally misjudged the Republicans. He found it hard to believe that they were seriously considering the experiment of emancipation, but still, he said, Virginians could not take "such a risk with the fate of the British West Indies before their eyes." For Virginia secessionists, as for Hunter, secession was about slavery. For Unionists, however, the issue was far more complex, and one does not have to go far into their ranks to find a significant difference of opinion. Governor John Letcher, though hardly unconditional in his Unionism, was deeply suspicious of South Carolina and Lower South secessionists in general and urged his state to be mindful of its own interests as the cotton states were of theirs. Pointing to the coerciveness of the new Confederate government's decision to ban any trade in slaves from border states that were not part of the new Confederacy, he warned against alliance. Instead, he imagined a fracturing of the United States into not two, but four, different confederacies, with Virginia safely nestled in a confederation of like states—the states of the "great valley" as he put it—those with commerce centered on the Ohio, Missouri, and Mississippi rivers. Letcher's "middle confederacy" would serve Virginia's distinct and varied agricultural and industrial interests.[69] For Virginia Unionists the choice between Union and secession was about a lot more than slavery.

Stark as they were, the differences between Hunter and Letcher did not even begin to indicate the range of positions in Virginia. In Richmond there were "immense meetings of the citizens," as the newspapers described them, raucous, divisive, democratic affairs at which every variety of disunion was aired right alongside unconditional commitments to the Union. One meeting called by Richmond's "working men," which drew more than fifteen hundred people, turned into an outright brawl between those "friends of the Union" and a crowd of secessionists who attempted to hijack the meeting and pass a disunion resolution. Demanding repeatedly that "none but mechanics and working men" could speak, the working men eschewed entirely the subject of slave property to pass a highly class-conscious resolution declaring their own interest as working men "that this Union should not be dissolved." The undisputed champion of the city's white working men was John Minor Botts—aka "the Bison"—an unconditional Unionist backed by street gangs who would end up in prison on treason charges. City papers regularly derided Botts as a Black Republican, and he was, in fact, on record in extreme opposition to the disruption of the Union "for so slight a cause" as imagined dangers to property. White men's property—he consistently refused to single out slave property—was perfectly safe in the Union, Botts insisted, even endorsing Lincoln's right to suppress secession. The interests of the city's white working men were well represented in the run-up to the convention and, although Botts did not win election, in the convention as well. With elections fast approaching on February 4, Richmond's public meetings regularly degenerated into rowdy brawls, with diverse constituencies pitted against each other in the confines of one urban hall, dueling speakers, resolutions, national anthems, and heckling shouts of "go it spread eagle" for the Unionists and chants of "fight, fight" for all and sundry.[70] Richmond, not surprisingly, returned a wholly divided delegation to the convention.

The countryside was no different. Resolutions sent in from public meetings there confirmed the diversity of opinion in rural Virginia and especially flagged the resolute opposition to secession in the northwestern part of the state. One resolution declared in no uncertain terms county citizens' rejection of the right of secession, opposition to the calling of a convention, and "immovable and unalterable attachment to the government under which we have grown and prospered." The contents of the Wheeling press revealed the extent and depth of unconditional Unionism: the area was a hotbed.[71] To urban working men's opposition in the convention, then, was surely to be added that of rural free-labor farmers in the section of the state beyond the Blue Ridge Mountains and, especially, in the northwest.

And indeed there was nothing random about the alignments revealed in the secession crisis between class and sectional interests in Virginia. The vote for convention delegates confirmed the divisions within the state, with support for secessionists mapping pretty accurately over the high slaveholding counties. But in Virginia, unlike the Lower South, that did not amount to anything close to a majority for secession. The northwest, to no one's surprise, returned a strong Unionist vote.[72] As a result the fundamental divisions already evident in the state were carried into the convention, where they played out at ridiculous length as secessionists and Unionists engaged in a standoff broken only by Lincoln's Force Bill.

In the convention itself, more dissent emerged from the Shenandoah Valley, where opposition to secession was also strong. One valley delegate, Samuel McDowell Moore, locked horns early and repeatedly with Henry Wise, ex-governor and secessionist from the eastern shore, over the interest of Virginia's manufacturing sector and its white mechanics. Mechanics, Moore insisted, were committed to free trade, low taxes, high wages (for white labor), and a robust white man's democracy, all of which were radically at odds with the articulated policy of the cotton South Confederacy. On whether secession was in Virginia's interests, Moore said bluntly, the valley simply differed from eastern Virginia. When charged with harboring openly antislavery views (a charge to which he was vulnerable), Moore would say only that he did not regard slavery as an evil "so far as the slaves are concerned." Wise's impassioned defense of the slaveholders' interest only confirmed the nature of the struggle.[73]

Ominous as those divisions were, none came anywhere close in scale and explosiveness to the division between the northwestern and eastern delegates over the particular interests of the northwest section. Northwest Unionists seized on the convention as a long-awaited opportunity to redress the structural injustice between the sections or, failing that, as they repeatedly insinuated, to impose a final settlement by a secession movement of their own—secession from the secessionists. Delegates like Morgantown's Waitman Willey aired all the region's grievances—about eastern politicians' willful arrogation of state tax money for transportation improvements and utter neglect of the region west of the Blue Ridge, about the way the state transportation system cut them off from the east and directed their commerce to the free states of the Ohio Valley, and about the vulnerability of the northwest in the likely event of war that secessionists were bringing down on them.

But if that litany of grievances were not enough, at the beginning of

March northwest delegates added an explosive demand: that eastern politicians agree to a fundamental revamping of the state's tax system to tax the full value of slaves like other (white men's) property. It was nothing less than a declaration of independence not just for the section but for the "western poor man," as one put it, against the eastern slaveholders or "rich men." Willey, who introduced the resolution, made no bones about the fact that the issue was fundamentally a "question between classes." "Until this thing is done by our eastern friends," one delegate said, "you might as well undertake to remove the Alleghany mountains from their base, as to undertake to induce the people of the Northwest, for present causes, to secede from the Union." Timed carefully for the day of the first secession vote, the west's tax reform program was shaping up as a down-and-dirty political quid pro quo. Bring it on, Samuel McDowell Moore said of the motion for secession, "I wanted to vote it down."[74] Even after the firing on Fort Sumter and Lincoln's call for troops as conditional Unionists finally threw in the towel, a core of Unionist opposition west of the Blue Ridge held on. That beautiful valley would "become the Flanders of the battle," one predicted hauntingly in explaining his opposition vote on April 17.[75] The fight between east and west, between the interests of slave labor and free labor, slaveholders and nonslaveholders, lasted—and outlasted—the convention.

From February 13 until April 17 the convention of the people of the state of Virginia sat in continuous session, controlled by a Unionist majority whose main strategy was delay. "What [is] the convention . . . wait, wait, waiting for," asked the people of Dinwiddie County in late March. Was it holding off, they wondered, until General Scott took up his headquarters in Richmond? By mid-March, secessionist delegates, still a minority in a convention elected in early February, were reduced to looking to the streets and the people for deliverance. In addition to big street demonstrations in Richmond that harassed Unionist delegates and the still-reluctant governor, they got up public meetings in rural parts of the state that, urging immediate secession, laid into the convention majority. Henry Wise, the hothead from the eastern shore, even organized an alternate convention—"a spontaneous Southern Rights Assembly"—to meet on April 16; rumors were rife in March and early April that Wise and his crew were plotting a coup to arrest Governor Letcher and forcibly organize a secession government. And indeed formal politics went on inside, but paramilitary schemes were clearly afoot out-of-doors.[76]

In Virginia, delegates fiddled while Rome burned. By the time South Carolina troops opened fire on federal troops at Fort Sumter, all hopes of acceptable compromise had been dashed. The convention had become a virtual Potemkin village of Unionism in Virginia—real enough inside the hall but bearing little resemblance to the political world out-of-doors. Not until April 17, after a delegate returned from a personal meeting in Washington with firm evidence of the president's intention to retain the Union by force if necessary, not until the governor was called on directly to provide his state's quota of the seventy-five thousand troops to put down the rebellion, did the Virginia convention finally submit to a vote on an ordinance of secession.[77] In Virginia the secession convention was entirely outrun by events. In the end, its protracted deliberations proved largely irrelevant to developments in either the state or the nation.

And so, on April 17, amid plaintive calls for unity and one last attempt at delay, the representatives of the people of Virginia voted 88 to 55 for the secession of their state from the Union. The long-sought harmony of the body politic was never going to be. Fifty-five men, a hefty 38 percent of delegates, voted against the secession of Virginia from the Union. For cooperationists it was finally time to prepare for war. But a significant number of other delegates held on in opposition; their Unionism turned out to be truly unconditional. Twenty-five northwestern delegates voted against the secession of their state, and five voted for it. A majority of delegates from the Shenandoah Valley—Samuel McDowell Moore's turf—also resisted to the end, although splitting more profoundly than the northwest: 16 valley delegates voted against the ordinance and 10 voted for. "To me the future looks dark—dark and dreary," Baldwin of the Shenandoah Valley county of Augusta said, sunk in foreboding.[78]

Implausibly, but according to the script, assertions of unity were made.[79] But the image of unity was far-fetched, and Governor Letcher was left to try to impose the will of the "people of Virginia" on the people of west Virginia. "All our people have voted," he wrote in a public letter "TO THE PEOPLE OF NORTHWESTERN VIRGINIA" in mid-June 1861, "you as well as the rest of the state have cast your vote fairly and the majority is against you. It is the duty of good citizens to yield to the will of the state." For more than two years thereafter, Letcher struggled to get the men of the northwest to make the state "one people" as before. "The troops are posted at Huttonsville," he rallied the men of the northwest, "come with your own good weapons and meet them as brothers."[80] But the people of Virginia never did become the band of brothers. In Virginia, as in the rest of the Upper South, secession involved differences so profound they entirely resisted political resolution even in the face of civil war.

In the end the state did secede from the Union and northwestern Virginia seceded from the Confederate state of Virginia, eventually creating the breakaway state or "restored" government (depending on your perspective) of West Virginia. But the secession of west Virginia only raised the issues of consent and democratic legitimacy all over again. For as the new state of West Virginia took shape, "loyal" citizens in Harrison County—loyal, that is, to Virginia and the Confederate States of America—refused their consent to the new government in Wheeling, and other citizens in the northwest called on Governor Letcher to recognize them as loyal men. There were double secessions up there, and matters of loyalty and treason, legitimacy, and illegitimacy became entirely contextual.[81]

In a process repeated across the Upper South, Lincoln's call for troops finally impressed on reluctant men that the middle ground was gone. But like Virginia, the Upper South split in every direction, showing just how divided the people were about the fundamental question of Union or Confederacy. In that threatening moment, every possible outcome was reached: alliance with the Confederate States of America, continued membership in the United States, even armed neutrality. When all was said and done, four Upper South states left the Union and four never would. Virginia (but not west Virginia), North Carolina, Tennessee, and Arkansas threw in their lot with slavery and the Confederacy—although persistent Unionism in east Tennessee presented a significant problem of allegiance for Confederate authorities throughout the war and the sectional basis for a reconstructed Union state in 1864. Maryland didn't get to choose. Its hard core of secessionists posed too much of a threat to the territorial integrity of the Union capital in nearby Washington, D.C., so federal forces occupied Maryland before the state could vote.[82] Without much trouble Delaware chose Union.

But Missouri and Kentucky, though initially settling on, respectively, the Union and armed neutrality, underwent fractures similar to those in Virginia, with rump Confederate governments establishing themselves in opposition to their parent Union states and seeking (and gaining) admission to the Confederate States of America. Like Russian nesting dolls, new smaller states, or parts of states, were carved out of old ones as questions about the legitimacy of democratic decisions—about the consent of the people—ramified outward. In Missouri, a secessionist governor, Claiborne Fox Jackson, openly defied the decision of a strongly Unionist state convention, seized control of the state militia, built it up as a pro-secession and pro-Confederate force, and declared Missouri out of the Union. By the summer of 1861 Missouri was in a state of guerilla war, and persistent conflicts about which armed forces counted as recognized combatants under the laws of war added a special ferocity to the course of war in that unfortunate state.[83]

In Kentucky, a breakaway Confederate government formed at a convention called by pro-Southern forces in November 1861, after the state declared its official allegiance to the United States in the war. Observing all formalities, it organized a provisional government and proceeded to write an ordinance of secession and "in the name of the people . . . declare Kentucky to be a free and independent State." There, the consent of "the people of Kentucky" had been seized by secessionists in a simulacrum of a democratic process. Clearly biding time for a change of military fortunes and the exertion of Confederate control over the state, the new government was admitted to the Confederate States of America on Jefferson Davis's recommendation, maintained representation in the Confederate Congress throughout the war, and was written into the budget for military appropriations. In reality, the provisional Confederate government was not much of a presence in Kentucky itself but operated as forces following Braxton Bragg's army. It was a government on the run. The provisional Confederate government of Kentucky never amounted to much more than a series of army camps and—not inconsequentially—a government legislative journal, now safely ensconced in archives where it continues to represent its authors' claims.[84] The Russelville rump, as the Kentucky Confederate government is called, offers a fascinating perspective on what constitutes democratic legitimacy. In Kentucky, secessionists' long-standing insistence on fabricating consent where they couldn't produce it culminated in a farcical production of truly Shakespearean proportions.[85]

"We few, we happy few, we band of brothers." The idea of a powerful male bond cemented in battle had passed down in the English-speaking and Shakespeare-reading world since the sixteenth century.[86] That it had currency in the precipice of disunion at which every Southern state arrived in 1860 and 1861 is not in doubt, but that it had utility—or effectiveness—is. For whatever its efficacy as a description of men in battle, it failed utterly as a political rallying cry in the secession crisis, serving more often to mark unbridgeable gulfs in the body politic than to describe the "harmonium" of it. Secession was an attempt to define a new nation as a band of brothers with similar interests, rights, and duties. But even among "the people," the white male voters soon to be soldiers, unity was elusive. In some sections and quarters significant questions of consent and legitimacy lingered on for the duration of the conflict, laying down the contours of political and military struggles on the ground.

Had secessionists won the consent of "the people"? Only a small minority of the Southern people—fewer than 2 million adult white men out of a population of 12 million—had ever been consulted about the wisdom of secession and the risk of war. In the crisis of the Union in 1860 and 1861, there were many more Southern men and women whose consent had never been solicited, never mind secured, and whose political salience was utterly discounted in the process. If that seemed an unremarkable aspect of Southern political life at the end of the antebellum era, it would not be so for long.

Secession was the high point of the Confederate founders' idea of the people. No sooner had they gotten their states out of the Union than they turned to the matter of perfecting the new republic, writing constitutions for the states and for the fledgling national government in Montgomery. Secessionists wasted no time, moving immediately to codify the assumptions about slavery and citizenship that had driven them out of the Union, to secure slavery beyond any possibility of government interference and to delimit democracy, as they hoped, permanently. The first task—to secure slave property for all time—fell to the provisional Congress of the Confederate States of America in Montgomery, Alabama, in late February 1861. The Congress attempted to dispense in one fell swoop with all the agitating issues concerning slave property and black citizenship of the antebellum period. Unlike the original U.S. Constitution, which delegates used as a template, the Confederate Constitution explicitly recognized the "sovereign and independent character" of states (and thus the right of secession), bound the Congress and territorial governments to recognize and protect "the institution of negro slavery," and guaranteed citizens the right of sojourn and transit in any state or territory of the Confederate states "with their slaves and other property." Purging their Constitution of the euphemisms for slavery adopted in the original U.S. Constitution, they struck out aggressively to secure the property in slaves, using the term "slaves" instead of "other persons" in writing their version of the three-fifths clause (Article 1, Section 2), the fugitive slave clause (Article 4, Section 2), and a wholly new part of Article 1, Section 9, which stated, categorically, "No bill of attainder, ex post facto law, or law denying or impairing the right of property in negro slaves shall be passed" by the Congress. Confederate founders moved to put slavery under positive constitutional protection and to render it a fundamental and permanent feature of the slaveholders' new breakaway state.[87] The new Confederate Constitution left no doubt that slavery was the foundation of the new republic; it was a *proslavery* Constitution for a proslavery state.

There was only so much the new federal government could do in defining and delimiting citizenship, given its form as a confederation of sovereign states. Years later when he wrote his extended defense of secession and the Confederate States of America, ex-president Davis would insist, as he had in January 1861, not only that slavery was a form of property "recognized and guaranteed" by the U.S. Constitution, but that Chief Justice Taney's decision in *Scott v. Sandford* had settled it once and for all that "persons of the African race were not, and could not be, acknowledged as 'part of the people,' or citizens, under the Constitution of the United States." When white Southerners got their chance to write a constitution for their new slave republic, they moved decisively to eliminate any and all questions about who had the right to vote and hold office, and to limit those privileges exclusively to "citizens" of the C.S.A., as all relevant articles of the Constitution specified. But citizenship itself remained ill-defined. The Confederate Constitution referred to three kinds of citizens—natural born citizens, those who were citizens at the time of the adoption of the Constitution, and those citizens born in the United States prior to December 20, 1860, drawing, one can only presume, on the definition of citizen rendered by Chief Justice Taney, which President Davis regarded as the "final" word on the matter. They made provision for the Congress to write "uniform laws of naturalization," but because they never did so, the terms of naturalization that would have revealed the Confederate government's notion of federal citizenship were never spelled out.[88] In practice, then, Confederate citizens were presumably those recognized as such by the separate states.

The work of defining citizenship and the identity of the people in the new Confederate States of America thus fell to the states in their sovereign capacity. They embraced the task with energy, seizing the opportunity nation making provided to delimit democracy explicitly and permanently. Immediately after secession, the states set to work writing new constitutions, most leaving their secession conventions in place to do so. In that welcome task Southern politicians moved to close down all the loopholes that had been used to corrupt the practice of politics in the original republic and to codify their own understanding of political membership in the sovereign people. South Carolina wrote the first, and what became standard, citizenship clause adopted in the new constitutions, which concluded with the injunction that the state bound itself to extend citizenship to "every free white person . . . born within the territory of this State or [who] may be born outside of that territory of a father who was then a citizen of this State" and to "every free white person" engaged in the military service of the state. It specified in addition that a man's citizenship extended to his wife and children but that women's extended only to their children, reflecting assumptions about the relationship of marriage and citizenship for women and about men's proper role as household head. In case anything remained unclear, South Carolina's Confederate-era constitution makers closed with the cover-all-bases warning that "in no case shall citizenship extend to any person who is not a free white person." That free white men could earn citizenship by engaging in military service further riveted the link between race, masculinity, and citizenship in the slaveholders' state. Confederate South Carolina's constitution rendered the racial and gender terms of citizenship finally explicit and thus was a fitting coda to the long history of contestation that had surrounded precisely those issues in the early national and antebellum United States. Georgia followed suit, also making the racial measure of citizenship crude and clear. They restricted citizenship to "free white persons" and explicitly proscribed "any person who is not a free white person."[89]

In Alabama also, delegates moved to make theirs the republic of white men in a literal sense. Indeed, Alabamians took the matter of the racial exclusivity of the people one step further, defeating, after extended debate, the proposition that only men who were citizens should be allowed to vote. There, race, it seems, mattered more even than nationality. The issue arose when delegates confronted the question of whether Alabama would disfranchise white men who were not citizens by birth or naturalization. The answer was a resounding no. "[We have now] separated ourselves from the old Union," and Alabama ought to keep free of the dangerous heresies that destroyed republican liberty before, one delegate insisted. "Let us commence by discountenancing distinctions among white men at the South. Let there be but two classes of persons here—the white and the black. Let the distinction of color only be distinction of class—keep all the white men politically equal—the superior race—let the negro be the subordinate and our government will be strong and our liberties secure." That argument was repeated in versions that grew ever more demagogic, and it won the day.[90] In Alabama, secessionists built an explicitly racial and patriarchal republic. Not only did their constitutional definition of citizenship proscribe membership of any person of African descent, free or slave; their effective conflation of citizenship and suffrage confirmed yet again the essential masculinity of citizenship and underscored how merely formal women's status as citizens was in the slaveholders' democracy.

But definitive as those constitutions were, there were plenty of new

Confederates who would have liked the states to go even further, to seize their chance to build a perfect republic by limiting suffrage to property holders as in days of old. David Gavin, a South Carolina planter and perennial complainer about "mobocracy," thought the convention delegates in his state missed their chance. "Property," he said, "does not have the proper constitutional influence," the vote should have been restricted to holders of property, which in the South Carolina system, he specified, means "land and negroes." Like conservatives and some old Know-Nothings in other states, including Georgia and Virginia, Gavin had been hoping for a much less democratic political system. But still, he admitted, the new Constitution was better than the old one, because in the Confederacy at least universal suffrage meant only white men "and a large portion, the slaves, are excluded."[91]

In the C.S.A., Southerners finally got to render explicit their assumptions about the people and the republic. Once secession was accomplished—in eleven, but not all fifteen, slaveholding states—and the C.S.A. was founded as a new nation under God, its leading politicians worked as promised to perfect the republic of white men. This was the vision of the new nation they offered to the world, one dedicated to the proposition that men were not created equal, a beacon of true liberty and a tribune of racial truth against the corruptions of modern liberal democracy and equality. "Confederates did not believe they needed to make new worlds," one historian has written; "they were more than content with the world they already had."[92] Jefferson Davis and other Confederate founders and latter-day propagandists of the Lost Cause cast secession as a wholly constitutional move designed simply to restore government as the founders conceived it. They thus obscure the historical nature of what Confederates attempted to do at such incredible risk of blood and treasure. For, as Davis for one knew, the world was hardly likely to recognize their breakaway nation-state unless it could sustain itself in war. Regardless of what they claimed about the conservative and restorationist nature of their national project, in seceding to perfect the republic they set out to make something that had, in fact, never existed before: a polity purged of the contestations, hedges, and ambivalences about slavery and representation that had defined the republic, the state, and the Constitution since the founding. No, Confederates' vision of a perfected republic of white men was something new unto this world, the only explicitly proslavery nation-state any agrarian elite ever attempted to build in the modern world.

The Civil War was conceived as the Brothers' War. It was the brothers who brought it on in their (divided) capacity as the people, and the brothers assumed it would be theirs to fight. Secession, war, and nation making were supposed to be the work of white men. "We will make a history for ourselves," Jefferson Davis gamely said as the war started. But that view of history as a field of exclusively white male subjects would prove to be a profoundly narrow and mistaken vision of what nation making, war, and history required. If that vision of the people seemed to secessionists not only adequate but ideal in March 1861, some Southerners could already glimpse its limits, and not just because of the painful divisions between the brothers that had already lacerated the Confederate body politic. The conflicts revealed in secession, especially the challenge from nonslaveholders, left important divisions and points of weakness in the Confederate body politic.

Historians and the public already know a great deal about this Civil War history of dissent, about its class and regional bases and political consequences in guerilla warfare, secret Unionist organizations, peace movements, and desertion. But the Confederate government would face a whole set of other challenges as well, arising not from the band of brothers but from the great mass of the Confederate people—women and slaves—who had been purposely disfranchised and excluded from the ranks of the political community. The challenges they posed would prove even more threatening to the political prospects of the regime and are more unknown to historians of it.

In the weeks right after Fort Sumter, there was a dawning recognition of the new political reality. As local newspapers commented on the heightened anxiety of "all classes, sexes and even colors" to hear the news, one correspondent began to articulate what war would require of the people of the Confederate South. "All, all of every name and every age to arms! to arms! My father go, my son go, my brother go, your country calls you." But the demands extended beyond the ranks of citizen-soldiers: "Mothers, wives and daughters buckle on the armor for the loved ones," the correspondent urged, "bid them, with Roman fairness, advance and never return until victory perches on their banner." Nor was the stoic sacrifice of white women, formerly bystanders to the conflict, the only new development. Slaveholders and their human property would each have their role to play as well. "Let the Governor call on the slave owners to furnish each . . . so many able-bodied negro men to proceed immediately . . . wherever they may be needed and aid in fortifying against the foe," the correspondent announced, as if that was a simple proposition; as if the slaveholders and slaves would simply acquiesce in such claims on slave property made in defense of slavery in the war now under way.[93]

By April 1861 a new nation had indeed claimed a place in the game of nations, a late proslavery nation launched at the high tide of commitment to abolition and the expansion of democracy. Choppy seas for a small reactionary state, rich in enslaved humans and (for the moment) cotton, poor in every other kind of wealth that mattered in the new age. Architects of the Confederacy took perverse pride in its out-of-step mission, saw it in grandiose terms, and linked it to the cause of reaction throughout the world: to the Transvaal Republic of South Africa, to Spanish slavery and Russian serfdom, to the remnants, that is, of slaveholding and agrarian elites' once powerful but now faltering regimes. Rising "phoenix like" from the ashes of the American republic, sanctioned by God, the Confederacy was, one minister said, a mighty new nation created by "three hundred and fifty thousand white men" commanding the labor of "four million African slaves." It was, Alexander Stephens said, "the first government ever instituted upon principles in strict conformity to nature, and the ordination of Providence, in furnishing the materials of human society."[94]

The hubris is stunning. Conceived as the perfected republic of white men, a beacon of conservative righteousness in the modern world, the Confederate States of America in its subsequent history would become a fiery trial not just of that national ambition but its impoverished political vision. The demands of nation building in war would unleash a new crisis of legitimacy and create a heightened context for political loyalty that would test not just the unity of the people but the very definition of the people itself. The Confederate body politic would be rent asunder by war. By war's end it would be a bloody remnant of its original self, its very corporate identity subject to violent contestation by precisely the people—women and slaves—it was designed to exclude. War and the experiment of nation making that brought it on would propel a profound transformation of Southern political culture. Confederates made history, all right, but the cast of characters went well beyond the band of brothers called for in the original script.

CHAPTER 3

Antigone's Claim

We do not make war on women and children.

Illinois private, 1862

RECALL ANTIGONE, THAT POWERFUL and enduring figure of woman in Western culture. Sophocles' fourth-century B.C. tragic character, she buried her brother against the express prohibition of the king whose city-state he had betrayed in war. For that she suffered the penalty of death. Antigone's primal commitment to her family seems to have been imagined precisely for the circumstances of civil war that pit brother against brother and render partisan choice horrific. In Sophocles' mythic Thebes, war had left both of Antigone's brothers dead, one an honored patriot, the other a dishonored traitor who had led a foreign army against his king. But not for Antigone the state's distinction: to her there was no "patriot" or "rebel," only "brother, my own flesh and blood," and woman's obligation to perform the death rites that honored both. Antigone's commitments were antecedent to those of civic life. She buried her brother, sprinkling a handful of dust over his exposed and mauled remains, and was mourned by the city for her "glorious action." Sophocles' Antigone is a powerful representation of women's primal obligation to the realm of kinship, not citizenship; household, not polity; family, not state.[1] It speaks, still, to issues of universal significance, touching on the human condition.

One finds expressed in many cultures a deeply human reluctance to see women as parties to war. The United States in the Civil War was no exception. Even there, where war and mobilization reached proportions not often matched in history, parties to the conflict on both sides retained and only partially surrendered, assumptions about women's nonparticipation in the struggle. Women were victims of war, often booty in it, but not perpetrators of it. In North and South alike in 1861, assumptions about women's position in the struggle were fundamental expressions of a commitment to gender difference itself. As in Antigone's Thebes, the conditions of civil war seemed particularly to demand the distinction: between soldier and civilian, combatant and noncombatant, partisan and nonpartisan, man and woman. In Civil War America, as in other times and places, the insistence on women's nonpartisanship and on the meaning of gender difference was, in an essential sense, about imposing limits on war's destructiveness. Given the human capacity for violence, the need was urgently felt. "It is the men with arms in their hands upon whom we make war," one Illinois private wrote his wife from Arkansas early in the war, "the women are entitled to protection even if they are the wives and daughters of rebels."[2] Men were the parties to war, women and children the parties to be protected. The Civil War record holds abundant evidence of that mythic need, of military men's repeated faith that women were not the enemy.

But part of the untold story of the American Civil War is how that evidence of faith accrued in the record as a litany of painful betrayals. For in ways no one anticipated at the outset, the deeply held assumptions about women's nature and proper role collided with a historically contingent set of developments bearing on their political behavior in the war. Indeed, for government officials and military men on both sides of the contest, the Civil War involved a series of startling confrontations with women engaged in what could only be called political acts. Envisioned as outside politics, as objects of male protection in war, women were instead encountered as intense parties to the struggle. They were met as fiercely partisan women in Union-occupied territory, as spies operating in both national capitals and territory, and as informers and "enemy abettors" in the guerilla warfare that ravaged the border states. In divided parts of Confederate states like east Tennessee, western Virginia, western North Carolina, and the Pearl River area of Mississippi, Confederate forces encountered women members of Unionist dissenter bands, operating as enemy collaborators and harborers of deserters and guerillas, and most common of all, as organized and demanding constituencies of soldiers' wives in all of the Confederate states. On occasion women were even encountered as soldiers in the Confederate ranks—about 250 at last count.[3]

Military men, state officials, and politicians alike struggled throughout the war with the strategic implications of women's partisan engagement. Although there remained considerable ambiguity in Union and Confederate views of women's political standing, and although the men retained an all-too-human desire to see women as members of a family world that was a sanctuary from war, there was also a growing recognition on both sides of women's political identity and capacity. One can see it in the myriad ways officials moved over the course of the war to hold white women accountable for their actions politically and militarily, and, most dramatically, in their growing willingness to "handle women speedily and roughly," as a Mississippi judge put it to President Davis. "Many of the men not liable to military service and nearly all the women are openly at work to weaken our army, procure desertion and assail the Confederacy," he raged about affairs in the area of Leake and Jones counties, Mississippi. There was to be no more leniency shown to women.[4] The new view of white women that evolved out of struggles on the ground represented a considerable departure from the secessionists' imagined national script. At worst it amounted, as some charged, to waging war on women.

That women were not outside war was recognized with the greatest reluctance. Nobody, North or South, began the war expecting to contend with women. In the antebellum period, white women, although citizens, had never been of much interest to state officials. The state had reached married women, if at all, through their husbands, men recognized as household heads for purposes of taxation and political representation. Even in the crisis of the Union, Southern authorities felt confident they could retain women's loyalties using only vague promises of protection. But the limits of that customary respect for coverture, of men's right to run their own households and rule their women without interference from the government, was quickly reached in the South as the scale of the state's activities increased, the demands on its citizens intensified, and it geared up for a war that would test the political loyalty of every man, woman, and child, slave and free, in the new C.S.A.

For white Southern women the war represented something new, not least a radically changed and far more direct relationship to the state. It is hard to exaggerate the growth of state power in the C.S.A. Emanating both from state capitals and from Richmond, government demands on citizens, subjects, and property expanded to previously unthinkable proportions and reached into the very heart of the household in search of men and matériel of war. One consequence was that white Southern women were driven into ever more intimate relationships with the myriad officials dispatched to execute the policies of these newly powerful and radically intrusive states. Then the recognition of women as a force in Confederate political life came into sharp focus. For in the daily struggles and negotiations brought on by war policies, white women forged not just a new relationship to the state but new and strategically useful political identities, individual and collective, by which to advance their interests.

The politics of protecting womanhood took some unexpected turns in the Civil War. Some involved matters of loyalty and treason and were worked out by both governments over the course of the war. Others involved domestic politics within the C.S.A. as that government struggled to extract the resources for a massive war out of its own diverse and largely disfranchised population. Women, it turned out, were critical to that effort and hardly the passive parties officials initially expected. Indeed, even as military men moved to hold women accountable to the state, women citizens moved to hold the state accountable to them. Out of the conventional promises of protection Southern politicians made in the secession crisis, white women forged something else altogether: a concrete politics of protection that framed many uneasy developments on the home front. In the massive public records generated by wartime governments, that story awaits us: about how multitudes of ordinary white women, some wealthy but most not, gave the lie to their political exclusion by pressing on the official arenas of Confederate life for the means of protection, survival, redress, and justice. In doing so they made themselves into a new political constituency—of soldiers' wives, as they would have said—whom politicians ignored at their peril. In that sense, as in so many others, the Confederate experience constitutes a vital new chapter in Southern political history.

In the American Civil War, white Southern women's politics and allegiance came to matter as never before. Taken as a whole, the swirling set of developments around the matter of women and war amounted to nothing less than an assertion and reluctant recognition of women's political personhood and capacity for treason. Then, the idea of women as outside war—Antigone's claim—was a mere illusion.

In the late spring and early summer of 1861, the secession campaign finally drew to a close and the new Confederate States of America moved immediately into a state of war. In the brief lull after Fort Sumter, the separate states and central government worked feverishly to organize, staff, finance, and equip armies to face the four hundred thousand Union men the U.S. president had called to arms. Enthusiasm for volunteering ran high; many Southern states had more men than guns to arm them with. As men poured into the armies of the North and South by the thousands, as towns and rural districts emptied of their young men, who could have doubted that war was men's work? But that civilizational touchstone—the one that marked the limits of war—was much less certain than it appeared to be. In the first summer of war, even as people retained an innocence about the scale of the conflict under way, there were a few developments that foreshadowed the boundless shape of the struggle to come.

"You have held me, Sir, to man's accountability." So charged Rose O'Neal Greenhow, ardent secessionist from Maryland to the U.S. secretary of war as she sat under house arrest in Washington, D.C., in the sweltering summer of 1861.[5] Mrs. Greenhow was not the only one shocked by that development. Just a few months before, nobody in either government was even vaguely worried about the political loyalty of female citizens. But here already was a respectable woman under arrest on charges of spying for the enemy. In fact Greenhow already had company, for on the same August day the federal Secret Service had also picked up Eugenia Levy Phillips, a married woman and mother of nine young children. Nobody mentioned Phillips's husband or the widow Greenhow's male family members. The crimes, and the political views that engendered them, were clearly the women's own. After two arrests, the second punished by incarceration in the Old Capitol Prison, federal authorities in Washington banished Greenhow to the Confederate South; Phillips, too, was removed beyond the lines upon her release from house arrest in September 1861.

Nobody made much of it at the time. The Greenhow and Phillips cases and relatively lenient punishment registered the novelty of the problem they posed and the unsettled state of Union thinking in the opening days of the war. In times of peace, women's detachment from the state was desirable and customary, a just recognition of men's authority over their wives. But it was not necessarily so in times of war. The arrest of two women accused of spying for the enemy was only the beginning; nobody in August 1861 could foresee the dimensions the problem of women's political loyalty would assume. Before much more time had elapsed, however, both governments would discover that they had a pressing state interest in forging a more direct relationship with married women: to identify women's individual political views, leverage their loyalty, and punish treason. "What is my crime?" Eugenia Levy Phillips asked defiantly in her journal. If her pro-Confederate sympathies constituted treason, she wrote, "then am I indeed a traitor."[6] The question of women's capacity for treason was posed from the first.

It was not supposed to be that way. At the outset of the Civil War, women's loyalty was entirely assumed, usually regarded as an attribute of femininity itself. In the South, politicians routinely offered paeans to women's patriotism, ascribing to them as a group a devotion to nation that was pure precisely because it was not partisan or self-interested. In the secession crisis and the early days of war, patriotism, not politics, was perceived as the ladies' domain.[7]

Southern women, especially the elite ones politicians and editors talked about, did little to disabuse anyone of that view. Planter women expressed strong political opinions about the wisdom of secession, and they divided over it too. They attended secession conventions in droves, cramming the galleries, volubly seconding the delegates (Union and secessionist) who advocated their positions on the floor, offering bouquets to their favorites. In fact, their diaries, correspondence, and occasional communications to newspapers reveal a complete absorption in national political affairs. What yeoman and poor white women made of national developments is far harder to know, but there is every reason to assume that they divided over the wisdom of secession and a risky independence as did other members of their political communities. Numbers of poor white women from Unionist parts of North Carolina would later charge that they had been taken out of the Union without their own consent. But notwithstanding the obvious differences of political opinion, secessionist politicians routinely touted the support of all the ladies as evidence of the righteousness of their cause. The idea that women were the most ardent of Confederates dates thus from secession, not from wartime. It was a view that never loosened its grip on the American imagination.[8]

The ladies were careful to make the gestures required of femininity. When they did make their views known in public they typically disavowed politics for patriotism. The forty ladies of the best families of Virginia (as they described themselves) who went pointedly into print with their demand that the state sever "all connection with the traitorous inhabitants of the North"—this in the midst of the state convention's protracted deliberations—carefully cast their intervention not as a political choice but an expression of "their patriotic spirit." Never mind that their patriotism yet lacked an object (they had no new country yet), they were, as they put it, "high priestesses in the temple [of liberty]" tending the "sacred fire of patriotism." Like all of their sex, the editor wrote approvingly the next day, this was a class "indifferent to political movement," motivated by the purest motives and by the "instinct of all domestic animals, which rouses them to resistance when hearth and home is menaced by a real danger."[9] These were no political women meddling in the domain of men, just genteel ladies pledged to the national cause in the way mothers guard their young.

As secession gave way to war in the summer of 1861, women's loyalty to the C.S.A. remained an article of public faith. So even as elite women embraced a new idea of patriotic service and usefulness, the work they typically volunteered to do reinforced their identification with symbols of the nation and riveted their identity as patriots. The favorite symbol was the flag. There was a perfect mania for flags among Confederate ladies: flag committees, flag making, and best of all, flag presentations. Women presented richly detailed flags of their own making to politicians in state secession conventions, to the provisional government of the Confederate States of America in Montgomery, and most often to officers who had raised companies of local troops in emotional ceremonies preparatory to waving men off to war. One young lady in rural Louisiana even made a Confederate flag and "presented it" to her slaves, who promptly accommodated her by marching around the house with it, or as she put it, marching "under their Confederate flag." It was as if their loyalty could be stimulated by it as her own was: "I presented it to them," she said, and "told them they must not let the Yankees get hold of it."[10] Women were so closely associated with symbols of the nation that when the Confederate House of Representatives solicited designs for the new national flag, nine out of ten submitted were from ladies. Ladies drew pictures in their diaries of the flags they had designed and sewn, wrote sentimental poetry about the Confederate flag, and like Sue McDowell of South Carolina, recorded with great emotion their witness to the first raising of the Confederate stars and bars. It was, she wrote, "the critical moment in the birth of the new nation." When New Orleans was occupied in April 1862, Sarah Morgan attached a homemade Confederate flag to her dress and paraded downtown in front of the federal troops. The time would soon come when men in Union-occupied territories were executed for raising the Confederate flag, and Union women risked arrest for keeping a U.S. flag under lock and key at home in Confederate cities, as secessionist women would in Union-occupied ones.[11] Flags were, of course, symbols of political allegiance, and the possession and display of an enemy flag in war was self-evident proof of treason. But in the early days, when no one was thinking much about the damage women could do, many elite Confederate women embraced the flag with abandon, treating it as a seemingly innocent part of the joyful ritual observance of the birth of their new nation.

Like flag making, Confederate women's other patriotic labors had mostly ritual and symbolic value at the outset of the war. Even sewing, though obviously useful, was as much about patriotic display as the value of the goods produced. Cut off from the New York garment industry, lacking an indigenous white working class of garment workers, the states and communities scrambled to outfit the hordes of men signing up. The states furnished uniforms mostly through outwork and volunteer labor. Ladies sewing societies were founded everywhere. Women gathered, each contributing their mite of labor and money, making tents and uniforms, knitting socks, rolling lint, and generally trying to outfit the volunteers for duty. The work did fill a need. Governor Joseph Brown of Georgia, for instance, specifically called on the ladies to make uniforms, promising to provide the cloth if necessary. Women wrote him for it: for jeans and woolen cloth, trimmings, buttons.[12]

But there was much playacting about elite young women's early ideas of duty, a search for sociability as much as usefulness. There was a flush of activity in the secession spring and early summer of 1861, but many quit when the novelty wore off. Some girls joined who couldn't sew; others took the work home for their slaves to do; some sewing societies raised money and paid poor soldiers' wives to do the rough work. Emma Holmes went to the founding meeting of one Charleston society, met thirty other women there, went for a stroll on the battery with one of her friends, joined up with some young men for a "frolic to the ice cream garden," and after picking up a few more friends went home in the buggy. There was a frenzy of activity: meetings and more meetings, fund-raisers, and tableaux were all the rage. Mary Boykin Chesnut was delighted with it all. "What marvelous experiences a little war begins to make," she crowed in May 1861. But her friend Louisa McCord, the dyspeptic South Carolina writer, was disgusted. Like Mary Wollstonecraft of old, she denounced the ladies' frivolity. "Day after Day, fresh rigged with the frippery of the new season," she sees them, she wrote, and doing what for their country in the war? "Talking of fight—giving bouquets wreaths and banners with mottos and good wishes, some of us scribbling for newspapers, all of us saying 'God speed to the great cause' . . . Nero fiddling while Rome burns." McCord called for a more austere patriotism of the Spartan mother variety, involving the abandonment of frolic and sacrifice of wealth and fashion.[13] But McCord was off-key in the summer of 1861.

The rush of elite women's activity at the beginning of the war thus did little to trouble conventional assumptions about the political standing of the sex. The antebellum view that women were not members of the political community held even as the view that they were important members of the new nation gained strength. Indeed, the association of elite women with the national cause only deepened the conventional view of women as objects of male protection. When the same Virginia ladies who came out for secession proposed to make a flag for their local cavalry unit, they said it would remind each man "to draw his sword bravely in her defense."[14]

The trope of protecting women, so familiar to our ears that it sounds natural, was a relatively new feature because it was associated with the rise of citizen armies in the Napoleonic era and with the particular challenges involved in mobilizing volunteer armies. Through the flag they presented, the Virginia women offered themselves as living symbols of the national cause. In the mobilization for war, as in the secession crisis, white Southern women—elite ones most prominently—functioned primarily to transfer men's political obligation to the state. In the C.S.A., as in so many other wars to come in the modern period, men were called to war to defend women.

That idea that men went to war to protect women was commonplace in 1861. It had been a staple of political talk in the secession crisis. But the mobilization that followed Fort Sumter and Lincoln's call for troops put new burdens on freemen's political obligation and engendered a dynamic politics of protection that played out over the whole course of the war. The protection of women, by which they meant white women, was placed at the heart of the glorious cause. Much of the talk was from young soldiers, sons, trying on a man's responsibility. They spoke as often of mothers and sisters as they did of wives and daughters. "A call has been made upon the young, brave and chivalrous sons of Georgia and the South to leave home and the endearments that bind us to our families to defend the rights and interests of our mothers and sisters and homes," young Edwin Bass puffed to his sister in April 1861. "Tis glorious to die for one's country and in defense of innocent girls and women from the fangs of lecherous Northern hirelings," another recruit, William Plane, wrote his wife in June of the same year. In the Civil War, as in other wars that would come after, talk of violence against women, children, and the family offered undeniable moral imperatives with which to urge reluctant recruits and to justify sacrifice from a population pressed to give up its husbands and sons.[15]

But as men entered military service, the talk about protecting women began to shape a new, war-born relationship between citizens, subjects, and the state. Confederate citizens of all sorts readily subscribed to the view that the Civil War was a defensive war waged for the protection of hearth, home, and womanhood. State officials subscribed to it, too, or at least said that they did. Citizens thus not unreasonably expected that military deployment would be shaped by, or at least accommodate, those social goals. But therein lay the problem. For men took their role as protectors of women seriously. From the first, the nature of the call to arms seemed to authorize a very local notion of defense—literally home protection—that made the task of military mobilization all the more tricky. In the innocence of the early months, before the staggering requirements of the war hit home, most volunteers worked on the assumption that service would be local *and* short term, allowing them to fulfill their obligations both to their family and to the Confederacy. "We are composed mostly of married men of families," the Magnolia Rifles of Randolph County, Georgia, explained to the governor. "We want a place in our own state and feel that 12 months will be best for us and our families."[16] Men expected war and military service to accommodate the farming cycle and their customary obligation to support and protect their dependents.

But already by May 1861 the Confederate War Department was facing up to the task of building a national army and authorized enlistment of as many as four hundred thousand men, not for twelve months as previously, but for three years or the duration of the war. The idea of a truly national army stirred up enormous resistance as men faced service out of their own locality and even out of the state. In Georgia men complained about being forced to go too far.[17] Once the Confederacy started mobilizing for war, it wasn't long before white men began to feel that the protection of womanhood was at odds with military service, the private duties of husband and father antagonistic to the political obligation of the citizen-soldier. "It is the greatest dilemma that mankind can feel to leave a family in . . . destitute condition," one enlisted man with a sick wife and three small children wrote his governor in 1862. "Still I know there is a great obligation resting on me to shoulder arms in defense of my country."[18]

Caught in the dilemma of conflicting private and public obligations, men turned the problem back to the state, demanding the reciprocity implicit in freemen's obligation to serve. The quid pro quo was widely understood. Jacob Blount of Attapulgas, Georgia, put it to his governor: "Sir," he wrote, "I am willing to defend my country but I as well as all other men want my wife and children protected." In calling repeatedly on state governors and the Confederate president and secretary of war to fill their shoes at home, new soldiers both expressed and deepened their vision of women as objects of protection. For if politicians and state officials cast women as objects of male protection (as the responsibility of their husbands), those men called to military service insisted on a more even exchange. In offering their military service to the state of South Carolina (as proof of their allegiance), two different groups of free blacks asked "only that if ordered off . . . our wives and children will be taken care of & provided for."[19]

The new reach of the state had profound implications for political relations and identities in the Confederacy, including those of women citizens. Throughout the war, male citizens would continue to press state authorities to make good on their promises to protect their women. It was an endless source of conflict as state demands on them for military service reached proportions utterly unthinkable at the beginning of the war, profoundly disrupting households *and* their customary relations of production and power. It would eventually produce a set of claims from soldiers' wives themselves that introduced a dynamic new element to Confederate political life. The promise of protection had a Confederate history all its own.[20]

But all of the new developments in the political culture proceeded from the view, universally held, that women were not parties to war, that they played no role in the politics that had brought it on and would take no part in waging it. Thus, far from girding themselves to do political battle with enemy or dissident women, far from anticipating treason, Confederate and Union authorities took it as an article of faith that women were outside war, that they were innocent parties, entitled to protection, even perhaps from enemy men.

The first real test of the cardinal principle of the right of white women to protection came when Confederate women faced enemy troops in areas under Union occupation, as they did in some places as early as the fall of 1861 and winter of 1862. Then began the painful education of all parties to the reality and consequences of Confederate women's partisan commitments. It was clear from the outset that Virginia would play an outsized role in the war, and, as state Unionists had insisted, that the Shenandoah and Kanawha valleys would prove to be the Flanders fields of the war. It was true of both places.[21]

Sigismunda Stribling Kimball was a planter woman who had the misfortune to live on a farm near Berryville, Virginia, a small town in the Shenandoah Valley not far from Winchester. Kimball lived in the very eye of the storm. For Winchester was critically located at the northern end of the Shenandoah Valley, close to Maryland on the one side and West Virginia on the other. It was also the headquarters of the Confederate army of western Virginia under Major General Thomas S. (Stonewall) Jackson and was violently contested terrain. The town changed hands as many as seventy times during the war, and Kimball's Berryville area went with it, usually a few days in advance. From the time the Yankees first took Winchester in March 1862, Kimball, her slaves, and all of her neighbors and their slaves lived alternately in United States and Confederate territory. The turnover could be rapid. "We are again in Dixie," Kimball wrote on December 6, 1862; "Yankees in Berryville," she corrected herself on December 27. Nothing held for long. The Yankees had been in Winchester less than two weeks when they made an appearance on Mrs. Kimball's farm. When three "yankees" rushed up to her door looking for "a rebel that belongs to this house," the mistress made her first foray out to meet the enemy. Although an avowed and open Confederate, she took the gendered high ground, revealing her own—and many other planter women's—assumptions about how this was all to go. "I told him there is no one at home but ladies of course they are always respected and protected." To Kimball's shock, the soldier, a private, would have none of it: "He said they had plenty of ladies prisoner and they were the worst traitors in the world." But Kimball was not through. Like the young Louisiana woman counseled by her soldier brother to use "cold politeness" to control "the impudent dog in blue cloth," and to request orders of protection from the resident enemy commanders, Mrs. Kimball redirected her appeal to the man's officers, counting on their gentlemanly instincts. "Immediately went to the Col, claiming his protection, which had been offered before," she noted.[22]

Remarkable as it might seem, many elite Confederate women saw their right to protection as an obligation that extended to enemy men. Nor were they wrong. Like many other Yankee officers in the occupied South, Kimball's colonel was not only solicitous, recognizing her as a lady deserving of respect, he committed to protect her against the rougher sorts in his own army. In actions repeated all over the occupied and battleground areas of the South in 1861 and 1862, Colonel McDowell issued an order of protection and posted a guard of five men at Kimball's gate until his troops withdrew from the area. "I had no idea I could feel so desolate without such protection," she wrote after they left. "We have been so fortunate in having gentlemanly officers to guard us and feel thankful for colonel MacDowel;s protection." "Victory to our arms," Sigismunda Kimball prayed, when the Yankee pickets withdrew from her gate.[23] The idea that women were entitled to protection (or at least that elite women were) held firmly on both sides in the first year or so of the war.

But orders of protection revealed more than the value of chivalry; they reflected something fundamental about the law of war. Sigismunda Kimball made no secret of her politics and national allegiance while she demanded the protection of Union officers. Clearly she thought herself entitled both to her own political opinions and national allegiances *and* protection as a woman. Like many other "secesh" ladies, as the soldiers called pro-Confederate women, she was alert to the strategic value of her identity as a lady, that elevated form of Southern womanhood. It was not at all unusual for planter women to lecture Union soldiers about their chivalrous obligations. But the obligation to protect women was also, as some knew, a more formal matter. Mary Greenhow Lee, a widow who lived just a few miles from Kimball in Winchester and shared the alarming experience of life in the combat zone, delivered an unusually acute speech in which she indicated her knowledge of what was required not just by gender customs but by army regulations. In January 1863 she sought an interview with the Union provost marshal. "I told Captain Alexander," she recorded in her diary, "that we were all rebels but that we expected as citizens to be treated according to the usages of civilized warfare, and as women, we demanded the courtesy that every lady has the right to expect from every gentleman."[24] In seeking orders of protection from enemy officers, as she did from General Milroy two months later, Mary Greenhow Lee demonstrated her knowledge of the laws of war and the obligations it imposed on occupying forces with respect to noncombatants.

The obligation to protect women was written into the Union army's laws of war, showing just how deep such ideas went in the Western world. All over the South, elite women like Kimball and Lee assumed an entitlement to protection and asserted it even to enemy troops. Most interpreted Union officers' compliance reflexively as respect for gender and gentility itself, and thus as confirmation of their own values.[25] And in fact, Union men, like their enemies, did bring to the fight a set of deeply embedded gender assumptions about women's nonpartisanship that proved hard to dislodge. But there was more to it than that, as Mary Greenhow Lee astutely indicated. For as the legal thinker Francis Lieber put it in 1863 when he prepared a formal set of instructions for the use of the United States army in the field, the laws or usages of modern war (unlike the barbaric practices of earlier times) specifically recognized the protection of "inoffensive citizens of the hostile country" as part of the larger object of limiting the severity of war itself and minimizing practices that "make the return to peace unnecessarily difficult." Section 27 of the "Instructions for the Government of the Armies of the United States in the Field" specifically enjoined officers to "acknowledge and protect, in hostile countries occupied by them . . . the person of the inhabitants, especially those of women."[26] In seeking—and getting—orders of protection, women like Kimball and Lee harnessed both individual men's gender assumptions and those embedded in the international laws of war. In that respect they traded not only on their gender but more consequentially, perhaps, on the United States army's need to see itself as a model modern army abiding by the principles of civilized warfare, including the protection of enemy women.

But there was much else in the laws of war that followed from the recognition that "war is not carried on by arms alone." The protection of noncombatants was a general principle. But modern usages allowed for the harsh treatment of civilians who fell into the orbit of combat in areas occupied by armies. Armies engaged in a siege could, as part of the tactics of war, starve hostile belligerents. And they could act harshly against noncombatants in a civil war who showed themselves to be partisans dangerous or detrimental to the state's cause though not members of the regular army. Those "enemy combatants, not belonging to the regular army," many of whom operated in occupied areas—the laws specifically listed scouts, armed prowlers, war rebels, spies, war traitors, captured messengers—could suffer penalty of death. And on this Lieber was explicit that womanhood did not matter: "The law of war, like the criminal law regarding other offenses, makes no difference on account of the difference of sexes, concerning the spy, the war-traitor or the war-rebel," he wrote.[27]

The tensions between women as a protected class in war and as non-regular parties to war accountable as other citizens for their acts, runs through Lieber's document as it would through the history of the American Civil War. In 1861 and 1862, Union officers issued many orders of protection in the Confederate territory they occupied. Most of that territory was still small enclaves on the Atlantic coast, places that Union troops had taken early, like the areas around Hampton Roads, Virginia, or Beaufort, South Carolina, but by the spring of 1862 it also included a large swath of southern Louisiana that fell into Union hands along with New Orleans. Kate Stone, a rich young Louisiana woman who lived through that occupation, claimed that so many women "were getting letters of protection from the general at the Bend," that her mother was one of only three who would not stoop to it.[28] But officers bound by the laws of war had conflicting obligations in relation to enemy women. As soldiers' recognition of Confederate ladies' dangerously partisan activity grew, as the rigors and scope of occupation generated new policies, women's demands for protection would increasingly go unanswered. In places like Winchester and New Orleans, "secesh" women would appeal in vain for protection and would find themselves held accountable for what Union officers increasingly regarded as treason. But in the early days of the war, the idea that women were outside war, that they were entitled to protection in it, held firm.

For both Confederate and Union military officials, a reckoning with elite women's politics and national allegiance started early. Given the ingrained assumptions men themselves brought to the encounter, it was a hard lesson learned through repeated and often dangerous encounters on the ground. The men who arrested Rose O'Neal Greenhow learned it quickly, by the middle of the first summer of the war, in fact, for the idea that women could pose a real threat to military operations arose first in reference to women spies. The problem would never abate: It persisted to the very end of the war. But already by the summer of 1861, governments North and South had to contend with what one Lincoln official called "fashionable women spies."[29] The arrests of Greenhow, Phillips, and the rest hardly prepared President Lincoln or his war department for what lay ahead, but it was a wake-up call.

The issue posed by the existence of female spies was an awkward one in American political thought: the idea of women as traitors, indeed of women as *capable of treason.* Theoretically, of course, as citizens white women bore the same obligation to refrain from treason as men. Treason statutes formally embraced them too. The government of the Confederate States of America lifted its treason statute directly from the American Constitution, including its gender-neutral language of "persons": "Treason against this Confederacy shall consist only in levying war against it, or in adhering to its enemies, giving them aid and comfort. No person shall be convicted of treason unless on the testimony of two witnesses to the same overt act, or on confession in open court." But the critical question was whether a married woman could levy war. Part of the issue as it had been posed in the key 1805 case, *Martin v. State of Massachusetts,* was whether a woman's allegiance was of any value to the state, or whether her disloyalty could impose any harm. Was she capable of treason? And if she was, did states want to prosecute married women for treason, and did it want to hold wives to exactly the same standard of allegiance as their husbands? The legislature in revolutionary-era Massachusetts had explicitly included women in each of the three statutes that demanded loyalty to the revolution (the statutes defining treason, requiring oaths of allegiance, and punishing traitors by the confiscation of property). But it was exceedingly rare for women to be so charged. Post–Revolutionary War governments, including the federal one, had backed away from the recognition of women's political sovereignty implied in wartime statutes. In the Martin case, where the defendant won, the peacetime state expressed a greater interest in a woman's obedience to her husband than in securing her loyalty and obligation as an individual citizen to the state. It seemed the greater wisdom was in the state keeping its hands off married women and upholding the privacy of marriage, the principle of marital unity, and a husband's legal authority over his wife. That postwar conservative gender order shaped the terms of women's citizenship throughout the first half of the nineteenth century, leaving in abeyance the larger matter of women and treason.[30]

The issue reemerged quickly in the Civil War. Like the state of Massachusetts in the 1780s, the Union and Confederate governments would have plenty of reason to reconsider the question of whether a married woman could levy war against the state and give aid and comfort to its enemies. Did the state's greater interest lie in the protection of marriage and a husband's legal rights? or in recognition of women citizens as political individuals capable of treason? The landscape of gender and treason in the Civil War has not been mapped, but it is critical territory to survey.[31]

When the issue was first posed by a few prominent women spies, Confederate women imagined it all a game. "It is so delightful to be of enough consequence to be arrested," Mary Boykin Chesnut quipped in August 1861 on news of the arrest of the alleged spies Mrs. Greenhow, Eugenia Levy Phillips, and a Mrs. Gwin. The majority of women eventually detained by the Confederate and Union governments on charges of spying were, in fact, poor women—Unionist women in Confederate east Tennessee, Richmond, and other parts of the C.S.A., and pro-Confederate women in Union Missouri, Kentucky, and Union-occupied parts of the C.S.A. Probably the greatest number of female spies were slaves, women critical to Unionist networks operating in Confederate areas and to Union military operations everywhere. But it was the sensational cases of "fashionable women spies" that caught the attention of Mary Chesnut and the public at large in 1861 and that have held it ever since.[32]

Already by July 1861 Chesnut's elite Richmond circle was buzzing with stories of women's daring exploits. Chesnut was excited by reports of beautiful young women riding into Confederate camps with "letters done up in their back hair," as Greenhow's young courier had apparently done in relaying news of federal troop numbers and movement to General Beauregard on the eve of the battle of Bull Run. And there were others less famous, like Hannah Townell, the young woman who claimed credit for transmitting "timely information" of the approach of the enemy in the battle of Big Bethel, Virginia, in June 1861. "They are our spies," Chesnut said proudly of Greenhow, Townell, and the rest.[33]

But the other side had theirs as well. From the very beginning of the war, Chesnut and her circle saw federal spies everywhere: Mary Todd Lincoln's mother and sister in the first Confederate capital, Montgomery, in April 1861 ("I should watch them," Chesnut wrote); an "ancient female" she sized up as a Yankee spy sitting across from her at a dinner table in a Richmond boarding house later that year; a couple of women too well dressed to be Confederates sitting across from her on a train en route to Alabama in the summer of 1862. And in the Confederate capital, Richmond, Unionist women were under suspicion and surveillance by Confederate authorities as early as July 1861. The *Richmond Dispatch* urged action—that they be "exposed and dealt with as alien enemies to the country." The authorities probably had their sights already fixed on Elizabeth Van Lew, the Richmond lady who had already initiated the complex of dangerous activities that would make her a central figure in the Unionist spy ring that operated in the city to the very end of the war. Though certainly the stuff of high drama, Chesnut's accounts were not all fiction. By the fall of 1861 Union and Confederate military men and state officials had women on their payrolls as spies and the U.S. government had enemy women under arrest for treasonable activity, including military espionage.[34]

From the beginning, women spies like Rose O'Neal Greenhow, Belle Boyd, and even Elizabeth Van Lew, had regarded their gender as disguise.[35] But the disguise was as much philosophical as physical, with the women strategically inhabiting a set of assumptions about women's nature and alienation from politics and war and making use of the ideological space those ideas opened up as much as the physical space for papers provided by the chignon or hoop skirt. No one, apparently, believed in women's nonpartisanship as fervently as the women themselves. Rose O'Neal Greenhow, though operating a covert spy operation, had the nerve to accuse Union secretary of state Seward of impropriety in "turning its arms against the breasts of women and children." Greenhow expected to have it both ways. Even as she took credit for her espionage work for the Confederacy ("my mischief," she coquettishly put it), she inveighed against the Lincoln government's violation of women's customary impunity. "My suffering will afford a significant lesson to the women of the South, that sex or condition is no bulwark against the surging billows of the 'irrepressible conflict,'" she chastised the Union secretary of state. The argument had great public resonance. The treatment of Greenhow was shocking, the *Richmond Whig Leader* declaimed. By August 1861, with Greenhow in jail, and women, or so at least Chesnut said, subject to physical search at federal borders—"false hair taken off and searched for papers, pistols sought for under 'cotillons reverses,' bustles suspect, hoop skirts ruthlessly torn off"—even elite women's ability to act under cover of gender was narrowing.[36]

Clearly unprepared, military officials North and South had to confront the dangerous evidence of women's political activity and to find ways to hold them accountable. In 1861 the response on both sides was tentative and reluctant. Even Greenhow, after repeated arrests, suffered only imprisonment, followed by banishment across the lines into Confederate territory. The reluctance to punish women as traitors would never disappear entirely: no woman was ever executed for treason in the American Civil War. Men apparently still shrank from that full accounting. But the reluctance would recede as state and military men's recognition of women's capacity for treason grew and a painful intelligence record accrued. By 1863 military prisons (Union and Confederate) had their share of women prisoners, Confederate women were being tried by military commission in Union-occupied territory (women accounted for about 4 percent of all Union court-martials), and state and military officials on both sides contended with the consequences of women's treasonous behavior on the ground and demanded action against traitors "without regard to sex."[37] "Fashionable women spies" were only the beginning. As the recognition of damage grew, so did soldiers' willingness to hold women perpetrators accountable.

Judging from the uproar in the press, the real wake-up call for Southern women came not so much with the arrest and banishment of a cluster of Confederate spies, but with the treatment of secesh women in the occupied South. The key development was the fall of New Orleans to Union troops in the spring of 1862. For then, as all the world would come to know, the head of the occupying forces, Major General Benjamin Butler, facing the constant public harassment of his troops by the secesh ladies of the city, vowed to treat future offenders as he would any "woman of the town plying her avocation." He planned to treat them, that is, as prostitutes. Benjamin Butler's General Order No. 28 reverberated all over the United States and the C.S.A., engendering a heated argument about the treatment of enemy women in war that was transatlantic in scope.[38]

The story of Butler's actions in New Orleans is often told in tones of moral condemnation that echo the contemporary coverage. New Orleans has thus been taken as a sui generis case, largely because of Butler's instantly infamous status.[39] But in fact there was nothing really unusual about New Orleans except the federal commander's wickedly acute response to pro-Confederate ladies' usual attempts to provoke occupying troops. At exactly the same moment in Winchester, Virginia, in the spring and summer of 1862, Union generals Nathaniel Banks and Robert H. Milroy grappled with exactly the same problem of open defiance from resident Confederate women. Like Butler, they too issued a raft of orders and proclamations calculated to control the ladies, though none so creative, admittedly, as Butler's famous "woman order."

It is in the broader context of the struggles in other occupied places that the real significance of what transpired in New Orleans emerges. For it was not so much Butler's single action or the outraged response to it that matters, but what the episode signaled about the new accountability imposed on Confederate women by enemy soldiers: a new estimation of the value of women's loyalty and of their political salience. All over the Confederate South, elite women in areas under Union occupation claimed their privilege as ladies to act politically while disowning responsibility.

By late April 1862, when New Orleans fell to federal guns, the process of Union occupation of Confederate territory had just begun, but it already encompassed much of northern Virginia, parts of eastern Virginia, points along the coast of North Carolina, South Carolina, and Florida, southeastern Louisiana along the Mississippi River, middle and western Tennessee, a part of Arkansas, northern Mississippi, and northern Alabama. To that would soon be added Baton Rouge and other areas of the lower Mississippi.[40] Already a cordon of federal power rimmed the Confederacy. The belligerent occupied population to be controlled was growing fast.

Even before federal troops marched off the ships and into New Orleans to take up quarters at the Custom House, Southern women's reputation for "violent secessionism," as U.S. General Thomas Williams put it, preceded them, the intelligence harvest of earlier encounters. "How do you account for the secession proclivities of the sex," General Williams wondered in a letter to his wife written aboard ship off Ship Island,

Mississippi, on March 29 as he awaited orders to move up the river to New Orleans. Williams braced for the encounter. But when he marched ashore, heavily armed amid a dense crowd of the disaffected, the women were missing in action. For three or four days the women laid low, fearful, as everyone was, of mob violence. Then they emerged.[41]

In New Orleans, a portion of the ladies were determined to express their political loyalties in the face of enemy occupation, and they did, in ways both trivial and treasonous. Their instinct was shared by ladies across the country in Winchester, Virginia, and in the numerous other places that had fallen into enemy hands that spring. As elsewhere they calculated their public actions to signal contempt for soldiers and officers: putting on a show to avoid contact, by the way they dressed, by verbal assaults and physical taunts. Elegantly dressed girls and ladies stormed off streetcars when federal soldiers got on, stepped into the gutter to avoid passing them on the sidewalk, switched their skirts aside as soldiers passed, and, so General Butler said, whirled on their heel in disgust as he approached, presenting him with a full view of their backsides. Ladies in Winchester, Virginia, had their own bag of tricks. They took to wearing thick veils and sunbonnets (what one Unionist woman derided as "Jeff Davis bonnets") to avoid eye contact and carrying parasols in front of their faces even on cloudy days. In New Orleans and Baton Rouge young women openly flaunted orders against the display of "all devices, signs, and flags of the Confederacy," attaching small homemade ones to their dresses. "Henceforth I wear one pinned to my bosom," Sarah Morgan Dawson boasted on May 9 after reading the order. "The man who says take it off will have to pull it off himself; the man who dares attempt it—well! A pistol in my pocket fills up the gap."[42] Dawson's was the braggadocio style of the teenager; she was only 16.

But whatever the style, some of the ladies in occupied cities were intent on provocation, watched carefully for a reaction, and prided themselves on landing their blows. "They seemed to feel the insult," Clara Solomon, a New Orleans teenager, reported triumphantly when she made a show of vacating her pew as soldiers entered her church one Sunday. Mary Greenhow Lee, a Winchester widow engaged in treasonous gender warfare, was delighted by reports that Union troops thought the Winchester ladies the worst. The soldiers boasted, she claimed, that they would "make the Secessionist women hold their tongues." But no. The violence of secesh women's political speech shows the sense of impunity the ladies felt. The billingsgate or fishwife style was much in evidence in Winchester, New Orleans, and elsewhere. One of Mary Greenhow Lee's neighbors earned her admiration for the verbal wars she waged with General Milroy, the commanding officer in Winchester in the spring of 1862. When soldiers camped on her neighbors' grounds, the woman told them they were "welcome to 6 feet of southern land but nothing else." She regularly got into shouting matches with Milroy, asserting once, for example, that John Brown was the cause of the war, which he called a lie. She shouted: "Don't you say I lie." And he, enraged, ordered her out. She seemed to relish the encounters, her little chance to wage war on the enemy. The ladies could be crude. One "handsomely dressed" Winchester lady laid into a Union soldier on the street, asking if "that son of a b—h (pointing to one of the Yankees) [was] going to make one our own men [pointing to a prisoner of war in his charge] dig a grave for a d—d yankee." And they were bloodthirsty, shocking themselves sometimes by the violence of their own utterances. One infantry sergeant in Tennessee recalled a young woman cursing him and his comrades up and down, saying "that if it were in her power she would kill us every one right there." Southern men sat in U.S. military prisons for less.[43]

But if most of this was just "annoyance," as General Butler wrote, some of it was hard for the troops to put up with and thus threatening to military discipline and civic peace. In Rome, Georgia, the students at a girls school emptied chamber pots from their balcony on the heads of passing soldiers; in New Orleans a group of women in the French Quarter hit Flag Officer Farragut with the contents of theirs as he passed in full dress uniform. In New Orleans, however, the straw that broke Butler's back was polite ladies' habit of spitting in the officers' faces. "Such venom one must see to believe," General Williams wrote. To him the violence of women's political beliefs was so unnatural it unsexed them. "Such unsexing was hardly ever before in any cause or country so marked and so universal," he mused, "I look at them and think of fallen angels."[44]

Harper's Weekly offered a hilarious spoof of the whole spitting episode. But if the ladies' spitting revue was good comic material, it was also deeply disturbing. In New Orleans, Winchester, and other occupied areas, federal officers and soldiers felt that they were fighting women, something they had clearly never bargained on. The violence of elite women's secessionism was doubly disturbing because it posed both a moral challenge to their assumptions about gender and a military challenge to occupying forces. One Union officer in New Orleans who had been spit on was at a loss as to the appropriate response. Asked by a friend why he didn't do anything, he said, "What could I do, Davis, to two women?"[45] That was the question Generals Milroy, Banks, and Butler faced all over the expanding territory of the occupied South in 1862. When it came to treasonous women, "the embarrassment is in knowing what to do with them," as one federal officer put it.[46]

By the late spring of 1862, when the Union took New Orleans, military commanders were less inclined to turn a blind eye to the secesh ladies' provocations, having reason to suspect by then that their rebel loyalties consisted of more than gestures. In Winchester, Mary Greenhow Lee's public gestures of contempt concealed activities explicitly defined as treason, some of them punishable by execution. Although it took the federals some time to figure it out, Lee was the center of a Confederate mail network that carried letters (sometimes fifty a month) and money across the lines. Lee was also a smuggler who stockpiled money and contraband goods (she called them her "treasonable supplies") for distribution to rebel soldiers; and she was a spy who gathered and transmitted military intelligence to Generals Stonewall Jackson and Turner Ashby commanding Confederate troops in the Shenandoah Valley. Strictly according to the laws of war, Lee's activities in conducting unauthorized intercourse between the territories occupied by belligerent armies, smuggling, communicating information to the enemy, and giving "positive aid and comfort to the enemy," marked her as a disloyal citizen, spy, and war traitor, the perpetrator of treasonous acts "highly punishable" even to "death and hanging." Commanding officers in Winchester kept her under close surveillance. But it was not until the war was nearly over, in early 1865, that General Sheridan finally banished her, giving her two days' notice before removing her behind Confederate lines.[47]

In some places, as federal officers reluctantly acknowledged, secesh ladies were dangerous enemies. In New Orleans, General Butler was not inclined to fool around. "We were 2,500 men in a city . . . of 150,000 inhabitants," he wrote shortly after the event, "all hostile, bitter, defiant, explosive, standing literally in a magazine, a spark only needed for destruction." The women, he feared, would provide the spark. As Butler saw it, the women challenged his ability to retain control of the conquered city. Everyone in New Orleans in the spring of 1862 feared mob violence, and no one underestimated the difficulties of holding the place. This place cannot "be held for the Union except by military force," General Williams said from his heavily fortified redoubt at the St. Charles Hotel on May 5. "A force of 6500 men is not in excess for the object of keeping so large a disaffected population as this in order." Butler's force was not nearly so large: the governor of Louisiana had accused Jefferson Davis of abandoning New Orleans. Butler, he said, "held possession of New Orleans with troops not equalling in number an ordinary city mob." Certainly Butler didn't underestimate the task. One of his first acts in taking the city was to execute a citizen, William Mumford, who had violated the terms of surrender by removing the federal flag from the U.S. Customs House. He "arrested the men who hurrahed for Beauregard," charging them with treasonous speech. Faced with hordes of "bejewelled, becrinolined and laced creatures calling themselves ladies," who "took every means of insulting my troops and inflaming the mob," Butler took a similarly hard line. How long, he asked, could his men be expected to put up with the insults before one snapped, inflaming the crowd, precipitating street violence, and requiring him to clear the streets with artillery fire? He could just see it, he said, the howl that would come up about how "we had murdered these fine women."[48]

To Butler the women posed a clear military threat. He was convinced that they acted deliberately to incite men to resistance and riot. And he repudiated directly their self-representation as patriots. "Women secessionists of the city," he always called them, defining them by their politics. As such, of course, they were patently guilty of disloyalty to the United States, if not outright treason. To Butler the women were partisans in war. What they called patriotism was to him not love of country but "acts which [they] think proper to do in carrying on the war." He engaged them as enemies and gave careful thought about how to do so. From a strictly military point of view the appropriate response was simple—"arrest and transportation." But that would be "a source of perpetual turmoil" and possibly "ripen into insurrection." This was a "a unique but dangerous entanglement." Butler refused to play the heavy and tried not to create martyrs. The trick, he explained later, had been to find an "order that would execute itself."[49]

Butler was hardly alone in the challenge he faced. In other occupied cities commanding officers also struggled for a means to combat the ladies, "to compel respect for the occupying troops," as General Philip Sheridan put it in the Shenandoah Valley, and to defuse the threats to their military regimes. In Winchester, General Banks passed a raft of orders and proclamations, warning men and women against "circulating flying rumors and creating false excitements," claiming that any women showing "exultation" at Confederate military victories would be shot, prohibiting the wearing of Jeff Davis bonnets, and prohibiting Winchester "ladies" from insulting "the soldiers." In August 1862, before it was common in the occupied South, he insisted that secesh women take an oath of allegiance to the United States government to earn rights to enter and exit occupied towns, conduct trade, or buy foodstuffs from army sutlers, the only provisioners left in town.[50]

Butler had the same objectives, but his response was so creative and offensive to settled gender views that its propriety is still passionately debated. In May he promulgated the now-famous General Order No. 28 that asserted that contemptuous women would be treated like prostitutes. Far from a "maladroit order," Butler had called the bejeweled ladies' bluff, forcing them to police themselves or to sit in the municipal jail with the other women of the town. Needless to say, most policed themselves.[51] In New Orleans, Winchester, and other parts of the Union-occupied South, military men moved to hold women accountable for their actions. "The law of war, like the criminal law, makes no difference on account of the difference of sexes, concerning the spy, the war traitor, or the war-rebel," Francis Lieber specified in 1863. By that point, the official instructions issued to Union armies only confirmed decisions already made in the field.[52]

No Union order in Virginia or anywhere else drew the media attention that Butler's did. It was a propaganda bonanza for the hard-pressed Confederate States. The outrage knew no bounds and extended from the mayor's office in New Orleans to Jefferson Davis's desk. It hit the Northern press hard and reverberated even across the Atlantic to Lord Palmerston's cabinet, where it briefly became a pawn in sensitive international discussions over the recognition of the Confederacy. Most, except Butler's defenders, seemed to interpret the order not as threatening elite New Orleans women with arrest as prostitutes, but as a license to rape: "turning over the women of New Orleans to his soldiers," as Mary Chesnut tersely put it. The mayor of New Orleans turned it into an affair of honor, defending the ladies' behavior as a manifestation of their displeasure (as if it were a personal matter). Calling the order a "war upon women and children," he determined to "vindicate the honor of the virtuous women of the city." After a couple of go-arounds, Mayor Monroe got a cell in Fort Jackson for his trouble.[53]

The Confederate press and President Davis latched onto the order as to a lifeline. From May 1862 to the end of the war, Davis never ceased to include it in his litany of Yankee barbarisms and as evidence of the Confederates' higher cause. In August 1862 he ranted to the Confederate Senate and House of Representatives about the episode as a violation of the usages of civilized warfare and the dictates of humanity. In December, he declared Butler a war criminal, marked for execution if captured. The grounds he specifically cited were the murder of William Mumford in New Orleans for raising the Confederate flag and the general orders that invited soldiers "to insult and outrage the wifes, the mothers and the sisters of our citizens."[54]

The order was also put to work in the field, rousing men to military valor. Butler's insult breathed new life into the old Southern line about protecting womanhood. In May, officials at the headquarters of the Western Department at Corinth, Mississippi, commanded that Butler's General Order No. 28 be read on dress parade. "MEN OF THE SOUTH," General G. T. Beauregard's appendage went. "Shall our mothers, our wives, our daughters, and our sisters be thus outraged by the ruffianly soldiers of the North, to whom is given the right to treat at their pleasure the ladies of the South as common harlots? Arouse, friends, and drive back from our soil those infamous invaders of our homes, and disturbers of our family ties." John Hunt Morgan printed it up on a broadside and distributed it in advance of his campaign in Kentucky to recruit men to the Confederate army. In 1864 it was still doing yeoman duty as one general, John B. Gordon, reminded his troops of the "proclamation of the infamous Butler" as they formed the line of battle near Richmond at the Williamsburg road "and of the fate which awaited us if defeated."[55]

For a brief moment it even looked as if the New Orleans flap might deliver the ultimate propaganda yield: British recognition of the Confederacy. After one Sir John Walsh made a parliamentary speech calling Butler's order an act "of barbarism akin to Ghengis Kahn or Nadir Shah" that warranted breaking British neutrality, the British prime minister, Lord Palmerston, got on board. Penning an indignant note to Charles Francis Adams, the American consul in London, he charged that Butler had violated international practice: that "it is the practice of the commander of the conquering army to protect to the utmost the inhabitants and especially the female part of them" and not, as Butler had done, to hand "over the female inhabitants of a conquered city to the unbridled license of an unrestrained soldiery." Adams, who saw the pro-Confederate Palmerston as spoiling for a fight, pulled out all the diplomatic guns, accusing the prime minister of diplomatic irregularity and ignorance. But he also pushed back against the idea of female innocence. Far from associating the streets with an invitation to sexual harm, Adams pointed out, New Orleans women took men's public deference as such a matter of course they "assumed on it." Instead of seeking the kind of "severe seclusion" European women had in occupied territory during their nineteenth-century wars, New Orleans women had instead taken to the streets, behaving in ways "indecent and intolerable," indulging in "grossly insulting speech," spitting on the objects of their detestation, and training children to disrespect the coffins of the federal dead. Butler's order, he said, was not only necessary, it worked, and "in less than 24 hours brought the 'ladies' of New Orleans to a wholsome realizing sense of the situation."[56] The diplomatic squall soon passed.

Butler's order drew ringing support in one other quarter: among the South's slaves. In Union Missouri, the slave Mattie Jackson recalled how hard her mistress, a rebel sympathizer, took the news of the fall of New Orleans. But not so her slaves, including Jackson's mother, who took to singing a new song they learned from Union soldiers.

That's the way Columbia speaks, let all men believe her
That's the way Columbia speaks, instead of yellow fever
He [Ben Butler] sent the saucy women up and made them treat us well
He helped the poor and snubbed the rich; they thought he was the devil
Bully for Ben Butler, then, they thought he was so handy
Bully for Ben Butler, then—Yankee Doodle Dandy.[57]

Well might Confederates, conservative British, and even the Northern press condemn Ben Butler and defend the right of the ladies of New Orleans to spit on Union troops. But slave women had a special perspective on the ladies—their mistresses, after all—and like Union soldiers, they took a particular pleasure in seeing Confederate ladies called to account.

In New Orleans, the unflappable Butler and after him General Banks (newly transferred from Winchester and so well versed in the challenges of gender warfare) continued to engage the enemy. In late June, Butler arrested and imprisoned Eugenia Levy Phillips, the old intimate of Rose O'Neal Greenhow, now resident in the city, for showing public disrespect to the funeral cortege of a Union officer. Butler had already warned Mrs. Phillips to desist from disloyal speech and acts, so whatever calculation went into her recklessness was seriously off. Informed, probably by one of her slaves, that she had been "laughing and mocking at [the] remains" of Lieutenant DeKay from her balcony as it passed below, Butler had her confined at Ship Island at the mouth of the Mississippi River.[58]

But the most dramatic evidence of the long-term meaning of developments in New Orleans and elsewhere came not with the increasingly harsh treatment meted out to individual women like Phillips but with

the general orientation toward enemy women as a class. In Winchester, as commanding officers of occupying Union forces took the full measure of women like Mary Greenhow Lee and her rebel neighbors, they ceased issuing orders of protection. As Lee's treasonous activity geared up, General Banks laid down the new law and refused the moral injunction to act the gentleman. When a Mrs. Strother Jones wrote to him in mid-1862 to complain about hay and corn seized by his quartermasters, she expressed the hope that he would be "willing to attend to the rights of

all helpless women." But Banks refused. "You are mistaken in supposing we come into Virginia for your protection," he lectured her. "We make no pretensions to that Chivalry which vilifies the major part of the American people and then abandons its own women and children to seek the protection of those they despise."[59] Politics, not womanhood, mattered to Banks. With experience in governing an occupied town, he came sooner than most Union officers to the recognition that some of the dangers his troops faced came from rebel women. Butler was not long behind him. By the end of 1862 the Union government had given up all illusion about how easy it would be to reclaim most Southerners to the Union. A policy of hard war included much harder attitudes toward rebel women. By 1862 one Union soldier moving south with the army through the Mississippi Valley anxiously observed that they had resorted to "making war on women and children." In May of that year, one plantation mistress in Louisiana wrote a local U.S. officer about whether her property would be respected. But this time instead of orders of protection she was given thirty minutes to clear out of her house and then it was burned before her eyes. By the time General William Tecumseh Sherman brought the policy of hard war to fruition, there was nothing left of the idea that women were entitled to protection. When Sherman's columns reached Fayetteville, North Carolina, at the very end of the war, one rebel woman politely asked for a guard. But this was not Berryville in early 1862. "You'll git no protection," one soldier shot back. "That's played out long ago."[60]

One marker of the new recognition of women's political personhood and salience came far earlier than Sherman's march: the insistence that women citizens of occupied territory take the oath of allegiance to prove their loyalty. Women citizens' *capacity* to take an oath had never been in doubt, as slaves' and free blacks' had been. But there is very little evidence that women were ever *required* to take oaths of allegiance after the Revolutionary War or that it was insisted on by Union forces in the early part of the Civil War.[61] But by June 1863 all "registered enemies of the United States" were required to take the oath of allegiance, and in New Orleans, at least, that order was enforced on women. In New Orleans those who refused to swear an oath of allegiance to the U.S. government had to leave the city and go within Confederate lines. Contemporary reporting suggested just how novel, and shocking, that was. General Bowen (the new commanding officer) intended to "out Butler Butler," the *Harper's Weekly* correspondent put it. *Harper's* offered an amazing sketch of the scene that ensued in General Bowen's office, as enemy ladies, still becrinolined and bejeweled, flocked in, in vain attempts to wrangle their way out of the requirement by dint of coquettish charm. Still sure that the commander would make an exception for them, they ran every trick in the playbook. Some were "despondent" and some "haughty," the *Harper's* correspondent wrote, as if they scorned the very favors they had come to try; some tried appealing "to the conscience of the venerable Captain Nott, as a father, while others vainly waste their bewitching smiles upon that fascinating young officer, Lieutenant Milner Brown, neither of whom can swerve one inch from the inexorable duty of swearing them in or banishing them from Dixie." Daughterly appeals, coquetry, scorn: to the women's shock, nothing worked, and like the other Confederate citizens they were forced to choose between hard exile in Dixie or humiliating subjection to the Yankee flag.[62] The insistence that rebel women take the oath marked federals' new estimation of how much coercion it would take to compel allegiance. In New Orleans, as in provost marshals' offices all over the occupied South, Confederate ladies were taught a hard lesson in their political accountability to a state they regarded as their enemy.

Requiring women to take the oath of allegiance posed a resounding answer to the question "Can a woman levy war?" Clearly women's loyalty was a valuable thing to a state at war. It could be cultivated; it could be coerced; but it could no longer be taken for granted.[63] Even for the rich ladies of New Orleans, marriage and gender no longer offered protective cover for political acts. Called out of coverture, the state now defined them as sovereign political individuals capable of dangerous partisan acts, answerable for their own beliefs and actions. If the women found it ludicrous, the state found it necessary: "Is it not absurd," Mary Greenhow Lee wrote, when she learned women would have to take the oath, "that we should be made of so much importance, treating us as if we were men." By 1862, Union forces had already been forced into a whole new estimation of women's political salience. Thereafter rebel ladies, hopeful of protection from enemy troops, would watch helplessly as their plantations burned, would stand trial before U.S. army military commissions on various treason charges, sit out considerable sentences in federal military prisons, and on occasion suffer sentence of execution for treason.[64] Not just Antigone anymore.

Jefferson Davis never tired of talking about the Yankee abuse of Southern womanhood, never missed an opportunity to offer it as proof of Yankee perfidy. This is becoming "a savage war," he wrote to Robert E. Lee right after Butler's order, "in which no quarter is to be given and no sex to be spared." Davis's righteousness on the subject never waned. But he might as well have been talking about his own army. The Yankee experience as an army of occupation had certainly drawn the United States into a dangerous encounter with enemy women. But the demands of mobilizing citizens on their own territory had also drawn Confederate military men and state officials into war against their own citizens, some of them women.[65] The landscape of gender and treason extended beyond the occupied cities and towns of the Civil War South into the heart of the Confederate state.

In the Confederate States of America, the question of loyalty was posed not only by enemy women in occupied territory but in far more unsettling ways by female citizens in their own national territory. That territory never expanded beyond the original eleven slave states, notwithstanding raids into Union territory and diplomatic attempts to acquire new territory in Cuba and Mexico. The C.S.A. never made good on its imperial ambitions. It had trouble enough holding its own ground. From the very outset of the war, Confederate civil and military officials encountered Southern white women acting in ways calculated to cause damage: women spies working for the Union were the obvious case. But while the numbers of women arrested as spies and for various kinds of treasonable conversation, correspondence, and trade continued to grow throughout the war, the problem of women's loyalty—or rather disloyalty—assumed wholly new proportions in the struggle against Southern Unionists and, by late 1862, against powerful bands of deserters and guerillas. It was in that ongoing fight that Confederates confronted large numbers of women, many avowedly Unionist, some not, but all in determined opposition to the Confederate state and its military agenda, who defied the state's authority to conscript and undermined its capacity to wage war.[66]

As the Confederate state moved against its new enemies, old prohibitions about violence against women went out the window and military men began to pursue a startlingly harsh, even brutal, policy on the ground. In Mississippi one judge who pressed Jefferson Davis for "an iron rule enforced with iron hand and hearts of stone" against deserter bands urged no quarter for the women. "The women and noncombatants must be handled speedily and roughly," he advised; against them, "the most radical and severe treatment is required." And indeed in Jones County, Mississippi, and in western and central North Carolina, East Tennessee, northern Alabama, Florida, and everywhere desertion reached militarily threatening proportions, the Confederate states waged war against its domestic enemies and they did not spare the women.[67]

But still a deep confusion about married women's political standing, their obligation to refrain from treason independent of their husbands, and their accountability to the state hounded Confederate officials for the duration of the war. The confusion left them open to politically damaging charges, not least from the women themselves, about the treatment of female citizens. A war against disloyal women might have been necessary, but every official involved scuttled away from the consequences. The politics of protection played out beyond anyone's capacity to foresee or control in the Confederate war.

The official Confederate position was that women were innocent parties, bystanders and victims in war, worthy recipients of male protection. Nobody thought they had anything of real value to offer the state. So even as the secretary of war, James Seddon, tried to squeeze every last man out of the Confederate population—even casting his eye jealously on slaves —the idea of using women was never entertained. Citizens periodically talked about fighting "every man, woman and child," but mobilization went on in reference exclusively to men (the whole "arms bearing population,"), maybe including black men. The only persons not citizens of the C.S.A. who were required to leave or be considered enemy aliens were "males aged fourteen and older." Women, it seems, not only couldn't help the state, they had little capacity to harm it. Instead they were grouped among those precious possessions men fought wars to defend: "all that is dear to humanity—property, honor, wives, children and homes . . . for us are staked on success," as Seddon put it in his one formulaic mention of women.[68]

But Seddon's views were seriously outdated. For if nobody included white women in calculations of Confederate manpower, they did start to take serious notice of women's political activity and of the damage they could inflict. By early 1862 the issue of citizens' loyalty to the Confederate States of America was pressing, and officials moved to enforce loyalty and punish treason. The problem was worst, not surprisingly, in areas where opposition to secession had been strong and where Unionism persisted after the onset of war. For the matter of loyalty in the Confederacy had something of a down-the-rabbit-hole quality—"loyal" Confederates were the traitors whom Generals Butler and Banks had battled in New Orleans and Winchester, while the disloyal, or "tories," were the men and women who never abandoned their original allegiance to the Union. The struggle against the Unionists straddled the chronology of United States and Confederate history. It dated from the secession crisis, that long political season of fear mongering, coercion, and violence, and it carried right on into and through the war. It didn't let up even with defeat, some said, but remained a vital aspect of the us-and-them politics of the American South into Reconstruction.

Nobody in the Confederate States of America underestimated the Unionist threat. From the very outset of the war, all of the governors and to some extent President Davis and his secretary of war were aware of the continuing significance of Unionist sentiment and organization in the states. And if they didn't know (they had all studied the election returns) every mailbag brought new reports, most of them from citizens informing on their neighbors. Reports rolled in from everywhere, but especially from areas that had been the heartland of Unionism in the secession crisis: west Virginia, western and central North Carolina, east Tennessee, northwest Georgia, piney woods Mississippi, and northern Alabama, where Yancey had promised to make the traitors pay. "Looke Sharpe" warned Governor Clark of North Carolina early in 1862 that loyalties in Rutherford County remained divided, that there were men in the county openly working against military enlistment, indeed, that the majority there was for the governor appointed by Lincoln to govern the occupied territories on the coast. Warnings poured in to Clark about the hostility to the war in the Blue Ridge counties and about local Unionists who continued to control local government, and of the number of men who said they would never go into the army.[69]

But the evidence of Unionism went beyond seditious speech and the avoidance of military service to embrace Unionist organizations, military companies, networks, and secret societies. In northern Alabama, where opposition to secession had been ferocious, one of the convention delegates, Robert Guttery, was subsequently accused of organizing "Union companies," of hoisting the Union flag and vowing to fight for Lincoln when federal troops made it to Alabama. Other reports confirmed in five northern Alabama counties the organization of military companies raised and equipped to defend the old government of the United States. In some, Unionists had apparently retained control of the local militia and thus had a ready-made force. In North Carolina, Governor Clark was alerted to the existence of secret Unionist organizations, including one organized by illiterate men and women at a prayer meeting. They had raised the white flag, the informant said, and declared themselves for peace. And in Georgia, as Governor Joseph Brown struggled both to win upcountry citizens to the Confederate cause and to protect them from the worst of the new Confederate state's demands, he contended with considerable treasonous activity. The Union men there had with "great success labored to keep up their Union party ever since the state seceded," a Mr. Campbell wrote him in 1862 about his neighborhood around Morganton. A very large majority (he estimated two-thirds) of the men "are Disloyal," not half a dozen had gone into service, and "nearly every one of the others have run away to E. Tenn," where they were lying out in the mountains.[70] In all of those places the evidence of disloyalty and its regional patterns traced divisions that originated in secession.

By late 1861 authorities in the individual states and the central government were already moving hard against the Unionists, jettisoning protections for freedom of speech and assembly, abandoning distinctions between sedition (disloyal speech) and treason (disloyal acts), encouraging vigilante action within communities, and moving anew to bring the power of the state down on its internal enemies. The approach was legal and military. The secretary of war authorized the imprisonment of men arrested for attending the Wheeling convention. Confederate prisons began to fill up with men and smaller numbers of women picked up on charges of sedition and treason, sometimes simply for hurrahing Lincoln. As early as July 1861 Governor Moore of Alabama categorized as seditious "any citizen declaring himself in favor of the Lincoln government, hoisting the United States flag, or declaring a readiness to fight on that side, or any other act of like character." He issued a variety of proclamations declaring his general intention to "use all the power of the state to suppress and curtail all acts of hostility to the state or to the Confederacy."[71] But from the first, in areas where Unionists posed a serious political threat, the response was also military, and even before the passage of the Conscription Act in April 1862 an open war was launched against the draft resisters and deserters, and the power of the state descended on dissident communities in the form of mounted militia companies and state and Confederate troops.

The situation was worst in western Virginia. Part of that territory was in the process of breaking off to become the state of West Virginia, a development the Confederate government fought hard. Hardly had secession been passed—over the strenuous objections of the northwestern delegates—before the governor, John Letcher, dispatched troops up into the Blue Ridge and Allegheny mountains to quell dissent and Unionist organization. In June 1861 he issued a proclamation pleading for unity and summoning the band of brothers; a month later he issued orders calling out the militia in six counties straddling what would become the dividing line between the states, ordering them to destroy all the railroad bridges on the major rivers and cut off communication to the free states to the north.[72]

But even as the devouring hordes of the Confederate army invaded northwest Virginia, Unionist organization flourished and by January the governor was inundated with pleas from loyal Confederate citizens begging more troops to defend the region. In Pocahontas County, which ultimately declared allegiance to the United States and the government of West Virginia, one citizen reported that Yankee troops had been guided into the area by local Unionists who fled over the lines and enlisted in the federal army. They maintained a steady flow of information through their friends still in the area who came and went with impunity from Confederate military camps. But others, worried more about social order than matters of national allegiance, simply begged relief from all of the mountain bands, plundering parties, and military expeditions that had already turned mountain Virginia into a civil war in miniature.[73]

It was in the early campaigns against the Unionists that Confederate authorities first were confronted by disloyal women in numbers large enough and engaged in acts damaging enough to be of concern. For the problem, as they discovered in West Virginia, was that Unionists operated not so much as individuals but as parts of political networks. Unionist men, those who went over the lines and those who remained near home, depended quite literally on their friends and families, a fact officials hunting them down soon recognized. "I fear we will never be able to destroy guerillas while we permit their friends to remain amongst us," a federal officer in Missouri told his superior. "Many men and women at home do us more damage than the regular soldier . . . [because] they feed, harbor and conceal the guerillas." In the Confederate South as in the Union border states, networks and circuits of political life were familial, no less for men than for women, and that put them all at risk when the army went after them.[74]

Sarah Thompson left a powerful account of how one of those Unionist networks operated in the area of Greenville, east Tennessee, and of the loyal white women, enslaved men and women, and white men who composed it. Greenville was in the heartland of Southern Unionism: the region had opposed the secession of the state by a ratio of two to one in the referendum of June 1861. Thompson's region of "upr est Tenesse was," by her estimation, "a good dele more than one half union." But after a highly dramatic raid in November 1861 by Unionist saboteurs who succeeded in burning five railroad bridges, the entire area was put under martial law. The pursuit of known Unionists started then and carried on without stop until the Union army occupied the area beginning in 1863. In fact, even as towns like nearby Knoxville were liberated (as the local Unionists saw it) in the fall of 1863, Greenville remained under Confederate control, contested militarily, for another year. Notwithstanding the original Unionist orientation of the area in the secession crisis, Thompson and her husband, Sylvanius, operated in a highly dangerous local context of Confederate military occupation and surveillance, in a region descending rapidly into guerilla war.[75]

It took some serious planning and organization to operate a Unionist network in that context. Thompson's account of theirs starts in September 1864 and circles back to the spring of 1862 when her husband went over the mountains to Kentucky and enlisted in the Union army. When he came back to raise more recruits for his company, he had to "ceep his self hid as a mater of corse" and he turned to her "to helpe him . . . as he had more confindens in me then eny one els." She was his "ade" (as she put it) or front man, moving about the countryside, approaching those she knew to be true to the Union cause, inquiring about their willingness to enlist and effectively serving as the local recruiting agent for the men her husband would guide over the mountains. She did not act alone but in league with other covert agents of the cause in east Tennessee: white Unionist men and women in the rural community around Greenville, and, as she was at pains to point out, "the colord pepell," slaves of Union men and rebels both. "We new who to trust," she explained later, wondering still at how "strange [it is that] these pore soles would worke all day in thare mastes servas and then goo all night for what thay caled thare ease of freedom." When the group of recruits was ready to go off, she would cook "a good lot of fude and put it in saks and then when the time wold come I wold meet them" at a place of her designating and "see that ore plans had not bin fond out by the enamy." Only then would she hand them off to her husband.[76]

Thompson also acted as intermediary and courier for the network, as many Union women in the border states did. One time her husband instructed her to go "see a colord man which was call alf and get him som men to take over the lings." After the men left she received whatever mail they sent back, once from a man who came in disguise to her home, then delivered it to other "union women," which is exactly how she identified them. Sarah Thompson was Sylvanius's partner. He was killed by Confederate soldiers in an ambush in early 1864. But from the spring of 1862 until his death, his ability to work as a federal recruiter depended crucially on a network of collaborators at home in Confederate territory marshaled by his wife.

Sarah Thompson was a "union woming" in her own right. She had a clear political identity and was known by it to rebel soldiers in the area. Like many others, she became a target of brutal harassment by rebel soldiers in Confederate east Tennessee who valued the military intelligence they knew the women had. As early as 1862, she says, rebel soldiers were "surchen ever house to whip and kill union men and forse them to goo in ther army" and in the process initiated a campaign of violence—she says it included murder—against Union women. Hers is a biblical account of the Unionists' passage through the wilderness. And as she tells it, modestly, as becomes a true Christian woman, women no less than men were engaged as the enemy. They were threatened, plundered, burned out, knocked about, and abused, she said, "in miny ways that wold not be proper for me to state here." "It was anuff for the rebels to cary off all youe had let it bee little or much it was yore all but thay much burn yor barns and a hass and ravis yor wifes and darts and hange by hes neck ar young boys to try to scare oute of them what thay did not knowe." Some of the sons were, in fact, hanged. She was threatened with the rope by soldiers in John Hunt Morgan's unit before she and her children were taken out by Union soldiers to the safe, federally occupied confines of Knoxville in the fall of 1864.[77]

In the end, Sarah Thompson would be known best for her role in the capture of Confederate raider John Hunt Morgan in September 1864, using precisely the network of local Unionists, male and female, black and white, she had long deployed against the rebels in Greenville.[78] But Thompson's account is more valuable for the quotidian than the spectacular. For what it offers is a rare ground-level account of how Unionist women in Greenville—key operatives in Unionist networks, possessed of valuable military intelligence, and out of the protection of their men—were engaged, as their counterparts were elsewhere in the front lines of the war against the domestic enemy. The recognition of women's salience in the treasonous politics of Unionist communities was already well advanced in some particularly divided places by 1862. By that point, in those places, Confederate authorities' reluctance to use violence against women citizens subsided fast.

For Confederate authorities, the turning point in the struggle with their own citizens came early, with the passage of the Conscription Act in April 1862. For as it did in Thompson's Greenville, the first draft act transformed Unionists' aversion to military service into a crime. After that, men aged 18 to 35, and later 17 to 50, who refused to submit to military service in the Confederate army, and all those who aided and abetted them, were criminals. No distinction remained between draft evaders, resisters, and deserters. From that point forward, all of them were pursued, sometimes in contexts of shocking violence, by the military forces of the states and the central government.

By late 1862 in many parts of the Confederate South the war against the deserters was on. Units of home guards and conscript cavalries went up into the fastnesses of the mountains, picked their way down into sheltered valleys, fanned out across the rolling Piedmont hills, and searched the dense river thickets in search of the tories and bushwhackers, as the deserters were called. And when they did, they found not just the men but the women arrayed against them.

The war with the deserters built steadily starting in 1862. By 1863 Jefferson Davis and his secretary of war were worried about draft resistance and desertion in many different parts of the national territory, and they were continually fielding reports from generals about the extent of desertion in their ranks. By May 1863 as much as one-fifth of the entire armed forces were absent without leave, a third by early 1864, and maybe two-fifths by early 1865. In response, Davis kept up a barrage of communication with state governors, urging firm enforcement of the law. At one point, for example, he urged Governor Vance of North Carolina not to suffer the actions of disloyal men too long in hopes of conciliating them. He must put such men "at defiance," Davis cautioned Vance, because "if the contrary policy be adopted I much fear you will be driven to the use of force to repress treason."[79] But like other governors faced with a major problem of desertion, Vance had already tried everything, from amnesty to execution, and the use of force against the traitors in the North Carolina mountains and Piedmont was already a well-tried part of his arsenal.

Governor Vance's strategy in the war against deserters marked a turning point in the relationship between women citizens and the Confederate state. North Carolina was a critical case because it contributed more men to the Confederate military than any other state (fully one-seventh of the total number of troops who served) and it had twice as many draft dodgers and deserters. As early as September 1862, the governor was sufficiently concerned about resistance to conscription in the old Unionist stronghold in the Piedmont counties in the center of the state (known locally as the Quaker belt), that he dispatched conscript officers on a cam-

desertion

paign to arrest the offending men. By early 1863 he acknowledged that desertion was "alarmingly on the increase," that deserters were increasingly well organized, more bold in their attacks on public officials and the troops sent to hunt them, and in their depredations on loyal citizens. Indeed, by that point Vance was inundated with demands from outraged citizens calling on him for protection from their own troops.[80] Along with periodic offers of amnesty to first-time offenders and pleas to President Davis to parlay for peace, Governor Vance unleashed a harsh military campaign against the deserters and the networks that sustained them.[81]

A broad understanding of the nature of the fight and of its participants developed on all sides. By early 1863 in North Carolina, troops sent to hunt deserters targeted women, especially wives, in their efforts to locate and bring in the men. As in Greenville, east Tennessee, wives, daughters, and other women played roles that were crucial to the operation of deserter networks. At first, men who evaded military service had been able to stay at home largely undisturbed. But by late 1862, as the problem reached critical proportions, they were literally hunted—"fleeing before us like rabbits before a fire," one conscript officer said—by home guard units and detachments of regular troops. Not safe at home, they took to lying out in the woods and mountains around their farms, as runaway slaves had long done. That left them necessarily dependent on family members, who not only provided all of the farm labor when the men were gone, but fed them when they came in, took food and clothing out to them when they could not, nursed the wounded, and provided security by alerting the men when troops approached and closely guarding, even under duress, all information concerning their whereabouts and hideouts.

Deserter networks were familial in shape, and women were key parties to their operations. In Randolph County, North Carolina, where original antisecession Unionism was a stronger force, arguably, than anywhere else in the state, the war divided the community, eventually pitting soldiers' hard-pressed families against those, equally hard-pressed, of deserters. One woman whose men were in the Confederate army complained bitterly to the governor about how she had made a little crop by her own labor only to see the green corn torn down nightly "and carried off to supply the families of these cowardly tories and deserters." In that woman's locality it seemed to be a war of one kinship group against another. But that left conscript officers fighting not individuals but whole family connections. One citizen, informing on his neighbor, denounced not just him but his entire lineage: "All his brothers have been in the woods and still are," he ranted, "and he is regarded as a dangerous man and his father and all his uncles, aunts, cousins, nephews and nieces are true representative descendants of their grandfather old Dick Miller of Tory notoriety in the Revolution." Unionist families like the Moores and Hulens of Randolph County, North Carolina, or the Knight family of Jones County, Mississippi, targeted in the war against the deserters, had traditions of religious and political dissent going back to the late eighteenth century.[82]

In the Civil War South, political allegiance ran in family lines. In that respect, women's politics were no more embedded in family loyalties, or derivative from them, than were men's. When Henry Thompson went hunting deserters in July 1862, he knew the men to be well armed, but the person he feared most was their father, who had threatened to kill the first man who took his sons prisoner. But disloyalty and danger also ran in maternal lines, and within neighborhoods the women's views could be as well known and worrisome as the men's. One citizen tellingly identified two bushwhackers who had killed a conscript officer as "Nance Drew's sons." When loyal Confederate men and women called for action against the deserters, many pointed specifically to the women. Informing on women in her mountain neighborhood who had publicly expressed the wish that Jeff Davis and his cabinet be hanged and that the Yankees would come through, one woman asked of the governor, "What can we expect but desertion from the army when mothers, wives, and sisters" openly broadcast such treasonous views. The people who "harbor deserters should be swung up and let hang," one young woman wrote the local conscript officer.[83]

By the time the military campaigns against the deserters swung into high gear, female collaborators were as much the target as the male deserters themselves. "Desertion can never be stopped while . . . they receive any countenance or protection at home," Governor Vance allowed in one proclamation. So while pleading with "all good citizens and true patriots" to arrest the evil, he also identified civilians as the enemy, moving to criminalize the act of harboring deserters and authorizing troops to arrest "parties of any age or sex" who have information about the deserters. In Mississippi, during an equally brutal campaign, a local judge openly blamed the women—"many of the men and nearly all the women are openly at work to weaken our army, procure desertion, and assail the Confederacy," he wrote—and urged President Davis to handle them roughly. In Mississippi authorities reported success. "The women are frightened and are working hard to get the men to come in, and are doing some good," one officer reported. By 1863, Confederate governments, like that of Governor Vance in North Carolina, were not only cracking down on treasonous women, they began to target women as a key part of their military strategy. "This was no mere war among men."[84]

What happened under those kinds of orders confirms just how far authorities had moved from the view of women as outside war or objects of protection. At the very beginning of the new year, in January 1863, Governor Vance dispatched more than three hundred troops, mounted and on foot, up into Madison County in the mountains of western North Carolina. They were in pursuit of a particular band of deserters, maybe fifty men who had, a few days previously, pulled off a bold early evening raid on government stores in the nearby town of Marshall. The hunt was personal: Colonel Laurence Allen, from the North Carolina 64th Regiment, one of the most affluent men in Marshall, had been personally targeted in the raid, his home plundered and wife and children threatened. Other officers involved in the campaign quickly picked up a handful of suspects, arrested them, and lodged them in the county jail. But Colonel Allen, commanding a separate group, picked his way down the icy mountain passes into the secluded Laurel Valley (the Shelton Laurel, as it was called, after the family who had settled it after the Revolution), a narrow valley gouged out of the Appalachian chain. The Shelton Laurel was a strong Unionist enclave in the mixed political terrain of the mountains. It was home to the openly Unionist and heavily armed deserter band led by Bill Shelton.[85]

When Allen and his men reached Bill Shelton's home, the men were nowhere to be found. But the women were there. Allen and his men went to work on the women, torturing them for information. They took two of the women, Sarah and Mary Shelton, wives of two suspected raiders, tied a rope around their necks, and hanged them from a tree until they nearly strangled; they did the same to 85-year-old Unus Riddle. They took four other women, one near 70 years old, and whipped them until the blood ran down their backs. They took one nursing mother, tied her to a tree, and put her child on the snowy winter ground in front of her and out of reach, threatening to leave the child there, exposed, until she talked.[86] When Allen and his troops finally got the men—the particular chain of events remains murky—they took them, thirteen in all, out to the Knoxville Road and two days later at a clearing by a creek summarily executed them all, including 13-year-old David Shelton.

The targeting of women in pursuit of male suspects is still a highly controversial anti-insurgency or antiterrorism strategy. The idea of making women turn state's evidence against their own men does not go down easily even now. Nor did it in the Confederate war. Confederate authorities found it necessary, but when it came to light they were hard-pressed to justify it. In September 1864 Colonel Alfred Pike, a deputy sheriff from Randolph County, North Carolina, and the colonel of a home guard unit, went out in pursuit of William Owens, the notorious leader of a deserter band that operated all over the lower central part of the Piedmont. Like Allen a year previous, Pike claimed to be operating under explicit instructions not to spare collaborators in the attempt to break up the Owens gang. When Colonel Pike arrived at Owens's place, he found only Owens's wife, washing at the spring house. He "inquired of her as to Owens's whereabouts," to which she replied that he was dead and buried. When they demanded to see the grave, Pike said, she began to "curse and abuse us for everything that was bad," at which point, he claimed, he yielded to the urgings of his men to work her over. Seizing up her infant in her arms, she swore resistance, at which point Pike "slaped her jaws until she put down her baby & went with them." His men "tied her thumbs behind her back & suspended her with a cord tied to her two thumbs fastened to a limb so that her toes could just touch the ground." That seemed to work. After a few minutes she admitted that her husband wasn't dead and promised to talk. They let her down. But once down, Pike said, she again refused to talk, so he dragged her "some fifty yards off to a fence & put her thumbs under a corner of the fence." Then, he said, she behaved very respectfully.[87]

From neighboring counties in the Piedmont in 1863 and 1864 came similar stories of women intimidated, threatened, plundered, burned out, clapped in jail, beaten, and tortured for information on the whereabouts of their husbands. Martha Hough complained to the governor that her son "had been gone nearly a year," but still the soldiers torment her as if "he were really about home." Recently they "dragged her off to camp" as punishment. Anny Beck claimed she did not have "Any Body in the wods Lying out" but still militia came to her house, "caught me . . . drug me a Bought scanless," and tore up her house. One citizen reported that a self-appointed deserter-hunting posse headed by a man called Adam Brewer was terrorizing the women of Moore County, robbing them even of their last provisions, dragging off their young sons, and when challenged, drawing bayonets on them and threatening to shoot them on the run.[88]

Two sisters, Clariday Hulin and Phoebe Crook, likewise reported constant abuse bordering on torture. They were of particular interest to the home guard as part of the devoutly Wesleyan, antislavery, and Unionist Hulin/Moore families, which had become one of the most powerful deserter bands in central North Carolina. Clariday Hulin claimed that a detail of troops took every scarce item of food she owned, down to the last hog, "tore up my Clotheing and tulk My Molasses and pord them over the flore . . . it ant only Me they air takeing from its is every boady," she wrote. "They take the womens horses out of the plows and riding them and beeting them scanless and destroying every thing that can lay hans upon." Phoebe Crook reported precisely the kind of physical abuse and torture dealt out to Owens's wife. The home guard was "taking up the woman," she wrote, "and keeping them under gard and Boxing thir jaws and nocking them a baut as if they ware Bruts," forcing them to jail when they have suckling infants, taking little children and "Hange them until they turn Black in the face trying to make them tell whear there fathers is." The men say, when challenged, that "they hav ardes from the governer to do this" and to "Burn up thir Barn and houses and Destroy all that that hav got to live on," Crook charged pointedly.[89]

By all accounts, the women did not exaggerate either the violence or the authority under which it was done. Thomas Settle was sent up to investigate the treatment of Owens's wife, and he confirmed the pattern and extent of the violence that had emerged as government policy. "I found in Chatham, Randolph and Davidson [counties]," he reported disapprovingly to Governor Vance, "that some fifty women in each county and some of them in delicate health and far advanced in pregnancy were rudely (in some instances) draged from their homes & put under close guard & there kept for some weeks." Some he said have been frightened into abortions under the eyes of their terrifiers. Not only were these not isolated incidents, they were understood by the officers perpetrating them to represent a faithful enactment of the governor's instructions. When arrested, Settle said, the militia officers "have shown me your orders as justification." "I know that your excellency never intended by any order to justify torture" and yet in many cases "equally as bad as it was in Owens case the officers boldly avow their conduct and say that they understand your orders to be a full justification."[90] War against women, not excluding torture, was state policy in the C.S.A.

To many of the public it looked exactly like a war on women, and the shock was obvious. Citizens, some of whom could barely write, inundated the governor with reports of the outrages, and almost everyone talked of the behavior toward women as entirely out of bounds. "Governor, such conduct is two bad and aught not to be allowed," one man wrote at the request, he said, of a group of citizens of Moore County, "let them go ahead and arrest the deserters and conscripts if they can and not destroy property and cary off horses and other property from the poor women who about to starve any how and to be treating women in such style." "The good people are looking to you for protection," he finished plaintively. Others threatened revenge from men in the army at the news that their wives were being preyed upon. "I have never bin in favor of the gard imposing on womming and children," one wrote. The women's outrage fairly lifts off the page in their descriptions of conscript officers, sometimes "half tite," whose behavior toward women, children, and "poore old grey headed fathers"—the war's innocents—was "shameful," "scanless," "too indecent to express." The tone in Thomas Settle's report on the Owens case for Governor Vance's office was one of shock and sadness; it communicated a sense that some fundamental moral code had been violated.[91]

Surely it had been. At the most fundamental level, the attacks represented an abandonment of the idea of women as outside war, engaging them instead as dangerous partisans and enemies of the state. More specifically, they violated the promise of protection of womanhood held up as a defining principle of the Confederate cause. And they tossed overboard the customary view of women as wives, whose first allegiance was to their husbands, insisting instead on their primary obligation as citizens to the state, demanding that they refrain from treason even if that involved rebelling against the authority of their husbands.

Behind all of these developments lay a wholly new estimation of women's political significance and a new view of women's standing in relation to the state. As in Butler's New Orleans, so in Vance's North Carolina, officials had been forced to find ways to hold women citizens accountable for treasonous activities. As in federally occupied areas where Southern women had been forced to take the oath of allegiance or face banishment, now Confederate officials subjected the women in their own nation to an array of legal and extralegal means, not short of torture, to punish treason and compel loyalty. Disloyal women were indeed handled "speedily and roughly." In Jones County, Mississippi, in Randolph County, North Carolina, and every other part of the Confederacy where Unionism and desertion were rampant, commanders got what they asked for: "an iron rule enforced with an iron hand and hearts of stone." Whatever Jefferson Davis might say to the contrary, in the C.S.A. "no sex was to be spared."[92]

But what proved necessary in practice was not always defensible in principle. Roughing up women was official policy but nobody wanted to own up to it. There remained a deep ambivalence in Confederate thinking about white women's political standing, and about the meaning of marriage and coverture for it, even in times of war. Governors and military men called to account for harsh policies toward women generally disowned responsibility and tried to put as much distance as possible between themselves and their minions, even when their own express orders were produced as authority. Colonel Pike was unusual in standing by his actions in torturing Bill Owens's wife. "If I have not the right to treat Bill Owens, his wife and the like in this manner I want to know it," he said defiantly, "and I will go to the Yankees or anywhere else before I will live in a country in which I cannot treat such people in this manner."[93] But the governor, Zebulon Vance, a mountain politician of modest origins himself, claimed to be (and perhaps genuinely was) appalled by the treatment of the women, even ones of known Unionist and anti-Confederate stripe. Calling immediately for investigations, he distanced himself as completely as possible from his own orders, quickly trying to reassert his populist position as the protector of women, whatever their political views and crimes.

It was an impossible position to sustain in practice. The tension Vance and others faced, between new necessities and old preferences, would abide—and maybe outlast—the war. The new views of women's political standing adopted in war were no less significant for being unwanted.

With respect to women, at least, the Confederate project was seriously off course. In the original vision of the nation—as the white men's perfected republic—women citizens had been a perfect nullity. But a new version of the body politic was taking shape in the South in the crucible of war. Its emergence and forms were owed in large part to the pressures exerted on the state by the dependent and the unfranchised, among them newly assertive constituencies of women. For as it turned out, it wasn't only the disloyal who made authorities take notice but a whole new group, self-identified as soldiers' wives, who turned old promises of protection into a new set of demands on the Confederate state.

CHAPTER 4

Soldiers' Wives and the Politics of Subsistence

THE AMERICAN CIVIL WAR TORE like an earthquake through the foundation of Southern life. The impact registered in every domain, from the high reaches of the central state and its military command to the most intimate recesses of the household. Transformation is the essential characteristic of modern war, because the calling in of long-standing private obligations fundamentally changes the citizen's relationship to, and expectations of, the state. In the Confederate war, the claims of the state reached proportions rarely matched in the history of modern nations. They went beyond the ranks of those white men called upon to serve to reach their dependents, the women, children, and slaves who made up the unfranchised mass of the Southern population. The American Civil War forged a new understanding of the relationship between citizens, subjects, and the state and a renegotiation of the social contract. When war was done, neither the vision of "the people" nor of the government was the same.

The Confederate nation was conceived in war, and with it came the necessity of a social contract between the people and their new government that would be adequate to the times. At the center of the contract, as in all republics, was citizen men's obligation to provide military service in defense of the state. The call-up of men in the spring of 1861 lent urgency and concreteness to the reciprocity implicit in the new government's charter. The version that emerged in the Confederacy was not so different from the one Southerners had lived under as American men: it spelled out the exchange of military service for government protection of the rights and property of citizen men. But there was one important difference: in the new version the government was explicit about its obligations to the citizen-soldiers who were asked to risk their lives on its behalf. Like many wars, the Confederate war created new political possibilities. At the outset it was a public article of faith that the government had entered a new social contract with soldiers for the support and protection of their families. It was simply conventional to say, as the *Confederate Baptist* did, that "our soldiers' families are entitled to our protection and care for those soldiers are our defenders." Or, as the Charleston Board for the Relief of Families of Soldiers did, that "the soldier in this terrible war . . . is rightly entitled to know and feel that . . . his loved ones at home are under the kind protection of his State Government and in the care and protection of those who regard them as part of their household."[1] The idea that the state had incurred an obligation to the soldiers to protect their families was tied to religious and secular conceptions of the nation, its people, and their cause. Variously referred to as a promise, a solemn duty, a sacred claim, a state imperative, an obligation, and a public trust, it was trumpeted from press box and pulpit, piously sworn to by government officials and private citizens alike.[2] Few ideas in Southern political life in the Civil War acquired more public legitimacy; few had a more unpredictable career.

By the end of the first summer of the war, the contract with the soldiers was already shaping local and state politics and transforming the tax burden on citizens. Initially Confederate officials did not anticipate any new relationship with soldiers' wives. The political relationship was with the soldiers whose dependents they now saw as being under the state's care. The state of Mississippi pledged "herself to her soldiers that those dear ones they have left behind shall not want," as the legislators put it. "Let them be adopted as the children of the State," the governor said of the soldiers' wives and children.[3] The state creation of a class of "soldiers' wives" thus reframed, rather than challenged, women citizens' political status as dependents, subject to the authority of particular men. The sacrifice was the soldiers' sacrifice, the claim on the state the soldiers' claim.

It did not take long for all of that to change. Two years into the war, hordes of angry soldiers' wives had blasted that notion to bits. Their arrival on the public scene helped transform the content and direction of social policy in the C.S.A. thereafter. Forced into a newly intimate relationship with government officials, subject to the unimaginable intrusions and demands of the wartime state, Southern white women, most of them poor, laid claim to a new identity as soldiers' wives and emerged, against all conceivable odds, as a critical constituency in Confederate politics. Brandishing their own undeniable sacrifice as a calling card, they moved individually and "as a boddy" to define the terms of protection for themselves, to construe protection as an entitlement of the state, and to hold that state accountable to them for its promises. As soldiers' wives, poor white Southern women found a means of self-representation and the makings of a politics—a way to intervene in the making and changing of worlds. As soldiers' wives, Southern white women made unprecedented claims on the state and in the process turned themselves into a powerful voice for social justice in the C.S.A. That "soldiers' wives" emerged as the term of self-description for the great majority of poor white Southern women tells us something very significant about the transformative possibilities of politics in war.[4]

For those Southerners—white women and slaves—who were not original parties to the social contract, the impositions and openings war created were especially historic.[5] One consequence of war showed in the reconfiguration of Southern political life and particularly in the way power on the home front shifted as white women emerged into authority and even leadership on a range of issues at the heart of popular politics in the Civil War South. That story has been hidden in plain sight. For every politician and government official was aware from the content of their correspondence that the war had caused a fundamental change in the very terms and practices of political life.[6] Their correspondence registers all the changes: the new penetration of the household by the state, but also the rearrangement of household relations, local political networks, and modes of communication during the war. What lies now in the archives captures the existence of a whole set of new, war-born political identities, individual and collective, chief among them that of "the soldier's wife." There were new issues in Civil War politics, but there were also new stories and new players.

Soldiers' wives' politics constitute a critical development in Civil War history and in the long history of Southern political culture. But they are not easily read through our usual lexicon of women's concerns. The political meaning of Civil War developments has long been a central question in women's history.[7] For the most part Southern historians have focused on planter women and defined Confederate women's politics in one of two ways: in relation either to their support for women's rights and women's suffrage or to Confederate nationalism and the Confederate cause. But it was not planter women who embraced the identity of soldiers' wives and made it a force in political life. And it was not as an assertion of their rights as citizens or their contribution to the military defeat of the Confederacy that the women made their claims.[8] Confederate soldiers' wives did not make predictable claims about women's rights or citizens' rights; in fact they did not much speak a language of rights at all. Nor did they align themselves clearly for or against the Confederate cause; in fact they did not much speak a language of nationalism at all.[9] Rather their new political significance was evident in their participation in community deliberations and in the actions they took to shape public and even military policy in their own interests. The central story of women's politics in the war is thus about their participation in the basic practices and organization of political life: the way the women intruded into local circuits of power and authority and claimed qualification to speak, power to act, entitlement to state resources, and in the relationships they developed with the state that claimed to represent and rule them. Their politics was important in the historical process that unfolded in the Civil War and not just in the outcome of it.

By 1863, soldiers' wives were a force to be reckoned with in the C.S.A. The vast majority of them were poor women pushed into political action by the deep disruption of their family and community life in the war. These were women who had been immured in their families, to use Mary Wollstonecraft's powerful image, their subordination to men and distance from the state long understood to be in the public interest.[10] But it was precisely these poor white, mostly rural, women who emerged from the private recesses of their households to speak for themselves in the public arena during the Confederate war. The Confederacy was not defeated until the spring of 1865, and there would be no white women's rights movement in the American South until the 1880s. But long before then, Confederate soldiers' wives had put their imprint on Confederate policy and on the practice of Southern politics. By that time, homegrown change had arrived long since in the perfected republic of white men.

In 1861 and 1862 the proliferating war policies of state and federal officials bore down on every rural community and town in the new C.S.A. As the web of relations between the state and citizens daily thickened, politics remained exclusively an affair of men. Citizen-men conducted the negotiations over what the community could sustain, defined and represented their vital interests, and pressed them on the state. From the very moment officials began to make demands on the population for the manpower and matériel with which to wage war, requests for relief and revision of government policy poured into the offices of state governors and the various Confederate secretaries of war. Most, predictably enough, concerned the recruitment, deployment, and after April 1862, conscription of men. Citizens demanded the return of military units to their home counties, the protection of their settlements from marauding Union troops and undisciplined Confederate cavalry, the exemption from conscription of crucial local men (millers, physicians, blacksmiths, overseers, teachers), the exemption of whole counties from the draft so that the wheat crop could be saved or the slaves kept in subjection, and military protection from their own slaves. But whatever the request, the "citizens" meant the men. When in April 1861 the "Citizens of the town of St. Mary's and of Camden County, Georgia" sent a panicked missive to Governor Joseph Brown about their exposure to attack from Florida slaves in the event of an enemy landing on ungarrisoned Amelia Island, they indicated their vulnerability by citing the "number of voters in the county [at] 230 to 250 and the number of slaves about 4,000." That shorthand for salient manpower equated the number of citizens, voters, and soldiers—the people—in a wholly conventional way. Forty-six "citizens" appended their signatures to the petition, every one of them male. As in St. Mary's and Camden County, it was rare for women citizens to participate in their community's public deliberations or petitions.[11] In the early days of the war, relations between citizens and the state meant citizen men. The pattern was so old it was hardly noticeable.

It took less than two years for the hoary gender patterns of American republicanism to show serious signs of strain. They first emerged when savvy men began to cite their service to local soldiers' wives in seeking exemptions from military service. By 1862, there were signs that women were encroaching on foreign gender terrain by presuming to represent themselves in negotiations with officials over the wisdom of the state's relentless demands on citizens. By the middle of the war, the accumulation of women's political activities amounted to a virtual rerouting of power and authority on the home front and the clear emergence of white women as a salient constituency in Confederate politics.

The change was tentative enough at first, with men merely conjuring up women's needs to serve their own wartime ends. In April 1862 the Confederate States of America showed their resolve by passing the first draft act in American history. But even before that, Southern men were finding it hard to duck military service. Not only were shirkers frowned on, but states set county quotas for volunteers, which, some claimed, so stripped the localities of men that there were not enough left behind to "make bread for the women and children." J. M. Cansler said as much to Governor Brown of Georgia in February 1862, promising that if exempted from his state's call he would remain here "giving my attention to the families of the soldiers which I have been doing for some time." With the passage of the Conscription Act, the situation became more dire, and the flood of demands for exemption was so great that by November the secretary of war forwarded a handful of them to President Davis to exemplify the need for a uniform policy. They were, he said, a mere sample of the many requests he had received that "exhibit bereavement and distress." With exemptions increasingly difficult to obtain, more men adopted Cansler's strategy, citing the state's obligation to protect and support soldiers' families as the basis of their particular claim. In petition after petition men promised service to soldiers' wives in exchange for their release from military service.[12] By late 1862, men seeking favors from the government knew to cite the public good and not just their own private interest.

The soldier's wife thus made her first appearance in the story of the Confederate war as a bit player in the men's drama, in her old guise as the isolated and dependent object of male and state protection. The young North Carolina soldier who begged the secretary of war to let him get back "to the plough handles where I was raised" to make a support for his desperate family, or the Citizens of Columbus, Mississippi, who begged Governor Pettus to mount sufficient local defense for "the protection and support of the families of our soldiers," seemed genuinely concerned about the effect of government war policies on dependents.[13] The civic recognition of soldiers' families as a constituency that the government must serve had its basis in real need. But the claim to provide service to soldiers' wives was also a strategic ploy, circulating currency in a new discursive economy. Many of the men's petitions were transparently opportunistic. Countless planter men distraught about the exposure of their valuable slave property to enemy troops demanded the diversion of military manpower to their localities to protect, as one put it, "our defenseless mothers and sisters" from rape and persecution by the enemy. When citizens cited the value of slave property at risk of marauders—three million dollars in their own precinct, one group of Georgia citizens pointedly informed the secretary of war—they showed their hand. James Brantley showed his hand when he tried to get a furlough to go home and tend his plantation in southwestern Georgia, explaining that he would serve his country better at home rendering "service to soldiers' needy families," supplying them with provisions and controlling emboldened local slaves. Brantley abandoned the high ground quick enough and revealed his real interests in enraged complaints about impressing officers who are "taking advantage of me in my absence from home to rob me of my property." Even Brantley's brother could not revive his benevolent image despite testimony that he "has been since the beginning of the war most abundant in patriotic deeds for the benefit of soldiers' families—for a long time giving corn to these persons, as your excellency also has nobly done, for a year past selling it at nominal prices—making glad many needy ones who have walked long distances to partake of his bounty."[14] However inauthentically, the claim of the "poor soldier's wife" on the state became the most powerful card in petitioners' hands.

In an important sense, of course, it mattered less whether men meant what they said about soldiers' wives than that they felt compelled to say it at all. There were certain postures it proved wise to adopt. Savvy men seeking exemptions, discharges, furloughs, and details increasingly engaged in a kind of ventriloquism, throwing the voices of soldiers' wives in making their case to state officials. "My nabor women has beg me" to request exemption, the North Carolina farmer, Joseph Roberson, informed Governor Vance in seeking to find a way out of the state militia. When a group of men and women from Coweta County, Georgia, petitioned their governor to exempt the local physician from a recent call-up, the voice was at once male and female: "Shall we after having given up our husbands, brothers, and sons, now be compelled to give up our Physician, and leave a large number of our women, children and negroes to suffer and die without medical attention?" they asked. The possessively male "our women" uttered at the end of the petition collided awkwardly with the allegedly female voice ("our husbands") with which it had opened.[15] No matter. Confederate men routinely marshaled women's sacrifices of their husbands and protectors as the grounds of their own claims on the state for relief.

By the second year of the war, in the face of official skepticism, it was no longer enough for men to gesture vaguely toward women's support. Now they had to produce the evidence, hoofing it around their neighborhoods, petitions in hand, to collect women's signatures. Like so many other petitions that went in to the secretaries of war and the governors of Confederate states by 1862, one from Coweta County, Georgia, carried five pages of signatures, many of them women's. The Coweta petition listed the signatures irrespective of gender. But others exhibited a more self-conscious strategy with petitioners' signatures divided neatly into columns, as if to draw attention to the difference. "Names of Women" said the heading on the left side of a Tallapoosa County, Alabama, petition to Governor Shorter, "Names of Men" said the heading on the right. A petition from the citizens of Stanhope, North Carolina, to the secretary of war separated the signatures by gender while explaining further that "the ladies names in this petition are the names of widow ladies and soldiers wives."[16] All endorsements evidently were not equal. By 1862 women's support was required to legitimate men's claims on the mercy of the state.

But more fundamental change was already under way in Confederate politics as white women, including poor rural ones, began to take matters into their own hands. Since the beginning of the war men had monopolized the deliberative and representative role in the increasingly dense thicket of relations with state officials. That started to change not only in the routine appearance of women's signatures on community appeals but when women began to speak for themselves. At the beginning of 1862 it was still rare for women to assume the responsibility of self-representation; a year later it was commonplace. By early 1863, their households and communities ravaged by the demands of a war policy that relentlessly mobilized men and goods, women's tentative foray into the male realm of politics shaped up as an angry and sustained encounter between soldiers' wives and the state.

The patterns are striking. For all intents and purposes women citizens' relationship with the state dates from the Civil War. In the antebellum period women's communications with government officials were few and far between and confined to a narrow range of issues. Antebellum women did, on occasion, approach their governors, usually in writing, sometimes through a third party, most commonly seeking clemency for themselves or family members.[17] But with the war, the necessity and frequency of citizens' communications with state governors increased exponentially and a growing portion came from women. In 1861 the antebellum gender pattern largely held. In 1862 women sent in only a trickle of the petitions war governors received. But by 1863 the number had increased significantly, and it remained so in 1864 and 1865 when a sizable proportion of the correspondence governors received from private citizens was from women.[18] While much harder to quantify (because of the volume), a similar pattern pertains to communications with the various secretaries of war.[19] In the voluminous 1861 correspondence to the secretary of war, there is scarcely a letter from a woman citizen. There was the odd one complaining about a husband who enlisted without her consent or seeking the release from the army of an underage son. But by the middle of the war the secretary received a steady stream of petitions and requests from white women, usually trying to get a particular man out of the service or raging against the inequity of the central government's conscription and exemption policies. The documents are thus an index to a new politics, a surprising archival record of the emergence of a collective public voice of poor white Southern women in the Civil War. What these documents represent is evidence that in the turmoil of war, white Southern women had found a means of self-representation and, with it, a strategic and efficacious kind of political agency they had never possessed before.

But new as they were, the terms of the women's new self-representation reveal the weight of the past. Confederate women never could claim the name of citizens. "This constitution was made for white men—citizens of the United States," Thomas R. R. Cobb of Georgia had proclaimed in 1860. Thus it seemed only to reflect the common sense of the matter when, in petitioning their governor, a group of men and women from Bulloch County, Georgia, divided their signatures neatly into two columns: "Citizens Names" and "Soldiers Wives Names."[20] Soldiers' wives did not make their claims under the sign of citizen.

Disempowering as it might seem, "soldiers' wives" was, in fact, a new identity and one replete with possibilities. Within a few years of the start of the war, Southern white women moved decisively out of the shadowy backspace of virtual representation to make a set of claims on their own behalf. They relied far less often on men to represent the community's interests or their own particular ones in negotiations with government officials. There was also a more coherent assertion of a class and gender identity. When forty-seven women from Green County, Mississippi, addressed the secretary of war, begging for the release of Private John Smith, they did so, they said, "for the purpose of assisting the distitute Famelies of Beat No. 3, greene County, Miss, of which we live, for there is not any person left to labour or provide in know shape." To be sure, the women still traded in their identity as dependents of soldiers, but they also managed to craft a useful corporate identity. Others used the same strategy when in signing petitions they identified themselves pointedly in relation to their sacrifice for the cause: "wife of deceast soldier," or "soldier's wife," women often wrote beside their names. Indeed by the middle of the war, women commonly annotated their signatures on petitions to government officials, as the women from Tippah County, Mississippi, did in theirs to the secretary of war: "Soldier's Wife," "Husband in the Army," "Husband in Service;" "2 sons in the army," the lone widow carefully noted.[21]

Soldiers' wives. The use of that identity was, to be sure, an indication of how tightly women's political identities and status were tied up with marriage and the practices of coverture that customarily defined their distance from the state. But in a world in which the state and its officers reached into the very heart of the household, there was little customary about marriage or white women's wartime experience of it. An idea of the new necessities and possibilities can be found in a letter that Mary Jones, a soldier's widow from Natchez, Mississippi, wrote Governor Pettus in mid-1862. She had gone to Yazoo City "to see if I could draw anything up there as you told me," she began. At that point Jones was on at least the second go-around with Pettus in an attempt to secure government support for herself and her three young children. But she got the runaround from officials there, who told her that she "could not draw anything yet as the Law had not allowed any thing for Soldiers Widows," and she could not get her husband's pay either as "only the Virginia Law Department" could authorize that disbursement. Caught between the state of Mississippi and the central government, Jones struggled to learn the bureaucratic ropes while doggedly sticking to her belief that someone owed her support. "Every Body say I must be taken care of by the Confederate States they did not tell my Deare Husband that I should Beg from Door to Door when he went to fight for his country." Jones's letters to Governor Pettus were pathetic and begging for sure, but they were also insistent. "You ar all that I can call on for protection," she wrote again in September 1862. "I hope you will act a Father's part towards me." Starting in 1862 Mary Jones and other desperate widows and soldiers' wives pressed on government officials their sense of themselves as a constituency entitled to support.[22] They began to define the social contract with soldiers for themselves.

Mary Jones was a leading indicator of soldiers' wives' politics in the Confederate South. For the possibilities and strategic uses of that identity did not emerge immediately or all in one piece. Rather they developed over time in dynamic relationship to the demands the state placed on Southern households. At first women's engagement with politicians and state officials was tentative, a mere trickle of females venturing onto male terrain. There was little to begin with that could be identified as a political language, corporate identity, or clear sense of entitlement from the state. Women's needs were real enough and pressing, but the practice of female self-representation was foreign indeed, especially for women from yeoman and poor white families.

Initially most of the women who approached government officials directly were from planter families, many of them widows seeking their sons' exemptions to manage their slaves. In October 1862 the Confederate Congress passed a highly controversial act that permitted the exemption from military service of one man for every plantation with twenty or more slaves. They were responding to a tidal wave of public concern about the likelihood of slave insurrection that arose with the Union invasion and occupation of large parts of the Mississippi Valley and the fall of New Orleans. Slaves were indeed seizing the opportunities war offered to challenge slavery and their masters' state, and the government was compelled to respond, both to shore up the foundational institution and to stanch slaveholders' protests. But this was one of those cases in which the simultaneity of domestic challenges facing the Davis administration complicated the policy response. Answering one threat, legislators exacerbated another—from soldiers' wives. First the government heard from wealthy women with property on the line. Planter women were quick to exploit the opening presented by the twenty-negro exemption, and a rash of petitions poured into the War Department.[23] Rebecca Campbell approached Secretary of War Randolph in November 1862, forthrightly requesting her son's release from the army "under the exemption law." She was the owner of a large plantation, she explained, could find neither a substitute for her son nor an overseer for the plantation, and she feared not only for her pecuniary interest but "more than all for the safety and well being of herself and her defenseless children without any man person on the place." Like Rebecca Campbell, planter widows usually appealed to sentiment, if at all, only at the end of a carefully drawn legal case. Many approached state officials as third parties, through lawyers and judges of probate, deploying the men who had always conducted legal business on their behalf. Their claims were empowered not by government promises to soldiers' wives but by the positive provisions of the law. They demanded only what they were legally entitled to as property holders in the slave republic. They knew the law: "I have seen from the papers that you have the power to exempt for widows etc," one slaveholding widow reminded President Davis, urging him to use the law to favor her.[24]

In the first year or so of the war, women from yeoman households or rural landless or urban working men's households hardly seemed to imagine, let alone initiate, any relationship with government officials. Cast outside the protection of the exemption act—the class character of that legislation was infamous from the moment of its first printing—they had no law to appeal to and no ready habit of doing public business to fall back on. On the rare occasion when poor white women did look to the state for help, they used the timeless weapon of the weak, the begging letter. Frances Brightwell pleaded with President Davis for the "discharg of my husband." In justification, she offered only pressing need and her identity as "a tinder female with a poor orfint child [with] no one to take care of me." Brightwell's sense that women were naturally owed protection and support seemed to emanate from the very bedrock of sex itself, as did her insistence that in her husband's absence the president himself "doo sumthing for me." In the beginning of the war most poor women simply pleaded for relief, not as part of a group of soldiers' wives created by the war's policies, but as individuals—just poor suffering women. They spoke of themselves not as citizens in relation to the state, but more particularly, as "a poor wife," "a poor widow," or more tellingly yet, a "female subject."[25] As they ventured onto the terrain of politics, they moved as strangers, intimidated interlopers, female subjects.

By late 1862 and 1863 that had changed, and the flood of petitions into governors' offices and to the secretary of war testified to the emergence of a group in Confederate political life self-identified as soldiers' wives. It was a historical development of some significance. For Confederate women's collective identification as soldiers' wives was part of a broad political reimagining. When, in February 1863, Margaret Smith, a North Carolinian, moved to get some relief for herself and the rest of the "Sufering . . . Soldiers' Familеys in Wayn County Dudley District," she introduced the basic elements of a new politics that poor Confederate women were bringing into being. Smith was blunt about the driving need facing her and her neighbor women in the absence of their men: "Without help we must starve." But Smith knew more than need. Like most soldiers' wives' petitions to government officials, hers invoked an official promise of protection only to turn it directly back on the state. "You our govner of north carlina has promust the soldiers that thare familieys shod sher of the Last," she said, quoting almost verbatim words from Governor Vance's recent proclamation to the people of North Carolina, and "wee think it is hie time for us to get help in time of our need." Smith's sense of entitlement, though new, was firm. She and her neighbor women were not accustomed to asking the government for help. But, she reminded him, the state had promised to protect them when it took their men. So Margaret Smith called in the soldiers' debt, on behalf, she noted carefully, of "all the Soldiers Famileys," and "ourselves . . . all Soldiers wives in Dudley desstrict, the righters as Sign thare name." Self-identified as "soldiers' wives," Margaret Smith and many others like her moved to redeem the promises of protection the government and public had made to their men.[26] It was hardly a robust claim to the rights of citizens, but it did lay claim to a collective public identity and to an entitlement from the state.

For poor white Confederate women to become soldiers' wives involved an act of deliberate and highly strategic self-creation. To the extent that a group called "soldiers wives" has previously been noted by historians, they have been cast either as figures in Confederate fiction, part of a class of poor whites, or as unruly poor white women in the war.[27] But soldiers' wives were neither a creation of the Confederate imagination, a submerged part of the broad poor, or a group emanating organically from the immiserated conditions of war. They were, rather, a particular *political* constituency of women self-identified as soldiers' wives, who emerged into salience in the Confederate body politic by the middle of the war. Soldiers' wives were a creation not of Confederate social life but rather of its politics, a point confirmed by the very specific class character of those who embraced the name.

Not every woman with a husband in the army embraced the name of soldier's wife. Needless to say, only white women were recognized as protected parties in relation to the Confederate state. Slave women were shut out of the possibilities or benefits inherent in that title, although when the Davis administration made its late decision to enlist slave men in the Confederate army, their "wives" would figure vaguely in discussions about what was owed to the slave soldier and his family.[28] But until that point, Confederate soldiers' wives were by definition white. Yet not all white women embraced the name. Elite women never saw the use in it. They did speak the language of protection; all Confederate women did.

"I claim the protection of our own Governor with the conviction that you will do all in your power for our relief," a Mrs. Let Page of Gloucester County, Virginia, wrote her governor confidently in late 1862. But like the other planter women who wrote state officials requesting the deployment of military units or the detail of particular men "to manage and assist in controlling our slaves," the protection she requested was from slaves —including from the necessity of managing them. Mrs. Page was from Gloucester County, Virginia, a section badly hit by the war and abandoned by the Confederate army after the evacuation of Yorktown. Now, their husbands pulled out with the army, the women were left, Page said, with no protection but their servants, which was worse than no protection at all. Slaves who had "stampeded" into adjoining counties awaited only the arrival of the Union army to "come down as an avalanche upon us [with] consequences . . . too terrible to dwell on." Page wanted Governor Letcher to send "a large body of cavalry down" to winter there and to "keep down insubordination and give notice of approaching danger."[29] Mrs. C. Clark and her neighbors in Washington County, Georgia, made a similar plea, asking their governor to detail a Mr. William Brian. "We the assign Ladys are prinsipaly owners of slaves," they told him, "and as we cannot have our husbands and sons to plan and manage and assist in controling our slaves," they wanted Brian. He had a good pack of negro dogs, they explained, and when at home he attended "to the Poor Soldiers' Wives." "Attend to this as early as possible," they concluded, a tone of instruction more appropriate to the overseer than the governor.[30]

By 1863, petitions from women citizens linking the protection of women to the violent control of slaves poured into government offices from all over the South, from Virginia to Texas. Again and again Southern ladies urged their governors—Joseph Brown of Georgia, Zebulon Vance of North Carolina, John Gill Shorter of Alabama, John Pettus of Mississippi, Moore of Louisiana, and John Letcher of Virginia—even the secretary of war and President Davis—to deliver the protection promised. Some were, as the literature has assumed, concerned about their personal safety and sexual virtue. "What I fear most is not the Yankees but the Negroes," Susan Jervey of coastal South Carolina put it.[31] But many others were concerned more about protecting their property in slaves and land from the emancipationist designs of the slaves themselves.

But if slaveholding women spoke the language of protection, they did not speak, or identify themselves, as soldiers' wives. "Mrs. Let Page," "Mrs. David Shipp," "Mrs. C. Clark," the "Ladies" signed off, adding no social signifier except marital status, a matter that acquires meaning in contrast to the signatory style of their poorer counterparts, who took care to justify their claims on the state in relation to their husbands' military service.[32] To these "ladies," in fact, soldiers' wives were the other—those "Poor Soldiers' Wives" they claimed their overseers would charitably assist.

When Mary Tisinger and her neighbors in Upson County, Georgia, petitioned their governor for the detail of some man in the service, they delineated the substance of protection and identified themselves in strikingly different terms than elite women did. The signers of the petition were "the wives and widows of deceased soldiers and mothers of soldiers in the Confederate Army," Tisinger and the other women specified in the opening line of their petition. "All of your Petitioners are very poor and dependent, there are only a few slaves in the neighborhood not exceeding four or five . . . that during peace or before the war your petitioners were dependent on white labor for support." With all the neighborhood men in the army "we are now," they said, "without protection or any one to gather our little crops of fodder, chinese sugar cane, or go to mill for us." Without male help, they said, they would starve. For Tisinger and her neighbors, it was the absence of slaves—not their numerous presence—that rendered them in dire need of protection. These poor white women made their demands on the state, like ladies, in the sanctioned language of protection, but the protection they claimed was not from slave men but from the sole burden of producing subsistence. Mary Tisinger signed first, "mary Tisinger with 6 chilrin, sldier wife." Mary Stilwell signed after her, "Mary Stilwell soldiers widow 6 children." Mary Taylor signed too, "mather of slder [unreadable] children." Sarah Kersy, "the mother to too soldiers," "Elizabeth Kimbalt One syster and Brother died in the Army," and so on down the list. Every woman who signed—there were twenty-three of them—specified her identity in terms of family relation to men in military service and the sacrifice made to the cause.[33] For these nonslaveholding women, like the many others who signed their letters as "Soldiers Wives," or sometimes just "sw" (so obvious was the shorthand), sacrifice was a grounds of entitlement, the soldier's wife a critical new identity in relation to the state.

The patterns and class differences in Confederate women's history thus emerge from the mass of letters lying in the archives, and so do the outlines of poor white women's new wartime politics. Elite women, self-identified as "ladies," interpreted the substance of protection out of their historical experience of sexual inviolability and leisure from labor. But yeoman and poor white women, self-identified as soldiers' wives, defined protection in relation to what marriage and coverture had meant for them, as white women in small and often poor farm households in the slave South and in relation to the new legitimacy their husbands' military service conferred. Huge numbers of women left at home, as one described it, with "no one but my four little children to work with [and] a large crop of small grain to cut and no one to cut it" begged for their husband's release "long enough to save my grain." "I have worked as hard as some of the rich men's darkey's," a North Carolina woman put it, "and din make much."[34] Elite women might speak as Southern ladies, particularly rich men's wives. But non-elite women spoke specifically as soldiers' wives, discerning in the historical moment something that had never existed in the past, not, at least, for women of their class, in their region, in their lifetimes. Such disruptions of yeoman divisions of labor, loss of household independence, scrambling of customary gender arrangements, and erosion of racial distinctions between free women and slaves constituted the very core of home-front politics in the Civil War South. In the quotidian details of rural women's lives, the original claim of protection was transformed into the political practice of the female unfranchised.

By 1863 government officials were beset with the demands of soldiers' wives. The term served as the most individual of identities and the most usefully collective. It was, surely, the most unpromising of materials. "Wife" had always been a ground for exclusion, virtual representation, and sacrifice, and "soldier's wife" seemed likely only to compound the effects.[35] Defined by their men's military service, the women never obscured that fact. But as they cast it, the sacrifice and the entitlement were clearly theirs. "The pore soldiers are in the army wading through wed [weed?] and water and fighting fore our bee loved cuntry," one North Carolina woman wrote, "while urthers at home a specerlating ove the pore women and soldiers wives." The palpable injustice charged in her account assumed a broad public understanding of the contract the public had made with the soldiers' wives. Sometimes women told tales of violation so deeply personal they were more stories of betrayal than anything else. "To think that my loved one had gone and suffered and died in defense of those who were at home living in plenty," one woman agonized, "and they could feel so indifferent about the wants of his family." They are so "close harted it was more than any ackeing heart could bear." We are owed more for the sacrifice of our men, the women said in a collective voice. Of that much they were sure. "We hav given our sons and husbands and brothers to the batle field," Sarah Halford and her neighbors bluntly put it, "an after so much we hav done," we have been preyed upon by the agents of their own government.[36] "We have given our men," "we have done so much," they said again and again in demanding relief. Soldiers' wives claimed the sacrifice of their men as their own unmatched contribution to the cause. And they brandished it as their calling card, turning the sacrifice of their men into a legitimate claim on the state's protection and resources.

Developments in the American South during the Civil War thus speak directly to the transformative possibilities, not so much of war itself, but of the cultural and political environment it creates. The issue is less the movement of the army and the logistics of peopling and supplying it, although those are not inconsequential, but more the efforts required to support and legitimate the military and political project. The Confederate war was not the only one in which a public emphasis on sacrifice created openings women managed to convert into political claims. In Britain in World War One, a new public rationale of service and sacrifice (associated with a volunteer army) was converted into the vote, earned, as feminists put it, "by the blood of our sons." In the North during the American Civil War, with an organized women's movement and a suffrage claim, leaders like Elizabeth Cady Stanton and Susan B. Anthony harbored real hope that they could do the same. They strategized openly about how to make their contribution pay. There was worry, but also real hope that war service could be converted into suffrage or some concretely expanded set of women's rights.[37] But in the South, where no such women's movement or leadership existed—where they lacked the antislavery movement always required to nurture them—no such fulsome claims to citizenship were possible.[38] Had not the Confederate band of brothers formed precisely to prevent such upstart imaginings? But the architects of the C.S.A. could not control the entire course of events on the home front any more than on the military front. So even there, in the perfected republic of white men, as the government struggled to meet the challenges posed by slaves, the war also provided white women opportunities to unsettle fixed conceptions of political belonging as partial payment of their sacrifice for the nation. In their hands, sacrifice became a means of self-representation and the basis of a new and more accountable relationship with the state.

In the Confederate States of America, as in other times and places, the meaning of sacrifice was fixed in the play of politics. Soldiers' wives moved ineluctably into the fray. Approaching the state, they turned a conventional ethic of sacrifice into grounds of entitlement, and a discourse of protection into a complex politics that involved local and state officials in extended negotiations with their demands. By the middle of the war, they had placed themselves squarely on the political agenda, authorized, as they usually put it, as "women [whose] husbands and sons are now in service or [have] died."[39] They had emerged as a salient new constituency in Confederate political life.

As the grounds of a collective political identity, the soldier's wife was a quintessential Southern figure, as much a product of the draft as her soldier husband. Soldiers' wives were creatures of the Confederate state. As a social group they were an index to the rapid process of state formation under way in the C.S.A. Their very existence attested to the new power and reach of the central state, to its intrusiveness and proximity, and to the structural problems faced by the slave republic at war. The key development was military service and especially conscription: the central state's decision, after only one year of war, to render mandatory the military service of adult white men. With 40 percent of the male population enslaved and unavailable for military service, President Davis and the secretary of war had no choice but to dig ever deeper into the ranks of the male citizenry for soldiers. In early 1862 they faced the loss of most of the men already in service, early volunteers whose twelve-month terms were due to expire in April, just as the spring military campaigns opened. Already outmatched by the Union's far greater population base, and anticipating a brutal onslaught especially in campaigns in the west, Confederate War Department officials made the fateful decision to adopt a draft of all white men aged 18 to 35 years. Conscription was the most statist policy the Confederate government adopted and the strongest measure of bureaucratic expansion.[40] Although President Davis appeared to take that decision fully in stride as what was required for the successful prosecution of the war, it would be hard to exaggerate its consequences in Confederate history, including for civilians.

The effects of that decision were felt in every household in the C.S.A. Initially military mobilization in the Confederate States, as in the Union, was entirely voluntary, and took off sons, brothers, and sweethearts, mostly men under 30 and with an average age of 18. Very few were married. In 1861 and into 1862, the labor implications for rural households, even those without slaves, thus were not dire, except for widows whose sons provided the only adult male labor on their farms. And it was widows, not surprisingly, who set up the first clamor for exceptions and policy revision. But in contrast to the Union, which continued to take sons and brothers while sparing husbands—up to 70 percent of Union soldiers were unmarried men—the Confederate War Department soon adopted a conscription policy that exempted virtually no one. With an estimated 750,000 to 850,000 men in service by the end of the war, the Confederate military machine ultimately claimed 75 to 85 percent of the nation's military-age white men. This in contrast to the Union's 50 percent. It was a level of mobilization unparalleled in their own era and probably unmatched until World War Two. It represented, to say the least, a considerable flexing of federal muscle, a wholly new conception of the power of the central state, and one that required the strongest measures of bureaucratic expansion.[41] "The conscription is being pressed mercilessly," the chief of the Confederate Bureau of War admitted in 1864; all exemptions were disallowed. By that point the Conscription Bureau offered its official opinion that no more men were to be had. Already by 1863 many Southern women could have said, as one did, "I have no head to my family."[42] The women who described a rural landscape literally stripped of men did not exaggerate.

The political consequences of conscription in the C.S.A. can be discerned in the emergence of the soldiers' wives, and in their effectiveness in shaping state policy. There were, of course, married men in the Union army and soldiers' wives on the Union home front. And there too the prosecution of the war generated a new terrain for women's politics on matters of welfare, draft resistance, and labor demands that requires us to think beyond the conventional focus on women's relief work. But for a variety of reasons—the lower numbers of married men enlisted, the greater relegation of war financing, supply, and relief to the private sector, the absence of an ideological framework for war focused on the protection of hearth, home, and women as in the South—the demands of the state did not nurture the emergence of the same collective identity and political mobilization of poor women as soldiers' wives in the Union as it did in the C.S.A. In the Union it was the soldier's mother who served as the representative figure for purposes of welfare claims, and not the wife. As a salient political force, soldiers' wives appear to have been a distinctly Confederate development.[43]

By 1863 soldiers' wives were legion in the Confederate States. As a political class the women attested to the new power and reach of the state. For as the central state executed its conscription policy—and added new policies, especially on taxation—it thickened immeasurably the network of extraction and bureaucracy within which ordinary citizens were enmeshed. Not only did conscription take off men and leave behind desperate women to work farms, plantations, mills, and workshops on their own; the law also had to be enforced. The ensuing expansion of state capacity and intrusiveness of the policies adopted by the C.S.A. can hardly be exaggerated. Historians have been consistently struck, by the irony for sure—this was a republic erected on the principles of states rights, after all—but also by the sheer scale of the state-building project undertaken. It has been called a "revolutionary experience," even an example of "state socialism." In terms of central state structure and policies, and especially the mobilization of national material and human resources, the C.S.A. was far more statist and modern than their counterpart in the Union, "almost futuristic" in its assumption of central state power. Indeed, so "well organized and powerful" was the Confederacy, one historian has argued, that the United States would not see a central government with comparable authority until the emergence of the New Deal.[44]

The implications for the history of American state formation and for the figuring of women within that process are intriguing, especially if we consider that the wartime experience of Southern citizen-state relations was not entirely rendered irrelevant by the military defeat of the C.S.A., as the literature assumes. It is now conventional for historians to talk about the birth of the modern American state in the Civil War. But the state they invariably have in mind is the one that won—the Union Republican Party state. If "of all dimensions of central state authority, the American Civil War most profoundly shaped future state-society development in the relations of individual citizens to the state," then perhaps we ought to entertain the notion of a dual origin of the modern state.[45] Certainly Southern men and women, enslaved and free, had considerable experience of a big state by the time their military leaders stacked arms at Appomattox. When they faced the new Republican Party state in the aftermath of the war, their expectations and sense of legitimate authority and entitlements surely owed something to that recent ordeal.

Before the war Southern citizens male or female had little experience of a big state. Their wartime introduction was fast and brutal. At the moment of secession there were few federal appointees of any kind in the interior of the Southern states; after the customs office and the post office, as Confederate vice president Alexander Stephens said in 1861, the loss of the federal government would be little noticed. But wars expand states, in large part because leaders are forced to improve their abilities to extract the resources—men, money, and matériel—with which to wage war, and they must build an effective administration to accomplish that. At its peak the C.S.A. had seventy thousand civil servants, 80 percent of them in the War Department, and that does not include the huge number of officers of the separate states designated by the central government to identify and round up conscripts, operate conscript camps, and hunt deserters and lie-outs.[46]

But soldiers were not the only needful thing, nor was conscription the only policy driving an expansion of the central state bureaucracy in the Confederate South. In addition to conscription, which required a virtual army itself of officers to enforce, the C.S.A. adopted a highly centralized taxation policy to feed and clothe the army. In April 1863 the Confederate Congress passed the infamous one-tenth tax or tithe, as it was called, which required citizens to surrender one-tenth of everything grown and raised on their farms and plantations beyond what was required for subsistence. Taxation, "the emblematic policy of state-building," was particularly onerous in the Confederate case. For in shaping the financial instrument closely to the forms of societal production, in this case agricultural goods, the federal government opted for a tax-in-kind, which required tax collectors, TIK men they were called, to go into each household, farm, workshop, and plantation and remove part of everything produced there. It was not only onerous, it was highly intrusive, forcing ordinary men and, more often, the women left to run those farms and plantations into regular confrontations with government agents. The stack of papers in South Carolina politician Lewis Malone Ayers's personal files records exactly the number of bushels of corn, head of cattle, and everything else produced on his plantation and specifies the exact amount of the government's one-tenth share, each receipt the remnant of a startlingly personal encounter with a government agent.[47] The government's increasing recourse also to impressment—the involuntary seizure of private property in exchange for currency, bonds, or promises to pay (all usually below market price)—further increased the presence and power of government agents in citizens' everyday lives. One Alabama man estimated that as of August 1863 there were "about one thousand government agents" in this state "under the new system of taxation and purchasing for the army." After passage of the April 1863 law, the Treasury Department named 1,440 appraisers and the War Department sent 2,945 agents into the Southern states to enforce the new law. You could hardly miss them.[48]

For people accustomed to a very small government presence in their lives, this was a tremendous shock. Like a swarm of locusts, the officers of the conscript bureau, TIK men, army procurers, press agents, home guardsmen, and countless others cloaked in federal authority spread out over the Southern landscape, thrusting men and women into a newly intimate relationship with government authorities. John Milton, the governor of Florida, drew a vivid picture of that power in late 1863. "Why," he asked state legislators, "should any citizen be clothed with military authority which would enable him to intrude himself into the sacred precincts of the family circle, and when reproved or repulsed for his intrusion, then with an armed force at his back, to return and make unlawful searches and seizures?" John Letcher, governor of Virginia, spoke for many in a public letter that railed against federal policies that flooded the country with "an army of impressing agents intruding into the homes of private citizens and searching them from top to bottom, to wrest from the proprietor the products of his labor." Men subject to the considerable power of enrolling officers complained bitterly to local politicians and state governors about "being prodded an halled about so much" to prove they were legitimately exempt from service; others raged about the power conscript officers had to treat men "worse than slaves," or to make them "the slave of the government," their language attesting to their outrage at the violation of long-standing rights and privileges accorded free white men in the slave South.[49]

But women, too, suffered under—and protested—the onslaught. They all lived with the consequences of conscription, and like the North Carolina woman whose husband was a prisoner of war and who managed to support her seven children on rented land, soldiers' wives all staggered under the weight of the new 10 percent tax in the fall of 1863. She had worked hard all summer to get a good corn crop, the woman wrote the governor, and would have "most enof to do yos if wee cod ceep it but I her that the presedent has one 10 of it and I have non to spare." Others wrote their governors asking if, really, the tax-in-kind was supposed to apply to soldiers' wives. One soldier forwarded a letter from his wife reporting that "the government has gone and taking the tenth part of her Bacan living her and the little children to Starve."[50] But whether it was the TIK man, the conscript officer hunting their husbands, or the army or cavalry impressing their goods as they went, soldiers' wives had to contend with "the government" as never before. The state was not simply out there, it was inside every household. It was not so much that white women emerged voluntarily out of the recesses of the household into public life during the war as that the state came barging in their front door, catapulting them into a relationship they had never sought but could hardly refuse.

Women's ability to turn vague promises of protection into concrete claims required a level of practical knowledge about the workings of the political system that not many possessed at the outset of the war; it also depended on the responsiveness of politicians, which was predictably uneven. So it is startling to see how quickly there took shape the outlines of a new politics, distinctive for sure but also deeply strategic in sensibility, as poor white women tried to manage and survive the demands of the big state now confronting them. Poor white women's new political culture was made out of the materials at hand.

Strategically speaking, women were at a great disadvantage compared with men. Poor white women had little experience in calling meetings, resolution writing, lobbying, jockeying, patronage seeking, violence, and the sheer horse trading that made up the regular practice of antebellum politics. But the bureaucracy and policies of the wartime world worked at a level of complexity that was new to everyone involved. State governors and the various secretaries of war fielded a constant barrage of inquiries from men and women alike, who wrote in complete confusion about the scope of particular policies or legitimate powers of state officers. In 1863 men wrote to ask whether they were covered by particular extensions of the Conscription Act if they had already paid for a substitute or if their appointment to a local office still rendered them exempt. Women wrote state governors to ask for the exemption of their husbands and sons only to be told that they had applied to the wrong branch of government and to be directed to the War Department, which had authority over all conscripts. Government officials spent half their time handing down lessons on the organization of the bureaucracy to confused citizens. Departments of government were so new and underfunded some of them simply scratched out "United States of America" on the antebellum forms and wrote in "Confederate."[51] The learning curve was steep for everyone involved, but for none quite as much as the soldiers' wives.

Poor white women had little experience to draw on in the world of wartime politics. Elite women who wanted something from the government often proceeded through the channels of patronage politics their men had customarily used, working their family connections as before. Eliza Lamb wrote a Dr. Murphy demanding to know "if you have writen Gov Vance about getting my son out of the army." A letter received around that time made "at the request of Mrs. Eliza Lamb, a widow lady of our County," referred the governor to a state senator "to whom all parties in this matter are well known." That was the way connected people operated. "When I tell you who I am, you will know that it is no stranger who needs your assistance," one planter woman assured the governor of Virginia. But poor white women had no choice but to write as strangers. And for the first time, and in surprising numbers, they did. With no connections to tap, they nonetheless went straight to the men at the top, to their governors, the secretary of war, and President Davis, with their appeals, recommendations, and demands. "Dear sir this is a graeate undertakeing for me as I never wrote to a man of authority before," Martha Coletrane began her letter to Governor Vance.[52]

Unfamiliar as such communications were, soldiers' wives' efforts clearly reflected a strategic sensibility, honed in local networks of information about the new state, its powers and obligations. "I was told t write a ltter to you and that you would see to it for me that it ws your bisiness to see to it," one woman began her letter to the governor of North Carolina. When a county commissioner was called to account by the governor in response to a woman's complaint about the allocation of state funds, he petulantly dismissed her: "she has herd of some women writing to you and getting help and no doubt thats the main cause of her letter." And indeed, women assiduously gathered and shared information about how to craft a successful appeal. One South Carolina planter woman, Meta Morris Grimball, wrote with some astonishment that not only did "the families of soldiers now take newspapers and if they don't read themselves they get people to read to them," but that some of them "have learned to read themselves" and even to write in order to get and exchange letters. When the Louisiana farm wife Mary Wilkinson decided to try to get her husband out of the army, she combed her neighborhood for information, conferring with local men about who had to go in the new call-up and who might still be exempt. She tried to identify the best category under which her husband might apply for a discharge. With him stuck in camp she had far better access to information about the activities of local conscription officers, and it was she who kept him informed about his chances of getting off. "All has to go that got two legs and two arms so says the law," she told him in the fall of 1862. If he came home then, she told him, he would "be drug about from piller to post and then sent off in the confederacy."[53]

Soldiers' wives were equally astute in the way they crafted petitions for exemptions. Most pointedly mentioned the service their husbands would provide not simply to them but to other soldiers' wives in the settlement (what they called their neighborhoods) or provided hard evidence of their physical unfitness to continue service. Catherine Miller knew better than to request her husband's release simply to support her. Instead she got fifty of her neighbors (mostly women) to attest to the fact that he was needed "for his famely and settlement use." One gets the distinct impression of neighborhoods aswirl with rumors about what worked and what did not. Some, not willing to waste their time on dead ends, just asked government officials straight out what kind of appeal would move them. "There have been a great many petitions sent up some to affect and some not herd from," Mrs. G. E. Cook wrote Governor Brown of Georgia. "If a petition will do any good," she wrote, "I can send up one as strong as it can be made."[54]

The petition was, not surprisingly, the women's preferred form of written address. It was the one political right possessed by the weak and dependent that had never been called into question. Few Southern women had ever written any before the war. Yet by early 1863 most soldiers' wives had a good handle on the nature of the petition as a political instrument, attempting not only to abide by the customary rules (getting signatures to testify to the truth of your claims) but to parry the suspicion with which they knew the claims were greeted in government offices. One strategy often employed was to accuse other local folks of being bald-faced liars: "They have names on there petitions seven miles from home where they could not get any around Home," a Mrs. Cook told Governor Brown about one that had been sent up by her neighbors. With governors and secretaries of war constantly alerted to "lying petitions" and men "crawling into shamshops under the pretense of shoemakers to git clear" (that is, claiming a false exemption), women tried everything to convey the truth and transparency of their own claims. "This is no false tale made up to save some one from the army as you may think," Eliza Thomas assured Governor Vance. "I would not tell a lie."[55]

Like everyone else in Civil War America, Southern soldiers' wives lived in a virtual force field of information and rumor generated by proclamations, newspapers, military orders, broadsides, and word of mouth.[56] But with the exception of battlefield lists of the dead and wounded, no information mattered more than the personal disposition of state officials toward them and their class. Who would look favorably on their requests? The women knew that they depended on the favor of the big men. And while there were hard limits to the personal nature of power in the Confederate South—governors could not exempt men from Confederate service, for example—soldiers' wives' instincts to appeal to government officials were not entirely wrong. It is no coincidence that they were able to operate more effectively in states with populist governors and legislatures than in those without, and that they had more success in terms of concessions and policy revisions with individual state governments than with the federal one. Their success depended on finding friends in high places.

Soldiers' wives were resourceful. They had no political patronage to trade, no votes to offer, collect on, or threaten to withhold. A few did try their hand at the usual quid pro quo of Southern politics. "You have dun well so fare," the self-designated Female Sect of Rutherfordton, North Carolina, lectured their governor. Now see to it that Samuel Norville "be releast." "You wer the choice of our Husbands and sons and we too look up to you Sir with perfect confidence [that you will] do something for us," Mary Moore and her neighbors put it.[57] But most soldiers' wives took a different approach, acknowledging their dependence on favors and appealing directly to power. In one communication after another, soldiers' wives acknowledged—even exaggerated—the vast new power of the state, while moving decisively to embody it in particular men. "I look on you as Sovering of this state," Ellen Congleton told her governor, Zebulon Vance. "Your majesty," Sophia Bowen, addressed him. "Relese him ser if you plese," Catharine Hunt told Vance, "I wont say if you can I now you can." It was an art powerless rural people had perfected over millennia of history when no rights had been established to which they might appeal. For women, such forms of traditional politics persisted long past the onset of Western democracies, even advanced ones such as those that had evolved out of the struggles of the nineteenth century in the United States and the C.S.A.[58]

But the bended knee and the begging letter revealed the imprint of the new forms of state power the war had engendered, and not just the weight of the past. For the two tactics the women used in approaching officials—

exaggeration and embodiment—were a measure of their attempt to exert some control over the remote and bureaucratized new powers that inhered in the state. Now, it seemed to them, *all* power lay with the state. Mary Bennett pleaded with Governor Brown to send her "a peas of riten that offers [enrolling officers] can [not] truble him." Mary Bennett had learned that paper had power, but there was surely something of magical thinking in her belief that the governor could deliver her simply by providing her with a piece of it. There was even an element of naive monarchism in soldiers' wives' sensibility, evident in the urgency with which some reported to higher-ups the doings in their neighborhoods: "I don't believe you are knowing to the way the Men is doing here," Elizabeth Coker wrote Governor Brown. "If so I think to be sure you would put a stop to it."[59] To Bennett, Coker, and the others, the Confederate state—whether the governments of the separate states or the federal one—had new power over life and death. By appealing to powerful political leaders, soldiers' wives summoned up the just and benevolent leader they needed in the moment, imagining him alternately as sovereign, majesty, father, husband, and always as a friend. "A Husband and a Father," Bettie Baylin called Senator R. M. T. Hunter.[60] State patriarchy was better than none at all. Soldiers' wives could practice a very literal politics of protection: you protect us, they said, you are the head to our family now. The big men had, after all, had promised them that.

Women tried their hand everywhere, even in places like Virginia where there was little encouragement to do so. Women sent petitions to Governor William Smith signed by "the soldiers' wives," and Smith did press their needs for family labor on military officials. No governor was entirely tone deaf. But soldiers' wives' politics flourished most in states with populist governors, where women knew the political conditions to be most opportune for holding state officials accountable. "I have heard you were a generous man (or I never should have written)," as one woman put it to Governor Pettus of Mississippi. "We could not or would not transmit this statement of affirs to you if we did not have your pledge that you will . . . provide for the helpless ones at home," Priscilla Allen said of Governor Allen of Louisiana.[61] Like everyone else in political life soldiers' wives tried to find allies. In the Confederacy's significant core of self-styled populist governors, they often did.

They had less luck with federal officials. After the beginning of the war, few letters got through to President Davis, though women did send them, and the many received by the Confederate secretary of war were answered, although often, as Elizabeth Mason's was, with the dismissive notation "explain as usual why request can not be granted." Women wrote anyway hoping for sympathy and compassion.[62] But much as soldiers' wives tried to hold those individuals accountable, their appeals fell mostly on deaf ears. Robert Kean, the chief of the Confederate War Bureau who was on the front lines of the exemption battles, said the cries of the women almost drove him mad. "It is agonizing to see and hear the cases daily brought into the war office, appeal after appeal and *all* disallowed," he observed in 1864.[63]

Yet with populist governors like Zebulon Vance of North Carolina, Joseph Brown of Georgia, and John Gill Shorter of Alabama, poor white Southern women managed to get an ally, especially in the struggle against the overweening powers of the central state. Vance, for one, never failed to answer a letter. He doled out small favors, including orders on factories for thread and cloth; he followed up women's complaints against local officials who failed to deliver the relief the legislature had promised; and he took up their fights with military officials, federal conscripting officers, and impressment agents, instructing his secretaries to send the women printed copies of his letters of protest to Davis, Seddon, and the rest. If he could do nothing else, he simply acknowledged the sufferings of the "ladies" as he invariably put it. "Answer some how," he wrote on more than a few.[64] In South Carolina the Confederate congressman Lewis Malone Ayers also went to work for the poor soldiers' wives, trying to advance their claims on the Confederate government for pensions when their husbands were killed in battle, writing letters, showing up at the relevant offices in Richmond, and tirelessly pressing for answers to his inquiries on their behalf.[65] Like Ayers, Governor Vance and other self-styled populist governors recognized soldiers' wives as an important new constituency in Southern political life and one to whom they now answered.

As soldiers' wives, poor white women put themselves squarely on the political agenda in the Confederate states. Theirs was a specifically political identity, born of war, embraced selectively, and deployed strategically. That soldiers' wives had more impact and success in some places than in others owed to the same constellation of broad political forces that bore on every constituent's chances. But what is striking is that these women were out there at all. For that is the truly remarkable thing: that in the identity of soldiers' wives, poor white Southern women found a way to make themselves count in Southern political life.

The issues at the core of soldiers' wives' politics were anything but narrow. As officials of the Confederate states struggled against increasing odds to wrest from their people the wherewithal to wage war, matters of labor, subsistence, relief, and social justice that soldiers' wives saw as their own gained desperate salience in the body politic as a whole. The nexus of issues women agitated—from the government's manpower policies, soldiers' wages, government prices for women's work, relief, federal taxes, impressment, and monetary policy, to name the main ones—were as comprehensive as the struggle to sustain life itself. Taken together they constituted a politics of subsistence. Poor white women's political vision and authority within their own communities and with the government officials who sought to retain their support followed from the issues war and its leviathan state had introduced. "The iron is gone deep into the heart of society," Robert Kean, chief of the Confederate Bureau of War, memorably put it. As the iron struck ever deeper, white Southerners pushed more fiercely back.[66] Soldiers, many of them privates earning $11 per month, pressed their commanders and civilian officials about the desperate condition of their wives and children and about government policies that spared slaveholders while leaving their women with no labor at all. But the women proved increasingly willing to fight their own battles. Empowered to make claims on the state, women left at home proved anything but reluctant to do so.

Up from the farmsteads, workshops, settlements, country towns, and bursting Confederate cities came a tidal wave of protest and resistance, much of it emanating from, and organized by, women. The emergence of soldiers' wives as a force in Confederate politics represented a significant rerouting of power and authority on the home front, and, at least for the duration of the war, a striking realignment of state-citizen relations. For even as women spoke specifically as soldiers' wives, and thus in a gendered voice, they spoke increasingly on behalf of the men of their class, taking leadership on a range of social justice issues at the heart of popular politics in the Confederacy. By the spring of 1863, women's claims on the government had not only increased in volume; they had become the main vehicles of demands on state officials, expressive of local knowledge and political opposition. "As gustic [justice] belongs to the people," one woman memorably put it, "let us have it."[67]

The basic issue was labor, as Margaret Smith, the North Carolina soldier's wife, made painfully clear. "We hav seen the time when we could call our Littel childen and our Husbun to our tables and hav a plenty, and now wee have Becom Beggars and starvers an now way to help ourselves," she told her governor, poignantly invoking yeoman women's loss of household independence as a consequence of the Confederate army's manpower policies. Without their husbands, the primary laborers on their small farms, Margaret Smith and the other soldiers' wives simply could not do enough field work to wrest subsistence from the land. "I have scuffled for them as long as I could," another poor woman wrote President Davis of her struggle to support herself and her three little children in the absence of her husband. Conscription and an exemption policy useful only to planters had destroyed their very way of life.[68]

The soldiers' wives were hardly confused about the source of their troubles and let government officials have it about military manpower policies that seemed deliberately calculated to break the poor. Even in the most traditional petitions, resentment, and knowledge of whom to hold responsible, came through. Almira Acors begged Jefferson Davis to discharge her husband, a boot and shoe maker from Thornburg, Virginia, to come home and take care of her and their three small children. She could get no help from "the rich people about here there hearts are of steel," she told him. Acors was in the Confederate service and, as his wife knew all too well, only the president or secretary of war could get him out. Acors begged only the relief of her own husband; she made no suggestions beyond her personal case. But still she made it perfectly clear that federal policy—she had in mind the notorious twenty-negro exemption law—had not been written in her interest. Why is it, she asked President Davis, "if widows ladies overseers are released who have servants working for them why not release a poor man to his suffering family." Acors must have known her petition was a long shot, and it was. Davis sent the petition over to his secretary of war, where it presumably languished in the files with the many other hopeless pleas they received in 1862.[69]

Labor, and the government-induced shortage of it, was the paramount concern of every soldier's wife who painstakingly spelled out or dictated a letter to a government official. It was not something they had done before. So it is all the more amazing to confront the tone and scope of those communications, and to puzzle out the local political developments that had encouraged poor white women to think that their opinion made a difference. In an incredible number of petitions—traditional begging letters—poor white Southern women presumed to chastise, instruct, warn, demand, and threaten government officials about everything from conscription to monetary policy that they regarded as ill-advised and unjust. Oftentimes they began with the narrow issue of labor in formulaic tones of neediness and respect, only to peel off seconds later into confrontational commentary on a whole complex of issues in state and federal politics. Soldiers' wives' outraged demands for consideration in the making of government policy were arguably unprecedented, certainly in Southern, and perhaps in American, history.[70]

Martha Coletrane, a North Carolina soldier's wife, exemplifies the pattern. Political novice, she nonetheless wasted no time on pleasantries. Necessity required her to write, she told Vance, "as we are nonslave holders in this section of the state [and] I hope you and our legislatur will look to it and have justice done our people as well as the slaveholders." Coletrane had a specific objective bearing on the condition of her family: she wanted to keep her husband out of the army now that conscription had been extended to men aged 35 to 45. "Without my husband we are a desolate and a ruined family," was how she put it. But Coletrane did not request a personal exemption. Instead she went after the policy, presuming to instruct Vance on his deportment in relation to the Confederate Congress, a body, as she well knew, heavily dominated (to the tune of 90 percent of delegates) by slaveholders. Coletrane took aim at the new Conscription Act, which had been passed in August 1862, as specious class legislation. "Hold the rane in your own hands," she lectured Vance, "and do not let the confederate congress have the full sway over your state[.] I appeal to you to look to the white cultivaters as strictly as congress has to the slaveholder"; leave the older men at home to "support their families," she advised. Coletrane articulated a politics of subsistence that spoke not just for her or the needs of women, but for their whole class of "white cultivators." "We trust in god and look to you for some help for our poor children so no more." Sole author, Martha Coletrane nonetheless spoke for an imagined community of soldiers' wives.[71]

There was a world of political change distilled in that "we." The politics of subsistence registered the conditions of impoverishment and misery the state had imposed on nonslaveholders. The range of issues was broad—as broad as the government war measures bearing on subsistence—and the critique sweeping. Yeoman women were enraged most by a conscription policy that forced poor men into the army while leaving rich men at home by dint of substitution, exemption to manage slaves, appointment to government office, and all manner of other loopholes. Lucy Shelton wrote the governor of South Carolina about the twenty-negro exemption law that "the people here don't like espeacily the poorer class that is exempting al men that has twenty negroes." If the law had made them pay "one thousand dollars for the poor men's wives that has been killed or that is in the field of battle," she pointed out, it would have "binn all right but it is not right as it is." "Call that to the floor again and make A mends on it for the benefit of the poor men wives." Now soldiers' wives presumed to tell governors how to make law. "I wish you would have all the big legislater men and big men about towns ordered into serviz," one South Carolina woman lacerated President Davis, "they [ain't] no serviz to us at home." Anger at the big men and a government that favored them underlay every communication. But so did an expectation of redress. Like so many of the others who pressed their case on government officials, she wrote as an individual but spoke for an imagined community of soldiers' wives.[72]

If conscription or military service was the root of the women's problems, it was hardly the sum total. For poor women's attempts to scrape out subsistence, absent the field labor or wages of husbands and sons, were immeasurably worsened by other policies to which government—especially the federal one—was driven in its efforts to extract the resources to feed, arm, equip, and pay an army. Confederate armies had been impressing slave labor and provisions in an ad hoc fashion since the beginning of the war and had moved in the fall of 1862 to regularize the practice. But things entered a critical new stage in April 1863 when the War Department imposed the tax-in-kind. The tax was supposed to be assessed only against surpluses, but that was a matter of bitter dispute in practice. That tax represented an extension of state authority and a burden on poor white people that far exceeded any other government levy. Planters could and did protest the government impressment of property, especially slaves, for the war effort. But to poor soldiers' wives, the 10 percent tax was, quite literally, an insupportable burden, the very difference between an eked-out subsistence and starvation. "They are gathering everything they can of the poor soldiers' wives and children," C. W. Walker protested to her governor about the TIK men in her community. "They are as grate enemys as the yankies."[73]

The women fought back, incredulous and enraged. "Do we wimmin ha[ve] to pay [tithes] whare our husbunds is in the war?" one wrote her governor in disbelief. "I tell you," Nancy Richardson told Governor Vance, "if such as we has to give the tenth our husbands ses thay in tend to dye at home that [they] are just waiting for the [tithes] to be takond from us thay will disert just as soon as it is dun." These were no empty threats. They came at precisely the moment governors, including Zebulon Vance, were enmeshed in an escalating battle with deserters and the women who supported them. When Mary Moore warned Vance that she had heard rumors about talk of desertion among men from Davidson County, all of whom were armed with "repeters" (repeating rifles), she laid the blame on the tax-in-kind. "Thare is one thing that should be look after soon," she lectured him, "that is the one 10 of it comes out of the poor soldiers that have only thir wife or mother and children to labor[.] the army will be brok some of the best soldiers I know say that they will come home if its taken from them."[74]

Increasingly, soldiers' wives saw themselves as the victims of a systemic, not personal, injustice, of a government policy that was literally consuming their substance. One political scientist who has studied Confederate war policy has offered the chilling view that the Confederate War Department "cannibalized the regional economy," that it pursued extraction policies that literally "and steadily consumed the material base of the economy." That was exactly how soldiers' wives saw it, and they said as much in the letters written to the officials they held responsible. Some insisted that the crisis of subsistence was part of a larger conspiracy to expropriate the poor people of their land; those views surfaced particularly in North Carolina, and there speculators were sometimes cast as the advance guard of a long-standing class war. To them, the erosion of yeoman independence was purposeful, a planned-for consequence of government policy. But in every state, soldiers' wives protested that private citizens were empowered to prey on the poor by the government's refusal to act to secure poor women's subsistence.[75]

"Speculators" distilled the palpable sense that everything about war policy in the C.S.A. advantaged the rich and victimized them. In North Carolina, Nancy Vines and some other women described how they walked almost fifty miles in search of yarn only to end up in a physical fight with the men at one factory. "He saide he did not cear hoo was slders wives and hoo wurt not who was wider an hoo was not an hoo was naked and hoo was not." Why would he sell to her, she reported the owner as saying, when he could sell the yarn for $15 to $20 to others and "make a speculation of it." Nor was the situation much different in Georgia. Men who have corn won't sell it to soldiers' wives at anything less than market prices and won't take the Confederate currency in which their soldier husbands were paid, a group of women alerted their ally, Governor Brown. "They can speculate of soldiers' wives make fortunes of them. Just look at the women and children that are begging bread husband in the war or perhaps dead." This was class injustice on a grand scale, they insisted, and it was enough to turn them against the war. "Those that brought the war on us is at home," they raged, "and our boys are fighting for there property. It has been an unholy war from the beginning," they concluded, "the rich is all at home makeing great fortunes"—the rich didn't care "what becomes of the poor class of people so that they can save there neggroes." So went the flood of letters across the governors' desks.[76]

Extortion and speculation emerged as a central theme in Confederate culture and politics. No issue registered more profoundly. As the *Montgomery Daily Advertiser* put it, "The whole country is ringing with denunciations of the extortioners."[77] But if historians have widely recognized the problem of speculation and acknowledged that women were particular victims, they seem not to have noticed that the public debate was largely stimulated by the actions of women as well. Speculation—and the expansion of public welfare in response—were put on the political agenda by the mass agitation of soldiers' wives. By 1863, the year in which public concern peaked, not only had soldiers' wives pressed the issue in masses of letters (individual and collective) to state governors, President Davis, and the secretary of war, letters that, increasingly ominous in tone, themselves demanded a political response; particular groups of soldiers' wives scattered across the country had also thrust the issue front and center in public consciousness by a series of spectacular and highly publicized seizures of food.

The wave of food riots, all apparently organized and led by women, that surged through the Confederate states in the spring of 1863 riveted public attention on soldiers' wives and their claims for justice for the Confederate poor.[78] But the food riots have a deep backstory, one not often told. It consists of a multitude of attempts by poor women like Martha Coletrane to alert their leaders to the vast gulf between their means and the price of subsistence, to convey their mounting rage at those who profited from their immiseration—the speculators, or big men, as they so often put it. They demanded policy that met governments' basic obligation to support soldiers' dependents. Soldiers' wives' politics of subsistence took increasingly collective, organized, and confrontational forms even before the violent demonstrations of late March and April 1863. Shocked as they were, state officials could hardly say they had not been put on notice.

Political danger loomed, not least in the way in which poor white women had begun to speak in a collective voice: in the name of soldiers' wives, nonslaveholders, and the Confederate poor more generally. This manifest collective identity suggested political possibility, a capacity for organization and a potential for mobilization by a population hardly known for either. It isn't easy to figure out how rural soldiers' wives organized their written protests, but the possibilities for collective organization were quite real. Clerks in government offices confronted with documents signed by hundreds of women must have wondered how they managed to achieve such numbers. Did someone carry the petitions around the neighborhood? Did they write them up at local meetings of women? Did they hire an agent to collect the signatures? All of these strategies appear to have been used at one time or another. The more than five hundred women who (in 1863) signed "A Petition of the Women of North Carolina" wanted it known that they had not used an agent. If they had, their cover letter said, "the signers would have been thousands instead of hundreds." Still, hundreds of women (522 to be precise) from the area around Rockingham did sign it, lining up their names in columns under the headings "Soldiers Widows Mothers" and "Wives Daughters Sisters Friends." The body of the petition was a searing protest against the exploitation of the poor by planter speculators. "Men who promised our Husbands, Sons and Brothers when they volunteered to do much to supply their places now turn a deaf ear to our entreaties and leave us prey to the merciless speculators and extortioners who have monopolized much of the produce of the county." "This is the voice of the women of North Carolina appealing to the Chief Executive of our state for justice and protection." "We ask for relief and protection," they repeated, and ominously, they asked for Vance to sue for peace. "Let this horrid war end! Let blood cease to flow."[79] The voice is stunning in its clarity, the numbers involved more stunning still. It is difficult to imagine five hundred Southern white women doing anything together before the Civil War. It took a great deal of coordination to produce such a document, and a small sea change to produce the sensibility it evinced.

Confederate soldiers' wives were clearly capable of some kind of political organization, if only what was required to get five hundred signatures on a piece of paper. They sent many mass petitions to government officials during the Civil War. The obvious counterpart is the women's mass antislavery petition campaign executed in the Northern states in the antebellum period and during the Civil War. But in clear contrast to that centrally organized campaign, not a single one of the Confederate petitions was on a preprinted form or followed any preauthored script such as those then (and now) mass-mailed to U.S. congresspersons.[80] To the contrary, all Confederate petitions were handwritten and used language so individual they obviously had no template. At the same time they often carried signatures or terms of self-description that identified the authors as collectivities of soldiers' wives.

There was no national organization of soldiers' wives with state or local branches organizing a petition campaign in the Confederate South.[81] But there was clearly something we might regard as an ad hoc local mobilization of soldiers' wives repeated in hundreds of settlements and towns across the length and breadth of the South. For the coordination required to produce those huge petitions and even their smaller counterparts suggests a prior process of political organization by poor white women that was hardly customary in that political culture. It also suggests that the groups of women (identified as mobs) that coalesced in various parts of the South in 1863 and 1864, and that drew press attention mostly during food riots, had their basis in a broader local political process expressed more commonly in written protests than out-of-doors actions.

It is not always easy to tell where one political form left off and another began. Women whose sense of the social contract had been violated were formidable enemies. In reading the mass of threatening letters pouring into governors' mailboxes and to the secretary of war, one gets the distinct sense of options being entertained—tried on—in ordinary conversations in neighborhoods across the Confederate states. Two women writing in November 1862 concluded a typical account of how "women cant make support for ther familys" by warning that "the women talk of Making up Companys going to try to make peace for it is more than human hearts can bear."[82] What did they mean by companies? Were those idle threats? Threats of various kinds were issued with more regularity thereafter, and the violence of the women's speech was stunning. Some threatened to bring down God's vengeance on those responsible for the suffering of the poor; others threatened to summon bands of deserters to beat stingy big men or to take their husbands out of the army; and others again, like those who took to the streets, threatened to take matters into their own hands. The means were varied, but the political threat was pointed and persistent in the rural, small-town, and urban South by early 1863.

The Confederate South, like the antebellum South, was a deeply evangelical culture. Women had always been a disproportionate share of churchgoers, and even as the ability to keep a minister and services deteriorated during the war and church attendance became impossible, many yeoman and poor white women turned desperately to their God. Like slave women who construed prayer as work for the Union cause, many poor white women could muster faith *only* in God. They turned their angry faces heavenward, confident that He would serve justice to the powerless. "An all wise God . . . will send his fury and judgment in a very grate manner [on] all those our leading men and those that are in power," a group of women threatened the secretary of war, "if thare is no more favors shone to . . . the mothers and wives of those in poverty who has with patriotism stood the ferce battles." "Do you suppose that God will ever give to such people the victory," a Mrs. Wellborn concluded a ten-page letter to the governor of Georgia, detailing the injustices and hardships visited by Confederate policy on the poor soldiers' wives and children.[83]

Evangelical women's Christian cosmology could turn apocalyptic in the firestorm of war, could even turn in antislavery and antiwar directions in certain settings. In North Carolina, one poor woman prophesied eternal ruin for the cause of slavery, the Confederacy, and its architects, begging the governor to "try and stop this cruel war . . . For God sake to try and make peace on some terms and let they rest of the poor men come home and make somethin to eat [for] the sake of suffering humanity and especially for the sake of sufering women and children." Slavery, the Confederacy—God had set his face against it all. By 1865 when she wrote, a highly organized—and to the Davis administration, dangerous—peace party had been operating in North Carolina politics for more than two years under the leadership of William Holden, and soldiers' wives and widows in that state were far more likely to urge their governor and legislators to make peace than in other states. But this North Carolina poor woman not only stood for peace, she stood against slavery, a highly unusual position even in that state. Soldiers' wives, like many soldiers, complained bitterly about slavery and slaveholders' privileges, convinced that they were being forced to sacrifice to protect and perpetuate that institution and its class privileges. Many, too, talked fearfully about the way the war was working a process of racial erasure. "I have worked as hard as some of the rich men's darkey's and din make much," as one woman put it. That kind of racial fear, of becoming as poor and disrespected as slaves, usually didn't turn in an antislavery direction. But there were some, like this North Carolina poor woman, who turned against slavery itself. "If we are to bee slavs let us bee slaves together," she implored Vance, "for ther is I see no other chance. I will only say for they sake of suffering women and children, let they niggar go, for we cant hire none to work." Hers was, to be sure, the painfully squinting antislavery vision of a religious woman, steeped in the practices, deprivations, and resentments of poor white people in the rural South. A few of her class, especially devout Unionists, managed to struggle toward common human cause with enslaved opponents of the Confederacy—Sarah Thompson and her husband, the Tennessee Unionists, had found their own religious way to that position. But this North Carolina woman was more typical of yeoman antislavery in her instrumental opposition to slavery and lack of fellowship with slaves. "We can't hire none to work": that was antislavery of the Southern white variety at the tail end of the American Civil War. Still, this woman was ready to abandon the foundational institution of Southern and Confederate life as a divine imperative. "I believe slavery is doomed to dy out," she wrote, "and that god is agoing to liberate niggars and fighting an longer is fighting against God." "Now sir," she wound up, "you and some of the rest of those big bugs will have to answer for they blood of our dear ones who have been slain, God will demand their blood at your hands." A widow, her husband killed in battle, she had nothing left. She put her trust only in God. "These are words badly written," she signed off, "but they are words not to be denyed by an God fearing man."[84]

There was plenty of violence implied in that woman's vision of justice. Some of it came to pass. Martha Sheets was indicted in county court in North Carolina for a personal threat made against the life and person of Aaron Saunders, a grist mill owner in her neighborhood who had callously turned her away from his door when she appealed to him for relief. Sheets, who recklessly signed her name to the written threat, thought her actions justified, legitimated even, by the broad context of class warfare the war had wrought, and by her outraged sense that he had violated the contract with soldiers' wives. Saunders had made public promises to help the families of soldiers who signed up as volunteers, Sheets reminded him. "When this ware brake out you sad goe Boys ill spend the last doler for your famerlys and drat your old sold you never have dun a thing for the pore wiming yet." "You nastly old whelp," she lacerated him, "you have told lys to get your suns out of this war and you don't care for the rest that is gon nor for ther famelyes." Her sense of fairness and entitlement violated, she turned menacing. Demanding two bushels of wheat and two bushels and a peck of corn, she warned that if he didn't deliver the goods in ten days, she would "send enuf deserters to mak you sufer that you never sufered before." "Send me good grain if you want to live . . . This from Martha A. Sheets." All of Martha Sheets's threats were recorded in the court documents prepared for her prosecution. There they lie still, in the North Carolina archives, a reminder to posterity that some Southern women were prepared to take justice into their own hands. Sheets was indicted only for writing a threatening letter. But clearly local officials had reason to take it seriously. Was it only coincidence that four months later Aaron Saunders's mill was attacked by a posse of armed women, some related to the state's most notorious deserter band?[85] Not all the soldiers' wives' threats were harmless, a recognition Confederate officials had arrived at long before Martha Sheets was hauled in.

There would be more violent episodes involving Confederate women before the Civil War was over. The terms in which that action would come were all rehearsed by many who themselves stayed on the peaceful side of the line. Groups of soldiers' wives found themselves in physical fights with mill owners for impossible-to-obtain yarn and contemplated raising a crowd and seizing it. After one such incident a Mrs. Brown warned the governor "to do something for us for if you do not somebody will burn it [the mill] up certain or els the soldiers' wives will rob it." Another North Carolina woman, worried about both foodstuffs and yarn and the impossibility of buying either on a soldier's salary, warned that "if they [the big men] don't use there [the soldiers'] wivs better they will rais a crowd take something to eat and I want your advice." Susan Wallee warned the governor to "press . . . provisions from these men that has it, for if you dont I am afraid the wamen will have to do it and I dont want to press anythin if I can help it." If women said those things in letters to lawmakers, what were they saying to each other? Some of the options being entertained were radical indeed.[86]

It is clear from the timing that some of the women's threats—those posted in late 1863 and 1864—imitated violent actions already taken and highly publicized. But others anticipated them. In Virginia, where the largest food riot would break out in the spring of 1863, there is no evidence of prior warning in women's letters to the governor. John Letcher was not perceived as a sympathetic figure by soldiers' wives. Whatever unrest was churning the waters in Virginia is hard to detect in his (possibly purged) correspondence. But in North Carolina, where Governor Vance had fully performed his part as the protector of the poor soldiers' wives, and where county clerks had already written him about the negligence of magistrates and destitution of the women, everything in his letter bags alerted him. "How can our Soldiers fight when they know their wives and children are destitute even of a peace [*sic*] of bread," the clerk of Green County wrote Vance in panic in January 1863.[87]

And then there was this: an anonymous letter that landed on Governor Vance's desk in Raleigh exactly six weeks before the wave of food riots broke out in nearby Salisbury, from a "company" (their term) of women in Bladen County. "Reglators"—"our company will be calld Reglators," the women wrote.[88] The term was calculated to place the authors in the state's long (formerly male) tradition of rural justice and direct action dating back to the late 1760s when a band of North Carolina farmers mounted armed attacks on British officials to protest high taxes, corrupt sheriffs, and the scarcity of hard currency. Purloined by a group of women, it spoke of a new female presence in a traditional history of dissent. They would have corn at $2 a bushel or they would seize it, the women informed Vance matter-of-factly in the opening line. "The time has come that we the comon people has to hav bread or blood and we are bound boath men and women to hav it or die in the attempt."

The Regulators' letter bore all the hallmarks of rural soldiers' wives' protests expressed in thousands of other letters written in the Confederate states by the end of the war. But the cry for bread or blood—which would echo eerily across the Confederate South in a rash of riots a few weeks later—that was new. Like Margaret Smith and countless others, the "Reglators" laid out the subsistence crisis soldiers' wives faced: the erosion of household independence with the conscription of their men, the impossible equation between their husband's pay and the prices planter speculators demanded for food, the need for state intervention to set prices in the interest of the poor. But to that they added a far more radical view of the war as a species of class warfare, a conspiracy by the rich to complete the work of expropriation of poor men's farms on which they had always planned. "The ideas is that the slave ones [owners] has the plantation and the hands to rais the bred stufs," they explained to Vance, "and our people is drove of in the ware to fight for the big mans negro and he at home making nearly all the corn that is made and then becaus he has the play in his own fingers he puts the price on his corn so as to take all the solders wage for a fiew bushels and then them has worked hard was . . . in living circumstances with perhaps a good little homestid and other thing convenient for there well being perhaps will be credited until the debt will take there land and every thing they have . . . and then they will have to rent thure lands of them lords." Like the poor women once able to call their little children to their own table and have plenty, they had become beggars and debtors, their yeoman independence entirely undone by the planters and their government friends who protected them and their property in slaves.

The crisis of subsistence in the C.S.A. clearly yielded some radical ideas, radical in diagnosis but also in agendas for action. For the "Reglators" put Vance on notice about their willingness to use violence if political solutions failed. Vance could either take them out of the Confederacy or he could set a fair price on corn. But if he failed—"if this is the way we comon people is to be treated in the confdercy"—then they would take matters into their own hands. If it was not enough that poor white women had come to speak for the people, to advance their collective demands for justice, this group was prepared to assume the final male prerogative and enforce their will by force of arms. "Sir," they told Vance, "we has sons brothers and husbands is now fighting for the big mans negro [and] are detirmined to have bread or blood out of there barns and that at a price that we can pay or we will slaughter as we go." Violence, or so they said, was part of the political repertoire of Confederate soldiers' wives.[89]

The Regulators' letter eerily predicted the violent action others carried out in Salisbury, North Carolina, six weeks later. The conditions were suspiciously similar, as if the "Reglators" wrote the script for the Salisbury crowd. That they had not speaks all the more powerfully to poor white women's politics of subsistence in North Carolina and other states. Nothing ties the Regulators to events in Salisbury. But a year later, in another starving spring, five women were tried and sentenced to jail for forcibly opening and seizing food from a government warehouse in Bladensboro, North Carolina. This time it was the "Reglators."[90]

The American Civil War represents a striking contravention of the usual social prescriptions against female violence. And although there is a long tradition of rough justice to which we might look to understand Confederate developments, Southern charivari had not been particularly a female practice. So although such behavior had been known in other times and places, the women who took to the public highways in 1863 armed with pistols and hatchets could hardly have felt buttressed by some long-ago precedent in another country and century.[91] No, the context for Southern women's Civil War violence was more immediate and local: a mass political movement of women, empowered as soldiers' wives, largely contained to nonviolent protests—and an emboldened minority who crossed the line from threats to violent direct action.

CHAPTER 5

Women Numerous and Armed

IN THE SPRING OF 1863, in a wave of food riots, soldiers' wives impressed the possibilities of their politics on a shocked nation. After that, no one questioned women's capacity for direct action or their willingness to pursue an out-of-doors politics. The riots were spectacular, and numerous. Mobs of women, numbering from a dozen to three hundred and more, armed with navy revolvers, pistols, repeaters, bowie knives, and hatchets, carried out at least twelve violent attacks (there are rumors of more) on stores, government warehouses, army convoys, railroad depots, saltworks, and granaries. The attacks occurred in broad daylight, and were all perpetrated in the space of one month, between the middle of March and the middle of April 1863. It was truly a Confederate spring of soldiers' wives' discontent.[1] The events were stunning in their boldness, organization, and violence, and in the rioters' management of the media and public opinion. For whatever the mayors and editors might say, the public simply assumed that the mobs were composed of soldiers' wives—as if prior developments had prepared them for the actions on the streets, as indeed they had.

The food riots, the most dramatic and well-known episodes of Confederate women's history, have drawn interest sporadically over the years and invited comparison to other like events in early modern European history. But lacking a context within which to make sense of the events of the spring of 1863, historians have been inclined to see them as isolated events and as an expression of a traditional female moral economy. But the key to understanding the food riots lies not in the example of crowds of rioting English women in the eighteenth-century transition to capitalism, as most historians, lacking any better alternative, have said. Rather the key lies closer to home, in events on the Confederate home front, in the breakdown of rural and urban household economies, and in women's assumption of leadership on the critical politics of subsistence that convulsed the C.S.A. Indeed, the food riots invite a directly political reading in which the legitimating idea came not from some far-off idea of the customary good, but from a discourse of protection with near roots in the secession crisis, and the idea of a social contract with soldiers' wives that had been brutally violated.[2] Then the riots come into focus as one highly public expression of soldiers' wives' mass politics of subsistence: the means by which, in written protest and direct action, poor white women registered, contested, and reshaped the insupportable demands of the wartime state. There was in the Civil War South a whole world of political communication and organization we do not know much about. To recapture it is to provide what has long been missing: a context within which to understand the food riots, the spectacular examples of violent direct action the poor white women's political culture yielded.

The women's riots of the terrible spring of 1863 occurred in the midst of a military crisis. The Davis administration in March and April of that year faced the challenge of fielding, feeding, and equipping an army adequate to the size and extent of the conflict. To meet the enemy facing the Confederacy strained every sinew of the body politic. In addition, all of the states and the central government were forced also to contend with a politically explosive crisis of subsistence on the home front. The challenges escalated: men for soldiers, slaves for labor, arms and factories to produce them or ships to run them through the blockade, corn and wheat for bread, beeves, pork and salt to preserve them, leather for shoes, uniforms, medicine, cavalry and draft horses, mules, railroad ties and labor to lay them, money to pay for it all. The thinness of the supply lines feeding the Confederate war machine worried every man in government and forced both the states and the central government into the kinds of central state policies that carried a high political price for democratically elected officials. But it was not just the soldiers and the voters who taught the Davis government and state governors the limits of what would be borne by the people in the name of war. Even as the Davis administration forced through a number of highly extractionist policies, including the one-tenth tax on the country's produce, and an extension of the age of military service upward to 45, they were also forced to divert food supplies from the army to starving soldiers' families on the home front, and the state governors were forced to undertake such a profound overhaul of the way they provided relief that it amounted to a complete rewriting of Confederate welfare policy. That was the immediate upshot of the food riots and the lasting mark soldiers' wives' politics left on Confederate war policy.

By the summer of 1863, after a long string of military losses in the western theater, including, critically, Vicksburg, the last Confederate holdout on the Mississippi River, Jefferson Davis acknowledged that the war had entered a new stage that would test the fortitude of the people and not just the armies. The war was now a civilian war. Davis acknowledged just how inextricably intertwined the social, political, and military fortunes of the country had become. The war secessionists had begun was now "eminently a war of the people," he said in October 1863.[3] The food riots of the previous spring, and the demonstrated political power of the women who led them in the name of every Confederate soldier's wife, were clearly part of President Davis's education.

Richmond's was the biggest of the food riots, but not the first. That was in Atlanta, on March 16. The next day was Salisbury, North Carolina, then Mobile, Alabama, and then Petersburg, Virginia, probably a copycat action, as was Richmond, the biggest street action of all, on April 2.[4] "Bread or blood," the Richmond women notoriously shouted, a trademark cry already seen in the written threats from the "Reglators" and on the banners Mobile's army of women waved in their rough procession through city streets: "Bread or Blood" they emblazoned on one side, "Bread or Peace" on the other.[5] The women meant business.

Everything about the riots in Atlanta and elsewhere reveals the connection between violent new developments and the local political culture of Confederate soldiers' wives. Atlanta set the pattern in miniature. There on the morning of March 18, fifteen or twenty women collected "in a body" and, led by a tall lady wearing a determined look, began to move through Atlanta's downtown streets. They stopped in front of a provision store on White Hill Street. All entered. The tall woman, apparently their spokeswoman, interviewed the merchant, asking him specifically about the price of bacon. Told it was $1.10 a pound, she protested, declaring the "impossibility of females in their condition" paying such prices for the necessaries of life. But that was all a set piece. When he refused to budge on price, the woman immediately drew a long navy pistol from her bosom and, holding the owner at bay, ordered the women to help themselves. They left the shop when they were done, stopping long enough to explain to some lookers-on that their families had "been deprived of anything to eat in the last few days, save a small portion of corn bread." It was "their suffering condition" that drove them to act as they did.[6]

Not very much is known about events in Atlanta. By midday the women had melted back into the masses of underfed folks crowded into that bursting Confederate city. Still, the Atlanta women's singular action introduced a pattern confirmed through repetition. The food riot had been a highly organized, premeditated, and disciplined affair. There was a designated leader, violence was part of the plan, and so was the management of public opinion, including an appeal to the public conscience on matters of just price and the needs of soldiers' wives and daughters. The social contract with its implied reciprocity was referenced. It was clear that everyone adjudicating the Atlanta riot (newspaper reporters and readers, mayors, local elites, city, state and national politicians, the broad public) knew—assumed even—that the rioters were "the wives and daughters of soldiers' families" and readily conceded the legitimacy of their claims. The gentlemen who had queried the women outside the White Hill Street store professed a "feeling of deep sympathy for the ladies" (the weaponry notwithstanding) and immediately raised a fund for their relief. Even the mayor and the city council, though denouncing the action, moved speedily to provide more aid "for the relief of soldiers' families." The fund was "the result," one editor plainly admitted, "of the recent women's *raid* in this city." "It is the duty of all men at home to look into the wants of these families," another editor put it, and most particularly "the wants of the wives, children, sisters and mothers of the gallant soldiers."[7] Atlanta acknowledged its debt to the soldiers' wives. Though criminal, the women's actions had obtained results.

In Salisbury, North Carolina, the next day, another mob of forty or fifty women mounted armed attacks on about eight merchant establishments. The same broad context was in evidence. In Salisbury, the female mob took to the streets, backed by a crowd of men and armed with hatchets. The women, self-described as "respectable poor women . . . all Soldiers wives or Mothers," targeted merchants they regarded as speculators. One was Michael Brown, who reported that they appeared in front of his store demanding cheap flour and, when refused, broke down the door with hatchets and forced their way in, leaving only after he bought them off with ten free barrels of flour. They repeated the action at numbers of other stores, amassing a supply of flour, molasses, and salt and twenty dollars in cash. The women were at the front of the mob, backed by a sizable crowd of men, and they took the lead both in the violent seizure of food and in the negotiations that preceded it. For not only were women the members of the community now clearly authorized—or self-authorized—to take the lead on matters bearing on the price and availability of foodstuffs, a central preoccupation of state and county government by 1863; they cast their violent action as a vehicle of social justice, and made a conspicuous display of their offer "to pay government prices for what we took," as one later told the governor. "We took our little money wit us . . . but the speklators refused us anything or even admittance into their premises." Only then, they insisted, did the women force their way into the shops and compel the owners to give them provisions.[8] The women's targeting of known speculators clearly had the approbation and perhaps prior permission of leading men in the community, as the gathering mob indicates. Women, however, were the ones now seen as best suited to do the dirty work the government had failed to do.

The new politics of subsistence implemented and led by soldiers' wives was prominently on display in Salisbury. Indeed, the perpetrators there justified their actions in precisely the language soldiers' wives ordinarily used in their petitions to governors and secretaries of war. As Governor Vance struggled to find an appropriate response, Mary Moore, a member of the mob (and perhaps the leader), wrote him a lengthy defense of the women's actions. Like many other North Carolina women, she looked to the governor as the people's champion and appealed to him, notwithstanding the violence, on behalf of the women rioters "for protection and a remedy of these evils." Her sense of legitimacy was keen. "We Gov are all soldiers Wives or Mothers," she began, "our Husbands and Sons are now separated from us by the cruel war not only to defend their humbly homes but the homes and property of the rich man." Forced into measures not at all pleasant by the "cruel and unfeeling Speculators" who have carried food out of the state, were their actions not "justifiable" under the circumstances? Laying out their identity as "respectable but poor women," and the conditions of their life and labor during the war, she, like many other women, reminded him of the impossibility of providing subsistence with their sole farm labor, a woman's pay in a government uniform factory, or a private's measly salary. "We . . . were from stern necessity compelled to go in search of food to sustain life." She admitted that they had stolen food and money at gunpoint—twenty-three barrels of flour, two sacks of salt, half a barrel of molasses, and twenty dollars in cash—but cast the riot as the seizure of what was rightly owed to the people, whose claims it had fallen on the women to enforce. "Now Sir, this is all we done," she finished, and assuming to speak for them all reminded him that "he was the choice of our Husbands and sons and we too look to you Sir with perfect confidence as being able and willing to do something for us." "This is the earnest and heartfelt prayer of many Soldiers Wives."[9]

Moore's defense of Confederate women's mob action was more matter-of-fact than defiant, and all the more extraordinary for it. It confidently tapped a sense of entitlement that went deep in popular political culture. What was owed to soldiers' wives? As in Atlanta, few argued with their views. Governor Vance issued an equivocal denunciation warning the women to leave forcible seizures to state agents. Michael Brown, one of the targeted merchants, complained to Governor Vance that the mayor and town commissioners had witnessed the attack on his store while offering no resistance. And the newspaper coverage in the state and, ominously, in Richmond, reiterated verbatim Mary Moore's claim that the action was aimed at known speculators, arose from "pinching want," and represented only what the community owed to soldiers' wives. "Do they suppose they will escape the fury of the devil their maladministration has helped to arouse," the *Carolina Watchman* asked, blaming the county commissioners charged with providing relief. "Many of the families in this town and vicinity . . . have not tasted meat for weeks and some times months together." The social contract had been violated, just as the women claimed.[10]

After Atlanta and Salisbury there were more riots, in Mobile, Alabama, Petersburg, Virginia, and Macon, Georgia, five or more in the space of two weeks. Then Richmond, then more. It was a strikingly coherent series of events, each organized and pulled off locally, yet so closely spaced, so similar in pattern, there was wild speculation about the connections. By the time the wave of springtime riots crested in Richmond two weeks later, conspiracy theories abounded. How could events so apparently coordinated and highly organized erupt spontaneously? Who was behind it? After three riots in Georgia, erroneously reported as simultaneous, the *Atlanta Southern Confederacy* described them as a "preconcerted movement among wicked and ignorant women."[11] "If it were the only thing of this sort which has appeared in Southern cities, it would not be worth much attention," the *Richmond Daily Examiner* wrote. But the paper had already reported on the riots in Atlanta, Salisbury, and Petersburg, "and the very next day" comes "this in Richmond." If these were "unconcerted tumultuous movements caused by popular suffering they would not, and could not have this regular gradation of time from one city to the another in the line of travel from South to North." Something and someone was behind it. "It is impossible to doubt," the *Examiner* speculated, "that the concealed instigators in each case were one and the same. Having done this work in one city they took the cars to the next. That they are the emissaries of the Federal Government it is equally difficult to doubt."[12] Such seemingly connected and highly organized events were far beyond the capacity of mere women. This had to be the work of professionals: the all-purpose Yankee operatives so active in secession were resurrected for the occasion.

But in its respect for the level of organization achieved, the conspiracy theory speaks powerfully to the political capacity of women. For even as various parties in the city and across the South indulged the comfortable assumption that women, like slaves, were not agents themselves, only pawns of Yankee agents or other "worthless men," the evidence accrued—a result of the Richmond city government's decision to bring criminal charges against the women—and the Confederate public learned just how the Richmond riot was organized and pulled off: of the leadership, recruitment, prior mass meetings, preparations, and collective discipline of women that culminated in the Richmond streets on the morning of April 2. That event may well have been a copycat crime; Richmond women seem to have borrowed a few plays from the Mobile book, and there is speculation that they were emboldened by the example of Salisbury, which was well covered in the Richmond papers. But Yankee conspiracy it was not.[13] In other riots there are suggestions of prior organization. But in Richmond, the sheer numbers—an estimated three hundred women followed by a crowd that may have been as big as a thousand—defied any possibility of spontaneous eruption. And the evidence that emerged at the women's trial confirmed it.

Eyewitnesses commented on the strange formality of the event. John B. Jones, a clerk in the War Department, described it as a procession. On the morning of April 2, around nine o'clock, Jones was pulled down to the street by an odd sight glimpsed from his office window: a mob of a few hundred women followed by a crowd that swelled until it was "more than a thousand," surging out of the western gates of Capitol Square and proceeding down Ninth Street, past "the War Department and crossing onto Main Street, increasing in magnitude at every step, but preserving silence and (so far) good order." They had appeared "as by concert" in the Capitol Square, he reported, "saying they were hungry and must have food." "Not knowing the meaning of such a procession," he stopped someone and asked. A young, emaciated woman "answered that they were going to find something to eat," to which he "remarked that they were going in the right direction to find plenty in the hands of the extortioners." Jones later learned that the women, armed with six-barreled pistols, bowie knives, and hatchets, forced their way into numerous stores, emptied them of their contents, impressing drays and carts in the street to haul off their loot, and holding off the police at gunpoint. The pillaging continued, Jones said, until the governor read them the riot act and threatened to open fire if they did not disperse. By three o'clock, he reported, the streets were quiet.[14]

It was a strange event Jones described: the numbers, the timing, the discipline and order of the crowd, the clearly planned route and obviously designated targets. Yet sympathetic though his account was (a perspective born from intimate familiarity with the appeals of soldiers' wives to an unresponsive War Department), it was sustained and amplified by subsequent testimony. If anything, Jones's account understated the degree of organization and discipline involved. He had not, for example, witnessed the highly choreographed beginning of the event when the women went first to the governor's mansion demanding an interview. The local papers quickly generated the handy conspiracy theory, and two days later Jones himself repeated the *Examiner's* charge that the riot "was a premeditated affair, stimulated from the North and executed through the instrumentality of emmisaries." The city government's decision to pursue criminal charges against the rioters, however, brought forth a body of evidence, daily reprinted in the city paper, that left the *Examiner* and all who subscribed to the conspiracy theory with egg on their faces.[15]

Richmond puts to rest all questions about Confederate women's political ability. For shocking as it surely was to many who read about it in the Richmond papers, what came out in court testimony was clear and indisputable evidence that the riot on April 2 was a highly organized and orchestrated event, in planning for at least ten days. And despite widespread assertions that it was instigated by men, it was, in fact, the work of one Mary Jackson, soldiers' mother, farm wife, and huckster in meat in Richmond's Second Market. "Mrs. Jackson is the [reputed] prime mover and chief instigator of the riot," the *Richmond Daily Examiner* flatly admitted a week or so into the investigation. Starting on April 4 and continuing into October, witnesses streamed into the mayor's court to give testimony in the case against the women: John B. Jones, the War Department clerk who had seen much of it firsthand testified, as did merchants and wagon driver victims of the rioters, clerks at the Richmond markets, police officers, governor's aides, and colonels of the city battalion called in to restore order. Most incriminating of all were the forty-four women and twenty-nine men under indictment for perpetrating the "thief and harlot riot," as the mayor took to calling it.[16] Surrounded on all sides by the evidence, the rioters' loot, which one reporter described as the usual inventory of a country store—sacks of flour, flitches of bacon, barrels of sugar and coffee, candles, bolts of silk, brogues, cavalry boots, ladies' white satin slippers—they stood up in the witness box and revealed how Mary Jackson and three hundred women had planned and pulled off what may have been the biggest civilian riot in Confederate history.[17]

The riot offers a stunning portrait of poor white women's mass political mobilization. Recruiting apparently began around March 22 when Mary Jackson began telling people in the market that "there was to be a meeting of the women in relation to the high prices." Jackson made no secrets of her plans. Her networks were rural and urban, and she worked them all. She recruited in the city, primarily in the market and among the women who worked in a government clothing factory, but she also worked the surrounding countryside recruiting women from Henrico, Hanover, and New Kent counties as well. She "sent word to all the women in Hanover [County] that they must come to town and participate in the proceedings," one woman testified. Others told of a stream of women coming in from the country on the day before the riot, some from a distance of eleven miles. One woman reported that "some women from the country" came by her house asking for directions to Oregon Hill, looking for the place Mrs. Jackson had appointed for a meeting. Mrs. Weasley was among those who came up from the country for the meeting on Wednesday night and later said that she was then "authorized to come up the next day and bring a hatchet."[18]

Jackson was a good organizer. More than three hundred women turned up for the meeting in the Belvidere Baptist Church on Oregon Hill on April 1 where the riot was planned. "All were women there except two boys," a Mrs. Jamison explained. "The object of the meeting," she told the court "was to organize to demand goods of the merchants at government prices; and if they were not given, the stores were to be broken open and goods taken by force." By all accounts it was a rowdy meeting. Jackson was clearly in command. In a stunning assumption of male authority and violation of fundamentalist practice, she "went up into the pulpit" to address the gathered crowd and to issue instructions about how the demonstration was to proceed. "She said she didn't want the women to go along the streets like a parcel of heathens," one woman testified later, "but to go quietly to the stores and demand goods at Government prices and if the merchants did not grant their demands they were to break open the stores and take the goods." Thus Jackson organized the troops, telling them to meet the next morning at nine o'clock, to leave their children at home, and to come armed.[19]

Unusual and violent as the riot was, Jackson and the women who planned and executed it were products of the same political culture and politics of subsistence as the mass of Confederate soldiers' wives. Jackson literally so. John Jones (the War Department clerk who had witnessed the riot firsthand, and whose job it was to vet the petitions of soldiers' wives and mothers to the secretary of war) said he recognized Mrs. Jackson "from her frequent application at the war office for a discharge for her son."[20] Before Mary Jackson took to the streets, she had been one of the mass of ordinary petitioning Confederate women. Her strategy for the riots suggests as much, too. She insisted that the rioters first make an offer of government price for the goods they planned to seize from speculators and that they seek an audience with the governor to air their grievances. It was an inspired bit of political choreography, and it showed the women's deep investment in the ideas and practices of poor white women's wartime political culture.[21]

But violence was planned for from the beginning. In that sense, too, Jackson's plan and leadership held. The day after the Oregon Hill meeting, she arrived at the market early but brought nothing to sell. She made no attempt to conceal news of the action, but rather continued recruiting, telling anyone who would listen what she was up to, waving weapons around recklessly. She told one police officer at the market that "he had better keep out of the street today for the women intended to shoot down every man who did not aid [them] in taking goods." When another man overheard her threatening violence against merchants, he thought it was a joke. But she "said it was no joke and asked me to lend her a pistol . . . she said she meant to be armed." Jackson was seen with a bowie knife and a six-barreled pistol as she left the market.[22]

All went according to plan. By eight a.m. Jackson and her crowd of armed women surged out of the market, heading first to Capitol Square for another "women's meeting," and then headed to the governor's mansion to demand an audience. Mrs. Mary Jamieson said that "the women wanted to go straight to the stores but I told them it would never do to go breaking into the stores without letting somebody know what we were doing." So over they went to the governor's house on Capitol Square, barged up the stairs to his office, and finding only his aide who asked them what they wanted, replied that they "wanted bread and bread they would have or die."[23] Like their subsequent offers to pay government prices for the merchants' goods, a strategy adopted in virtually every Confederate food riot, the women's delegation to the governor was part of a larger morality play calculated to communicate the reasonableness of their action. In that sense it was a bid for legitimacy. But it was also a clear signal of whom they held responsible for their condition: not just the merchants, but the state government who failed to curb speculators, who paid government wages but did not enforce government prices. The government had failed to provide adequate relief to those whose male protectors they had taken. When reasonableness failed, was not violence warranted? The women had guns, but like the crowd in Atlanta and the women in Salisbury, they also had a public relations strategy.

After that, in Richmond on April 2, violent direct action was the order of the day. After a brief and threatening speech from Governor Letcher, which didn't deter them one bit, the women took to the streets. The mob —now numbering in excess of three hundred women and trailed by an ever-growing crowd of men and boys—surged out of the western gates of Capitol Square up into Ninth Street, marching silently as Jackson had instructed. The women were heavily armed, one eyewitness noted in shock, with both domestic implements and the rejected contents of an old armory: axes and hatchets, "rusty old horse pistols . . . clubs, knives . . . bayonets stuffed in belts . . . and specimens of those old home made knives with which our soldiers were wont to load themselves down in the first part of the war." For a good two hours they wreaked havoc on the streets of Richmond, targeting known speculators, smashing their way into stores with hatchets and axes, looting them at gunpoint, and loading the stolen goods onto wagons they impressed on the street. Many of the women eventually arrested were caught on top of those wagons driving off their haul or in possession of it in working-class neighborhoods and farms in and around the city. One merchant claimed they cleaned him out in ten minutes, taking three thousand dollars' worth of goods, including five hundred pounds (!) of bacon. At least twelve stores in all were looted before the public guard was called out and, threatening to fire on the rioters, managed to put the riot down.[24]

Then the arrests started.[25] Among those caught in the dragnet were ordinary women who distinguished themselves in the fray: Mary Duke, a soldier's wife left at home with four children, her husband in Lee's army. She had leveled a navy revolver at several men who had tried to stop her from looting a store. Minerva Meredith, six feet tall, rawboned and muscular, who had thrown a hospital steward off his wagon, jumped in, and driven off with his load of beef. She had been seen on the corner of Main Street and Locust Alley in the heat of the riot, pistol "uplifted in the air, inciting the women to riot." In court, when confusion arose about her identity, she confirmed, "I was the woman that had the pistol." Mrs. Mary Woodward, a young, genteel married woman only 18 years old, caught in a wagon with loads of stolen goods, who admitted to being in the riot. When the officer tried to arrest her, she struck him in the face and drew a pistol on him. It was quite a crew they dragged in. And they also got the ringleaders: Mary Jamieson or Johnson, she of the governor's mansion plan, fingered by Robert S. Pollard for leading the first attack on Pollard and Walkers on Shockhoe Slip. And, of course, Mary Jackson, there to the bitter end, picked up around noontime in a mob of women trying to break into a store, still unbowed, brandishing a bowie knife, shouting, yes, "Bread or blood!"[26]

There would be more riots in 1863—six more at least—and as in Atlanta, Salisbury, and Richmond, they played out in violent form the politics of subsistence that soldiers' wives had forged.[27] In all of them, too, women's anger was turned as much against government officials as merchants and planters, had as much to do with the inadequacy of welfare as with speculation. That, as it turned out, was one of the key elements and critical policy implications of the women's riots and the larger politics out of which they grew. And it is the chief measure of its efficacy in Confederate politics and policy. For it was really only after—and largely in response to—the riots that local, state, and even federal officials undertook a systematic reform and extension of the traditional antebellum system of delivering relief that had proved entirely inadequate to the needs of the population in wartime.

There has been no lack of attention by historians to these events. Social historians tend to read them as the disaffection of the Confederate poor; cultural historians as a public expression of a deep customary idea of the common good. Rich ideas all. But what they miss is what is most striking about the riots: the deep context, savvy politicking, strategic thinking, and collective organization they involved, and the political leadership and mass participation of women they announced. The food riots were thus not just social phenomena, rising organically out of the immiseration of war; nor were they just cultural phenomena that spoke to deep residual female moral values. They were manifestly political events—a highly public expression of soldiers' wives' mass politics of subsistence—events in an American, Southern, and Civil War women's political history that historians are only now beginning to write.[28]

Given the numbers of women involved in the food riots, it would be easy to dismiss them as relatively insignificant events. But as a wake-up call to the press and public, the riots pointed right to the intersection of civilian and military developments in a critical moment two years deep into the kind of war never before seen. The press played it precisely this way, casting the riots as symptomatic of a crisis in the management of the war. In that sense, the riots and rioters connect downward to a grassroots politics of subsistence and mobilization at work in every county in the Confederacy; but they also connect upward, directly to problems at the top, about how to sustain the level of troop mobilization the war required and how to organize society to support and survive it. In agitating issues of civilian concern, the women rioters, though few in number, created change absolutely salient to the prosecution of the war.

If efficacy is the gold standard of political salience, then soldiers' wives achieved it in the spring of 1863. That was obvious in the way mayors, city councils, state legislatures, governors, and even federal authorities moved to expand the provision of public welfare in the immediate aftermath of the riots and in direct response—none tried to conceal it—to the actions of soldiers' wives. Discussion of the significance of poor white and yeoman women in the Confederacy has usually focused on the women's role in encouraging desertion and, thereby, in military defeat. And there can be little doubt that women played their part in driving up the desertion rate. Civil and military officials repeatedly warned against the effects of wives' expressed views on their husbands' willingness to serve. Just four days after the riot in Atlanta, one city editor issued "A Solemn Warning to Wives," delivering a moral tale about a good soldier driven to desertion by the exaggerated complaints of his wife. Governor Allen of Louisiana urged rich men to open their corncribs to "the soldier's wife and children," warning that "most of the desertions that take place are caused by news from home that the soldier's family is starving." And most striking, in January 1865 "North Carolina Soldiers of Lee's Army" urged their governor to do more for their wives and children: Yankee armies could not make them run, they insisted. But "Sir, we cannot hear the cries of our little ones and stand . . . Do something for them and there will be less desertion." The idea that soldiers' wives' desperate letters were driving men to desertion was widely held by the Confederate public and officials alike.[29] Yet the argument that dissent equals desertion equals military defeat resists definitive proof. However, if the effect of women's politics on desertion and defeat cannot be quantified, its considerable measure can be taken in another realm of political life: in public policy, especially on welfare.[30] For it was only after the food riots that city, state, and federal officials really attended to the problems of the nation's noncombatant poor, moving in the spring of 1863 to revise and reconsider a variety of policies from taxation to impressment, conscription, and exemption that bore on the problems of labor and subsistence. With some support from the central government, the states of the C.S.A would build a welfare system on a scale that was unprecedented in the history of the South or the North in terms of budget and administrative commitment. That welfare system was a direct product of poor white women's mass politics and direct actions on the country roads and town and city streets of the Confederacy in the spring of 1863.[31]

In many places city officials promised aid even as rioters ran the streets. In Atlanta, a group of gentlemen expressed a deep sympathy for the ladies by raising a fund for their relief, which they delivered on the day of the riot itself. In Richmond, Governor Letcher appeared in the midst of the action promising to distribute food. Everywhere there were riots, the response was the same: immediate public acknowledgment of the claims of social justice and legitimacy of the women's demands. There was, to be sure, official disapprobation from mayors, governors, and the Confederate president himself. But those statements were strictly for public, and especially Northern, consumption. Davis tried and failed to ban the telegraph office from relaying news of the riot out of the city. The true and lasting response was revision and redress. All of the city councils and Southern legislatures—even the Confederate Congress, which had long regarded social provision as the domain of the states—quickly took it up as a matter of public policy.[32]

City governments responded immediately. In Atlanta, the *Intelligencer,* which covered the riot under the heading "RELIEVE THE DISTRESSED," immediately announced the creation of a fund for the relief of the "wives and daughters of soldiers' families who are in extreme want." In addition the editor urged the city council to call a county meeting and, publicizing the legitimacy of the need and inadequacy of support, soon reported that within two days the city had raised and distributed more than $1,300. Some city papers took the opportunity to rail against the Confederate government for its attacks on the rights of private property, in the spirit of "You seized our property and so did they." But mostly the women's pleas struck a resonant chord. "It is the duty of all men at home to look into the wants [of] . . . the wives, children, sisters and mothers of the gallant soldiers," one man in the service of the Confederate Quarter Masters' Department proclaimed.[33]

The quantities of money involved varied from the local and small to the state and significant in terms of budget share. All of the governments in the C.S.A. were highly strapped. Carving out significant chunks of money for welfare thus had to be a huge political priority. Clearly it was. In the cities the aid poured in and took numerous forms. In Mobile the city council appropriated $15,000, created a Citizen Relief Committee to scour the countryside for food, and thereafter attended carefully to ensuring the provision of food at reasonable prices to the poor. In Richmond, prosecution of the rioters proceeded in tandem with a massive expansion of the system of public relief. Only two days after the riot, the mayor formed a citywide committee to investigate the needs of soldiers' dependents, and by April 9 they had appropriated "$20,000 for the relief of the families of soldiers." By April 13 the city council had written and passed new laws establishing a free market in food for the poor.[34] The response of every city government constituted a substantive acknowledgment of the legitimacy of soldiers' wives demands and a fiscally difficult effort to deliver relief.

It was far less obvious how, and if, the states and central governments would respond. But they did, and here, in the legislative realm, it was clear that women's actions forced a significant revision of public policy.[35] There had, of course, been a system of poor relief prior to 1863. A carryover of the traditional policies of social provision aimed at widows and the disabled poor, the burden was carried by local governments, with funds raised typically from a tax levied on polls and property. Steady increases in the numbers on the rolls in the first two years of the war drove the tax up past anything individual counties could sustain. Local officials were alarmed by the extent of the need. By 1863 many states (North Carolina, Georgia, Louisiana, Mississippi, Alabama) had shifted the fiscal burden of providing for the poor to state governments. Already in 1861 and 1862 numbers of states had ramped up their relief programs, distributing salt free or at cost to indigent soldiers' families, massively increasing the amount of money distributed by county authorities, or even (as in Louisiana) establishing a system of state stores. A number of cities (Charleston, Augusta, Richmond) opened free markets. It was the inadequacy of those free markets, among other things, that the Richmond women had protested so violently. "The applicants for aid are mostly ladies," the Charleston Board for the Relief of Families of Soldiers politely put it in October 1862 when it was already supporting six hundred soldiers' families and urging the state government to do more.[36] "Salt, Salt! I have a lot of salt sent to Rome by Governor Brown for distribution to soldiers' wives and destitute widows," one Georgia salt agent broadcast in 1862.[37] Soldiers' wives were the most visible of the new clamoring poor, and it was explicitly to them that local officials directed the aid.

But notwithstanding the expansion of local programs in 1861 and 1862, the amount of relief was clearly inadequate, a fact widely acknowledged at the beginning of the new year. As the prospect of another reduced harvest (1862 had been a bad year) bore down on the C.S.A. in the spring of 1863, public officials, journalists, and citizens alike warned that the situation was dire. In the Mississippi Valley, the drumbeat of battles was near. The Confederacy was still reeling from a series of military disasters in the winter and spring of 1862, the fall of Forts Donelson and Henry at the head of the Tennessee river system and the towns of Nashville, Corinth, and Memphis. Huge Union armies marched steadily southward. With states in the Mississippi Valley losing men (to both armies) and huge swaths of agriculturally rich territory, a "subsistence crisis" loomed ominously in the region as 1863 began. As early as May 1862, the governor of Alabama, John Gill Shorter, not usually an administration critic, had pleaded with the secretary of war to delay conscription of yeoman soldiers in northern Alabama, concerned about the suffering of women and children if their men were taken before the grain and provision crops were harvested. Shorter was reacting to a series of letters he had received from soldiers, soldiers' wives, and military commanders describing neighborhoods stripped of men, counties in which the whole food supply was in the hands of three hundred women, and others in which women were "left to plow and sow and reap and mow on the principle of 'root hog or die.'" He had also been warned by county relief commissioners that their limited means were exhausted. Already by 1862, Shorter and other governors east and west, were worried about poor soldiers' wives and what they perceived to be the real danger of desertion if the women's needs were not met.[38]

Even in the east where General Robert E. Lee continued to hold off far larger Union armies, it is clear that 1863 was a moment in which most civilian and military men alike acknowledged that the war had entered a phase that tested the people and not just the armies. Few denied that home front and military conditions were inextricable. A debate about the equity of conscription had already erupted in the Confederate Congress in the session of August 1862. But in that moment of military collapse in the Mississippi Valley, with Union navies and armies penetrating by river into the very heart of the black belt South, concern for the Confederate poor was overridden by concern about how to maintain control of slaves. Congressmen, overwhelmingly slaveholders themselves, yielded to the demands of planters and the plaintive letters of planter women claiming protection and passed the notorious "twenty-negro law." Secretary of War Seddon said defensively that the law was designed "not to draw any distinction among classes but simply to provide a . . . police force, sufficient to keep our negroes in control." Defended as a measure that would free up planters and their slaves to grow food for the armies and destitute civilians, the exemption was resisted from the outset as the very essence of class legislation, as the government's blatant preference for the rich and its abandonment of the poor left to fight their wars. "Why not let the poor men stay at home to protect his own family against the slaves of the rich men," Mississippi senator James Phelan raged during the debate. "If we are to have class legislation . . . let's legislate in favor of the poor." But they did not. By December of 1862 public outrage over the law threatened to spill over into civil disobedience and mass desertion. The popular novelist Augusta Jane Evans tried to warn her friend Senator Jabez Lamar Curry that the new law was already linked to an upturn in desertions in General Pemberton's Army of Mississippi. With court-martials "everywhere in session," she wrote Curry, men were pleading in "palliation of desertion, the cries of hungry wives and starving children." Even officers could be sympathetic to men who received letters "urging them to come home at every hazard." Evans urged Curry to amend the law before popular insubordination proved "potent in completely dividing our people." Seddon effectively acknowledged Evans's point when he urged President Davis to modify a law now reviled as "exempt[ing] the rich from military service" and forcing "the poor to fight the battles of the country."[39] Thus did the "twenty-negro law" speak directly to the dilemma of the slave regime at war: how to protect the property of slaveholders without putting undue service burdens on backcountry yeomen—and on their women, left at home to shoulder the plow.[40]

In autumn 1862, as planter women rushed to take advantage of the exemption to get their sons home, yeoman women faced another hard prospect of making a crop alone. The food crisis the law was designed to avert arrived nonetheless. By January 1863 newspapers were filled with outraged expressions of public concern about the food supply and planters' self-interested practices of planting cotton when what was needed was corn. General Joseph Johnston, commander of the Department of the West, warned of a shortage of food for his army after the military loss of the rich agricultural territories of Kentucky and Tennessee. His army was already on short rations. By March—in fact on the very day Atlanta women took to the streets—Governor John Gill Shorter issued a proclamation "to the Planters of Alabama" that blamed cotton producers for the imminent "famine" and the state government's inability to relieve the distress among soldiers' families. So dire was the situation that Secretary of War Seddon, perhaps affected by the deluge of desperate pleas from soldiers and their wives, actually recommended to President Davis that the Confederacy "exempt soldiers on whom several helpless dependents relied for food." Although denied, it was a telling request from one usually charged with finding more men for the army. The east was in no better shape. In North Carolina, in February, a worried Governor Vance assured one woman that he "will see that they ('the wimmin') do not starve in the absence of their husbands," and ordered county officials to enter soldiers' wives on the relief rolls. On March 16, presumably with no knowledge of the riot in Atlanta, Virginia governor and Richmond resident John Letcher, pleaded with the secretary of war to stop the impressment of cattle on the way to the city market.[41] That there was a shortage of food in the Confederate capital was no secret. What was lacking was the political will to deal with it.

The women's riots changed all that. The competition for resources, human and material, was great, but women's priorities rose to the top. In the spring of 1863 the women on the street drove policy. "The great question in the revolution is now bread," Georgia governor Joseph Brown bellowed in an official message delivered nine days after the Atlanta riot, pretty much confirming the point. With no political context in which to place the riots, historians remain ill-attuned to the response, noting the public debate in April 1863, the ensuing uproar over the substitutes bill, the systematic reform of welfare policy in the spring and summer of 1863, while not noticing the timing or the cause. The Confederate public erupted in urgent debate about the starving poor in April 1863. It was then, and only then, that state governors and federal officials issued a series of public resolutions about the food crisis, and moved, finally, to revise and reconsider a variety of social and even military manpower policies bearing on the food crisis faced by the nation's now legion crew of indigent—and mobilized—soldiers' wives. When Zebulon Vance agitated with Jefferson Davis for a change in the conscription policy ten days after the riots in Salisbury and elsewhere, he did so not only on behalf of the soldiers' wives but in the very language of the soldiers' wives themselves. Indifference to the gender of Confederate politics is a contemporary, not historical, problem.[42]

The effect of the soldiers' wives' actions coursed through the Confederate body politic in late March and early April 1863. It registered in the public debate about the justness of the women's ends, in a series of official resolutions and messages issued in the month following the riots, and, more concretely, in a historic revision of welfare policy in the C.S.A.[43] The response was most direct at the level of state government. And nowhere with more urgency than in Georgia, where the governor jumped into action. Just nine days after the riot in Atlanta, Governor Brown called the legislature back into session early and delivered a message, reprinted all over the state, that "recommend[ed] the passage of an Act" severely restricting the cultivation of cotton and requiring planters to supply soldiers' wives. The women's need for food was the first order of business in Brown's message, and he was blunt. In whole sections of the state where land is cultivated almost entirely by white labor, that labor was now in the army, he told the assembled legislators, and "the women and children are destitute of bread." Scenes of suffering must ensue and desertion run rampant if planters are not made to do their duty. Action was imperative or the consequences unthinkable: "Attempt to conceal it as we may, the fact is undeniable, that the great question in this revolution is now a question of *bread.*" "Bread or blood." Brown, at least, had heard the women's demand.[44]

In Georgia, policy was fleshed out in the notable numbers of dollars committed in state budgets. Georgia soldiers' wives set Brown's agenda. After the Atlanta riot, securing subsistence for soldiers' wives emerged as a policy and budgetary priority in Brown's administration and remained so for the duration of the war. No state would do or spend more. Brown delivered property tax exemptions, free salt, free corn, and so much aid in money to the counties that, as a share of the state budget, it almost equaled that expended on wartime military costs. The legislature appropriated $2.5 million in 1863, $6 million in 1864, and $8 million in 1865, and delivered it to the counties for distribution, as the law specified, to "assist soldiers' families, the children and widows of deceased soldiers and disabled veterans." It was never enough. After another women's riot in Savannah in the spring of 1864, part of a second wave that hit the C.S.A., one low-country editor railed against Georgia's failure to "come up to the full measure of their duty" to wives and children of soldiers. Governor Brown met that and other like criticism by publicizing his efforts—to the tune of $10 million in 1864, he said—"to feed and clothe the suffering wives, and widows and orphans of soldiers." The political will to deliver aid, the amount delivered, the administrative system by which it was delivered, and the embrace of poor white women as part of the governor's core constituency—that was all new. Not so much a reflection of Brown's "overriding concern for the little man," as one historian has put it, the unprecedented expansion of state welfare was a political response to the mobilization of yeoman and poor white women in that and other states of the Confederacy.[45]

Like Georgia, at least six other Confederate states transferred the fiscal burden of welfare from counties to state legislatures in 1863, a systematic reform of welfare policy that usually followed the riots and owed a great deal to them. North Carolina passed four different acts in a losing effort to keep up with the need, spending as much as $20 million on the needy in the course of the war.[46] Before the war the state did virtually nothing by way of social provision for the poor: it did provide pensions for widows of deceased soldiers, which taken together never exceeded a couple hundred dollars per year of the public budget. In 1861 and 1862, it was still only widows who qualified, and the budget commitment remained minuscule: $370 in 1861, and $230 in 1862. It was not until February 1863 that the state legislature amended the law to reach the wives of living soldiers as well. That law shifted the fiscal burden from the counties to the state and authorized an appropriation of $1 million for welfare. The "Act for the Relief of the Wives and Families of Soldiers in the Army" identified the soldier's wife—not the widow or the family—as the primary recipient of the new state funds. From mid-1863 on, the state funded that act to the tune of $1 million a year, although the treasurer often struggled to meet the fiscal obligations. As elsewhere the budget commitment was never sufficient to meet the need. In the second legislative session in 1864, a bill proposing to raise the appropriation for relief to $3 million failed to pass, but in 1864 and 1865 the state, like others in the C.S.A., changed the law to allow counties to borrow additional money or levy additional taxes for the relief of soldiers' wives, and many counties were forced to those ends as well. Innovation continued into the desperate last days of the war. On January 31, 1865, the North Carolina legislature, still struggling to provide sufficient food aid to soldiers' wives, proposed a tax-in-kind of their own to match the one the federal state had levied since 1862.[47]

To Governor Zebulon Vance, like his compatriots Brown in Georgia and Pettus and Clark in Mississippi, nothing assumed more importance than the state's obligation to "feed the poor whose supporters and protectors are in the army."[48] That commitment propelled the expansion of state bureaucracy and introduced a whole series of entitlements—maybe even the very concept of entitlement—all predictably generative of new political relationships, processes, and practices.

Much of the new welfare politics was played out at the county level, where state funds were disbursed and decisions about eligibility were made. All of the new systems focused on serving the soldiers' wives. North Carolina adopted a system, a version of which pertained in other Confederate states, that left the administration of relief to the county courts, which were regarded as best informed of the condition of the people. Each county court appointed a subcommittee to oversee relief, elected a county relief "agent"—a position that carried an exemption from military service—to purchase provisions for disbursement, and in "each captain's district" a committee of three men whose duty it was to report to the executive committee on who was entitled to relief and in what amount. From the outset, then, the administrative unit for the disbursement of aid was a military one—the beat or militia district—that had long served as the smallest administrative unit of state and local government in the American South. In building up from that available structure, the new welfare system tied women's "entitlement" directly to their husbands' service; if the men were discharged, the women's entitlement immediately ceased.[49]

A considerable number of people and amounts of money passed through the system. In Orange County, North Carolina, 508 women and 735 children were on the rolls in late 1863; by 1865 more than 600 women and 800 children, 20 percent of the adult female population of the county and a whopping 35 percent of the children. In Duplin County even more white women met the official criterion of indigence, meaning "not enough food to sustain life." In the terrible year that spanned November 1863 to November 1864, agents in Randolph County collected and disbursed roughly $55,000, most of it distributed in small amounts. Local committeemen received detailed instructions upon appointment: "The allowance for each *woman* shall not exceed three dollars per month, children under eight years of age, one dollar and fifty cents," one set read. "Needy fathers" and widows and children of deceased soldiers to "receive the same as a lone woman."[50] Indeed, as the court instructions assumed, women constituted the vast bulk of recipients of relief and received most of the welfare dollars. One Orange County list named 41 "persons who got the county corn," every one of them a woman or a woman with children. A separate but apparently concurrent list named another 17 persons who paid for their corn (but were entitled to buy it at the below-market government price) all but four of them women. "Not soldiers' orders," the county officer noted at the top of the second list, indicating that the women who got their corn free were soldiers' wives. Other lists of "soldiers' families" include small numbers of men—the "needy fathers" presumably—among far larger numbers of women recipients. Another Orange County committeeman, who kept a list of tithe corn delivered to George Ray's Mill for "the benefit of soldiers wives and other needy persons," started to write "sol wife" beside the name of every such woman who collected her allotment but then gave up and used ditto marks, so common was the designation, and noted only those who were other: "sol, children," he identified the lone man, John Wagoner, "sol. mother" he noted beside two names, and just plain "needy" after three.[51]

As the local instructions indicate, the Confederate welfare system was made in the image of the soldier's wife. Even the needy father had to fit the mold cast for her. The printed form announcing the new corn regulations of Orange County, North Carolina, in December 1863 gave these instructions to millers about distributing government corn: "First To soldiers' wives at six dollars a bushel and take in payment the county order issued by the proper Committee man." "Second, They will sell corn to such other needy persons as bring orders in writing from the committee man." Commissioners instructed to determine who was entitled to financial aid from the Soldiers' fund were issued the same guidelines. Find "First, what soldiers' wives shall have orders for their monthly allowance from the Committee men of their respective Tax district"; only then "other *needy persons.*" In all of the instructions issued, the soldier's wife was the main client, entitled others likened to her. Mississippi legislation enacting the Military Relief Fund followed precisely the same logic.[52]

In the most literal sense the soldier's wife provided the political model for the new welfare system and its entitlements. She was the very prototype of the legitimate welfare client. Others—soldiers' widows and mothers, and indigent men—were left to plead for inclusion. "It seems to be forgot that widows have all their sons gone to war leaving their Mothers old and infirm it is worse than soldiers' wives."[53] Worse than soldiers' wives but calculated, all the same, in relation to the one who had the most political clout.

The response to the springtime wave of riots was nothing short of remarkable. In all of the states one can discern in policy a new concern about the soldiers' wives. In some, the welfare of indigent soldiers' wives emerged as *the* budgetary and policy priority. That was certainly the case in Georgia, in North Carolina, and in Mississippi, where after 1862 the first wartime governor, John Pettus, and his successor, Charles Clark, pursued a policy of aggressive expansion of the welfare system, even as they faced the daunting task of heading a government in exile. Forced out of the antebellum capitol in Jackson in May 1863, minutes ahead of an invading federal force who put the torch to the city, and on the run thereafter, first to Enterprise, Meridian, and then Macon, Governors Pettus and Clark nonetheless acted on a commitment to soldiers' wives and families, "one class of our citizens whose claims upon the state [are] as imperative and as sacred as any claim the State can have upon the soldier in this perilous hour." With policy framed explicitly for "soldiers' wives" by November 1863, no issue thereafter occupied more of his—or the legislature's—attention. When the new governor, Charles Clark, addressed the legislature, he devoted only one brief paragraph of his address to a discussion of monies in the state treasury before turning to the matter of relief for soldiers' wives; "DESTITUTE FAMILIES" took priority in his mind even over the matter of "STATE TROOPS AND MILITIA."[54]

Behind all of the expansion, innovation, and desperate maneuvering lay primal need but also a new web of political relationships. That web had its own connections that ran between governors and soldiers' wives, that pulled in legislators, local relief officials, even federal tithing officers and conscript officers. But it was, in the first instance, a product of the dynamic interplay of gubernatorial leadership, soldiers' wives' activism, and the obligations of welfare provision. In Mississippi, Governors Pettus and Clark responded as well as led; responded to the deluge of letters and complaints from soldiers' wives pushing them to deliver more and more just welfare, and pressing their version of the governors' obligations to them. For those governors, the women had become an important political constituency. "There is no subject on which I feel a deeper interest," Governor Clark once said. When the legislature first met after events of the spring 1863, Pettus reminded members of their obligation to provide "that support and protection [soldiers' wives] *have a right to demand* for the sacrifices now being made by their lawful protectors." Governors Pettus and Clark were fixed in that web of political rights and obligations soldiers' wives created with their demands. That might be why the Mississippi legislature was careful to order the printing and distribution in pamphlet form of a thousand copies of the act they passed in December 1863 "to better provide for the families of our soldiers."[55] There must have been some political value in advertising their attention to an issue so critical to their new women constituents.

The Confederacy would never centralize welfare under federal authority. The development of that kind of centralized welfare system would come only after the war in the full flush of power exerted by the Republican Party state and from which ex-Confederates would, initially, be excluded.[56] But the Confederate government was not immune to the pressures issuing from below and, unable to risk all that it portended, redirected some of its incredibly scarce resources from military to civilian use and finally accepted a revision to the Conscription Act designed to secure the food supply for soldiers' wives. Even the Confederate state was forced to act decisively in the face of the political threat. With about one-third of their national territory occupied by the enemy and a huge proportion of adult white men already in the army by the end of 1863, any concession to civilian welfare was a sure sign of political necessity.

From its capitol in Richmond, the government of the C.S.A. had a bird's-eye view of developments on the street. It was just as well, too, for on civilian welfare the Davis administration proved reluctant to act. As president, Jefferson Davis had long regarded the diplomatic and military spheres as his primary responsibilities and home front activities as being the domain of state governments. But the subsistence crisis that rocked the Confederacy in the spring of 1863 was not born of conditions governors and state legislators alone controlled. In fact, as Governor Brown made plain in his April message, the root cause, as soldiers' wives said, was a conscription policy that exempted male laborers on plantations already well stocked with slave workers while depriving poor white and yeoman farm women of the male labor necessary to work their farms. On March 31, 1863, as the wave of food riots ripped through the Confederacy, North Carolina governor Zebulon Vance pleaded the women's case to Jefferson Davis, trying to force revision of conscription policy. Conscription had swept off "a large class whose labor is, as I fear, absolutely necessary to the existence of the women and children left behind." The only solution, Vance advised Davis, was to exempt from the draft all men who were the sole support of dependents.[57] Like the proposal of the secretary of war the year before, this one fell on deaf ears. In the circumstances of 1863, with Lincoln's government enacting a draft to put even greater numbers of men into service, it was literally impossible to adopt such a broad class of exemption. Married men released from service simply could not be replaced.

Still, Davis came under intense pressure to act, from governors, private citizens, and some members of his own administration. None of the governors who pleaded with Davis managed to move him on exemptions to conscription in 1863 or later, although he did occasionally suspend conscription in particularly overtaxed areas of the country. Nor would he move initially on the matter of substitution, the abolition of which was, by the summer of 1863, "a noisy and portentous demand." Governors, state legislators, even General Braxton Bragg and seventeen other generals in the Army of Tennessee recommended the reversal of that policy, which, like the twenty-negro law, exempted from service precisely those men whose wives had slaves to make subsistence for them. Even the secretary of war conceded that "the poorer classes" resented it. Just weeks before the Richmond riots, one soldier in Lee's army alerted John Letcher that the men got "along as well as four ounces of rancid hog fat" would permit, but that "wide discontent and disgust" were brewing in the ranks over the matter of substitutes. "The community is crystalysing into two classes—those who make fortunes by the war and those who starve and die by it," he warned, a feeling immeasurably deepened by the "prospect of starvation for the families of the soldiers." There was a clear recognition in the army that the suffering of soldiers' families had political and military consequences. Although they would never enact any categorical exemption on conscription for the husbands of nonslaveholding women, Congress did, finally, abolish substitution in the session of December 1863.[58]

The pressure exerted by women rioters and by the men who pressed their cause did tell in one other important revision of federal policy: a new willingness to use the central government and the military to secure the food supply. Immediately after the food riots—only two days after the Richmond riot, in fact—Congress wrote and passed a joint resolution "relating to the production of provisions." Like state laws, this one obligated planters to forgo the planting of cotton and other cash crops in favor of "such crops as will insure a sufficiency of food for all classes and for every emergency." "Is no power vested in the rulers of this government to help the starving population?" one Virginian demanded of Davis in 1863. Even Jefferson Davis had to act. On April 10, the president addressed the "People of the Confederate States" and finally used his bully pulpit to press planters to grow more food for "the people and the army." To be sure it was the army that Davis was mostly worried about—soldiers were already on half meat rations—but he made no bones about the food crisis that afflicted the Confederacy, and that, as the entire Confederate public now knew, had driven women all over the country into violent action.[59] By mid-1863, even President Davis could no longer deny that the home front and military conditions were inextricably linked, materially and politically. Women rioters had played their part in that recognition and in forcing a redirection of federal power and resources.

When it came to President Davis's personal recognition of women citizens as part of the body politic, the riots and the spring of 1863 were only modestly effective, like a small wave hitting up against a massive levee of culture and history. For Davis, women citizens had always been an abstraction, a group his political eye simply did not take in. In one perilous moment in 1862 when Governor Pettus called on the Mississippi legislature to match more stringent conscription with liberal provisions for the soldiers' wives, Davis, who was in attendance at the session of his home state legislature, commended the governor on the aid to the ladies, whom he described as key "objects of his [the soldiers'] affection."[60] Davis's sentimental language was a dead giveaway that he had not yet come to regard the women as living political subjects.

But after the spring of 1863, even Davis knew something important had occurred. In 1864, on a cross-country sweep to confer with his commanders in the west, he gave a series of speeches in which he acknowledged the significance of women's support (and opposition) and bid openly for their loyalty and leadership in a campaign against desertion. This time "the women" citizens were critical to his endeavor, and moving well beyond his usual passive idea of sacrifice to insist that they "must do more," he urged women to use their influence to propel men back into service. In effect, he was asking Confederate women (and not just the ladies) to constitute a "public opinion" that mirrored state goals and to do what conscription officers could not.[61] It evidenced a new regard for women's clout. Davis's patriarchal conception of the people had proved too limited for war, and even he, myopically, acknowledged as much.

In the end, most of the material concessions the Davis government made came on the impressment of food and the so-called tax-in-kind and, in February 1864, in revision of conscription legislation that effectively turned those exempted by the twenty-negro law into government growers. Even as the administration started in April 1863—the timing was hardly auspicious—to collect one-tenth of everything grown or raised on the farms, they had to start giving it back in particularly hard-hit places. Secretary of War Seddon, who once referred to impressment as "a harsh, unequal and odious mode of supply," yielded to pressure and authorized specific counties (some in North Carolina and Georgia) to purchase food from quartermasters at government prices for the "use of soldiers families and other poor people."[62] By November 1863 he was in receipt of letters directly from county officers in North Carolina describing conditions so severe from drought and labor shortage that county corn agents could find no corn to buy for the hundreds of soldiers' wives on the relief lists. What was difficult in 1863 was impossible in 1864 and 1865 because the Confederate government effectively controlled the corn market. J. W. Norwood, the corn agent for Orange County, North Carolina, reported in January 1865 that the government had issued orders that it would claim by purchase or impressment three-quarters of the corn crop of eastern North Carolina "for the use of the army." No planters could sell or deliver their remaining corn until the government agents got their three-quarters. The net effect, he said, was that the army quartermaster had effectively "closed the corn market." As a result, county courts in North Carolina and elsewhere turned repeatedly to the federal government requesting permission to buy back the tithe corn.[63] In this desperately ad hoc way, local officers acting on behalf of huge numbers of welfare clients hammered the federal government to assume its necessary role in providing for the welfare of Confederate soldiers' wives and children.

The Confederate government moved only by fits and starts, unable or unwilling to mount the kind of massive overhaul of military manpower and taxation policies real reform would have required. The new tax bill of February 1864 did enact some progressive reforms, exempting poor families with less than $500 in property from the tax-in-kind. Although Congress would never repeal the twenty-negro exemption law, eventually it attached a provision obligating its beneficiaries to sell surplus grain and provisions to the government or to soldiers' families at government prices—precisely what the Richmond rioters had demanded. In 1864, broadsides posted in the Virginia countryside by General Jubal Early assured soldiers' wives that wheat and corn purchased for them by county welfare committees would not be subject to impressment by Confederate agents as it had been previously.[64] In the end even the federal government had to address the subsistence crisis on the Confederate home front. What they did was extracted under tremendous political pressure—pressure that, it is now clear, originated in no small measure in soldiers' wives politics of subsistence and in its public expression in the wave of Confederate food riots in 1863.

What are we to make of the welfare system built in the image of the soldier's wife? In the C.S.A. the soldier's wife was the very prototype of the welfare client and provided the political model for the new welfare system and its entitlements. That raises a whole series of interesting questions about the relevance of the Confederate case to the history of welfare in the United States. In the Confederate states during the American Civil War, state and local politicians built a welfare system that was entirely unprecedented in terms of budget commitments, numbers of clients, and administrative infrastructure. Nothing in the Union seems to compare. Georgia alone appears to have spent as much on welfare in one year as Massachusetts did during the whole war. Far more of the Union welfare net issued from private sources and soldiers' bounties and served far fewer clients. Certainly, there is nothing in Union governors' papers or other government records to suggest a comparable mobilization of women to demand welfare reform.[65] Confederate developments are all the more remarkable in light of the constraints of manpower and money under which those states operated by the middle of the war, and in the face of a Union army and society seemingly unlimited in its resources to make war. All of this was new, and little of it accords with anything we already know about Confederate politics or about women, war, and welfare in U.S. history.

It is a truism that victors write history, and that is certainly the case in accounts of the origins of the American welfare state now routinely traced back to the Union pension system that originated in the 1870s, and to the maternalist and child-saving politics of its advocates. As in so much else, the Confederate experience of state welfare left no trace in American political life. The Confederate juggernaut of war, massive expansion of state responsibility for the welfare of its citizens, and special significance of the soldier's wife in the formulation of welfare policy figures nowhere in the American history of welfare and the making of the modern American state. Perhaps it shouldn't. That American welfare system was built up through a system that started with Civil War pensions paid by the U.S. government, mostly to the mothers of Union soldiers for the loss of support of their dead or disabled sons.[66] The Confederate system was never federal and never represented the power of "the state" in that classic liberal centralized sense. And its idiomatic figure was not the mother but the soldier's wife. It left little or no trace in policy.

But the historical significance of Confederate welfare might lie less in policy than in politics. Even if the Confederate experience of early and expansive welfare provision never imprinted the logic of American welfare policy in any permanent sense, the political relationships and practices it involved—particularly the intimate relationship between female citizens and the states, their sense of entitlement, expectation of state support, and strategic knowledge about how to make it happen—left a strong imprint in the South. Southern citizens' early experience of a big state was hardly rendered obsolete with reunification. When female citizens in the occupied or defeated Confederate states lined up outside the Union provost marshal's office, the Union army commissary, or the office of the freedman's bureau agent to take the oath and get relief, they carried over from their recent past a host of assumptions, skills, and expectations of the relationship into which they were entering. White women often outnumbered ex-slaves among those lining up for relief. One woman, who with her husband, a Freedmen's Bureau agent, was stationed in Summerville in the South Carolina low country, noted immediately after the war that as a result of his harsh self-help regime "only ninety whites and eighty colored persons were receiving rations and these were entirely women and children." In Wilmington, more ex-Confederates than slaves appeared at the Union commissary for relief and received the bulk of the government help. And that pattern appears to hold for the federal poor relief disbursed by the Freedmen's Bureau in various parts of the just-defeated C.S.A.[67] Most female citizens of the newly powerful reconstructed Union state were not beginners in working the bureaucracy. The Confederate experience reminds us that the relation between women and the state and welfare traces back to the Civil War itself and thus has its origins in two states and two histories.

The formative moment in Confederate welfare policy was clearly in 1863. But poor white Southern women kept themselves on the political agenda through local activism until the last days of the war, mobilizing to secure the entitlements already established. The network of agents, clients, committees, legislators, gubernatorial leadership, and federal negotiation built up around civilian welfare propelled bureaucratic expansion and intensified women's contact with government agents. But it also added new contentious dimensions to local political life, not least because at a moment of extensive mobilization local relief agents were among the last state officers whose elections or appointments carried exemptions from military service. By 1864, when men aged 15 to 50 were subject to conscription, these were valuable and desperately sought after positions, and that added urgency to men's usual claims to represent the women's preference of agents. For relief agents, providing service to soldiers' wives was, after 1863, about exemption.[68] And that made women players in the routine game of patronage politics for the first time.

After the big expansion of programs in 1863, women all over the South battled local officials or agents over eligibility and the adequacy of relief, insisting ferociously on their entitlement to aid. Those battles included further threats of violence. In Randolph County, Alabama, where there were seventy-five thousand white men in military service and eight thousand persons (all women and children) on the relief rolls, a group of farmers alerted Jefferson Davis to the reports "of women riots . . . in several parts of the Country in which government wheat and corn has been seized to prevent Starvation of themselves & Families." Another Alabama hill county, Talladega, reported more than fourteen thousand whites on relief where before the war there had been thirty. Where relief was insufficient, as it was everywhere, some soldiers' wives were still prepared to exert political pressure through the instrument of violence. Reports of food riots surfaced in various parts of the Confederacy in 1864, in another starving Confederate spring. There were reports of riots in Bladensboro, North Carolina, and Savannah, Georgia, among other places. But interestingly, there was nothing on the scale of the year before and what there was did not ignite Confederate public opinion in the same way, perhaps because the revision and expansion of the welfare system focused anger about food and attempts to extract it on the agencies and agents charged with providing it.[69] All over the South soldiers' wives proved willing to challenge local officials, complaining regularly to higher-ups about those who did not serve them well. Where governors remained alert to women's complaints, local officials had no choice but to be accountable to that constituency. It was an uncomfortable situation, to say the least—the disfranchised, or so it seemed, calling the shots.

Like so much else in Confederate political life, this struggle was local in origin, although it did hinge crucially on women's access to governors and tied them into statewide political networks. The picture that emerges from the localities is of complex and fraught negotiations between agents appointed or elected to serve the women, and angry, underserved, but highly entitled female clients. Even the archival detritus of those relationships—scrawled notes demanding aid, slips noting how much (or little) so-and-so was entitled to, lists of names, highly intimate assessments of crops in the field, food in the corncrib, and amounts of money and food given out—tell a new story. In Richmond County, North Carolina, where one planter politician kept in his private papers, safe for the ages, all the little pieces of papers by which women communicated with him, it is clear that at the beginning (1862) the men giving out the aid regarded the soldiers as their clients and not the wives. He listed the eligible women by their husbands' names and company affiliations and used the military company as the administrative unit for distributing relief. So "John Kelly's wife" and five small children show up on a "List of the Wives and mothers of the Volunteers in the Black Jack District, Jn Littles Company"; they had "a supply of bread for 1862, some Hogs but without Bacon," the agent J. C. Ellerbe noted of Mrs. Kelly.[70]

But however the men in charge construed the deal, it is obvious even at that early date that in dealing with the committee the wives acted as empowered parties. Though stating clearly their need, they offered no flattery, did no groveling, but simply demanded the support due them. Send "what is comeing to me," one said bluntly. That phrase—the customary directness of plainspoken farm women?—is repeated oddly in the messages local women sent to county agents. "I want you to send me what money there is comin to me," Elizabeth McJaffee put it to the agent in her district. "Pleas Sire send me my money" cut a slightly more polite note but conveyed the same sense of entitlement. Some of the women who could not write signed their demands with an "X," but illiteracy hardly dulled the voice. Mrs. McKinnon explained that "I would a went to see you but the wether is to war[m] to cary my chile." Instead a Mr. Gibson made the request for her. Even in the third person, the demand to "send her allowance" comes through loud and clear. Local agents in that North Carolina welfare unit fielded a constant stream of demands and complaints from soldiers' wives about the inadequacies of the system: about how they had fallen through the cracks because their husbands were conscripts and not volunteers, because the men had enlisted in another county, because the woman had moved, and on and on; and endless complaints about the equity of the process, about how it could be that "you [the county committee] have helpe sum that is not as neady of help as I are." Like the last woman, every one of them was sure she was "entitle."[71]

Local officials were the line of first attack in a system the inequities and inadequacies of which no one denied. But soldiers' wives also took their complaints to their friends in high places. "I have been lauft at by our agent for saying I would complain to the govner," Arabella Davis wrote Vance in 1864. Like Mrs. Davis, many soldiers' wives did just that. Davis alerted Vance to the misdirection of funds intended by the legislature "for the soldiers wives," others to the negligence of local agents. "I am intitled to a support but I am not getting it," Elizabeth Sampson reported: "I have got to have more done for me than is done." These women were empowered. They had reason to be, too, for Vance, Brown, even the second Virginia war governor, William Smith, all held local officials strictly accountable to the women. Not a letter of complaint went across Vance's desk but he followed it up. When Martha Allen complained to Vance about how little aid was available from commissioners in her county, she named the guilty party: "Mr Pahial Atwater is the man that is appointed to pay over what the county allows to soldiers wives." "Col Barnes will please write the comrs [commissioners] and ask that they look after this lady," "ZB Vance" noted on the cover of the letter. And so Atwater was called on the carpet. Less than two weeks later he offered the governor a full account, contesting Mrs. Allen's charges by insisting that the last time he checked on her she got twenty pounds of good bacon and fifteen dollars in cash to buy corn. She was a chronic malcontent and troublemaker, Atwater charged. But Vance's sympathy for the women was a matter of public knowledge, and Atwater knew it would not do to blow off their complaints. "We are not going to let soldiers wives suffer as long as it can be helped," he wrote the governor defensively, "but some cant be satisfied."[72] A government official was held accountable by and to a yeoman farm woman. That message came from the top as well as the bottom.

A very telling indication of the extent of women's empowerment is the assumption of women married to deserters that the state had an obligation to support them too. In many of the Confederate states, legislation explicitly excluded the families of deserters from eligibility for aid.[73] But even amid statewide campaigns to root out desertion, some wives denied by local officials felt sufficiently entitled to aid and representation that they also took their case to the higher-ups. But here Vance's legendary sympathy for the female poor found its limit. When Anstio Carver complained to him in writing about the local commissioner of relief who was denying her "my just dues," she didn't say anything about her husband's desertion. She was a constituent of Governor Vance, confident that he would help her find support. "And now best friend of the soldier what shall I do I ask you in gods name must I starve?" she wrote him. When Vance got the report from the chairman of the board of relief for Randolph County where she lived, he learned that she was denied relief because her husband was a substitute and a deserter. Clearly Carver thought this no grounds of disqualification. But she was wrong. As the local official put it to Vance, "In this County . . . we will help no family while they are deserters and in the second place we will help no family that gives aid and comfort to deserters by feeding . . . the same. If we are wrong in these premises I would like to know as all others that are destitute we help." It is fair to say that Vance, engaged at that very moment in a brutal campaign against deserters in Randolph County, concurred on that one.[74]

The confidence even of deserters' wives gives some indication of women's sense of power in the new welfare politics. Yes, they were desperate—little ones left to look after each other while mothers worked in the fields, a minimal diet and no reserves of corn or meat, no money coming from their soldier husbands either. But for once they had some leverage. Their trump card was the exemption that came with appointment or election to local welfare offices. Such exemptions became more precious with every new call-up: of substitutes, men aged 45 to 55, nonessential civil servants. Even as the Confederate Conscription Bureau cut the list of exempted offices and occupations to the very bone, governors refused to concede critical state officers. The Georgia governor was especially aggressive. In fact, Brown was accused of padding the civil service rolls to deny the central state and its army any more Georgia bodies. But even in Georgia, welfare officials were among the last state officers to lose their exemptions. Appointment or election as agent to the soldiers' wives was a precious lifeline. Soldiers' wives knew it and so did the agents themselves. In that context the men became craven in their attention to the women on whose sufferance they served. In seeking appointment or continuation in office they filed petitions loaded with soldiers' wives' names and produced testimonials to the "entire satisfaction" the women clients expressed in their service. Joseph Phillips has been acting commissioner of relief in his Georgia district for two years, one member of the inferior court reported to Governor Brown, and had given such complete satisfaction that "the families in that district have unanimously petitioned us to retain him in that position."[75] By late 1863 service to soldiers' wives was fully enmeshed in the high-stakes politics of exemption.

But if the men were craven, some of the women showed a taste for hardball politics. Agents who served—or claimed to—on the sufferance of women could also be fired. Lucy James had had enough of her relief commissioner, who, she said, issued unequal rations and cursed women when they complained. James wanted him out: "You will have him removed" was her recommendation to Vance, adding the coup de grâce: "if possible have him sent in the field next to the Enemy of our country with the husbands of those women that he has treated with so much injustice," she added maliciously.[76]

Whether they liked it or not—and most didn't—local officials were accountable to the women, forced to treat them as significant members of the political constituency they had been elected or appointed to serve. Poor white women, for their part, had learned how to hold the men accountable, how to make the system respond to their needs to some extent, to insist on a measure of self-representation. All of which is to say that they had entered fully into the practice of politics in the Civil War South.

In 1857 Supreme Court Justice Roger Taney had been able to define citizenship without any reference to women. The architects of the Confederacy had been able to effect secession and declare war without their consent. But war had expanded the terms of consent and legitimacy, created new political identities, expanded the concept of the body politic, widened the conception of citizenship, rerouted the paths of power and patronage, and engendered new political subjects and constituencies. This war, the Confederate war, had its own unexpected developments, the significance of which intensify in light of the original Confederate vision. Far from perfecting the republic of white men, fixing forever the exclusion of black and female dependents, the Confederate war had proved its undoing, most unpredictably, perhaps, in the way it brought white women—especially poor white women—to a position of unquestionable salience in Confederate politics.

That much was strangely confirmed in 1866 when, in the face of unmanageable confusion in the postwar courts, the North Carolina legislature (like a lot of other states) wiped the docket clean of all political crimes left over from the war by passing a blanket amnesty law that covered the political acts of "soldiers of North Carolina, the Confederate States of America, or United States of America." Three months later, with a docket still stacked with cases of women who had made "raids upon any county, state or Confederate States Commissaries or Quartermasters, or other person or persons"—women like Martha Sheets, who threatened to bring down deserters to attack Aaron Saunders's mill, and Sarah Hulin, the wife of a notorious leader of a deserter band, indicted for riot at Saunders Mill—they extended the amnesty to include women, writing into law an explicit recognition of women's "crimes" as political acts. In doing so they offered an official acknowledgment of women as political subjects.[77]

It would be tempting to cast this history of Confederate women as an episode in the history of citizenship in the United States, to slot it into the dominant liberal framework of American political history by which disfranchised people progressively claimed citizenship and its attendant rights. And there is some reason to see it that way, especially given the current emphasis on "social citizenship" (the claim to state entitlements) and not just political citizenship (the franchise).[78] But there is also reason to entertain a less predictable view of Confederate women's politics in American and comparative political history. For it is significant that notwithstanding the obviously strategic nature of their political style and language the women so rarely deployed the identity of citizens or the language of rights. "Citizen" was a term rarely used by soldiers' wives, or even, for that matter, planter women. Unlike the masses of female petitioners who sought the abolition of slavery in the Union, Confederate soldiers' wives did not move to make their claims based on perceived rights as citizens of the nation.[79] The importance of citizenship changed fundamentally with the Fourteenth Amendment, but it was already a salient concept in political life before the war, especially for the excluded. It is also true that the ideals of popular sovereignty and equal citizenship were enshrined in the Confederacy, as in other modern nation-states. But the C.S.A. was no ordinary nineteenth-century experiment in nation building. It was an explicitly proslavery nation in conception and design. It had a deep investment in limiting democracy, and it was committed, as a matter of ideology, to the exclusion of free women and enslaved men and women from political life. White women occupied a peculiar position in Confederate political life in that, unlike slaves, they did have civil standing as citizens. But not only did they lack the attendant political rights of citizens; most of the legal and civil rights of the married majority were vitiated by coverture: wives remained their husbands' property. Their membership in the political community thus was explicitly denied. In entering the political arena, Confederate soldiers' wives did not—could not—advance a universal claim to the equal rights of citizens.[80] That lay entirely outside the politics of the possible. The history those women made defied Jefferson Davis's imagination, and it issues a pretty considerable challenge to ours as well.

But if Confederate soldiers' wives cannot simply be cast as a chapter in American political history as we usually tell it, they might prompt us to rethink the story outside national boundaries. For the mobilization of poor, mostly rural women in the Confederate South during the Civil War bears resemblance not to the process of gradual extension of citizenship around which most American political history is framed, but far more to the way politics was practiced by poor rural and urban people in the modern world: what one historian has called the politics of the governed in most of the world. Indeed, in some respects Confederate women's behavior is so strikingly like that of the poor in twentieth-century India that it reminds us that the strategies of the governed (including violence) are needful and practiced—perhaps particularly by women—not just in non-Western, postcolonial societies with huge subaltern populations but in modern Western nation-states as well, long after the formal introduction of so-called universal suffrage, which meant, of course, suffrage only for men.[81]

Seen in this broad context, the situation as it unfolded in Confederate political life was strikingly like that in other modern, formally democratic societies in which the mass of people are "not proper members of civil society or of the republican body of true citizens," have no right of representation or to hold office, but manage nonetheless to mobilize as particular communities to influence government policy in their favor. Unable to participate in the political life of the nation as equal citizens, not properly part of "the political fraternity of citizens" (a painfully revealing phrase), they instead take categories the state uses to govern the population—refugees, the poor, or "soldiers' wives"—and infuse them with moral content.

In doing so, they effectively invest those categories with the imaginative possibilities of community and produce a new rhetoric of political claims. Although not advanced on the terrain of nation and citizenship, these claims are irreducibly political and constitute a separate and critical arena of political society.[82] It is hardly likely that Confederate state actors would have conceded that point of view, but it can hardly be denied that in their own creative, instrumental, if limited, way one female part of the Confederate governed had managed to widen the field of popular democratic practice and rendered suspect the practicality of the strictly delimited Confederate vision of the people so foundational to that national political project.

CHAPTER 6

"Amor Patriae"

> And with what execration should the statesman be loaded, who permitting one half of the citizens thus to trample on the rights of the other, transforms those into despots, and these into enemies, destroys the morals of the one part, and the amor patriae of the other. For if a slave can have a country in this world, it must be any other in preference to that in which he is born to live and labor for another.
>
> Thomas Jefferson, *Notes on the State of Virginia*

THE PROBLEM OF SLAVES' political allegiance arose with the birth of the republic. At the very dawn of the nation Thomas Jefferson admitted that slavery destroyed slaves' love of country: that it turned slaves into enemies and nurtured traitors at the American breast. It was a harrowing thought, never more so than in war. The problem it names runs through the history of not one but two slaveholding republics in North America.

The problem of slaves' political allegiance was posed with stunning sharpness in the second North American republic—the Confederate States of America—an explicitly proslavery nation-state, born in the crucible of war. The idea that slaves were excluded from the polity was foundational in Confederate political life, as close to a founding principle as the Confederacy had. Jefferson Davis had said as much in explaining Mississippi's secession from the Union; and Justice Roger Taney's view that slaves were rejected from the duties and obligations of citizenship was a matter of everyday assumption in law, the practice of politics, and the behavior of white Southern citizens. Unlike white women, who were under the protection of the state, slaves were domestic enemies against whom the state adopted a posture of self-protection. Few white Southerners in 1861 would have quarreled with Davis's description of slavery as a form of civil government for a class of people not fit to govern themselves. Slaves were part of a separate polity, masters—not the state—being the authority to whom they owed allegiance.[1] The roughly four million men, women, and children enslaved in the new Confederate republic knew that better than anyone. Lifetimes of subjection to the personal power of masters had rendered clear instruction on where power lay.[2]

But if slavery shaped slaves' standing as outsiders to the state, then that was a system far better suited to peace than war. For slaves who had no rights also had none of the duties or obligations of citizens and other members of the political family, including the burden of national allegiance. Even white women owed allegiance to the government under which they lived. It was hardly noticed at the time, but in relegating slaves to their masters' authority, slavery also left them beyond the reach of the state. Slaves' standing in relation to the state and the way slavery shaped the state thus were two sides of the same Confederate coin. It was not of much concern to anyone in the antebellum South, but slavery compromised state authority and left whole subject populations outside its grasp. Where masters' power was paramount, the slave owed no service to the state, James A. Seddon, the Confederate secretary of war, said bitterly in 1864. "The government knows him only as the property of his master."[3] Confederate authorities would have much reason to regret that fact.

The problem of slavery and state formation was not particular to the C.S.A. In the ancient world, slavery made the state weak against the household.[4] Wherever the institution of slavery existed, it required the relegation of considerable personal authority to the slaveholder to control his property. Usually cast as the right of the household head to govern his dependents unimpeded, slavery established those households as realms of private power and put fast limits on state control of slave property. Like other forms of servile labor claimed traditionally by landed elites, slavery perpetuated into the modern period precisely the kinds of petty sovereignties that monarchs and then "the people" sought to dismantle in building sovereign states.[5] In slave states, the household typically constituted a parallel realm of government, precisely what President Davis said in 1861.

Although slavery does not figure much in the history of modern state formation, the emancipation of servile populations has long been recognized as a central feature of that process in western and eastern Europe. Indeed, so protracted was that process that a great deal of what Confederates faced in building a state adequate to war was playing out almost simultaneously on the other side of the Atlantic. One after another since the Napoleonic period, European governments had undertaken servile emancipations in the context of war and explicitly for reasons of state. Emancipation was always part of a critical "struggle for supremacy between absolute monarchs and their nobles." It was not until the crisis of the Crimean War in the 1850s that the struggle to end serfdom reached its conclusion in Russia. In Russia, as in Prussia and in France, servile emancipations had been undertaken largely for military reasons, often in the wake of military defeats, as states sought to shore up their own weakened claims to territorial sovereignty by developing more effective armies. Whether monarchies or republics, those sovereign states sought the destruction of systems of servile labor to augment the power of the central state over and against individual masters and, especially, to assert their right to the military service of peasant men. Servile emancipations in eastern Europe, that is, were tied to political struggles for the loyalty of the peasantry—especially military-age men—in contexts of war and revolution. After emancipation everyone was born free and was a subject of the state and, as such, owed the same obligations to the state.[6] Emancipation was crucial to the growth of state power, the unity of the state, and the authority of the monarch or sovereign people.

But what of the American republics born in war and revolution in the eighteenth and nineteenth centuries, and what of African slavery and its meaning for the shape of those modern states? That question emerged as a critical one in the Spanish American republics, all of which shed slavery, although gradually and unevenly, in the process of nation making.[7] Not so the United States of America and its breakaway, the C.S.A. Both of those republics countenanced slavery and perpetuated and extended the petty sovereignties of the masters within the borders of the nation-state. In doing so, they limited the reach, authority, and absolute sovereignty of the state, left whole populations under the authority of masters, rendered slaves nonparties to the social contract, and foreclosed the relation of rights and obligations members had to their governments. Slavery perpetuated elements of the old order into new world republics and fragmented the very public authority on which the sovereignty of the people was alleged to reside. In the modern period at least, slavery made for weak states.

That much was obvious in the United States from 1787 to 1861, which purposely built a weak central state, dispersing the power to govern and tax from the center to the constituent (some would have said still sovereign) parts: *These* United *States* of America. Even as the United States grew as a powerful imperial power with respect to federal control over the territories, it continued to exercise limited power over domestic policy within the separate states. The necessity of that arrangement owed in no small measure to the need to satisfy slaveholders that their peculiar forms of property would be safe in the Union. It was the ability of those slaveholding states subsequently to limit central state growth that underscore the significance of the Civil War in American state development. It was not until the destruction of slavery in the American Civil War that the leviathan American state—the Republican Party state built by the Union war government—took off. The destruction of slavery, and with it the power of the slaveholders as a class in American political life, was the one needful thing.[8]

The C.S.A.—the only explicitly *pro*slavery nation-state formed in the modern period—inherited all of the contradictions and liabilities of the older slaveholding states of America. With independence the slaveholding states got their wish, shaping their new government to establish rights of property in slaves as wholly within the control of the individual states. Sitting down to write their Constitution in Montgomery, Alabama, members of the provisional government crafted a document that defined slaves explicitly as property, put slaves definitively outside the boundaries of the political community, prohibited the incorporation of any new state that did not sanction slavery, and put it beyond the power of their federal government to limit, revoke, or otherwise interfere with the legality of slave property or rights of slaveholders.[9] These were the purposes for which the C.S.A. was formed. Governor Brown of Georgia described the Confederacy as a "league between sovereigns," and the central government as "the servant of several masters, not the master of several servants."[10] Slaveholders had finally gotten the state they wanted.

That was the state with which they would have to wage war. With 40 percent of their adult male population enslaved and unavailable for military service, Confederates faced a structural problem from the outset. "The seven Confederate states have not more than double the number of the male population capable of bearing arms, which has been offered to this [U.S.] government as volunteers since the 15th of this month," John A. Campbell, the recently resigned associate justice of the U.S. Supreme Court, secretly advised President Davis in April 1861.[11] The problem would hardly abate, even with the addition of eight Upper South states. The Confederacy would pay a high price for its commitment to slavery.

In their judgment of what war would involve, Confederate founders and ordinary citizens counted slaves out. They could not have been more wrong. Among the four million people enslaved in the American South in 1861, most of them in Confederate territory, were many who moved with great determination to make their political loyalty count, prove the truth of Jefferson's fear that slavery destroyed slaves' love of country, made them into traitors and enemies, and nurtured allegiance to any country that countenanced their emancipation. Stripped of any standing in relation to the state, excluded definitively from the political community, enslaved men and women nonetheless embraced the possibilities the moment offered in their own long political history. They put themselves on the Confederate and not just Union agenda, made Confederates bid for their political allegiance, and showed up the weakness of a state that had no way to claim their loyalty or service. It was, ironically enough, as "enemies within" that slaves managed to assert themselves as a political force in the C.S.A. Slave men and women would of necessity take very different paths through war to emancipation, but each group would prove formidable enemies of slaveholders and their new national government. There would be a reckoning.

Thomas Jefferson notwithstanding, Confederates launched their national career heedless of the dangers slaves posed, instead gloating over the advantages slavery conferred on a society at war. Slaves might be outside political life, but Confederates meant to make them count (as labor) in the national project. From the very beginning of the war, white Southerners talked about slaves as "one of our most potent elements of strength." "Both our wars with England and the whole history of the world, demonstrate that a slave population is an element of strength in war, and not of weakness or insecurity," the editor of the *Richmond Dispatch* crowed just days before Fort Sumter. Far from the insurrectionary volcanoes Northerners had predicted they would become, "the servile classes were in perfect order and quiet." "The southern negro has no sympathies with Northern abolitionists," he boasted recklessly.[12]

With slaves counted out, Confederates proceeded to scheme about how best to deploy them in war. Most, habituated by years of proslavery instruction, seemed to think of slaves as part of the nation's natural resources, like the size of its territory or value of its cotton crop. Vice President Alexander Stephens indicated the usual approach when he excluded slaves from the body of "the people" but counted them as population and taxable property in his itineration of the wealth of the nation in his attempt to woo Virginia into the Confederacy.[13]

Plans "to avail ourselves of our peculiar population" flowed steadily into the War Department in the early months. Most people believed that slaves ought to be left on plantations to raise supplies, freeing more white men for the army. But given Southerners' habit of deploying slaves to do their dirty work, it is hardly surprising that they also turned quickly to the use of slaves for military labor. When a Georgia senator and other citizens of coastal Georgia seized Fort Pulaski on the governor's orders in January 1861, they "carried a large negro force to clear out the ditches." Jefferson Davis and others trained in the entrenchment school of warfare at West Point quickly proposed the use of slaves to help build fortifications and called on planters for contingents of their male slaves to begin almost immediately.[14]

Confederates' enthusiasm for using slaves to their advantage knew few bounds. Some proposed deploying slaves with regiments of white soldiers to serve as laborers, draymen, craftsmen, and military police. In late April an Alabama man, recognizing that the government would need "all the effective force" it could muster, offered twenty of his slaves as mechanics to the army. The obvious scarcity of white mechanics in the South led another to propose to raise a corps of artificers using skilled slaves contributed by their owners.[15] The idea that slaves were an inexhaustible resource waiting to be tapped engendered other more serious plans, including the use of slaves as soldiers. More than a few such plans were pitched to the secretary of war, to President Davis, and to state governors in the first few months of the war. W. S. Turner wrote from Helena, Arkansas, to ask the secretary of war if he could get "negro regiments received for Confederate service, officered of course by white men." He would want arms, clothing, and provisions, he said, the "usual pay for officers, and not one cent for negroes." George Gardner suggested to Governor Brown the wisdom of accepting "companies composed partly of negroes, say one third or one fourth" of the whole, although discerning the weird direction in which it would take Confederate policy, added perceptively, unless it is against the law or "derogatory to the dignity of our commonwealth." Confederates intended to make slaves count in the cause.[16]

Whatever the particulars, all proposals evinced slaveholders' instrumental view of enslaved men and women in disposing entirely with the matter of their consent. In all of the plans it was the masters' consent that mattered; slaves were so many pawns on the planters' chessboard to be moved at will. No one asked if slaves would cooperate. Racial thinking provided all the proof needed of slaves' willingness to serve the masters' cause. "I know one man that will furnish and arm 100 of his own [slaves] and his son for their captain," an Arkansas slaveholder told Walker, as if the man in question was sending out a gang to the fields. He had long experience "with negro character," he assured Walker, and was "satisfied that they are easy disciplined and less trouble than whites in camp and will fight desperately as long as they have a single white officer living." Knowledge of "negro character"—millions of enslaved men, women, and children reduced to one racial type—was the only assurance required. Albert T. Bledsoe, chief of the Bureau of War, answered, and although rejecting Turner's offer, carefully registered his agreement to the racial assumptions. "This Department is not prepared to accept the negro regiment tendered by you," he wrote, "and yet it is not doubted that almost every slave would cheerfully aid his master in the work of hurling back the fanatical invader."[17] Early plans about how to make slavery an element of strength in the war showed shockingly little consideration of slaves' own political stake in the crisis of national affairs. Even the practicality of arming slaves as soldiers was regarded as a matter of masters' willingness to cooperate, not slaves' willingness to serve.

In planters' talk about how to wage war, there was a great deal said about slavery and very little about slaves. When slaves broke the horizon of consciousness it was as subjects of racial theory, in easily offered assurances about the Negro character, the Negro's disposition, or the natural inferiority of negroes. "Many governments have been founded upon the principle of the subordination and serfdom of certain classes of the same race," Alexander Stephens said in March 1861. But "our system commits no such violation of nature's law. With us, all of the white race, however high or low, rich or poor, are equal in the eyes of the law. Not so with the negro. Subordination is his place." Stephens's modernizing scientific racism came just in time to steel slaveholders' nerves in their new, risky undertaking. "One salutary result of the movement in favor of Southern independence has been the awakening of Northern minds to the true relations existing between the negro and the white man," wrote a Louisiana editor in March 1861. The editor relished the ideological battle enjoined. "The idea of the equality of race is a figment . . . The negro," he said, "is happiest" when in servitude.[18]

Amid the optimistic din there were, to be sure, a few panicky voices registering a note of caution. It was evident in the heightened surveillance and police activities planter woman Sarah Lawton reported from Savannah in December 1860. Whatever the official line about slave passivity, planters took no chances. With fortunes at stake, they geared up the slave patrols, formed home guards, and urged state politicians to retain enough troops at home to keep the "Negroes" in subjection. Fears of slave insurrection surfaced in relation to the prospect of invasion, especially in places like South Carolina, which had a few scary months of independence before the C.S.A. was formed. Governor Pickens informed President Davis in early March 1861 that because of the vulnerability of the slave population on the coast around Beaufort in the event that South Carolina was "dragged [*sic*] into a sectional war," he would have to retain enough men at home to garrison the harbor forts and "run an efficient police boat" between the islands. Still it was the Yankees and not the slaves who presented the real threat. When Alabama farmer William Lee said bluntly to President Davis in early May that "the Negroes is very Hiley Hope up that they will soon Be Free," he sounded a shockingly cacophonous note.[19] Slaves' hopes were not yet much on any one's minds.

At the beginning of the American Civil War, slaves were racial ("negroes"), not political subjects, seen simply as property to be made available to the cause. But early confidence notwithstanding, the struggle to make slaves material to the cause would prove to be protracted and massively revealing of the structural problems of a slave regime at war. As late as 1863, War Department officials were still trying to find the combination that would unlock slavery's power and access the South's wealth on the nation's behalf. In counting out slaves politically, white Confederates showed uncommonly little sagacity about the dilemma war provoked.

Secessionists had no sooner begun trumpeting the advantages of slavery to a society at war than slaves registered their challenge to that flatly instrumental view. The slaves' war opened simultaneously with—some would have said predated—the Confederate war for independence. "Your late and [our] *all time* enemies," a group of South Carolina freedmen pointedly said of Confederates when talking to Union soldiers in October 1865, succinctly conveying slaves' different chronology of, and political stakes in, the American Civil War.[20]

Even before war began, enslaved men, women, and children had read the signs and omens of consequence for their struggle against slavery. William Webb, the prophetic Mississippi slave autobiographer who spoke of "free life" as "the light," said he began to build a movement among the enslaved during the Fremont campaign in 1856: "That was the first the colored people knew about another Nation wishing for the slaves to be free." Webb went into Kentucky like a prophet: "I told them Fremont was a small light and it would keep burning until it spread all over the world." During the election the people held "great meetings and had speeches among themselves in secret," he said, "and would pray." But when Fremont was defeated, prayer gave way to more martial forms of political mobilization. At one secret meeting in Mississippi some present determined "to rebel and kill." It was at that meeting that Webb and others resolved to build a secret slave communication network in preparation for a possible rebellion of all the slave states. "We cannot do much unless we can send word all over," as he put it. The idea was to build up a network of departments linked at twelve-mile intervals, each with its designated "head men," providing a road "to carry news from post to post from Mississippi to the Headquarters at Kentucky." That way, "if we were to rebel we would rebel in all the States at one time, so the white people would not have a chance." By the time Lincoln was elected, he claimed, the network could move news over three states. "The blessed news flew from one State to another, and the colored people all over the State knew who was their friend and we understood the whole matter."[21]

William Webb's story was corroborated time and again in its broad outlines by the testimonies of other slaves: the existence in the antebellum period of secret networks of communications that could move news over long distances; the combination of martial and prophetic traditions that governed their politics as slaves; the dating of political awakenings from the moment (whether the emergence of Garrison, Fremont, or Lincoln) at which slaves could see *two* nations coming into being, one of which took up their antislavery cause; and about the election of Lincoln as a critical event. In account after account, slaves told about those moments when they first recognized that the nation had divided over them and that the parties had arranged themselves in adversarial relation to the slaveholders and their new nation.

Extensive black communication networks had existed in the slave period and laid the foundation for the politics of freedpeople.[22] In responding to the new opportunities secession and war opened up, enslaved men, women, and children mobilized strategies they had long used to communicate, organize, and resist. In 1860 and 1861, when slaves went to meet their friends at their fish traps on the river, stole away to a church meeting on the outskirts of Savannah, or went into the swamp by lamplight to hold a secret meeting, they did what they had always done, hoping that this time the balance of forces—and the outcome—would be different. Ex-slaves left graphic accounts of the strategies they had relied on under slavery. Chief among them was the ability to get and relay information of personal and political significance by assembling the required elements into one human network.[23] William Robinson said that his access to news established him "as almost a prophet among my people." He was a driver and house servant on a North Carolina plantation, the kind of slave whose mobility and access to white conversation gave him valuable information and the means to relay it. Robinson was illiterate, but he specialized in reading the masters nonetheless, by learning how to "listen carefully to every conversation held between white people" and by stealing newspapers and mail, which he took to a black neighbor who could read and write, a tactical pairing slaves relied on all over the South. "A Colored man who could read was a very important fellow," Henry Clay Bruce confirmed.[24]

Literacy was a dangerous secret under slavery. For obvious reasons, slaves' networks were clandestine and built upon tests of trust. Yet in many cases those networks included antislavery white men. For Henry Clay Bruce that man was Gather Ashby, a preacher and small slaveholder who told Bruce during the Fremont campaign that "he believed slavery to be wrong." In North Carolina, the slave William Henry Singleton recalled various encounters with antislavery white people and Underground Railroad men, who sympathized with the slaves and gave them information about what the North was trying to do. Those contacts were crucial and their existence is confirmed by criminal prosecution records. "We knew little about the outside world," Singleton recalled. One thing they did learn was "that a man named Wendell Phillips and a man named Garrison were getting slaves into Canada and we were told that once you got into Canada . . . you were free." "We were," he added, "anxious to be free too." In virtually every locale ex-slaves described, those "grapevine telegraphs," as Booker T. Washington later called them, were in place and used trusted people, mostly black but including a few whites, to convey news of personal and political significance.[25]

Slaves' networks were spatial as well as human, and involved maps of places known only to them. Such maps included the trails slaves took when they needed to lie out, move stolen goods, hold a secret prayer meeting, or deliberate in groups of more than two or three. These were not the straight roads planters took between plantations, easy for horsemen to patrol, the kind that showed up on slaveholders' maps. They were the shortcuts and winding paths that crisscrossed the land and plantation boundaries and led out into the woods, along which people and goods moved clandestinely. Slaves' politics were grounded in an alternative geography that mapped their secret networks in the landscape.[26]

Some of the places were hard to get to, the places slaves headed for when they wanted to go missing. Southern slaves left frequent reference to secret "camps" where slaves could lie out for a time. All slaves seemed to know where such places were. When William Robinson needed to run—he had struck his owner with an axe handle in reprisal for hitting his mother—he headed straight to a hideout he had heard about as a child. The camp was remote. He reached it only after traveling through the night. Crawling on his belly through a thick cane brake and crossing a stagnant pond, he finally reached the cave and, after passing security at the entrance, joined the sixteen people already there. One had been there already for eleven months.[27] One ex-slave from Louisiana described his resistance during the Civil War as a direct outgrowth of a period spent at a camp four miles back of his plantation. There were thirty people in that camp, ten of them women. They roped cattle for food and exchanged the meat with fellow slaves for cornmeal. Octave Johnson spent a year and a half in those woods before he made it to Union lines. As in the Caribbean, marronage was part of enslaved men and women's strategies of resistance, and it was a strategy especially drawn upon by slaves in societies at war.[28] In the dangerous times ahead, slaves would make increasing recourse to those places of refuge.

Slaves' maps also led to secret meeting places closer to home. Time and again slaves told how, in the crisis of the Union, they returned to their secret places to share the news, interpret it, and try to shape it. Reaching for Bible passages to shed light on specific political developments, trusting in the efficacy of prayer to bring change, they often prayed that "the day would dawn soon." William Webb wasn't the only one awaiting the light. "The negroes that had prayed so hard to God said that was the cause of the war," Kate Drumgoold recalled, "for [their] prayers . . . seemed to reach up to heaven, and the answer had come for their deliverance."[29]

Virtually every slave who left any account of the times recalled Lincoln's election as a major development. Large numbers of slaves plotted their personal political histories primarily in genealogical time, crediting their parents for their political education. The slave John Quincy Adams clearly had very brave parents. From them he got not only his name but the knowledge that his people would not always be slaves. The newborn Abraham Lincoln—so named by his mother, a slave on a plantation in Confederate South Carolina—got the same message as his birthright too.[30] But long before Lincoln, slaves also watched elections closely, attempting to discern any meaning they might hold for their war against the slaveholders. "When an election was going on," John Quincy Adams explained, "they [the owners] did not want the negro to know anything . . . but I tried to learn all I could do that I might tell father and mother." Like Webb, the Missouri slave Henry Clay Bruce remembered the Fremont election as particularly important. "I had learned to read and could understand enough of the political situation at that date to be a 'Fremont man,' but a very silent one." Bruce and Webb developed partisan identities. But Bruce's political education had started in the "hard cider Campaign" of 1840, the same moment from which another slave, Peter Still, dated his antislavery hopes. As Booker T. Washington would later say, long before Lincoln's election and by means common to enslaved people, slaves were "able to keep themselves . . . accurately and completely informed about the great National questions that were agitating the county." In this respect, he said, secession and war were part of a longer "movement" of agitation "for freedom" that slaves had kept close track of from Garrison on.[31]

Slaves read other signs, too, in the fate of slavery in the Western Hemisphere and plotted their own history in that transatlantic one. Lewis Clarke, a Kentucky slave who ran to freedom in the early 1840s, insisted that slaves in his neighborhood learned of British West Indian emancipation shortly after it took place. "It was the occasion of great joy," he wrote. "They expected they would be free next. This event has done much to keep up the hopes of the slave to the present hour." Masters never could repress knowledge of the great black republic in the Caribbean, Haiti, which even slaves in the remote new territory of southwest Georgia had learned of before the war.[32] These national and international developments gave American slaves hope that their day would come and kept them alert to the moment and means of their own deliverance.

But the scale of the openings that came with Lincoln's election was unprecedented, as all acknowledged. The election of 1860 "created more excitement probably than any that had preceded it," Henry Clay Bruce recalled, "because greater questions and issues had to be met and settled." Bruce recalled speeches by "Bob Toombs of Georgia" that alerted him to the depths sectional divisions now went. Toombs said he intended "to call the roll of his slaves on Bunker Hill and would do so if the South was successful." Booker T. Washington said much the same thing, that during the campaign when Lincoln was first a presidential candidate, "the slaves on our far-off plantation . . . knew what the issues involved were . . . and knew that the primal [issue] was that of slavery."[33]

There was no shortage of information; slaveholders could not quarantine the news. They were so fired up to hear and relay every development, so consumed by electioneering and speechifying, that they could not cut slaves out of the loop. If whites on a farm in southwest Virginia or a plantation in southwest Georgia could get the news, so could their slaves, often by the same means. James Henry Hammond admitted that slaves got a good deal of their political news at home, at slaveholders' own "tables and . . . firesides," and at political meetings: "[At least] ten percent of the audience at political rallies and meetings were slaves," he noted anxiously. In South Carolina in December 1860 the Spartanburg grand jury called for legislation barring all negroes from musters and political meetings.[34]

In January 1861 in Richmond, Virginia, a state that had not yet seceded, Lincoln's election fed rumors among some area slaves that war had already begun. In the combination of news and rumors (not easily distinguished) Richmond slaves openly struggled to interpret events. The editor of the *Richmond Dispatch* reported uneasily on testimony extracted from one slave woman of the news just brought from Richmond to her plantation, that "a great crowd of people was standing around the telegraph office in this city, intelligence having arrived that the colored people of the state would be free in two months; that war would soon be here, and that a vessel ladened with silver was now on its way from the North for the use of the colored people." To that another slave on the plantation allegedly replied that "he would bring a paper and read the news to them, if it proved to be true." Prophetic rumor, we might call this particular aspect of slaves' antislavery politics.[35]

In the activity around telegraph offices, militia musters, and political meetings, and the information conveyed in conversations, political speeches, electoral results, newspapers, or purloined mail in late 1860 and early 1861, slaves everywhere discerned news of significance. Using established networks, old strategies, and secret meeting places, they gathered, read, relayed, and deliberated on developments, struggling to interpret and respond to Lincoln's election, Southern secession, and the likelihood of war. Like William Webb, they took many of their cues from the behavior of the whites, simply reversing the signs. Susie King Taylor said she heard so many "warnings to the North" issuing from the whites during the secession months in Savannah that she grew certain that "the Yankee was going to set all the slaves free." "I wanted to see these wonderful 'Yankees' so much," she remembered. Louis Hughes said simply that the slaves he knew took the masters' blowhard talk about whipping the Yankees as a good sign for them.[36] Mattie Jackson's mother used the same tactic in her personal war with her mistress, a Missouri rebel. "The days of sadness for mistress were days of joy for us," Jackson recalled. In that household, a struggle between two nations—Union and Confederate—played out over the kitchen table between two women with conflicting national loyalties.[37]

Like Mattie Jackson's mother or the self-appointed prophet William Webb, enslaved men and women forged their own, directly adversarial interpretation of secession. One night in early 1861, William Robinson hid himself, determined to overhear the discussion under way among the leading men of Wilmington in his master's dining room. "I heard one of them say if the Yankees whipped them, every negro would be free." Then, Robinson said, his understanding of secession was set. He "became convinced that the negro was the bone of contention, and that the light of liberty was about to dawn."[38] Taking their masters' enemies to be their friends, Robinson, Mattie Jackson, William Webb, and countless other slaves attached themselves and their historic hopes to what they construed as the antislavery nation.

As Jefferson had feared and slaves had long hoped, they were now a people with a nation. Whatever the masters said, enslaved men and women had their own interpretation of secession, understood it as a major event in their own political history. That much was obvious pretty quickly to slaveholders as well, and it would shape not just the history of the Union in the war but of the Confederacy as well.

It was on plantations that slaves' politics registered first. Take Gowrie, the rice plantation in the Georgia low country where the war-time battle between masters and slaves reached epic proportions. "The people," as the owner Charles Manigault called his slaves, had been actively resisting his government for a long time before Confederate independence. But with secession Manigault immediately recognized the new stakes: the destruction of slavery itself. "They have very generally got the idea of being emancipated when 'Lincon' comes in," he said in January 1861.[39] With its ninety-eight enslaved men, women, and children, and one powerful white slaveholding family, the struggle on Gowrie was old but the political terrain was new.

Charles Manigault, the patriarch, owned two plantations and a small farm: Gowrie, on Argyle Island, eight miles upriver from Savannah; Silk Hope, a rice plantation on the Cooper River, forty miles inland from Charleston; and Marshlands, a farm seven miles from Charleston. The slaves on Gowrie were managed by Louis, Charles's oldest son; most had been moved there in 1844. Another son, Gabriel, managed Silk Hope, where about 126 slaves lived when the war began.[40]

1860 had been a rocky year in slave management for the Manigault men, especially on Gowrie, even before the shock of political events registered. "Mr. Capers our overseer tells me that he had had much trouble with the Negroes last summer and several runaways," Louis wrote. That was something of an understatement. In June, one Gowrie slave had committed suicide, declaring in full view of the overseer, driver, and assembled slaves that he would drown himself before he would submit to a whipping. William Capers, the overseer, ordered that his corpse be left to float in the river as a lesson to the other slaves. Capers also recommended that Charles Manigault sell the driver, who had refused a direct order to stop London, saying "he would not dust his feet to stop him."[41] Manigault regarded both of his drivers as "broken," kicked both of them down to field labor, and bought and installed a new man he thought more pliable. Several children died that summer, too; there were suspicions that they had been poisoned by Old Betsey. In August two slaves, Hector and Daniel, had taken to the woods, and in October, two more, Big Hector and Carpenter George, "left the plantation . . . without one word being said to them." Hector kept showing back up at the plantation, wearing a "pr of Pistols and a sword," he "says he will not be taken."[42] Carpenter George had probably run to protest his demotion.

Late January 1861 thus found South Carolina grappling with the consequences of its secession from the Union, and Louis Manigault still trying to bring in five Gowrie slaves. Yet chronic as the struggles were, Charles Manigault and his sons were sure that something fundamental had changed. Casting developments on Gowrie as part of a much larger political pattern, they began to talk of an epidemic of runaways on the Savannah River as a whole. "It is seriously the case in various sections of the Country far from Charleston," Charles alerted Louis, attributing it to slaves' interpretation of Lincoln's election and expectation of emancipation.[43] The war between the masters and slaves had entered a new phase, and even the masters' acknowledged it.

As the new phase opened, Louis Manigault managed a few wins on Gowrie. He brought in the five runaways still out in January. But the correspondence makes it clear that the Manigault men regarded their slaves as formidable adversaries. They worried most about slaves' communication networks. Gabriel alerted his brother Louis to the scale of the problem. In November he had gone with a parcel of overseers and professional Negro hunters to search the woods near Gordon's brickyard, a refuge for runaways in the vicinity of Silk Hope. But notwithstanding their knowledge of the location of the hideout, they "saw no one at all." The experience taught him a few things: that he had to go armed and be prepared to shoot any Negro who attempted to resist or escape after being caught. Even more important, he had to observe "the utmost secrecy and caution" in making plans, "as it is extremely difficult to prevent the runaways from being informed of a search after them." Gabriel attributed the failure of his mission to "their intention having been communicated by house negroes." "No overseer or Planters should speak on such subjects before a small house boy or girl." Because rice planters did practically nothing without the aid of their slaves, that was a tall order. It always proved difficult for planters to make preparations without revealing themselves to the enemy.[44] The Manigault men clearly saw themselves arrayed against not just particular runaways but the collectivity of slaves now imbued with emancipationist hopes and potentially powerful allies.

What ensued on Gowrie after Confederate independence can only be described as a war. Few, if any, Manigault slaves made it to Union lines before Savannah fell, despite the plantation's proximity to the coast and the Union fleet. Confederates fortified the city early in 1862, and Savannah River plantations were thereafter more secure than those elsewhere in the low country.[45] Jack Savage, Big Hector, and the other Gowrie slaves thus had to wage their war with their master behind Confederate lines, on Confederate terrain, using strategies and networks built up under slavery. Nonetheless, from January 1861 until Christmas 1864, when the low country fell to Sherman's troops, Gowrie was in a state of barely suppressed insurrection and marronage. Developments on plantations like Gowrie threw a significant wrench into Confederate officials' plans to use slaves to national advantage, if only because they made planters extremely cautious about anything that disrupted routine or diminished surveillance. From early on, planters like Charles Manigault were under no illusions about their slaves' intentions.

In November 1861, after the "day of the gun shoot at Bay Point" (as low-country slaves called it) when Union troops took Port Royal and all of Savannah was packed to run upcountry, a number of Gowrie slaves made their move. Louis Manigault had no sooner finished congratulating himself that "the Negroes give no trouble" than Big George, Jack Savage, and at least two other slaves tried to reach Union lines by canoe. When a search of the plantation quarters revealed that another slave, Jack Savage's younger brother Ishmael, had stockpiled a "quantity of plantation guns and powder," Ishmael openly confessed "his intention to go with the Yankees."[46] From that point on, Louis Manigault was, and knew himself to be, in a state of open warfare with at least a portion of his slaves.

What ensued on Gowrie was a relentless campaign to suppress revolt by removing "bad negroes"—identifying the ringleaders and rebels, sending them to the workhouse, selling them away, but most commonly moving them inland to Silk Hope, "sufficiently remote," they hoped, "from all excitement." Admitting that the slaves' heads had been "turned by recent military events," the Manigaults responded with an intensification of the usual violence. After the November 1861 escape attempt, they removed ten Gowrie slaves, three by force; caught in the act of running away, the slaves went to Silk Hope in handcuffs and soon thereafter to the Charleston workhouse, where they spent three months. The overseer, William Capers, advised Louis to sell Big George and send him to Cuba: "Let him go or you will lose him," he wrote, "he should not be among a gang of negroes." The logic of infection and quarantine was quite explicit. Louis thought about returning the remaining seven to Gowrie over Christmas (he resented the loss of their labor) but decided against it, worried that "Christmas is always a very bad time for Negroes . . . any year but far more so this."[47] But on Gowrie, the ever widening circle of Manigault's quarantine testifies only to the increasing intensity of the struggle. By February 1862 Charles Manigault was convinced that planters had learned a valuable lesson: that "the Government of our Negroes" was far too slack and that many of the slaves had "got their heads more or less turned by recent military events and intercourse with bad Negroes." At the end of the month, Louis removed more slaves from Gowrie to Silk Hope, where he intended to keep them until the declaration of peace.[48]

The identity of the twenty-three he removed is telling and a bit surprising, given the prominence of women among those identified as rebels and leaders. The original ten prime hands removed included the usual suspects but also "Jenny." And among the eighteen more removed in February 1862 were "Bess and her Infant," "Betty and infant," "Catherine," "Betty," "Amey" (Jack Savage's wife), "Louisa," "Tilla," "Polly," "Katrina," and "Kate." Fully ten of the eighteen and almost half of the total twenty-three finally removed to Silk Hope were women, two with infants. Indeed, like a lot of planters, Louis Manigault believed that women house servants were the chief conduits of political intelligence: they are "often the first to have their minds polluted with evil thoughts," he observed. His father Charles never got over the fact that when the Yankees took Charleston, "every one of our house and yard Negroes immediately left us." Indeed, his sense of betrayal by women slaves was so strong that in April 1865 he was "looking for a white woman to do the drudgery . . . resolved never to have a Negro in our house again." Like planters everywhere the Manigaults were accustomed to viewing women as laborers—and recalcitrant ones at that. Almost a third of the slaves who ran away from Gowrie before and during the war were women, and so were four of the twelve judged so incorrigible as runaways that they suffered the ultimate Manigault punishment: sale. Women were regularly found among the runaway slaves who tried to survive in swamp settlements or maroon colonies before and during the war. Dissidence was not the preserve of men alone.[49]

Discussion of slaves' politics almost always focuses on slave men, because in war it was the men whom state officials saw as a threat. But that was not how it looked to planters. None of the Manigaults ever made the mistake of underestimating the Gowrie women. Nor did they show any reluctance to deal with them roughly. Those who proved hard to break were sent to the workhouse or jail, where they were subjected to courses of professional whipping, just like the men. In 1863 William Capers found himself in a brutal struggle with Rose, the slave nurse of Louis's child, who not only resisted a whipping, she fought him, he said, "until she had not a rag of clothes on." "Before she is turned loose," Capers wrote his boss, "she will know she is a negro." Like planters all over the South, the men who managed Gowrie developed a distinct view of slave women's capacity for resistance and struggled throughout the war with the evidence of their betrayal and leadership in revolt.[50]

The plantation was a school of political instruction during the Civil War, although it was the masters who struggled to learn the lessons slaves were teaching. Jack Savage did his part. Only weeks out of a stint in the workhouse and under constant surveillance, he made a successful break in February 1862, the very night he was to be removed to Silk Hope with his wife, Amey. Savage managed to stay out for "upwards of a year . . . in the dense Carolina swamp near the McPherson plantation in company with 'Charles Lucas' [another Gowrie slave] and other runaway Negroes." In this, obviously, he had help. Jack Savage emerged from the swamp after a year, half starved, his owner said. But he stayed only a month before he threatened to run again, saying "he had not come home to be killed up with work." Manigault, whose family had owned Savage since 1839, finally sold him in the fall of 1863, allegedly to a man in Columbus, Georgia, for the hefty sum of $1,800. Rumors persisted that Savage had foiled the sale and was still in the area.[51] On Gowrie, marronage was an antislavery strategy used especially by slaves—men and women alike.

In the epic struggle of Louis Manigault and Jack Savage, sale was not the final chapter. More than two years after the Savannah River plantations fell to Sherman's troops, Louis Manigault was still exiled from Gowrie, reduced to scrounging for river news from "negroes" he bumped into in the Savannah rice mills. He did not get back to Gowrie until March 1867. But when he arrived, who was there to receive him but Jack Savage, "the last one I should have dreamt of," as he put it, advancing to meet him, hand extended in greeting.[52] "We Southerners knew nothing of the Negro character," the exiled master finally acknowledged on his one brief return to the home place. In the struggle for Gowrie, Jack Savage outlasted the master.

Like countless other planters in the eye of the Confederate storm, the Manigaults could not escape the recognition of their slaves' oppositional politics. Nor could they confine its significance to the plantation, although that was the primary terrain of struggle. After Louis moved the first ten dangerous men and women to Silk Hope in November 1861, his brother Gabriel hastened up there, worried that "if not rigidly watched" they were "likely to be talking sedition to the others." Something had indeed gone seriously awry with "the Government of our Negroes."[53] In the Civil War on the Manigault plantation, "the people" were in rebellion against the masters' state, and the masters knew it.

Almost everywhere after Lincoln's election, slaves' willingness to fight their masters increased. The plantation quickly emerged as a crucial site of local politics across the Civil War South: crucial because there "the people" taught the masters some hard lessons about the relevance of their own politics in the war; crucial also because the intensely local politics of masters and slaves shaped and bedeviled Confederate military policy from the outset of war down to its radical modification in 1864 and 1865. It was on plantations and farms that the pressures of the Confederate project registered first. Despite official talk about slaves as an element of strength, planters struggled with evidence of a different sort, in epidemics of sedition that preceded, and continued in the wake of, slaves' "stampedes" to the enemy. The volatility of the military situation introduced dangers on all sides. In many places it was not long before planters were stripped of all illusion about slaves' passivity and became well tutored in their intentions to pursue all avenues war offered for the destruction of slavery and the masters' state.

There was infinite variety to the way the process unfolded in the vastness of Confederate territory, much of it calibrated in relation to the positions of Union and Confederate troops, to be sure, but also to the temperaments of individual masters and slaves.[54] Still, from everywhere from Virginia to Texas in the spring of 1861 came reports about "the alarming attitude of our slave population" and about "signs of insurrection." As the mania for volunteering reached its height and thousands of white men were deployed out of their neighborhoods, the shift in the balance of power was not lost on anyone, enslaved or free. Slaveholders and local officials reported unprecedented levels of slave activity, discerning evidence of all sorts that slaves were poised for action. Violence and surveillance had always been central to the operations of the slave regime. In 1861 planters everywhere became anxious about drawing off too many men and losing the means to keep the "negroes in subjection." One Alabama planter expressed his concern about too much volunteering to President Davis in May, warning that one-third of the voters in his county were already in the field and beseeching him on "behalf of the women and children of our county" to instruct the War Department to receive no more of their troops. "We need the remainder of them to keep the slaves down," he pressed Davis, "and save ourselves from the horrors of insurrection, which may be incident of war." The battle with military officials over the recruitment and deployment of troops began then and never let up. If the protection of women was the avowed reason, that was because planters expected their plantations to become the site of war. From the outset, Confederates prepared to wage war on two fronts.[55]

Their fears were not unfounded. Charges of slave insurrection were ubiquitous. In the area of Second Creek and Natchez in Adams County, Mississippi, in the spring of 1861 a group of planters came to the conclusion that a significant number of slaves, draymen prominent among them, were organizing militarily for their own war. Worry surfaced as early as May, when one planter wrote the governor of Mississippi about a planned "outbreak," urging him to retain as many troops as possible in the river counties. The fears did not subside. In September local planters undertook an "examination" and extracted, almost certainly by torture, a whole series of testimonies from slave men implicated in the plot.[56] The terms of what emerged highlight the convergence of planter fears and slave opportunity. This was a slave insurrection plot with a difference, and the difference was the political context.

What emerged from "testimony" is a picture of slaves' organizing to take advantage of the new local balance of power. A planter reported that the "insurrection"—slaves referred to it as "the war"—was first discussed by the slaves "on the night of the 14th of April 1861 as they came up the hill from sending the Quitman Light Artillery off." This, just two nights after the firing on Fort Sumter, was a propitious moment for slaves, to be sure, and a worrisome one for heavily outnumbered slaveholders. But if the departure of the whites was one circumstance, the anticipated arrival of Union troops was equally relevant. For the confessions extracted under torture confirmed that the slaves involved—from at least eight plantations in a fifteen-mile radius—were trying to coordinate the timing of their "war" on the whites in relation to the arrival of enemy troops. The slaves even claimed to have received dispatches from the enemy. One reported vaguely that they planned "to kill the white folks when the Northern Army got to Natchey." But Orange, the man identified as the leader, claimed more precise information that "[General] Scott would be here [in Natchez] 10th Sept." In that, Orange and the other slaves were drawing on the same rumors of imminent invasion in which local whites trafficked. As always rumor crossed the color line. Amelia Montgomery, a plantation mistress at neighboring Belmont, wrote her husband in panic in early October that "New Orleans is in immediate danger of falling to Yankees" and Natchez with it. They were all wrong, of course. There would be no Union occupation until April 1862. But in September 1861 one implicated slave claimed only to repeat "what the white man said—that Genl Scott would eat his breakfast in New Orleans" around September 10.[57]

With that information some slaves in Second Creek began "talking of freedom . . . rais[ing] a company," collecting arms, and getting ready to "fight the white people" with axes and hoes. The company appeared to involve organizing sworn members into ranks variously as governor, general, captain, lieutenant, even "head," titles that combined labor with political and military hierarchies. Their goal was to fight their way to a new condition of "freedom." Along the way they planned to settle some old scores. Nelson planned to rape Miss Mary "because she poured water on his daughter." Another offered as his reason to join that "Master whips our children." Wounds to children were much on the minds of Second Creek men. Harry Scott said "Hell kicking up." "Orange says whipping colored people would stop." So it poured out. The grievances were old but the possibilities new: "Simon said the Northerners make the South shit behind their asses."[58] At Second Creek the rumors of impending Union invasion worked on black and white alike, and converged, as in many other places, in insurrection. Whites dreading the arrival of Union troops feared, and eventually uncovered, a slave insurrection; slaves hopeful of their arrival organized for that eventuality.[59]

The anticipated approach of the Northerners did change a few things in the vicinity of Second Creek, Mississippi. Slaves increased their planning and activity, and slaveholders unleashed a campaign of violence. They hanged ten on September 24, but the repression continued into 1862 as Confederate slaveholders attempted to stamp out black underground networks and dissent. Years later local slaves and freedpeople insisted to anyone who would listen that the Second Creek slaves were executed not for plotting insurrection but for Union sympathy.[60] To Confederate planters that was a distinction hardly worth making: Union sympathy was petty treason, the plantation version of rebellion against the state. Events at Second Creek confirmed what slaves were up against in their war against the slaveholders and what internal enemies slaveholders had to contend with in their war against the Union.

In other places, of course, slaves' plans to coordinate with enemy advances were not just made but executed. In those instances, planters' unwelcome knowledge of the lengths to which slaves went to meet the enemy obliterated proslavery fictions of passivity and loyalty and propelled them into a frontal acknowledgment of slaves' will for freedom. Such episodes are significant in and of themselves because they represent a stunning moment of truth in the history of American slavery, but also because of the way they informed slaveholders' responses to state demands in the formulation of military policy and prosecution of the war.[61]

One such drama played out up and down the Atlantic coast between May 1861 when the federal fleet captured Fortress Monroe on the tip of the Virginia peninsula and November when they took Hilton Head, South Carolina. By the early part of 1862, coastal areas of Virginia, North Carolina, South Carolina, Georgia, and Florida were all under Union occupation and plantation districts on the periphery of the Union zone were under constant threat of invasion. With federal gunboats steaming up and down low-country rivers, slaves could hazard attempts to reach Union lines. Indeed, Union general Benjamin Butler had no sooner taken command of Fortress Monroe in May 1861, when a scouting party of slave men managed to make it by boat to the fort, where they inquired about the commander's receptivity to fugitives. They had come, they told him, from the Confederate batteries at Sewall's Point. A few days later another "squad" came in, this time "bringing," as Butler put it, "their women and children." Alert to the advantage such defections represented, Butler not only let them stay but began to justify their status as "contrabands," property confiscated to deny the Confederate government use of it as labor in support of the rebellion.[62]

Near Hilton Head, South Carolina, where the Union fleet landed in early November 1861, slaves knew it was coming. In the days before the landing, as the fleet massed in Port Royal Sound, slaves impressed for military labor went singing down to Hilton Head to build fortifications they hoped would prove inadequate. South Carolina fire-eaters had sworn that their slaves would "drive out the Yankees," but instead the slaves did everything in their power to join forces with them. Resisting their owners' attempts to herd them onto the Beaufort ferry, slaves pushed off to the Union boats in their own canoes, took off for the woods and swamps, or just sank down low into the tall corn rows until their panicked masters gave up and left. Then in a pattern much like that of the north plain of Saint-Domingue in 1791, they sacked the plantations and town houses so the owners had nothing to return to. When Union troops arrived, slaves told terrible stories of masters who burned their slaves to death in their cotton houses rather than leave them for the Yankees, or shot them as they ran for the woods.[63]

William Elliott knew his slaves were active parties in his loss. Scion of the great Beaufort planter family, he owned two plantations on Port Royal Island and another on the mainland. For the five days, between the time the Union fleet arrived off Hilton Head until they disembarked troops, slaves on his Port Royal plantations were insubordinate, refusing to work, and "communicating with the enemy," a point confirmed by Union officials. His attempt to get Confederate forces detailed to help him control his slaves was futile, and he had to abandon his plantations, slaves and all, and retreat inland. Elliott's slaves stayed put to welcome their Union allies. William complained bitterly to a commander stationed nearby about the abandonment of the Beaufort planters by the Confederate military. By that point, he admitted with no apparent irony, he needed an army to control his slaves. Unless the Confederate army was deployed against them, he argued, "every able bodied negro man" would go over to the enemy and become a "recruit in his ranks."[64] Already by 1861, planters in the coastal zones were in conflict with Confederate military authorities over which enemy to array their army against.

Further inland, on the periphery of the Union-occupation zone, slavery hung on in some places as it did on Gowrie, until virtually the end of the war, in others for a year, or two years. The excruciating contingency of the process was an essential aspect of the Civil War, setting the destinies of slaves, masters, and to some extent the Confederate military and nation. From the minute the Union took Hilton Head, the area just back of the islands on the mainland, including the Grove, John Berkley Grimball's plantation in Colleton district, was on military alert. "I find everything up here on a military footing," Grimball noted on November 12, 1861, "pickets at the landing at night, the Home Guard about in all directions." By December, as Union troops moved northward toward Charleston, a company of South Carolina troops was stationed on Pineberry, the smaller of Grimball's two plantations. Slaves on the Grove knew the Union army had landed; they also knew that planters were making preparations to remove them inland. Slaves had always operated in a police environment: Grimball retained a private police force to hunt runaway slaves in addition to the slave patrol.[65] But with Confederate troops massing in areas of Union advance, the slaves' historic opportunities were matched by escalated danger. Slaves in the orbit of Union and Confederate troops operated in a militarized zone.

Slaves were not, however, the only ones contending with the Confederate military. Operations on Grimball's plantations were fundamentally disordered, not least because Grimball now operated under the authority of local military officials. A company of South Carolina troops was stationed on his place. The state had established a beachhead on his plantation, interposing a substantial authority between him and his slaves. He did not take well to that, and his resistance to their orders for removal of his slaves cost him dearly. He complied with the requisitions for slaves to work on fortifications, and of his flatboats and carts to haul materials. But when Grimball began to receive recommendations, and then direct orders, for planters "to remove their negroes from the threatened sections," presumably because the slaves would go to the enemy, he dragged his feet. "To move or to stay seems to be equally ruinous to my prospects," he wrote. "I have never been more harassed and perplexed in my life—the future for me as black as night—nothing visible but impending poverty."[66] As his neighbors evacuated, as Confederate troops swarmed around the Grove, he dithered, every bad piece of news for him received no doubt with jubilation by the 140 or so slaves on the Grove and Pineberry plantations. Where he saw darkness, they surely saw light.

On the Grove, the slaves made the first and decisive move. On March 3, as Grimball sat down to dinner in his elegant Charleston townhouse, his slave man arrived with the news that eighty slaves had fled the plantation overnight. "Nearly all the Negroes—and the best of them," he recorded that night, "about 80 of them according to Adams account—men women & children. He says that the pickets reported that a Steamer had come up to Jehosses mill during the night—and that Mr. Carroll [the overseer] on being informed—went out to hurry the Negroes to a place of safety but found them already gone—they may have gone in the Steamer."[67] This was clearly a collective undertaking, preceded by extensive communication and planning, and executed with stealth. The Grimball slaves' knowledge of events—their network of information—and perhaps even their ability to shape them, had proved superior to that of the Confederate military, the white overseer, and their owner.

Similar mass escapes occurred at the same time and the following year when the Union again raided up the Pon Pon River. In some of those raids, as Union and Confederate officials confirmed, gunboats had moved on specific intelligence about Confederate troop movements provided by local slaves. The Confederate officer in charge of investigating the 1862 raid on the Pon Pon concluded that slaves had been in communication with the enemy. "The enemy seems to have been well posted as to the character and capacity of our troops and . . . well guided by persons thoroughly acquainted with the river and the county. Their success was complete." The masters' education in slaves' politics was painful, and Grimball detailed his in a series of compulsive lists. In 1862 and again in 1863 when his father-in-law's slaves also managed a mass escape, Grimball struggled with financial and cognitive collapse. Like a man picking through the ruins of a house after a bomb blast, he made and annotated lists of "those that remain," the sixty or so slaves who had not hazarded the run to the steamer. On March 8 he made a list "of the Negroes belonging to J. B. Grimball who left the Grove and Pineberry Plantation on the night of the 2nd March 1862 and deserted [an appropriately military term] to the Yankees at Edisto Island." Again on March 12 he made a list "of my absconding negroes." Grimball was worried that the slaves had ruined him financially. But his distress went beyond the financial. "This is a terrible blow," he admitted. But it was his wife who took the proper measure of it all: "Mr. Grimball is quite unstrung by it," she said.[68]

There was little comforting to Grimball in the patterns discerned in those lists, but much of interest to those attempting to grasp the extent and nature of slave insurrection in the American Civil War. On the Pon Pon a whole people got up and left. On the Grove, the youngest to depart was a baby, just two months old, carried in her mother's arms, the oldest a slave of 62. Eighteen were children under 15 years of age. Indeed, the group included virtually every family formation imaginable. The families in the exodus were mostly two-generational, including grown children and their parents. There were mothers and children: Daphne, a 45-year-old woman, and her children, one son aged 13 and a daughter aged 18; Affy, who was 40 years old, and her three sons, one touchingly called "hard times." There were fathers and their children: Poyas John, who was 38, and his daughter Julia, who was only 10. Siblings stuck together, Isaac who was 35 leading his younger brother and two sisters; Rose who left with her son and younger sister, who were her whole family. Sons took their aged mothers, as did Richard who took Old Tyrah. In Grimball's lists virtually every family group could be seen, except, strangely enough, husband and wife. Meta Morris Grimball noticed the pattern: "Wives leave their husbands, the men their wives, but they all seem to cling to their children."[69]

In the first big exodus from the Grove, many of the slaves braved Confederate pickets to make the dangerous run to the gunboat and the unknown existence that awaited down the Edisto River. Women were just as likely to take that risk as men. When morning came, more than half of the women on the Grove had gone. Grimball was especially distressed by the disappearance of Kit, the cook, who was, he noted scathingly, the first to go off: she absconded from town on November 11, 1861, just days after the federal fleet arrived. And the whole family obsessed over Diana, one of his father-in-law's slaves, whose decision to leave her husband behind in another mass escape a year later seemed somehow to hold the key to the whole affair.[70]

Whatever the particulars, it is the pattern that speaks most powerfully. For it directs attention to the central role slave women played in the destruction of slavery on Confederate plantations during the Civil War, a part rarely registered by the military authorities or the historians who rely on their records. It was obvious to all on the Grove on the morning of March 3, 1862, and to the federal authorities who received them on the boat, that women were at the very center of slaves' political networks and strategies of resistance, as much a part of the destruction of slavery as men were. That was as true of the Civil War South as it was of every other slave rebellion or liberation struggle in the slave zone in the late eighteenth and nineteenth centuries. In Saint-Domingue, Guadeloupe, Jamaica, Cuba, and elsewhere, women were "equal and active participants in . . . insurrectionary conspiracies," party to all of the tactics used by slaves, not excluding membership in armed maroon bands. Nor were women spared the violence that everywhere attended resistance. In Saint-Domingue, women regularly showed up on lists of rebels and leaders, including those targeted for execution, just as the women on Gowrie, the Grove, and other Civil War plantations were not spared the retributive violence of planters, Confederate guerillas, and the military.[71]

That dimension of slave emancipation would be lost as state authorities' competition for the military labor of slave men came to dominate events. Even as contraband policy was formulated during the war, Union authorities began to construct the "contraband"—and thus "the slaves in rebellion"—as male, a process that masculinized the emancipation struggle and conceived of women as dependent parties or political minors in it. The view from plantations like Gowrie or the Grove is thus significant, not least because it affords a strikingly different perspective from the statist one.[72]

In 1863 John Berkley Grimball had his real moment of truth. Faced with another mass escape of slaves, this time from his father-in-law's plantation, Grimball's desperate attempts to insist that they had "been taken off" by the Yankees collapsed. Meta Morris Grimball stopped talking about slaves being forced off and finally admitted what they all now knew: the slaves wanted freedom. "The poor creatures have all gone wild with the idea of being free." Slaves on the Pon Pon River had left their putative owners no illusions about their intention to adhere to the nation's enemies and destroy slavery in the process.[73] Grimball's investment in the Confederate project of perpetuating slavery for future generations was destroyed. In 1863 he sold his remaining slaves. His, at least, would not count as an element of strength in war. So even as Confederate military officials went on demanding slaves, executing orders of impressment, planters like Grimball struggled to contend with the forces secession and war had unleashed, not least of which was the new salience of their slaves' politics and adherence to their enemies.

The strategies slaves used in plantation politics differed by region. In the South Carolina or Georgia low country, slaves could make contact with the Union navy and arrange a mass exodus from a plantation. That was much harder in places like the Upper South, where even if the Union army was willing, slaves were often dispersed across a landscape of much smaller farms. But Virginia was different, too, because it was, as nowhere else, the seat of war, and with two massive armies encamped on the peninsula, and numerous smaller ones contending for control of the critical Shenandoah Valley, slaves and masters alike faced complex considerations about how to act in relation to the location of enemy armies. In places like Winchester, which changed hands as many as seventy times during the war, everyone read the movement of the armies as the only reliable indicator of their own prospects. Slaveholders tried to move their slaves into safe Confederate areas, but in Virginia, and especially in the valley, that was almost impossible. Areas that were safe one month, or even one day, were occupied the next. For enslaved men, women, and children, life in the very vortex of war demanded the utmost in political intelligence and skill. For Virginia slaves, as later for those in the Mississippi Valley, the proximity of the Union army in the Confederate interior meant heightened danger but also powerful and proximate allies. The fugitive slave who returned to his elderly master's house to reclaim his wife and children and brought the federal cavalry with him delivered a blunt message about the future of slavery. Flourishing his sword over the old man's head, he declared that "he now had the power and intended to use it."[74]

In 1862 and 1863, especially after the Emancipation Proclamation, slaves struggled to harness, and masters to contain, the volatile new possibilities of political life in the war zone. Sometimes the rhythms of ordinary life gave way within seconds to moments of world-historical significance. There was one such moment on a farm near Berryville, Virginia, in February 1863. The owner was Sigismunda Stribling Kimball, the slaveholding woman whose family owned two farms in the vicinity. With her husband deployed nearby in the valley in Stonewall Jackson's army, she and her elderly relatives were left to run the farms and control the slaves on them. That was no easy task, for Berryville was only about eight miles from Winchester, and in 1862 and 1863 Kimball's farm was occupied alternately by two armies. In early November 1862, Confederate troops were quartered on her farm; in late November, Yankees were. Turnovers were quick: "We are again in Dixie," she wrote ecstatically on December 6; "Yankees in Berryville," gloomily on December 27.[75]

The slaves in Kimball's household understandably proceeded with caution. Their very household was a militarized zone, and even Union soldiers when encamped there were hardly predictable allies. Indeed, in April 1862, during a period of Union occupation, their mistress was one of the women who had succeeded in getting orders of protection from the local Union commander, Colonel McDowell, who posted a five-man guard at her gate "to protect us" from a marauding unit of Michigan cavalry. The men and women enslaved on Kimball's farm surely learned, as did she, that the soldiers posted were "no abolitionist[s]" and had no stomach for a war of emancipation. But they would also have learned that the troops had recently been read an order from the U.S. secretary of war instructing all of them "that fugitives should not be returned to their masters." Mixed but promising messages. Unsure about the reception they would receive, slaves on Kimball's farm appear to have bided their time through at least three different periods when the locality changed hands. The first ones to claim a tenuous freedom in attachment to the Union army made their move only when General Banks, Colonel McDowell, and their men were forced to retreat from Berryville to Winchester in April 1862 and then from Winchester after two months of Union occupation. Perhaps thinking it was their last chance, some felt they had to make a choice, and three of Kimball's slaves, all men, took off, one stealing a wagon and two horses, which he used to gather up family members from two other farms in the neighborhood before he "put off to Winchester." It seemed to be a family exodus, but given the marital and family patterns of Upper South slaves, it was imperfectly accomplished before the window of opportunity closed and they were "again in Dixie," as Kimball crowed.[76]

But the real drama of emancipation on Sigismunda Kimball's farm came six months later when Kimball's slaves or their relatives returned, fully possessed of the awesome power of the Union state: the Emancipation Proclamation and troops to enforce it. Then, in what can only be called a moment of truth, Kimball was instructed in the new terms on which the struggle with her slaves was henceforth to be conducted. High drama it was, too, in late January 1863 when the Yankees rode back in and white Union soldiers "piloted by negro men" appeared at local plantations with official orders to remove the men's wives and children. Rumors flew around the neighborhood of slaves seized by orders of General Milroy. Kimball noted one such set of orders sent to her neighbor to "release to Mr. John Washington his wife and six children . . . persons once slaves but now free by the president's proclamation of January 1st." The strategy was not confined to Virginia. In other places where slaves could reach the Union army, they tried to enlist white soldiers in their project of liberating family members. One slave in Florida wrote a Union general providing directions to the plantation on which three generations of his family were held, asking him the "small favor" of detouring his troops by there. "Sir it isent mor then three or four Hours trubel . . . Sir, my Farthers Name Adam Harris he will Call them all to gether & tel him to take Cousan janes childarn with hime."[77] In Berryville it was rare to find three generations on one plantation. But in Berryville, unlike some other parts of the Confederacy, the Emancipation Proclamation had immediate local meaning.

Two weeks after her neighbor, it was Kimball's turn. On February 24, 1863, two Yankees piloted by two enslaved men she knew appeared in her yard with a wagon, "dashed up to the Negro house," and began to load other slaves onto the wagon. Kimball's mother went to the door because Kimball was, she said, "too mad to speak." "Mother said, I would like to ask what you came for. He replied, pointing to William [a slave who belonged to a neighbor] I came to take that man's brother's wife away," pointing now to Farinda, Kimball's slave, whose husband Phill had run to the Yankees the previous week and sent his brother back with troops to get her. "By what authority," Kimball said, asking the million-dollar question. "The authority of the Commanding General, Gen. Milroy," the officer answered. Milroy "has no right to take them," Kimball stormed, "they do not belong to him." "O," he replied, a historical transformation condensed in a second, "they do not belong to any one, the government has fixed that." And with that he hitched up four horses to a wagon, put Farinda and her child in, and prepared to go. Asked by the white soldiers what she wanted to take of plantation property, Farinda—in her one appearance in the historical record as the teller of her own tale—replied memorably that "she did not want anything but herself."[78]

Some slaves would continue to bide their time, lacking confidence in Union motives or anticipating reversals that could turn deadly. Kimball smugly recounted the interview between the Yankees and her elderly slave man George, who when asked why he did not go North reportedly said, "There are more people north now than ought to be there." Folks had plenty of reasons to stay put. One South Carolina woman explained that she could not leave because her master had her teenage son hidden away in the swamp. On many farms and plantations, as on Kimball's, some slaves stayed put while others went off. Of Virginia planter William Wickham's 268 slaves, 56 went off to the Yankees in 1863. As usual about 40 percent of the fugitives were women. But in Virginia, as in the coastal areas of other Atlantic states, many planters lost all their slaves to the enemy.[79]

Seizing the opportunities of war, Virginia slaves, like those on Kimball's farm, established themselves as allies of the enemy army, always and everywhere in clear pursuit of their own war aims, not least emancipation and family reconstitution.

In the seat of war such moments as those on Kimball's farm could be anything but definitive. Slaves, including Phill and Farinda, struggled desperately to stick close to the federal army, the only basis yet of any real claim to status as free persons. Theirs was a highly precarious freedom, easily revoked in the exigencies of war and, in places like the Shenandoah Valley, the constant turnover of territory. Winchester-area slaves were regularly recaptured when Confederates seized Union units and supply wagons and faced the summary justice that went with that reversal of fortune. When one Confederate soldier asked for instructions on what to do with runaways caught by his scouts, his commanding officer told him to proceed at once to hold a drumhead court-martial and if guilty to hang them on the spot. It was especially difficult for women and children whose presence in the rear of moving columns of troops or in ramshackle camps around the outskirts of encamped armies was entirely unwanted.[80]

All over the C.S.A. enslaved men and women worked toward the destruction of slavery tactically and in stages, emboldened by the post-1862 turn in Union policy that brought Union war aims more closely in line with their own. Planters, whether in Union-occupied territory, in contested territory, or in areas solidly under Confederate control, all struggled with the consequences of the diminishment of their authority and what they perceived to be the expansion of their slaves' arena of choice. To John Houston Bills, a Tennessee planter caught in the river war of 1862 and 1863, plantation life and labor went on, but he felt entirely at the mercy of his slaves' decisions: "I have got possession to day of all my servants," he wrote in September 1862. "How long they will stay out of the federal lines no one knows." "I have no confidence when all our authority is gone," he concluded. Bills tried to resign himself to a situation, common in the Mississippi Valley by mid-1862, in which planters could not rely on the state or Confederate government to back up their authority as masters. Without the means of state violence at their control, planters could hardly operate. Bills just called it a mutiny. Of the slaves he said, "Many of them I think do all they can to have us destroyed and delight in seeing the work of destruction done."[81] The mutiny played out in a multitude of ways, but few Confederate masters would have doubted the truth of Bills's observation.

The plantation emerged as a critical site of Civil War politics because it grounded a struggle that radiated out and up through the various levels of power and sovereignty in the C.S.A. The war between slaves and masters on Confederate plantations could hardly be contained to those allegedly private domains. From the earliest signs of trouble, planters had expected the army to buttress their authority as masters and had railed against particular commanders when they did not. In southern Louisiana after the fall of New Orleans in April 1862, and in the Mississippi Valley with the fall of Forts Henry and Donelson in February 1862, slaves' resistance to their masters and adherence to the enemy assumed such proportions that planters looked desperately to the military power of the Confederate state to shore up their crumbling authority. Then slaves' oppositional politics began to register off the plantations, and plantation politics became a matter of public concern. At that moment, planters abandoned their usual claims to domestic sovereignty and, like Bills, acknowledged the critical role the state had always played in securing the means of violence by which they asserted personal domination. Offering a sorry tale of openly insubordinate slaves refusing to work and claiming control of local plantations, one Louisiana planter explained to a local Union officer, "Our family has owned negroes for generations and we never before had any difficulty with them being supported by the government, but now that the government in the parish of Plaquemines . . . is turned against us, we have no one but yourself and Genls Shepley and Butler to protect us against these negroes in a state of insurrection." State power had always been crucial to the maintenance of slavery and slaveholders' power: it was not a good sign for the government of the C.S.A. that these and other southern Louisiana planters cared not which state protected them, so long as their property in slaves was sustained. As elsewhere in the hemisphere, war wreaked havoc on masters' claims to sovereignty.[82]

It certainly made for high drama that among those Mississippi and

Louisiana plantations in a state of insurrection were ones owned by high-ranking Confederate officials—General Braxton Bragg, Governor Thomas O. Moore of Louisiana, and President Davis himself among them. That was surely inevitable in a Confederate republic in which the interests of Confederate slaveholders merged into the persons of its statesmen-politicians so fully that they were, for all intents and purposes, one and the same. General Robert E. Lee suffered the occupation and confiscation of his plantation in Alexandria, Virginia, early in the war and had to watch it turned into a contraband camp and freedmen's village. When the Union army opened the Mississippi River to invasion in 1862, key Confederate politicians and military men struggled to answer the blow in their private and public capacities simultaneously. Then planters' recognition of slaves' anti-Confederate politics necessarily reached the highest levels of state authority and left planter-statesmen and military men contending with the challenge it issued to their plans to make slaves an element of strength in the war. In Mississippi and Louisiana, few doubted that the war had become a slave rebellion.

After the fall of New Orleans, the situation in Mississippi and Louisiana was complex in the extreme for slaves and masters. As the Union army exerted control over most of the Mississippi River, occupied territory on both sides of the river, waged campaigns to extend that territory, and sent detachments of troops out scouting for black laborers on outlying plantations, the entire region became a patchwork of Union and Confederate land, a two-state state that, for slaves, represented opportunity and danger in about equal measure.

In Mississippi, the state government was on the run, shifting the capital from Jackson to the small town of Macon, then to Columbus, and again to Meridian, the territory and number of citizens under its control shrinking by at least a third. In Louisiana, too, whole swaths of the state fell into Union hands: the city of New Orleans, the surrounding sugar parishes, and areas adjacent to the Mississippi River by the summer of 1862, parts of central Louisiana as well by the next summer. But in the Mississippi Valley, not only was the landscape divided between enemy states and armies; before January 1, 1863, Union policy toward slaves was in such a state of flux that fugitive slaves might find allies in one Union camp but be turned away from another. One officer manning the lines entering Camp Parapet four miles above New Orleans sought advice from his commander about what to do with the slaves gathering near the upper picket station on the river road who sought admission: men, women, and children, he said, now destitute, who had come from various points within a one hundred mile range. The slaves had come to the right place. The camp commander, Brigadier General J. W. Phelps, was a known abolitionist who saw the harboring of fugitive slaves as part of the process by which slavery would be destroyed and the authority of the national government extended over all its subjects. But in admitting slaves to camp, and later in arming black male fugitives for service as soldiers, Phelps acted against Union policy and, constantly thwarted by his superiors, he finally resigned, declaring that he would not serve "as a mere slave driver." Even at Camp Parapet, an abolitionist stronghold, slaves were not safe from recapture or return.

Nor did the Emancipation Proclamation resolve the dilemma, because the southern Louisiana parishes, with their cohort of Unionist sugar planters, were officially exempt from its provisions. Planters there might appeal to Union commanders to return their slaves or assist in putting down rebellion on their plantations. But they might also find themselves appealing to the wrong officer at the wrong moment. They might also simply arrive one day to find their plantations overtaken by the combined forces of their own slaves and Union soldiers, their slaves mostly gone, big houses sacked, plantations inoperable, and slavery effectively destroyed.[83]

As elsewhere, in the Mississippi Valley the fundamental contest between states and armies registered first and intensely in the politics of masters and slaves on individual plantations. One such plantation belonged to Confederate General Braxton Bragg, the highly unpopular commander of the Army of Tennessee. While Bragg was preparing for an anticipated battle in Tennessee in November 1862, his plantation just north of New Orleans was seized by enemy troops and fugitive slaves; then his own slaves seized their chance. With symptoms of "servile insurrection . . . becoming apparent," as the local commander put it, and planters "in terror of a general rising," Mrs. Bragg appealed to U.S. Brigadier General G. Weitzel for protection from her own slaves. It was a nervy move for a high-ranking Confederate general's wife. Weitzel was inclined to oblige; he wanted to send out troops to put the slaves down. But Weitzel's superior, George C. Strong, said sharply that he was putting down the wrong rebellion. Turning aside concerns about slave rebellion and terrified women and children, Strong reminded Weitzel that he was in a country in which the blacks outnumbered the whites by ten to one, and in which the whites "are in rebellion against the Government or in terror seeking its protection." When rebels laid down their arms against the United States and called upon its army for protection, they will get it, he raged, "because from that moment between them and him war would cease." Until that time, Mrs. Bragg was on her own.[84] Sometimes the personal struggles of planters with their slaves had public meanings so obvious they resonated all the way through the system.

That was certainly the case across the river in Mississippi, where the most dramatic plantation battle played out for all the world to see. Starting in May 1862, Jefferson Davis watched helplessly from Richmond as his elder brother, Joseph, struggled vainly to beat back the challenge of their slaves' bid for freedom in the maelstrom of the war his state's secessionist action had brought on. Davis and his brother were longtime owners of a pair of plantations located in a bend of the Mississippi River—Davis Bend as it was called—twenty miles below Vicksburg. As early as February 1862, President Davis's worries about the fate of the Confederate west was tied up with concern about his own home and property. In February, noting his special vulnerability to enemy attack, he urged his brother to remove their slaves and all their valuables (cotton included) into the interior of Mississippi, should a descent of the river be attempted by the federals. In May, after the fall of New Orleans, Joseph removed the family and so-called "family slaves"—house slaves presumably—to Vicksburg by flat boat, initiating a forced migration that eventually took him to Choctaw County, Alabama.[85]

Then the Davis slaves made their move, responding not to the immediate presence of the Union army (which was not yet near), but to the signal Joseph Davis had sent about the shifting balance of power. No sooner had Joseph pushed off from the dock than the remaining slaves seized control of the two plantations, sacking the big house on Hurricane, destroying the cotton, carrying off every article of value, and refusing to work. They would retain control of the plantation, indeed would refuse to be forced off even later by federal troops, seizing a rough-and-ready freedom while still on their home plantation.[86] On Davis Bend, the slaves moved not with, but in advance of, the arrival of Union troops. By the end of May 1862, Jefferson and Varina Davis received a series of lurid accounts of events on Brierfield. "Negroes at Brierfield . . . said to be in a state of insubordination," one telegram said. Charles Mitchell, a nephew-in-law, was even more blunt, offering Davis an account of his slaves' refusal to work or submit to the overseers who were still resident on the plantation, or to any attempt to carry them inland. They had declared "that on no conditions would they agree to leave the places." All of a sudden, as John Houston Bills had said, slaves were exercising their right to decide. With still no Yankees in sight, some of the Brierfield slaves ventured to the Union navy's boats stationed below Vicksburg, undoubtedly to check out their reception by potential but, as they discovered (when they were turned away), unreliable allies. Nonetheless, Mitchell said, "I am sorry to say that I think the Yankees would be offered any facilities in the power of the negroes to grant on your place and the Hurricane." "The negroes and their friends the Yankees," was how Mitchell described the new alliance sought by the Brierfield slaves with the enemy of their master, the Confederate president.[87]

The men, women, and children held as slaves of Jefferson Davis would fight on during the war. Some left with the Union army when a raiding party arrived seeking to carry off male slaves to the army. As on so many Mississippi River plantations, men and women both left; "their departure was sudden and in the night," Joseph told his brother. But even after Vicksburg fell they were still at risk. Joseph never quit scheming about how he could remove them to safer Confederate territory. He even tried to convince General Van Dorn to detail troops to capture Union marauders and liberate the plantations at Davis Bend. And indeed, at least fifteen Davis slaves were recaptured in a raid by a detachment of Confederate troops. The slaves did not go easily. Some were killed in the raid, to Joseph Davis's horror. The raiders reported that the Brierfield slaves shot at them as they approached from the river. The plantations apparently now included among their residents a party of sixty armed blacks led by a Captain Horace and a Captain Henry. Much in the way slaves in Second Creek had imagined it would be, the slaves at Davis Bend knew it would take military force and organization to claim freedom in Civil War Mississippi. The Confederate lieutenant who led the raid insisted that almost all the slaves on the Davis plantations had guns and newspapers, the requisite armaments of a people at war. Having claimed a tenuous freedom in the wake of their owners' flight, in a no-man's land of state authority, Jefferson Davis's slaves had obviously prepared to defend it by force of arms.[88]

While the battle was raging, Jefferson Davis retained his composure, at least publicly. But the blow had to have been staggering. His slaves had led federal soldiers to the farm where his private family possessions were concealed, despoiling his property and pointing out place after place where his valuables were hidden. A crowd of thousands (so it was said) had gathered to watch the boxes torn open and emptied of their contents, books and papers strewn all over the yard and through the woods for miles, fine carpets cut to pieces and carried off for saddle blankets, everything "plundered and destroyed with a ruthlessness worthy of Attila himself." His image—the image of the Confederate president—had been desecrated by Union soldiers who stabbed it repeatedly with a knife, items had subsequently been sold at the Great Western Sanitary Fair in Cincinnati, and the Brierfield slaves had celebrated the fourth of July alongside, not their masters, but the "school marms and other disciples of the Freedman's cause." Davis and his neighbors had been reduced to reading about events at Brierfield through clippings from the *Vicksburg Daily Herald*.[89]

The effects of Jefferson Davis's—and the nation's—trial over slavery would eventually register in official policy, in the acknowledgment of the necessity to secure the loyalty of slave men to the Confederate state. But that would come later, when his slaves had won the battle on Brierfield and Jefferson Davis was no longer Massa Davis. In 1862 and 1863, before the Union army took Vicksburg, Jefferson Davis stuck to the official proslavery story about slaves' fidelity to their masters. Until his abrupt *volte-face* in 1864, Davis reserved the term *slave insurrection* strictly for Lincoln and his government, charging repeatedly that they were "engaged in exciting servile insurrection" among "peaceful and contented laborers." Never mind that the slaves on Brierfield and Hurricane, as in so many other places in South Carolina, Louisiana, Mississippi, and elsewhere, had acted in advance of the arrival of Union troops in their areas. It was a calculated bid for foreign recognition, and Davis reached for that argument repeatedly in his addresses to the Confederate Congress. In January 1863, just days after its promulgation, he denounced the Emancipation Proclamation in an address to the Senate and House of Representatives, calling those who would execute the law criminals subject to prosecution. A year later he denounced it again as "a mere brutem fulmen." "President Lincoln has sought to convert the South into a San Domingo by appealing to the cupidity, lusts, ambition, and ferocity of the slave," he raged, his dangerous invocation of Saint-Domingue cutting decisively against his continued insistence on the fidelity of the slave (always carefully singular) and showing just how close he came, in this post-Brierfield moment, to acknowledging the slaves as actors in the drama of emancipation.[90]

But if President Davis struggled, implausibly, to adhere to the orthodox view of slaves as loyal to their masters, few of his planter neighbors in the Mississippi Valley were buying it. And like Union and Confederate officials with responsibility for administering the region, they all called it what it was: a slave rebellion. Governor Moore of Louisiana suffered a similar personal assault on his authority as master of his Red River plantation. His slaves seized control of the plantation as soon as the overseers left in fear of a Yankee raid, conducted a weeklong "jubilee" during which they sacked the plantation, and then suffered through Confederate military reoccupation of the neighborhood, the reinstitution of plantation labor, and the hunting of fugitive slaves by the Confederate cavalry.[91] Needless to say, in Governor Moore's neighborhood proslavery pieties were abandoned as so much old junk; there, planters had too much knowledge of what happened when vigilance slackened even momentarily or the balance of power appeared likely to shift.

In Rapides Parish, the local newspaper made no bones about the blow that slaves had struck or about the fact that this was no longer a private matter. "The uppermost thought in every one's mind before the Yankee invasion of our Parish was what will be the conduct of the slaves," the *Alexandria Louisiana Democrat* wrote in the aftermath. Now that they knew, the question became "What conduct are we to pursue to them?" Faced with slaves who had "taken possession of their masters' property, pointed his place of refuge out to the enemy . . . voluntarily acted as guides to them in their marauding overspreading of our country," or were "seen armed or participat[ing] in active demonstrations," the editor called for a military commission to mete out justice. "It may be said that each individual owner will be the best judge of the matter of his slaves' offences and the best executioner of his sentence," the editor opined, but "this is a matter of too much public concern to be left to such uncertain control."[92] Events in Governor Moore's neighborhood demonstrated just how slaves' politics had become a matter of public, indeed state and military, concern. For these planters and local officials, including the governor, it was impossible to continue to think about slaves as an element of strength in war.

That the Civil War was, among other things, a massive slave rebellion seems clear in hindsight. Many at the time said so: planters whose operations were destroyed and officials on both sides, especially in Mississippi and Louisiana, for reasons particular to that region, including the scale of plantation slavery, hugely disproportionate numbers of blacks to whites, the powerful presence of enemy troops, and the sharp local memory of the great slave rebellion in Saint-Domingue. In addition to reports of "demoralization" and descriptions of jubilees, sacking, burning or seizure of plantations, punishment of captured Confederates, armed self-defense, the organization of slave companies, and massive "stampedes" to the enemy, planters in the vicinity of New Orleans also wrote Union commanders about their experience of servile outbreaks and slave insurrection using those highly charged terms. One planter ominously described cartloads of slaves coming in from the country to the city, exciting all in their path "to insurrection and mentioning Christmas as being the time set for the emancipation of the Slaves." "Already scenes similar to those . . . that were perpetrated on the Isle of St Domingo have transpired here," as another put it, no doubt for effect. John Wederstrandt, the southern Louisiana planter who sought protection from a Union officer for his sister and her children resident on his New Orleans area plantation, said matter-of-factly that in his parish of Plaquemines the "negroes were in a state of insurrection."[93]

But for bluntness and perspicacity, few matched Union Major George C. Strong, who offered a brilliantly clear statement about the relationship of war and emancipation in the Civil War South. To the argument that the white community had already experienced several "outbreaks" and lived in "hourly expectation and terror of a general rising" since the arrival of black troops, General Strong retorted, "Have you not mistaken the cause?" "Is it the arrival of a negro regiment, or is it the arrival of United States Troops, carrying by the Act of Congress freedom to this servile race? Did you expect to march into that country, drained, as you say it is, by conscription of all its able bodied white men, without leaving the negroes free to show symptoms of servile insurrection? Does this state of things not arise from the very fact of war itself?" It did not take black troops to incite slaves to rebellion, he pointed out: "Did you not see the same thing on the plantations here when we arrived, although under much less favorable circumstances for a revolt?" General Banks made the same point a different way: "The boldest Abolitionist is a cipher when compared with the leaders of the rebellion."[94] In southern Louisiana, at least, by 1862, Union commanders and planters seem not to have doubted that the Civil War involved a slave rebellion.

Indeed, in that region planters and Union officers often went further and spoke of the war explicitly in terms of Saint-Domingue. In doing so, of course, they meant to invoke the greatest slave rebellion in history: the one that began on the island of Saint-Domingue in 1791 in the context of the French Revolution and that not only destroyed slavery in the richest sugar colony of the Caribbean but established the first independent black republic in the hemisphere.[95] It was not only planters in Louisiana who invoked the image of Saint-Domingue. For if they did so to summon white protection against fiendish slaves, some Union officials invoked it to summon slaves to protect the Union government against planters in rebellion against its authority and sovereignty. When Adjutant General Lorenzo Thomas went to southern Louisiana in 1863 to recruit black soldiers, he cast the Union's war as a black revolution in the mold of Haiti and invoked the figure of Touissant L'Ouverture, the great black general of a slave army. In doing so, he meant to direct black men's attention to the obvious comparison between the two historical events: the Union government's willingness, like that of the French republican government, to link emancipation and black enlistment as a way to secure black men's loyalty and service to the state.[96] Evidence that the Civil War became a massive slave rebellion is to be found in every Confederate state where slaves seized the opportunity of war to rise against their masters, destroy slavery where they lived, and claim allegiance to a nation that had never really been theirs. It was not the existence of slave rebellion that makes the difference between say, South Carolina and Virginia, on the one hand, and Louisiana, on the other. It was only that in Mississippi and southern Louisiana, people were more likely to admit it and to make the searing historical analogy to Saint-Domingue.

Historians have been loath to notice the analogy deployed during the war itself and have shied away from any description of the Civil War as a slave rebellion. But that owes to the explosive politics of the analogy for slaves themselves during the war, for their leaders in the postwar period, for Union officials (charged with inciting it), and for Confederates and their lost-cause descendants bent on denying it, far more than it does to historical conditions in the Confederate South during the Civil War. It is quite true that no single movement in the Civil War South matched the scale and destructiveness of the slaves' rising on the north plain of Saint-Domingue in August 1791. But it is also true that in Saint-Domingue, as in the C.S.A., emancipation was a process, regionally uneven, temporally protracted, dynamic, and reversible, and in which the proximity to abolition armies was crucial to slaves' prospects of freedom.[97]

That was true everywhere slaves fought for and won emancipation in the context of war. In Saint-Domingue in 1791, even as the north plain went up in flames, slaves in the south and west were still mostly on their plantations; as late as 1793 there were large numbers of slave men under arms but many more men and women still enslaved on the plantations, in maroon bands in the hills, or trapped in the British-occupied zone where the sole new route to emancipation—military service—could be taken only by select men. A full four years after the revolt in the north and a year after the defeat of the Spanish and the French Republican proclamation of general emancipation, as many as sixty thousand were still slaves on plantations in the British zone.[98] The pattern held in other parts of the Americas too. In Spanish America, where slavery did not survive the wars for independence, the process of abolition nonetheless extended over forty years and was intimately tied up with military emancipation and the conditions and reversals of war itself. In Cuba, in historical conditions most like those in the C.S.A., emancipation came late, after the defeat of

Confederate slaveholders and any hopes of Cuban planters' salvation by annexation. But still it came slowly and unevenly, first in the eastern part of the island where anticolonial insurgents offered emancipation in exchange for military service, and much later and in proximity to insurgent armies in the western sugar districts where planters and the Spanish state were forced into a competition for the military services of slave men, and where they fought emancipation every step of the way. All told, emancipation there took twenty years.[99]

There was nothing particularly unusual about the way emancipation unfolded in the Confederate States of America. The unevenness of the process over space and time hardly invalidates the specific comparison to Saint-Domingue or the larger comparative argument for the Civil War as a slave insurrection. Nor does the obvious recognition that much of the opportunity Southern slaves grasped to work the destruction of slavery and claim freedom arose in the context of war and in alliance with enemy armies. In the Civil War South slaves moved tactically and by stages, men and women both, equal and active participants in the whole array of insurrectionary activities calculated to destroy the institution of slavery, their masters' power, and the prospects of the C.S.A. as a proslavery nation. Emancipation there was indeed regionally uneven, temporally protracted, and linked to the Union army's invasion and federal emancipation policy. But to planters and slaves alike, it was unmistakably, too, the consequence of a massive rebellion of the Confederacy's slaves.

CHAPTER 7

"Our Open Enemies"

THE SLAVES' WAR WITH their masters quickly overspilled the bounds of Confederate farms and plantations. The questions of loyalty, allegiance, and treason it raised radiated out from those initial sites of struggle into the theater of war. Excluded from political life as a matter of foundational principle, slaves' politics registered profoundly nonetheless, not just in Union policy where we have been trained to look, but in Confederate policy, as state and federal officials attempted to make slaves count as labor for the cause.[1] It shaped slave impressment, the deployment of military forces, and the conduct of the war more generally, and complicated every Confederate attempt to make slaves an element of strength.

In the C.S.A. slaves were legally construed as property. The state knew them, and had access to them, only as the property of their masters. It did not take long for that essential fact of Confederate political life, the slaves' alienation from the state, to emerge as a military liability. For even as the states and central government attempted to draw on slave property to sustain the war, slave owners attempted to draw on the state to protect slave property in the war. The problem of mobilizing slaves *as slaves* proved intractable in the face of the linked resistance of slaves and masters both, and pushed Confederate officials onto rapidly shifting and dangerous terrain. Enslaved men and women's efforts to destroy slavery and willing adherence to the enemy touched off a powerful struggle between slaveholders and Confederate officials: about rights of property and state access to slaves, slaves' status as persons or property, and where sovereignty lay in the slaveholders' nation. The struggle to make slaves material to the cause was deeply revealing of the structural problems faced by a slave regime at war. Long before Confederate officials contemplated the enlistment of slave men in the national army, they had faced the problem posed by slaves' politics in attempts to harness their labor for the cause. As early as 1862 slaves had made their loyalty count and provoked intractable questions about allegiance and treason in the C.S.A.

It was an article of faith in the Confederacy that slavery would be a great element of strength in the war. "This it is which makes our 8 million of productive fighting material equal to the 20 m of the North," Major Samuel W. Melton, assistant adjutant general, explained to James A. Seddon, Confederate secretary of war. Melton's plan sounded reasonable enough: Southerners could counter the demographic power of the North by putting every eligible fighting man in the army and those "unfit for service by reason of servitude" to work at everything else. With 40 percent of the nation's adult male population enslaved and ineligible for service, it was a salient consideration. "The problem which must be worked out," Major Melton noted, "is so to adapt our peculiar system of labor as most effectually to relieve the fighting population" and place the burden on slaves where "it is our peculiar happiness to place it."[2] That Melton was still trying to work out the problem of how to use slaves' labor two and a half years into the war was not an auspicious sign. What seemed simple in theory clearly proved difficult in practice.

Slave impressment emerged early in the war as the key policy by which to harness slaves' labor to the service of the state.[3] "There is nothing so military as labour," General Robert E. Lee declared, unwittingly flagging the murky territory ahead. If much of soldiering was labor, then what distinguished military labor from military service? The endless innovations in impressment policy were a clear prologue to the debate on "Confederate emancipation," as the decision to enlist slave men is mistakenly called.

Lee made the observation in distress over the evident disparity in Union soldiers' recognition of the value of pick and shovel and Southern boys' prejudice against it. Given the emphasis on entrenchment and earthworks in nineteenth-century warfare—or "West pointism and spades," as Jefferson Davis called it—it is hardly surprising that Confederate military men turned quickly to slaves to provide the military labor white soldiers shunned.[4]

At the outset, state and Confederate officials confidently followed the old proslavery script, calling on planters to volunteer their slaves to labor on the public works. In January 1861, slaves offered by their owners were already at work on batteries in Charleston, Savannah, and Mobile. John Berkeley Grimball sent 16 slave men down to work on the fortifications on Edisto Island for one week with his son as their guard. By the end of February there were 250 slaves working on Morris Island, "loaned by their owners," Charles Manigault noted. "Several of the Planters owning them are there also, living in tents nearby," a caution he could appreciate given the recent discovery of guns and powder on his Savannah River plantation. The use of slaves for military labor involved a few peculiarities, not least the need to send other men to guard the laborers, and planters' assumption that service would be brief.[5] Still, the general expectation seemed to be that slave labor would be forthcoming as needed.

As war began in earnest and military officials scrambled to build fortifications at the Confederacy's many vulnerable points, the demand for slave labor escalated. Within weeks the limits of planter voluntarism were reached, and the state's power to command the labor of slave property was put to the test. One has only to look at Virginia in the first summer of the war, when General John B. Magruder, commander of Confederate forces on the peninsula, attempted to acquire a sufficient force of slaves to erect fortifications at the entrance to the James River. In July 1861, with the Union navy already in control of Fort Monroe and Confederates facing Union maneuvers at Gloucester Point, Magruder issued a call on the citizens of neighboring counties for one-half of their male force of slaves to finish the works around Gloucester Point. Between May and September identical calls were made on slaveholders in four other counties to work on the Williamsburg and Yorktown fortifications.[6]

From the first, requisitions specified adult male slaves, a pattern that was laden with meaning for slaves themselves. Magruder did once ask to hire black women "at very cheap rates" to work in military hospitals, and slave women were employed by the military, especially in quartermasters and medical departments. But no government ever considered impressing slave women, notwithstanding their recognized value as laborers. Planters tried periodically to send women to fulfill their quotas, and many complained about a system in which agents are "prohibited from . . . taking any female slaves," but "count in all the women [aged 17 to 50] . . . & take one third of the total number in men" of that age. Unmoved, Confederate officials confirmed that the state wanted only the men.[7] Women slaves were hardly absent from the struggles on the ground. But their uselessness to the Union and Confederate states for military labor had far-reaching consequences in the war, engendering an official disinterest that is continually replicated in the absence of slave women in histories of emancipation. As the competition for the military labor of slave men heated up, it carried crucial meanings for slave women, configuring men as potential political subjects in relation to the two warring states and putting men and women on different paths through war to emancipation.

Nothing in planters' previous experience prepared them for the demands the new state made on their property. Magruder's July 1861 requisition was so unprecedented in scale—half of the male slaves of the county aged 17 to 50—that it signaled something altogether new in terms of central state power and the interposition of government authority into the delicate relation of master and slave. In Virginia, planter resistance was quick and effective. Some simply ignored the orders. Others shot off incredulous letters of complaint to President Davis and the War Department. But in Charles City and New Kent County discontented planters empowered their congressman, the ex-president John Tyler (himself an owner of thirty-nine slaves), to lodge an official protest with the War Department about the "legality of this proceeding on the part of the General." The legality of impressment was on the table from the outset. And so was the government's touchiness on the subject of executive tyranny and invasion of property rights. Faced with a string of complaints from highly placed Virginians, the secretary of war issued a stinging rebuke to

General Magruder, reminding him that "however urgent and obvious the necessity the power [to impress slaves] should be exercised only in subordination to the ultimate rights of the owners."[8]

In the first instance, then, in the C.S.A. slaves were impressed as property plain and simple, and as behooved the slaveholders' republic the masters' claim was paramount. But the difficulties of that approach were already evident in Virginia in 1861 and 1862 and only intensified with further Union incursions as commanders in other regions made similar calls on planters for their slaves. Indeed, Magruder's initial call set off an intractable series of conflicts between slaveholders and the central state over the rights that attached to property in slaves and about the state's power to abrogate those rights and the petty sovereignties they created. It raised far-reaching legal and political questions about the legitimacy of the state's claim on privately held property in slaves and the trajectory of military service that starts with impressment.

From the outset, planters cited slaves' own objections to that labor as the key impediment to compliance. Ironic as it might seem, slaves' consent emerged as a critical factor in Confederate impressment policy. From 1861, when the policy was initiated, down to the very end of the war, planters' opposition proved a real obstacle to government plans to use slaves. That opposition issued from a variety of grounds: the removal of slaves from agricultural production in the high season; the inequity of requisitions; the treatment of slaves on the government works. But the most common ground of opposition planters offered was slaves' refusal to comply and propensity to escape if coerced. Slaves, state senator Thomas Urquhart reported in seeking exemption for his eastern Virginia county, "have a perfect horror of working on entrenchments." They have been "[running] to the enemy in the adjoining counties of Isle of Wight and Nansemond . . . I feel certain that if they hear of another impressment, we will lose nearly all of our men." Planters and military men on both sides knew these to be no idle threats. "The last time the general called for laborers," Urquhart added, "200 left the county in 3 days." If men who were owners of chattel property saw any irony in quoting the property's opinion about government policy, they did not acknowledge it. A year later in response to another complaint from Urquhart, the secretary of war made the damaging admission that slaves do tend to run away when forced to work on the fortifications. General Joseph Johnston likewise confessed that he had never been able to hold impressed "negroes" with an army near the enemy. "They desert," he said. In the sizable body of literature on impressment in the C.S.A., there is no clear grasp of the significance of the slaves' own role in shaping the policy, or the peculiar triangulating of power—between slaves, masters, and the state—that policy inevitably involved.[9]

The personhood of slaves and evidence of their political agency veered up in the face of Confederate officials at every turn during the war, despite their determination to impress them simply as property. And in truth, planters' fears accorded pretty closely with conditions on the ground, as Virginia legislators knew all too well and military commanders themselves sometimes acknowledged. In October 1862, Brigadier General Henry Wise relayed a report from the engineers corps at Chaffins Bluff, Virginia, that nine slaves had escaped a few nights previous and were presumed to be heading either back to their homes or to the enemy massing on the other side of the river. The bluff must be strictly guarded, Wise instructed, and all boats hauled up to some safe place above the batteries to prevent slaves' use of them in escape. In the face of constant communications of that sort, President Davis exempted a number of Virginia counties from slave impressment.[10]

State congressmen like Urquhart and Tyler proved powerful allies of slaveholders in their resistance to military requisitions, seeing the protection of their constituents' property as one of the chief objects of government itself. But that set them on a collision course with military officers who regarded slave property as so much matériel of war. Virginia slaveholder James Cook wrote his congressman in August 1861 demanding military intervention to stanch the flow of slaves to the enemy from his area near Newport News, Virginia. Raising the specter of slaves providing military intelligence to Union forces, he demanded to know whether in view of their "treasonable correspondence" "*every means* should [not] be used by our Forces in the field to check these evils." "Is not the protection of property one of the duties of an army in the field?"[11] It was a reasonable question and a troubling one, and it shaped not just Confederate impressment policy but other aspects of the conduct of the war as well.

The Confederate government had no choice but to access slaves as property. Chattel property was, after all, a constitutionally protected form of property in the C.S.A., the raison d'être of the government itself. But the property status of slaves cut against military commanders' attempts to use their labor in the national defense. This was because the property insisted on acting as persons, pursuing their own political ends to the detriment of Confederate operations. It was also because the owners not only refused to surrender their property but demanded that the military be deployed to shore it up. "A government that does not protect its subject in the enjoyment of their property . . . is not the kind of government to command respect," one Georgia slaveholder railed in September 1862.[12]

Such were the elemental conflicts involved in any attempt to use slaves as property in the war effort. General Magruder was up against them all, and as he saw it, they fatally undermined his attempt to build adequate defenses on the Virginia coast. In September 1861 he complained to General Samuel Cooper about the wealthy men of Gloucester and Surry County who refused to send their slaves on requisition from him. He sent out a detachment of dragoons to bring them in. "If these gentlemen are sustained in their refusal no negroes can be had when wanted," he said in his own defense. In January 1862 he tried to hire slaves for the works, but when his agents went out they found "that it was a very difficult matter to do so." Again he resorted to compulsion, calling on several counties for one-third of their working male force, again the counties protested to the War Department, and again the War Department upheld the planters. Directed to countermand his order, Magruder protested to no avail. Even as Magruder struggled to get the labor he needed, he grew increasingly incensed at the War Department's empowerment of shirkers. "The people have got an idea that the influence of the Government will be cast against my efforts," he complained to General Cooper.[13]

Magruder was surprisingly blunt about the cost of planter and slave resistance to the defense of Virginia. When ordered to dispatch troops to reinforce another commander on the peninsula in March 1862, he sent only one regiment, explaining that he could not spare more because his fortifications were inadequate to the defense of his own position. "The reason why I cannot do more, is that notwithstanding all my efforts to procure negroes I have rec'd but eleven from the Counties in my district

... I supposed that by this time I would have had negroes enough to have fortified my positions sufficiently to have enabled me to spare . . . 2000 men." Fearful that his flank would be turned because he had no position to fall back to, he could not spare any more men.[14]

On the Virginia peninsula the imagined equation between fighting men and slave men's labor collapsed at first trial. Slave impressment failed to provide the needed element of strength. Undermined by planters suspicious of the loyalty of their own slaves, and themselves upheld by local magistrates, congressmen, district attorneys, and even the secretary of war, General Magruder failed to get the slave bodies he needed to compensate for the C.S.A.'s decided disadvantage in numbers of eligible fighting men.

If, in a concrete sense, attempts to impress slave men foundered on the shoals of property rights and personhood, some Virginia planters also objected to it on more existential grounds as a practice dangerously transformative of slaves' status and destructive of slavery itself. If nothing was more military than labor, one Virginia slaveholder fretted in December 1861, what did it mean to subject *slave* men to military duty? That planter, John Speice, was concerned about the practical meaning of impressment for the already tenuous management of his own slaves and blunt about the danger that deployment to military works in northwest Virginia would present by advancing his slaves' political education. They will "get to talking with Union men in disguise" and turn impressment into the occasion of escape, he worried. Men who had always feared the assembly of their slaves in groups of more than two or three hardly welcomed the collection of hundreds of them in one lightly supervised place. But Speice was also convinced that the state's seizure of slave men had profound implications for the slaveholders' republic, concerns he expressed in a letter to the attorney general of the Confederate States in August 1861. "Whilst I do not controvert the right of the Government to impress into its service *wagons and teams,*" he declared, "yet I do controvert the right to impress *Slaves:*—It does seem to me that no one can be impress'd into military service of any kind unless he is subject to military duty: because this whole business is relating to the Army, and is a purely military matter."[15] If slaves were subject to military labor, then were they not subject to military duty, and presumptively persons and maybe even citizens in the eyes of the state?

Speice was not entirely alone in his concern about the road the Confederate military had started down. Other slaveholders protested the power of the Confederate government to initiate a change in the status of slaves. These were hardly unwarranted questions, given the difficulties they faced. Could slaves really be impressed as property plain and simple, or did impressment for military labor already suggest something else? A penetrating statement of the problem was offered by John M. Gregory, a former governor of Virginia, in two lengthy letters to the secretary of war. Gregory claimed that he had always deprecated the use of negro slaves in the army for any purpose whatever and Magruder's actions raised his worst fears. A Confederate commander given the power to impress might use it to abolish slavery, he warned bluntly in March 1862. The new power the state claimed on the ground of military exigency had no obvious limit.  What if emancipation proved a military necessity? In March 1862 and again in March 1863, when, he estimated, 50 to 70 percent of slaves in his Virginia county had already escaped to the enemy, Gregory issued the disturbing warning: "if negroes were employed by us to do such work as soldiers ought to do, the Yankees would use that as a pretext to interfere with them and emancipate them." Once the Confederate military moved to use slave men, had not "yankees denounced negroes as contraband of war and offered them protection in their camps?"[16] It was their own government, he insisted, that had initiated the dangerous transformation attributed so often, then and now, to the Union.

Gregory was right. The contraband policy, now understood as foundational to the Union government's emerging emancipation policy, was made possible by the Confederate state's decision to turn slave men into military laborers. That was precisely what Union general Benjamin Butler charged in justifying the holding of fugitive slaves at Fortress Monroe on the Virginia peninsula in May 1861. For the thousands of enslaved men, women, and children of Confederate owners who eventually found shelter there, and the many more in other Union forts, camps, and rears of armies, claimed the status of "contraband," property legitimately confiscated from the enemy because they had been used as "matériel of war." Butler had received the first such escaped slaves at Fort Monroe in Magruder's backyard just weeks into the war. The men had come to him, Butler emphasized, "from the Confederate batteries at Sewall's Point." The Virginians are "using their negroes in the batteries and are preparing to send the women and children South," he insisted in May 1861. "The escapes from them are very numerous and a squad had come in this morning to my pickets bringing their women and children."[17]

Impressed to work on Confederate fortifications, slaves had, by their willingness to risk escape, opened up a new possibility in their war against the slaveholders. Butler was alert to the opportunity: "As a military question it would seem to be a measure of necessity to deprive the master of their services," he argued of the able-bodied men subject to Confederate impressment who had come from the fortifications. The women and children not subject to impressment posed a thorny problem for Butler's quickly improvised policy, although he did initially attempt to pull the adult women under the cover of military necessity by claiming to deprive masters of the services of "able bodied men *and women* who come within my lines." Of the children he worried, "How can this be done? As a political question and a question of humanity can I receive the services of a Father and a Mother and not take the children?" But despite Butler's initial inclusion of women slaves as labor denied the enemy, that logic failed in the face of the Confederacy's male-only impressment. Most Union officers would quickly come to see women and children as a welfare problem, "incapable of army labor, a weight and incumbrance," as one federal commander later put it when struggling to support the massive numbers of escaped slaves, three-quarters of them women and children, flooding into camps in the Mississippi Valley.[18]

Those kinds of distinctions, between men who were wanted and women who were not, proved crucial to enslaved women's attempts to claim freedom in the orbit of the Union army. The women fit neither the logic of Union contraband policy about subtracting slave men from the Confederate war effort, nor the practical goals of Union officers interested in recruiting slave men as laborers or as soldiers for their armies. Enslaved men and women's war goals only partially ever fit with those of the Union government and its army of liberation, and that was true even after the Emancipation Proclamation and Union recruitment of black soldiers.

However, regardless of what Union commanders wanted, whatever the orders sent out to pickets to keep out the dependents, whatever the distinctions between loyal and disloyal owners, or requirements of military service for the Confederacy embedded in Union Confiscation Acts, still slave women and children arrived, unbidden and unwanted, along with the men at Union camps and outposts.

By May 1863 there were an estimated ten thousand contrabands at Fortress Monroe alone and twenty-three thousand inside Union lines in occupied parts of the Virginia tidewater, about 45 percent of them women. Union policy quickly settled on treating women slaves as the *wives* of contrabands—another poor fit for a population denied the rights of legal marriage and arriving out of slavery inhabiting a multiplicity of family forms. No matter that marriage was illegal for slaves or that many of the women who made it to Union lines or camps had come on their own or as heads of families themselves. The "woman who came through 200 Miles in men's clothes" to Fortress Monroe had no husband, or at least none with her when she arrived. Nonetheless, marriage was part of the basic template of federal emancipation policy from its earliest imaginings in the American Civil War and the solution to the problem of contraband women and dependency most often reached for in federal policy. The recourse to marriage reflected deep-seated assumptions about adult women's dependency and the normative position as wives, of course, but it was also animated by a host of pressing concerns, chief among them the specter of a huge welfare population and government insistence on slave men's responsibility for their dependents as a condition of emancipation. With "contraband" imagined as male, and the women as their "wives," Union policy cast slave women as dependent parties in the project of emancipation, a role they have never managed to escape.[19]

The transformation of slavery initiated by slaves on the Virginia peninsula in the spring of 1861 was far-reaching indeed. As ex-governor Gregory had predicted, Confederate impressment of slave men for the military duty of soldiers opened that avenue to the destruction of slavery. What Gregory missed, but General Butler made no attempt to conceal, was that Union contraband policy did not initiate the competition for the military labor of slave men; that was initiated by the thousands of slave men, women, and children in "delivering themselves up" to the Union. The ex-slave Harry Jarvis insisted on that point in describing his escape by canoe and sail from the eastern shore of Virginia to Fort Monroe in the spring of 1861, before "Gin'ral Butler had 'lowed we war contraban'." Having made it to Union—and, he hoped, free—territory, Jarvis asked Butler if he could enlist. "But he said *it warn't a black man's war.* I tol' him it *would* be a black man's war 'fore dey got fru."[20]

What that early experience made abundantly clear was that the transformation of Confederate slavery did not simply work from the outside in. The internal workings of the institution generated plenty to worry about, as the massive resistance to slave impressment confirmed. Impressment of slaves was a matter of urgent debate in the C.S.A. during the American Civil War. Confederate officials dutifully cited precedent to obscure the innovation: "The slaves liable to this call shall be the same that are liable to road duty in this state," they would serve for one month and be administered by the commissioner of roads, one state requisition put it in 1862. A call is made on the citizens of the county "for one fifth of the road hands to labour on the fortifications at Weldon," another specified. But road duty was a shaky basis for the newly muscular intrusions of the wartime state. "You are aware that one fifth of the road hands is practically one half of the able bodied men upon most farms," a North Carolinian rebuked his governor in response to a call. "Estimating the number of hands liable to road service at 85,000," General P. G. T. Beauregard protested that the 4,000 currently called for constituted only "5 percent of the male negro-labor of the state, leaving out of view the large number of negro women available for and actually employed in field labor."[21] But however the general cut it, the numbers involved violated all previous understandings of the government's right to reach into the household and claim private property in slaves for public use. It represented a newly immediate relationship with a central government whose former authority over slavery, and even more so over individual slaves, had been strictly delimited.

For a nation established to give greater security and permanence to slaveholders' enjoyment of their peculiar property, impressment came as a terrible blow. It cut against the power masters had always claimed to govern slaves as their personal property. By subjecting master and slave to the orders of state agents, it called into question the masters' sovereignty.

Juridically speaking, the idea of property was the key to the definition of slavery in the antebellum period, and everything about the antebellum law was designed to give security to that property.[22] However carefully handled, impressment was a revolutionary intrusion on rights of property.

Alert to the political dangers, Confederate officials trod gingerly, reluctant to assert controversial powers. Nobody doubted the need. But what emerged as impressment policies were belated, piecemeal, and often unenforceable. Federal impressment legislation was slow in coming; state legislation slow and partial. The swift rebuke of Magruder in the summer of 1861 signaled the War Department's approach. Notwithstanding the inadequacies of the voluntary program, they did not attempt to pass a general impressment act until March 1863, and that obligated them to work in compliance with state legislation where it existed. First they tried to get the states to take the lead. In November 1862, President Davis urged governors to sponsor legislation that would lend support to commanders in the field. But the states, too, trod gingerly on the subject of slaveholders' property rights, relying initially on voluntary offerings under the inducement of hiring contracts. Only six of eleven Confederate states ever passed legislation empowering governors to impress slaves, and one of the six, South Carolina, stalled until 1864. In Georgia attempts to pass such legislation failed entirely in the face of the strenuous objections from the planter class, supported by Governor Brown, a perennial Davis administration foe. Where it did pass, state legislation imposed strict limitations. Virginia's Act for the Public Defense limited requisitions to a maximum of ten thousand slave men for sixty days labor. Owners were compensated at $16 per month. In Virginia, site of unceasing military operations by the Union army and navy, counties rarely met their quotas and repeatedly applied for and received exemptions because of heavy losses of slaves "in consequence of their escape to the public enemy."[23]

But no approach, however tentative, could forestall planter opposition or elicit ready compliance. In most states, governors and legislators did not take up their role as crucial allies of a federal government attempting to sustain its beleaguered armies. Instead they lent legitimacy and vital support to constituent resistance, casting themselves as the protectors of planter interests against federal tyranny. A few governors would prove staunch allies of the administration in their attempts to give commanders the labor they needed. Governor William Smith, who took office in Virginia in 1863 fought bitterly with planters and local officials until the fall of Richmond. But in most states, especially in the east, slaveholders found powerful allies in state legislators and governors and even among some members of the Confederate Congress and secretaries of war. In South Carolina, Brigadier General John S. Preston warned the secretary of war, "members have been sent to the Legislature avowedly to protect the people and their slaves from the Confederate authorities."[24]

Given the patterns, it is not too much to say that what the parties—and historians—have often cast as a principled issue of states' rights was actually an issue of slaveholders' rights. What looked like a struggle between state and federal power was really a struggle over the right of the central state to abrogate the sovereign rights of slaveholders.[25] For in most cases, governors' denunciations of central state tyranny simply kicked up the chain of command complaints they had received from slaveholders with property subject to impressment. In North Carolina, Governor Vance waged a bitter struggle with Brigadier General W. H. Whiting, the Confederate commander of operations, over the provision of slaves for the works, fighting for the return of slaves even as Wilmington was under siege. After a round of blistering exchanges in June 1863, Whiting exploded at Vance, telling him that "all but about 30 of the negro laborers here have been returned," and demanding more. "Surely in the 300,000 negroes belonging to N.C. 500 might be spared for so important a purpose. I beg of you to consider this—there are many counties which have not furnished any." A year later, it was the same thing. Wilmington was about to fall, but Vance was still harassing Whiting with demands for the return of his constituents' slaves. "Both the transportation of troops and provisions and the defense of this place are of far more importance than the return of two hundred and fifty negroes," Whiting raged, "if it has not been done before it has been from impossibility."[26]

It proved almost impossible to work through the states, as federal officials had hoped, because governors and legislators saw it as their role to protect their constituents' interests. That had long been the function of state government. Like so many other governors, Vance was deluged by complaints from voters about the impressment of their slaves and invasion of their rights: about how the harvest was suffering and promises to soldiers' wives going unfulfilled in the absence of their hands; about the inequity of military calls on counties; about the holding of men beyond the specified time; about the treatment of slaves on the government works; and above all, about the "ease with which they [the slaves] can make their escape to the enemy." Impressment was an insupportable blow to planters' already tenuous hold on their slaves in wartime eastern North Carolina. Slaves made no secret of their opposition to labor on the public works, and deployment only provided additional incentives and opportunities to escape, either before they went to the works or while they were there. No reassurances from the military—no promises of compensation or beefed-up guards—could allay planter fears. "I was about to send one man off," a Mr. B. B. Walker told Governor Vance in December 1864 at the height of the crisis at Wilmington. I "fixed him with $30 to encourage him [to come home]" but he "dodged before I delivered him at Graham," and now wants "some assurance of being released from the present call."[27] Walker's note underscores the dilemmas of the Confederacy's slave impressment policy in its obvious confusion of volition. Who dodged? Who wants to be released?

Slaves, planters, and in too many cases their governors as well were arrayed against the military use of slaves' labor as a direct attack on the security of slave property. Under pressure from slaveholders who charged him with "indifference to owners' rights," Vance and the North Carolina legislature moved from obstruction into open opposition. In the starving spring of 1863, as he faced the revolt of the women, Vance tried and failed to get slaves returned from the works in time for harvest. By 1864, he empowered magistrates to refuse to enforce General Whiting's orders and directed state military commanders not to execute orders for additional slaves to replace those who had run away from the works. In state legislatures traditionally beholden to planter interests, there was little daylight between the issues of slaveholders' rights and state rights. In the face of those still-robust rights of property, any attempt to put the burden of impressment on the separate states proved a total failure.[28]

If slave men were to make up the difference of numbers between eligible fighting men in the Union and the C.S.A., the central government would have to take matters into its own hands. Finally in March 1863 it did. Building on a congressional act of April 1862 that allowed for the enlistment of small numbers of slaves or free blacks in the army as cooks or musicians, the Confederate Congress passed an act authorizing the general impressment of private property for use by the army and, in Section 9, treating slaves as a particular species of that property subject to impressment. No law, including the Conscription Act, was so widely reviled by the Confederate population, for the impressment of human property seemed to slaveholders to strike at the very vitals of the republic. Anticipating the opposition, the law obliged the Confederate government to operate in submission to state laws where they existed.[29]

That necessary but highly costly genuflection to state and slaveholders' rights was telling of just how difficult it was for the War Department to mobilize slave men for military labor in their legal status as property. Planters' rights of property were hard to invade, even when the War Department found the political will. The Confederate government had the legal right to claim private property for public use—"an extraordinary exertion of power," as one Virginia judge put it—in what was manifestly a clear public emergency. But the mass seizure of property in slaves was so widely resisted, and so politically unpalatable, that as late as March 1863 even the secretary of war hesitated. Only a series of repeated failures convinced him to act.[30] Legislation would become more comprehensive and authoritative, enforcement more muscular and punitive, but the status of slaves as property—and the behavior of that property—would confound all attempts to use slaves for military labor in large numbers.

The federal government's impressment policy went through endless modifications in the face of increasing resistance from slaves and planters both. The law of March 1863 was no sooner written than it was revised and augmented. In July, admitting the impossibility of voluntary compliance, the secretary of war sought enforcement orders: a general order explicitly locating authority to determine the necessity of impressing slaves with the commanding general or officer of engineer, and rendering those men who accompanied slaves to the works "subject to the control of the officer in charge." That new legislation of October 1863 represented, at least in theory, a significant undercutting of the individual masters' authority by the agents of the central state and a fundamental reconfiguration of the master-citizen's position in relation to state authority.[31]

But that didn't work, and manpower shortages in the army only worsened. Shortly after the October efforts, Assistant Adjutant General Samuel Melton attempted to "work out" the problem in a long and bleak report about the structural disparity between the Confederacy and the Union with respect to manpower and recruitment. Slavery had to be made to pay for the C.S.A., Melton insisted, because "the conscription laws now in force will be utterly inadequate to restore to our armies the numbers they contained last January, and to preserve this strength during the coming year." They needed an additional hundred thousand men, he told Secretary of War Seddon, just to hold their own. The only possible solution was to substitute slave labor for every—and he meant every—home front and military task and to call in all of the men exempted from service or who had paid for substitutes. Seddon acknowledged the obvious: that to command slaves in anything like the number required for government works, "compulsion in some form would be necessary." "There may be difficulties and embarrassments in enforcing the service of slaves," he went on, in one of the most colossal understatements of the war, "but they might be overcome on the principle of impressing them as property" as opposed, he presumably meant, to persons.[32]

Seddon, of course, was right. In the Confederate slaveholders' republic, slaves *could* only be impressed as the property of their masters. "The slave [is] an item of property, is not a member of the body politic; he owes no service on his own account to the Government," he pronounced at one point, "the Government knows him only as the property of his master." And therein lay the problem. Slaves' alienation from the state was a major liability to a slave regime at war. As one South Carolina agent put it, "the aid and authority of the master is indispensable and as the Confederate authorities possess no control over him can impose no pain or penalties, they must in the present condition of affairs be powerless to act effectually." The aid and authority of the master was not forthcoming, Lieutenant General Kirby Smith explained as he scrambled for labor after the fall of Vicksburg, because of "a feeling of distrust in the loyalty of their slaves."[33]

Slaves may have had no standing in relation to the state, but their actions, desires, and objectives weighed heavily on Confederate impressment. Behind slaveholders' noncompliance (and expedient collusion) was slaves' mass resistance to labor for the Confederate cause. From all over the South reports poured into the War Department of counties already emptied of slave men who had gone to the enemy, of slaves impressed to work on the fortifications dodging off before they could be sent, running away from the works, turning up at Union picket lines, camps, and forts and occasionally at home, making no secret of their unwillingness to serve and intention to escape. Planters deep into a four-year war with their slaves, some already financially destroyed by the escape of large numbers of their slaves to the enemy, inundated the president and secretary of war with frank talk about how their slaves' actions limited the government's new impressment policy. Few bothered to obscure slaves' volition. "Numbers of them say that while they have no disposition to leave yet before they will go to Richmond during the winter season to work on the fortifications . . . they will go to the Yankees—and we believe numbers of them will go—. . . [and] will take with them their wives, children, etc," one Virginian repeated without embarrassment. The new interest in what slaves wanted, including from the agents charged with making them work, only encouraged "this spirit of insubordination now so dangerous & general in our country," as one slaveholder put it. Some citizens of Sussex County, Virginia, wrote to President Davis in the fall of 1864: "They are going constantly," and if the new requisition were to go through "it will cause a stampede among those men who are not now disposed to go. We believe that for every man the government would obtain . . . the enemy would add ten or twenty to his ranks."[34]

Suddenly slave consent figured in private calculations and official ones. It was another of those fundamentally contradictory revisions of political practice and policy making the Confederate war required. Slaves' consent mattered to slaveholders desperate to retain the property the new nation had been established to secure; and it mattered to federal officials desperate to make planters comply with their requisitions *and* to make slave men's labor effective when they got it. Planters, of course, had the head start, but the recognition of slaves' political agency eventually penetrated the consciousness of military men and government officials as well. Despite their obligations to orthodoxy, Confederate officials eventually abandoned the customary proslavery grammar by which slaves were always "forced off" by the enemy (but never went of their own accord), and admitted what planters had long known: that slaves' resistance to impressment and flight to the enemy both aimed at the destruction of slavery and issued from a broader set of allegiances, principled and strategic. Slaveholders understandably focused on the former, talking constantly about how "the Negro is demoralized *as a slave*," by which they meant that slaves were more intent on freedom than labor. But Confederate officials, and especially military men, took a broader view of slaves' resistance, concerned about its political implications. For bluntness, few matched W. G. Turpin, captain of engineers and acting chief of construction in the Department of Northern Virginia, who, charged with managing slaves on the works, was surely in a position to judge. County planters generally say "that the negroes would run to the Yankees [if impressed]," Turpin allowed in 1864, "showing the utter demorealization [*sic*] of the slaves and showing that owners regarded their right and authority over their slaves was so frail as to preclude all attempts at controll [*sic*] or discipline." But Turpin thought that too narrow an interpretation of slaves' actions; he saw more at stake than the masters' interests, and he made the political meaning dangerously clear: "I believe there is a disinclination on the part of the slaves to labor on the defensive works resulting not from hard labor or starvation but from a disinclination to do labor that will thwart the Federals, who they look upon as fighting for their freedom and to which all are looking forward as being near at hand."[35]

It was as much the refusal of slaves to act as property as the refusal of planters to yield that property up that thwarted Confederate attempts to make impressment work. Owners who feared the loss of their slaves would not voluntarily comply even with federal legislation. That much was pretty obvious to President Davis and the War Department, who struggled from March 1863 to get the numbers of slaves the legislation was intended to supply. Constant revisions, expansions, and toughening of policy were all pronounced a failure. All "produced less result than anticipated," as Davis admitted at the end of 1864.[36] So even as the Confederate Conscript Bureau admitted they could enroll no more white men and engaged in outright competition with the Union for the labor and loyalty of slave men, the C.S.A. tried and failed to make up the military difference with slave men. In January 1864, General Joseph Johnston, hunkered down with the Army of Tennessee in winter quarters in Dalton,

Georgia, begged for more slave laborers. He wanted ten or twelve thousand to substitute for soldiers on detached or daily duty. Thomas Hindman, one of Johnston's corps commanders, wanted even more, enough, he said "to swell our ranks, at once, about 20,000 men." But those kinds of numbers were never forthcoming. In Georgia the number of slaves working on fortifications under federal impressment legislation ranged from 160 to a temporary maximum of 2,000, and even after General Sherman's advance on Atlanta the Confederate Congress was still trying to get that state's share of the 20,000 slaves authorized by legislation a year previous. In Virginia in early 1865 when General Lee requested 5,000 slaves, he got about 500. There were never 20,000 slaves made available at one time to any Confederate army.[37]

By 1864 the Confederate War Department was in a no-win situation. Every flexing of federal muscle intensified the opposition of slaveholders. The February 1864 legislation hewed carefully to the description of slaves as a species of property, pledging compensation to the owner for slaves who ran away, were killed, or died in service. But it also transferred responsibility for the execution of the law to the "Bureau of Conscription," suggesting a dangerous elision between slaves and soldiers, the management of property and persons, military labor and military service. There were practical reasons for that, including conscription agents' knowledge of locations and the network of conscript camps already set up to capture reluctant white men. But when the Department of War sent out conscript agents to round up slave men, when they arrested them over the protests of their owners or came with cavalry to compel compliance, and marched those slave men off to Conscript Bureau camps for deployment to the army, when they organized black conscripts into labor battalions with all the trappings of military order and discipline, it seemed to many—including slaves—that the slaveholders' paramount claim was in real jeopardy and that a key distinction between slaves as persons and as property had been eroded. Did the Bureau of Conscription not recruit soldiers, citizens with obligations to serve?[38]

That the Confederate state was forced into dangerous—even revolutionary—innovations is what lends the story of that breakaway republic its drama. Historians and others grasped the irony. But in confining their accounts to the state and the citizens, in taking no notice of the women and the slaves, they missed some of the most dramatic reversals of the war.[39] For just as the mass of Confederate white women, yeoman and poor white—supposed to be subjects of household governance—ended up more, not less, politically engaged in the slaveholders' new republic, so slave men and women—whose perpetual enslavement that republic aimed at—ended up with more, not less, political leverage in relation to the slaveholders' state.

Enslaved men and women had long ago learned the brutal lesson that under slavery the ultimate power of life and death lay with their master and not in an abstraction called "the state." For them, impressment was a key experience in a new wartime view of the reality of the government. Even the limited intrusions of central state authorities in attempts to reach past the master to the slave were meaningful in slaves' awareness of the instability of contemporary political life. For people who had long looked for such openings, the war represented a speeding up of history itself. When his master was tapped for a contingent of slaves to work on the fortifications at Vicksburg, the Natchez slave Jeff Claiborne recalled that the man immediately struck an uncharacteristic tone. He told us he was sorry to see us go and "expressed hope that we would not run away." When he came down to the works to check on them, he offered an object lesson—one Claiborne never forgot—in the possibilities of war. "He said he would do all he could to get us home, *but it was not in his power* to release us." So if Confederate impressment policy must be judged a failure, still it created unprecedented cracks in the masters' power to dictate terms, and introduced elements of dangerous (but exploitable) instability into the old horrifying edifice of the masters' sovereignty at home.[40]

Enslaved men and women's introduction to the idea of the state, to its powers and potential to shape their future for better or worse, did not all come by way of Lincoln and the Union government. Many slaves watched their masters' personal power wither away or collapse dramatically with the arrival of the Union army in their neighborhoods. Almost every slave who later gave testimony to federal commissions recalled exactly where they were when Union troops arrived on their places. But most slaves never made it to Union lines, didn't live in places under Union occupation. The state they had to contend with was the Confederate one. The C.S.A. might have lost its wartime battle to curtail the sovereignty of masters, but by introducing a new outside element into the traditional relation of personal domination between master and slave, the Confederate state came to figure in slaves' political calculations as no previous one had ever done.[41]

Still, as slaves knew, there were real limits to what the Confederate government could do in abrogating masters' property rights in slaves, limits characteristic of state action in slave societies. Even as some military men and the president contemplated radical changes to the law of slavery to make slaves' labor effective in the war, the government as a whole lacked the power and political will to reach past the master and access slave men directly. Instead they tried time and again to mobilize slaves as the property of individual masters. In February 1864, in December 1864, and again in February 1865, the War Department tried to make impressment work, to find some way, as Lee put it, "to use our negroes in this war, if we would maintain ourselves, and prevent them from being used against us."[42] Slavery may have been a source of strength in war, but the endless modifications of federal policy suggested how impossible it was to put into practice.

"The sacrosanctity of slave property in this war has operated most injuriously to the Confederacy," the assistant secretary of war said bluntly in July 1863. And so it had. "The planter is more ready to contribute his sons than his slaves to the war," the *Mobile Register* declared in outrage during one impressment campaign. It was a damning accusation, and one that at this distance seems palpably true. Slaveholders offered more opposition to slave impressment than to conscription. F. S. Blount, chief impressment agent in the Department of Alabama, Mississippi, and East Louisiana, talked of his failures to get enough slaves "to complete a road so vitally important to the protection of the very individuals, whose highest patriotic impulses never ascend above their own petty . . . schemes for the accumulation of wealth." "You cheerfully yield your children to your country, how you refuse your servants?" one broadside blasted.[43] Slavery, as it turned out, was a form of property that dangerously attenuated citizens' allegiance to the state and submission to its authority. Planters colluded with their slaves in thwarting impressment agents, giving them passes or running them into the woods at the first approach of government agents. They took oaths of allegiance in occupied territory to hold onto their slaves and guided Yankee detachments back to their plantations to repossess their worldly wealth in cotton and slaves. They attacked military commanders who did not make it a priority to protect their property or prevent its escape, and they demanded that politicians represent their interests against the demands of the War Department and the Davis administration. For some, any state would do—Union, Confederate, Brazilian—if it adequately protected their property in slaves.[44]

Slaveholders, it seems, were more concerned with property than nation. Do historians' robust assertions of the strength and endurance of Confederate nationalism take that into account? How else are we to explain the actions of a group insane enough to take a region and all its people into a perilous war, but not patriotic enough to do what it took to fight it?[45] Everywhere in the C.S.A. the policy on slave impressment was resisted. In some places that resistance reached a scale that could only be called massive civil disobedience. In Georgia and North Carolina, legislatures battled the tyranny of the federal government on behalf of slaveholders' inalienable rights of property in slaves. In South Carolina, that struggle went to extremes as planters who had long been "ready with excuses for not furnishing labor to defend Charleston" stacked the legislature with their own and then wrote legislation designed, as Brigadier General John S. Preston charged, "as an explicit declaration that this State does not intend to contribute another slave or soldier to the public defense." As chief of the Bureau of Conscription, Preston, himself a Carolinian, had been out trying to procure "men and labor for the public defense." But there was no military situation so dire as to prevent quibbling. In 1863 Preston had managed to get only 450 of the 2,500 slaves requisitioned by the Engineer's Department, while the governor and legislature ignored the War Department's urging to pass relevant legislation. And again in 1864, even as General Sherman advanced toward Charleston, he could not get the 2,500 men called for. Then in late 1864, with Sherman's legions virtually at the gates, the legislature of South Carolina passed two acts—one asserting ultimate state authority over conscription and another over impressment—so in conflict with the instructions of the War Department that Preston denounced them as "treason to the Confederate States." "May you be endowed with strength and wisdom to overcome enemies stronger than yankee armies—the folly and wickedness of our own people,"

Preston wrote his president.[46] Planters would not sacrifice the very property they had created the government to protect.

The Confederate government's struggle to make impressment work was coterminous with the war itself. It reached its climax right where it started, in Virginia. As Lee and the Army of Northern Virginia fought for the nation's very survival in the trenches of Richmond and Petersburg from December 1864 to April 1865, Governor Smith fought and lost another battle to deliver the slave labor Lee repeatedly requested. In that last attempt, Smith leveled the full power of the state and federal government against scofflaw planters. He used data from the Engineer's Bureau to draw up detailed charts of the number of eligible slaves in each county, harassed local sheriffs and clerks of county courts to comply, threatened punitive action against those who did not, and sought and got additional legislation to compel enforcement.[47] No other governor pushed as hard. Still, Smith failed in the face of a campaign that combined slaveholders' usual resistance with the calculated refusal of local officials to enforce his orders. No sooner had Smith's call on the counties gone out than he was "overwhelmed" with requests for exemption or suspension of the orders. Some came from individual planters, but most were official remonstrances. The county court of Caroline protested its obligation to send a hundred male slaves, offering the usual explanation that citizens had already lost three-quarters of their slaves and another call would result in "a much larger acquisition of slaves to the enemy than to the Confederate Government." As usual, slaves' opposition to impressment was the reason for noncompliance. Others claimed that the cavalry had destroyed the county, that soldiers' wives would starve, that slaves had been abused, and always that slaves would escape rather than go. And so it went on, at least nine counties and the city of Lynchburg making formal application for release from the call.[48]

In Virginia, even as the enemy advanced on the capital, the governor faced a level of resistance, not just from civilians but civil authorities, that he regarded as treasonous. "Entire communities and not just individuals resisted the call." Smith was withering in his denunciation of slaveholders so preoccupied with petty property interests, so narrow-minded and shortsighted, they could not see the larger national picture. "At a time when the slave institution is itself in peril & our ability to hold Richmond would make our interests in slave property worthless," he charged, slaveholders had responded with "coldness and reluctance" to Lee's call for slaves to hold the city. Their action was enough to fill "the hearts of those anxious for our liberty and independence with anguish if not with despondency." In March 1865 Smith was still trying to get the men Lee called for. He sent out a circular to the courts of the counties and cities reiterating their obligation to comply with the requisitions and trying to elicit a patriotic, or failing that, self-interested response from slaveholders, "involving as it does the safety of the capital of our State, and, it may be, the institution of slavery itself."[49]

Governor Smith fought hard to the end. His fight with the slaveholders and the counties over the impressment of slave men for military labor went on so long, it gave way seamlessly to the struggle to enroll slave men in the Confederate army. In mid-March 1865 he sent out an angry circular calling for 20 percent of the slaves between 18 and 55 and giving notice that his order "will be rigidly enforced" and official "malfeasance" punished. March 25 found him compiling numbers of slaves in the counties available for military service and corresponding with Lee about the "importance of making a right commencement in the business of enrolling for military purposes." Nor was he alone. A few months earlier General Joseph Johnston had responded to the critical shortage of soldiers by proposing to Davis that they substitute slaves for soldiers on detached or fatigue duty. As an incentive he suggested that slaves receive a portion of a soldier's pay. This scheme, while falling within the parameters of impressment, sounds like military enlistment; it treated slaves as the property of masters while addressing the issue of slave men's willingness to serve.[50] Even as they failed to get slave laborers, they moved on to getting slave soldiers.

In the Confederate States of America, the struggle over impressment was not simply prologue to, but continuous with, the struggle over slave enlistment. All of the critical questions tied up with slave enlistment had been faced in attempts to impress slave men's labor: the status and security of slave property, the locus of sovereignty in a slaveholders' state, and above all, the personhood and political allegiance of slave men. None of these issues were new when the Confederate government turned to consideration of enlisting slave men in its armies. They would reach new proportions when the government proposed to extract the ultimate obligation of the citizen—military service—from the slave. But the key questions had already been faced. The Confederate state in its desperation for labor had already been forced into a revolutionary intrusion of its authority on the master-slave relation. The Confederate debate over arming slaves did not begin de novo in 1864 as historians assume, but was part of a much longer struggle to harness slaves' labor to the cause, one concurrent with the war itself.

In a remarkable address to Congress in November 1864, President Davis admitted that impressment had been a failure and called for a radical modification of the law of slavery to recognize slaves as persons and not just property as a way to secure their loyalty and allegiance to the cause. That was a recognition slaves themselves had extracted by their determined refusal to labor for the military forces of C.S.A. When President Davis raised the possibility that the "private right of property" could no longer be maintained, he was still just trying to find a way to get access to slave men—forty thousand he said—to use for every military task short of shouldering the rifle. It was not just the failure of every previous policy of impressment that had driven him to that juncture, but the impossibility of any that sought to mobilize slaves as property.[51]

In the end, efforts to make the policy work were thwarted by the actions of the slaves themselves. Impressed as property, slaves instead acted as political subjects, confounding every government attempt to make them an element of strength in war. In doing so, they forced a whole set of awkward questions about the political allegiances of slave property. The C.S.A. was not rich in railroads, factories, financial capital, or diplomatic allies. It did not even boast the North's population. But it did have one treasure trove of wealth, one peerless natural resource in its slaves. Or so Confederates thought, until it was transformed by the alchemy of war.

The recognition of slaves' personhood and political subjectivity eventually registered at every level of the Confederate regime, from the plantation to the highest reaches of central state authority. The slaves' actions in pursuit of emancipation shaped impressment policy, profoundly undercut its effectiveness, and showed the weakness of a slave state with limited access to a whole subject population. But it did more. It set off a competition between military powers for the labor and loyalty of slave men that played out in the military policies of the Confederate state no less than it did the Union.[52]

In the C.S.A. the practical recognition of the danger slaves posed forced a series of significant adjustments in the conduct of the war. Among planters and state officials, it generated demands for the diversion of scarce military resources from the battlefront to domestic needs, to protect slave property, suppress revolt, and curtail escape to the enemy.[53] For commanders in the field, it posed an impossible issue of loyalty and treason that propelled them and the War Department into a perilous reconsideration of the political status of slave men in the Confederate body politic long before the president was pushed to that juncture.

On the Atlantic coast and on the Mississippi River, Union incursions and occupations wrought havoc. In eastern North Carolina, planters' struggles started early with the mass escape of slaves following the capitulation of Forts Clark and Hatteras in the first summer of the war. In Hyde and Martin counties on Pamlico Sound, scores of slaves escaped every day, some taking their masters' horses to the enemy. Coastal planters attempted to stem the tide, begging local military commanders to find a way to cordon off their slaves from the Yankees. Even as the battle for eastern North Carolina raged the following year, planters raised a mounted patrol to establish a line of defense against their slaves on the Tar River, and commanding officers chronically short of men and trying to guard against Union advance, faced additional civilian demands that their troops attend to the protection of slave property. The state legislature, meeting in secret session, acknowledged the extent of the problem: "Facts of a startling nature are existing—The slaves unanimously refuse to be removed . . . They are fully aware of the causes of the invasion and know that involves their freedom." Nobody underestimated the problem. "I am decidedly of the opinion it would be best if our pickets would take no more negroes prisoners that runaway to go to Newbern but would shoot them on the spot," one citizen instructed the governor. "They are our open enemies & are well calculated to do us immense injury."[54]

The recognition of slaves as the enemy within was hardly lost on local military commanders. The military costs or benefits of slaves' adherence to the enemy were readily apparent on both sides of the Civil War divide. Union soldiers regularly testified to the value of slaves' military intelligence. In Kentucky, Union soldiers relied on slaves for information about which local whites were loyal men. Escaped Union prisoners of war were guided out of Charleston by slave men. A Savannah waiter provided the Union commander at Fort Pulaski detailed information about the location and number of rebel batteries, ships, and guns and the conditions of roads for moving artillery. A Union officer at Huntsville, Alabama, posted slave spies on river plantations to get the kind of intelligence he needed to "defy the enemy" on the 120-mile stretch of river he guarded. A lieutenant was able to defend against an attack on a supply train because a slave named Johnston came to his pickets in the night with information gleaned at his master's dinner table. "The negroes are our only friends" was how Brigadier General O. M. Mitchel put it when requesting permission to offer government protection to those fugitives who "furnish us valuable information." Secretary of War Stanton was not inclined to quarrel: "The assistance of slaves is an element of military strength," he said, assuring Mitchel that he was fully justified in making use of it. The ex-slaves who detailed their services to the Union in postwar hearings had plenty of corroboration to the truth of their claims.[55]

For every piece of intelligence, equipment, or manpower slaves delivered to Union forces, Confederate planters and military men paid. The threat slaves posed to Confederate military operations had to be met on the ground and involved a commitment of forces that could hardly be afforded anywhere in the C.S.A. But the effort to assert military control over slaves who proved subversive of military success posed other, more existential problems, as became clear to local commanders on the coasts of Georgia and Florida in the spring and summer of 1862. Then when a committee of citizens of Liberty County, Georgia, past frustration at their inability to prevent the flow of their slaves to the enemy, pushed the local commanding officer to punish captured slaves under *military law,* it was clear that slaves had forced a practical acknowledgment of what had long been denied: that "the Negroes constitute a part of the body politic, in fact, and should be made to know their duty . . . to the government under which they live." Listing with outrage the various acts of local slaves and their military value to Union troops as "spies," "guides," "pilots," and even soldiers in blue, the Georgia men declared "the absconding Negroes . . . Traitors" and demanded that they be subject to capital punishment under martial law. Slaveholders and Confederates themselves, they acknowledged the obvious problem, that in the case of "Negroes," it would be hard to mete out such a punishment because of the "absence of the political ties of allegiance and the peculiar status of the race." But found in "rebellion against the power and authority of their owners and the Government under which they live," with no relief adequate under civil law, they had to be recognized for what they were—traitors.[56]

Nobody in the Confederacy was seeking a redefinition of slaves as persons and citizens obligated to allegiance. But the Liberty County planters' recognition of slaves as members of the body politic marks precisely the distance war had taken such men and much Southern thinking. To measure it, one has only to recall the views Chief Justice Taney offered as legal convention in 1857: that slaves were "no part of the people" or the political community, were "repudiated, and rejected from the duties and obligations of citizenship."[57] By 1862 in some parts of the Confederacy, slaves—men in particular—had emerged as a force in Confederate politics in their political identity as the enemy within.

To find a way to hold slaves accountable for their treason was no simple matter in the C.S.A. Brigadier General Mercer acknowledged the dilemma in forwarding the Liberty County men's memorial to the secretary of war. He hardly minimized the impasse commanders found themselves in, dealing with the consequences of slaves' aid and support to the enemy but unable to pursue them as they would other citizens and subjects of the nation. "The subject presented . . . is one that demands the early notice of the Congress," he wrote, "and the Instructions of the War Department." "The evil and danger alluded to may grow into frightful proportions unless checked . . . it is likely to become of portentous magnitude if the war continues, and I do not see how it can be properly dealt with except by the supreme legislature of the country."[58] The matter of slaves' allegiance was a huge and looming problem for commanders like Mercer. Slaves' allegiance counted, as Jefferson knew it would.

The problem was not merely legal and theoretical, but posed huge problems for commanders in the field. Indeed, the recognition of slaves as "open enemies" compelled the Confederate military to fight on two fronts. From the beginning of the war, local governments had demanded the retention of troops at home to keep the slaves in subjection. Reports of official committees set up in late 1860 and 1861 to put states on a war footing prominently included in their calculation of "military need" sufficient means to fight "sudden invasion from abroad *and* insurrectionary movements at home." That two-front logic continued to govern official thinking and planning throughout the war and was a constant feature of negotiation among local, state, and federal officials. One striking pattern was the way planters and governors repeatedly presented evidence of slave conspiracies in requesting the retention of military forces at home. Charges of slave insurrection could surface at any time, but as in the antebellum period, Christmas was "the most critical time of the year as it concerns insurrections," as one Georgia citizen put it in 1860. By the next Christmas the usual anxiety about slaves converged with frightening new circumstances, none more important than the departure of so many soldiers and the resulting scarcity of armed men at home.[59] Wherever charges of slave insurrection arose at Christmas, as they did every year of the war, they were invariably tied to appeals to state or federal officials to retain at home troops scheduled to depart.

The pattern was especially clear in North Carolina at Christmas 1864. It was a critical moment in Confederate fortunes as Fort Fisher, entrance to the last open Confederate port, first survived and then fell under bombardment from the Union navy massed on the coast. As citizens anticipated the advance of Sherman's army on their state and the battle of Wilmington raged, officials called up every white man, including the home guard and boys aged 10 to 15. At that exact moment, whites in a cluster of southern Piedmont counties smack in what they thought was Sherman's path, produced evidence of a massive slave insurrection—including the building up of a slave army—as urgent proof of the need to keep troops at home. One citizen, reporting the "discovery of a war planned . . . and most diabolical scheme of Insurrection among the negroes," urged Governor Vance to "call the attention of the Legislature . . . to the subject of local defence and protection against such enemies" and to keep a sufficient number of men at home to preserve "the government of negroes." Even as every man was required at the front, Confederate citizens pressed their need for men at home to fight the slaves. So insistent were Southern planters on retaining their monopoly on the means of violence that even planters in occupied Mississippi and Louisiana routinely raised charges of slave insurrection at Christmastime as justification for the rearming of local militias and home guards. This long-standing battle to retain guns and mastery in the hands of whites preceded the American Civil War and would continue long after it was over.[60]

The need to fight the domestic enemy shaped manpower policy in the Confederacy in fundamental ways. First it required the withholding of men from the front. The exemption added to the first Confederate conscription law, which authorized the retention at home of one man for each twenty slaves owned, was the most concrete—and controversial—measure of the cost of fighting the enslaved. Adopted, tellingly, after the penetration of the Mississippi Valley by the Union in the spring and summer of 1862, and in response to the screams of planters about the need to put down the slaves' revolt, it cost the Confederate military heavily, not just in men but political support among nonslaveholding whites, especially after the food riots of 1863. President Davis made no bones about the logic of that law. It had gotten more criticism than it deserved, he noted in a speech in Jackson in December 1862, on a rare trip to the western theater. "The object of [it] . . . was not to draw any distinction of classes, but simply to provide a . . . police force, sufficient to keep our negroes in control. This is the sole object of the clause."[61] The need to retain military force at home to fight domestic dependents was one of the key structural problems faced by slave regimes at war, and the C.S.A. was no exception. The government's lack of access to men "ineligible by reason of servitude"—the fact that the population from which they could recruit was only 60 percent of military-age Southern men—was another significant toll on the military.

In the literature on the Confederacy, the cost of slavery to the war effort has figured mostly in arguments about military defeat: about whether the C.S.A. was simply overpowered by an enemy with superior resources in men and arms or was weakened from within; and the related argument about whether the commitment to slavery was a critical foundation of Southern nationalism (including among nonslaveholders) or served to erode nonslaveholders' nationalism and will to fight.[62] Slavery, in other words, has figured mostly in argument about why Confederates lost, not how they fought. But that hardly takes the military measure of slavery in the C.S.A., because slavery figured not just in the causes and outcomes of the war, but in the conduct of it as well. As planters grasped the scale of their war with the slaves, the slaves' intention to turn the Union army to their own account, and the upending of order in whole districts with even rumors of Union advance, they turned expectantly to the Confederate army to restore the balance of power.[63] Planter demands that local commanders calibrate military strategy to protect their investment in slaves —that they deploy their forces to accomplish that end—set up a struggle between planters (and the governors and state legislators who represented them) and local military men over the conduct, and even object, of the American Civil War.

Planters' demands on the military were constant and unyielding. Some seemed to regard the Confederate army as little more than a giant slave patrol. "The conscript army should not be prostituted into a police guard for the slaves," one outraged Virginia senator protested early in the war. He hardly exaggerated. In South Carolina, as Union gunboats advanced on Port Royal in November 1861, planters like William Elliott applied to the local commander for a military force to restrain their slaves, and railed against him when he failed to make that a priority. "The abandonment of Port Royal was no military necessity," Elliott raged, recounting the losses in slaves and crops. A few months later Francis Pickens, the governor of South Carolina, complained bitterly to President Davis about a Confederate general (Pemberton) whose strategy of withdrawal from the coast around Georgetown saved cannon and men but "exposed some sixty thousand negroes and entirely destroyed the prospect of a rice crop of one million five hundred thousand bushels." It would only take "ten negro men to have paid for their cost," he expostulated, grossly computing the value of military hardware and manpower in the market value of slaves, slaveholders' common currency. In 1863 one prominent citizen reported the existence of a squad of slaves armed with swords and guns in the upper reaches of his parish and asked the local general to detail men to capture the slaves with dogs. Again in 1864, Georgetown planters alerted President Davis to the need for twelve thousand troops to guard the coastline, keep the slaves inland, and prevent them from communicating freely with the blockaders, as if a request for twelve thousand troops was realistic in 1864. No military situation was too pressing to override planters' private needs.[64] Even Jefferson Davis's brother, Joseph, was not above requesting the deployment of a Confederate unit to try to retake his plantation, Hurricane, after the slaves took control of the place. Even some military men continued to think as planters, conflating the national interest with their own petty property concerns. When General Wade Hampton heard that his plantations in Mississippi would be destroyed by advancing federal forces, he requested reassignment to Mississippi with "cavalry, sharpshooters, and Arty to protect the prominent landings on the river."[65]

Planters' calculations of their interests were so narrow that some refused to comply with military orders to remove slaves in communication with the enemy. When a Major Jeffords ordered the removal of the slaves of an Ashepoo River planter in November 1862 on "incontestable proof" that they were "in continual intercourse with the enemy" and endangering his picket line, "the proprietor . . . refused to remove them." His commanding officer confirmed the truth of the charges against local slaves. When he sent out a scout "who pretended to be a Yankee" to test "one or two old negroes near the enemy's lines . . . they gave him all the information an enemy could desire in regard to the position and strength of my pickets." Union naval men operating on the South Carolina rivers relied on that kind of intelligence to plan their operations, as Commander P. Drayton confirmed to Flag Officer DuPont in December 1861. The slaves assisted them voluntarily, he reported, of a successful expedition up the Ashepoo, where so many slaves approached his boat that he could not take them all. "I overheard one of them say that it was but fair that they should do for us as we were working for them."[66] Slaves' insistence on their own interpretation of the war, and demonstration of their military value to the Union, cost the Confederate military heavily.

The necessity of fighting on two fronts was an ineluctable condition of war in the slaveholders' republic. The need to contain the damage slaves could inflict shaped military men's calculations about what was necessary, no less than it did planters'. In view of what everyone came to regard as slaves' potentially treasonable correspondence with the enemy, commanders of vulnerable forces had no choice but to divert troops to fight slaves as a matter of strategy. In coastal South Carolina the destruction of slavery on local plantations in 1861 was of sufficient significance to warrant a telegram to the governor from his aide-de-camp. It isn't clear what military action was taken at that point. But a year later, as slaves from Beaufort and Savannah arrived at Union lines carrying valuable information threatening the safety of local Confederate units, instructions went out from headquarters to "make a reconnaisance [using the 'Rebel Troop'] up the country around Summerville, S.C." because of the "disturbance and alarm . . . caused by gangs of run away negroes, leagued with deserters in that neighborhood." A few months later Colonel Lawrence Keitt confirmed the continuing need for troops in coastal South Carolina to guard all of the inlets along the coast because "numbers of negroes intimately acquainted with the network of Bays, inlets, creeks and narrows along the coast, have deserted to the enemy and are known to have passed frequently between the fleet or the islands and the parishes of Christ church and St. James Santee." It was knowledge of those kinds of inland waterways and the number and precise position of Confederate troops, pickets, fortifications, and guns on them that Robert Blake had recently conveyed in astonishing detail to federal forces in Beaufort. Little wonder, then, that Keitt felt compelled to assign more men he couldn't afford to join the "three cavalry companies . . . and two infantry companies" already assigned to guard and patrol the coast. Keitt's pointillist map of vulnerable points of exit and entry suggests just how difficult it was to keep the enemy out when there was another enemy at hand to guide them in. Like Governor Wise in Virginia, Keitt ordered the "removal of all the small Boats" from the local rivers, because they could be used by the slaves in their escape.[67]

That the war against the slaves materially shaped Confederate military strategy was something Union military men acknowledged in time and place. Keitt's orders lend credence to the charges Union colonel Thomas W. Higginson prominently expressed before a Senate committee: in South Carolina, rebel "pickets are stationed with a view to keeping slaves in rather than others out—disposed more with reference to internal than external approaches." "I often find pickets posted up rivers at points where slaves would be likely to come," he testified. In December 1862 federal naval commanders reported that the coastal islands were "infested with gangs of rebel cavalry whose principal if not sole object is to drive the negroes into the interior." As late as February 1865 that was still true. For even as the Confederacy fell, as black soldiers started to appear in interior districts, as slaves on interior plantations waited out the last agonizing weeks of war, Confederate military authorities were still dispatching troops to "suppress disorder among the negroes," and Confederate scouts were still waging a campaign of murderous violence against local slaves that shaded seamlessly into the postwar terrorizing of freedpeople by paramilitary remnants of that same army.[68] If Confederate planters expected the national army to function as a giant slave patrol, sometimes they got their wish. Given the value of fugitive slaves to the enemy, Confederate military men faced their own imperatives to play slave-catcher.

The interests of planters and military authorities were hardly the same. But the slaves' determined war against their masters and their masters' state opened an internal front in the Confederate war and demanded the diversion of military resources to fight it. The significance of winning on that front increased exponentially once the Union government and military moved from simply confiscating slave property and using it for military labor to waging an explicitly emancipationist war in which they enlisted black men as soldiers. At that point—with the Emancipation Proclamation and Militia Act—the Confederate military's battle with the South's four million slaves entered a new, more critical phase, and the competition with the Union for the bodies and political allegiance of slave men became overt. "The policy of our enemy in arming and organizing negro regiments, is being pushed to formidable proportions," Kirby Smith put it from his post in the beleaguered trans-Mississippi west. "Our plantations are made his recruiting stations . . . When we fall back as little as possible should be left for the enemy." Endorsing a policy of slave removal that became general throughout the C.S.A., he rendered the military logic brutally clear: "Every sound male black left for the enemy becomes a soldier whom we have afterwards to fight."[69]

The calculus was entirely defensive, the goal to deprive the Union army of loyal slave recruits, and in the absence of planter cooperation, the policy required the detachment of cavalry to execute it. In northern Mississippi, General Order No. 70 called for planters to remove their slaves in advance of Union troops and dispatched cavalry to do so. "Detachments will be sent from each Brigade into the District of Country adjacent to the enemies lines to arrest and remove within our lines all able bodied negroe men who are liable to be captured by the enemy . . . No others than those capable of performing Military duty will be taken." "Old women and children will be allowed to remain," another officer noted. Thus did the Confederate military make the same kinds of distinctions between men and women as the Union did in the policy of sorting by gender—siphoning men off to the army and assigning women to the plantations—which it applied concurrently in the same region.[70]

Removal of slave men was clearly a military imperative. But the policy was hardly calculated to appeal to planters and states. The Confederate War Department and individual military commanders were left to contend with the consequences of civilian opposition and to summon sufficient authority to control the movement of slaves and insist on their removal. Slaves were, after all, the private property of Confederate citizens, and planters generally regarded themselves as the ultimate authority over them. Inevitably, with the military policy of slave removal, as with impressment, the masters' paramount claim—sovereignty—was sharply at issue.

In some states, governors and legislators recognized that private property—slaves—was now a matter of urgent public interest. In November 1863, as Mississippi was overrun with Union troops and the government fled the capital, Governor Pettus reiterated the logic of removal. "Every able bodied negro man that falls in to the hands of the enemy is not only a laborer lost to the county," he insisted, "he is also, under the current policy of the U.S. government, a soldier gained to its army." He urged the passage of legislation that would authorize officials to make such disposition of slaves as may "be deemed best for the public good." South Carolina passed legislation that empowered military commanders to execute the removal of slaves even over the objections of owners.[71] But as with impressment, planter opposition was widespread and planters were hard to best. Commanders tried to harness planters' concern about the value of slave property to their own military objectives. One circular distributed in South Carolina in 1863 warned planters that their property was in more danger than at any time since the commencement of the war, and made the case that it was the "duty of every plantation owner to remove every negro whose age and strength fit them" for military service. Planters were not convinced. One public letter of protest, composed at a public meeting, offered the familiar objection that removal was "impractical and especially impolitic" because slaves would not consent to it. Planters in Mississippi responded in precisely the same way, offering evidence that those who tried removal lost nearly all the men and many of the women and children. Secretary of War Seddon was firm in his response, his backbone stiffened, perhaps, by the reports of Assistant Secretary of War Campbell and others in November 1863 describing the absolutely dire prospects of replenishing the armies. "If the negroes remain on the estates," Seddon wrote the Mississippi protesters, "they will be subject to Yankey control and the males may at any time be Drafted into their Armies—is it not the duty of the Confederate government to prevent this and instead of allowing the male slave to be converted into armed soldiers against us to preserve them as useful laborers for their owners and the Confederacy?"[72]

In Mississippi and South Carolina, Seddon's appeal worked and legislatures fell in line, conceding to the War Department the authority it needed. It still cost them in scarce manpower to enforce the policy, and planters never cooperated voluntarily or ceded authority over their slaves to military commanders. The issue of sovereignty was everywhere pressing. But some states were recalcitrant, Virginia critically so. There the legislature again construed itself as the ultimate defender of the slaveholders' interests and put the protection of their property claims above the demands of patriotism. In January 1864, Wyndham Robertson, chairman of the Virginia legislative committee on Confederate relations, wrote a letter to Seddon conveying the legislature's vehement opposition to his recent removal policy. He made no bones about the effect of slaves' politics on the state's slaveholders; there weren't many male slaves left, he claimed, and "efforts to remove the rest into Confederate lines would be met by flight to the woods or to the enemy." In Virginia slaves were again setting the terms of slaveholders' support for Confederate military policy. Gentlemen had expressed the fear, Robertson told Seddon, that "the loss of their still remaining slaves occasioned by such an intervention of the Government might lead . . . to alienating from our cause persons now friendly to it." It was a startling and potentially treasonous admission: that slaveholders' loyalty to their own country was contingent on that state's protection of their property in slaves. It cuts against the view that the C.S.A. was prepared to sacrifice slavery for nation.[73] It was not clear where the greater threat of treason lay in Confederate Virginia: among the slaves or their owners.

In the standoff with Virginia, the weakness of the central state in slave republics was again in evidence. Seddon bowed to the pressure. Heretofore "the enemy used mainly seduction [to gain slave recruits] and have not, so far as known, drafted or forced slaves into military service," he wrote Robertson, in what constituted a blunt acknowledgment of slaves' political volition for a high official of a proslavery state. The Confederate War Department would defer to the wishes of Virginia slaveholders and the state legislature for now, he said. But if the United States moved to recruitment by compulsion, then Confederate forces would be justified in acting even over the objections of owners.[74]

In the C.S.A., even in the most difficult days of the war, when every resource was stretched to the limit, the War Department struggled to exert sufficient authority over slaveholders to get the access to slave men crucial to military operations and prospects. Having gone to war to protect and extend claims to property in slaves, they had to live, and fight, with the consequences. In the American Civil War, all parties to the conflict attempted to turn the mass of adult slave men into a "beneficent element of governmental power," as one Union advocate of slave enlistment put it, and all understood slaves' lack of relation to the state as the central problem in their ability to do so. "They are of that 4,000,000 of our colored subjects who have no king or chief, nor in fact any Government that can secure to them the simplest natural rights," the same U.S. military officer wrote. "A small class of owners . . . stand between them and their Government, destroying its sovereignty." Union Brigadier General Phelps was fighting his war from southern Louisiana. It was the sovereignty of the Union government he had in mind, but he could as well have been speaking about the Confederate one too.[75]

The mix of compromised state sovereignty and slaves' political agency proved lethal in the C.S.A. Conditions on the ground sounded a constant drumbeat of trouble not just for planters in their daily operations but for military commanders in theirs. The slaves' insurrection loomed over it all. As officers routinely complained, the problem of loyalty and allegiance slaves posed was acutely pressing but impossible to resolve at the level of an individual command. Charles Manigault could casually acknowledge his slaves' sedition; planters all over the South could rail about their slaves' lack of fidelity and intention to desert to the enemy; North Carolina authorities could arrest white men for treasonable conduct in exciting a slave to insurrection; individual citizens could bluntly identify slaves as the enemy; and groups of citizens, like the one Colonel Colcock Jones was part of in Liberty County, Georgia, could flat out call them "traitors." "They are traitors who may pilot an enemy into your *bedchamber,*" he wrote his son. "They know every road and swamp and creek and plantation in the country, and are the worst of spies." Radical Union commanders might reverse the equation, putting the stigma of treason on the masters. "Fugitive rebels," David Hunter famously called them, men who "everywhere fly before the appearance of the National Flag." What was needed instead was a "fugitive master law," he wrote sarcastically. But from the Southern point of view, it was slaves who were the traitors, slaves whose "absence of the political ties of allegiance" posed a threat to the very existence of the Confederate republic. Confederate citizens from all walks of life looked to the government and the military to establish slaves' accountability. "Can we find protection under Military Law?" the Liberty County planters asked. "This is the question we submit to the General in Command."[76]

But it was one thing for private citizens to call slaves traitors and quite another for the government or military to formally acknowledge them as such, given the Pandora's box it would open about their standing in the slaveholders' republic. And yet that is precisely the position to which the Davis administration was driven by the actions of a military officer in Pensacola, Florida, when, in responding to conditions much like those in Liberty County, he initiated a court-martial of six slave men in March 1862. The charges? "Attempt to violate the 57th Article of War," "holding correspondence with, or giving intelligence to, the enemy." "Who ever heard of a negro slave being arregned before a court martial for a violation of the Articles of War?" their incredulous master railed. Who indeed? In charging slaves with treason, the officer posed a profound question about their political status and membership in the body politic. A "traitor," after all, was one who would "overthrow the government or impair the well-being of a state to which one owed allegiance." Did slaves owe allegiance to the state? Could slaves be traitors? Were they subject to military law?[77] The settlement of those questions went all the way up the chain of command to the secretary of war, raising fundamental questions about slaves' changing relation to the state.

The officer in command, Colonel Thomas Jones, had his views, although he knew he was on shaky ground. Jones and his troops, the 27th Mississippi, were in a highly exposed condition, holding Pensacola Harbor while positioned directly across the bay from Fort Pickens, which was in Union hands and to which slaves were constantly escaping. "Colonel Jones was left at Pensacola under very trying circumstances," his superior officer, Major General Samuel Jones, reported to a War Department official after all hell broke loose, "and strong measures were needed to prevent spys whether white or black conveying information of his true condition to the enemy." Planters from that area of the Florida panhandle, and even the governor, John Milton, were simultaneously pleading with President Davis for troops to stem the tide of slaves "defect[ing] to Pensacola, where they are constantly giving information to the enemy." In fact, Colonel Jones identified runaway and insurgent slaves as the greatest threat to his "little army." Convinced of their "treasonous designs," he had already issued a proclamation making known his intention to apprehend slaves detected in escape to Santa Rosa Island. Jones did not seek to revolutionize the condition of slaves, only to contain the military threat they posed. On March 26, when his men picked up six slaves, five belonging to Jackson Morton and another belonging to a Mr. R. L. Campbell, he subjected them to a court-martial under the 57th Article of War. All six were convicted on all counts, three sentenced to death and three others to multiple rounds of whipping, all to be carried out by April 14.[78]

And there it might have ended, in the invisible torture and death of six slave men, six more added to the innumerable count piled up by Confederate troops and guerillas during the American Civil War. But Colonel Jones was a proper military man. He initiated a legal procedure, allowed the slaves a defense lawyer, and produced a record of the court-martials that Jackson Morton then used to challenge the legitimacy of the proceedings. As well he might. Could the court-martials of slaves under the Articles of War stand up to official scrutiny? Could the War Department really sanction it? Morton had his views, and he played them out in full with the War Department. Denouncing the court's proceedings as "irregular and improper," and the officer as the "autocrat of Pensacola," he insisted that his slaves were just slaves, subject as such to punishment only by him. "The negroes should have been delivered to me when apprehended, I should have had them properly punished and removed to a place of safety," he railed. To him this was simply a matter of slave fidelity concerning only their loyalty to him. But if the master Morton still regarded slaves as subjects of the household state and the masters' law—just runaways—Colonel Jones thought them by necessity subjects like other citizens of the Confederate state and military law. To him and the court that convicted them, they were five "intelligent beings, possessing the faculties of conveying information which prove useful to the enemy and detrimental to the Confederate states." Traitors, that is, not runaways. Testimony produced at trial confirmed the Morton slaves' knowledge of the local waterways, troop strength, recent reductions in numbers, and lack of arms.[79]

The court-martials of the slaves put Colonel Jones and, as it turned out, the Confederate War Department on uncharted—and very precarious—ground. It was, as Morton charged, a clear departure from the army's customary policy, which stipulated the holding of recaptured slaves in depots in each state to be reclaimed by, or delivered to, their owners. That policy, although a drain on military resources, was entirely in keeping with the constitutional obligation to treat slaves as the private property of their owners.[80]

There was simply no precedent for charging slaves with treason under civil or military law. The treason law the United States had adapted from English law retained the essential principle that acts of treason aimed at the overthrow of the government. The new federal and state laws, like the colonial statutes, encompassed "domestic insurrection" or "domestic disturbance" within the offense of treason, but the threat posed by alliance with, or adherence to, an external enemy was clearly the main concern. More important, in every case when writing treason acts or clauses, the new government entities—the Continental Congress, Congress, and the individual states—explicitly tied allegiance to the laws of the United Colonies or States to the "protection" derived from those laws.[81] One had to be under the protection of the laws to owe allegiance to the state. Because of the obligation to personal obedience incurred by those in subjection, even free married women were questionable cases with respect to charges of treason. Legal citizens, clearly under the protection of the law, they were shackled by coverture and the competing legal obligation of submission to their husbands. States that had rendered explicit women's obligation to refrain from treason during the Revolutionary War beat a fast retreat in its aftermath, remanding married women to the legal jurisdiction of coverture.[82]

Slaves were a far more clear-cut case. Understood by almost any standard as being outside the protection of the law, they were bound instead by ties of subjection to a particular master, owing obedience and allegiance exclusively to him. The nineteenth-century record leaves very little evidence of treason charges ever being brought against slaves. There were a few cases reflecting an older view, probably still held in the war years, that slave insurrections threatened the social order and thus constituted a crime not just against the master but against the people and the state. But the majority of those charged specifically with treason in relation to slave insurrections were white men, and slaveowners were careful not to treat slaves as guilty of high treason, "thereby avoiding . . . any problem about *allegiance* due to society." Instead slaveowners believed that the allegiance slaves owed had a private object (their owners) and that slaves were capable only of petit treason—willful murder committed by one who is in subjection to and owes duty and obedience to the party murdered—not high treason. To apply the treason act to slaves in the event of rebellion was to treat them as citizens of the state in some fashion or another. The idea of slave treason was legally incoherent.[83]

The year of war that preceded Colonel Jones's court-martials offered manifold evidence of slaves' revolt against their masters, intent to levy war and adhere to their enemies, but little by way of precedent for treason charges against the perpetrators. The climate of vigilantism and summary justice that prevailed in 1861 and continued throughout the war explains that. Ad hoc committees of safety, or the kind of "examination committees" to which the Second Creek slaves were subjected, did the work of trial and punishment that would otherwise have reached the courts. "I saw a Negro hung in Jackson for being hired to the Yankees to go in our breast works and see how many big guns we had," a soldier in a Jackson regiment reported. "He undertook the task for the promise of 40 Dollars and was hung for it rite before our Regt." Slaves constituted only about 5 percent of the 4,100 or so political prisoners held in Castle Thunder in Richmond in 1862–63 (the only prisoner census available); most at risk of indictment were presumably spared that formality and dealt with out on the roads and waterways by extralegal means, as was the Jackson slave. The military mostly operated the same way. Of the few slaves accorded the privilege of imprisonment, the majority were simply listed as runaways and held for return to their owners. The handful captured on their way to or from the enemy were held on specific charges, including informing to the enemy, but only one for "disloyalty."[84] None were charged with treason, which explains the furor that arose around Colonel Jones's decision to court-martial Morton's slaves under the 57th Article of War.

Colonel Jones did not purport to try Peter, William, George, Robert, and Stephen in state court. He exercised his authority as a commander under military law. But even that elastic domain was unpromising to Jones's case, his decision a departure from usual practice and, in an official sense, untested. The legitimate reach of military law was hotly disputed during the Civil War, North and South, and in the C.S.A. the issue of whether a civilian could be tried by court-martial was fiercely contested, with civilian lawyers, politicians, at least one state supreme court justice (North Carolina) and even the Confederate vice president, Alexander Stephens, denying that they could. "The Constitution is made for war as well as peace," he famously said. The Articles of War under which Jones issued the indictments applied most explicitly to members of the armed forces, governed the conduct of soldiers in the field, although some of its provisions did extend to allied civilian hirees of the army. In fact, when the War Department was forced to rule on one such case in November 1862—at the exact moment when Colonel Jones's case hit the War Department—Adjutant General Samuel Cooper sided with the civilian lawyer in the case, agreeing that the military could not try his client.[85] But the civil liberties of slaves were nowhere at issue in the Confederacy during the war. None of the previous legal wrangling settled the question of whether the military could try slaves, men who were not citizens of the C.S.A. Colonel Jones was on his own.

In attempting to administer slaves as traitors, Colonel Jones's court-martial bore far more directly on the matter of slaves' political standing than their legal standing. It is true that in recent years historians have moved past the brittle picture of the master-slave relation in statutory law and appellate decisions to a view of the legal personhood of slaves in the Southern law of slavery: the double character of slaves as property and persons. One recent reading of the way the law operated at the local level even makes the case that slaves were part of the legal order, that they were understood to be under the protection of the law and thus had status, if not rights. Statutes holding masters criminally liable for the murder of their slaves and the introduction of information by slaves at civil trials or magistrate hearings all speak to the nuances of the legal order that evolved in the antebellum South. But homicide statutes proved impossible to enforce, and far more slaves went to law as pieces of property itemized in bills of sale, turned into cash, and divided up in estate settlements, or sold under the sheriff's hammer—than ever did as participants in hearings. Whatever the evolution of the law over time in the antebellum period, it is still hard to avoid the conclusion that little interfered with the treatment of slaves at law as property. It was "the property element in the slave that was 'juridically' significant," one legal historian has insisted.[86] This was certainly the view Morton took and the one he pressed on the secretary of war in demanding review of the legality of Colonel Jones's action.

In the slave South, enslaved peoples' absolute and permanent exclusion from the body politic—their lack of political standing—was not in doubt. Whatever the limited concessions made in law to accommodate the necessity of administering justice in cases involving human property, no such concessions had been necessary in political life. Alexander Stephens might have been right when he said that the Confederate Constitution was made for war as well as peace. But war created precisely those circumstances in which the political alienation of slaves became a liability. This was the point made by the Liberty County planters and many others in similarly exposed circumstances, and it was Colonel Jones's point in insisting on the court-martial of Morton's slaves as a "high military necessity."[87]

Recognizing slaves as traitors was part of "the stern logic of events" in war. But it was also profoundly at odds with the political project of the Confederate republic. In attempting to deal with slaves as traitors, Confederate military authorities were tripped up, as impressment officers had been, by the limited sovereignty of the state over slave subjects, by the way the master stood between the state and the slave. This was precisely what Colonel Jones said when he learned of Morton's attempt to thwart the proceedings by appeal to the secretary of war. "Strong influences had been interposed to protect and shield those who had been detected and apprehended," he complained to the adjutant and inspector general from his post in Pensacola. "Since this citizen is unwilling to make a sacrifice of his personal interests to the public welfare, and has had the power to interfere with the interior of my command and what I conceive to be the proper execution of my duties, I beg that I may not be held responsible for the difficulties & escapes which will most certainly follow."[88]

It was those two fundamental issues—the masters' paramount claim and, most explosively, slaves' status as property or persons—that Jones's court-martial raised. "Two questions are presented in these cases," Samuel Cooper noted by way of précis, in forwarding the record to the secretary of war for review. The first was practical: Can men be convicted for an "attempt" to correspond with or give intelligence to the enemy, the issue raised by the defense. The second was profound: "The parties are *slaves.* Can they be guilty of a violation of the military code, even when extended to the civil community by the proclamation of martial law?" Colonel Jones knew he was on new ground. Convinced that the exigencies of the service demanded his action, he also expressed relief when the matter was taken out of his hands, "as it was a case about the strict legality of which I had some doubt."[89] But Colonel Jones's relief became the secretary of war's dilemma, as he tried to figure out a way to exert state control over treasonous slaves while not recognizing them as part of the body politic.

When seven months later the Confederate secretary of war was forced to adjudicate the question of whether slaves can be guilty of treason under military law, the new politics and political subjects the war had called into being were perfectly in evidence. No ultimate legal ruling, only the confusion of Confederate states' attorneys, can be found in the record. Indeed what ruling *was* possible? Clearly, as Major General Jones said,

Confederate commanders needed to recognize slaves as traitors. But how could that be adopted as an official position without profound damage to slaves' status as property and masters' rights to it in the C.S.A.? Developments in Pensacola show the profound dilemma war—and, in this case, six Pensacola slaves—had launched them into. If slaves were traitors, they were no longer just slaves.

The Confederate state's willingness to concede slave men's membership in the body politic proceeded from the need to establish accountability, to counter slaves' treasonous activity with state violence. Such efforts, as in Pensacola, drew the Confederate state and military into increasingly intractable conflicts with slaveholders over the rights that attached to private property and contributed a great deal to the radically shifting terrain of Confederate politics. It is hard to overstate the distance covered in the C.S.A. in a few short years of war. Having first been seen as an element of strength, slaves had become the enemy within; having begun with an instrumental view of slaves, Confederates had come to recognize their political agency; and having at first insisted on slaves' political exclusion, they had come instead to insist on the necessity of their incorporation. These were hardly minor concessions. Although entirely pragmatic in origin, they were a direct repudiation of foundational Confederate principles. It was not simply that white Southerners had found nothing to complain about in Taney's view of slavery as the natural status of people of African descent in the United States and his insistence on the complete exclusion of slaves from the body politic; they had gone to war—and expended hundreds of thousands of citizens' lives—to extend those principles into perpetuity.

But the logic of change did not remain entirely negative and disciplinary. Some civilians and military men, particularly in the western theater, calculated the price of slave disloyalty differently and began to engage issues of volition and consent that went to the very heart of the Confederate republic. In September 1863, a Jackson, Mississippi, editor summed it up when he said, "We must either employ the negroes ourselves, or the enemy will employ them against us . . . They are no longer negative characters, but subjects of volition as other people." A plainer statement of the problem and its imperatives could not be found. They must be taught that the C.S.A. was their country, and "he [the negro] must further be taught that it is his duty, as well as that of the white man's, to defend his home with arms, if need be." To this man the trajectory of Confederate politics was clear. "It is the duty of this Government to forestall Lincoln and proceed at once to . . . the emancipation or liberation of the negroes itself. Let them be declared free, placed in the ranks, and told to fight for their homes and country."[90]

By making their political and military value clear, enslaved men and women had presented the Confederate republic with an impossible problem of allegiance. That much was clear by the beginning of 1863. But the consequences were only beginning to play out. In time the pressure slaves exerted on the proslavery C.S.A. would move beyond delimited groups of citizens, editors, and military men in embattled corners of the republic to the office of the president himself. When it did, it would force Davis and his cabinet to do the unthinkable: to move to undermine the owners' paramount claim to their slaves, to claim state access to privately held property in slaves, and to contemplate the enlistment of some slave men to save the slaveholders' republic.

CHAPTER 8

The Fall

> If slavery is what we believe it to be—the best form of society—it is not only fitted for peace but for the exigencies of war.
>
> *Houston Telegraph,* March 29, 1865

THE CONFEDERATE STATES OF AMERICA was a proslavery nation. Founded in defiance of the spirit of the age, it aimed to turn back the tide of abolition that had swept the hemisphere in the Age of Revolution. Trusting that major powers had had their fill of the failed experiment in emancipation, Confederate founders proposed instead to perfect the slaveholders' republic and offer it to the world as the political form best fitted to the modern age.

The C.S.A. was inextricably part of the broad hemispheric history of slavery and emancipation. But the war Confederates launched to escape history only confirmed their place in it. For as it turned out, they could not escape the fate that befell so many slave regimes at war. War, as one historian has observed, was often part of larger crises in which slaveholding regimes were pressed to take "account . . . of social forces hitherto excluded from political life."[1] Among the most powerful of those social forces was the slaves themselves.

Like so many other slave regimes that turned to emancipation in the context of war, the Confederate States of America was driven by "the stern 'logic of events'" into a process of slave enlistment and partial emancipation that literally eviscerated the original national project. Independence "is about the preservation of our political institutions, the principal of which is slavery," the governor of North Carolina reminded President Davis in late 1864. We would pose the question of whether Confederates were still fighting "for our system of civilization," the original fire-eater, Robert Barnwell Rhett, put it in January 1865. "We intend to fight for that or nothing."[2]

There is an important pattern in the history of slave emancipation in the Western Hemisphere, one of considerable significance for the Confederate States of America: and that is the intimate association of war, slave enlistment, and emancipation. From the American War of Independence to the last surrender of slavery in Brazil in the aftermath of the Paraguayan war, to virtually everything in between—Saint-Domingue, the Spanish-American Wars of Independence, the U.S. Civil War, the Ten-Years War in Cuba—slaves fought for and won their freedom in the context of war.[3] It was in the context of war that slave men became the objects of state interest and the focus of intense competition between warring states for political loyalty and military service. In this respect, the American Civil War was hardly unique. In its two warring states as in so many others, military service and emancipation were temporally and causally linked, as manhood and citizenship would be in the aftermath of Union victory.

If that pattern of war and emancipation emerges so strikingly from the record, historians have not accorded it much significance. Yet the circumstances of war, including crises of state, the slaves' antislavery, and the necessity of widening the conception of citizen, all point to a crucial condition clearly at work in the American Civil War: the reaching into the ranks of the male slave population by various states in the competition for soldiers. The lack of authority over, and access to, whole segments of the male military-age population was one problem of slavery and state formation that assumed critical proportions in times of war. Was this not what the *Richmond Whig* meant, in the midst of the debate over whether to arm slaves, when it referred to "the natural development of the necessities of the crisis?"[4]

The C.S.A. was not the first slave state to arrive at that juncture, and it would not be the last. The long history of arming slaves stretches back to the ancient world.[5] But the practice assumed new dimensions in the late eighteenth century when, with the rise of antislavery movements, some parties proved willing to make offers of general emancipation to slaves in exchange for military service. In this respect, no case was more critical than that of Saint-Domingue. Confederates were haunted by the history of that island. No other history seemed more relevant to their own experience, and arguably none was.

Events as they unfolded in Saint-Domingue tell a great deal about the circumstances and choices faced by other slave regimes at war, including the staunchly proslavery C.S.A. In fact, given Confederates' habit of comparative thinking, it is surprising that historians have been loath to adopt that perspective themselves, consistently favoring a national framework in interpreting Confederate developments. The revolutionary dynamic of war was certainly grasped by some in time and place. The history of Saint-Domingue and other slave societies past, Jefferson Davis said, was a reminder to Confederates "to use the greatest circumspection in determining their course."[6] But even as Confederates struggled to escape what had been the fate of slaveholders in the world's richest slave society and first black republic, they were caught in the same problems of state and currents of war that had propelled the process of slave enlistment and emancipation there.

The pattern emerged early in the French colony in the revolutionary struggle initiated in 1789 and transformed decisively in 1791 by a massive revolt of slaves on plantations in the northern part of the island. The onrushing course of events yielded a many-sided struggle between free colored men, insurgent slaves, and planters, and after Britain declared war in 1793, between France, Spain, and Britain. All those powers then moved to arm slaves in a war of imperial competition that played out across the Caribbean for more than a decade.[7] A full accounting of the arming of slave men in Saint-Domingue would be a lengthy affair, but a few key moments, all following the slave revolt in 1791, are suggestive of the key and persevering patterns involved, including in Civil War America.

As early as 1790 some parties in the revolutionary struggle in Saint-Domingue had moved to arm and train their own slaves, notably the wealthy *gens de couleur* emboldened in their demands for equal citizenship by events in Paris. From the outset, factional conflict led to the arming of modest numbers of slaves.[8] But the real competition for slave soldiers was set in motion by the massive self-arming of slaves in August 1791 as they rebelled against planters, slavery, and the French republican state. By the end of the year black leaders had built substantial slave armies, which continued to grow in numbers in part through alliance with existing maroon bands. It was from that position of strength that the black generals proceeded to negotiate the terms of their service between contending European powers, first with the Spanish invading Saint-Domingue and then with the beleaguered French republican forces scrambling to repulse and defeat them.

In the early years of the Haitian Revolution, as in the American one before it, universal emancipation was an unthinkable goal, liberty at issue only in the most delimited way, available only to men directly under arms, and not to all of them. Even at that early point, the gender terms of the struggle for emancipation come into focus: where freedom was traded for military service, it necessarily opened up greater opportunities for men than for women. In early negotiations with French republican commissioners in late 1791, the black generals demanded freedom for themselves and four hundred of their followers. The deal would have obligated them to force the remainder of their own insurgents, men and women both, back into plantation labor as slaves. Even that limited deal was refused. By late 1792, facing French republican forces allied with *gens de couleur* in the project of restoring slavery on the island, leaders of the largest slave armies in the north cut deals with the Spanish, in exchange for official recognition of the freedom of the black soldiers. A full two years after the slave insurrection in the north there were massive numbers of slave men under arms and a new route to emancipation had been opened up—military service—albeit one that could be taken only by men.[9] Wherever emancipation emerged in the context of war, as a specifically *military* policy, it had those same fundamental gender patterns.

In this highly militarized context, French republicans offered the terms that changed the course of history. For centuries slave soldiers had been able to offer military service in exchange for personal freedom, and in moments of danger slave regimes had found it necessary to cut the deal. Slavery itself had never been at issue. But all of that changed in June 1793, when Léger Félicité Sonthonax, one of the French commissioners sent by the Republic, faced a coup by the governor general of the colony. Then he made a desperate bid for the loyalty and military service of the *mass* of slave men in the colony, offering liberty to *all* slave insurgents who would fight for the Republic. Only the timely arrival of republican reinforcements under the control of two black generals and the sack of Le Cap turned the military tide. Emboldened by success, Sonthonax extended the offer, issuing a proclamation in Creole and French promising freedom also "to the womenfolk of black warriors as long as they were prepared to go through a Republican marriage ceremony."[10] Sonthonax's emancipation policy thus was, among other things, a critical reflection of the centrality of marriage and patriarchal authority in French republican policy, as would be the case fifty years later in the American Civil War. Issued without authorization from the General Assembly, Sonthonax's decree of general liberty profoundly changed the stakes in the bidding war under way for the military service of the island's slaves.

For French radicals, especially Sonthonax, emancipation was a principled act. But it was the conditions of war and, crucially, slave insurrection that necessitated it in 1794 as they would also in the American South. Slaves in Saint-Domingue had seized the opportunity of war to make their allegiance, and willingness to bear arms, count. In the competition that ensued, many slave soldiers extracted guarantees of freedom in exchange for their service, including from the proslavery Spanish. But it was Sonthonax who declared *all slaves* free. In 1794, amid the chaos of revolution, the French Assembly officially decreed the abolition of slavery—the first universal emancipation decree in history—and forever changed the deal. It was only after the passage of the decree that the great military leader Toussaint L'Ouverture took his huge slave army over to the French (he had been allied with the Spanish), calling on his "brothers" to unite with him in the fight for freedom and equality in Saint-Domingue.[11] Born in war, it could sometimes seem as if the very nation was male.

Despite the great document, there was nothing final about emancipation in Saint-Domingue in 1794. As in the United States more than half a century later, it took military victory to secure emancipation. Until 1803, when Napoleon and the French were defeated by the black armies of Saint-Domingue, the restoration of slavery still threatened, and the military service of formerly and still potentially enslaved men was required in the extended process by which Saint-Domingue's slaves could finally call themselves free.[12] But after 1794, with universal emancipation official, the terms of slave men's military service were forever changed. The similarities to the American case were not lost on anyone, least of all Confederates.

When, more than half a century later, American slaves made their own bid for emancipation, in the context of a war that surpassed in scale even that which had convulsed the Caribbean in the 1790s, many of the same conditions and patterns were in evidence. In the American Civil War, Southern slaves' insurrection against both slavery and the slaveholders' state alerted Union men to the potential utility of their labor, loyalty, and military service, and put emancipation on the agenda, as Lincoln put it in the Emancipation Proclamation, as a "fit and necessary war measure."[13]

What war measures would Confederates find necessary? "The real question," Mississippi congressman Ethelbert Barksdale put it at the height of the crisis, "is how to make him available as a soldier?" One opponent of the measure warned of the danger in arming slaves. "That you dare not do, remembering it was the free negroes of St. Domingo who had been trained to arms that excited the insurrection of the slaves."[14] Saint-Domingue haunted Confederates' political imagination. Even as they struggled to escape the fate of slaveholders in Saint-Domingue, they were caught in the same dangerous currents of war, slave enlistment, and even emancipation.

The pressure of numbers weighed on Confederate officials from the outset. It was not easy for a slave society to wage modern war.[15] After all, the C.S.A. lacked access to 40 percent of its adult male military-age population, men enslaved and thus ineligible for service. With a total population roughly one-third that of the Union, that left only 965,000 free white men between the ages of 18 to 45 to draw on for armed service. And that was if every adult white man served, which they could not. George Randolph, the first secretary of war, thought that at most they could put an army of five hundred thousand men in the field, which would still have the Confederacy committing a larger proportion of its population than any European power had ever done. Slavery may have been the only true foundation of republican government, but it came with a political price. It was one thing to keep the political community small and exclusive in times of peace, to sequester power in the hands of a privileged minority. That was the point of a slave republic, after all. But when it came time to bear arms, there weren't many male citizens to do it. Out of a "voting population" (the proxy term for free white men) of about 47,000, the governor of South Carolina complained in 1862, the state had already fielded "at least 33,000 men." The Union, by contrast, could draw on a pool of men three times the size. "We have entered upon a conflict with a nation . . . vastly superior to us in numbers," President Davis said in 1862, and "in the face of these facts the wonder is not that we have done so little, but that we have done so much."[16]

Confederates tried strenuously to counter the deficit. As early as April 1862 the disparity in troop levels propelled the government into the first draft in American history, compelling service of every white man aged 18 to 35. A few months later they extended the age limit to 45, and they would extend it again in both directions, prompting critics to observe that the Confederate army robbed the grave as well as the cradle. By the end of the war, military age was 17 to 50. They had also tried to make slave men count for the war even if they could not be soldiers, calling on owners to volunteer slaves to work on the defenses and trying over time to substitute slave men for every labor of the soldier short of bearing arms. Slaves were always a big part of the Confederate manpower equation. The population of the Southern states is "a complex one consisting of two races . . . and in this state the slave element preponderating," one Mississippian observed in April 1862 as things turned dicey there. Under the circumstances would it not be well to ask "whether it is prudent to attempt the defence of the country with only one of these elements of its power?" The man thought slaves should be requisitioned to work on the fortifications, a policy the government and military tried desperately to make work, but, he also suggested, "is not impossible that they might on occasion of great exigency be relied on in the ranks." By the end of 1862 the Union had already fielded 740,000 men.[17] The shortage of soldiers put incredible pressure on Confederates to make up the difference with slaves.

The problem grew ever more intractable. For if it proceeded from the peculiar character of the slave republic, the disparity in men was exacerbated by the Union's growing willingness to stake all on the war. Much of what the Confederacy had to contend with was unforeseeable at the beginning: the level of Union mobilization, willingness to conscript, and size of the armies they managed to field. Who could have imagined an army of 100,000 such as that McClellan commanded on the Peninsula, or the 120,000 Grant had outside Petersburg? At the end of the war the Union had one million men under arms, a number that exceeded the total who had ever served in all of the armies of the Confederacy over the entire course of the war. The scale of death was another unimaginable development, 620,000 dead, sometimes as many as 7,000 in one battle.[18] By 1863 the saturation of the Confederacy's own military population, the failure of slave impressment, the growing recognition of their slaves' open adherence to the enemy, and above all—after January 1, 1863, when President Lincoln issued the Emancipation Proclamation—their recruitment by Union armies, all these escalating conditions of war brought the C.S.A. to a self-acknowledged crisis by the summer of 1863.

The Emancipation Proclamation changed everything, much as Sonthonax's policy had in Saint-Domingue. After that, the competition between powers for the political loyalty and military service of the South's slave men was overt and, on the Confederate side, desperate. If the Emancipation Proclamation did not bring freedom to the more than three and a half million slaves still stuck in rebel territory in 1863, it certainly confirmed that they had a powerful military ally in the war. The proclamation likely hardened their ideas about political allegiance, reconfigured calculations of the risks involved in flight to Union lines and service in the Union army. "Some men who came here [to Fortress Monroe, Virginia] from North Carolina knew all about the Proclamation," Captain C. B. Wilder testified to Congress in May 1863, "and they started on the belief in it." "I sympathized with the Union cause," a South Carolina slave would later testify. "I wanted to be free—and wanted my race to be free—I knew this could not be if the rebels had a government of their own."[19] The freedom promised by the Emancipation Proclamation could be secured only by the military defeat of the C.S.A. None were more acutely aware of that fact than the Confederacy's slaves.

The link between emancipation and enlistment in Union war policy was explicit. That the emancipation of American slaves was taken for reasons of state and specifically to gain access to a population of slave men for military service was hardly something President Lincoln attempted to obscure. To the contrary, he proclaimed to the world that he took the radical action in his capacity as "Commander in Chief of the Army and Navy of the United States, in time of actual armed rebellion against the authority and government of the United States, and as a fit and necessary war measure for suppressing said rebellion." To that end, he further declared his intention to receive "into the armed service of the United States" all "such persons of suitable condition . . . to garrison forts, positions, stations, and other places, and to man vessels of all sorts in said service." The text of the great document inscribed the process that made it possible. "No human power can subdue this rebellion without using the Emancipation lever as I have done," Abraham Lincoln declared in one of the most gripping images of the war. "Freedom has given us the control of 200,000 able-bodied men, born and raised on southern soil."[20] If Lincoln left the mistaken impression that there was no action until he turned the lever, still, liberating slave men to be soldiers was what the Emancipation Proclamation was about. What lever could the Confederacy use?

The Emancipation Proclamation profoundly upped the ante for the C.S.A. in their battle for the hearts and minds of their own slaves. The abolitionist U.S. brigadier general John W. Phelps insisted to his superiors that the slave men in his camp were "willing to submit to anything rather than to slavery." "If we reject his services," he added, "any petty military chieftain, by offering him freedom, can have them for the purpose of robbery and plunder." But that kind of random assignment of national allegiance and free-for-all bidding for slave soldiers—the sort that pertained in Saint-Domingue before 1793—was rendered obsolete by the Emancipation Proclamation. For even before it was issued, when Lincoln made known his intention to do so with the Preliminary Emancipation Proclamation, his commitment to immediate and universal slave emancipation as a matter of official Union policy profoundly shifted the political and military landscape. Jefferson Davis was thus not far off the mark in charging that by the Emancipation Proclamation ("the most execrable measure recorded in the history of guilty man") "President Lincoln has sought to turn the South into a San Domingo."[21] It would take the rest of the war for the logic of that observation to play out.

When all was said and done, about 180,000 African American men served in the U.S. army or navy during the American Civil War; about 98,500 of them were slaves from the Confederate states. The recruitment of black soldiers had reached a certain level of maturity in policy circles by January 1863 when the Census Office began to tabulate numbers of free blacks and slaves of arms-bearing age. By that point the estimated 750,000 male slaves in the United States—the vast majority of them in states in rebellion—figured centrally in Union military calculations, just as Southerners feared. When the Union government formed the Bureau of Colored Troops in May 1863, the policy was official.[22]

By the spring of 1863 the Union army was recruiting aggressively in Confederate territory. With large swaths of the Mississippi Valley and coastal areas of Virginia, North Carolina, South Carolina, and Florida under occupation, they had plenty of scope for their operations. Thereafter the army recruited as it moved, purposefully attempting to exert pressure on Confederates, whom they knew to be chronically short of men. As Union general in chief Henry W. Halleck put it in March 1863, "every slave withdrawn from the enemy is equivalent to a white man put hors de combat." To that end, Secretary of War Edwin Stanton authorized black recruiters and recruitment fees of two dollars per head, and army units were soon out in the field operating on explicit instructions to bring back slave men from military forays organized for that purpose. Instructions to Union officers confirm the pattern. "All Africans, including men, women and children, who may quit the plantations and join your train, are not to be driven back but to be protected by you," went one set of orders to a commander of a black brigade in North Carolina. All the able-bodied men were to be enlisted, he was told, and all the others turned over to the superintendent for Negro affairs in the Norfolk area.[23]

As aggressive recruiting of Confederate slaves emerged as official Union policy, officials faced en masse the problem first presented by contrabands at Fortress Monroe. As the numbers of slaves in the orbit of the Union army assumed vast proportions, recruiters like Adjutant General Lorenzo Thomas worried about what to do with those "unfit for military service, including the women." In response, the Union government, like the French Republic before it, reverted to the policy of marriage to administer the slave women who came into their lines. As General Butler explained from his post in Fortress Monroe, "the theory . . . is that every

negro able to work who leaves the rebel lines . . . diminishes by so much the producing power of the rebellion . . . and the United States thereby gains either a soldier or a producer. Women and children are received because it would be manifestly iniquitous and unjust to take the husband and father and leave the wife and child to ill-treatment and starvation. Women and children are also received when unaccompanied by the husband and father, because the negro has the domestic affections in as strong a degree as the white man, and however far South his master may drive him, he will sooner or later return to his family." Butler thus adhered to the fiction that every slave woman, however single, was in fact a wife, and proposed, as French republican officials had done before, to tuck women slaves into the tidy confines of marriage. It was a way to stretch a military policy to cover a nonmilitary population, to bid for the loyalty and service of black soldiers (hardly likely to enlist if their families were turned away), and perhaps most of all, to manage a huge population of potential welfare dependents in an unwieldy transition from slavery to freedom. That settled, Butler ordered "all officers commanding Expeditions and raids [to] bring in with them all the negroes possible, affording them transportation, aid, protection and encouragement." As in Mississippi and Louisiana, the policy of military sorting was adopted: the slave women brought in by recruiting expeditions were sent to plantations or contraband camps, while any man who could pass muster as a soldier was siphoned off to the army. "Our plantations are made his recruiting stations," Kirby Smith howled in panic from Shreveport, Louisiana, in September 1863.[24]

By the summer of 1863, under the additional pressure of Union emancipation and recruitment, the problem of manpower in the C.S.A. reached critical proportions. Even as President Davis, his cabinet, and War Department officials attempted to lay their hands on every last white man for the nation's armies, they knew it would never be enough. Caught in a relentless competition for their own slave population, the C.S.A. edged toward more radical solutions to the intractable problems faced by their slave regime at war.

A turning point came in July 1863. The news coming into the Confederate War Department was devastating. On July 3, Davis received word of defeat at the battle of Gettysburg, with 28,000 men killed or wounded, fully one-third of General Lee's proud Army of Northern Virginia. On

July 4 he got news of General Pemberton's surrender at Vicksburg and the loss of a whole army of 30,000 men. Robert E. Lee put his finger on the problem a few days later when he wrote Davis asking, without much expectation of success, for reinforcements. "Conscious that the enemy has been much shattered in the recent battle," he admitted, "I am aware that he can easily be reinforced, while no addition can be made to our numbers." Davis answered in a long letter itemizing the losses and the demands for more troops coming in from all quarters. But in a tone different from that of earlier communications, he also conveyed his sense that the war had entered a new stage that would test the people and not just the armies. "Our people have proven their gallantry and patriotic zeal," Davis informed Lee, "their fortitude is now to be tested."[25]

A sense of crisis pervaded every discussion of national affairs in the summer and fall of 1863, including in the War Department. In internal correspondence, officials spoke frankly about the dire straits into which they had been pushed by Union recruitment policy, about the inadequacy of their numbers, and about how to survive in the new environment of overt military competition for their slaves. It is one measure of the crisis that officials took so seriously an Alabama slaveholder's offer of a quarter of his slaves for service in the army. As William Bibb's offer made its way up the chain of command—gathering endorsements from Assistant Secretary of War James Campbell, Secretary of War James A. Seddon, and Davis himself—it elicited shocking admissions about the state of the army, the failure of slave impressment and the necessity of doing something, anything, to prevent military defeat at the hands of their own slaves. Accept the offer, Davis noted on the letter, further instructing Seddon to order quartermasters to procure slaves for teamsters and ostlers, company and hospital cooks, as suggested.[26] It was the first time the Confederate government had accepted the need to use slaves' labor *in* the army itself.[27]

As President Davis's call for more stringent impressment legislation made its slow way through the Confederate Congress in the fall of 1863, the War Department attempted to rebuild the nation's armies. In early November, in a report solicited by the secretary of war, Samuel Melton, the assistant adjutant general, bluntly responded that "the conscription laws now in force will be utterly inadequate to restore to our armies the numbers they contained last January and to preserve this strength during the coming year." They would need one hundred thousand additional men just to wage a defensive war, he said, and many more to change the situation radically by going on the offensive. In his own bleak report to Davis a few weeks later, Seddon went further, emphasizing "the superior numbers and more abundant resources of the enemy," the weakness of Confederate armies whose "effective force is generally a little more than half, never two thirds, of the numbers in the ranks" and the inadequacy of every measure at hand to generate adequate numbers of men. They had already extended conscription to age 45 (to little effect), as he pointed out, and they had to move immediately to repeal both the substitution and exemption laws and to take harsh action against deserters.[28]

But like Melton, Seddon also believed they had no choice but to impress slaves aggressively and by compulsion. And this he cast as the necessary response to the Union recruitment and enlistment of slave men. There were thirty thousand black troops already in arms for the Union, he told Davis, "regiments of the slaves they have seduced or forced from their masters," and the number grew daily. Confederates now faced the prospect of being exterminated "through the insolent lordship of our slaves to the mastery of his brutal despotism." The only way to avoid that fate was for the Confederate government to claim those slaves, both to get the labor for their own cause and "from the plainer necessity of preventing the enemy from recruiting their armies with our slaves." The C.S.A. needs to mobilize its whole "arms bearing population," Seddon said, with no exaggeration.[29]

The new logic of events unleashed by Union emancipation policy cast slave men into the middle of a desperate military calculus. In the C.S.A. every man counted, whether white or black. Officers in the field, like Colonel Jones in Pensacola, already knew that, but now the men at the top of the military chain of command came to the same recognition. Speaking privately, they made no bones about the fact that the battle for the labor and service of slave men was on. So in the fall of 1863 the War Department cracked down, attempting to lay hands on every white man capable of bearing arms for the republic. They extended the age of conscription in both directions, eliminated substitution, scaled back exemptions, fought state governors over their power to exempt state officers, offered amnesty to deserters, and pressed governors to send out troops to hunt down those who refused to return to service. Enlistment was pressed past the point poor white households could sustain, the welfare rolls grew past what the localities and states could manage, and the howls of protest that came up from the farms and workshops of the South generated their own new political constituencies and pressures on the states and central government. But even with the memory of the food riots of the previous spring fresh in their minds, the War Department had no choice but to go after every last white man for the army. Enlistment rates would eventually reach as high as 75 to 85 percent of eligible men.[30]

Inevitably the Confederate government turned its sights on slave men too, initiating new policies of slave removal and impressment calculated to do two things: deny slave men to the Union armies and harness them to their own. They moved on the first front by a policy of slave removal. But given the need to mobilize the whole arms-bearing population, it is hardly surprising that some proposed to go still further. A series of radical proposals floated up from the Mississippi Valley, from men desperate in the face of Grant and Sherman's massive armies.[31] Members of the Alabama legislature gathered in late August 1863 to debate steps the government might take to avert the disaster bearing down on them. About a month before, right after the fall of Vicksburg, a Confederate congressman from Mobile had warned officials in the capital that Mississippi and Alabama were almost subdued and urged them to entertain abolition in exchange for foreign recognition. Another urged enlistment of black men because the number of available white men "is so much exhausted that we cannot raise a force sufficient to meet the enemy on equal terms."[32]

But it was one thing for citizens or even congressmen to make such recommendations privately, another for a state legislature to issue a public resolution on the matter. Yet that is exactly what happened in Montgomery in August 1863. With south Alabama about to be invaded, a legislative committee debated a series of emergency measures about compulsory impressment of slaves for military service as "pioneers, sappers, and miners, cooks, nurses, teamsters, or as soldiers," as the *Montgomery Weekly Mail* shockingly reported. The House and Senate issued a set of joint resolutions "in relation to the increase of the Army of the Confederate States" to be sent to the president, secretary of war, and their own representatives in Congress. Those resolutions proposed that because "the Government of the U.S. has determined to put in the field negro soldiers and are enlisting and drafting the slaves of the people of the South, this General Assembly submits for the consideration of Congress the propriety of using in some effective way a certain percentage of the male slave population of the Confederate States, and to perform such services as Congress may by law direct." If they did not use the term "slave soldiers" in that resolution, the newspaper coverage of the debate left no doubt that was precisely what they proposed.[33]

In Alabama a newly aggressive discussion about slave impressment for military labor shaded over into one about military service. By the late summer of 1863 some officials were ready to talk about arming slaves. The *Montgomery Weekly Mail* reported the astonishing debate and the range of opinion expressed. What no one discussed was whether slave men would be willing to serve the C.S.A.: the issue of emancipation did not come up. The editor worried about the implications of arming slaves for "our historical position on the slavery question," as he delicately put it. "The argument which goes to the exclusion of negroes as soldiers is founded on the status of the negro." Negroes, he asserted, are "racial inferior[s]," but "the proposition to make them soldiers . . . [would be but a] practical equalization of the races." Nonetheless, they had to do it. "The War has made great changes," he insisted, and "we must meet those changes, for the sake of preserving our very existence." They should use any means available to defeat the enemy, and "one of these, and the only one which will checkmate him, is the employment of negroes in the military service of the Confederacy."[34]

The late summer of 1863 was the real beginning of the slave enlistment debate in the C.S.A., as "the Confederate emancipation debate" might more accurately be called.[35] The question arose as an aspect of the manpower problem in the slave republic, one massively compounded by the pressures of military defeat and the Union turn to slave emancipation and black enlistment. It was, as one Richmond paper later put it, simply a matter of military necessity, and emancipation was simply incidental to the main expedient of arming the slaves.[36] Even as military labor shaded over into military service, as some Confederate officials contemplated the enlistment of slave men in their armies, the question of slaves' willingness to serve was not broached: emancipation was not much part of the discussion.

If Confederates thought they could sidestep the question of slaves' political allegiance—that they could simply compel military service as they compelled labor—military commanders had no such illusions. Watching the Union recruitment of slave men in Jackson, Mississippi, one editor put the matter of slaves' treason and urgency of securing their allegiance directly on the table. They must be taught that "this is their country" and that they had a duty to fight for it. Any battle for the hearts and minds of slaves could head in only one direction by September 1863, and the Jackson editor went there, urging Confederate officials to meet the slaves' own war objectives by proposing emancipation.[37]

As the idea of mobilizing the *whole* arms-bearing population earned serious consideration in the military, individual military men and even the War Department found themselves contending directly with the consequences of slaves' politics, including the war they had waged relentlessly since Confederate independence. If that war had started with acts of resistance on the nation's farms and plantations, if it had thwarted military policy and even military operations on the ground before, by the fall of 1863 it was clear that slaves' politics had penetrated decision making at the highest reaches of the slaveholders' regime. The necessity of engaging slaves' politics was starting to be faced where it mattered most: in the military.

One small tremor that started in northern Georgia augured a full-blown earthquake in Confederate military affairs. In December 1863 an Irish-born officer in the Army of Tennessee, hunkered down in winter quarters in Dalton and brooding on the string of devastating defeats suffered by his army, came to the conclusion that only one thing could save the slaveholders' republic. On January 2, 1864, standing before fellow officers, Major General Patrick Cleburne made his heterodox views known, recommending that the C.S.A. arm and emancipate its own slaves. It was an astonishing proposal from a senior military officer of the hemisphere's only independent slave republic. In that sense Cleburne's memorandum spoke to the stern logic of events in that slave regime at war. Although it was never adopted and Cleburne did not live to see a slave enlistment policy, he staunchly predicted both the terms that required it and the terms under which it would work. Most stunning was the central role he attributed to slaves and their politics in the Confederate military dilemma. For Cleburne's core contention was that to get slaves' military service, the C.S.A. first had to win their political loyalty with the promise of freedom.[38]

The men Major General Cleburne addressed needed no primer in the "exigency in which our country is now placed." Every last one of them was a survivor of Missionary Ridge and Chattanooga. One of them, Thomas Hindman, a fellow officer and antebellum law partner of Cleburne's, had already made a similar proposal anonymously in a Georgia paper. But Cleburne put his name on his memorandum and shared it with other officers of the Army of Tennessee. Addressing the commanding general, the corps, division, brigade, and regimental commanders, he recounted the humiliating history of their army and country. "Every soldier in our army already knows and feels our numerical inferiority to the enemy," he said bluntly. "If this state continues much longer we must be subjugated." The stakes clear, Cleburne proceeded coolly to identify "the three great causes operating to destroy us." After the numerical inferiority of Southern armies, and the poverty of their supply sources, he came to the third: "the fact that slavery, from being one of our chief sources of strength at the commencement of the war has now become, in a military point of view, one of our chief sources of weakness."[39]

Cleburne's unflinching analysis of the military weakness of the slave state was so complete, it serves as an historian's index to the subject. It touched on every vulnerable point: the Union's superiority in numbers of white men and ability to augment their armies with Confederate slaves; the defection of slaveholders to save their property on the approach of the enemy; the scattering of Confederate forces to prevent Union raids and slave escape so that they were "not free to move and strike like the enemy"; the fact that slaves were useless to them but valuable to the enemy. Slavery is an "omnipresent spy system," he charged, with slaves "revealing our position, purposes and resources, and yet acting so safely and secretly that there is no means to guard against it." On every approach the enemy found recruits awaiting him with open arms, guides ready to supply a complete history of the neighborhood, and men to resupply the enemy's already massive armies. Cleburne hardly underestimated slaves' effect on Confederate military operations. Slaves, he said, are the enemy within. Because of slavery the C.S.A. was forced to wage war with the Union army in front and "an insurrection in the rear."[40]

Cleburne's was a merciless critique of the liabilities of a slave regime at war and as blunt a description of the damage slaves were wreaking on the Confederate military effort as one will ever read. But Cleburne rehearsed that military history to show not just what the C.S.A. was up against but what it would take to change it. His most shocking contention was not that the Confederacy needed slave men to fill its armies, but that it could do so only by recognizing slaves' own objectives in the struggle under way. The logic was military, the goal more men in uniform, but the political vision was radical indeed. Cleburne looked slaves' anti-Confederate politics squarely in the face. "For many years, ever since the agitation of the subject of slavery commenced, the negro has been dreaming of freedom," he acknowledged. "It has become the paradise of his hopes. To attain it, he will attempt dangers and difficulties not exceeded by the bravest soldier in the field." It was "the chronic irritation of hope deferred" that alienated the "sympathies of his whole race" from the South, raised insurrection in the rear, and filled the ranks of Union armies. Only one thing could change that. "We must bind him to our cause by no doubtful bonds," he declared, and the only bond sufficient was the "hope of freedom." "It would be preposterous to expect him to fight against it with any degree of enthusiasm." Whatever anyone else thought, Cleburne recognized that the paramount challenge for the C.S.A. was to win slaves' loyalty, and he was prepared to do what it took. "When we make soldiers of them we must make free men of them beyond all question," he said, "and thus enlist their sympathies also." From that heretical truth of slaves' Civil War politics Cleburne shrank not a whit.[41]

Slave emancipation arose in Confederate history, as in so many other slave societies, as a military imperative. And like other such military emancipations this one figured slave women as marital recipients of a freedom earned by their men. Cleburne always spoke of the slave as a male. But like republican commissioners in Saint-Domingue and officials of Lincoln's government, Patrick Cleburne recognized the necessity of extending freedom to women as a condition of the political loyalty and military service of slave men. Like those officials, he turned to marriage to make that work. Recognizing how the Emancipation Proclamation had changed the terms of the competition for men, he said, the Confederacy had "to give the negro not only his freedom but that of his wife and child." To that end, Cleburne proposed they make "his [the slave's] marriage and parental relations sacred in the eyes of the law." He proposed, that is, that they first create marriage and then free slave women into it as a gift to their soldier husbands. In his scheme, slave women would be delivered directly from the legal regime of property into that of coverture. For Cleburne, as later for General Lee, President Davis, and the War Department, the slave who dreamt of freedom was male, and it was the black man—husband, father—who would earn emancipation for his wife and children. As in so many cases of military emancipations before, Cleburne proposed that men take the military route to emancipation through the war and its devastation, and slave women, somehow, the marital route. Even in this most progressive Confederate proposal the usual terms of military emancipation were exposed, showing the pattern in official views across time and space.[42]

Cleburne's assessment of the Confederacy's military prospects showed the weight of history. He knew the relationship between war, slave enlistment, and emancipation, and he knew too that the C.S.A., overmatched, desperate for men, could not escape the pull of those historical tides. "Will the Slaves Fight," he asked rhetorically. "The helots of Sparta stood their masters good stead in battle. In the great sea fight of Lepanto . . . the galley slaves . . . were promised freedom and called on to fight at a critical moment of the battle . . . The negro slaves of Saint Domingo, fighting for freedom, defeated their white masters and the French troops sent against them . . . and the experience of this war has been so far that half trained negroes have fought as bravely as many other half-trained Yankees." With the "allurement of a higher reward," Confederate slaves would fight for their masters, too, he concluded. Unlike President Davis, Patrick Cleburne extracted the salient message from the complicated history of war and emancipation: slaves will fight when they are fighting for their freedom.[43]

It was a discomforting message to deliver to men fighting on a proslavery platform. To think of slave men as soldiers was to think of them as freemen and members of the state. To Cleburne, emancipation was the only right and reasonable term on which to demand slave men's military service, because they would not fight for less and because principle demanded it. "It is a first principle with mankind that he who offers his life in defense of the State should receive from her in return his freedom and his happiness and we believe in acknowledgment of this principle."[44] Freedom from slavery, membership in the body politic, standing in the state, marriage, and the rights of husbands: by their resistance slave men and women were pressing nothing short of a revolution in Confederate political life.

It was a revolution for which most Confederates were not ready. Many would never be desperate enough to embrace its revision of Confederate society and politics. Was that the republic they had seceded to establish? One that emancipated its own slaves? Cleburne's proposal—brilliant, impolitic—was immediately suppressed, almost to the point of being lost to history. Some of the men present when he first read it exploded in anger. Among them were a few who sought to punish Cleburne for his heresy. A year later others would get behind the idea of arming slaves, but virtually no one else, with the telling exception of General Robert E. Lee (who said little and wrote less), came as close as Cleburne to calling for a general emancipation of the nation's whole slave population. A great many serious proposals to arm the slaves, including one from the president himself, contemplated emancipation only of those who served, and there were many people inside government and out who thought it entirely feasible to arm slaves *as slaves.*

The kind of radical thinking Cleburne offered would not be seen again. Davis immediately ordered the document suppressed, deeming it "injurious to the public service that such a subject should be mooted, or even known to be entertained by persons" in authority. The best policy was to "avoid all publicity." No copy of it resurfaced until the 1880s. On orders from General Johnston, Cleburne destroyed all personal copies and endured the consequences of his apostasy until he was killed in the service of his country in the battle of Franklin ten months later.[45]

President Davis managed to suppress Cleburne's proposal. But one can hardly help thinking about how its harsh truths and radical recommendations played on the president's mind between January (when he received it) and November 1864 when, facing the utter failure of slave impressment policy and an even more desperate military situation, he made his own radical proposal to the Confederate Congress. President Davis never would take Cleburne's broad agnostic view of the matter of slave emancipation—constitutional issues alone assured that he would not—but like him, he could not avoid the problem of slaves' political loyalty and the necessity of securing it to the slaveholders' republic. In that respect Davis's proposal, although far more politic, shared historical ground with Cleburne's brilliant proposal. The Confederate political project was undergoing a powerful test and no little tempering in the crucible of war.

The suppression of Cleburne's proposal did not buy the Davis administration much of a reprieve. By 1864 the subject of arming slaves was irrepressible in the Confederacy, especially in Virginia and the western states, all the scene of harrowing campaigns. After Atlanta fell in September, calls from citizens in Georgia joined those from Mississippi, Alabama, and Louisiana urging Davis and his administration to act. Women fighting the recent call-up of detailed men urged President Davis to "send us protection in the shape of our sons & husbands and we will send you able bodied negroes." Others pressed to arm slaves and spare what remained of the nation's white men. "Is it not time now to enlist the negroes?" one Georgia citizen bluntly inquired of Davis shortly after the disaster at Atlanta. Do it now or "the cries of starving women & children will make of us all cowards."[46]

As the military situation deteriorated, eyes turned to the only untapped military population source remaining in the C.S.A. In mid-September President Davis acknowledged that two-thirds of the army was absent, most without leave. By that point, the South had only about a quarter as many soldiers present for duty as the North. The head of the Conscription Bureau reported that the recruitment of white men had reached its limit and that "the functions of this Bureau may cease with the termination of the year 1864." In November Seddon again did the dismal math, concluding that the Confederacy simply could not compete with the Union in the size of its armies. We have limited exemptions and details, impressed slave men, and pushed conscription to its limits, he admitted, "[and yet] it is not to be disguised that they must still leave those armies relatively weak to encounter the hosts being summoned by the enemy for our subjugation . . . additional legislation is necessary."[47]

By the time Seddon offered his recommendations for more aggressive slave impressment, the public debate had moved far out ahead of the administration. Even as Davis and the Congress remained mum on the subject of arming slaves, citizens and the press noisily debated the merits of doing just that. During the fall of 1864 there was a clear sense of a public anticipating a decision. The discussion was single-handedly jump-started by the governor of Louisiana, Henry W. Allen, in September 1864 when a very pointed letter he wrote to the secretary of war was intercepted—and published—by the Union authorities. Governor Allen having been driven out of his state capital in Baton Rouge, his intercepted letter was datelined Shreveport, and his sense of urgency and readiness for radical change in military policy jumps off the page. Responding to a request from Richmond to send troops to Georgia and Virginia, Allen said he could spare none. "The time has come for us to put into the army every able-bodied negro man as a soldier," he told Seddon abruptly in the middle of the letter. "This should be done immediately" by Congress. "The negro . . . must play an important part in this war. He caused the fight & he will have his portion of the burden to bear . . . I would free all able to bear arms & put them into the field at once. They will make much better soldiers with us than against and swell the now depleted ranks of our armies." Picked up by Union forces, Allen's incriminating letter was forwarded to Generals Halleck and Grant. In October Allen conferred with other governors, who together recommended "a change of policy on our part" in the use of slaves for the public service; newspaper editors, private citizens, and Confederate politicians all staked out their position on the decision they were sure was coming. Union newspapers in the occupied South hooted about the arming of slaves as conclusive evidence that the rebellion was in its death throes.[48]

Like so much else in the Confederate war, the enlistment debate started out in the hinterlands and arrived late in Richmond. By the time it erupted in the capital—in October 1864—Governor Allen's position, that slave men should be enlisted and freed, was only one among many about how to make such a policy work. The *Richmond Enquirer* took a pro-enlistment position that was widely regarded as a trial balloon floated by the

Davis administration. Other papers endorsed the *Enquirer's* view, some talking in starkly racist terms about how Confederates had already sacrificed the flower of their population and about negroes as "good enough for yankee bullets." For these advocates of enlisting slaves no general emancipation of the sort Cleburne had envisioned was talked about at all, but at most a partial emancipation covering only those who served: the sacrifice of some slaves to save the rest.[49]

But while that position occupied the center of the political spectrum in the Confederate debate, it was not uncommonly the view that slaves should be enlisted as slaves, with no change in their social condition or standing in relation to the state.[50] Following Cleburne, most historians have cast the choice faced by the C.S.A. in stark ideological terms—as a choice *between* independence and slavery—and thus as a referendum on emancipation and a test of the strength of Confederate nationalism.[51] But many Confederates, including politicians, believed that they could have their cake and eat it too: that they could choose independence and slavery, arm slaves and retain slavery. Indeed, the parties most likely to acknowledge a necessary or inevitable connection between arming slaves and general emancipation were those most strongly opposed. "Those who fight for freedom are entitled to freedom, and we say so too," the *Lynchburg Republican* barked on its editorial page, before refusing the terms of the deal they believed they were being asked to make—slavery for independence. "If the white men of the South . . . claim rights in slaves which they are incapable of maintaining by force of arms, then we say we deserve no other fate than to be leveled to the equality of our negroes." "This is the monstrous proposition. The South went to war to defeat the designs of abolitionists and behold! In the midst of war, we turn abolitionists ourselves."[52] Most advocates of arming slave men seemed perfectly sanguine, by contrast, about the ability to enlist slave men and emancipate only those who served (and perhaps their families) while retaining slavery as a social institution governing the vast majority. Some diehard proslavery types even believed that slaves could be made to fight without any promise of freedom. Most Confederates were for independence and slavery until the bitter end.

That much became apparent in Richmond in the fall of 1864. As the public debate rose to a fever pitch, a Confederate senator from Virginia,

Allen Caperton, worked out his views in anticipation of a congressional debate. It was, he said, "the most serious social proposition that has been presented since at least the commencement of the eighteenth century to the people of Virginia: Whether to conscript the male slaves of the country between the ages of eighteen and fifty." Caperton was weighing a particular proposal, probably the one floated in the *Richmond Enquirer:* to conscript two hundred thousand slave men, to give them the pay of soldiers, and to enlist them on the promise that the conscripts "shall henceforth be free." General emancipation was not on the public agenda. The question, as Caperton put it, was whether it was "not better to part with a portion of our property than the whole of it and our liberty besides."[53]

It tells a great deal about the so-called "Confederate debate on emancipation" that even that proposition was too much for Senator Caperton. "This would be abolition with a vengeance," he protested, going immediately, as so many others would, to the specter of a black army nestled in the heart of a slave country. The Confederacy should hesitate to undertake such a dangerous experiment, Caperton protested, spinning out a postwar scenario of such horror it hung the peace and security of Confederate families forever in the balance. Caperton did not dispute the need to arm the slaves. In that he occupied the middle of the political spectrum in the C.S.A. Arm them, he said, but don't free them. "Is the proffer of freedom necessary or proper," he asked. "May not this step be taken without invoking the permanent interests of white man and the slave?" "I answer it may." Slaves will fight more gallantly for their masters *as slaves,* he assured himself, than as freemen.[54] The Virginia senator imagined that Confederate slaves could be made to fight as slaves for hearth, home, and slavery just as white men did.

Senator Caperton's views on arming slaves in the C.S.A. were not particularly extreme. They were shared by far more of his compatriots than ever considered a general emancipation as the necessary condition of enlistment. But the dismissal of the matter of slave men's will to fight as slaves—for slavery, presumably, and Confederate independence—was a whole lot easier for Caperton and newspaper editors than for their counterparts in the administration and the military who would be charged with making such a policy work.

President Davis, a rigid constitutionalist and no radical, proved an unlikely protagonist in this regard and thus a perfect vehicle for the historian's assessment of the late-war fate of the Confederate political project. Throughout September and October 1864 the public debate raged. Congressman William Porcher Miles, chairman of the House Military Affairs Committee, quietly solicited the view of General Robert E. Lee, who in turn made it known that he supported the use of slaves in the armies of the C.S.A. Lee's view would not be publicly known for some time, but the solicitation of it shows how imminent Miles considered the decision to be. As citizens exchanged views, newspaper editors hammered out positions, senators prepared speeches, and important committee chairmen took the temperature of the military, the president of the C.S.A. likewise took the matter under consideration.[55] Sometime in October he solicited the advice of the secretary of war. On October 27, Seddon delivered to him "two rolls, which will be found to contain views . . . in reference to the employment of Slaves in our Armies. The roll bound with white string," Seddon said in the cover letter, "was prepared by myself as making the popular views on the subject and presenting my own convictions, and would probably be most politic at this time." "The other," he said more ominously, "presents a fuller and more exhaustive consideration of the subject, and comes from the pen" of Assistant Secretary Campbell, who gave "a good deal of reflection to the subject and prepared the paper for my use."[56]

If Seddon's report is anything to judge by, the politic position was for the administration to reject association with a project so radically transformative of the status of slaves and institution of slavery in the slaveholders' republic. Seddon did not gainsay the need. His report offered a dire account of military affairs and the state of the armies relative to the hosts summoned to destroy them. Under the circumstances, Seddon reasoned, the country was certainly justified in arming slaves in its own defense. But that was neither necessary or desirable. "For the present it seems best to leave the subordinate labors of society to the negro, and to impose the highest, as now existing, on the superior class," Seddon summed up.[57] By November 1864 the possibility of arming the slaves was on the table and in advising Davis Seddon spoke vigorously against it.

Davis moved toward a different conclusion. On November 7, in his annual address to the Congress, Davis made his views on the explosive question of arming slaves publicly known for the first time.[58] His speech represented such a radical departure from any proslavery or administration orthodoxy—such a threat to the security of slave property—that it shook the very foundation of the slaveholders' republic. Davis's position was nothing short of a *volte-face*. Standing before the assembled members of the Confederate Congress conveying the dire military situation—the unlikelihood of foreign recognition, impossibility of a negotiated peace, and utter failure of slave impressment—he invited their "consideration . . . of a radical modification in the theory of the law" of slavery. Delivered in measured tones, Davis's proposal was nonetheless shocking. The slave, he declared flatly, can no longer be "viewed merely as property" but must be recognized instead in his other "relation to the State—that of a person." As property, Davis explained, slaves were useless to the state, because without the "loyalty" of the men nothing of value could be gained from their labor. "The duties required of them [in the army] demand loyalty and zeal," he insisted, describing a whole series of tasks slave men had been asked to undertake. "In this respect, the relation of person predominates so far as to render it doubtful whether the private right of property can consistently and beneficially be continued."

Thus Davis came face to face with slaves' politics in confronting the failure of impressment, and like Cleburne he did not flinch. The state, he said, had to bid for the loyalty of slave men. The government needed to purchase forty thousand male slaves for labor in the armies, and it was quite possible, he admitted, that the state might have to hold out "his emancipation . . . as a reward for faithful service." To make slaves an element of strength in the C.S.A., in other words, they would have to destroy the master-slave relation. As Davis acknowledged, it was slaves themselves who had brought a founding father and the sitting Confederate president to that juncture.

To many congressmen seated in the hall, the president's speech must have seemed incredible. Although the specific proposal was hybrid in nature, it was perfectly clear to everyone that he was laying ground for a more radical step. His own language and analysis—the salience of slaves' allegiance, the recognition of their standing in relation to the state, the necessity of emancipation—suggested as much, marking a radical modification in the theory of slavery such as would be needed to enlist slave men as soldiers in the nation's armies. On that question Davis was publicly cautious. To use slaves as soldiers was a policy that should be regarded "solely in the light of policy and our social economy," he said evenly. There was no moral problem in doing so and they would be justified if they did so decide. Davis carefully kept his options open. But for that step he was not ready. "I must dissent from those who advise a general levy and arming of the slaves for the duty of soldiers," he announced. "But should the alternative ever be presented of subjugation or of the employment of the slave as a soldier, there seems no reason to doubt what should then be our decision." As of November 7, President Davis's radical modification stopped short of arming the slaves, for reasons that bore directly on the political nature of the Confederate republic.

The direct infringement on the master's paramount claim that Davis proposed was, even with compensation, too much for the majority of congressmen. That body refused, to the bitter end, to enact the radical modification Davis urged. But from Davis's point of view, arming slaves violated principles more fundamental even than that of "pecuniary interest." For him, it was the "social and political question" that was preeminent. To arm slaves, he explained, had far-reaching implications embracing "the stability of our republican institutions—resting on the actual political equality of all its citizens."[59] To do so required either the admission of black soldiers as equal citizens in the republic or the abandonment of the principle of the equality of republican citizens admitted to membership in the body politic. In a republic it would be impossible, he seemed to say, to extract military service—the highest duty of the citizen—without extending the rights and privileges that were usually exchanged for it. The nexus of manhood, military service, and citizenship was so tight in the nineteenth century, even in a proslavery republic, that Davis balked at violating it.[60]

The political implications of arming slaves were abhorrently clear to Davis. They involved a repudiation of foundational political precepts going back to the vision of the slave republic that Chief Justice Taney had articulated in *Dred Scott* and Southern men had offered as grounds for secession. Slaves, U.S. Senator Davis had said four unimaginably long years ago, were never part of the political community. To admit them as such, as Northerners proposed, was to threaten both the right of property in slaves and the principles of republican government itself. To enlist slaves as soldiers in the C.S.A. was thus to overthrow the very republic the South had seceded to perfect. On November 7 Davis teetered on the brink, recognizing the stern logic of war but loath to admit to the world the failure of the Confederates' ambitious political project at the hands of their own slaves.

Judging by the public reaction, no one was reassured by the president's disavowal of the idea of arming slaves. Although his immediate recommendation concerned slave impressment, few doubted that this was exactly where the Confederacy was headed. Davis's message opened the floodgates. In the ensuing weeks, the wisdom of arming the slaves was furiously contested in army and civilian life.

The press reaction mirrored the divisions that would become legislatively critical. The *Charleston Mercury* went straight to the million dollar issue of what, if emancipation was in order, secession had been for. The paper was already on record with its view of the move as apostasy: "Assert the right in the Confederate Government to emancipate slaves, and it is stone dead," it editorialized days before Davis's speech, charging administration advocates with "treachery to our cause itself." In the aftermath the paper amplified its role as keeper of the flame, handily measuring the distance between what the government "was created to protect and perpetuate" and what it now claimed the "power to destroy." By that Robert Barnwell Rhett and the *Mercury* did not just mean slavery but, like Davis, the republic they had set out to build on that foundation. Nobody would have voted for a Constitution that gave the government "the power to emancipate our slaves," Rhett raged in an open letter. "The true view of the Constitution seems clearly to be, that it establishes a Confederacy of *freemen.* Freemen constitute the militia of the States. Freemen made—freemen own—and freemen who made and own the Confederate Government, alone can be called on by the Government to defend it." To the Rhetts, nothing had changed in war. Slaves, he insisted, "are a part of the domesticity of the States exclusively under their jurisdiction and their control."[61] Slaves, Rhett said, as Chief Justice Taney and Senator Davis had in 1860, were not counted among the men of the political community called on to defend the state and never could be.

In his vehement adherence to foundational principles, Rhett brilliantly illuminated the pace of change in Confederate political life such that the matter of slave men's political status was now on the table. What kind of republic was it, the *Mercury* asked repeatedly, in which slave men were trained to arms, made free, and endowed with the rights of citizen-soldiers? What would this be but "a mongrel, half-nigger, half white-man, universal freedom, beggarly Republic not surpassed even by Hayti." Haiti was again the coup de grâce. As one Richmond paper put it, "the existence of a negro soldier is totally inconsistent with our political aim and with our social as well as political system."[62]

Other papers took more middling ground, trying to follow the administration's signal about what was required to avert military disaster. The *Richmond Enquirer* was the administration organ in this regard. It set up at the opposite pole from the *Mercury* and advocated tirelessly for the use of slave soldiers and an emancipation limited to those who served. The issue, the *Enquirer* reiterated, was numbers and military necessity, not abstractions like proslavery ideals or constitutional theory. Arming slaves was not a matter of choice but necessity, and freedom for the soldier at the end of the war was the term on which it could be had. "The negro wants his freedom," the paper acknowledged bluntly, "whether a boon or a curse he wants it, and for it may be willing to serve in the army of his country. That country stands in need of those services; one is offered for the other." On the subject of freedom for the wives and children or other kinfolk of slave soldiers, the *Enquirer,* like Davis earlier, said nothing; even freedom for the soldiers was to be withheld until the end of the war.[63]

Scanning the political spectrum right to left, one thing was clear: no one publicly advocated the kind of general emancipation Cleburne had envisioned. Some editors did point out the absurdity of the idea that slave men would fight to leave their wives and children in slavery, especially when the slaves who went over to the enemy fought for the freedom of all their people. Free black men trained to arms would certainly rise up and overthrow such a republic in the postwar period, William Holden of the *North Carolina Standard* insisted. Was it possible that the government was holding up "for our imitation the example of heathen Sparta or insane France in 1792? . . . What would such independence as Hayti be worth to us," invoking again the specter of the colony that armed slaves of necessity only to see it turn into a black republic. Between those who opposed arming slaves and emancipation because they were necessarily linked, and those who advocated arming slaves and the manumission of those who served as a way to preserve slavery and independence, there was a range of positions. As before there were even people who believed that slaves should be made to fight for their country with no change in their status at all.[64]

As the Confederate public fought it out in the newspapers and on the streets, as men and women leaned over their gates in conversation with neighbors or whispered with each other in the slave quarters at night, the Davis administration maneuvered to advance its position and congressmen girded for the fight to come. President Davis operated by proxy. But it was his policy, and he moved it forward against formidable opposition in the last months of the Confederate republic. He said nothing to contradict his public position until the middle of March when he rebuked Confederate senators for moving too slowly on a bill to arm slaves that had already passed the House. If it was once regarded as apostasy to say so, there remains little doubt about Davis's advocacy of a policy his administration began to pursue aggressively in December 1864 and with greater urgency in January and February 1865, after the talks at Hampton Roads and a secret diplomatic mission to England failed to achieve a negotiated peace. By December key members of his administration—notably Benjamin and Seddon—were reaching out to prominent men seeking public support and political cover for precisely such a move.[65]

Judah P. Benjamin, Davis's controversial secretary of state, was the administration front man, charged with drumming up support among key figures. In December he approached the South Carolinian Frederick Porcher about writing articles for the Charleston papers in support of "the policy foreshadowed in the president's message," as he put it, confirming all suspicions. Benjamin spoke for Davis and presented himself as such. In consultation with Porcher, moreover, he hewed closely to Davis's view that enlistment include the emancipation of any who served. The administration policy under discussion in December was to make the Confederate government owner of as many negroes as were required for the public service and to emancipate them as a reward for faithful service;

that the states act upon the status of the families of the men so manumitted to find a way for their "ultimate emancipation after an intermediate stage of serfage or peonage," following the British model of apprenticeship. States were to provide legal protection for the marital and parental relations. By those various means, Benjamin suggested, the C.S.A. might at once gain many slave soldiers and while "vindicating our faith in the doctrine that the negro is an inferior race and unfitted for social or political equality with the white man yet so . . . ameliorate the existing condition of that inferior race" as to relieve the country "of the odium and reprobation of civilized man." Invoking the blessing of General Robert E. Lee, who was strongly in favor of using "the Negroes" for the national defense and emancipating them if necessary, the secretary of state urged Porcher to write a series of articles posing the question "Is it better for the negro to fight for us or against us?"[66] Necessity was pushing the Davis administration hard in a radical direction. If this was the state of Davis's thinking in December 1864, it suggested an arming and emancipation of slave men and their immediate family members far more expansive than anything he would be able to get Congress or the state legislatures to adopt.

Frederick Porcher was on board, and most importantly so too was Robert E. Lee. But that gives a far too encouraging impression of the state of opinion on the subject among the political and military elite. When Seddon approached the Georgia general Howell Cobb to ask him to lend support to the administration's policy, he gave a frontal rebuff to the whole idea. "I think that the proposition to make soldiers of our slaves is the most pernicious idea that has been suggested since the war began," Cobb exploded. "You cannot make soldiers of slaves, nor slaves of soldiers." In the aftermath of his recent defeat at Macon, and in the very midst of the struggle for control of southwest Georgia, Cobb knew the military odds Confederate armies faced and the number of requests for reinforcements that had gone unfulfilled. Still, like the editors of the *Mercury,* he regarded the turn to arming slaves as a "suicidal policy," the very death of all for which they contended. "The day you make soldiers of them is the beginning of the end of the revolution," he proclaimed.[67]

The Davis administration did have one powerful arrow in their quiver: the endorsement of Lee. If any man could clinch the deal for the administration, it was him. In December Judah Benjamin casually referred to Lee's views as "well known." In the new year, as legislators began to take up the issue, Lee's views were repeatedly solicited and became public. In January, Virginia senator Andrew Hunter solicited Lee's advice on whether to use the military strength "supposed to be found in our negro population." As the question suggests, Senator Hunter was opposed and would remain so to the bitter end. Lee declared himself a robust supporter of the policy and, like his predecessor Cleburne, insisted that it include a plan of emancipation. This despite Senator Hunter's leading suggestions about how to do it without disturbing the institution of slavery. Slavery, Lee said bluntly, was done for, one way or another. What they must decide, he said, is "whether slavery shall be extinguished by our enemies and the slaves be used against us, or use them ourselves at the risk of effects which may be produced upon our social institutions. My own opinion is that we should employ them without delay . . . they can be made efficient soldiers."[68]

But if General Lee made the case for "negro soldiers" on the basis of necessity, he was entirely practical, too, about what it would require. The only way to make it work, he insisted, was first to bind slaves to the Confederate cause. "Our chief aim should be to secure their fidelity," he told Hunter. The surest foundation on which the fidelity of an army can rest is the "personal interest of the soldier in the issue of the contest," presenting as natural something that was in fact historical. Generals had fought with hireling armies for time out of mind. But those were not the armies of a free man's republic. Lee's soldiers were freemen and citizens, men with a personal stake in the contest. That they could give to the slaves only by granting "immediate freedom to all who enlist, and freedom at the end of the war to the families of those who discharge their duties faithfully (whether they survive or not) together with the privilege of residing at the South."[69]

One would have to go all the way back to Cleburne to see a proposal that went so far on the matter of emancipation as a reward for service. Davis had never gone that far. He had not publicly mentioned the extension of freedom to the families of slave recruits, although judging by the plan Benjamin was floating, it was under consideration. But Lee followed Cleburne in a call for the gradual emancipation of all the slaves. They could not "expect slaves to fight for prospective freedom when they can secure it at once by going to the enemy," he told Hunter, so "the best means of securing the efficiency and fidelity of this auxiliary force would be to accompany the measure with a well-digested plan of gradual and general emancipation." It would come to that one way or another, Lee assured him; they should do it themselves and "obtain all the benefits that accrue to our cause."[70] Lee presented his plan as an eminently practical response to the crisis of the Confederacy. But the radicalism of it—gradual general emancipation of the nation's slaves—was stunning nonetheless. Abraham Lincoln himself would have found those terms acceptable as late as 1862.[71]

It was clear from the statements of Lee and everyone else who supported the administration plan that nobody chose this path out of principle. Every one yielded to necessity. Every man who made the case recited the numbers, obsessively reiterating the disparity in population and troops between the C.S.A. and the enemy. At a huge public meeting in Richmond in February, Benjamin went out to make the case, reeling off antebellum population figures for the North and the South and comparing the North's 3 million men to the 1.6 million Confederate men, enslaved and free. "Look in the trenches below Richmond," he declaimed, "is it any time now for antiquated patriotism to argue a refusal to send them aid, be it white or black."[72] John H. Stringfellow came to the conclusion that the war had shown slavery to be "an element of weakness" in a military sense. "The history of this war demonstrates the wonderful fact, that the Confederate states mainly subsists both of the immense armies engaged in the conflict," as he put it to Davis, "and actually after furnishing all the soldiers to our army, contributes about one half of those making the army of its enemies." These men were not abolitionists at heart or by choice. "The principle of slavery is a sound one," the *Richmond Daily Examiner* insisted even as it abandoned opposition and got on board in late February. The exchange of freedom for military service was at war with the first principles of this relation, they still believed, and the beginning of abolition. They yielded, they said, only "to this imperious necessity."[73]

Alone among the architects of administration policy, Robert E. Lee believed in the necessity of gradual general emancipation. The rest talked about a policy (still undefined) that would manumit only those who served and survived, and *maybe* the members of their immediate families. But still, those who embraced the idea of arming slaves *and* who were serious about making it "effective," as Lee put it, acknowledged that the policy would work only if it engaged the political will of slaves themselves. Proslavery they all were, but still the matter of slave consent, volition, and allegiance—which is to say, the recognition of slaves as political persons—pressed in from every side. By 1865 it really did matter "what the Negroes think."[74]

Elements of that long-standing problem of allegiance—one that began with Jefferson and ended up in the necessity of the enlistment and emancipation of slave soldiers—would survive the brutal vetting process required to make the Davis administration's plans into Confederate law. But only just. For if Davis's key allies thought the policy of arming slaves to be crucial and emancipation indispensable to its terms, that view was not shared by many in Congress. The idea of enlisting slaves proceeded on two tracks after the administration started to push it in December 1864. First, and most promising, was the track that went through the Virginia legislature, which took up the measure in December upon the vigorous urging of Governor Smith. Smith acknowledged the mountain of opposition and the profound division in the state and legislature over it. When the question "becomes one of liberty and independence on the one hand," he said in addressing the legislature, "or subjugation on the other . . . every man will agree to this." "Has the time arrived?" he asked on December 7. Men, he said, must be blind not to see that it has. Smith, who was the strongest ally Davis and Lee had during the last months of the war, managed to get the Virginia legislature to take up the issue in early January. After much delaying, reminiscent of how they went out of the Union in 1861, they finally passed a bill in March. It authorized Confederate authorities to call on Virginia for "as many of her able-bodied slaves between the ages (18–45) as may be deemed necessary for the public defense" up to a maximum of 25 percent of the state's slave population. Notwithstanding Smith's insistence that the bill include an emancipation provision and legislators' knowledge of General Lee's views, the bill did not require the consent even of the owners of the slaves and did not seek the consent of slaves themselves. It involved no incentives for slaves, never mind promises of manumission.[75] The issue of slaves' political consent and allegiance was crucial but politically difficult.

The second track went through the Confederate Congress. But so reluctant were members to wade into those treacherous waters that they could not be persuaded to do so until early February, after months of public agitation. Despite administration urgings and pointed leaking of Lee's urgent desire for black troops, the Congress could not be moved. It took another series of military and political disasters to concentrate their resolve. As Congress stalled in December and January, Davis, his cabinet, and generals contended with a perfect storm on the military front. Davis daily fielded calls for reinforcements from commanders at Macon, Wilmington, and Richmond, then Savannah and Charleston, as General William T. Sherman pushed through Georgia into South Carolina. In Wilmington, the Union navy pounded Fort Fisher into submission using the largest Union fleet ever assembled in the war, while six thousand Union troops attacked by land. As if to draw a map of the bleeding body politic, rumors of a massive slave insurrection emerged along the northward path of Sherman's troops into the southernmost counties of the vulnerable state. In the trenches outside Richmond, General Lee and his men held on against wave after wave of assaults from Grant's forces, fearing the moment when he would be further reinforced by the arrival of Sherman's army from the Shenandoah Valley. As Davis corresponded desperately with his commanders about shifting limited troops from one vulnerable point to another, about the relative merits of holding Charleston over Richmond, various diplomatic missions undertaken out of desperation also failed. It took the fall of Macon, Savannah, Charleston, and Fort Fisher, the closing of the last Confederate port at Wilmington, and the collapse of diplomatic initiatives to the North and England to finally bring the Confederate Congress to the table.[76]

The congressional track would eventually, reluctantly, and over powerful—almost fatal—opposition produce a piece of legislation authorizing the use of slaves in the Confederate army. But it took a severely delimited view of what was required to make the policy work. To the critical matter of slave consent and allegiance, to the matter of emancipation however partial or gradual, the Confederate Congress turned its back. On that problem, the Davis administration, the War Department, and the general in chief of the armies of the C.S.A. were on their own.

The outlines of the Davis administration plan for arming slaves, the plan that involved the emancipation of those who served, did have a real test in the congressional battle. It came in the Senate. The first motion to "call negroes into the field" was introduced in the House on February 6, and after an attempt to kill it failed, it was referred to the Committee on Military Affairs. The following day the Senate submitted a resolution instructing the committee to report out a bill on the subject. Their instructions are worth noting because of their close kinship to the terms previously advanced by President Davis and Secretary Benjamin. The committee was instructed to report a bill "to take into the military service of the Confederate States a number of negro soldiers, not to exceed two hundred thousand, by voluntary enlistment, with the consent of their owners, or by conscription," if that proved necessary. But the committee was also instructed to provide for "the emancipation of said negroes in all cases where they prove loyal and true to the end of the war," with compensation to their owners. That bill was voted down the same day, 13 to 3.[77]

The bill was debated, tellingly enough, in secret session, but Senator Graham of North Carolina, a confirmed opponent, revealed the nature of the opposition that killed it. In a letter to an old friend he boasted that he "argued it at length as unconstitutional, according to the Dred Scott decision as well [as] inexpedient and dangerous." How a U.S. Supreme Court decision could constrain men no longer part of the United States nor bound by its Constitution is a mystery from the point of view of law. But politically it makes perfect sense. Chief Justice Taney's malignant notion of the republican political community hung over Confederate senators' deliberations. Graham voted against every bill that sought the enlistment of slave men in the national armies. The Senate bill was the only one ever considered in the Confederate Congress that included some form of emancipation, and it fell far short of General Lee's preferred plan of general gradual emancipation. Still it was voted down. Its immediate and utter defeat speaks volumes about the political resistance to change in the Confederate Congress and arguably in the nation at large.[78]

When they finally acted, the members of the House did not make the

Senate's mistake of overreaching. In early February, shortly after the Senate bill failed, Ethelbert Barksdale, a congressman from Mississippi and staunch ally of Davis and Lee, introduced a very different bill. This narrow, circumscribed one went the distance. Named "A Bill to Increase the Military Force of the Confederate States," it was defensively crafted. It simply authorized the president to ask for and accept from slaveowners the services of able-bodied slave men to perform military service in whatever capacity he might decide. It not only avoided any and all mention of manumission, gradual, immediate, or otherwise: it explicitly stated that nothing in the act shall "be construed to authorize a change in the relation which the said slaves shall bear toward their owners as property, except by consent of the States in which they may reside, and in pursuance of the laws thereof."[79] That constitutional brake on emancipation would survive into the final act. In the Barksdale bill there was no mention of manumission or emancipation, not for the slave soldiers in question or their immediate families, and not of the slave population in general on any timeline at all. Thus did Barksdale try to steer the ship of state safely across the shoals of slavery in war.

In the Confederate Congress no one was asked to chose between slavery and independence. When the issue was finally taken up, Congress was asked only to allow the president to use slave men in the military with the permission of their owners. Even to this highly circumscribed proposition the opposition was furious and almost lethal. William Porcher Miles tried immediately to kill it by insisting on an open test of house opinion. William Wickham, a Virginia congressman, likewise wanted to dispose of the question "finally and forever." Barksdale fought back, urging Miles not to prejudge. The bill had been introduced "under a solemn conviction of his duty to his country." "It raises no irritating issues," he insisted, but rather provided for the possibility that gentlemen "have the privilege of contributing their slaves as a free-will offering to aid in repelling the savage foe . . . The bill provides nothing more." Barksdale managed to get the bill advanced to a select committee. As late as March, Confederate senators would try to force an adjournment before the bill made it to a vote.

The nature of congressional opposition to the bill authorizing the arming of slaves was remarkably congruent. The most powerful (and common) opposition concentrated on the political consequences for a nation that might survive the struggle for independence by the use of black troops. What political arrangements would it necessitate? In that sense it went right to the matter of political equality of citizen-soldiers that had constrained Davis a few months before. Davis might have been willing to take his chances. But a great many congressmen were not and never would be. Again and again they made the argument that military service was the obligation of the free citizen and slaves who provided it could not be denied the rights that went with it. Mr. Wickham gave a shorthand version when he tried to kill the bill, saying "it were idle to say that if negroes were put into the army they would not be upon an equality with our soldier. They would be compelled to."[80] That was the basic objection. Customary nineteenth-century assumptions about the relationship between manhood, military service, citizenship, and suffrage proved a powerful ground of opposition to the arming of slave men in the C.S.A.

That opposition view got a full airing on the floor of the house in a speech by another Virginian, Thomas Gholson. Gholson's speech was critical because it was repeated almost verbatim in the minority report filed in dissent to the bill that eventually passed. Like every opponent of arming slaves, Gholson's objections concentrated on the specter of race war in a postwar South. They were being asked whether "the boon of freedom is to be given at the termination of the war." The bill did not say so, he acknowledged, but every thinking man knew that slaves would have to be offered freedom to get them to fight. "What is this," he raged, "but abolition?" It was not only a surrender of the ground on which they defended slavery—"we hold that the slave . . . is incapable of self-government"—it was a surrender of the political future they were fighting to secure. "What then is to become of these freedmen," he asked. "What will become of their wives and children?" Would they not fight for the freedom of their wives and children? For opponents of arming slaves, the wives and children were always the entering wedge of abolition and race war. "What would be the character of the returned negro-soldiers," Gholson asked, "familiar with the use of fire-arms and taught by us that freedom was worth fighting for?"[81] The political consequences of military service, the fear of freedmen trained to arms, and the political meaning and power of guns ran through the Confederate debate over slave enlistment like a fault line on the tectonic plates of the past and the future. In that sense the debate over arming slaves really did rehearse a postwar future.[82]

President Davis's old objection to the idea of arming slaves—that the political price would be too high—was at the very center of congressional opposition. Five men signed their names to the report that insisted that the C.S.A. could never compete with Lincoln in the inducement of emancipation. Who could really believe that two hundred thousand armed men would be willing to "remain forever disfranchised," they asked, inevitably confronting the nation with the question Davis had confronted a few months before. "Would we ever be willing to admit them to the rights of citizenship? The imagination recoils from its consideration."[83] The very nature of the Confederate republic was at stake in the debate over arming slaves, Gholson and his allies insisted. And indeed it was. "It sounds the death knell of slavery and with it, all that is conservative in Southern institutions and most valuable in our political and social system." "A Democratic Republic without the balance wheel, which our disfranchised laboring class affords must soon degenerate as the experience of the Northern states has proved, into a Mobocratic despotism."[84] Was not this precisely what they had seceded to escape?

As congressmen like Gholson worked against the bill, fellow Mississippian and Davis ally Ethelbert Barksdale tried to make the case for it in the house. In February as the various bills wound their torturous way through the Congress, Benjamin and Davis maneuvered from the outside. On February 9, Benjamin made his push for the policy in a massive public meeting at the African Church in Richmond. R. M. T. Hunter, the senator from Virginia, and others spoke too. Hunter was adamantly opposed and along with Senator Graham was key to the opposition in the Senate. But Benjamin pressed on, and in this he got the aid of General Lee, who produced evidence of the army's support for the initiative as a way to counter the opposition. This would prove crucial. With Lee's approval known and his express solicitation of soldiers' opinion circulating among troops outside Richmond, soldiers' resolutions were soon forthcoming. Pretty quickly too they entered into the stream of debate in the House and Senate as advocates of the bill rose on the floor to read them into the record.[85]

Barksdale, who had introduced the slave soldier bill, remained its chief advocate. In the congressional debate Barksdale reserved his fire until the very end, giving a long speech in its defense just before the bill came up for a vote. Yet while Lee had insisted that any bill to employ slaves as soldiers had to include an emancipation clause to be effective, the bill that passed said nothing of the sort. Far from a bill that advised the general arming and emancipation of slaves, Barksdale assured his fellow representatives, the one before them eschewed conscription and left it up to the "master to select from among his slaves those who would become serviceable soldiers." "It is not the plan of the pending measure to interfere with the status of the negro," he reassured them. "No abolition is proposed." The question is left "where it belongs, with the owner himself, under such laws as his state may enact." About the wives and children of black Confederate soldiers, Barksdale pointedly said nothing. Most important, Barksdale shied away from discussion of the postwar period to focus narrowly on what war required. "The real question is how to make him available as a soldier," he said, showing just how far war had driven the Confederate state, as it had other slave regimes in the past. By that means, he insisted, they sought not to abolish slavery but to preserve it, as one might throw "part of [the] cargo of a vessel in a storm at sea . . . overboard to save the remainder." "If we triumph in the end, the institution itself will be preserved." For Barksdale and those he convinced to vote with him, the act of arming slaves required no choice between slavery and independence. Men are driven to embrace this measure, Barksdale said in summation, not by choice but by "the stern logic of events occurring in the present war." "The enemy are employing all the slaves he can steal or entice away from their owners for service as soldiers . . . the contest must then be, who can arm them fastest." It was as ever a battle of numbers, and they had to compete. Then Barksdale read Lee's letter as his final peroration for the Confederate decision to arm the slaves.[86] In the end, the Confederate Congress would give General Lee what he needed, but not, on the matter of emancipation, exactly what he had asked for.

The vote in the House could not have been closer. It passed by a margin of three: 40 to 37. Then it languished in the Senate for more than two weeks. As Davis and Lee tried desperately to anticipate and forestall the movement of Union troops toward Richmond, senators balked, then demanded an amendment limiting the number of slaves that could be called up to a maximum of 25 percent of the military-age men of each state. Hunter voted for it only under instruction from the Virginia legislature and even then spoke out against it. "If we are right in passing this measure," he railed, "we were wrong in denying to the old government the right to interfere with the institution of slavery and emancipate slaves." Senator Hunter says Southerners think "slavery was the best and most desirable condition for the negro," the *Richmond Whig* quoted him as saying, but the question is not "what we might think on the subject of emancipation, *but what the negro thinks.*"[87] What the negro thinks? There was no concealing the fact that slaves had managed to define the terms of Confederate military policy.

On March 8, 1865, kicking and screaming the whole way, the Confederate Congress finally passed "An Act to Increase the Military Forces of the Confederate States." In the Senate the bill passed by a margin of exactly one coerced Virginia senator's vote. On March 13, in the capital of the slaveholders' republic, President Davis did the unthinkable and signed into law an act making soldiers of slaves. That act cut the narrowest path possible to the desired end. It permitted him "to accept from the owners of slaves the services of such number of able-bodied negro men as he may deem expedient . . . to perform military service in whatever capacity he may direct." It preserved the sovereignty of the master, which had done so much to compromise the state in the war. And it made no provision whatsoever for emancipation. Indeed, the text of the law expressly stated that it did "nothing . . . to authorize a change in the relation which the said slaves shall bear toward their owners" except by the consent of the owners and the states in which they reside.[88] The Confederate Congress, in other words, proposed to enlist still-enslaved men as soldiers in the nation's armies. Far from choosing independence over slavery, as so many historians continue to insist, the Confederate Congress refused, even at the eleventh hour, to write an emancipation clause.[89]

But General Lee would have none of that and neither would President Davis. In the end they prevailed, and Confederate slaves proved themselves the architects of a new political era. On March 23 Jefferson Davis signed and released General Order No. 14, a piece of enabling legislation that contained the revolutionary clause that "No slave will be accepted as a recruit unless with his own consent and with the approbation of his master by a written instrument conferring, as far as he may, the rights of a freedman." The Confederate army would enroll no slaves, only freemen, by their own consent.[90] It was a momentous development in Southern and Confederate political life. The opposition was ferocious and telling. But key political and military figures in the Confederate States of America had been forced to recognize the relationship between political allegiance, military service, and emancipation. Enslaved men and women had managed to make their foundational political exclusion unsustainable, to make their political consent count, and to force the Confederate government to contend for their loyalty with emancipation. General Order No. 14 inscribed the new political realities the South had arrived at through the devastation of war, including and especially the necessity of the political inclusion of slaves. In that crude but very real sense, those male slaves they wanted as soldiers were now recognized as part of the political community, part of the nation, necessarily part of the Confederate people. If the damages inflicted by the slaves' war against the slaveholders' state was to be contained, if slave treason was to be curbed, if slave men were to be soldiers, they would have to be free and the men among them perhaps eventually recognized as citizens. This was what independence and war had wrought in the slaveholders' republic.

The Confederate States of America had been envisioned as the perfected republic of white men, a racial and patriarchal state for the modern age. The significance of the Confederate experience in arming slaves lies not in the fact that what they undertook was so radical—for, comparatively speaking, it was not—but that they were forced to undertake it at all. In that respect it not only belongs in a long hemispheric history of war, enlistment, and emancipation, but illuminates that history in a way that has never been appreciated. Even historians expert in comparative history, who put Union developments in a hemispheric frame, dismiss it as a desperate and meaningless last move. But the fact that the Confederacy, an explicitly proslavery state, was pushed to the extremity of arming its own slaves tells us a great deal about the structural problems of slave regimes at war, about the problems of state formation they invariably faced, and about the terms and logic of military emancipations over space and time. It also tells us a good deal currently not available for comparative analysis about what happened in Cuba and Brazil, the only two slave regimes left in the hemisphere by 1865, when they found themselves at war. Cuban and Brazilian slaveholders as well as colonial and imperial officials watched Confederate developments anxiously and tried to extract their own lessons from the collapse. But there was much about the policies of the colonial government in Cuba, pushed to arm their slaves in the Ten Years War, that was similar to the path already taken by the C.S.A. Indeed, the policies of both the Cuban and the Brazilian governments in the Ten Years War and the Paraguayan War of the 1860s and 1870s bear a far more striking resemblance to those of the Confederate side in the American Civil War than to the Union side, with which they are usually compared. The fate of the C.S.A. resonated across the hemisphere and put the remaining slave powers on notice about the stern logic of war.[91]

Within the crumbling national borders of the C.S.A. in March 1865, the turn to slave soldiers was indeed a "'bitter pill' to swallow, "an abandonment of the cause for which we entered upon the contest" as a couple of Virginians put it. The meaning was widely understood, hence the utter divisiveness of the public response. "If slaves will make good soldiers," General Howell Cobb of Georgia wrote as the necessity neared, "our whole theory of slavery is wrong."[92] Of course the theory was wrong, but rarely were so many owners of slaves and citizens of a slaveholding republic brought so publicly to admit it. Arming slaves on the condition of even partial emancipation represented the utter failure of the Confederate political project.

All through March 1865 Jefferson Davis, his generals, and what was left of his cabinet struggled to hold the collapsing republic together. Every day another frayed string broke. At the beginning of the month he fended off rogue efforts to negotiate a peace proffered by Confederate senators and the governor of Georgia. General Lee wrote to say he would seek an interview with General Grant. At mid-month he faced the loss of Raleigh and "the region of supplies" in North Carolina upon which the C.S.A. relied for its armies. At that point Davis was reduced to begging Lee to "avert so great a calamity." Lee was himself horrified at the idea of losing Raleigh, fearing, as he openly admitted, that if Raleigh fell, "both armies would certainly starve." But he was more horrified about the idea of losing the men and cautioned General Johnston to fight only if he could win. "The greatest calamity that could befall us is the destruction of our armies," he said. By this point Johnston's army was a mere sixteen thousand in the face of Sherman's sixty thousand, and Lee could spare no men from the thin line he had spread out to protect the capital. If he dispatched any men, he told Johnston, "the city [Richmond] must be abandoned." Throughout March, word leaked out from officials in Richmond that "the thing is up with us and so regarded and admitted privately by every thinking man and many of the Jeff Davis extreme secessionists." By March 21, Davis and Lee were engaged in a highly anxious conversation about Sherman's movements north and the expected movement of Union troops from east Tennessee into Virginia. "Unless troops can be speedily gotten from the trans-Mississippi," Lee told the president, "I see no other way of averting this new disaster." Send no more property from Richmond toward Lynchburg, he warned him. "[If] obliged to retire from Richmond," "[we have] but one outlet" left. Thus did Lee and Davis watch the escape routes close.[93]

Amid it all President Davis, Robert E. Lee, and their ally Governor Smith struggled to get "Negro" soldier enlistment up and running. Even as calls went out for slave men to fill up companies of "negro troops," even as they managed to get two companies filled up and drilling on the streets of Richmond, even as the governor of Virginia took the lead in recruiting, Governor Smith continued to prosecute slaves for treason in deserting to the enemy, to lash them to the whipping post, and to aggressively pursue the impressment of slave men against their will for labor in the same army that their compatriots were supposed to enter voluntarily as soldiers. On the streets of Richmond, two "negro soldiers" in Captain Boisseaux's company, still referred to as "slaves," were picked up as runaways because they had no pass. Governor Smith, although stalwart in support of recruiting slaves, accepting of the need to gain their consent and of emancipation as the terms of service, still expressed profound discomfort at the idea of large assemblies of such slaves in recruiting camps or depots. Even as he moved to mobilize them as soldiers, he still sought to control them as slaves.[94] Such was the incoherent state of the Confederate republic in its last days.

The political status of the slave men sought and even recruited as soldiers in the Confederate army was never resolved in the C.S.A. The act was signed into law on March 13 and War Department regulations were written three days later. Lee had been asking about the availability of black soldiers all month and was still insisting that the enlistment be "entirely voluntary on the part of the negroes." But by March 24, desperate for bodies to hold the lines outside Richmond, he dispensed with the requirements of slave consent and manumission and called on the governor of Virginia to draft all Negroes "slave and free between the ages of eighteen and forty-five, for services as soldiers" authorized by the state's legislation.[95] Finally even Lee was desperate enough to take slave soldiers.

But that was not the end of the matter. A call went out from Majors J. W. Pegram and Thomas P. Turner "to raise a company or companies of Negro soldiers . . . Composed of persons of Color, free and slave, who are willing to volunteer under the recent acts of Congress and the Legislature of Virginia." The call left much unclear—the status of the slaves who volunteered, for example. It was more a call to slaveholders to offer up their slaves to the cause than an appeal to slaves themselves. Indeed, one has to wonder about their grasp on reality, for the pitch to slaves called on them to "rally with enthusiasm for the preservation of the homes in which they have been born and raised, and in which they found contentment and happiness." They only wanted men who came voluntarily, but it was entirely unclear who was to volunteer them and on what terms. It was Pegram and Turner's men who were picked up as runaways, asked for passes, and dragged into court. And it was their men who Richard Maury, a diehard rebel, saw on the streets of Richmond and described in terms more fitting of a Confederate theatrical than a national army. He had never yet seen them under arms, he noted of the two companies of "negro soldiers" drilling in Richmond, but, he said, "I have met them walking on the street with their uniform belts and side arms on—they looked quite military with their grey jackets and caps and their blue pantaloons quite military I say but ah! How funny." "I hate the idea of having to lug Cuffee and Sambo into the ring very much," he said, describing the little boys who follow the "Darkies in crowds wherever they appear," and the citizens of Richmond who stop and smile as "the Corps of Negroes goes shuffling past." To Maury the companies of black soldiers were a carnival sideshow in which slave men appeared dressed up as soldiers. In regard to these black soldiers, one Richmond paper advised, "there should be some definite understanding . . . Sambo is going through the crucible at present" and they need some system to relieve him of the supposition of being runaways—"at least upon the city streets if not upon the tented field."[96]

On March 25, as General Ulysses S. Grant tightened the net around Richmond, Davis forwarded Lee's request for black troops to Governor Smith, but appended a statement of his reservations about "compulsory enlistment." On March 30, as they struggled to make the law operational, he still urged Smith to stick to getting volunteers rather than issuing a requisition; he also noted again the absence of any emancipation clause in the Virginia law and urged Smith to get one passed. "I am happy to receive your assurance of success," he wrote the governor, "as well as your promise to seek legislation to secure unmistakable freedom to the slave who shall enter the army, with a right to return to his old home when he shall have been honorably discharged from military service." As late as April 1, as Lee's troops fell back toward Richmond, Jefferson Davis still labored, though "without much progress," he admitted, "to advance the raising of negro troops" and extract the "most liberal provisions for those who volunteer to fight for the safety and independence of the State."[97] Whatever anyone else thought, the Confederate president regarded consent and emancipation to be the only right and reasonable terms on which to recruit slave soldiers.

In the end, two companies of black troops were raised in Richmond and sent to battle on the fortifications in front of Petersburg days before the end. Little remains by which to ascertain their status. Whether they fought as slaves, as slaves promised freedom, or as men already possessed of manumission papers, we do not know. There is no doubt that many Confederates, including white men in the military, were happy enough to leave things, legally and politically speaking, where they stood in 1861.

There is little surprising about that, and it certainly puts to rest any lingering idea that most Confederates would have surrendered slavery for independence.

But what is more interesting from a historical point of view is the practical impossibility of that position by 1865. If nothing else the slaves' war had rendered it moot. Some historians insist on the possibility that slave men would have rallied to the Confederate call to arms. Two companies of men, most of them attendants at Winder Hospital, apparently did. But those men were already in the grip of the Confederate state and military.[98] Far more impressive is the evidence of the thousands of other slaves still trying in the last days of the war to break out of Confederate lines or to advance the Union's military fortunes, risking arrest and execution or gruesome ad hoc murder at that pregnant historical moment. In Richmond, slave men continued to hide slave compatriots in their carts and tried to spirit them out of the city and into Yankee lines under cover of night. The slave Peter did that and was sentenced to stripes and banishment; he had suffered the stripes and was up for a pardon (on the application of his master) when Richmond fell on April 2. In the South Carolina low country, which descended into a state of guerilla war after Christmas 1864, slaves continued to pilot Yankee soldiers to the swamp hideouts of Confederate troops and were hunted mercilessly in return. In the last days of March 1865, as black Union troops occupied the plantations in St. John's, Berkeley Parish, told the slaves there they were free, and distributed planters' personal belongings as proof of new ownership, Confederate scouts rode out to order slaves back to work and murdered those who resisted. On March 22, Confederate scouts in that lawless, two-state parish, hanged Harry, a driver on Hanover Plantation.[99]

The violent repression of slaves-turned-freedpeople continued into the postwar period, but still slave men and women risked their lives to bring Union victory and Confederate defeat. Well might Majors Pegram and Turner call on slaves to fight for their country. To that, one Virginia slave gave the only possible answer: "I never felt at liberty to speak my mind until they passed an act to put colored men into the army," he would later say. "That wrought upon my feelings so I couldn't but cry . . . They asked me if I would fight for my country. I said, 'I have no country.'"[100]

On April 1 President Davis still struggled to avert military disaster by recruiting slave men into the army of the C.S.A. On April 2 General Lee ordered the evacuation of Richmond. As President Davis, his cabinet, and War Department employees hauled out the remaining contents of the Treasury and loaded boxes of archival materials onto the last train out, Lee and his army tried and failed to make it to Danville, Virginia. As the Army of Northern Virginia, the last best hope of the C.S.A., melted away on the run, Robert E. Lee came to terms with General Grant, and President Lincoln entered Richmond.[101] The crowds of slaves who lined the streets to receive him were not the same people who had watched as their masters and mistresses declared independence four brief years before. And neither were the whites who now lined the streets, peered out nervously from behind shaded windows, or lined up for Union relief, silently contemplating the price they would pay for their treason. War had transformed them all. The Confederate political project had been tried before the eyes of the world and it had failed. The poverty of Confederates' proslavery political vision had been proved once and for all time.

EPILOGUE

Confederate Reckoning

By April 1865 the Confederacy was in ruins. A nation founded in a risky bid to render slavery and the power of American slaveholders permanent had failed spectacularly, bringing down not just slavery and the Confederate States of America, but the most powerful slave regime remaining in the Western world. To say it changed the terms of history is not to claim too much.

Standing on the brink of war four short years before, recklessly contemplating secession, no one in the American South could have anticipated what lay ahead. The scale of war, the demands of waging it, the level of mobilization for it, and the dominion of death it ushered in, all this was unimaginable in 1861. Among the least expected developments was the way the war tested Confederates' national project from within as well as without. For in terms of the practicality and justice of its national ambitions, the C.S.A. was subjected to the judgment of its own people even as it attempted to survive the military test it faced from a Union government that grew stronger in men, arms, and territory with every year. It was the dynamic interplay of those two elements that accounts for the plot of war and transformation that unfolded over the course of the Civil War with such profound consequences for the nation, the South, and the people in it. For unlike secession, the four-year experiment in Confederate nation making it launched involved a reckoning with the political will of all of the Southern people, including the mass of unfranchised women and slaves, and not just the white male voters originally counted and consulted.

The plot of war and transformation that played out over the short national history of the C.S.A. joined the destruction of slavery to the failure of the Confederate experiment, with all of its meanings for civil and political life. Secession was difficult enough. It was no easy task to unite nonslaveholders behind the slaveholders' project, and the map of the Confederacy's war against the Unionists confirms that those were lasting divisions within the body politic. But the polity itself underwent a powerful reconfiguring in the crucible of war. The force of military arms and numbers brought against the C.S.A. by the Union—armies 120,000 strong and constantly replenished, a national force totaling more than two million men, and the evolving commitment of Lincoln and his party to the destruction of slavery and of slaveholders as a force in national life—all this created pressures not easily answered by the Confederacy.

The structural problems faced by the C.S.A. as a slave regime at war, including the lack of access to a significant segment of its adult male population, the need to wage war while protecting slave property and retaining the support of slaveholders, required it to take measures drastic even by the standard of mobilization set in the North. Every attempt to meet military need, every policy innovation, imposed a new toll on the population and set in train a dangerous political dynamic. When the C.S.A. adopted a draft of white men, when it enlisted 85 percent of adult white men and stripped the countryside of labor, when it attempted to create a tax base and supply the army by a levy on the "surplus" agricultural production of farms and plantations, it extracted the means of war from a population of women and children staggering under the burden of farm labor and, by 1863, facing starvation. Those women passed powerful judgment on the viability of the government's policies and its demands on the poor. And putting themselves at the very center of political life on the home front, they insisted that the slaveholders' nation serve justice and not just power. For a moment the conditions of war and difficulties of waging it in a slave society meant that Confederate politicians and officials answered to soldiers' wives.

Every move the Confederate government took to shore up the institution of slavery, starting with secession itself, moved them deeper into a war that worked its destruction. Attempting to use slaves' labor to wage war, the government and military only ensured slaveholders' noncooperation and outright resistance. Slaveholders' arrayed themselves against any measure that weakened their claims to property, even colluding with their slaves against the government. But the dynamic of war, including the policies Confederates forged to wage it, so profoundly shifted the balance of power that slaves gained unprecedented opportunities to resist their enslavement. History opened up to them. In the C.S.A., slaves quickly emerged as powerful enemies of the government, working to destroy slavery and the slaveholders' state from within even as the Union army pressed on them from without. It is telling of its significance that some of the best descriptions of the dynamic came from within the military leadership of the C.S.A. When the Confederate president and Congress were forced to permit the enlistment of slave men in the national army, the Confederate project was undone. By that point it was also clear that the C.S.A. had recapitulated the whole dangerous history of war and emancipation that had plagued slaveholders in the hemisphere since the American and French revolutions. From secession to defeat, Southern slaveholders' war for a proslavery nation played out in a highly charged international arena.

The C.S.A. had been built on a very slim foundation of democratic consent. That may have been its greatest weakness. When war came, its goal of building a proslavery and antidemocratic nation was tested and found wanting by its own people, only this time "the people" was a far more representative cast of the Southern population. Given its goal of preserving a highly restrictive body politic, it was a fitting judgment on the slaveholders' state. War transformed precisely the social and political relations it was designed to preserve. The poverty of Confederates' proslavery political vision had been proven once and for all.

In the defeated South in 1865 and 1866, ends and beginnings were all tangled up. The end of slavery as a system of organizing labor and social relations unhinged the system of political representation as well. It was not that white Southern politicians stopped invoking the *Dred Scott* decision as the last word on "negro" citizenship, for they did not. Now, however, their efforts were met by volleys fired from the other side, from ex-slaves no longer clandestine in their opposition, but open, forceful, organized, and empowered by their claims as the loyal people arrayed against the traitors. The brutal violence of political life in the postwar South was testament not to a continuity with the past of slavery but to the rupture the war represented and to the fundamental nature of the new negotiations about the future under way between old enemies. The struggle to define the composition of "the people" and the republic in the new postwar and post-emancipation South was hardly settled by the American Civil War. But there was no going back. It was not just that slavery was abolished and the Confederacy destroyed, but that the slaveholders' stunning experiment in proslavery and antidemocratic nation building was over. Their vision of the future had been tried, and it had failed in the face of enemy armies and the determined resistance of its own people to it. There would be new experiments in Southern political life, including ones in which formal freedom coincided with aggressively antidemocratic politics. But the firm ground slavery had long provided for Southern conservatism was gone for good. Southerners would struggle to put together a new society without the foundation of slavery. It would trace its history through bloody Confederate ground. It would arise out of the ashes of the old, but it would be new.

The history of the Confederate States of America offers an invaluable perspective on the workings of power and politics, the possibilities of change, and the writing of history. Founded at the height of the slaveholders' power in the United States, constructed as a national testament to the ambition of that class, the Confederacy instead sealed the destruction of slavery and of slaveholders as a viable political force in Western history. The Confederacy turned into a moment of profound historical reckoning, and the forces reckoned with bore little resemblance to the people who were supposed to make history.

Notes

ABBREVIATIONS

AHR	*American Historical Review*
DU	Archives and Special Collections, Perkins Memorial Library, Duke University, Raleigh, N.C.
FHS	Filson Historical Society, Louisville, Kentucky
GDAH	Georgia Department of Archives and History
GHQ	*Georgia Historical Quarterly*
GSF	Governor's Subject Files, Georgia Governor's Office, Georgia Department of Archives and History, RG 1-1-5
HU	Dearborn Collection, Houghton Library, Harvard University
LC	Library of Congress, Manuscripts Division, Washington, D.C.
LRCSW	Letters Received by the Confederate Secretary of War, National Archives, Washington, D.C.
LSU	Hill Memorial Library, Louisiana State University, Baton Rouge, Louisiana
LVA	Library of Virginia, Richmond
MDAH	Mississippi Department of Archives and History, Jackson, Mississippi
NA	National Archives, Washington, D.C.
NCDAH	State Archives, Division of Archives and History, Raleigh, North Carolina
O.R.	United States War Department, *The War of the Rebellion: A Compilation of the Official Records of the Union and Confederate Armies* (Washington, D.C., 1880–1901)
PJD	*The Papers of Jefferson Davis* (Baton Rouge: Louisiana State University Press, 1971–), 11 vols.
RASP	Kenneth M. Stampp, ed., *Records of Antebellum Southern Plantations from the Revolution through the Civil War* (Frederick, Md., 1985)

SCC	Southern Claims Commission, NA
SCL	South Caroliniana Library, Columbia
SHC	Southern Historical Collection, Wilson Library, University of North Carolina at Chapel Hill
UVA	Special Collections, University of Virginia, Charlottesville
VHS	Virginia Historical Society, Richmond
ZBV	Zebulon B. Vance, Governor's Papers, State Archives, Division of Archives and History, Raleigh, North Carolina

PROLOGUE

1. Emory Thomas has insisted that Southerners formed the Confederacy "not to accomplish something new, but to defend something old—the 'Southern way of life'" (Emory M. Thomas, *The Confederacy as a Revolutionary Experience* [1971; Columbia, S.C., 1991], 1). For the idea of emancipation as a failure, see Eric Foner, *Nothing but Freedom: Emancipation and Its Legacy* (Baton Rouge, 1983), and Edward Bartlett Rugemer, *The Problem of Emancipation: The Caribbean Roots of the American Civil War* (Baton Rouge, 2008).
2. On the crisis of legitimacy in Confederate ideology, see Drew Gilpin Faust, *The Creation of Confederate Nationalism: Ideology and Identity in the Civil War South* (Baton Rouge, 1988), 55.
3. Thomas Jefferson, *Notes on the State of Virginia,* ed. Frank Shuffleton (New York, 1999), 168.
4. The relationship between war and emancipation, although not explicitly analyzed, emerges clearly from Robin Blackburn's commanding survey of emancipation in the colonies. See Robin Blackburn, *The Overthrow of Colonial Slavery, 1776–1848* (London, 1998). On the history of arming slaves, see Christopher Leslie Brown and Philip D. Morgan, eds., *Arming Slaves from Classical Times to the Modern Age* (New Haven, 1996). On Cuba, see Rebecca J. Scott, *Slave Emancipation in Cuba: The Transition to Free Labor, 1860–1890* (Princeton, 1985), and Ada Ferrer, *Insurgent Cuba: Race, Nation and Revolution, 1868–1898* (Chapel Hill, 1999). On Saint-Domingue, see C. L. R. James, *The Black Jacobins: Toussaint L'Ouverture and the San Domingo Revolution* (1938; New York, 1963); Blackburn, *Overthrow of Colonial Slavery;* Carolyn Fick, *The Making of Haiti: The Saint Domingue Revolution from Below* (Knoxville, 1990); Laurent Dubois, *Avengers of the New World: The Story of the Haitian Revolution* (Cambridge, Mass., 2004). On Brazil, see Hendrik Kraay, "Slavery, Citizenship and Military Service in Brazil's Mobilization for the Paraguayan War," *Slavery and Abolition* 18, no. 3 (Dec. 1997): 228–256. On Confederate slaves, see Steven Hahn, *A Nation under Our Feet: Black Political Struggles in the Rural South from Slavery to the Great Migration* (Cambridge, Mass., 2003); Matthew Clavin, "American Toussaints: Symbol, Subversion, and the Black Atlantic Tradition in the American Civil War," *Slavery and Abolition* 28, no. 1 (April 2007): 87–113.
5. The new interpretation builds on the foundational work of W. E. B. Du Bois,

Black Reconstruction in America (New York, 1935), and Benjamin Quarles, *The Negro in the Civil War* (1953; New York, 1989). For key recent contributions, see Ira Berlin et al., *Slaves No More: Three Essays on Emancipation and the Civil War* (Cambridge, UK, 1992), and the volumes of the series *Freedom: A Documentary History of Emancipation, 1861–1867,* ed. Berlin et al. It is not uncontroversial. For an introduction to the issues in dispute, see James McPherson, "Who Freed the Slaves?" in *Drawn with the Sword: Reflections on the American Civil War* (New York, 1996), 192–207; and Ira Berlin, "Emancipation and Its Meaning in American Life," *Reconstruction* 2, no. 3 (1994): 35–44. For a popular manifestation, see Ken Burns, *The Civil War,* PBS, produced by Ken Burns, Oct. 1990.

6. Jefferson Davis, Farewell Address, Jan. 21, 1861, in *The Papers of Jefferson Davis,* vol. 7: *1861,* ed. Lynda L. Crist and Mary S. Dix (Baton Rouge, 1992) (hereafter cited as *PJD,* vol. 7), 21.
7. The military-defeat paradigm dates back at least to Frank L. Owsley, *State Rights in the Confederacy* (Chicago, 1925), and continues unabated. For reviews of the literature, see Richard E. Berringer, Herman Hattaway, Archer Jones, and William N. Still, *Why the South Lost the Civil War* (Athens, Ga., 1986), 4–34; James L. Roark, "Behind the Lines: Confederate Economy and Society," in *Writing the Civil War: The Quest to Understand,* ed. James McPherson and William J. Cooper Jr. (Columbia, S.C., 1998), 203–221. The nationalism-and-defeat paradigm is also venerable and still contested. See the early contributions of Charles H. Wesley, *The Collapse of the Confederacy* (1937; New York, 1968), and more recent, post-Vietnam contributions, including Paul Escott, *After Secession: Jefferson Davis and the Failure of Confederate Nationalism* (Baton Rouge, 1978), and, on the other side, Gary W. Gallagher, *The Confederate War: How Popular Will, Nationalism and Military Strategy Could Not Stave Off Defeat* (Cambridge, Mass., 1997).
8. Thomas, *Confederacy,* 136–137.
9. Ann Laura Stoler, *Race and the Education of Desire: Foucault's History of Sexuality and the Colonial Order of Things* (Durham, 1995), 7–8, 52.
10. For a sample of the feminist theories and histories, see Carole Pateman, *The Sexual Contract: Aspects of Patriarchal Liberalism* (Stanford, 1988); Joan Wallach Scott, *Gender and the Politics of History* (New York, 1988); Linda K. Kerber, *No Constitutional Right to Be Ladies: Women and the Obligations of Citizenship* (New York, 1998); Nancy F. Cott, *Public Vows: A History of Marriage and the Nation* (Cambridge, Mass., 2000); Hendrik Hartog, *Man and Wife in America: A History* (Cambridge, Mass., 2000); Reva B. Siegel, "'The Rule of Love': Wife Beating as Prerogative and Privacy," *Yale Law Journal* 105, no. 8 (June 1996): 2117–2207; and Begona Arextaga, *Shattering Silence: Women, Nationalism and Political Subjectivity in Northern Ireland* (Princeton, 1997).
11. James Scott, *Domination and the Arts of Resistance: Hidden Transcripts* (New Haven, 1990), and Scott, *Weapons of the Weak: Everyday Forms of Peasant Resistance* (New Haven, 1985); Ranajit Guha, *Elementary Aspects of Peasant Insurgency in Colonial India* (Durham, 1999), and Guha, "The Small Voice of History," in *Subaltern Studies IX: Writings on South Asian History and Soci-*

ety, ed. Shahid Amin and Dipesh Chakrabarty (New York, 1996), 1–12; Partha Chatterjee, *The Politics of the Governed: Reflections on Popular Politics in Most of the World* (New York, 2004).

12. The new story traces out a particular historical dynamic focused on slaves' flight to Union lines, military labor for the Union army, and the eventual enlistment of black men in the Union army and navy. For a few important contributions, see Berlin et al., *Slaves No More;* Eric Foner, *Reconstruction: America's Unfinished Revolution, 1863–1877* (New York, 1988); and Hahn, *A Nation under Our Feet.*
13. For the numbers of black men in the Union army, see Berlin et al., *Slaves No More,* 52. The estimate of the numbers behind Union lines is from James M. McPherson, *The Negro's Civil War* (New York, 1965), ix. The most careful reconstructions are in Ira Berlin et al., eds., *Freedom: A Documentary History of Emancipation, 1861–1867,* ser. 1, vol. 3: *The Wartime Genesis of Free Labor: The Lower South* (Cambridge, UK, 1990), 77–80; and Hahn, *A Nation under Our Feet,* 82–83. The estimate of the number who ended the war in Confederate territory was arrived at by deducting the number of slaves in the Union border states and occupied territory from the total slave population of the United States. See Donald B. Dodd and Wynelle S. Dodd, *Historical Statistics of the South, 1790–1970* (Tuscaloosa, 1973), 10, 22, 30.
14. Ira Berlin et al., eds., *Freedom: A Documentary History of Emancipation, 1861–1867,* ser. 1, vol. 1: *The Destruction of Slavery* (Cambridge, UK, 1985), 196. On their view of the Confederate decision to arm slaves as "a desperate last gamble to forestall defeat," see 682.
15. On arming slaves in the C.S.A., see Emory Thomas, *The Confederate Nation: 1861–1865* (New York, 1979); Robert F. Durden, *The Gray and the Black: The Confederate Debate on Emancipation* (Baton Rouge, 1972); Philip D. Dillard, "Independence or Slavery: The Confederate Debate over Arming the Slaves" (Ph.D. diss., Rice University, 1999), and Bruce Levine, *Confederate Emancipation: Southern Plans to Free and Arm the Slaves during the Civil War* (New York, 2006).
16. Stephanie McCurry, "War, Gender and Emancipation in the Civil War South," in *Lincoln's Proclamation: Emancipation Reconsidered,* ed. William Blair and Karen Younger (Chapel Hill, 2009); Elizabeth Colwill, "'Fêtes de l'hymen, fêtes de la liberté': Marriage, Manhood, and Emancipation in Revolutionary Saint-Domingue," in *The World of the Haitian Revolution,* ed. David Patrick Geggus and Norman Fiering (Bloomington, 2009), 125–155. For an introduction to the literature on gender and emancipation, see Pamela Scully and Diana Paton, eds., *Gender and Slave Emancipation in the Atlantic World* (Durham, 2005).

1. WHO ARE THE PEOPLE?

1. The phrase "game of nations" is Robert M. T. Hunter, "Speech . . . on the Resolution Proposing to Retrocede the Forts . . . Delivered in the Senate of the

United States, Jan. 11, 1861," in *Southern Pamphlets on Secession: November 1860–April 1861,* ed. Jon L. Wakelyn (Chapel Hill, 1996), 283; Alexander H. Stephens, "Cornerstone Address," in Wakelyn, *Southern Pamphlets,* 408–409.

2. Stephens, "Cornerstone Address," in Wakelyn, *Southern Pamphlets,* 405–406. Stephens's claim was not without merit, given the rise of scientific racism in the late antebellum period.
3. W. H. Trescot to [W. P.] Miles, Feb. 8, 1859, William Porcher Miles Papers, Southern Historical Collection, Wilson Library, University of North Carolina at Chapel Hill (hereafter cited as SHC); J. L. M. Curry, "The Perils and Duty of the South," in Wakelyn, *Southern Pamphlets,* 44; Henry Benning in *Secession Debated: Georgia's Showdown in 1860,* ed. William W. Freehling and Craig M. Simpson (New York, 1992), 120. On the context in Europe, see Jerome Blum, *End of the Old Order in Rural Europe* (Princeton, 1978), and E. J. Hobsbawm, *The Age of Revolution, 1789–1848* (London, 1962). On the context in the United States, see Eugene D. Genovese, *The Political Economy of Slavery: Studies in the Economy and Society of the Slave South* (New York, 1965). On the idea of failed post-emancipation states, see Thomas C. Holt, *The Problem of Freedom: Race, Labor and Politics in Jamaica and Britain, 1832–1938* (Baltimore, 1992); Eric Foner, *Nothing but Freedom: Emancipation and Its Legacy* (Baton Rouge, 1983); and Edward Bartlett Rugemer, *The Problem of Emancipation: The Caribbean Roots of the American Civil War* (Baton Rouge, 2008). On the colonial, and not national, history of most Western slaveholding societies, see Robin Blackburn, *The Overthrow of Colonial Slavery, 1776–1848* (London, 1988). Neither Anderson nor Hobsbawm considers the possibility of a proslavery nationalism. See Benedict Anderson, *Imagined Communities: Reflections on the Origin and Spread of Nationalism,* 2nd ed. (London, 1991), and Eric J. Hobsbawm, *Nations and Nationalism since 1780: Programme, Myth, Reality* (Cambridge, UK, 1990).
4. Thomas E. Schott, *Alexander H. Stephens of Georgia: A Biography* (Baton Rouge, 1988).
5. Jefferson Davis, Farewell Address, Jan. 21, 1861, *PJD,* 7:18–23, quotation at 21. For a first-rate account of Davis's antebellum political career, see William J. Cooper, *Jefferson Davis, American* (New York, 2002).
6. Davis, Farewell Address, *PJD,* 7:21.
7. Ibid., 7:21–22, and Jefferson Davis, Reply to William Seward, Feb. 29, 1860, in *The Papers of Jefferson Davis,* vol. 6: *1856–1860,* ed. Lynda L. Crist and Mary S. Dix (Baton Rouge, 1992) (hereafter cited as *PJD,* vol. 6), 283.
8. Davis clearly thought that secession would bring war. See Jefferson Davis to Robert Barnwell Rhett, Jr., Nov. 10, 1860, *PJD,* 6:368–371, and editors' note at 370.
9. *Scott v. Sandford,* 60 U.S. (19 How.) 393, 410, 405, 420 (1857); Jefferson Davis, Speech at Jackson, Nov. 4, 1857, *PJD,* 6:158–159. On the Dred Scott case, see Don E. Fehrenbacher, *The Dred Scott Case: Its Significance in American Law and Politics* (New York, 1978).
10. George Blake quoted in Linda K. Kerber, *No Constitutional Right to Be Ladies: Women and the Obligations of Citizenship* (New York, 1998), 25; *Scott v. Sandford,* 60 U.S. (19 How.) 393, 422 (1857). The exclusion of women from "the

people" was repeatedly rendered explicit in political theory, including social contract theory. On ancient republics, see Susan Miller Okin, *Women and Western Political Thought* (Princeton, 1979); Wendy Brown, *Manhood and Politics: A Feminist Reading in Political Theory* (New Jersey, 1988); and Hannah F. Pitkin, *Fortune Was a Woman: Gender and Politics in the Thought of Niccolo Machiavelli* (Berkeley, 1984). On social contract theory, see Carole Pateman, *The Sexual Contract: Aspects of Patriarchal Liberalism* (Stanford, 1988).

11. Jefferson Davis, Inaugural Address, Montgomery, Alabama, Feb. 18, 1861, *PJD,* 7:45–51, quotations at 46–47; Dunbar Roland, ed., *Jefferson Davis, Constitutionalist: His Letters, Papers and Speeches* (Jackson, 1923), 5:48; Jefferson Davis, Speech at Richmond, June 1, 1861, *PJD,* 7:184.
12. Jefferson Davis, Speech at Richmond, *PJD,* 7:184–185.
13. Benedict Anderson says that "the nation is always conceived as a deep horizontal comradeship," and that it is "this fraternity" that makes so many people willing "to die for such limited imaginings." Nowhere in his text is the fraternal form of the national bond subjected to analysis. The gender of nationalist belonging is thus naturalized, a taken-for-granted part of the political landscape of the modern world. See Anderson, *Imagined Communities*, quotation at 7.
14. Alexander Keysaar, *The Right to Vote: The Contested History of Democracy in the United States* (New York, 2000), tables A-2 to A-5. The trend was away from black voting in the antebellum period. North Carolina rescinded the right of free black men to vote, and many Northern and midwestern states would continue to reject the policy in elections and referendums during the Civil War. In fearing a racial redefinition of the people by the Republican Party, secessionists created precisely the set of conditions—war and military service—under which it was likely to be accomplished.
15. Stephens, "Cornerstone Address," 408; George H. Reese, ed., *Proceedings of the Virginia State Convention of 1861* (Richmond, 1965), 1:349–350, 368–369, and 2:631. For an overview, see Ralph A. Wooster, *The Secession Conventions of the South* (Princeton, 1962), and David M. Potter, *The Impending Crisis, 1848–1861,* ed. Don E. Fehrenbacher (New York, 1976).
16. *Message of the Governor of Virginia and Accompanying Documents* (Richmond, 1861), iii–iv, xxv; William R. Smith, ed., *The History and Debates of the Convention of the People of Alabama, Begun and Held in the City of Montgomery, on the Seventh Day of January, 1861* (Atlanta, 1861), 17. Benning in Freehling and Simpson, *Secession Debated,* 116.
17. Robert Toombs in Freehling and Simpson, *Secession Debated,* 50. Curry said framers had "no such sickly philosophy as Lincoln and the Chicago program avow." See Curry, "Perils and Duty," 37–38. "American Congo" is in Smith, *Convention of the People of Alabama,* 83.
18. Thomas R. R. Cobb in Freehling and Simpson, *Secession Debated,* 8. For similar charges in Alabama, see Curry, "Perils and Duty," 37–38; Smith, *Convention of the People of Alabama,* 223–224.
19. The resolutions are reprinted in Allen D. Candler, ed., *The Confederate Rec-*

ords of the State of Georgia, 6 vols. (1909–1911; repr., New York, 1972), 1:58–156. For Merriwether County, see 87–88; Spalding County, 102–103; Habersham County, 119–120; and Bibb County, 131.

20. Smith, *Convention of the People of Alabama,* 286.
21. Kerber, *No Constitutional Right;* Hendrik Hartog, *Man and Wife in America: A History* (Cambridge, Mass., 2000), 100. Riva Siegel says the common law established the family as a kind of "gendered jurisdiction." See Riva B. Siegel, "She the People: The Nineteenth Amendment, Sex Equality, Federalism and the Family," *Harvard Law Review* 116, no. 4 (Feb. 2002), 947–1046, quotation at 982. On marriage and women's public standing, see Nancy Cott, *Public Vows: A History of Marriage and the Nation* (Cambridge, Mass., 2000); on feminists' midcentury presence, see Norma Basch, *Framing American Divorce: From the Revolutionary Generation to the Victorians* (Berkeley, 1999). On the antislavery context of all known women's rights activities, see Lori Ginzberg, *Untidy Origins: A Story of Woman's Rights in Antebellum New York* (Chapel Hill, 2005). On the proslavery use of marriage, see Stephanie McCurry, *Masters of Small Worlds: Yeoman Households, Gender Relations, and the Political Culture of the Antebellum South Carolina Low Country* (New York, 1995). On the paradox of the citizen-wife, see McCurry, review essay in *Signs* 30 (Winter 2005): 1659–70.
22. Governor Joseph E. Brown, "Special Message," Executive Department, Milledgeville, Georgia, Nov. 7, 1860, in Candler, *Confederate Records,* 1:33–34.
23. John Adams to James Sullivan, Philadelphia, May 26, 1776, reprinted in Alice Rossi, ed., *The Feminist Papers: From Adams to de Beauvoir* (Boston, 1988), 13–14; Reese, *Virginia State Convention,* 1:429, 432.
24. Ann Laura Stoler, *Race and the Education of Desire: Foucault's History of Sexuality and the Colonial Order of Things* (Durham, 1995), 7–8, 52. Political historians treat the exclusion of women as a natural fact of the nineteenth-century landscape. I am arguing that the most fundamental aspects of Southern political life lay outside the realm of party politics to which political historians attend.
25. The phrase "fusion of national and feminine" is Eavan Boland's, from her remarkable book, *Object Lessons: The Life of the Woman and the Poet in Our Time* (New York, 1995), 128.
26. Henry Wise quoted in Reese, *Virginia State Convention,* 1:36; Cobb in Freehling and Simpson, *Secession Debated,* 6; *Charleston Mercury,* Sept. 28, 1860, Sept. 21, 1859. For "genius of liberty," see Smith, *Convention of the People of Alabama,* 31–33; for "old lady in hoop skirts," see John S. Palmer to Simmons, Charleston, Dec. 19, 1860, Palmer Family Papers, South Caroliniana Library, Columbia, S.C. (hereafter cited as SCL).
27. Joseph E. Brown in Freehling and Simpson, *Secession Debated,* 155–156. On the use of women as objects of political obligation, see Robert B. Westbrook, "'I Want a Girl, Just Like the Girl That Married Harry James': American Women and the Problem of Political Obligation in World War II," *American Quarterly* 42 (Dec. 1990): 587–614; Stephanie McCurry, "The Soldier's Wife: White Women, the State, and the Politics of Protection in the Confederacy," in

Women and the Unstable State in the Nineteenth Century, ed. Alison Parker and Stephanie Cole (College Station, 2000), 15–36.

28. Smith, *Convention of the People of Alabama,* 83–84, 90; Reese, *Virginia State Convention* 1:147.
29. "An Immense Public Meeting of the Citizens of Richmond," *Richmond Enquirer,* Jan. 1, 1861. John Townsend's speech was reprinted in the *Charleston Mercury,* Oct. 31, 1860. See the similar analyses in Craig M. Simpson, *A Good Southerner: The Life of Henry A. Wise of Virginia* (Chapel Hill, 1985), esp. 225, and Lynn A. Hunt, *The Family Romance of the French Revolution* (Berkeley, 1992), 139–140.
30. On charges of rape as war propaganda, see Nicoletta Gullace, "Sexual Violence and Family Honor: British Propaganda and International Law during the First World War," *American Historical Review* (hereafter cited as *AHR*) 102, no. 3 (June 1997): 714–747.
31. Cobb in Freehling and Simpson, eds., *Secession Debated,* 29, 11, 23.
32. Printed circular, Robert N. Gourdin [Chairman of the Executive Committee] to Honorable R. F. W. Allston, Nov. 19, 1860, 1860 Association, SCL; John Townsend, *The Doom of Slavery in the Union, Its Safety Out of It,* 2nd ed. (Charleston, 1860), 22; John Townsend, *The South Alone Should Govern the South and African Slavery Should Be Controlled Only by Those Who Are Friendly to It,* 3rd ed. (Charleston, 1860); *Charleston Mercury,* Oct. 31, 1860; May Spencer Ringold, "Robert Newman Gourdin and the '1860 Association,'" *Georgia Historical Quarterly* (hereafter cited as *GHQ*) 55 (1971): 501–509.
33. From that perspective, historians' preoccupation with elite women's nationalist identification looks like a contemporary extension of the figurative landscape set in the secession crisis itself. Drew Faust's recent interpretation is thus a feminist inversion of the nationalist ideal. See Drew Gilpin Faust, *Mothers of Invention: Women of the Slaveholding South in the American Civil War* (Chapel Hill, 1996), and Faust, "Altars of Sacrifice: Confederate Women and the Narratives of War," *Journal of American History* 76 (Mar. 1990): 1200–1228; but the pattern goes back to Bell Irvin Wiley, *Confederate Women* (Westport, 1975).
34. For analyses that reiterate secession discourse, see James M. McPherson, *What They Fought For, 1861–1965* (Baton Rouge, 1994), 19–21, and Gary W. Gallagher, *The Confederate War: How Popular Will, Nationalism, and Military Strategy Could Not Stave Off Defeat* (New York, 1997), 79–80. For a description of the Virginia flag, see Reese, *Virginia State Convention,* 1:214; for the sword, see the illustration from the Filson Historical Society, Louisville, Kentucky (hereafter cited as FHS), in author's possession.
35. Submissionists wear "the federal collar about their neck with the badge of their master engraved upon it," from speech by John Townsend, *Charleston Mercury,* June 14, 1860.
36. William Lowndes Yancey, speech on the African slave trade in Smith, *Convention of the People of Alabama,* 251.
37. *Charleston Mercury,* Nov. 11, 1859.
38. Brown, "Special Message," 52–54. See also Governor A. B. Moore, Nov. 14, 1860, in Smith, *Convention of the People of Alabama,* 21–23.

39. For "no holiday work," see Benjamin H. Hill in Freehling and Simpson, *Secession Debated,* 102; Jonathan Worth to D. G. Worth, Asheboro, May 15, 1861, in *The Correspondence of Jonathan Worth,* ed. J. G. de Roulhac Hamilton (Raleigh, 1909), 1:144–145.
40. *Richmond Dispatch,* Apr. 2, 1861, reprinted in Robert F. Durden, *The Gray and the Black: The Confederate Debate on Emancipation* (Baton Rouge, 1971), 14; Jeremiah Morton in Reese, *Virginia State Convention,* 1:270; Curry, "Perils and Duty," 52.
41. Waitman Willey in Reese, *Virginia State Convention,* 1:360, 367.
42. Governor John Letcher "To the People of Northwestern Virginia," originally printed in *Richmond Dispatch,* June 17, 1861, in John Letcher Papers, ser. 6, Virginia Historical Society, Richmond (hereafter cited as VHS).
43. Hunter, "Speech . . . on the Resolution Proposing to Retrocede the Forts," in Wakelyn, *Southern Pamphlets,* 283; Reese, *Virginia State Convention,* 1:495; *Richmond Enquirer,* Jan. 29, 1861.
44. *Charleston Mercury,* Sept. 28, 1860.
45. Reese, *Virginia State Convention,* 1:184; *Richmond Enquirer,* Jan. 29, 1861. On Wise and Hunter, see the analysis in Simpson, *A Good Southerner,* 241; Simpson interprets the familial pattern in Oedipal terms.
46. *Richmond Enquirer,* Feb. 3, 1861. On the intimacy of citizenship, suffrage, and military service, see Kerber, *No Constitutional Right,* 221–302, and Keysaar, *The Right to Vote.*
47. Hunt, *Family Romance,* 13; *Charleston Mercury,* June 18, 1860.

2. THE BROTHERS' WAR

1. L. M. Keitt to Sue, Orangeburg, n.d., Lawrence Massillon Keitt Papers, in Archives and Special Collections, Perkins Memorial Library, Duke University, Raleigh, N.C. (hereafter cited as DU).
2. Governor Gist of South Carolina called for people to have "one heart and one mind" in the crisis. See Gist's "Proclamation," *Southron,* Nov. 14, 1860.
3. Jonathan Worth to D. G. Worth, May 15, 1861, in *The Correspondence of Jonathan Worth,* ed. J. G. de Roulhac Hamilton (Raleigh, 1909), 1:144–145.
4. Historians tend to see secession as either/or. For the first view, see J. Mills Thornton, *Politics and Power in a Slave Society: Alabama, 1800–1860* (Baton Rouge, 1978); for the second, see Manisha Sinha, *The Counter-Revolution of Slavery: Politics and Ideology in Antebellum South Carolina* (Chapel Hill, 2000). See also Stephanie McCurry, *Masters of Small Worlds: Yeoman Households, Gender Relations, and the Political Culture of the Antebellum South Carolina Low Country* (New York, 1995). Stephen Kantrowitz described secession as "a coup d'état against anti-secession majorities" in *Ben Tillman and the Reconstruction of White Supremacy* (Chapel Hill, 2000), 34.
5. *Journal of the Convention of the People of South Carolina Held in 1860, 1861, and 1862* (Columbia, S.C., 1862), 3–4, 11–12, 22–23, 43, 49; *Charleston Mer-*

cury, Dec. 21, 1860; C. Vann Woodward, ed., *Mary Chesnut's Civil War* (New Haven, 1981), 40. For the sequence of events, see Charles Edward Cauthen, *South Carolina Goes to War, 1860–1865* (Chapel Hill, 1950), 63–77.

6. John Palmer to Simmons, Dec. 19, 1860, Palmer Family Papers, SCL; John Berkley Grimball Diaries, Dec. 17, 1860, SHC; Simms quoted in Steven A. Channing, *Crisis of Fear: Secession in South Carolina* (New York, 1970), 251.
7. *Southron,* May 21, 1856. On the peculiarities of the state's political system, see Chauncey Samuel Boucher, *South Carolina and the South on the Eve of the Secession Crisis* (Washington University Studies, vol. 6, no. 2, 1919); Rachel N. Klein, *Unification of a Slave State: The Rise of the Planter Class in the South Carolina Backcountry, 1760–1808* (Chapel Hill, 1990); Lacy K. Ford Jr., *Origins of Southern Radicalism: The South Carolina Upcountry, 1800–1860* (New York, 1988); McCurry, *Masters of Small Worlds;* Sinha, *Counter-Revolution of Slavery.*
8. William Grimball to My Dear Elizabeth, Nov. 20, 1860, John Berkley Grimball Papers, DU. For a different view, see Sinha, *Counter-Revolution of Slavery,* 187–258.
9. James Henry Hammond to Miles, Nov. 17, 1858, Benjamin Evans to Miles, Mar. 8, 1858, D. H. Hamilton to Miles, June 28, 1860, Alfred Huger to Miles, Sept. 30, 1858, Feb. 18, 1858, Dec. 12, 1859, all in William Porcher Miles Papers, SHC; David Gavin Diary, Apr. 28, 1860, SCL.
10. *Charleston Mercury,* Sept. 22, 1860; Hammond in Carol K. Bleser, ed., *Secret and Sacred: The Diaries of James Henry Hammond, a Southern Slaveholder* (New York, 1988), 220.
11. The Ayers-Elliott dispute lasted through at least two congressional races. See *Southron,* May 21, 28, June 4, 1856, and *Charleston Mercury,* Feb. 29, Mar. 24, 30, Apr. 6, 1859, Sept. 7, 22, 1860. On reopening the slave trade, see *Charleston Mercury,* July 28, 1860; *Southron,* Mar. 14, 1860; Sinha, *Counter-Revolution of Slavery,* 125–186. On the negro trading law, see *Charleston Mercury,* July 14, 1858.
12. D. H. Hamilton to Miles, Jan. 23, Feb. 2, 1860, William Porcher Miles Papers, SCL; C. B. Harrison to Lawrence O'Bryan Branch, Dec. 2, 1860, reprinted in W. Buck Yearns and John G. Barrett, eds., *North Carolina Civil War Documentary* (Chapel Hill, 1980), 11–13.
13. On the first secession crisis in South Carolina, see Ford, *Origins of Southern Radicalism,* 338–343; John Barnwell, *Love of Order: South Carolina's First Secession Crisis* (Chapel Hill, 1982); McCurry, *Masters of Small Worlds,* 283–286; Sinha, *Counter-Revolution of Slavery,* 95–124.
14. See "Address of the Honorable C. G. Memminger," *Richmond Enquirer,* Feb. 3, 1860, and C. G. Memminger to Miles, Dec. 27, 1859, Jan. 16, 1860, William Porcher Miles Papers, SCL. See also Cauthen, *South Carolina Goes to War,* 12–13.
15. R. B. Rhett to Miles, Apr. 18, 17, 1860, William Porcher Miles Papers, SCL; Sinha, *Counter-Revolution of Slavery,* 240, 200–220; Ford, *Origins of Southern Radicalism,* 365–373.
16. Robert Nicholas Olsberg, "A Government of Class and Race: William Henry

Trescot and the South Carolina Chivalry, 1860–1865" (Ph.D. diss., University of South Carolina, 1972), 248; Printed circular, Robert N. Gourdin [Chairman of the Executive Committee] to Honorable R. F. W. Allston, Nov. 19, 1860, 1860 Association Papers, SCL; *Charleston Mercury,* Oct. 19, 1860. On the 1860 Association, see Cauthen, *South Carolina Goes to War,* 34–41; Channing, *Crisis of Fear,* 261–264, 280–283; Sinha, *Counter-Revolution of Slavery,* 232–235.

17. James D. B. DeBow, *The Interest in Slavery of the Southern Nonslaveholder* (Charleston, 1860), 3, 9, 11. For the echo, see *Camden Weekly Journal,* Nov. 6, 1860.
18. *Charleston Mercury,* Oct. 31, 1860, and John Townsend, *The Doom of Slavery in the Union: Its Safety Out of It* (Charleston, 1860). On public meetings in Barnwell and Williamsburg districts, see *Charleston Mercury,* Nov. 12, 13, 1860.
19. Nicoletta F. Gullace, "Sexual Violence and Family Honor: British Propaganda and International Law during the First World War," *AHR* 102, no. 3 (June 1997): 714–747. Gullace calls it "a battle between good and evil to be fought out at the very threshold of every home" (725–726); *Charleston Mercury,* Oct. 31, 1860.
20. On the militia beat, see McCurry, *Masters of Small Worlds,* pp. 265–271. For the muster field as political hall, see David Gavin Diary, July 6, 1859, SCL; James F. Sloan Journal, vol. 2, July 16, 1859, SCL.
21. D. H. Hamilton to Miles, Columbia, Dec. 9, 1859, William Porcher Miles Papers, SCL. See also McCurry, *Masters of Small Worlds,* 277–304; Cauthen, *South Carolina Goes to War,* 45–48; Channing, *Crisis of Fear,* 23–38, 269–273.
22. *Charleston Mercury,* Nov. 11, 1859; Branchville Vigilant Association, Minute Book, 1860–1863, 3rd Saturday in Dec. 1860, Nov. 17, 1860, SCL; Preston quoted in Channing, *Crisis of Fear,* 36 n. 33; W. L. Garrison, *The New Reign of Terror in the Slaveholding States* (1860; repr., New York, 1969).
23. *Charleston Mercury,* Jan. 12, 1860. The social identity of the members was calculated using the 1860 Census (M653) Beaufort Dist., St Peter's Parish, S.C. (Population Schedule: roll 1214; Slave Schedule: roll 1231), National Archives, Washington, D.C. (hereafter cited as NA). On the organization of vigilant committees, see *Charleston Mercury,* Jan. 20, 1860.
24. "Constitution of Minute Men for the Defence of Southern Rights," Minute Men, Oct. 7, 1860, SCL; *Charleston Mercury,* Nov. 13, 12, 1860. See Cauthen, *South Carolina Goes to War,* 46–47; Channing, *Crisis of Fear,* 269–271.
25. Cauthen, *South Carolina Goes to War,* 47; *Charleston Mercury,* Nov. 21, 1860; Claim of Felix W. Tuten, Beaufort, Southern Claims Commission (hereafter cited as SCC), RG 233, NA; Claim of Charles Brandt, Barnwell, SCC, RG 217, file #7798, NA; Claim of Richard A. Taylor, Beaufort, SCC, RG 217, file # 6795, NA; Claim of Lawrence McKenzie, Beaufort, SCC, RG 233, NA.
26. Claim of William Harvey, Beaufort, SCC, RG 217, file #6796, NA.
27. James M. Banner, "The Problem of South Carolina," in *The Hofstadter Aegis: A Memorial,* ed. Stanley Elkins and Eric McKitrick (New York, 1974). See also Mark O. Kaplanoff, "Making the South Solid: Politics and the Structure of Society in South Carolina, 1790–1815" (Ph.D. diss., Cambridge University, 1976); Klein, *Unification of a Slave State;* Ford, *Origins of Southern Radicalism;* Sinha, *Counter-Revolution of Slavery.*

28. *Beaufort Enterprise,* Sept. 26, 1860.
29. H. Judge Moore to Miles, Oct. 16, 1858, William Porcher Miles Papers, SCL; Lawrence Keitt quoted in Channing, *Crisis of Fear,* 245; Josiah Johnson quoted in Claim of Mary B. Tuten, Beaufort, SCC, RG 217, file #9390, NA. On fusion tickets, see Cauthen, *South Carolina Goes to War,* 63–66; McCurry, *Masters of Small Worlds,* 297–302.
30. William Elliott to Ralph Elliott, n.d. [1860], Elliott-Gonzales Papers, SHC; Cauthen, *South Carolina Goes to War,* 52–54, quote on 53.
31. Cauthen, *South Carolina Goes to War,* 60.
32. *Charleston Mercury,* Nov. 8, 1860; William Grimball to My Dear Elizabeth, Nov. 20, 1860, John Berkley Grimball Papers, DU. For Gist's call, see *Southron,* Nov. 14, 1860. For other calls for unity, see *Southron,* Nov. 14, 1860, and *Charleston Mercury,* Nov. 21, 1860. See also Olsberg, "Government of Class and Race," 20–21.
33. For a handy index of developments, see "Chronology of Events, November 1860–April 1861," in *Southern Pamphlets on Secession: November 1860–April 1861,* ed. Jon L. Wakelyn (Chapel Hill, 1996), xi–xii.
34. See, for example, the contrast Daniel Crofts draws in opening his analysis of the Upper South in *Reluctant Confederates: Upper South Unionists in the Secession Crisis* (Chapel Hill, 1989), 90–91; for a similar representation, see William A. Link, *Roots of Secession: Slavery and Politics in Antebellum Virginia* (Chapel Hill, 2003), 244.
35. For results in Florida and Louisiana, see Ralph A. Wooster, *The Secession Conventions of the South* (Princeton, 1962), 68, 104. For Mississippi, see William L. Barney, *The Secessionist Impulse: Alabama and Mississippi in 1860* (1974; repr., Tuscaloosa, 2004), 277, "Do Nothings" on 201.
36. Governor Perry quoted in Edward E. Baptist, *Creating an Old South: Middle Florida's Plantation Frontier before the Civil War* (Chapel Hill, 2002), 270. James Lusk Alcorn quoted in Barney, *Secessionist Impulse,* 309.
37. On Pettus's efforts and Davis's arms purchases, see Barney, *Secessionist Impulse,* 189, 201–204; John K. Bettersworth, *Confederate Mississippi: The People and Policies of a Cotton State in Wartime* (Baton Rouge, 1943), 1–21. On Davis's activities in Dec. 1860, see *PJD,* 6:374.
38. G. P. Whittington, "Thomas O. Moore, Governor of Louisiana, 1860–1864," *Louisiana Historical Quarterly* 13 (Jan. 1930).
39. For the votes, see the following: Mississippi—*Journal of the State Convention and Ordinances and Resolutions* (Jackson, Miss., 1861), 16; Florida—Baptist, *Creating an Old South,* 271; Louisiana—Wooster, *Secession Conventions,* 111; Texas—Walter L. Buenger, *Secession and the Union in Texas* (Austin, 1984), 148.
40. "Journal of the Convention of the People of Georgia," in Allen D. Candler, ed., *The Confederate Records of the State of Georgia* (1909–1911; repr., New York, 1972), 1:245–246. The cover-up was revealed, and the more likely result calculated, by Michael P. Johnson, "A New Look at the Popular Vote for Delegates to the Georgia Secession Convention," *GHQ* 56, no. 2 (1972): 259–275.

41. Anthony Gene Carey, *Parties, Slavery and the Union in Antebellum Georgia* (Athens, Ga., 1997), 228; Candler *Confederate Records,* 1:19–57; Wooster, *Secession Conventions,* 83.
42. All of the speeches in the Milledgeville debate are collected and reprinted in William W. Freehling and Craig M. Simpson, eds., *Secession Debated: Georgia's Showdown in 1860* (New York, 1992), including Benjamin Hill's "Unionist Speech," quotation at 102.
43. Thomas R. R. Cobb, Robert Toombs, and Joseph E. Brown in Freehling and Simpson, *Secession Debated,* 29–30, 73, 145–159.
44. Candler, *Confederate Records,* 1:79, 11, 122, and for county resolutions, 58–156; Thomas R. R. Cobb to Howell Cobb, Dec. 15, 1860, in Ulrich B. Phillips, ed., *The Correspondence of Robert Toombs, Alexander Stephens, and Howell Cobb* (Washington, 1913), 522; Howell Cobb quoted in Michael P. Johnson, *Toward a Patriarchal Republic: The Secession of Georgia* (Baton Rouge, 1977), 22.
45. Candler, *Confederate Records,* 1:245; for the votes, see 1:236, 256. The other state was Alabama.
46. Johnson, "New Look at the Popular Vote," 260, 270. Johnson's numbers were accepted by subsequent scholars. See Freehling and Simpson, *Secession Debated,* xxi; Carey, *Parties, Slavery and the Union,* 242.
47. Candler, *Confederate Records,* 1:269, 304.
48. J. R. Earle to Governor Joseph E. Brown, Apr. 18, 1861, Governor's Subject Files, Georgia Governor's Office, Georgia Department of Archives and History RG 1-1-5 (hereafter cited as GSF), box 29; N. A. Campbell to Gov. J. E. Brown, Feb. 23, 1861, GSF, box 26; F. D. Claiborne to Gov. J. E. Brown, Feb. 5, 1861, GSF, box 27; Candler, *Confederate Records,* 1:305–306. See also Paul Escott, "Joseph E. Brown, Jefferson Davis and the Problem of Poverty in the Confederacy," *GHQ,* 61 (Spring 1977): 63.
49. Barney, *Secessionist Impulse,* 115–116; William R. Smith, ed., *The History and Debates of the Convention of the People of Alabama, Begun and Held in the City of Montgomery, on the Seventh Day of January, 1861* (Atlanta, 1861), 73.
50. Smith, *Convention of the People of Alabama,* 17, 40–42; Margaret Storey, "Southern Ishmaelites: Wartime Unionism and Its Consequences in Alabama, 1860–1874" (Ph.D. diss., Emory University, 1999), 30.
51. See Wooster, *Secession Conventions,* 52, for convention election results. For votes showing cooperationist strength in the convention, see Smith, *Convention of the People of Alabama,* 55, 77, 80, 118, and Wooster, *Secession Conventions,* 55–60. On voter intimidation and the suppression of the cooperationist vote, see Storey, "Southern Ishmaelites," 28–29, and Barney, *Secessionist Impulse,* 201–219.
52. Smith, *Convention of the People of Alabama,* 28, 25, 27, 28–29. My analysis here departs from that of J. Mills Thornton, who emphasizes the unanimity of its ultimate adoption and not the argument and testy process of revision that preceded the vote; see Thornton, *Politics and Power,* 416.
53. Smith, ed., *Convention of the People of Alabama,* 64, 67–69.
54. Ibid. 68–69.

55. Ibid., 68–69, 72–73, 74, 116; for cooperationists' pursuit of a ratification resolution, see 55, 73–74, 77, 80, 116. See also Barney, *Secessionist Impulse,* 236. Reports continued to be made to the Confederate War Department of local officials still loyal to the Union government. See Addison White to Hon. L. P. Walker, Feb. 25, 1861, Letters Received by the Confederate Secretary of War, National Archives, Washington, D.C. (hereafter cited as LRCSW), RG 109 (M437), roll 1, no. 6.
56. Zebulon Vance to G. N. Folk, Jan. 9, 1861, in Frontis W. Johnston, ed., *The Papers of Zebulon Baird Vance* (Raleigh, 1963), 1:81–83, quote on 81; Robert Hatton quoted in Crofts, *Reluctant Confederates,* 103.
57. George Reese, ed., *Proceedings of the Virginia State Convention of 1861* (Richmond, 1965), 1:349, 368; Vance to Folks, Jan. 9, 1861, in Johnston, *Papers of Zebulon Baird Vance,* 1:81–83.
58. Zebulon Vance to William Dicson, Dec. 11, 1860, in Johnston, *Papers of Zebulon Baird Vance,* 1:71–73. Vance was a Whig from western North Carolina; he had been a Bell supporter in Nov. 1860.
59. Governor John Ellis, "Message to the General Assembly of North Carolina," Nov. 20, 1860, reprinted in Yearns and Barrett, *North Carolina Civil War Documentary,* 5–7, quotation on 7. The course of secession can be traced in David M. Potter, *The Impending Crisis, 1848–1861,* ed. Don E. Feherenbacher (New York, 1976), 505–513; Wooster, *Secession Conventions;* Crofts, *Reluctant Secessionists;* Link, *Roots of Secession;* Henry T. Shanks, *The Secession Movement in Virginia, 1847–1861* (1934; repr., New York, 1971); Joseph Carlyle Sitterson, *The Secession Movement in North Carolina* (Chapel Hill, 1939).
60. C. B. Harrison to Lawrence O'Bryan Branch, Dec. 2, 1860, reprinted in Yearns and Barrett, *North Carolina Civil War Documentary,* 11–13.
61. Unidentified to Zebulon Vance, in Johnston, *Papers of Zebulon Baird Vance,* 91; Crofts, *Reluctant Confederates,* 194; Holden quoted in *North Carolina Standard,* Dec. 5, 1860, reprinted in Yearns and Barrett, *North Carolina Civil War Documentary,* 8–10. For the Apr. 4 vote, see Reese, *Virginia State Convention,* 3:163.
62. "Speech of Mr. [George] Davis at Thalian Hall—The 'Peace Congress' and Its Failure," reprinted in Yearns and Barrett, *North Carolina Civil War Documentary,* 19–22, quotations on 20, 21–22; C. C. Jones to Zebulon Vance, Feb. 4, 1861, in Johnston, *Papers of Zebulon Baird Vance,* 95. On the Crittenden Compromise and its failure, see Potter, *Impending Crisis,* 530–533. On Crittenden as the most common terms of Upper South Unionism, and for the definition of Unionists, see Crofts, *Reluctant Confederates,* 197, 187.
63. Potter, *Impending Crisis,* 508, Lincoln quote on 526, and on the Republican Party platform commitment to nonextension of slavery to the territories, see 328–355; Eric Foner, *Free Soil, Free Labor, Free Men: The Ideology of the Republican Party before the Civil War* (New York, 1970); and Crofts, *Reluctant Confederates,* 195–214. The reading of Lincoln is informed by Lincoln's writings in the 1850s. See Michael P. Johnson, ed., *Abraham Lincoln, Slavery, and the Civil War: Selected Writings and Speeches* (Boston, 2001), 55–59, 101–102.

On the middle ground, see Crofts, *Reluctant Confederates,* 139; Crofts overstates Unionist strength. On the "morally attenuated" position of Unionists and the idea of the middle ground, see Barbara Fields, *Slavery and Freedom on the Middle Ground: Maryland during the Nineteenth Century* (New Haven, 1985), 90–95.

64. Jno Gallagher to My Dear Sir [John Letcher], Apr. 6, 1861, John Letcher Papers, ser. 6, VHS; C. B. Harrison to Lawrence O'Bryan Branch, Dec. 2, 1860, reprinted in Yearns and Barrett, *North Carolina Civil War Documentary,* 11–13; *Richmond Dispatch,* Jan. 22, 1861; *Journal of the House of Delegates of the State of Virginia, for the Session, 1861–62, Message of the Governor of Virginia and Accompanying Documents* (Richmond, Public Printer, 1861), Executive Department, Jan. 7, 1861, xxiii; Sitterson, *Secession Movement in North Carolina,* 196–197.
65. Worth to Springs, Oak and Co., May 13, 1861, in de Roulhac Hamilton, *Correspondence of Jonathan Worth,* 1:143.
66. Daniel Crofts, for example, views party politics as defined by party competition itself and separates party politics from material grounding in political economy. See Crofts, *Reluctant Confederates,* 53, 95.
67. *Richmond Dispatch,* Mar. 8, 1861. One North Carolinian agreed: "If Virginia goes out, North Carolina will have to follow her" (C. C. Jones to Zebulon Vance, Feb. 4, 1861, in Johnston, *Papers of Zebulon Baird Vance,* 1:95).
68. *Richmond Whig* quoted in Link, *Roots of Secession,* 223. Link's recent book provides the best account of sectional politics in the state during the secession crisis.
69. R. M. T. Hunter to James R. Micou, Thomas Croxton, and Others Signing the Call, Dec. 10, 1860, in "Correspondence of Robert M. T. Hunter, 1826–1876," reprinted in Charles Henry Ambler, ed., *Annual Report of the American Historical Association for the Year 1916* (Washington, 1918), 2:346; *Message of the Governor of Virginia,* xvii, xi.
70. *Richmond Enquirer,* Jan. 25, 1861; *Richmond Dispatch,* Jan. 30, 1861. For further descriptions of big public meetings, also see *Richmond Enquirer,* Jan. 1, 1861; *Richmond Dispatch,* Dec. 29, 1860; and the account in Link, *Roots of Secession,* 226. For Bott's views, see *Richmond Dispatch,* Jan. 10, 1861, and Link, *Roots of Secession,* 225.
71. Resolutions of Mass Meeting, Harrison County, Virginia, n.d. [1860], John Letcher Papers, ser. 6, VHS. But see the conflicting opinions in correspondence received by Letcher in P. A. Bolling to Gov. Letcher, Jan. 11, 1861, and James Powell to Gov. Letcher, Mar. 4, 1861, both in John Letcher Papers, ser. 6, VHS. The representation of the Wheeling press is in Link, *Roots of Secession,* 222.
72. For the convention election results, see Crofts, *Reluctant Confederates,* 175, and Link, *Roots of Secession,* 226–227.
73. For the Wise-Moore exchange, see Reese, *Virginia State Convention,* 1:43–47, and for Moore's extended case, 1:172–184.
74. See Reese, *Virginia State Convention,* 1:352–373 for Willey's major speech, 1:317 for the tax proposal, and 3:115 for "western poor men." For Willey, "ques-

tion between classes," see Link, *Roots of Secession,* 237. For "until this thing is done" and the rest of the debate on Apr. 4, see Reese, *Virginia State Convention,* 3:116, 160–161.

75. Reese, *Virginia State Convention,* 4: 51, 111.
76. *Richmond Enquirer,* March 23, 1861. On Wise's plots, see Craig M. Simpson, *A Good Southerner: The Life of Henry A. Wise of Virginia* (Chapel Hill, 1985), 241–245, 248–250; Link, *Roots of Secession,* 240–241.
77. For the vote, see Reese, *Virginia State Convention,* 4:14.
78. Ibid., 4:142; for the vote, see 4:144. For the geographical breakdown, see Link, *Roots of Secession,* 350 n. 79. Baldwin is quoted in Reese, ibid., 4:28.
79. Gov. John Letcher to William King, May 10, 1861, John Letcher Papers, ser. 6, VHS; James M. Mason to Jefferson Davis, Richmond, Apr. 21, 1861, in *PJD,* 7:113–115, quotes on 113.
80. Gov. John Letcher "To the People of Northwestern Virginia," *Richmond Dispatch,* June 17, 1861, in John Letcher Papers, ser. 6, VHS.
81. Proceedings of State-Rights meeting in Harrison, Harrison County, Apr. 21, 1861, and G. W. Berlin Esq. to Gov. John Letcher, July 4, 1862, both in John Letcher Papers, ser. 6, VHS. On West Virginia's path to statehood, see Link, *Roots of Secession,* 252–254; Richard Orr Curry, *A House Divided: A Study of Statehood Politics and the Copperhead Movement in West Virginia* (Pittsburgh, 1964).
82. Fields, *Slavery and Freedom,* 100. On the Confederate struggle with persistent Unionism in east Tennessee, see Jefferson Davis to T. R. Nelson, Aug. 13, 1861, *PJD,* 7:282–283; W. R. Hurley to Gov. John Letcher, Apr. 21, 1861, John Letcher Papers, ser. 6, VHS. On the secession of Virginia, North Carolina, and Tennessee, see Crofts, *Reluctant Confederates;* on Arkansas, see Wooster, *Secession Conventions,* 155–173. On Confederate aspirations in Maryland, see James M. Mason to Jefferson Davis, May 6, 1861, *PJD,* 7:148–152.
83. Missouri was admitted as the thirteenth state of the C.S.A. For the views of Missouri's secessionist and pro-Confederate governor, Claiborne Fox Jackson, see C. F. Jackson to My Dear Shields, n.d. [but before Jan. 1861], in Smith, *Convention of the People of Alabama,* 407–408. On Missouri, see William E. Parrish, *A History of Missouri,* vol. 3 (Columbia, Mo., 1973), and Christopher Phillips, *Missouri's Confederate: Claiborne Fox Jackson and the Creation of Southern Identity in the Border West* (Columbia, Mo., 2000), 242–296; Michael Fellman, *Inside War: The Guerilla Conflict in Missouri during the American Civil War* (New York, 1989). My thanks to Aaron Astor for his help on the Missouri developments. See Aaron Astor, "Belated Confederates: Black Politics, Guerilla Violence, and the Collapse of Conservative Unionism in Kentucky and Missouri, 1860–1872" (Ph.D. diss., Northwestern University, 2006).
84. Records of Secession Convention, State of Kentucky, Nov. 18, 19, 20, 1861, FHS. Regarding the funding for ten Kentucky regiments, see Telegram from George W. Johnson, Jan. 1, 1862, in *The Papers of Jefferson Davis,* vol. 8: *1862,* ed. Lynda L. Crist, Mary S. Dix, and Kenneth H. Williams (Baton Rouge, 1995) (hereafter cited as *PJD,* vol. 8), 3. James Holmberg of the Filson Historical Society calls it a "government on wheels."

85. Records of Secession Convention, State of Kentucky, FHS.
86. William Shakespeare, *The Life of King Henry the Fifth,* act 5, scene 3, in Alfred Harbage, ed., *William Shakespeare: The Complete Works* (New York, 1977), 767.
87. See the side-by-side copies of the U.S and Confederate constitutions provided by Jefferson Davis in his constitutional defense of the Confederacy, *The Rise and Fall of the Confederate Government,* 2 vols. (Richmond, n.d.,), 1:559–582. Davis understates the difference, saying the C.S.A. Constitution made only such changes as "experience suggested for better practical working or for greater perspicuity" (223). Emory Thomas echoes Davis's characterization. See Emory Thomas, *The Confederate Nation: 1861–1865* (New York, 1979), 62–65. Thomas says, "The permanent Constitution prescribed for the Confederacy much the same kind of union which the Southerners had dissolved" (64). Richard Bensel also underestimates the difference between the constitutions of the two states, which provides the basis of his side-by-side comparison of state building and centralization. See Richard Franklin Bensel, *Yankee Leviathan: The Origins of Central State Authority in America, 1859–1877* (Cambridge, Mass., 1990), 99.
88. Davis, *Rise and Fall,* 1:70 (art. 1, sec. 2), 559, 572–573 ("uniform laws of naturalization"), 565.
89. *Journal of the Convention of the People of South Carolina,* 765; Candler, *Confederate Records,* 1:306–307.
90. Smith, *Convention of the People of Alabama,* 223–224.
91. David Gavin Diary, May 18, 1861, in *Records of Antebellum Southern Plantations from the Revolution through the Civil War,* ed. Kenneth M. Stampp (Frederick, Md., 1985) (hereafter cited as *RASP*), ser. J, pt. 3, South Carolina. See also Johnson, *Toward a Patriarchal Republic,* and Drew Gilpin Faust, *The Creation of Confederate Nationalism: Ideology and Identity in the Civil War South* (Baton Rouge, 1988), 34–38.
92. Thomas, *The Confederate Nation,* 65.
93. *Richmond Dispatch,* Apr. 20, 1861.
94. Reverend William O. Prentiss quoted in Sinha, *Counter-Revolution of Slavery,* 246–247; Stephens, "Cornerstone Speech," in Wakelyn, *Southern Pamphlets,* 407. For the comparisons, see Sinha, *Counter-Revolution of Slavery,* 244, 227.

3. ANTIGONE'S CLAIM

1. Sophocles, *The Three Theban Plays: Antigone, Oedipus the King, Oedipus at Colonus,* trans. Robert Fagles (New York, 1982), quotations at 84, 95. This is not to deny Judith Butler's recent reading, which challenges the Hegelian opposition between kinship and the state. On this she and I agree, as will become clear. See Judith P. Butler, *Antigone's Claim: Kinship between Life and Death* (New York, 2000).
2. Illinois private quoted in Michael Fellman, *Inside War: The Guerilla Conflict*

in Missouri during the American Civil War (New York, 1989), 203. Fellman emphasizes the psychology of individual men's investment in the idea of women as being "outside" war, but the point is also embedded in the rules of war. See General Orders No. 100, "Instructions for the Government of the Armies of the United States in the Field," prepared by Francis Lieber, L. L. D., War Department, Adj. General's Office, Washington, Apr. 24, 1863, in U.S. War Department, *The War of the Rebellion: A Compilation of the Official Records of the Union and Confederate Armies* (Washington, D.C., 1880–1901) (hereafter cited as *O.R.*), ser. 3, 3:148–164.

3. For a count of the number of women soldiers, see Elizabeth D. Leonard, *All the Daring of the Soldier: Women of the Civil War Armies* (New York, 1999), 165; Drew Gilpin Faust, *Mothers of Invention: Women of the Slaveholding South in the American Civil War* (Chapel Hill, 1996), 202.
4. R. S. Hudson to Jefferson Davis, Mar. 14, 1864, *O.R.,* ser. 1, vol. 32, pt. 3, 625–627, quotation at 626.
5. Rose O'Neal Greenhow to William Seward, Nov. 1861, Rose O'Neal Greenhow Papers, DU. www.scriptorium.lib.duke.edu/greenhow; Ann Blackman, *Wild Rose: The True Story of a Civil War Spy* (New York, 2006).
6. On Eugenia Levy Phillips, see Leonard, *All the Daring of the Soldier,* 75–80, quotation at 77.
7. See *Richmond Daily Examiner,* Mar. 19, 1861, where the editor wrote that the feeling for honor and country expressed by the ladies in the preceding day's paper was "well known to be that of all their sex in this State of Virginia."
8. For crowds of women at secession conventions, see George H. Reese, ed., *Proceedings of the Virginia State Convention of 1861* (Richmond, 1965), 1:3, and William R. Smith, ed., *The History and Debates of the Convention of the People of Alabama, Begun and Held in the City of Montgomery, on the Seventh Day of January, 1861* (Atlanta, 1861), 119; on women presenting Smith of Tuscaloosa with a U.S. flag, 120–121. For women's privately recorded views, see Meta Morris Grimball Diary, Dec. 15, 1860, SHC; John F. Marszalek, ed., *The Diary of Miss Emma Holmes, 1861–1866* (Baton Rouge, 1979), 1–50. For newspapers, see "The Daughters of the Cockade," *Richmond Daily Examiner,* Mar. 21, 1861. The idea of elite Southern women as ardent patriots had such currency in the Civil War that Northern women felt compelled to defend their own patriotism. See Judith Giesberg, *Army at Home: Women and the Civil War on the Northern Home Front* (Chapel Hill, 2009), chap. 5. For the North Carolina women's charge, see Anonymous, Reglators to Gov. Vance, Feb. 18, 1863, box 162, Zebulon B. Vance, Governor's Papers, State Archives, Division of Archives and History, Raleigh, North Carolina (hereafter cited as ZBV).
9. "The Daughters of Virginia," *Richmond Daily Examiner,* Mar. 18 and 19, 1861.
10. Marszalek, *Diary of Miss Emma Holmes,* 37, 44, 249; Smith, *Convention of the People of Alabama,* 120–121; C. Vann Woodward, ed., *Mary Chesnut's Civil War* (New Haven, 1981), 19; Priscilla M. Bond Diary, Dec. 30, 1861, Hill Memorial Library, Louisiana State University, Baton Rouge (hereafter cited as

LSU). Robert E. Bonner, *Colors and Blood: Flag Passions of the Confederate South* (Princeton, 2002).

11. Drew Gilpin Faust, *The Creation of Confederate Nationalism: Ideology and Identity in the Civil War South* (Baton Rouge, 1988), 8; Sue McDowell Diary, Mar. 20, 1861, SCL; Sarah Morgan Dawson, *A Confederate Girl's Diary* (Boston, 1913), 65–67; Jefferson Davis to Robert E. Lee, *PJD,* 8:318; Elizabeth Varon, *Southern Lady, Yankee Spy: The True Story of Elizabeth Van Lew, a Union Agent in the Heart of the Confederacy* (New York, 2003), 152; Sheila R. Phipps, *Genteel Rebel: The Life of Mary Greenhow Lee* (Baton Rouge, 2004), 122.
12. Thomas Allen to His Excellency [Governor Joseph Brown], May 29, 1861, *GSF,* box 22; Lizzie Gaines to Gov. J. E. Brown, Nov. 30, 1861, *GSF,* box 31.
13. Woodward, *Mary Chesnut's Civil War,* 195, 203, 216–217, quotation at 63; Meta Morris Grimball Diary, Aug. 10, 1861, SHC; Marszalek, *Diary of Miss Emma Holmes,* 65; L.S.M., *Charleston Mercury,* Nov. 23, 1860.
14. *Richmond Daily Examiner,* Mar. 18, 1861.
15. Mills Lane, ed., *"Dear Mother, Don't Grieve about Me—If I Get Killed, I'll Only Be Dead": Letters from Georgia Soldiers in the Civil War* (Savannah, 1977), 4; "Letters of William Plane to His Wife," *GHQ* 48 (1964), 217; Nicoletta F. Gullace, *The Blood of Our Sons: Men, Women, and the Renegotiation of British Citizenship during the Great War* (New York, 2003), 18.
16. Jno R. Allen to "Sir," Sept. 7, 1861, GSF, box 22; E. N. Allen to "His Excellency," Nov. 16, 1861, GSF, box 22; A. M. Barrett to His Excellency J. E. Brown, Sept. 23, 1861, GSF, box 23.
17. William M. Brooks to Jefferson Davis, May 13, 1861, *PJD,* 7:164–166; William D. Brown to Gov. Brown, Aug. 25, 1861, *GSF,* box 25; J. Oscar Howells to Jefferson Davis, Dec. 29, 1861, *PJD,* 7:448.
18. Jason L. Dupress to Governor Brown, Mar. 5, 1862, *GSF,* box 29.
19. Jacob Blount to Gov. Brown, Aug. 12, 1863, *GSF,* box 24; William Mishaw et al. to J. H. Boatright, Jan. 10, 1861, and Joseph Randall et al. to Thomas T. Gantt, Esq., Jan. 10, 1861, Pickens-Bonham Papers, Library of Congress, Manuscripts Division, Washington, D.C. (hereafter cited as LC).
20. This is the subject of the next two chapters.
21. Stephen V. Ash, *When the Yankees Came: Conflict and Chaos in the Occupied South, 1861–1865* (Chapel Hill, 1995), 38–75; Mark Grimsley, *The Hard Hand of War: Union Military Policy toward Southern Civilians, 1861–1865* (Cambridge, UK, 1995). On the war in the Shenandoah Valley, see James McPherson, *Battle Cry of Freedom: The Civil War Era* (New York, 1988), 454–489.
22. Sigismunda Stribling Kimball Journal, Dec. 6, 27, Mar. 14, Apr. 8, 1862, Special Collections, University of Virginia, Charlottesville (hereafter cited as UVA); J. Gaillard Foster to Miss Sarah Foster, Feb. 11, 1864, James S. Foster Papers, box 1, folder 4, LSU.
23. Sigismunda Stribling Kimball Journal, Apr. 8, Apr. 15, Apr. 20, 1862, UVA.
24. Mary Greenhow Lee quoted in Faust, *Mothers of Invention,* 198; Phipps, *Genteel Rebel,* 187–188.

25. Historians have generally agreed, accepting their subjects' reports. See Faust, *Mothers of Invention,* 200; Phipps, *Genteel Rebel,* 175–198.
26. General Orders No. 100, "Instructions for the Government of the Armies," 148–164, quotations at 151, 158.
27. Ibid., 150, 157, 159.
28. John Q. Anderson, ed., *Brokenburn: The Journal of Kate Stone, 1861–1868* (Baton Rouge, 1955), 182.
29. Franklin A. Dick, Provost Marshall General of the Department of the Missouri to Montgomery Blair, Dec. 19, 1862, Abraham Lincoln Papers, 1774–1948, reel 45, LC. I thank Mark Neely Jr. for this reference.
30. Mark E. Neely Jr., *Southern Rights: Political Prisoners and the Myth of Confederate Constitutionalism* (Charlottesville, 1999), 18; Confederate Constitution, art. 1, sec. 3; Linda K. Kerber, *No Constitutional Right to Be Ladies: Women and the Obligations of Citizenship* (New York, 1998), 28, 3–46. The question posed in the case was "Cannot a *feme covert* levy war and conspire to levy war?"
31. The literature on treason in the Civil War is still quite small, and that on the C.S.A. is even smaller. What there is omits discussion of women and gender. See Mark E. Neely Jr., *The Fate of Liberty: Abraham Lincoln and Civil Liberties* (New York, 1991), and Neely, *Southern Rights,* for the most important examples. Nothing like Linda Kerber's sweeping treatment of the revolutionary era yet has been tried for the Civil War. See Linda K. Kerber, *Women of the Republic: Intellect and Ideology in Revolutionary America* (New York, 1986). For one book based on the 120 cases of Southern women tried and convicted in U.S. military courts during the Civil War, see Thomas P. Lowry, *Confederate Heroines: 120 Southern Women Convicted by Union Military Justice* (Baton Rouge, 2006).
32. Woodward, *Mary Chesnut's Civil War,* 162–163. On Unionist spies in east Tennessee, see Sarah E. Thompson Papers, DU, scriptorium.lib.duke.edu/thompson/; on Confederate women spies arrested in Union territory, see Elvira A. W. Scott Diary, Western Historical Manuscript Collection, Columbia, Missouri. Kristin Streater, "Patriotism or Impropriety? Gendered Constructions of Loyalty in Civil War Kentucky," paper presented at the Fifth Southern Conference on Women's History, Richmond, Virginia, June 2000; and Diary of Mrs. Mary E. Terry, Written While a Prisoner, 1864–1865, VHS. About one hundred women were incarcerated in Castle Thunder, in Richmond, Virginia, most of them poor women. See Varon, *Southern Lady, Yankee Spy,* 101.
33. Woodward, *Mary Chesnut's Civil War,* 92–93, 99; Hannah Townell to President Davis, June 8, 1864, in *The Papers of Jefferson Davis,* vol. 10: *October 1863–August 1864,* ed. Lynda L. Crist, Kenneth H. Williams, and Peggy L. Dillard (Baton Rouge, 1999) (hereafter cited as *PJD,* vol. 10), 457.
34. Woodward, *Mary Chesnut's Civil War,* 57, 92, 460–461; *Richmond Dispatch* quoted in Varon, *Southern Lady, Yankee Spy,* 60; for Van Lew, also see Varon. For evidence of women spies on government payrolls, see E. P. Alexander to Jefferson Davis, Sept. 11, 1861, *PJD,* 7:356; Varon, *Southern Lady, Yankee Spy,* 74–76; and Leonard, *All the Daring of the Soldier.*

35. This argument has been made by a number of historians, notably Faust, *Mothers of Invention;* Varon, *Southern Lady, Yankee Spy;* Phipps, *Genteel Rebel;* and Leonard, *All the Daring of the Soldier.*
36. Rose O'Neal Greenhow to the Hon. William H. Seward, Nov. 17, 1861, and Rose O'Neal Greenhow to Alexander Boteler, Richmond, June 19 [1863], in Rose O'Neal Greenhow Papers, DU, www.scriptorium.lib.duke.edu/greenhow. *Richmond Whig Leader,* Nov. 29, 1861; Woodward, *Mary Chesnut's Civil War,* 172.
37. For the prison inmate figures, see Varon, *Southern Lady, Yankee Spy,* 101; Neely, *Southern Rights;* and Neely, *The Fate of Liberty,* 136–137. For U.S. court-martial records, see Lowry, *Confederate Heroines,* and Thomas P. Lowry, "Research Note: New Access to a Civil War Resource," *Civil War History* 49, no. 1 (2003): 54, 58. Lowry notes that 200 women were subjected to military commissions, 120 were convicted, and a handful were sentenced to hang, but he found no indication that any sentence of execution was carried out. For two fascinating cases, see the military commissions convened to try Bettie Jackson, RG 153, LL 1229, NA, and Fannie Houx, RG 153, NN 2733, NA.
38. For the order, see Benjamin F. Butler, *Butler's Book: Autobiography and Personal Reminiscences of Major General Benjamin Butler* (Boston, 1892), 418.
39. Butler's "woman order" is by far the best-known episode in women's history of the Civil War and often the only story about Confederate women that makes it into books.
40. Ash, *When the Yankees Came,* 16.
41. "Letters of General Thomas Williams, 1862," *AHR* 14 (Jan. 1909): 320, 310, 316–317.
42. Butler, *Butler's Book,* 414–416; Phipps, *Genteel Rebel,* 177–179; Dawson, *Confederate Girl's Diary,* 24–25. See Elliott Askenazi, ed., *The Civil War Diary of Clara Solomon: Growing Up in New Orleans, 1861–62* (Baton Rouge, 1995), 354–428; George N. Carpenter, *History of the Eighth Regiment Vermont Volunteers, 1861–1865* (Boston, 1886).
43. Askenazi, *Diary of Clara Solomon,* 356; Phipps, *Genteel Rebel,* 179, 184, 183; Ash, *When the Yankees Came,* 43. See also the evidence in Faust, *Mothers of Invention,* 196–219; Neely, *The Fate of Liberty,* 140–145; and Ash, *When the Yankees Came,* 62.
44. Faust, *Mothers of Invention,* 202; "Letters of General Thomas Williams," 320.
45. "Letters of General Thomas Williams," 320–322; Butler, *Butler's Book,* 417–418.
46. Lowry, *Confederate Heroines,* 5–6.
47. Phipps, *Genteel Rebel,* 157–175; General Orders No. 100, "Instructions for the Government of the Armies," 158–164, quote on 164, 157, 158.
48. Butler to J. G. Carney, July 2, 1862, in Benjamin F. Butler, *Letters of Butler* (Norwood, 1917), 2:35; "Letters of General Thomas Williams," 315–317; T. O. Moore to Jefferson Davis, June 12, 1862, Dearborn Collection, Houghton Library, Harvard University (hereafter cited as HU); Butler to Hon. E. M. Stanton, May 16, 1862, in Butler, *Letters of Butler,* 2:403; Butler to J. G. Carney, July 2, 1862, in Butler, *Letters of Butler,* 2:35.

49. Butler, *Butler's Book,* 417–419.
50. Phipps, *Genteel Rebel,* 177: Sigismunda Stribling Kimball Journal, Mar. 7, Mar. 30, 1863, UVA; Ash, *When the Yankees Came,* 60.
51. Butler, *Butler's Book,* 418. The quote is from McPherson, *Battle Cry of Freedom,* 552.
52. Historians have rightly identified the significance of Butler's order in the way, contrary to custom, it held women accountable for their political actions. See Faust, *Mothers of Invention,* 210. But Faust does see Butler's decision as atypical. General Orders no. 100, "Instructions for the government of the armies," 159.
53. Woodward, *Mary Chesnut's Civil War,* 243; Mayor John T. Monroe to Butler, May 16, 1862, in Butler, *Letters of Benjamin Butler,* 1:498; James Parton, *General Butler in New Orleans: History of the Administration of the Department of the Gulf in the Year 1862* (New York, 1864), 330–338.
54. Jefferson Davis, "To the Senate and House of Representatives of the Confederate States," Richmond, Aug. 13, 1862, *O.R.,* ser. 4, 2:52–56; "General Orders No. 111, Adjutant and Inspector General's Office, Richmond, December 2, 1862," in James D. Richardson, ed., *A Compilation of the Messages and Papers of the Confederacy* (Nashville, 1905), 1:271–273.
55. General Orders No. 44, May 19, 1862, *O.R.,* ser. 1, vol. 10, pt. 2, 531; uncatalogued collection of Civil War broadsides, FHS; General John B. Gordon, *O.R.,* ser. 1, vol. 11, pt. 1, 979.
56. *Hansard's Parliamentary Debates,* ser. 3, vol. 167 (1862): 614; Charles Francis Adams, *Charles Francis Adams* (1900; repr., New York, 1972), 249, 247.
57. *The Story of Mattie Jackson,* written and arranged by Dr. L. S. Thompson as given by Mattie Lawrence (1866), 11, docsouth.unc.edu/jacksonm/jackson.html.
58. Butler to Carney, July 2, 1862, in Butler, *Letters of Butler,* 2:37; "General Orders No. 111," 272.
59. Banks quoted in Phipps, *Genteel Rebel,* 187–188.
60. P. A. Willis to S. E. Carry quoted in Erik Mathisen, "Pledges of Allegiance: Obligation, Sovereignty and State Formation in Mississippi between Slavery and Redemption" (Ph.D. diss., University of Pennsylvania, 2009), chap. 3; Priscilla Bond Diary, May 13, May 16, 1862, LSU; quoted in George Rable, *Civil Wars: Women and the Crisis of Southern Nationalism* (Urbana, 1989), 179, and see also the analysis at 154–180.
61. On the Revolutionary War, see Kerber, *No Constitutional Right,* and Nancy Isenberg, *Sex and Citizenship in Antebellum America* (Chapel Hill 1998), 24, 34; on the oath in Civil War America, see Rogers Smith, *Civic Ideals: Conflicting Visions of Citizenship in U.S. History* (New Haven, 1997), 274–275.
62. *Harper's Weekly,* June 6, 1863; see also Priscilla M. Bond Diary, Aug. 25, 1864, LSU, and "Oath Prescribed by Act of July 2, 1862," in Elizabeth Hargrave Papers, DU.
63. Stephanie McCurry, review essay in *Signs,* 30 (Winter 2005): 1659–70.
64. Lee quoted in Faust, *Mothers of Invention,* 214; Priscilla M. Bond Diary, May 16, 1862, LSU. For two examples of military commissions trying women, see

RG 153, LL 1229, NA, and RG 153, NN 2733, NA. For women imprisoned, see Diary of Mrs. Mary E. Terry and Elvira A. W. Scott Diary. For sentences to hang, see Lowry, "Research Note," 58.

65. Jefferson Davis to Robert E. Lee, July 31, 1862, *PJD,* 8:310.

66. For the arrest of women on charges of treasonous correspondence, trade, and spying, see W. A. Parham to Governor Vance, Nov. 25, 1864, ZBV, box 182; Mary Caroline Allen to Jefferson Davis, July 17, 1863, *PJD,* 9:284–285; Israel Welsh to Jefferson Davis, June 22, 1864, *PJD,* 10:478; R. G. Farley to James A. Seddon, Feb. 2, 1863, LRCSW, RG 109 (M437), roll 91.

67. R. S. Hudson to Jefferson Davis, Mar. 14, 1864, *O.R.,* ser. 1, vol. 32, pt. 3, 625–627; Ella Lonn, *Desertion during the Civil War* (1928; repr., Lincoln, Neb., 1998). On the context in Mississippi, see Victoria E. Bynum, *The Free State of Jones: Mississippi's Longest Civil War* (Chapel Hill, 2001).

68. James A. Seddon, Sec. of War, to His Excellency Jefferson Davis, Nov. 26, 1863, *O.R.,* ser. 4, 2:990–1018, quotation at 1018; Proclamation, *PJD,* 7:284–285; C. Wooten to Governor Clark, Mar. 10, 1862, box 157, Walter M. Clark, Governors Papers, State Archives, Division of Archives and History, Raleigh, North Carolina (hereafter cited as NCDAH).

69. "Look Sharpe" to Gov. Clark, Mar. 31, 1862, Henry M. Earle to Gov. Clark, Mar. 8, 1862, J. A. McDowell to Gov. Clark, Mar. 28, 1862, all in box 157, Walter M. Clark, Governors Papers, NCDAH. Women filed their share of reports. See report of Mary A. Peters of Greenbrier County, Va., Jan. 28, 1862, LRCSW, RG 109 (M437), roll 31.

70. Margaret M. Storey, *Loyalty and Loss: Alabama's Unionists in the Civil War and Reconstruction* (Baton Rouge, 2004), 60; Jefferson Falkner to President Davis, Mar. 14, 1864, *PJD,* 10:279; Elvira Worth Jackson to Fannie Long, Asheboro, Mar. 15, 1862, in *The Correspondence of Jonathan Worth,* ed. J. G. de Roulhac Hamilton (Raleigh, 1909), 1:163–164; William A. Littlejohn to Gov. Clark, Aug. 16, 1861, in *North Carolina Civil War Documentary,* ed. W. Buck Yearns and John G. Barrett (Chapel Hill, 1980), 26–27; W. A. Campbell to Gov. Brown, July 12, 1862, *GSF,* box 26.

71. Report of S. S. Baxter to Secretary of War, Mar. 1862, LRCSW, RG 109 (M437), roll 31; Storey, *Loyalty and Loss,* 61–62.

72. Gov. John Letcher, "To the People of Northwestern Virginia," *Richmond Dispatch,* June 17, 1861, and "Order of Virginia Council, Re: Militia in Bath and Adjacent Counties," June 1, 1861, both in John Letcher Papers, ser. 6, VHS.

73. Paul McNeel to Gov. Letcher, Jan. 4, 1862, and G. W. Berlin to Gov. Letcher, July 4, 1862, both in John Letcher Papers, ser. 6, VHS.

74. W. T. Leeper to Brig. Gen. C. B. Fisk, Feb. 1, 1864, *O.R.,* ser. 1, vol. 34, pt. 2, 213.

75. Sarah E. Thompson Papers, "Sarah Thompson's Account of Morgan's Defeat, Sept. 3, 1864," DU, scriptorium.lib.duke.edu/thompson/. On East Tennessee, see Robert Tracy McKenzie, "Prudent Silence and Strict Neutrality: The Parameters of Unionism in Parson Brownlow's Knoxville, 1860–1863," in *Enemies of the Country: New Perspectives on Unionists in the Civil War South,* ed.

John C. Inscoe and Robert C. Kenzer (Athens, Ga., 2001), 73–96; Noel C. Fisher, *War at Every Door: Partisan Politics and Guerilla Violence in East Tennessee, 1860–1869* (Chapel Hill, 1997).

76. Sarah E. Thompson Papers, "Sarah Thompson's Account of Morgan's Defeat, Sept. 3, 1864," DU.
77. Ibid.
78. Fisher questions the veracity of Thompson's claim while acknowledging that a number of Union military commanders sustained it in her pension application. See Fisher, *War at Every Door,* append. B, 186–187.
79. Yearns and Barrett, *North Carolina Civil War Documentary,* 94; Jefferson Davis to Zebulon B. Vance, Jan. 8, 1864, *PJD,* 10:161.
80. Yearns and Barrett, *North Carolina Civil War Documentary,* 94; Jonathan Worth to Zebulon B. Vance, Sept. 16, 1862, in de Roulhac Hamilton, *Papers of Jonathan Worth,* 1:187–188; Zebulon B. Vance to Jefferson Davis, May 13, 1863, *PJD,* 9:182; J. C. Kirkman, Capt, to Gov. Vance, Aug. 27, 1863, Marmaduke Swain Robins Papers, SHC; "Special Orders No. 52," Feb. 15, 1863, box 162, ZBV. For a few examples of the many citizen requests, see Jennette E. Loudermilk et al. [27 women] to Capt. T. A. Branson, Co. F, 46th N.C. Regt., July 21, 1863, box 168, and F. Munroe to Gov. Vance, Apr. 17, 1863, box 164, both ZBV.
81. For two examples of pardons, see "Proclamation of Governor Vance, May 11, 1863," in Yearns and Barrett, *North Carolina Civil War Documentary,* 100–101, and Z. B. Vance to Col S. G. Worth, Sept. 12, 1863, Marmaduke Swain Robins Papers, SHC.
82. Nancy Royal to Gov. Vance, Aug. 9, 1863, box 168, ZBV; [?] to J. Hoover, Esq., Sept. 14, 1863, Marmaduke Swain Robins Papers, SHC. On the Hulin/Moore families, see Victoria E. Bynum, *Unruly Women: The Politics of Social and Sexual Control in the Old South* (Chapel Hill, 1992), and Bynum, *Free State of Jones.*
83. Henry Thomson to Gov. Clark, July 27, 1862, box 157, Walter M. Clark, Governors Papers, NCDAH; J. L. Henry to Gov. Vance, Sept. 30, 1864, box 180, ZBV; Mrs. Moore to Gov. Vance, Sept. 10, 1863, box 169, ZBV; Miss M. M. McMaster to Marmaduke Swain Robins, Feb. 16, 1863, Marmaduke Swain Robins Papers, SHC.
84. "Proclamation of Governor Vance, May 11, 1863," 101–102; Phillip Shaw Paludan, *Victims: A True Story of the Civil War* (Knoxville, 1981), 71; and for evidence of criminal prosecution, *State v. James Blake* and *State v. John Wright,* both fall term, 1864, in Criminal Action Papers, Montgomery County, NCDAH; R. S. Hudson to Jefferson Davis, Mar. 14, 1864, *O.R.,* ser. 1, vol. 32, pt. 3, 626; H. Maury to My Dear General, Mar. 12, 1864, *O.R.,* ser. 1, vol. 32, pt. 3, 633. For "no mere war among men," see Bynum, *Free State of Jones,* 94.
85. The fullest account of events is in Paludan, *Victims.*
86. The torture of the women is documented in a subsequent investigation. See A. S. Merrimon [solicitor for the Western District] to Gov. Vance, Feb. 24, 1863, and A. S. Merrimon to Gov. Vance, Feb. 16, 1863, both in *O.R.,* ser. 1,

18:881, 893; Paludan, *Victims,* 95–96; Bynum, *Unruly Women,* 135. The horrifying scenes in Charles Frazier, *Cold Mountain* (New York, 1997), are retellings.

87. Again the details came out in an investigation. See Thomas Settle to Gov. Vance, Sept. 4, 1864, Thomas Settle Jr. Papers, NCDAH; Thomas Settle to Gov. Vance, Sept. 21, 1864, box 180, ZBV; Bynum, *Unruly Women,* 143–144. For a statement of federal concern about the scale of desertion in North Carolina, see Report of G. W. Lay to Maj. Gen. W. H. C. Whiting, Sept. 6, 1863, LRCSW, RG 109 (M437), roll 101.
88. Martha Hough to Gov. Vance, Sept. 28, 1864, box 180, Anny Beck to Gov. Vance, box 172, and Thomas W. Ritter to Gov. Vance, Jan. 25, 1864, box 173; all ZBV.
89. Phoebe Crook to Gov. Vance, Sept. 15, 1864, box 180, ZBV; Clariday Hulin to Gov. Vance, Nov. 20, 1864, box 171, ZBV.
90. Thomas Settle to Gov. Vance, Sept. 4, 1864, Thomas Settle Jr. Papers, NCDAH.
91. Thomas W. Ritter to Gov. Vance, Jan. 25, 1864, box 173; D. L. May to Gov. Vance, Nov. 13, 1863, box 171; Phoebe Crook to Gov. Vance, Sept. 15, 1864, box 180; Anny Beck to Gov. Vance, Dec. 7, 1863, box 172; all ZBV. Thomas Settle to Gov. Vance, Sept. 4, 1864, Thomas Settle Jr. Papers, NCDAH.
92. Jefferson Davis to Robert E. Lee, July 31, 1862, *PJD,* 8:310.
93. Thomas Settle to Gov. Vance, Sept. 4, 1864, Thomas Settle Jr. Papers, NCDAH.

4. Soldiers' Wives and the Politics of Subsistence

1. *Confederate Baptist,* Mar. 11, 1863; *Report of the Board for the Relief of Families of Soldiers in the Parishes of St. Phillip and St. Michael* (Charleston, 1863), 9.
2. For a sample of the language, see John J. Pettus, Dec. 14, 1861, in *Journal of the House of Representatives of the State of Mississippi at a Regular Session . . . Oct. and December, 1861 and January 1862* (Jackson, 1862), 238; John J. Pettus, Dec. 20, 1862, in *Journal of the House of Representatives of the State of Mississippi, December Session of 1862 and Oct. Session of 1863* (Jackson, 1864), 10; John J. Pettus, Oct. 3, 1863, and Charles Clark, Governor Elect, Inaugural Address, Oct. 16, 1863, both in *Journal of the House of Representatives of the State of Mississippi (1862–63),* 96, 160.
3. *Laws of the State of Mississippi, Passed at a Called and Regular Session of the Mississippi Legislature, . . . December 1862 and Oct. 1863* (Selma, 1864), 227; Charles Clark, Inaugural Address, Oct. 16, 1863, 160.
4. For the definition of political agency, see Begoña Aretxaga, *Shattering Silence: Women, Nationalism and Political Subjectivity in Northern Ireland* (Princeton, 1997), 8.
5. For women's membership in the sexual, but not the social, contract, see Carole Pateman, *The Sexual Contract* (Stanford, 1988).
6. Historians routinely cite the evidence of women's new participation without noticing its meaning for political life. Escott and Robinson use yeoman and

poor white women's letters to state officials without noting that they are from women, thus assimilating them to the suffering poor in general and missing the changed patterns of political communication they represent. See Paul Escott, *After Secession: Jefferson Davis and the Failure of Confederate Nationalism* (Baton Rouge, 1978), and Escott, "The Moral Economy of the Crowd in Confederate North Carolina," *Maryland Historian* 122, no. 1 (Spring/Summer 1982): 1–17; Armstead Robinson, *Bitter Fruits of Bondage: The Demise of Slavery and the Collapse of the Confederacy, 1861–1865* (Charlottesville, 2005).

7. On the North, see Lori D. Ginzberg, *Women and the Work of Benevolence: Morality, Politics and Class in the 19th Century United States* (New Haven, 1990); Jeannie Attie, *Patriotic Toil: Northern Women and the American Civil War* (Ithaca, 1998), 46–49; Nina Silber, *Daughters of the Union: Northern Women Fight the Civil War* (Cambridge, Mass., 2005); Judith Giesberg, *Civil War Sisterhood: The U.S. Sanitary Commission and Women's Politics in Transition* (Boston, 2000); Elizabeth D. Leonard, *Yankee Women: Gender Battles in the Civil War* (New York, 1994).

8. In the first paradigm the war either turned women into suffragists or engendered a retreat to patriarchy; in the second, women were either the backbone of Confederate nationalism or a significant factor in military defeat. The literature has long been characterized by historiographic mirroring. For the first paradigm, see Anne Firor Scott, *The Southern Lady: From Pedestal to Politics, 1830–1930* (Chicago, 1970), and Drew Gilpin Faust, *Mothers of Invention: Women of the Slaveholding South in the American Civil War* (Chapel Hill, 1996). For the second, see Bell Irvin Wiley, *Confederate Women* (Westport, 1975), and more recently, George Rable, *Civil Wars: Women and the Crisis of Southern Nationalism* (Urbana, 1989), and Faust, *Mothers of Invention.* Both sets of questions have been worked out almost exclusively in relation to planter-class women. The practice of women's history has moved beyond such univocal categories; we can no longer talk coherently of "Southern women."

9. There is no doubt that poor white women's politics was part of a larger stream of disaffection on the home front that historians link to the collapse of Confederate nationalism. But the debate over Confederate nationalism is too binary and reductive to illuminate much about women's wartime politics. My interest is not in taking sides but in trying to gauge the changes that underlay the emergence of soldiers' wives as a political force in the Confederacy. For a sample of the literature, see Gary Gallagher, *The Confederate War: How Popular Will, Nationalism, and Military Strategy Could Not Stave Off Defeat* (New York, 1997), and Escott, *After Secession.* For a rare focus on poor white women, see Victoria Bynum, *Unruly Women: The Politics of Social and Sexual Control in the Old South* (Chapel Hill, 1992). The literature on women and Confederate nationalism goes back to Bell Wiley, but see the recent contributions of Faust, *Mothers of Invention,* and Anne Sarah Rubin, *A Shattered Nation: The Rise and Fall of the Confederacy, 1861–1868* (Chapel Hill, 2005).

10. Mary Wollstonecraft, *A Vindication of the Rights of Woman,* ed. Carol H. Poston (New York, 1988), 5; Aretxaga, *Shattering Silence,* 61 and throughout.

11. Citizens of St. Mary's and Camden County to Gov. Joseph E. Brown, Apr. 25, 1861, LRCSW, RG 109 (M437), roll 1; Petitioners of Panola County, TX to Honorable G. W. Randolph, Secretary of War, Oct. 12, 1862, LRCSW, roll 41. For one exception, see Citizens of Courtney, TX to General P. W. Herbert, Aug. 8, 1862, LRCSW, roll 41.
12. J. M. Cansler to Gov. Brown, Feb. 20, 1862, GSF, box 26; Davis, on Memorandum by John A. Campbell, Oct. 21, 1862, *PJD,* 8:507.
13. Patrick A. Stevenson to Secretary of War, May 1, 1862, LRCSW, roll 71; Resolutions of Citizens of Columbus, Feb. 10, 1862, roll 6, ser. 757, Gov. John Jones Pettus, Correspondence and Papers, 1859–1863 and Undated, Mississippi Department of Archives and History, Jackson, Mississippi (hereafter cited as MDAH).
14. W. G. Murat to Secretary of War Randolph, June 16, 1862, LRCSW, roll 61; James M. Brantley to Gov. Brown, Jan. 16, 1864, GSF, box 24; M. A. Brantley to Gov. Brown, Feb. 5, 1864, GSF, box 24.
15. Joseph Roberson to Gov. Vance, June 21, 1863, box 166, ZBV; J. G. Bowles et al. to Gov. Brown, July 27, 1862, box 1, Executive Department, Petitions, Georgia Department of Archives and History (hereafter cited as GDAH); Captain John Bragg to Gov. Brown, Mar. 13, 1863, GSF, box 24.
16. Citizens of Hearalson and Vicinity to Governor Brown, July 27, 1862, box 1, and O. D. Gray et al. to Governor Brown, Feb. 18, 1862, box 3, both Executive Department, Petitions, GDAH; Women and Men of Tallapoosa County to Governor Shorter, May 5, 1862, LRCSW, roll 71; Citizens of Stanhope to the Secretary of War, May 25, 1862, LRCSW, roll 51.
17. This generalization is based on earlier research in petitions to the South Carolina legislature, 1820–1860, and was confirmed by a sample of the correspondence to the governor of North Carolina in 1860. See John W. Ellis, Governor's Papers, box 148 (Jan.–Apr. 1860), NCDAH.
18. The generalizations in the text are based on a sampling of the North Carolina and Georgia Governor's Papers. In both cases those papers categorized (by the archives) as petitions contain higher proportions of documents authored by women, but the pattern is also clear in the general correspondence in North Carolina, although those papers contain a promiscuous mix of official government (including military) business and correspondence from constituents. The North Carolina sample consisted of one box from each year, 1861–1865: box 150 [1861], John W. Ellis, Governor's Papers, NCDAH; box 158 [1862], Henry T. Clark, Governor's Papers, NCDAH; box 164 [1863], box 176 [1864], box 183 [1865], ZBV. I also read box 184 [labeled "Petitions," n.d.], ZBV. By 1865 the correspondence was almost entirely official, much of it telegrams. In Georgia 40% of petitions to the governor (in one sample box) were from women or mixed groups of men and women; the vast majority (over 75%) were dated 1864. See Governor Joseph Brown, Executive Department Petitions, box 3, GDAH.
19. My research, and the generalization in the text, is based on a one-tenth sample of the microfilm reels of the Letters Received by the Confederate Secretary of War (LRCSW), RG 109 (M437).

20. "Substance of Remarks Made by Thomas R. R. Cobb Esq., before the General Assembly of Georgia, Oct. 12, 1860," in *Confederate Records of the State of Georgia,* ed. Allen D. Candler (1909–1911; New York, 1972), 1:160; A. B. Briggs, Sr. et al. to Governor Brown, Aug. 8, 1863, Executive Department, Petitions, box 1, GDAH.
21. Mrs. Annie Breeland et al. to Secretary of War, June 7, 1863, LRCSW, roll 111; Citizens of Shelby County, Alabama to the War Department, LRCSW, roll 101; Citizens of Tippah County to the Military Authorities of Both Mississippi and the Confederate States, Apr. 3, 1863, LRCSW, roll 111.
22. Mary Jones to Governor Pettus, Apr. 16, 1862, roll 6, Pettus Correspondence, MDAH. See also "Destitute Woman" to Gov. Pettus, Sept. 3, 1862, roll 7, Pettus Correspondence, MDAH.
23. On the "twenty-negro act," see Albert Burton Moore, *Conscription and Conflict in the Confederacy* (New York, 1924), and Robinson, *Bitter Fruits of Bondage.*
24. Rebecca K. Campbell to George W. Randolph, Oct. 3, 1862, and Jane Crutchfield to President Jefferson Davis, Oct. 4, 1862, both LRCSW, roll 41. On widows, see Kirsten E. Wood, *Masterful Women: Slaveholding Widows from the American Revolution through the Civil War* (Chapel Hill, 2004).
25. Frances J. Brightwell to Mr. President Jefferson Davis, Mar. 17, 1862, LRCSW, roll 31; Martha J. Bell to Secretary of War, Apr. 1, 1862, LRCSW, roll 31; Ellen Congleton to Gov. Zebulon Vance, Apr. 15, 1863, box 164, ZBV.
26. Margaret M. Smith et al. to Gov. Vance, Feb. 4, 1863, box 162, ZBV. For the text of the promise, see Michael Bollinger to Gov. Vance, Mar. 3, 1863, box 163, ZBV. James Scott identifies this as the dialogic form commonly used by the weak. See Scott, *Domination and the Arts of Resistance: Hidden Transcripts* (New Haven, 1990), 92.
27. Here I am thinking of, in order, Drew Gilpin Faust, *The Creation of Confederate Nationalism: Ideology and Identity in the Civil War South* (Baton Rouge, 1988); Paul D. Escott, "The Cry of the Sufferers: The Problem of Welfare in the Confederacy," *Civil War History* 23 (Sept. 1977): 228–240; and Bynum, *Unruly Women.*
28. The subject of slave women is taken up in Chapters 6–8. But for evidence of the difficulties black soldiers' wives faced in relation to the Union government, see Ira Berlin, Joseph Reidy, and Leslie Rowland, eds., *Freedom: A Documentary History of Emancipation, 1861–1867,* ser. 2: *The Black Military Experience* (Cambridge, UK, 1982), 656–732.
29. Mrs. Let Page to Gov. Letcher, Nov. 17, 1862, John Letcher Papers, ser. 6, VHS.
30. Mrs. C. Clark to Gov. Brown, n.d., and Mrs. David Shipp et al. to Gov. Brown, July 21, 1864, both box 3, Executive Department, Petitions, GDAH.
31. Miss Susan R. Jervey, Diary, Feb. 27, 1865, in *Two Diaries from Middle St. John's Berkeley, South Carolina, February to May 1865* (Charleston, 1921), 7.
32. Mrs. Let Page to Gov. Letcher, Nov. 17, 1862, John Letcher Papers, ser. 6, VHS; Mrs. David Shipp et al. to Gov. Brown, July 21, 1864, and Mrs. C. Clark to Gov. Brown, n.d., both box 3, Executive Department, Petitions, GDAH.

33. Mary C. Tisinger et al. to Gov. Brown, Aug. 15, 1864, box 3, Executive Department, Petitions, GDAH.
34. C. W. Walker to Gov. Vance, May 8, 1863, box 165, J. C. Keener to Gov. Vance, Apr. 18, 1864, box 176, Anonymous to Gov. Vance, Oct. 9, 1863, box 170, all ZBV.
35. On marriage and citizenship, see Linda K. Kerber, *No Constitutional Right to Be Ladies: Women and the Obligations of Citizenship* (New York, 1998); Nancy F. Cott, *Public Vows: A History of Marriage and the Nation* (Cambridge, Mass., 2000); and Stephanie McCurry, review essay, *Signs* 30, no. 2 (Winter 2005).
36. Unsigned to Gov. Vance, Aug. 17, 1864, and Susan Halford et al. to Gov. Vance, Dec. 23, 1863, both box 172, ZBV.
37. Nicolleta Gullace, *"The Blood of Our Sons": Men, Women, and the Renegotiation of British Citizenship during the Great War* (New York, 2002); Attie, *Patriotic Toil; Proceedings of the Meeting of the Loyal Women of the Republic Held in New York, May 14, 1863* (New York, 1863).
38. For recent confirmation of the point, see Lori G. Ginzberg, *Untidy Origins: A Story of Woman's Rights in Antebellum New York* (Chapel Hill, 2005).
39. M. H. Bray and others to Gov. Brown, Jan. 26, 1864, Martha Warren et al. to Gov. Brown, n.d., both box 1, Executive Department, Petitions, GDAH.
40. Richard Franklin Bensel, *Yankee Leviathan: The Origins of Central State Authority in America, 1859–1877* (Cambridge, Mass., 1990), 131. On the adoption of the draft and conditions preceding it, see Moore, *Conscription and Conflict,* and Robinson, *Bitter Fruits of Bondage,* 145–162. For estimates of the number of male slaves of military age in the Confederate States, see Berlin et al., *Black Military Experience,* 12.
41. By 1864 military age was defined as ages 17–50. On the marital profile of Union soldiers, see Silber, *Daughters of the Union,* 16–18. For the enlistment figures, see Gallagher, *The Confederate War,* 28–29, 16–18. Enlistment rates were as high as 90% of eligible white men in parts of Virginia. See Aaron Sheehan-Dean, *Why Confederates Fought: Family and Nation in Civil War America* (Chapel Hill, 2007), 3. I thank Tom Childers for information on the broader perspective.
42. Bensel, *Yankee Leviathan,* 136; Jemima Ann Diggs to Gov. John Letcher, Jan. 17, 1863, John Letcher Papers, ser. 6, VHS.
43. Judith Giesberg, *Army at Home: Women and the Civil War on the Northern Home Front* (Chapel Hill, 2009); Ginzberg, *Women and the Work of Benevolence;* Attie, *Patriotic Toil;* Silber, *Daughters of the Union;* Giesberg, *Civil War Sisterhood;* Leonard, *Yankee Women;* Elizabeth Young, *Disarming the Nation: Women's Writing in the American Civil War* (Chicago, 1999).
44. Emory M. Thomas, *The Confederacy as a Revolutionary Experience* (Englewood Cliffs, 1971); Raimondo Luraghi, *The Rise and Fall of the Plantation South* (New York, 1978); Bensel, *Yankee Leviathan,* paraphrase and quotations on 6, 97, 14.
45. Eric Foner, *Reconstruction: America's Unfinished Revolution, 1863–1877* (New York, 1988); Bensel, *Yankee Leviathan,* quotation on 135.
46. Alexander Stephens, "Cornerstone Speech," in *Southern Pamphlets on Seces-*

sion: November 1860–April 1861, ed. Jon L. Wakelyn (Chapel Hill, 1996), 410. For the numbers of Confederate civil servants, see Bensel, *Yankee Leviathan,* 103.

47. Robinson, *Bitter Fruits of Bondage,* 149; Docs. #686, 687, 688, 689, Louis Malone Ayers Jr. Papers, SHC, in *RASP,* ser. A, pt. 2 (Tax in Kind Receipts). How subsistence was calculated is unclear; women charged officials with taking one-tenth of everything.
48. George Lynch to Honorable John A. Campbell, Aug. 17, 1863, LRCSW, roll 101. For the numbers of agents, see Paul Escott, "Poverty and Governmental Aid for the Poor in Confederate North Carolina," *North Carolina Historical Review* 61 (Oct. 1984): 472. Escott estimates that tax-in-kind agents collected $5 million worth of crops between July and Oct. 1863, two-thirds of it from North Carolina, Georgia, and Alabama. Bensel, *Yankee Leviathan,* 159, for the definition of impressment.
49. John Milton, Governor of Florida, "Fellow Citizens of the Senate and House of Representatives," Executive Chamber, Tallahassee, Fl. Nov. 23, 1863, *O.R.,* ser. 4, 2:974–975; John Letcher, Letter to Editor [Draft], 1864, John Letcher Papers, ser. 6, VHS; John Brackett to Gov. Brown, May 11, 1863, GSF, box 24; Garret Hallenbeck to Gov. Brown, Oct. 20, 1863, GSF, box 33; "A Southern Woman" to Governor Vance, Dec. 24, 1864, box 182, ZBV.
50. Elizabeth Jones to Gov. Vance, Sept. 2, 1863, box 169, and Calvin Pippin to Gov. Vance, Apr. 12, 1864, box 176, both ZBV.
51. Warrant for the arrest of three North Carolina men wanted for the murder of a slave in Spartanburg, S.C., encl. in State of South Carolina, Executive Department to Gov. Zebulon Vance, Aug. 5, 1864, box 179, ZBV.
52. Eliza A. Lamb to Dr. Murphy, Jan. 27, 1863, H. F. Murphy to Gov. Vance, Jan. 31, 1863, both box 161, ZBV; Columbia A. Herr to His Excellency William Smith, Oct. 16, 1864, folder 5, box 4, Governor Smith Papers, Library of Virginia, Richmond (hereafter cited as LVA); Martha Coletrane to Gov. Vance, Oct. 18, 1863, box 160, ZBV.
53. Lydia Hines to Gov. Vance, May 5, 1864, box 177, Martha Allen to Gov. Vance, May 6, 1863, box 165, and J. Atwater to Gov. Vance, May 18, 1863, box 165, all ZBV; Meta Morris Grimball Diary, Sept. 5, 1862, SHC; Mary Wilkinson to Micajah Wilkinson, [unreadable month] 19th, 1862, folder 2, Micajah Wilkinson Papers, LSU.
54. Catherine Miller to His Excellency Joseph E. Brown, July 11, 1864, GSF, box 40; Mrs. G. E. Cook to Gov. Brown, Aug. 16, 1864, GSF, box 27.
55. Mrs. G. E. Cook to Gov. Brown, Aug. 16, 1864, GSF, box 27; J. S. M. Cable to Gov. Clark, July 14, 1862, box 17, Papers of Gov. Henry T. Clark, NCDAH; Eliza Thomas to Gov. Vance, Oct. 25, 1864, box 181, ZBV.
56. Jason Phillips, "The Grape Vine Telegraph: Rumors and Confederate Persistence," *Journal of Southern History* 72, no. 4 (Oct. 2006): 753–788.
57. Female Sect of Rutherfordton to Gov. Vance, June 15, 1863, box 166, Mary C. Moore to Gov. Vance, Mar. 21, 1863, box 163, and Harriet S. Briles to Gov. Vance, Dec. 30, 1864, box 182, all ZBV.

58. Ellen Congleton to Gov. Vance, Apr. 15, 1863, box 164; Sophia Bowen et al. to Gov. Vance, May 27, 1863, box 165; Catharine Hunt to Vance, Jan. 15, 1863, box 161, all ZBV. The women observed a political form or strategy astutely analyzed by scholars of the non-Western rural poor especially in agrarian and subaltern studies. For a few key examples, see Scott, *Domination,* and James C. Scott, *Weapons of the Weak: Everyday Forms of Resistance* (New Haven, 1985); Ranajit Guha, *Elementary Aspects of Peasant Insurgency in Colonial India* (Durham, 1999).
59. Mary Bennett to Gov. Brown, Oct. 13, 1864, GSF box 23; Elizabeth Coker to Gov. Brown, Dec. 14, 1863, GSF, box 27. My thinking was stimulated by Gregory Downs's dissertation on vernacular conceptions of the state. See Gregory Downs, "Declarations of Dependence: Popular Politics in North Carolina from Reconstruction to the New Deal" (Ph.D. diss., University of Pennsylvania, 2006).
60. Bettie A. Baylin to Hon. R. M. T. Hunter, Mar. 15, 1862, LRCSW, roll 31.
61. Mrs. Ann. C. Bausman et al. to Hon William Smith, Governor of Virginia, Oct. 14, 1864, William Smith Papers, box 4, folder 5, LVA; William Smith to Braxton Bragg, June 6, 1864, HU; President Davis to Braxton Bragg, June 6, 1864 [endorsing Smith's request], *PJD,* 10:452; Josephine Martin to Governor Pettus, Mar. 30, 1861, roll 2, Pettus Papers, MDAH; Priscilla Allen to Governor Allen, Jan. 17, 1865, folder 10, box 1, James Calvert Wise Papers, LSU.
62. Elizabeth Mason to James A. Seddon, Secretary of War, Dec. 30, 1864, LRCSW, roll 101; Mrs. Maggie A. Smith to Hon. Secretary of War, July 8, 1862, LRCSW, roll 71; Louisa Stone to President Davis, Aug. 15, 1864, *PJD,* 10:611.
63. Bensel, *Yankee Leviathan,* 136.
64. Almost any Vance document confirms the point. For a sample, see the notations signed "ZBV" on: Sallie Wright to Gov. Vance, Apr. 26, 1863, box 164, G. H. White, County Commissioner to Gov. Vance, Oct. 4, 1864, box 182, Z. B. Vance to Colonel C. M. Avery, 33rd NCT, Oct. 21, 1863, box 170, and Mrs. E. Walters to Gov. Vance, Apr. 17, 1863, box 164, all in ZBV; Zebulon Vance to President Davis, Feb. 9, 1864, *PJD,* 10:227.
65. For one example, see Lewis Malone Ayers Jr. to W. H. S. Taylor, Second Auditor, Treasury Department, Richmond, Virginia, Sept. 13, 1863, Lewis Malone Ayers Papers, folder 82, box 111, SCL.
66. Bensel, *Yankee Leviathan,* 136.
67. Sarah Halford to Gov. Vance, Dec. 23, 1863, box 172, ZBV.
68. Margaret M. Smith et al. to Gov. Vance, Feb. 4, 1863, box 162, ZBV; Almira P. Acors to President Davis, Mar. 23, 1862, *PJD,* 8:112.
69. Almira P. Acors to President Davis, Mar. 23, 1862, *PJD,* 8:112. Armstead Robinson says that President Davis read the correspondence that came to him. Amy Murrell says that in 1862 many more petitions to the secretary of war went unanswered than in 1864. See Amy E. Murrell, "Of Necessity and Public Benefit: Southern Families and Their Appeals for Protection," in *Southern Fami-*

lies at War: Loyalty and Conflict in the Civil War South, ed. Catherine Clinton (New York, 2001), 77–99.

70. On the petitions of soldiers' wives in the American Revolution, see Linda Kerber, *Women of the Republic: Intellect and Ideology in Revolutionary America* (New York, 1980). Kerber calls the petitions "prepolitical," mentions only one from non-elite women (Charleston seamstresses), and does not document any particular coherence of women as soldiers' wives. The forms of the state were obviously quite distinct in the Revolutionary and Civil War periods. The other relevant comparison is to the petition campaigns of Northern women for the abolition of slavery in the antebellum and Civil War period. On this, see Susan Zaeske, *Signatures of Citizenship: Petitioning, Antislavery and Women's Political Identity* (Chapel Hill, 2003). But these women were not making demands for policy change in their own interest, and it was not a grassroots political movement of poor rural women. Judith Giesberg argues that some Northern rural women saw relief as an exchange with the state for a "wright" that followed their husbands' military service and that they became a constituency of soldiers' wives. But the evidence is, rather, of individual requests for relief and strikingly little by way of response on the part of government officials. See Giesberg, *Army at Home,* chap. 1.
71. Martha Coletrane to Gov. Vance, Oct. 18, 1863, box 160, ZBV. The law extending the age of men subject to conscription was passed at the momentous congressional session of Aug. 1862. See Robinson, *Bitter Fruits of Bondage,* 183–188.
72. Lucy Shelton to Milledge Luke Bonham, Oct. 28, 1862, Pickens-Bonham Papers, box 4, folder 130, LC; Sophia E. Bowen et al. to Gov. Vance, May 27, 1863, box 165, ZBV; Mrs. L. E. Davis to President Davis, Aug. 22, 1864, quoted in Rable, *Civil Wars,* 107.
73. Louisa Stone to President Davis, Aug. 15, 1864, *PJD,* 10:611; Nettie H. Edwards to Hon. Joseph E. Brown, July 28, 1864, GSF, box 29; C. W. Walker to Gov. Vance, May 8, 1863, box 165, ZBV.
74. Elizabeth Jones to Gov. Vance, Sept. 2, 1863, box 169, Nancy Richardson to Gov. Vance, Oct. 1, 1864, box 182, and Mary P. Moore to Gov. Vance, Sept. 3, 1863, box 169, all ZBV.
75. Bensel, *Yankee Leviathan,* 223–224; Anonymous, Reglators to Gov. Vance, Feb. 18, 1863, box 162, ZBV.
76. Nancy Vines et al. to Gov. Vance, Sept. 6, 1863, box 169, ZBV; Anonymous, from the Ladies of Spaulding County to Governor Brown, June 25, 1864, GSF, box 22.
77. Faust, *Confederate Nationalism,* 44–45, quote at 45.
78. The most extended popular treatment of extortion in the Civil War South was an 1864 novel called *The Trials of the Soldier's Wife;* see Faust, *Confederate Nationalism,* 48. But the genteel women of that story bear little resemblance to the enraged women in the street version of the drama.
79. "A Petition of the Women of North Carolina" to Gov. Zebulon Vance, n.d [Oct. 9, 1863], box 184, ZBV. The date is identified by the accompanying cover

letter, Delphina Mendenhall to Gov. Vance, Oct. 9, 1863, box 170, ZBV. See also M. F. Hopkins et al. to Vance, n.d. [probably Sept. 1864], box 184, and Saley An Dixon and others to Gov. Vance, n.d. [Sept. 1864], box 180, both ZBV.

80. See Zaeske, *Signatures of Citizenship.* The title indicates the interpretive emphasis.
81. Like the American Antislavery Society or The Loyal Women of the Republic as in the Union.
82. Nancy Vines et al. to Gov. Vance, Sept. 6, 1863, box 169, ZBV; Jeptha Clarke and Mrs. Martha A. Painter to Governor Vance, Oct. 8, 1862, ZBV.
83. Escott, "Poverty and Governmental Aid," 63; Mrs. D. Wellborn to Brown, Oct. 16, 1862, GSF, box 49. On elite women's religious chastening, see Faust, *Confederate Nationalism,* 29–40, and Faust, *Mothers of Invention,* 179–195.
84. "A Poor Woman" to Gov. Vance, Jan. 10, 1865, box 183, ZBV; "Sarah Thompson's Account of Morgan's Defeat, September 3, 1864," Sarah E. Thompson Papers, DU, scriptorium.lib.duke.edu/thompson/. On peace politics in North Carolina, see Chandra Manning, *What This Cruel War Was Over: Soldiers, Slavery, and the Civil War* (New York, 2007), 136, 173. There were other women who wrote urging Vance to make peace. See "A Petition of the Women of North Carolina" to Vance, n.d., box 184, Anonymous to Vance, Oct. 9, 1863, box 170, and W. P. Bynum to Vance, July 24, 1863, box 168, all ZBV. On peace politics and the war against the deserters, see L. S. Gast to Vance, Sept. 7, 1863, box 169, ZBV.
85. Indictment of Martha Sheets, Feb. 15, 1866, and *State v. Penina Hogden, Mary Lucas et al.,* Spring Term, 1866, both in Criminal Action Papers, Montgomery County, NCDAH.
86. Nancy Vines et al. to Gov. Vance, Sept. 6, 1863, box 169, Mrs. Brown and Company, Sept. 23, 1863, box 169, Mrs. Yellan to Gov. Vance, Apr. 19, 1863, box 164, and Susan C. Wallee [?] to Gov. Vance, Apr. 3, 1864, box 176, all ZBV.
87. R. W. Rest, County Court Clerk to Gov. Vance, Jan. 2, 1863, box 161, ZBV. The Virginia Governors' papers for the Civil War period are so bureaucratic in nature that one suspects a purging of constituent correspondence. I thank Joseph Glatthar for a helpful conversation about this. On Virginia, see William Blair, *Virginia's Private War: Feeding Body and Soul in the Confederacy* (New York, 1998), and Sheehan-Dean, *Why Confederates Fought.*
88. Anonymous, Regulators to Gov. Vance, Feb. 18, 1863, box 162, ZBV.
89. Ibid.
90. J. W. Ellis and others to Vance, Apr. 13, 1864, box 176, ZBV. For confirmation of the link, see Bynum, *Unruly Women,* 134.
91. Bertram Wyatt-Brown, *Southern Honor: Ethics and Behavior in the Old South* (New York, 1982). For Europe, see Natalie Davis, *Society and Culture in Early Modern France* (Stanford, 1965). The French Revolution was the example that came most readily to mind to literate observers, but women perpetrators themselves never invoked the comparison. See the image from *Leslie's Illustrated Newspaper* reproduced in Faust, *Confederate Nationalism,* 53.

5. WOMEN NUMEROUS AND ARMED

1. On Atlanta, see *Atlanta Intelligencer,* Mar. 19, 20, 23, 26, 1863; *Atlanta Southern Confederacy,* Mar. 19, 1863; *Augusta Chronicle and Sentinel,* Apr. 5, 1863; Paul Lack, "Law and Disorder in Confederate Atlanta," *GHQ* 66, no. 2 (Summer 1982). On Salisbury, see Mary C. Moore to Gov. Vance, Mar. 21, 1863, and Michael Brown to Gov. Vance, Mar. 18, 1863, both box 163, ZBV; *Richmond Daily Examiner,* Mar. 27, 1863; Paul Escott, "The Moral Economy of the Crowd in Confederate North Carolina," *Maryland Historian* 13 (Spring/Summer, 1982): 1–18; Victoria Bynum, *Unruly Women: The Politics of Social and Sexual Control in the Old South* (Chapel Hill, 1992), 125–126. On Mobile, see Harriet E. Amos, "All Absorbing Topics: Food and Clothing in Confederate Mobile," *Atlanta Historical Journal* 22, nos. 3–4 (Fall/Winter 1978): 17–28. On Petersburg, see *Staunton Spectator,* Apr. 7, 1863; on Richmond, see *Richmond Daily Examiner,* Apr. 3, 4, 6, 8, 15, 24, Oct. 12, 1863; Louis H. Manarin, ed., *Richmond at War: The Minutes of the City Council, 1861–1865* (Chapel Hill, 1966); Douglas O. Tice, "Bread or Blood!: The Richmond Bread Riot," *Civil War Times Illustrated* 12 (Feb. 1974); Michael V. Chesson, "Harlots or Heroines? A New Look at the Richmond Bread Riot," *Virginia Magazine of History and Biography* 92, no. 2 (Apr. 1984): 131–175; Drew Gilpin Faust, *The Creation of Confederate Nationalism: Ideology and Identity in the Civil War South* (Baton Rouge, 1988), 52–57. On Augusta, Milledgeville, and Columbus, Georgia, see *Savannah Republican,* Apr. 13, 1863, *Turnwold Countryman,* Apr. 12, 1863, and *Atlanta Southern Confederacy,* Apr. 16, 1863. For Macon, Georgia, see *Atlanta Southern Confederacy,* Apr. 24, 1863, and *Macon Confederate,* Apr. 1, 1863, reprinted in *Atlanta Intelligencer,* Apr. 5, 1863. On St. Lucah and other sites in Georgia, see *Confederate Baptist,* Mar. 11, 1863; Faust, *Confederate Nationalism,* 52; George C. Rable, *Civil Wars: Women and the Crisis of Southern Nationalism* (Urbana, 1989), 108–111.
2. For the major contributions, see the secondary sources cited in the preceding note. E. P. Thompson's idea of moral economy has been very influential; see Escott, "Moral Economy of the Crowd," and Faust, *Confederate Nationalism,* 52–57. The groundbreaking article is E. P. Thompson, "The Moral Economy of the English Crowd in the Eighteenth Century," *Past and Present,* 50 (Feb. 1971).
3. Jefferson Davis, "Remarks at Savannah," Oct. 31, 1863, *PJD,* 10:44; Jefferson Davis to Robert E. Lee, July 28, 1863, *PJD,* 9:307–311. The insistence of some historians on the causational primacy of developments on the battlefield has contributed to needless division between social and military historians, and the binary nature of arguments over Confederate defeat. For one example, see Gary Gallagher, *The Confederate War: How Popular Will, Nationalism, and Military Strategy Could Not Stave Off Defeat* (New York, 1997), 11. Perhaps the bridging role belongs to political historians focused on policy making.
4. On Atlanta, see *Atlanta Intelligencer,* Mar. 19, 20, 23, 26, 1863; Atlanta *Southern Confederacy,* Mar. 19, 1863; *Augusta Chronicle and Sentinel,* Apr. 5, 1863; Lack, "Law and Disorder." On Salisbury, see Mary C. Moore to Gov. Vance,

Mar. 21, 1863, and Michael Brown to Gov. Vance, Mar. 18, 1863, both box 163, ZBV; *Richmond Daily Examiner,* Mar. 27, 1863; Escott, "Moral Economy of the Crowd"; Bynum, *Unruly Women,* 125–126. On Mobile, see Amos, "All Absorbing Topics," 17–28.

5. *Richmond Daily Examiner,* Apr. 4, 24, 1863. On Mobile, see Amos, "All Absorbing Topics," 23.
6. *Atlanta Intelligencer,* Mar. 19, 20, 23, 26, 1863. On the numbers, see *Atlanta Southern Confederacy,* Mar. 19, 20, 25, 1863. Newspapers say the riot was Mar. 18; historian Michael Chesson, "Harlots or Heroines?" 136–137, says Mar. 16. Little is written about Atlanta, but see Lack, "Law and Disorder."
7. *Atlanta Intelligencer,* Mar. 19, 23, 26, 1863. The phrase "wives and daughters of soldiers" was repeated in other papers. See *Jackson Daily Southern Crisis,* Mar. 24, 1863; *Athens Southern Watchman,* Apr. 8, 1863. The *Atlanta Southern Confederacy* specifically identified the women as workers in government clothing factories and used the episode as an opportunity to rail against government seizures of private property; see Mar. 19, 1863.
8. On Salisbury, see Brown to Gov. Vance, Mar. 18, 1863, and Moore to Gov. Vance, Mar. 21, 1863, both box 163, ZBV.
9. Moore to Gov. Vance, Mar. 21, 1863, box 163, ZBV.
10. For Vance's response, see *Greensboro Patriot,* Apr. 9, 1863, quoted in Bynum, *Unruly Women,* 125–126; Brown to Gov. Vance, Mar. 18, 1863, box 163, ZBV; *Carolina Watchman,* Mar. 23, 1863, quoted in Escott, "Moral Economy of the Crowd," 9. The Salisbury riot was covered sympathetically in *Richmond Daily Examiner,* Mar. 27, 1863.
11. *Atlanta Southern Confederacy,* Apr. 6, 1863.
12. *Richmond Daily Examiner,* Apr. 4, 1863.
13. On previous reporting of the Salisbury riots, see *Richmond Daily Examiner,* Mar. 27, 1863. A number of historians have speculated that the Richmond women were inspired by the example of Salisbury, although the newspaper coverage comes later than reputed organizing. See Chesson, "Harlots or Heroines?" 136–137, and Tice, "Bread or Blood!" 14. For court proceedings, see coverage in *Richmond Daily Examiner* cited below, and Manarin, *Richmond at War.*
14. John B. Jones, *A Rebel War Clerk's Diary* (Philadelphia, 1866), vol. 1, 284–286. Jones's estimates of numbers (three hundred women and about a thousand followers) were upheld by Chesson, "Harlots or Heroines?" 138.
15. Jones, *Rebel War Clerk's Diary,* vol. 1, 286.
16. From the first, eyewitness accounts of the riot identified Mary Jackson as the organizer and leader. See *Richmond Daily Examiner,* Apr. 4, 1863; for "prime mover," "thief and harlot riot," lists of witnesses, and numbers of people indicted, see *Richmond Daily Examiner,* Apr. 4, 15, 3, 1863; Tice, "Bread or Blood!" 19; and Chesson, "Harlots or Heroines?" 162. All agreed that disproportionate numbers of men were arrested.
17. *Richmond Daily Examiner,* Apr. 6, 1863.
18. Ibid., Apr. 8, 24, 1863; Chesson, "Harlots or Heroines?" 161.
19. *Richmond Daily Examiner,* Apr. 24, 1863.

20. Jones's testimony reported in *Richmond Daily Examiner,* Apr. 6, 1863.
21. See the testimony of Colonel Bassett French and Mrs. Jamieson (who claimed it was her idea) in *Richmond Daily Examiner,* Apr. 6, 24, 1863. Government price was the rate paid for impressed goods, usually about half the market rate.
22. *Richmond Daily Examiner,* April 4, 13, 1863.
23. Ibid., Apr. 6, 8, 24, 1863.
24. Chesson, "Harlots or Heroines?" 144; *Richmond Daily Examiner,* Apr. 4, 6, 24, 1863.
25. Forty-four women and 29 men, according to Chesson, "Harlots or Heroines?" 156.
26. *Richmond Daily Examiner,* Apr. 4, 6, 7, 8, Oct. 12, 1863. On Mary Duke, see Chesson, "Harlots or Heroines?" 165. Jamieson got prison time, Jackson, inexplicably, did not.
27. For riots in Augusta, Milledgeville, and Columbus, see *Savannah Republican,* Apr. 13, 1863; *Turnwold Countryman,* Apr. 21, 1863; and *Atlanta Southern Confederacy,* Apr. 16, 1863. For Macon, see *Atlanta Southern Confederacy,* Apr. 24, 1863, and *Macon Confederate,* Apr. 1, 1863, reprinted in *Atlanta Intelligencer,* Apr. 5, 1863. On St. Lucah and other sites in Georgia, see Faust, *Confederate Nationalism,* 52, and Rable, *Civil Wars,* 108–111.
28. For social historians' readings, see especially Paul D. Escott, *Many Excellent People: Power and Privilege in North Carolina, 1850–1900* (Chapel Hill, 1985), 128; Escott, "Moral Economy of the Crowd"; Escott, "The Cry of the Sufferers: The Problem of Welfare in the Confederacy," *Civil War History* 23 (Sept. 1977): 228–240. Also see Bynum, *Unruly Women;* Bynum focuses on the particular victimization of the female poor. For cultural history readings, see especially Faust, *Confederate Nationalism; Faust* draws explicitly on Thompson, "Moral Economy of the English Crowd." Among other historians of the Richmond riots, there is mostly interpretive confusion. Douglas Tice calls the riots "a significant footnote to the history of the Civil War" (Tice, "Bread or Blood!" 19); Michael Chesson, who conducted the fullest inquiry, struggles to establish the significance of the events, suggesting in the end that the riots had some "slight" military effect "on the movements of the Army of Northern Virginia" ("Harlots or Heroines?" 173).
29. *Atlanta Intelligencer,* Mar. 20, 1863; *Inaugural Address of Governor Henry Allen to the Legislature of the State of Louisiana,* Jan. 25, 1864, LSU; North Carolina Soldiers of Lee's Army to Gov. Vance, Jan. 24, 1865, box 183, ZBV. On desertion and defeat, see Faust, *Mothers of Invention,* 243, and Faust, "Altars of Sacrifice: Confederate Women and the Narratives of War," *Journal of American History* 76 (Mar. 1990): 1200–28. But see also Ella Lonn, *Desertion during the Civil War* (New York, 1928), and Armstead Robinson, *Bitter Fruits of Bondage: The Demise of Slavery and the Collapse of the Confederacy, 1861–1865* (Charlottesville, 2005).
30. It is striking how little work has been done on public policy in the Confederacy or in Southern history in the Civil War era. One exception is Peter Wallenstein, *From Slave South to New South: Public Policy in Nineteenth-Century Georgia* (Chapel Hill, 1987). There is also no book on welfare or relief policy, although there are some article-length treatments of particular states. For

those, see Paul Escott, "Joseph E. Brown, Jefferson Davis and the Problem of Poverty in the Confederacy," *GHQ* 61 (Spring 1977): 59–71; Escott, "Poverty and Governmental Aid for the Poor in Confederate North Carolina," *North Carolina Historical Review* 61 (Oct. 1984): 462–480; William Blair, *Virginia's Private War: Feeding Body and Soul in the Confederacy, 1861–1865* (New York, 1998), 94–106; William Frank Zornow, "Aid for the Indigent Families of Soldiers in Virginia, 1861–1865," *Virginia Magazine of History and Biography* 66 (Oct. 1958): 454–459; and Zornow, "State Aid for Indigent Soldiers and Families, Louisiana, 1861–1865," *Louisiana Historical Quarterly* 39 (July 1956): 375–380. A full treatment of Confederate welfare would have to be reconstructed from widely dispersed state and county records.

31. There is no comparative study of wartime relief policy in the Union and Confederate states, so comparisons are difficult to make with confidence. One study of Massachusetts claims that that state distinguished itself with the level of public assistance provided, but the author offers no evidence and assumes, quite wrongly, that the Confederate states failed to develop a comprehensive welfare program; indeed, based on the numbers the author cites of monies spent and clients served in Massachusetts, arguments about the greater scale of Southern welfare programs seem warranted. See Richard F. Miller, "For His Wife, His Widow, and His Orphan: Massachusetts and Family Aid during the Civil War," *Massachusetts Historical Review* 6 (2004): 71–106. This judgment seemingly is confirmed by Judith Giesberg's recent study *Army at Home: Women and the Civil War on the Northern Home Front* (Chapel Hill, 2009), chap. 1. Historians of the Confederacy have mostly missed the connection between the riots and welfare policy. See Escott, "Poverty and Governmental Aid," 466; Escott, *After Secession: Jefferson Davis and the Failure of Confederate Nationalism* (Baton Rouge, 1978); and Robinson, *Bitter Fruits of Bondage,* 204. Both miss the timing of the calls for reform and amplified welfare.

32. *Atlanta Intelligencer,* Mar. 19, 1863; Chesson, "Harlots or Heroines?" 149. On the upsurge of activity around welfare, see Faust, *Confederate Nationalism;* Escott, "Moral Economy of the Crowd"; and Robinson, *Bitter Fruits of Bondage.*

33. *Atlanta Intelligencer,* Mar. 19, 20, 26, 23, 1863. On Atlanta, see also Lack, "Law and Disorder."

34. Amos, "All Absorbing Topics," 23–26; Manarin, *Richmond at War,* 312, 314–315, 317, 320; *Richmond Daily Examiner,* Apr. 23, 1863 (reprinting an account of riot in the *New York Herald*); Tice, "Bread or Blood!" 19, calls the responses in the cities "forerunners of the modern welfare system." On the police response, see also Chesson, "Harlots or Heroines?" 173, and Jones, *Rebel War Clerk's Diary,* vol. 1, 286, where Jones claims that the secretary of war declined permission to move troops into Richmond from camps near the city to "suppress the women and children by a summary process."

35. Faust noticed "the public debate" that erupted over "the justness of [the women's] ends" (*Confederate Nationalism,* 55).

36. Wallenstein, *Slave South to New South,* 42, 111, 114, 116–117; Escott, "Poverty and Governmental Aid," 464; Escott, *After Secession,* 157–159; Zornow, "Aid," 455–457; and Zornow, "State Aid." For one local set of records, see *Report of*

the Board for the Relief of Families of Soldiers in the Parishes of St. Philip and St. Michael (Charleston, 1863), 8.

37. *Rome Weekly Courier*, Jan. 3, 1862, quoted in Escott, "Problem of Poverty in the Confederacy," 64.
38. Robinson, *Bitter Fruits of Bondage*, 118–131, 202–205, 215–216; John Gill Shorter to Randolph (Secretary of War), May 30, 1862, LRCSW, roll 71. For a description of the letters Shorter was receiving, see Robinson, *Bitter Fruits of Bondage*, 121–124, quotation on 122.
39. Robinson, *Bitter Fruits of Bondage*, 184, 186–187, 185; Secretary of War Seddon to President Davis, Jan. 3, 1863, *PJD*, 9:6–7, 568–569. On the congressional debate, see also Faust, *Confederate Nationalism*, 54, and Albert Burton Moore, *Conscription and Conflict in the Confederacy* (New York, 1924), 70.
40. Robinson, *Bitter Fruits of Bondage*, 185, spoke only of the men.
41. Ibid., 130, 203, 125; Escott, *After Secession*, 151; Mrs. Silia Hoge to Vance, Feb. 15, 1863, box 162, ZBV; Escott, "Poverty and Governmental Aid," 471; F. N. Boney, *John Letcher of Virginia: The Story of Virginia's Civil War Governor* (Tuscaloosa, 1966), 187.
42. Governor Joseph Brown, *Message of March 25, 1863*, in Allen Daniel Candler, ed., *Confederate Records of the State of Georgia*, 6 vols. (1909–1911; New York, 1972), 2:370; Zebulon Vance to President Davis, Mar. 31, 1863, HU. For the emphasis on disaffection and defeat, and the failure to note the political pressure exerted by rioting women, see Bell Irvin Wiley, *Confederate Women* (Westport, 1975); Rable, *Civil Wars;* Faust, *Mothers of Invention;* Faust, "Altars of Sacrifice"; Escott, "Poverty and Governmental Aid."
43. On the public debate, see Faust, *Confederate Nationalism*, 55.
44. Candler, *Confederate Records of the State of Georgia*, 2:367–395, quotations on 369–370; *Atlanta Intelligencer*, Mar. 24, 1863.
45. Wallenstein, *From Slave South to New South*, 105; Escott, "Problem of Poverty in the Confederacy," 65, 69; *Turnwold Countryman*, May 3, 1864. On welfare policy in the Confederate States more generally, see Escott, *After Secession*, 156.
46. Paul Escott, "Poverty and Governmental Aid," 462–480 (number on 480).
47. The evolution of the law can be traced in the following: *Public Laws of the State of North Carolina Passed by the General Assembly at the Session of 1858–59* (Raleigh, 1859); *Public Laws of the State of North Carolina Passed by the General Assembly at the Adjourned Session of 1862–1863* (Raleigh, 1863), 63–64; *Public Laws of the State of North Carolina Passed by the General Assembly at Its Session of 1862–1863* (Raleigh, 1863), 33–35; *Public Laws of the State of North Carolina Passed by the General Assembly at the Session of 1864–1865* (Raleigh, 1865), 12–13, 66–67. On the 1865 proposal for a state tax in kind, see *Journal of the Senate of the General Assembly of the State of North Carolina at the Adjourned Session of 1865* (Raleigh, 1866), 52. The line item in the North Carolina budget for widows pensions in 1856 was $180. See *Public Laws of the State of North Carolina Passed by the General Assembly at the Session of 1856–1857, Statements of the Comptroller of Public Accounts for the Two Fiscal Years Ending Oct. 31, 1855 and 1856* (Raleigh, 1857), 159. The evolution of welfare policy in Mississippi followed much the same pattern.

48. *Journal of the House of Commons of the General Assembly of the State of North Carolina at Its Adjourned Session, 1863* (Raleigh, 1864), 10.
49. Special Term of Randolph County Court (Convened to Implement Act of General Assembly), June 21, 1861, folder 1, Randolph County, Misc. Records (Civil War Records), Court Order for Aid, NCDAH.
50. For the Orange County and Duplin County numbers (1863), see Escott, "Poverty and Governmental Aid," 477–480. For 1865, see J. W. Norwood, Report of the County Corn Agent, Jan. 4, 1865, folder 3, Orange County, Misc. Records, NCDAH; Randolph County financing in Report of the Committee on Finance, folder 3, Randolph County, Misc. Records (Civil War Records), NCDAH. For the instructions to the agent, see Provisions for Families of Soldiers, folder 1, Orange County Court, Feb. term, Mar. 3, 1863, Orange County Misc. Records, NCDAH.
51. Provisions for the Families of Soldiers, 1863–1865, "A List of persons who got county [corn] and the amount got by each person" and "A List of soldiers families in C. Hill District and No. Children," folder 1 (1863), Orange County Misc. Records, NCDAH. See also "A List of the Tithe corn deliverd at the mill of the heirs of George C. Ray decs for the benefit of soldiers wives and other needy persons," Apr. 18, 1864, folder 2 (1864), Orange County Misc. Records, NCDAH.
52. Provisions for Families of Soldiers, 1863–1865, County Corn Regulations, folder 1 (1863), and Provisions for Families of Soldiers, folder 1 (1863), Orange County Court, Feb. term, Mar. 3, 1863, both Orange County Misc. Records, NCDAH. For Mississippi, see *Laws of the State of Mississippi* (Selma, 1864), esp. "An Act to Better Provide for the Families of Soldiers" (approved Dec. 2, 1863), 113.
53. Mary K. Walker to Gov. Zebulon Vance, June 7, 1863, box 166, ZBV.
54. Governor's Message, Dec. 20, 1862, in *Journal of the House of Representatives of the State of Mississippi* (1862), 10; Governor's Message, Nov. 3, 1863, and Inaugural Address [Governor Clark] Nov. 16, 1863, both in *Journal of the House of Representatives of the State of Mississippi* (1864), 36; Governor's Message, Feb. 20, 1865, in *Journal of the Senate of the State of Mississippi* (1865), 6–8.
55. Governor's Message, Nov. 3, 1863, in *Journal of the House of Representatives of the State of Mississippi* (1864), 96, and *Laws of the State of Mississippi* (1864), 32; Governor's Message, Feb. 20, 1865, in *Journal of the Senate of the State of Mississippi* (1865), 8; *Journal of the Senate of the State of Mississippi (1862–63),* entry for Dec. 1, 1863.
56. Theda Skocpol, *Protecting Soldiers and Mothers: The Political Origins of Social Policy in the United States* (Cambridge, Mass., 1992).
57. Zebulon B. Vance to President Davis, Mar. 31, 1863, HU.
58. A. M. Keilry to Governor Letcher, Mar. 20, 1863, John Letcher Papers, ser. 6, VHS; William Smith to Braxton Bragg, June 6, 1864, HU; Moore, *Conscription and Conflict,* 39, 42, 44.
59. *O.R.*, ser. 4, 2:468, 475–477; Thomas S. Terry to President Davis, Nov. 18, 1863, *PJD*, 10:78; *Richmond Daily Examiner,* Apr. 15, 1863. On Davis's recognition of the new conditions, see, for example, Jefferson Davis to Robert E.

Lee, July 28, 1863, *PJD,* 9:307–311. Robinson, *Bitter Fruits of Bondage,* 204–205, discusses Davis's address with no consideration of the timing of the food riots.

60. Jefferson Davis, Speech at Jackson, *PJD,* 8:565–584, quotation at 569.
61. "Speech of Jefferson Davis at Augusta," in Dunbar Rowland, ed., *Jefferson Davis, Constitutionalist: His Letters and Speeches,* 10 vols. (1923; New York, 1973), 6: 359–360; William J. Cooper, *Jefferson Davis, American* (New York, 2002), 493–494.
62. Escott, *After Secession,* 141–142.
63. S. S. Harney et al. to Honorable James A. Seddon, Nov. 4, 1863, folder 4, Marmaduke Swain Robins Papers, folder 4, SHC; J. W. Norwood, Report of the County Corn Agent, Jan. 4, 1865, folder 3, Provisions for Families of Soldiers, 1863–1865, Orange County Misc. Records, NCDAH.
64. Wallenstein, *From Old South to New South,* 121–128; "General Early's Orders to Protect Soldiers' Families Supplies," Nov. 12, broadside, box 2, McDowell Family Papers, UVA.
65. Miller, "For His Wife"; Giesberg, *Army at Home,* chaps. 1–2.
66. Skocpol, *Protecting Soldiers and Mothers;* Megan McClintock, "Civil War Pensions and the Reconstruction of Union Families," *Journal of American History* 83 (Sept. 1996): 456–480. McClintock's article says virtually nothing about the wartime provision of relief to the wives of *living* soldiers. On the maternalist politics and origins of the welfare state, see Linda Gordon, ed., *Women, the State and Welfare* (Madison, 1990).
67. Frances Beecher Perkins, "Two Years with a Colored Regiment: A Woman's Experience," *New England Magazine,* Jan. 1898, James C. Beecher Papers, Schlesinger Library, Radcliffe Institute for Advanced Study, Harvard University; William McKee Evans, *Ballots and Fence Rails: Reconstruction on the Lower Cape Fear* (Chapel Hill, 1967), 38; Eric Foner, *A Short History of Reconstruction, 1863–1877* (New York, 1990), 69. See also Stephen V. Ash, *When the Yankees Came: Conflict and Chaos in the Occupied South, 1861–1865* (Chapel Hill, 1995). One American Missionary Association agent was disgusted by the demands of ex-Confederate refugees who came for aid; they were in desperate condition, displaced and living on the levees, but were disinclined to work, "proud, arrogant and self-important." See Bardwell to Strichey, Vicksburg, Dec. 24, 1864, American Missionary Association Manuscripts, Mississippi, roll 1 (originals at Fisk University). The AMA records make it clear that agents were prepared to provide welfare only to women and children.
68. F. N. Adams to Honorable Jos. E. Brown, July 28, 1863, box 22, and State of Georgia, Houston County, Clerk's Office, Inferior Court, July 26, 1864, box 23, both GSF. The governor's papers are full of requests for clarification, confirmation of exempt status, or petitions for appointments that carry exemption by men who claimed soldiers' wives wanted them to serve. For Louisiana, see E. C. Smart to Gov. Allen, Apr. 8, 1865, box 1, folder 1, James Calvert Wise Papers, LSU. For Virginia, see Henry Haskins [Justice of the Floyd County Court] to Gov. William Smith, Jan. 16, 1865, folder 1, box 5, Governor William Smith Papers, LVA.

69. William N. Harris et al. to His Excellency Jefferson Davis, May 6, 1864, in Ira Berlin et. al., eds., *Freedom: A Documentary History of Emancipation, 1861–1867,* ser. 1, vol. 1: *The Destruction of Slavery* (Cambridge, UK, 1985), 756–758, quotation at 757; Harrison A. Trexler, "The Opposition of Planters to the Employment of Slaves as Laborers by the Confederacy," *Mississippi Valley Historical Review* 27, no. 2 (Sept. 1940): 218; H. M. Gray to Col. S. Blount, June 1, 1864, in Berlin et al., *Destruction of Slavery,* 758–760. On Bladensboro, N.C., see J. W. Ellis and others to Governor Vance, Apr. 13, 1864, box 176, ZBV.
70. List of the Wives and others of the Volunteers in the Black Jack District, in Littles Company, signed J. C. Ellerbee, Aug. 22, 1862, in folder 4 (Relief Committee for Volunteers Families, Richmond County, N.C. 1861–1863), Leak-Wall Papers, SHC.
71. Lidia Smith to Mr. Robert Bostick, Aug. 18, 1862; Elizabeth McJaffee to Mr. Robert L. Steele, Sept. 26, 1862; Mary Driggers to Mr. R. L. Steel, n.d.; D. W. Gibson to R. L. Steele [re: Mrs. Margaret McKinnon], Aug. 1862; ? to Webb Lane, Aug. 17, 1862; all in folder 4 (Relief Committee for Volunteers Families, Richmond County, N.C., 1861–1863), Leak-Wall Papers, SHC. The handwriting is very hard to read on these documents; citations of names represent my best efforts at deciphering.
72. Arabella Davis to Gov. Vance, Jan. 11, 1864, box 173, Elizabeth Sampson to Gov. Vance, July 19, 1863, box 168, and Martha A. Allen to Gov. Vance, May 6, 1863, box 165, all ZBV.
73. See *Laws of the State of Mississippi Passed at a Called Session Held in Macon, August 1864* (Meridian, 1864), 9.
74. Anstio Carver to Vance, "Near the 1st of October 1863," box 170, and S. S. Horner to Vance, Nov. 3, 1863, box 171, both ZBV. Brown was in receipt of letters about the indigent families of deserters in the fall of 1863. See J. W. Booth to Governor Brown, Sept. 14, 1863, box 24, GSF.
75. N. B. Dozier to Joseph E. Brown, Governor, Sept. 2, 1863, box 29, and G. R. Brown to Governor of the State of Georgia, Nov. 2, 1863, box 25, both GSF; Henry Haskins to Governor Smith, Jan. 16, 1865, William Smith Papers, box 5, folder 1, LVA.
76. Lucy S. James to Gov. Vance, Sept. 1, 1864, box 180, ZBV.
77. *Public Laws of the State of North Carolina Passed by the General Assembly at the Sessions of 1866–67* (Raleigh, 1867), 8–9; *State v. Martha Sheets* and *State v. Jemima Hogden, Mary Lucas,* et al., both spring term, 1866, Criminal Action Papers, Montgomery County, NCDAH.
78. For "social" citizenship or citizenship as a "social standing," see esp. T. H. Marshall and Tom Bottomore, *Citizenship and Social Class* (London, 1992), 3–51; Judith N. Shklar, *American Citizenship: The Quest for Inclusion* (Cambridge, UK, 1991). See also Rogers M. Smith, *Civic Ideals: Conflicting Visions of Citizenship in U.S. History* (New Haven, 1997), for an even broader approach.
79. Susan Zaeske, *Signatures of Citizenship: Petitioning, Antislavery and Women's Political Identity* (Chapel Hill, 2003).
80. On the salience of citizenship as a postwar development, see William J. Novak, *The People's Welfare: Law and Regulation in Nineteenth Century America*

(Chapel Hill, 1996); and Michael Vorenberg, *Final Freedom: The Civil War, the Abolition of Slavery, and the Thirteenth Amendment* (Cambridge, UK, 2001). Historians have been much more open to exploring alternative historical narratives and ways of making political claims when it comes to slaves. See Laura F. Edwards, "Status without Rights: African Americans and the Tangled History of Law and Governance in the Nineteenth-Century U.S. South," *AHR* 112, no. 2 (Apr. 2007): 365–392; Steven Hahn, *A Nation under Our Feet: African American Political Life from Slavery to the Great Migration* (Cambridge, Mass., 2003).

81. Partha Chatterjee, *The Politics of the Governed: Reflections on Popular Politics in Most of the World* (New York, 2004); on gender, see 76. Attention to gender and the particular practices of women's politics thus sharpens the analysis and establishes its reach. See also Ranajit Guha, *Elementary Aspects of Peasant Insurgency in Colonial India* (Durham, 1999), and a very moving short essay by Guha, "The Small Voice of History," in *Subaltern Studies IX,* ed. Shahid Amin and Dipesh Chakrabarty (Oxford, 1996), 1–12; James Scott, *Domination and the Arts of Resistance: Hidden Transcripts* (New Haven, 1990).

82. Chatterjee, *Politics of the Governed,* 47, 35, 59–60, 46, 69. Here I mean only to indicate the usefulness of Chatterjee's idea of political society and the politics of the governed, and not to dismiss in any way the difference in the context and forms of the two democracies.

6. "AMOR PATRIAE"

1. Farewell Address, *PJD,* 7:18–23; *Scott v. Sandford,* 60 U.S. (19 How.) 393, 427 (1857).
2. Anthony E. Kaye, *Joining Places: Slave Neighborhoods in the Old South* (Chapel Hill, 2007); Thomas D. Morris, *Southern Slavery and the Law, 1619–1860* (Chapel Hill, 1996); Charles S. Sydnor, "The Southerner and the Laws," *Journal of Southern History* 6 (Feb. 1940): 3–23.
3. James A. Seddon to President Davis, Nov. 28, 1864, *O.R.,* ser. 4, 2:851–853.
4. M. I. Finley, *Ancient Slavery and Modern Ideology* (New York, 1980), 38.
5. R. R. Palmer, *The Age of Democratic Revolution: A Political History of Europe and America, 1760–1800,* 2 vols. (Princeton, 1959); Eric Hobsbawm, *The Age of Revolution: 1789–1848* (1962; repr., New York, 1969); Jerome Blum, *The End of the Old Order in Rural Europe* (Princeton, 1978); Jeremy Adelman, *Sovereignty and Revolution in the Iberian Atlantic* (Princeton, 2006).
6. Blum, *End of the Old Order,* 373, 371.
7. Robin Blackburn, *The Overthrow of Colonial Slavery, 1776–1848* (New York, 1988); C. L. R. James, *The Black Jacobins: Toussaint L'Ouverture and the San Domingo Revolution* (1938; repr., New York, 1989); Carolyn E. Fick, *The Making of Haiti: The Saint Domingue Revolution from Below* (Knoxville, 1990); Rebecca J. Scott, *Slave Emancipation in Cuba: The Transition to Free Labor, 1860–1899* (Princeton, 1985).
8. Donald Robinson, *Slavery in the Structure of American Politics* (1971; repr.,

New York, 1979); David Brion Davis, *The Problem of Slavery in the Age of Revolution, 1770–1823* (Ithaca, 1975). On the Civil War, see Steven Hahn, "Class and State in Postemancipation Societies: Southern Planters in Comparative Perspective," *AHR* 95 (Feb. 1990): 75–98; Eric Foner, *Reconstruction: America's Unfinished Revolution, 1863–1877* (New York, 1988); Richard Franklin Bensel, *Yankee Leviathan: The Origins of Central State Authority in America, 1859–1877* (Cambridge, UK, 1990). William Novak's recent challenge to the idea of the United States as a "weak state" is interesting but says nothing about slavery and state formation in the antebellum United States. See Novak, "The Myth of the 'Weak' American State," *AHR* 113, no. 3 (2008): 752–772.

9. Confederate Constitution, reprinted in Emory M. Thomas, *The Confederate Nation, 1861–1865* (New York, 1979), 307–322 . See also the state constitutions discussed in Drew Gilpin Faust, *The Creation of Confederate Nationalism: Ideology and Identity in the Civil War South* (Baton Rouge, 1988).
10. Governor Joseph E. Brown to Jefferson Davis, June 21, 1862, *PJD,* 8:262–263.
11. John A. Campbell to Jefferson Davis, Apr. 28, 1861, *PJD,* 7:136–141, quotation on 138.
12. *Richmond Dispatch,* Apr. 2, 1861, in Robert F. Durden, *The Gray and the Black: The Confederate Debate on Emancipation* (Baton Rouge, 1972), 14.
13. Alexander H. Stephens, "Cornerstone Address," in Jon L. Wakelyn, ed., *Southern Pamphlets on Secession, November 1860–April 1861* (Chapel Hill, 1996), 408.
14. A. P. Hayne to His Excellency Jefferson Davis, Aug. 8, 1861, in Ira Berlin et al., eds., *Freedom: A Documentary History of Emancipation, 1861–1867,* ser. 1, vol. 1: *The Destruction of Slavery* (Cambridge, UK, 1985), 695–696; Sarah Lawton to ? [sister-in-law], 1861, Alexander Robert Lawton Papers, SHC, in *RASP,* ser. J, pt. 3, reel 26; Jefferson Davis to Gustavus W. Smith, Oct. 10, 1861, *PJD,* 7:355–356.
15. G. M. Figh to Hon. L. P. Walker, Apr. 26, 1861, no. 477, roll 1, RG 109 (M437), LRCSW, 1861–1865; Joseph L. Dutton to Hon. L. P. Walker, Apr. 22, 1861, LRCSW, roll 1.
16. W. S. Turner to Hon. L. P. Walker, July 17, 1861, and A. T. Bledsoe to W. S. Turner, Aug. 2 1861, in *O.R.,* ser. 4, 1:482, 529; George A. Gardner to His Excellency Joseph Brown, June 30, 1861, box 31, GSF.
17. W. S. Turner to L. P. Walker, July 17, 1861, *O.R.,* ser. 4, 1:482; A. T. Bledsoe to W. S. Turner, Aug. 2, 1861, *O.R.,* ser. 4 1:529.
18. Alexander Stephens, "Cornerstone Address," and *New Orleans Bee,* Mar. 16, 1861, in Durden, *The Gray and the Black,* 8, 10–11.
19. Sarah Lawton [to her sister in law], Dec. 30, 1860, in Alexander Robert Lawton Papers, SHC, in *RASP,* ser. J, pt. 3, reel 26; Francis W. Pickens to Jefferson Davis, Mar. 17, 1861, *PJD,* 7:70–71; William H. Lee to Jefferson Davis, May 4, 1861, in Ira Berlin, Joseph Reidy, and Leslie Rowland, eds., *Freedom: A Documentary History of Emancipation, 1861–1867,* ser. 2: *The Black Military Experience* (Cambridge, UK, 1982), 282.
20. Henry Bram et al. to Major General O. O. Howard, quoted in Ira Berlin et al.,

"The Terrain of Freedom: The Struggle over the Meaning of Free Labor in the U.S. South," *History Workshop Journal,* no. 22 (Autumn 1986): 127.

21. William Webb, *The History of William Webb, Composed by Himself* (Detroit, 1873), docsouth.unc.edu/neh/webb/webb.html, 13, 26, 16, 18, 23, 30.
22. Steven Hahn, *A Nation under Our Feet: African American Political Life from Slavery to the Great Migration* (Cambridge, Mass., 2003). But see also Walter Johnson, *Soul by Soul: Life inside the Antebellum Slave Market* (Cambridge Mass., 1999), and Julius Sherrard Scott III, "The Common Wind: Currents of Afro-American Communication in the Era of the Haitian Revolution" (Ph.D. diss., Duke University, 1986).
23. Steven Hahn calls this "the social division of politics" (*A Nation under Our Feet,* 4).
24. Rev. W. H. Robinson, *From Log Cabin to the Pulpit, or, Fifteen Years in Slavery* (Eau Claire, 1913), docsouth.unc.edu/fpn/robinson/robinson.html, 76, 92–93; Henry Clay Bruce, *The New Man: Twenty-Nine Years a Slave, Twenty-Nine Years a Free Man* (York, 1895), docsouth.unc.edu/fpn/bruce/bruce.html, 86.
25. Bruce, *The New Man,* 85; William Henry Singleton, *Recollections of My Slavery Days* (Peekskill, 1922), docsouth.unc.edu/neh/singleton/menu.html, 6; Booker T. Washington, *Up from Slavery: An Autobiography* (Garden City, 1900, 1901), 8. For confirmation of those alliances in criminal prosecution records, see *State v. Peter Shartle* [?], Aug. 10, 1861, Criminal Action Papers 1777–1941, Richmond County, County Records, NCDAH.
26. Erskine Clarke, *Dwelling Place: A Plantation Epic* (New Haven, 2005), 49; Laurent Dubois, *A Colony of Citizens: Revolution and Slave Emancipation in the French Caribbean, 1787–1804* (Chapel Hill, 2004), 30–84.
27. Robinson, *From Log Cabin to the Pulpit,* 25–28.
28. Testimony of Corporal Octave Johnson before the American Freedmen's Inquiry Commission, in Berlin et al., *Destruction of Slavery,* 217. *Marronage* is a French word for "desertion." On marronage in the Caribbean and its use by women slaves, see Barbara Bush, *Slave Women in Caribbean Society, 1650–1838* (Kingston, 1990); Fick, *The Making of Haiti,* 6, 110, 152; Blackburn, *Overthrow of Colonial Slavery,* 55–56. Carolyn Fick quotes Orlando Patterson's claim that "all sustained slave revolts must acquire a Maroon dimension," using guerilla warfare to counter superior force of their masters. David Geggus is more skeptical. See Geggus, *Haitian Revolutionary Studies* (Bloomington, 2002), 69–80.
29. Bishop L. J. Coppin, *Unwritten History,* docsouth.unc.edu/church/coppin/coppin.html; Kate Drumgoold, *A Slave Girl's Story, Being an Autobiography of Kate Drumgoold* (Brooklyn, 1898), docsouth.unc.edu/neh/drumgoold/drumgoold.html, 32.
30. John Quincy Adams, *Narrative of the Life of John Quincy Adams, When in Slavery, and Now as a Freeman* (Harrisburg, 1872), docsouth.unc.edu/neh/adams/adams.html, 6; David Gavin Diary, Apr. 4, 1862, SHC, in *RASP,* ser. J, pt. 3, reel 10; Jacob Stroyer, *Sketches of My Life in the South, Part 1* (Salem, 1879), docsouth.unc.edu/neh/stroyer/stroyer.html, 26; Washington, *Up from Slavery,* 7–8.

31. Adams, *Life of John Quincy Adams,* 6; Bruce, *The New Man,* 85, 93; Mrs. Kate E. R. Pickard, *The Kidnapped and the Ransomed: Being the Personal Recollections of Peter Still and His Wife "Vina," after Forty Years of Slavery* (Syracuse, 1856), docsouth.unc.edu/neh/pickard/pickard.html, 159–160; Washington, *Up from Slavery,* 7–8.
32. Clarke, *Narrative of the Suffering of Lewis Clarke* (Boston, 1845), docsouth .unc.edu/neh/clarke/clarke.html, 82; Susan E. O'Donovan, *Becoming Free in the Cotton South* (Cambridge, Mass., 2007), 54.
33. Bruce, *The New Man,* 93; Washington, *Up from Slavery,* 8.
34. Steven A. Channing, *Crisis of Fear: Secession in South Carolina* (New York, 1970), 39–40.
35. *Richmond Dispatch,* Jan. 3, 1861. For prophetic rumor, see Dubois, *A Colony of Citizens,* 85. On rumor in the Civil War and the nineteenth-century South, see Steven Hahn, "'Extravagant Expectations' of Freedom: Rumour, Political Struggle, and the Christmas Insurrection Scare of 1865 in the American South," *Past and Present* 157 (Nov. 1997): 122–158; Yael Sternhell, "Communicating War: The Culture of Information in Richmond during the Civil War," *Past and Present* 203 (Feb. 2009): 175–205.
36. Susie King Taylor, *A Black Woman's Civil War Memoirs,* ed. Patricia Romero and Willie Lee Rose, eds. (New York, 1988), 32; Louis Hughes, *Thirty Years a Slave: From Bondage to Freedom* (Milwaukee, 1897), docsouth.unc.edu/fpn /hughes/hughes.html, 111.
37. Mattie J. Jackson, *The Story of Mattie J. Jackson: Her Parentage, Experience of Eighteen Years in Slavery,* written and arr. by Dr. L. S. Thomson, as Given by Mattie (Lawrence, 1866), docsouth.unc.edu/jacksonm/Jackson.html, 11.
38. Robinson, *From Log Cabin to Pulpit,* 76–77.
39. Charles Izard Manigault to My Cher Louis, Jan. 19, 1861, box 4, Louis Manigault Papers, DU.
40. On the Manigault operations, see William Dusinberre, *Them Dark Days: Slavery in the American Rice Swamps* (New York, 1996). In Dusinberre's view, the Manigault plantations epitomize the overweening power of the masters and the severely limited scope of agency of the slaves. "Not a single substantial slave insurrection occurred in the United States between 1831 and 1865," Dusinberre argues (122–123).
41. Louis Manigault, Slave List, Apr. 22, 1860, Manigault Family Papers, ser. 1, folder 5, SHC, reprinted in James Clifton, ed., *Life and Labor on Argyle Island: Letters and Documents of a Savannah River Rice Plantation, 1833–1867* (Charlottesville, 1978), 295–297; William Capers Sr. to Charles Manigault, June 13, 1860, box 4, Louis Manigault Papers, DU.
42. Louis Manigault, Slave List, Apr. 22, 1860, ser. 1, folder 5, Manigault Family Papers, SHC; William Capers to Louis Manigault, Aug. 19, 1860, William Capers to Louis Manigault, Oct. 31, 1860, William Capers to Louis Manigault, Nov. 3, 1860, and William Capers to Louis Manigault, Nov. 10, 1860, all box 4, Louis Manigault Papers, DU.
43. Charles Izard Manigault to My Cher Louis, Jan. 19, 1861, box 4, Louis Manigault Papers, DU.

44. G. E. Manigault to My Dear Brother [Louis], Jan. 21, 1861, Charles Manigault to My Cher Louis, Jan. 19, 1861, both box 4, Louis Manigault Papers, DU.
45. Dusinberre, *Them Dark Days,* 167.
46. Louis Manigault to Fannie Habersham Manigault, Nov. 11, 1861, box 4, Louis Manigault Papers, DU; Louis Manigault, Statement of Sales, Gowrie Plantation, June 12, 1862, ser. 1, folder 5, Manigault Family Papers, SHC; Willie Lee Rose, *Rehearsal for Reconstruction: The Port Royal Experiment* (New York, 1964), 11.
47. Louis Manigault to Charles Manigault, Gowrie Plantation, Nov. 24, Dec. 5, 1861, both reprinted in Clifton, *Life and Labor,* 326–327; Louis Manigault, Statement of Sales, June 12, 1862, ser. 1, folder 5, Manigault Family Papers, SHC; Charles Manigault to Mr. Capers, Jan. 26, 1862, William Capers to Charles Manigault, Nov. 14, 1861, both box 4, Louis Manigault Papers, DU.
48. Charles Izard Manigault to Mr. Capers, Jan. 26, 1862, box 4, Louis Manigault Papers, DU; Louis Manigault, Statement of Sales, June 12, 1862, ser. 1, folder 5, Manigault Family Papers, SHC.
49. Slave list, "List of Negroes who were sent from Gowrie to Silk Hope 21st Feb. 1862 and are there to remain for the present," Louis Manigault Papers, DU, and Charles Manigault to Louis Manigault, Apr. 30, 1865, both reprinted in Clifton, *Life and Labor,* 340, 353–354; Louis Manigault, June 12, 1862, ser. 1, folder 5, Manigault Family Papers, SHC; Dusinberre, *Them Dark Days,* 147, 130–131.
50. Dusinberre, *Them Dark Days,* 128.
51. Louis Manigault to Charles Manigault, Dec. 5, 1861, in Clifton, *Life and Labor,* 326–327; Slave list, "List of Negroes who were sent from Gowrie to Silk Hope 21st Feb. 1862," Louis Manigault Papers, DU; Louis Manigault, Mar. 13, 1863, Plantation Records, folder 5, ser. 1, Manigault Family Papers, SHC; William Capers to Charles Manigault, Sept. 15, 1863, and William Capers to Charles Manigault, Sept. 28, 1863, both in Clifton, *Life and Labor,* 345; Dusinberre, *Them Dark Days,* 165.
52. Louis Manigault, Visit to Gowrie and East Hermitage Plantations, Mar. 22, 1867, ser. 1, folder 5, Manigault Family Papers, SHC.
53. Gabriel E. Manigault to Louis Manigault, Dec. 11, 1861, Charles Izard Manigault to Mr. Capers, Jan. 26, 1862, both box 4, Louis Manigault Papers, DU.
54. The most comprehensive account is contained in the series *Freedom: A Documentary History of Emancipation, 1861–1867,* edited by Ira Berlin et al., but see also the host of excellent regional studies cited in notes below.
55. G. W. Gayle, to Hon. Jefferson Davis, May 22, 1861, in Berlin et al., *Destruction of Slavery,* 781–782; Capt. J. P. A. DuPont to Gov. Brown, July 29, 1861, box 29, GSF.
56. How [?] Hines to Governor J. J. Pettus, May 14, 1861, roll 3, ser. 757: Gov. John Jones Pettus, Correspondence and Papers, 1859–1863 and Undated, MDAH. "Trial testimonies" are recorded in Lemuel Conner Papers, ser. 5, folder 329, "Slave Uprising Testimony," LSU, and in William J. Minor Papers, Plantation Diary, 1858–1861, LSU. For the fullest analysis and reprint of key documents,

see Winthrop D. Jordan, *Tumult and Silence at Second Creek: An Inquiry into a Civil War Slave Conspiracy,* rev. ed. (Baton Rouge, 1995), 268–352.

57. "Testimonies" of (in order of quotations): Alfred, Nelson, George, George, Alfred, Harvey, and John, in "Slave Uprising Testimony," Lemuel Conner Papers, LSU; William J. Minor Plantation Diary, Oct. 3, 1861, William J. Minor Papers, LSU; Amelia Montgomery to My Dear Husband, Oct. 14, 1861, folder 5, box 1, Joseph A. Montgomery Papers, LSU.
58. "Testimonies" of (in order of quotations): John, Harry Scott, George, Wesley, George, Harvey, and Dennis, in "Slave Uprising Testimony," Lemuel Conner Papers, LSU; Thavolia Glymph, *Out of the House of Bondage: The Transformation of the Plantation Household* (Cambridge, UK, 2008).
59. Justin J. Behrend, "Building Democracy from Scratch: African-American Politics and Community in the Postemancipation Natchez District" (Ph.D. diss., Northwestern University, 2006), 37.
60. Ibid., 45–48; William J. Minor Plantation Diary, 1858–1861, Sept. 25, 1861, William J. Minor Papers, LSU.
61. "Moment of truth" is Eugene Genovese's moving phrase; see Eugene D. Genovese, *Roll, Jordan, Roll: The World the Slaves Made* (New York, 1974), 97–112.
62. Berlin et al., *Destruction of Slavery,* 72, 70–72, 88–90; John Blassingame, ed., *Slave Testimony: Two Centuries of Letters, Speeches, Interviews and Autobiographies* (Baton Rouge, 1977), 606–611; Robert F. Engs, *Freedom's First Generation: Black Hampton, Virginia, 1861–1890* (Philadelphia, 1979). On the problem of women as contrabands, see Leslie Schwalm, *A Hard Fight for We: Women's Transition from Slavery to Freedom in South Carolina* (Urbana, 1997); Thavolia Glymph, "'This Species of Property': Female Slave Contrabands in the Civil War," in *A Woman's War: Southern Women, Civil War, and the Confederate Legacy,* ed. Edward D. D. Campbell Jr. and Kym S. Rice (Richmond, 1996); Stephanie McCurry, "War, Gender, and Emancipation in the Civil War South," in *Lincoln's Proclamation: Emancipation Reconsidered,* ed. William A. Blair and Karen Fisher Younger (Chapel Hill, 2009).
63. Rose, *Rehearsal for Reconstruction,* 122, 106, 108–109.
64. William Elliott to Dear Ralph, Dec. 15, 1861, Elliott-Gonzales Papers, SHC, in *RASP,* ser. J, pt. 3, reel 21; Rose, *Rehearsal for Reconstruction,* 106–107.
65. John Berkley Grimball Diaries, Nov. 12, Dec. 29, Feb. 6, 1861, and May 13, 1862, SHC.
66. John Berkley Grimball Diaries, Nov. 20 and Dec. 7, 1861, Feb. 4, 19, 21, 1862, SHC; enclosure, letter from S. N. Carroll, Jan. 1, 1862, vol. 12, Grimball Family Papers, SHC; William H. Grimball to J. B. Grimball, Jan. 27, 1861 [1862], John Berkley Grimball Papers, DU; William H. Grimball to J. B. Grimball, Feb. 19, 1862, John Berkley Grimball Papers, DU.
67. John Berkley Grimball Diaries, Mar. 3, 1862, SHC.
68. Rose, *Rehearsal for Reconstruction,* 246; John Berkley Grimball, "List of the Negroes, belonging to J. B. Grimball who left . . . on the night of the 2nd March 1862," Slave Material [1828–1861], ser. 2, folder 81, Grimball Family Papers, SHC; John Berkley Grimball Diaries, Mar. 5 and 8, 1862, SHC; Meta Morris

Grimball Diary, Mar. 6, 1862, SHC. For confirmation of slaves' communication with the gunboats, see Berlin et al., *Destruction of Slavery,* 115–117.

69. The portrait follows the list of Mar. 8, 1862, in John Berkley Grimball Diaries, SHC.
70. See "List of the Negroes belonging to J. B. Grimball . . . on the night of the 2nd March, 1862," Slave Material, ser. 2, folder 81, Grimball Family Papers, SHC; John Berkley Grimball Diaries, Mar. 8, 1862 [List of slaves who escaped to the enemy], Mar. 5, 1862 [List of "those that remain"], SHC.
71. Elizabeth Colwill, "'Fêtes de l'hymen, fêtes de la liberté': Marriage, Manhood, and Emancipation in Revolutionary Saint-Domingue," in *The World of the Haitian Revolution,* ed. David Patrick Geggus and Norman Fiering (Bloomington, 2009), 125–155; Fick, *The Making of Haiti,* 226, 152; Diana Paton, *No Bond but the Law: Punishment, Race, and Gender in Jamaican State-Formation* (Durham, 2004), 80 and throughout. See also Bush, *Slave Women in Caribbean Society;* Blackburn, *Overthrow of Colonial Slavery;* Dubois, *A Colony of Citizens;* Scott, *Slave Emancipation in Cuba;* and Ada Ferrer, *Insurgent Cuba: Race, Nation, and Revolution: 1868–1898* (Chapel Hill, 1999).
72. This gendered history of emancipation is currently being written by historians of the United States and other slave societies. For the Civil War, see McCurry, "War, Gender and Emancipation." For the comparative landscape, see Pamela Scully and Diana Paton, eds., *Gender and Slave Emancipation in the Atlantic World* (Durham, 2005). On the United States, see Schwalm, *A Hard Fight for We;* Nancy Bercaw, *Gendered Freedoms: Race, Rights, and the Politics of Household in the Delta, 1861–1875* (Gainesville, 2003); Noralee Frankel, *Freedom's Women: Black Women and Families in Civil War Era Mississippi* (Bloomington, 1999); and Glymph, "'This Species of Property.'"
73. Meta Morris Grimball Diary, Aug. 4, 1863, SHC; J. B. Grimball to My Dear Wife, July 11, 1863, M. M. G. [Meta Morris Grimball] to J. B. Grimball, July 18, 1863, Lewis M. Grimball to J. B. Grimball, Aug. 30, 1863, M. M. G. to My Dear Husband, July 15, 1863, and J. B. Grimball to My dear Wife, July 17, 1863, all in John Berkley Grimball Papers, DU.
74. James A. Evans to Governor Smith, Dec. 14, 1864, Governor William Smith Papers, folder 8, box 4, LVA; Richard R. Duncan, *Beleaguered Winchester: A Virginia Community at War, 1861–1865* (Baton Rouge, 2007), ix; Yael Sternhell, "Revolution in Motion: Human Mobility and the Transformation of the South, 1861–1865" (Ph.D. diss., Princeton University, 2008), 72.
75. Sigismunda Stribling Kimball Journal, Nov. 5, 29, 1862, Dec. 6, 27, 1862, UVA.
76. Ibid., Apr. 8, 19, 23, May 1, 1862. On patterns of slaveholding, abroad marriages, and the dispersal of families in Virginia, see Brenda Stevenson, *Life in Black and White: Family and Community in the Slave South* (New York, 1996), 206–225.
77. Sigismunda Stribling Kimball Journal, Jan. 27, Feb. 24, 1863, UVA; Berlin et al., *Black Military Experience,* 691–692.
78. Sigismunda Stribling Kimball Journal, Feb. 24, 1863, UVA; Berlin et al., *Black Military Experience,* 157–158; Berlin et al., *Destruction of Slavery,* 98–99.
79. Sigismunda Stribling Kimball Journal, Mar. 29, 1863, UVA; Hahn, *A Nation under Our Feet,* 84; "List of Slaves—January 1863," William Wickham Diary,

vol. 8 (1862–1864), William Fanning Wickham Papers, VHS. See also the account of Virginia developments in John R. Woods to My Dear Son, Holkham, July 2, 1863, box 1, Micajah Woods Papers, UVA, and J. H. Hankins to My Dear Son, n.d. [1862], Hankins Family Papers, VHS.

80. See, for example, John R. Woods to Micajah Woods, July 18, 1863, Micajah Woods Papers, UVA; Minrose Gwin, *A Woman's Civil War: A Diary with Reminiscences of the War from 1862* (Madison, 1992), 64–65; Berlin et al., *Destruction of Slavery,* 300, 88–90, 141–142.
81. John Houston Bills Diary, Sept. 13, 1862, June 4, Oct. 17, 1863, and Feb. 11, 1864, John Houston Bills Papers, SHC, in *RASP,* ser. J, pt. 8, reels 15, 16. On the "river war," see James M. McPherson, *Battle Cry of Freedom: The Civil War Era* (New York, 1988), 392–427.
82. Wederstrandt to Shepley, Sept. 19, 1862, in Berlin et al., *Destruction of Slavery,* 219–221. On state power and the law of slavery, see Morris, *Southern Slavery and the Law.* I take up this issue more fully in Chapter 7.
83. Berlin et al., *Destruction of Slavery,* 209–217, quotation at 216, 225–231, 187–199. The literature on slavery and emancipation in southern Louisiana during the Civil War is quite rich. In addition to the volumes of the Freedom Project, see, especially, C. Peter Ripley, *Slaves and Freedmen in Civil War Louisiana* (Baton Rouge, 1976), and John C. Rodrigue, *Reconstruction in the Cane Fields: From Slavery to Free Labor in Louisiana's Sugar Parishes, 1862–1880* (Baton Rouge, 2001).
84. General Braxton Bragg to President Davis, Nov. 24, 1862, *PJD,* 8:509–514, quotation at 511; Berlin et al., *Destruction of Slavery,* 225–231, quotation at 225, 228, 229–230.
85. Jefferson Davis to Joseph Davis, Feb. 21, 1862, and Joseph Davis to Jefferson Davis, May 2, 1862, *PJD,* 8:53–54, quotation at 53, 159–161. On the history of the Davis plantations during the war, see Janet Sharp Hermann, *Pursuit of a Dream* (Jackson, 1999); William J. Cooper, *Jefferson Davis, American* (New York, 2000); and Joan E. Cashin, *First Lady of the Confederacy: Varina Davis's Civil War* (Cambridge, Mass., 2006).
86. Joseph Davis to Jefferson Davis, May 22, 1862, and Charles J. Mitchell to President Davis, June 7, 1862, both *PJD,* 8:196–197, 231–233.
87. David Porterfield to Jefferson Davis, June 5, 1862, and Charles J. Mitchell to Jefferson Davis, June 7, 1862, *PJD,* 8:227, 231–233.
88. Joseph E. Davis to Jefferson Davis, June 14, 1863, and Joseph Davis to Jefferson Davis, June 25, 1863, *PJD,* 9:216–217, 240–241; Joseph Davis to Jefferson Davis, July 10, 1862, *PJD,* 8:285–286; Joseph E. Davis to Jefferson Davis, Nov. 11, 1863, *PJD,* 10:61–65.
89. Robert E. Melvin to Jefferson Davis, July 22, 1863, *PJD,* 9:298–303; George Barnes to President Davis, July 16, 1864, *PJD,* 10:531.
90. President Davis, Address to "The Senate and House of Representatives of the Confederate States," Richmond, Jan. 12, 1863, *O.R.,* ser. 4, 2:336–350, quotation at 345–346; Jefferson Davis, Address of Congress to the People of the Confederate States, Joint Resolution in Relation to the War, Jan. 22, 1864, *O.R.,* ser. 4, 3:126–137, quotations at 132, 133.

91. J. R. Mainor to T. O. Moore, July 7, 1864, vol. 1, folder 14, Thomas O. Moore Papers, LSU. Events on Moore's plantation can be traced in the following correspondence: John H. Ransdell to Dear Governor, May 24, 1863, Ransdell to Moore, May 26, 1863, J. C. Younger to Governor Moore, May 27, 1863, Ransdell to Moore, May 31, 1863, Ransdell to Moore, June 3, 1863, and Ransdell to Moore, June 12, 1863, all in box 1, folder 12, Thomas O. Moore Papers, LSU. Moore moved sixty hogsheads of sugar into Texas before he ran there himself. See General E. Kirby Smith to Moore, Sept. 22, 1864, box 1, folder 14, Thomas O. Moore Papers, LSU.
92. "LOOK TO THE FUTURE," *Louisiana Democrat* (Alexandria), June 3, 1863, reprinted in G. P. Whittington, "Concerning the Loyalty of Slaves in North Louisiana in 1863," *Louisiana Historical Quarterly* 14 (Oct. 1931): 487–502, quotation at 489–490.
93. Thomas D. Hailes to Lieut. Colonel Richard B. Irwin, Dec. 20, 1862; Affidavit of J. Curcard and G. Chabaud, Dec. 22, 1862; and John C. P. Wederstrandt to Brigadier General Shepley, Sept. 19, 1862, all in Berlin et al., *Destruction of Slavery*, 232–233, 233–235, 219–221. See also Matthew J. Clavin, "American Toussaints: Symbol, Subversion, and the Black Atlantic Tradition in the American Civil War," *Slavery and Abolition* 28, no. 1 (Apr. 2007): 87–113.
94. Brigadier General G. Weitzel to Major George C. Strong, Nov. 5, 1862, and A. A. General George C. Strong to Brig. Genl Weitzel, Nov. 6, 1862, both in Berlin et al., *Destruction of Slavery*, 225–231; N. P. Banks, To the People of Louisiana, Dec. 24, 1862, *O.R.*, ser. 1, 15, 620.
95. On slave insurrection and war in Saint-Domingue, see Fick, *The Making of Haiti;* Blackburn, *Overthrow of Colonial Slavery;* Colwill, "Fêtes de l'hymen"; David Patrick Geggus, *The Impact of the Haitian Revolution in the Atlantic World* (Columbia, S.C., 2001); Dubois, *A Colony of Citizens*; and Laurent Dubois, *Avengers of the New World: The Story of the Haitian Revolution* (Cambridge, Mass., 2004).
96. On Lorenzo Thomas, see Erik Mathisen, "Pledges of Allegiance" (Ph.D. diss., University of Pennsylvania, 2009), chap. 4; Clavin, "American Toussaints," 95.
97. Steven Hahn, *The Political Worlds of Slavery and Freedom* (Cambridge, Mass., 2009), 55–114; Fick, *The Making of Haiti*, 91–119.
98. Blackburn, *Overthrow of Colonial Slavery*, 234, 161–264; Fick, *The Making of Haiti;* David Patrick Geggus, *Slavery, War and Revolution: The British Occupation of Saint Domingue, 1793–1798* (Oxford, 1982); Colwill, "Fêtes de l'hymen."
99. On Spanish America, see Blackburn, *Overthrow of Colonial Slavery*, 331–380; on Cuba, see Scott, *Slave Emancipation in Cuba*, and Ferrer, *Insurgent Cuba.*

7. "OUR OPEN ENEMIES"

1. The idea that slaves' politics shaped the course of the war through its impact on Union policy has been soundly established. For influential contributions, see the volumes in Ira Berlin et al., eds., *Freedom: A Documentary History of*

Emancipation, 1861–1867; Ira Berlin et al., *Slaves No More: Three Essays on Emancipation and the Civil War* (Cambridge, UK, 1992); Eric Foner, *Reconstruction: America's Unfinished Revolution, 1863–1877* (New York, 1998); Steven Hahn, *A Nation under Our Feet: Black Political Struggles in the Rural South from Slavery to the Great Migration* (Cambridge, Mass., 2003). There has been less interest in how slaves shaped Confederate policy. One exception is Armstead L. Robinson, *Bitter Fruits of Bondage: The Demise of Slavery and the Collapse of the Confederacy* (Charlottesville, 2005), although even Robinson focuses more on slavery than on slaves, and more on the meaning of slavery for military defeat than for Confederate politics and policy.

2. Samuel W. Melton to Hon. James A. Seddon, Secretary of War, Nov. 11, 1863, *O.R.,* ser. 4, 2:944–952, quotation at 946–947.
3. See Harrison A. Trexler, "The Opposition of Planters to the Employment of Slaves as Laborers by the Confederacy," *Mississippi Valley Historical Review* 27, no. 2 (Sept. 1940): 211–224; Bernard H. Nelson, "Confederate Slave Impressment Legislation, 1861–1865," *Journal of Negro History* 31 (Oct. 1946): 392–410; Clarence L. Mohr, *On the Threshold of Freedom: Masters and Slaves in Civil War Georgia* (Athens, Ga., 1986), 121–128, 162–163, 171–172; Ervin L. Jordan Jr., *Black Confederates and Afro-Yankees in Civil War Virginia* (Charlottesville, 1995), 49–68; Robinson, *Bitter Fruits of Bondage;* William Blair, *Virginia's Private War: Feeding Body and Soul in the Confederacy, 1861–1865* (New York, 1998), 41–43, 78, 121–124.
4. R. E. Lee to President Davis, June 5, 1862, and Jefferson Davis to Varina Howell Davis, June 11, 1862, *PJD,* 8:225–226, 235–237, quotations at 225, 236. On the Confederate "emancipation debate," see Robert Durden, *The Gray and the Black: The Confederate Debate on Emancipation* (Baton Rouge, 1972); Emory M. Thomas, *The Confederate Nation: 1861–1865* (New York, 1979), 261–264, 290–297; Bruce Levine, *Confederate Emancipation: Southern Plans to Free and Arm Slaves during the Civil War* (New York, 2006); and Philip D. Dillard, "Independence or Slavery: The Confederate Debate over Arming the Slaves" (Ph.D. diss., Rice University, 1999). I take up the subject in Chapter 8.
5. John Berkley Grimball Diaries, Jan. 14, 1861, SHC; Charles Manigault to Louis Manigault, Feb. 28, 1861, Louis Manigault Papers, box 4, DU; Nelson, "Confederate Slave Impressment Legislation," 393.
6. G. B. Cosby to Colonel Crump, July 28, 1861, and John Tyler, M. C. C. and Hill Carter, Colonel of 52nd Regt Va. Militia, to Secretary of War, Richmond, Aug. 28, 1861, in Ira Berlin et al., eds., *Freedom: A Documentary History of Emancipation, 1861–1867,* ser. 1, vol. 1: *The Destruction of Slavery* (Cambridge, UK, 1985), 686, 686–687; Jordan, *Black Confederates,* 58.
7. Brigadier General J. B. Magruder to Sir, July 18, 1861, and William N. Harris et al. to his Excellency Jefferson Davis, May 6, 1864, in Berlin et al., *Destruction of Slavery,* 685, 756–758, quotation at 757; Hiram Yuger et al. to Governor Smith, Nov. 2, 1864, Governor William Smith Papers, box 4, folder, 5, LVA; Jas. H. Binford to Local Enrolling Officers, circular no. 70, Oct. 22, 1864, *O.R.* ser. 4, 2:745–746. On the hiring of women slaves, see Leslie Schwalm, *A Hard*

Fight for We: Women's Transition from Slavery to Freedom in South Carolina (Urbana, 1997), 81–82, 86–88; Jordan, *Black Confederates,* 63.

8. John Tyler, M. C. C. and Hill Carter, Colonel of 52nd Regt Va. Militia to Secretary of War, Aug. 28, 1861, and L. P. Walker, Secretary of War to Brigadier General J. B. Magruder, Aug. 26, 1861, both in Berlin et al., *Destruction of Slavery,* 686–687, 687.
9. James B. Mallory to President Davis, Jan. 13, 1862, *PJD,* 8:18–19; Senator Thomas H. Urquhart to Hon Geo W. Randolph, Oct. 2, 1862, and James W. Cook to Hon. J. M. Mason, Aug. 27, 1861, both in Berlin et al., *Destruction of Slavery,* 701, 77; General Joseph Johnston quoted in Benjamin Quarles, *The Negro in the Civil War* (1953; New York, 1989), 275. On the literature, see Trexler, "Opposition of Planters"; Nelson, "Confederate Slave Impressment Legislation"; Jordan, *Black Confederates;* Mohr, *Threshold of Freedom;* Schwalm, *A Hard Fight for We.*
10. Henry A. Wise, Brig. Genl. to Coln. T. J. Page, Oct. 27, 1862, in Barron, Waring and Baylor Family Papers, Papers of Samuel Barron, box 2, UVA.
11. James W. Cook to Hon. J. M. Mason, Aug. 27, 1861, in Berlin et al., *Destruction of Slavery,* 77.
12. Joseph M. White to Hon. Geo W. Randolph, Sept. 8, 1862, in Berlin et al., *Destruction of Slavery,* 699–700, quotation at 699.
13. Brig. Genl J. Bankhead Magruder to Genl. S. Cooper, Sept. 20, 1861, Mjr. Genl. J. Bankhead Magruder to Genl. S. Cooper, Jan. 22, 1862, and Maj. Genl. J. Bankhead Magruder to Genl. S. Cooper, Mar. 1, 1862, all in Berlin et al., *Destruction of Slavery,* 688–689, 689–691, 691–692.
14. Maj. Genl. J. Bankhead Magruder to Genl. S. Cooper, Mar. 1, 1862, in Berlin et al., *Destruction of Slavery,* 691–692.
15. John. B. Speice to Attorney General of the Confederate States, Dec. 4, 1861, in Berlin et al., *Destruction of Slavery,* 782–784, quotations at 783, 782. On owners' fear of slave assembly in impressment, see Mohr, *Threshold of Freedom,* 161.
16. Jno. M. Gregory to Honbl. James A. Seddon, Mar. 7, 1863, and Jno. M. Gregory to Honbl. J. P. Benjamin, Mar. 12, 1862, in Berlin et al., *Destruction of Slavery,* 748–754, quotations at 748, 749.
17. Benj. F. Butler to Lieutenant Genl. Scott, May 27, 1861, in Berlin et al., *Destruction of Slavery,* 70–72, quotations at 71; John Blassingame, ed., *Slave Testimony: Two Centuries of Letters, Speeches, Interviews and Autobiographies* (Baton Rouge, 1977), 606–611. On the significance of contraband policy, see Berlin et al., *Slaves No More;* Foner, *Reconstruction;* Hahn, *A Nation under Our Feet;* and Robert F. Engs, *Freedom's First Generation: Black Hampton, Virginia, 1861–1890* (Philadelphia, 1979). The estimate of numbers of contraband in Fort Monroe is calculated from the table in Berlin et al., *Destruction of Slavery,* 91.
18. Benj. F. Butler to Lieutenant Genl. Scott, May 27, 1861, and Maj. Genl. S. A. Hurlbut to the President of the U. States, Mar. 27, [1863], in Berlin et al., *Destruction of Slavery,* 71, 304–306, quotation on 304. On the gender problem inherent in the logic of contraband, see Schwalm, *A Hard Fight for We,* 90 and throughout; Thavolia Glymph, "'This Species of Property': Female Slave

Contrabands in the Civil War," in *A Woman's War: Southern Women, Civil War and the Confederate Legacy,* ed. Edward. D. Campbell Jr. and Kym S. Rice (Richmond, 1996); Nancy Bercaw, *Gendered Freedoms: Race, Rights and the Politics of Household in the Delta, 1861–1875* (Gainesville, 2003); Noralee Frankel, *Freedom's Women: Black Women and Families in Civil War Era Mississippi* (Bloomington, 1999); and Stephanie McCurry, "War, Gender and Emancipation in the Civil War South," in *Lincoln's Proclamation: Emancipation Reconsidered,* ed. William A. Blair and Karen Fisher Younger (Chapel Hill, 2009).

19. The numbers are from Excerpts of Testimony of Capt. C. B. Wilder before the American Freedmen's Inquiry Commission, May 9, 1863, in Berlin et al., *Destruction of Slavery,* 88–90, table at 91, quotation at 89. The willingness to embrace marriage and its responsibilities was always part of the assessment of whether slave men were fit for freedom and citizenship in the age of emancipation. On the United States, see American Freedmen's Inquiry Commission, Preliminary Report, Senate Executive Document no. 53, 38th Congress, First Session, 1–24; Willie Lee Rose, *Rehearsal for Reconstruction: The Port Royal Experiment* (1964; Athens, Ga., 1994), 236; Amy Stanley, *From Bondage to Contract: Wage Labor, Marriage and the Market in the Age of Slave Emancipation* (Cambridge, UK, 1998); Linda Kerber, *No Constitutional Right to Be Ladies: Women and the Obligations of Citizenship* (New York, 1998), 47–80. On eighteenth-century England, see Christopher Leslie Brown, *Moral Capital: Foundations of British Abolitionism* (Chapel Hill, 2007), 206, 236. On France, see Elizabeth Colwill, "'Fêtes de l'hymen, fêtes de la liberté': Marriage, Manhood, and Emancipation in Revolutionary Saint-Domingue," in *The World of the Haitian Revolution,* ed. David Patrick Geggus and Norman Fiering (Bloomington, 2009), 125–155. For a fuller treatment, see my review essay on marriage and women's citizenship in *Signs* 30, no. 2 (Winter 2005).

20. Berlin et al., *Destruction of Slavery,* 72; Blassingame, *Slave Testimony,* 606–611, quotation at 608.

21. W. D. Porter and A. P. Aldrich to Hon. James A. Seddon, Dec. 30, 1862, *O.R.,* ser. 4, 2:267–269, quotation at 267; Richard H. Smith to Governor Vance, Oct. 13, 1864, box 181, ZBV; General P. T. Beauregard to Wm. Henry Trescott, Dec. 10, 1863, in Berlin et al., *Destruction of Slavery,* 714–717, quotation at 714.

22. As Thomas Morris put it: "The master-slave relation is so delicate that it was intruded upon only in extreme or unusual circumstances." Thomas D. Morris, *Southern Slavery and the Law, 1619–1860* (Chapel Hill, 1996), 181, 206; Mohr, *Threshold of Freedom;* Schwalm, *A Hard Fight for We.*

23. Nelson, "Confederate Slave Impressment Legislation," 392–410; Jordan, *Black Confederates,* 60. For state legislation, see *O.R.,* ser. 4, 2:267–270 (S.C.), 278–279 (La.), 296–297 (Miss.), 426–430 (Va.). For Davis's appeal, see Jefferson Davis to Governor J. E. Brown, Richmond, Va, Nov. 16, 1862, *O.R.,* ser. 4, 2:211–212. The exemption of Virginia counties is noted in *O.R.,* ser. 4, 2:426–430, quotation at 427.

24. Jno S. Preston to James A. Seddon, Columbia, S.C., Jan. 15, 1865, *O.R.,* ser. 4, 2:1018–19, quotation at 1019.

25. Nelson, "Confederate Slave Impressment"; Trexler, "Opposition of Planters"; and Frank L. Owsley, *State Rights in the Confederacy* (Chicago, 1925), 254–265.
26. W. H. Whiting to Governor Vance, Feb. 23, 1863, box 162, W. H. Whiting to Vance, July 3, 1863, box 167, W. H. Whiting to Vance, Mar. 21, 1864, box 175, W. H. Whiting to Col. G. Little, Telegram, Apr. 26, 1864, box 176, all ZBV.
27. E. J. Blount to Governor Vance, Oct. 18, 1864, box 181, B. B. Walker to Governor Vance, Dec. 21, 1864, box 182, both ZBV.
28. Richard H. Smith to Governor Vance, Mar. 24, 1864, box 175, Zebulon Vance to Brig. Genl L. S. Baker, Nov. 22, 1864, Letter Book, James McRae to Governor Vance, Sept. 9, 1863, box 169, and J. W. James to Governor Vance, May 24, 1863, box 165, all ZBV. The failure of impressment as a policy is noted by all historians who have studied it.
29. For the text of the Mar. 1863 legislation, see *O.R.*, ser. 4, 2:469–472 (sec. 9 is on 470); Nelson, "Confederate Slave Impressment Legislation," 403.
30. Samuel Melton to James A. Seddon, Nov. 11, 1863, *O.R.*, ser. 4, 2:944–952; James A. Seddon to the President of the Confederate States, War Department, Richmond, Nov. 28, 1864, *O.R.*, ser. 4, 3:851–853, quotation at 852; James A. Seddon to Jefferson Davis, Nov. 26, 1863, *O.R.*, ser. 4, 2:990–1018, quotation at 998. On the opposition of the Attorney General, see Nelson, "Confederate Slave Impressment Legislation," 400.
31. General Orders No. 139, *O.R.*, ser. 4, 2:897–898.
32. Saml. W. Melton to Hon. James A. Seddon, Nov. 11, 1863, James A. Seddon to His Excellency Jefferson Davis, Nov. 26,1863, *O.R.*, ser. 4, 2:944–952, quotation at 946, 990–1018, quotation at 998.
33. James A. Seddon to the President of the Confederate States, Nov. 28, 1863, R. B. Johnson to Governor A. G. Magrath, Columbia, S.C., Jan. 10, 1865, *O.R.*, ser. 4, 3:851–853, quotation at 852, 1020–23, quotation at 1023; Lt. Gen. E. Kirby Smith to Maj. Gen. Magruder, Sept. 5, 1863, in Berlin et al., *Destruction of Slavery*, 804–805.
34. Hiram Yuger et al. to Governor William Smith, Nov. 2, 1864, Governor William Smith Papers, box 4, folder 5, LVA; Robert R. Sotwell to Lieut. Coln. T. B. Lamar, Jackson, Mississippi, July 5, 1863, in Berlin et al., *Destruction of Slavery*, 800–802, quotations on 801; William D. Taylor and other citizens of Sussex County, Virginia, to President Davis, Oct. 13, 1864, *PJD*, 11:104; John Randolph Chambliss to His Excy the President of the Con. States, Jan. 27, 1863, John Randolph Chambliss Letters, VHS.
35. W. G. Turpin, Capt Engr & acting Chief Consn, D. N. V., Dec. 16, 1864, in Berlin et al., *Destruction of Slavery*, 727–728, quotation at 728; John Bowen et al. to Hon. Sec. of War, Sept. 26, 1863, in Ira Berlin, Joseph Reidy, and Leslie Rowland, eds., *Freedom: A Documentary History of Emancipation, 1861–1867*, ser. 2: *The Black Military Experience* (Cambridge, UK, 1982), 174. "Demoralization" was part of a transatlantic planter language. For Cuba, see Rebecca J. Scott, *Slave Emancipation in Cuba: The Transition to Free Labor, 1860–1899* (Princeton, 1985), 165, 177.
36. Jefferson Davis, Address to the Senate and House of Representatives of the

Confederate States, Richmond, Dec. 7, 1863, *O.R.,* ser. 4, 2:1024–49, quotations at 1041, 1047; "An Act to Increase the Efficiency of the Army by the Employment of Free Negroes and Slaves in Certain Capacities," *O.R.,* ser. 4, 3:208; Thomas C. Hindman to Jefferson Davis, Jan. 16, 1864, *PJD,* 10:180–183, and, on Davis's acknowledgment of failure, see editors' note at 183.

37. Joseph E. Johnston to President Davis, Jan. 2, 1864, and Hindman to Davis, Jan. 16, 1864, *PJD,* 10:144–150, 180–183; Mohr, *Threshold of Freedom,* 127; Jordan, *Black Confederates,* 65. It is impossible to offer any real estimate of the number of slaves impressed for military service, but all historians confirm that the numbers always fell short of what was requisitioned and were "minuscule" in comparison to the numbers of white men conscripted. See Mohr, *Threshold of Freedom,* 163; David M. Potter, "Jefferson Davis and the Political Factors in Confederate Defeat," in *Why the North Won the Civil War,* ed. David Herbert Donald (1960; New York, 1996), 100–101.

38. S. Cooper, Adjutant and Inspector General, General Order No. 32, Mar. 11, 1864, *O.R.,* ser. 4, 3:207–209; Jordan, *Black Confederates,* 62. See also Schwalm, *A Hard Fight for We,* 85, and Mohr, *Threshold of Freedom,* 162. Confederate use of slaves for military labor might have blurred the lines sufficiently that Northern blacks thought slaves were enlisted in the Confederate Army. See Berlin et al., *Black Military Experience,* 80–81.

39. There is virtually no discussion of slave impressment or resistance to it in Emory Thomas's *Confederate Nation.* Thomas says that "slaves never fought the Confederacy from within" (237); Raimondo Luraghi, *The Rise and Fall of the Plantation South* (New York, 1878); Richard F. Bensel, *Yankee Leviathan: The Origins of Central State Authority in America, 1859–1877* (Cambridge, UK, 1990).

40. Anthony Kaye, "Slaves, Emancipation and the Powers of War: Views from the Natchez District of Mississippi," in *The War Was You and Me: Civilians in the American Civil War,* ed. Joan Cashin (Princeton, 2002), quotation at 64.

41. A few historians have recognized the significance of slaves' encounter with the Confederate state. See Schwalm, *A Hard Fight for We;* Justin Behrend, "Building Democracy from Scratch: African American Politics and Community in the Postemancipation Natchez District" (Ph.D. diss., Northwestern University, 2006), chap. 1.

42. Jefferson Davis, Speech to the Senate and House of Representatives of the Confederate States of America, Nov. 7, 1864, J. F. Gilmer to General R. E. Lee, Nov. 19, 1864, R. E. Lee to Gilmer, Nov. 21, 1864, all in *O.R.,* ser. 4, 3:790–800, 829–831, 838–839. For subsequent laws, see General Orders No. 86, Dec. 5, 1864, *O.R.,* ser. 4, 3:897–899; "An Act to Provide for the Employment of Free Negroes and Slaves to Work upon the Fortifications and Perform Other Labor Connected with the Defenses of the Country," Feb. 28, 1865, *O.R.,* ser. 4, 3:1114–17; R. E. Lee to Hon. Secty of War, Petersburg, Virginia, Sept. 20, 1864, in Berlin et al., *Destruction of Slavery,* 723–725, quotation at 723. For the comparative claim, see Hendrik Kraay, "Slavery, Citizenship and Military Service in Brazil's Mobilization for the Paraguayan War," *Slavery and Abolition* 18, no. 3 (Dec. 1997): 228–256, quotation at 249.

43. J. A. C., Endorsement enclosed with W. C. Bibb to James A. Seddon, July 23, 1863, in Berlin et al., *Destruction of Slavery,* 704–706, quotation at 705; C. D. Melton to General John Preston, Jan. 14, 1865, *O.R.,* ser. 4, 3:1024–25, quotation at 1024; *Mobile Register,* Nov. 13, 1863, in Durden, *The Gray and Black,* 40–41, quotation on 40; F. S. Blount to Major P. Ellis Jr., June 23, 1864, and Broadside by the Chief Quartermaster of the Confederate Trans-Mississippi Department, Sept. 15, 1863, both in Berlin et al., *Destruction of Slavery,* 738–742, quotation at 741, 712.
44. Governor Charles Clark to Jefferson Davis, Nov. 18, 1863, *PJD,* 10:78, and Lt. Comdg. S. L. Phelps to Flag Officer A. H. Foote, Dec. 10, 1861, in Berlin et al., *Destruction of Slavery,* 520–522; Estill Belen to Jefferson Davis, May 1, 1864, William Roberts to Jefferson Davis, Dec. 18, 1863, and Zebulon Vance to President Davis, Apr. 18, 1864, *PJD,* 10:377, 114, 355.
45. For all of the continuing insistence on the strength of Confederate nationalism, I know of no account that considers slaveholders' willingness to surrender their property as a measure of their patriotism or nationalism. See Gary Gallagher, *The Confederate War: How Popular Will, Nationalism, and Military Strategy Could Not Stave Off Defeat* (New York, 1997); Blair, *Virginia's Private War;* Anne Sarah Rubin, *A Shattered Nation: The Rise and Fall of the Confederacy, 1861–1868* (Chapel Hill, 2005); Chandra Manning, *What This Cruel War Was Over: Soldiers, Slavery and the Civil War* (New York, 2007); Jason Phillips, *Diehard Rebels: The Confederate Culture of Invincibility* (Athens, Ga., 2007).
46. Chief of Staff Thomas Jordan to Jno S. McDaniel, Sept. 1, 1863, in Berlin et al., *Destruction of Slavery,* 710–711, quotation at 710; Jno. S. Preston to James Seddon, Jan. 15, 1865, *O.R.*, ser. 4, 3:1018–19; John S. Preston to Jefferson Davis, Dec. 28, 1864, HU; R. B. Johnson to Governor A. G. Magrath, Jan. 10, 1865, and Jno. S. Preston to Mr. Seddon, Dec. 29, 1864, *O.R.*, ser. 4, 3:1020–23, 979.
47. Broadside, Dec. 16, 1864, Requisition of the Governor, William Smith, UVA. See also the correspondence from the War Department: J. F. Gilmer to Hon. James A. Seddon, Dec. 14, 1864, James A. Seddon to the President of the Confederate States, Dec. 15, 1864, Jefferson Davis to His Excellency William Smith, Dec. 15, 1864, J. H. Alexander to Hon. G. W. Mumford, Dec. 21, 1864, and Circular to the Clerks of the County Courts, Dec. 16, 1864, all in Governor William Smith Papers, box 4, folders 7, 8, 9, LVA.
48. Application of County Court of Caroline, Dec. 28, 1864, William Smith Papers, box 5, folder 1; Cumberland Courthouse, Jan. 16, 1865, Greenville County Court, Jan. 7, 1865, William Smith Papers, box 5, folder 2; R. A. Scott, Clerk, Franklin County Courthouse, Jan. 11, 1865, Floyd County Court House, Jan. 7, 1865, Louisa County, Jan. 17, 1865, Orange County, Dec. 26, 1865, William Smith Papers, box 5, folder 1, all LVA.
49. Blair, *Virginia's Private War,* 123; William Smith to the General Assembly, Feb. 10, 1865, William Smith Papers, box 5, folder 4, LVA; William Smith to the Clerk of the Hustings Court of the City of Lynchburg, Richmond, Jan. 23, 1865, William Smith Papers, box 5, folder 1, LVA; William Smith, Governor of Virginia to the Honorable the Courts of the Counties, Cities etc Named in the Annexed Schedule, Mar. 14, 1865, *O.R.,* ser. 4, 3:1138–39.

50. Undated circular of William Smith to County Courts, [Mar. 5, 1865], William Smith Executive Papers, Mfm, misc. reel 5025, LVA; William Smith to Genl R. E. Lee, Mar. 25, 1865, William Smith Executive Papers, Mfm, reel 5024 [chart enclosed], LVA; General Joseph Johnston to President Davis, Jan. 2, 1864, *PJD,* 10:144–150.
51. Davis, Address to the Senate and House of Representatives of the Confederate States of America, Nov. 7, 1864, *O.R.,* ser. 4, 3:790–800, quotations at 799.
52. That the Confederate government was forced to contend for the loyalty of slave men is not much recognized in the literature on the Confederacy, although Drew Faust references it in popular culture. See Drew Gilpin Faust, *The Creation of Confederate Nationalism: Ideology and Identity in the Civil War South* (Baton Rouge, 1988), 58–81.
53. Armstead Robinson, *Bitter Fruits of Bondage,* linked the problem of slavery to military defeat. I am more interested in its political (and policy) consequences within the C.S.A.
54. H. A. Gilliam to Governor Clark, June 14, 1862, box 157, Colonel William Clarke to Governor Clark, Mar. 1, 1862, box 157, Henry T. Clark, Governor's Papers, NCDAH; David Schenck Diaries, vol. 3, Feb. 22, 1862 ["Secret Session"], SHC; C. Woaten to Governor Clark, June 28, 1862, box 157, Henry T. Clark, Governors Papers, NCDAH.
55. George Van Valkenberg to Dear Wife, Jan. 18, 1863, Van Valkenberg Papers, FHS; excerpts from testimony of Alonzo Jackson, Mar. 17, 1863, Capt Alured Larke and Capt. R. H. Day to the Provost Marshall, Dec. 7, 1864, Statement by Robert Blake, Sept. 1862, Brig. Gen. O. M. Mitchel to E. M. Stanton, May 4, 1862, and Stanton's reply, Statement of Lieut. Col. Josiah Given, Dec. 19, 1862, all in Berlin et al., *Destruction of Slavery,* 813–818, 809–810, 132–133, 275–276 (quotation at 276), 297–298.
56. R. Q. Mallard, P. W. Fleming, E. Stacy, Committee of Citizens of the 15th District, Liberty County, Ga., to Brigadier-General Mercer, in Mercer to Randolph, Aug. 5, 1862, *O.R.,* ser. 4, 2:36–38.
57. *Scott v. Sandford,* 60 U.S. (19 How.), 421.
58. H. W. Mercer, Brigadier-General Commanding, to Hon. George W. Randolph, Secretary of War, 1862, *O.R.,* ser. 4, 2:35–36, quotations at 35, 36.
59. J. Foster Marshall, Report, Committee on Military and Pensions, n.d., Papers of F. W. Pickens, LC; Citizens of Bolivar, Washington and Isaquena to President of the C.S.A., Feb. 1863, LRCSW, RG 109, roll 91; Garrett Andrews, Sr., to His Excellency, J. E. B., Dec. 20, 1860, box 22, GSF.
60. Henry Nutt to Vance, Dec. 12, 1864, box 182, ZBV; Citizens of Bolivar, Washington and Isaquena to President of the C.S.A., Feb. 1863, LRCSW, RG 109, roll 91; Thomas D. Hailes to Lieut. Col. Richd B. Irwin, Dec. 20, 1862, Affidavit of J. Burcard and G. Chabaud, Dec. 22, 1862, Pre Soniat to General, Dec. 20, 1862, all in Berlin et al., *Destruction of Slavery,* 232–233, 233–235, 231. A soldier in Sherman's army confirmed the existence of a network of slaves in southern North Carolina attempting "to force their way to our lines." For the key documents, see James P. Leak, J. P. to Governor Vance, Dec. 9, 1864, Henry Nutt to Vance, Dec. 12, 1864, Anonymous ["We Ladys"] to Vance, Dec. 13,

1864, Ralph Buxton to Vance, Dec. 14, 1864, R. J. McDonald to Vance, Dec. 17, 1864, all box 182, ZBV; "State v. Jack, a slave, Asa a Slave," indictment, Jan. 1865, "State v. Judy, 1865," both in Criminal Action Papers—Slaves and Free Persons of Color, Richmond County, N.C., NCDAH, and Richmond County, Superior Court Minute Docket, 1865, NCDAH; *The North Carolina Argus,* Dec. 15, 1864; Capt. David P. Conyngham, *Sherman's March through the South* (New York, 1865), 355; Conyngham claims that twenty-five slaves were hanged. On Christmas 1865, see Steven Hahn, "'Extravagant Expectations' of Freedom: Rumour, Political Struggle, and the Christmas Insurrection Scare of 1865 in the American South," *Past and Present,* no. 157 (Nov. 1997): 122–158.

61. Jefferson Davis, Speech at Jackson, Dec. 26, 1862, *PJD,* 8:565–584, quotation at 569. Repeal of the exemption was tied up with a growing political recognition of the necessity of aid to soldiers' wives. See Chapter 5.

62. This has long been the central debate among historians of the Confederacy, and it shows no sign of flagging. On one side is Paul Escott, *After Secession: Jefferson Davis and the Failure of Confederate Nationalism* (Baton Rouge, 1978); Armstead Robinson, *Bitter Fruits of Bondage;* Faust, *Confederate Nationalism;* and Steven Hahn, *The Roots of Southern Populism: Yeoman Farmers and the Transformation of the Georgia Upcountry* (New York, 1983), 86–133. On the other side is Gallagher, *The Confederate War;* Blair, *Virginia's Private War;* Rubin, *Shattered Nation;* Manning, *This Cruel War;* Philips, *Diehard Rebels;* and Aaron Sheehan-Dean, *Why Confederates Fought: Family and Nation in Civil War Virginia* (Chapel Hill, 2007).

63. Jas. W. Cook to Hon. J. M. Mason, Aug. 27, 1861, in Berlin et al., *Destruction of Slavery,* 77.

64. William Elliott to Dear Ralph, Dec. 15, 1861, Elliott-Gonzales Family Papers, *RASP,* ser. J, pt. 3, reel 21; Francis Pickens to Jefferson Davis, June 12, 1862, *PJD,* 8:239–243, quotation on 240; N. Goethe to Capt. Ed. H. Barnwell, Jan. 14, 1863, Pickens-Bonham Papers, LC; Allard B. Flagg and John Izard Middleton to Jefferson Davis, Apr. 9, 1864, *PJD,* 10:331–332; H. A. Gilliam to Governor Clark, June 14, 1862, box 157, Henry T. Clark, Governor's Papers, NCDAH.

65. Wade Hampton to President Davis, Oct. 23, 1862, *PJD,* 8:463; W. G. Murat to Secretary of War Randolph, Camp Richmond, Virginia, June 16, 1862, LRCSW, RG 109 (M437), roll 61.

66. Brig. Genl. W. S. Walker to Brig. Genl. Thomas Jordan, Nov. 18, 1862, A.A.I.G. E. W. Fraser to Condg. Officer of Our Posts, Nov. 7, 1863, and Commr. P. Drayton to Flag Officer S. F. Du Pont, Nov. 28, 1861, all in Berlin et al., *Destruction of Slavery,* 124–136, quotation at 133–134, 116–118, quotation at 118.

67. M. A. Moore to Governor Pickens, Mar. 5, 1861, Pickens-Bonham papers, LC; A.A.G. R. W. Memminger to Brig. Genl. Johnson Hagood, Aug. 16, 1862, and Col. Lawrence M. Keitt to General, Jan. 9, 1863, in Berlin et al., *Destruction of Slavery,* 132, 134–136.

68. Statement by Robert Blake [Sept. 1862] and Excerpts from Testimony of Col. Higginson before the American Freedmen's Inquiry Commission, June 1863, both in Berlin et al., *Destruction of Slavery,* 132–133, 138–139, quotations on 138, 139; *Two Diaries from Middle St. John's Berkeley, South Carolina,*

February–May 1865 (St. John's Hunting Club, 1921), 17; Julie Saville, *The Work of Reconstruction: From Slave to Wage Laborer in South Carolina, 1860–1870* (Cambridge, UK, 1994).

69. Lt. Gen. E. Kirby Smith to Maj. Genl. Price, Sept. 4, 1863, in Berlin et al., *Destruction of Slavery,* 772–773, quotation at 772.
70. General Order No. 70, Head Qtrs Cav. Northern Miss., Nov. 7, 1863, in Berlin et al., *Destruction of Slavery,* 776–777. On the Union policy of sorting by gender, see Bercaw, *Gendered Freedoms;* Frankel, *Freedom's Women;* and McCurry, "War, Gender and Emancipation."
71. John J. Pettus to Gentlemen of the Senate and House of Representatives, Nov. 3, 1863, *Journal of the House of Representatives of the State of Mississippi, December Session of 1862 and November Session of 1863* (Jackson, 1864), 94; B. F. Arthur to General G. T. Beauregard, Oct. 20, 1862, *O.R.,* ser. 4, 2:133–136.
72. Circular, Adj. Gen. 3rd. Military District, Dec. 8, 1863, Alexander Robert Lawton Papers, *RASP,* ser. J, pt. 3, reel 26; Jno. Pearce to Honl. Jas. A. Seddon, Nov. 3, 1863, and Endorsement, Jas. A. Seddon, both in Berlin et al., *Destruction of Slavery,* 775–776.
73. Wyndham Robertson to James A. Seddon, Jan. 13, 1864, *O.R.,* ser. 4, 3:25–27, quotation at 26. That slaveholders sacrificed slavery for independence is a position associated with Emory Thomas, contested by Robert Durden, but sustained in more recent accounts. See Thomas, *Confederate Nation,* 263; Durden, *The Gray and Black,* 287; Gallagher, *Confederate War,* 81–85; Dillard, "Independence or Slavery."
74. James A. Seddon to Wyndham Robertson, Jan. 24, 1864, *O.R.,* ser. 4, 3:41–42.
75. Brig. Genl. J. W. Phelps to Capt. R. S. Davis, July 30, 1862, in Berlin et al., *Black Military Experience,* 62–63, and Phelps to Davis, June 16, 1862, in Berlin et al., *Destruction of Slavery,* 210–217, quotation at 211.
76. Jones quoted in Eugene D. Genovese, *Roll, Jordan, Roll: The World the Slaves Made* (New York, 1974), 104; R. Q. Mallard, P. W. Fleming, E. Stacy, "Committee of Citizens of the 15th Dist., Liberty County, GA," to Brig. Genl. Mercer, Savannah, Georgia, Aug. 5, 1862, *O.R.,* ser. 4, 2:35–38, quotations at 37. David Hunter to Edwin Stanton, June 23, 1862, in Berlin et al., *Black Military Experience,* 51.
77. Proceedings of a General Court Martial Convened at Pensacola, Apr. 5th 1862, and Apr. 6, 1862, Enclosed in Col Tho. M. Jones to Maj. Genl. Sam Jones, LRCSW, RG 109, roll 97; C.S.A., War Department, Army Regulations Adopted for the Use of the Army of the Confederate States (New Orleans, 1861), 414; Jackson Morton to Capt. E. Farrand, Pensacola, May 6, 1862, LRCSW, roll 97; *Random House College Dictionary,* rev. ed. (New York, 1982), 1399. The Articles of War were the same in the C.S.A. and the U.S.A., presumably because the Confederate army adopted the extant U.S. manual. For the Union army, see Orville J. Victor, *The Military Handbook and Soldiers' Manual of Information, including the Articles of War* (New York, 1861). Part of the record of this case is reprinted in Berlin et al., *Destruction of Slavery,* 785–794.
78. Saml. Jones, Maj. Gen. to Genl. S. Cooper, Adjt & Insp. Genl., Apr. 22, 1862, LRCSW, roll 97; Willis Sturdivant to Jefferson Davis, Jan. 10, 1863, *PJD,* 9:20; John Milton to Jefferson Davis, Tallahassee, Aug. 20, 1862, *PJD,* 8:349–350;

Ths. M. Jones to S. Cooper, Hq Qrs. Army of Pensacola, Apr. 12, 1862, LRCSW, roll 97; Genl. S. Cooper, Adjt. & Insp. Genl. to Secretary of War, enclosing report of Col. Thos. Jones, LRCSW, roll 97.

79. Jackson Morton to Honorable A. E. Maxwell, Apr. 17, 1862, Jackson Morton to Capt. E. Farrand, May 6, 1862, and Proceedings of a Court Martial Convened at Pensacola, Apr. 6, 1862, all in LRCSW, roll 97.

80. Adjutant and Inspector General's Office, General Orders No. 25, Mar. 6, 1863, *O.R.*, ser. 4, 2:420–421; Mark E. Neely Jr., *Southern Rights: Political Prisoners and the Myth of Confederate Constitutionalism* (Charlottesville, 1999), 137.

81. U.S. Constitution, art. 4, sec. 4; Willard Hurst, *Treason in the United States*, reprinted from the *Harvard Law Review* 58, nos. 2, 3, and 6 (1945): 258–259, 247, 396.

82. Hurst, *Treason in the United States*, 258–259, 247, 396; Kerber, *No Constitutional Right*, 3–46; McCurry, review essay in *Signs* 30, no. 2 (Winter 2005): 1659–70. Reva Siegel uses the term "gendered jurisdiction." See Siegel, "She the People: The Nineteenth Amendment, Sex Equality, Federalism, and the Family," *Harvard Law Review* 115, no. 4 (Feb. 2002): 982.

83. Morris, *Southern Slavery and the Law*, 273, 275, 265, quotation on 275; Hurst, *Treason in the United States*, 439; *Report on the Trial of Castner Hanway for Treason in the Resistance to the Execution of the Fugitive Slave Law of September, 1850* (Philadelphia, 1852); *State v. Peter Shartle*, Criminal Action Papers—Slave, Richmond County, N.C., Fall term 1861, NCDAH.

84. Adjt Pleas Smith to A.A.G. J. Thompson, Jan. 8, 1863, in Berlin et al., *Destruction of Slavery*, 300. For the number of political prisoners, see Neely, *Southern Rights*.

85. Neely, *Southern Rights*, 49–50, quotation at 49.

86. Ariela J. Gross, *Double Character: Slavery and Mastery in the Antebellum Southern Courtroom* (Princeton, 2000); Laura F. Edwards, "Status without Rights: African Americans and the Tangled History of Law and Governance in the Nineteenth Century U.S. South," *AHR* 112, no. 2 (Apr. 2007); Morris, *Southern Slavery and the Law*, 55–56, quotation at 2, and passim.

87. Proceedings of a General Court Martial Convened at Pensacola, Apr. 5, 1862, and Apr. 6, 1862, LRCSW, roll 97.

88. Thos. M. Jones to S. Cooper, Apr. 12, 1862, LRCSW, roll 97. For "stern logic of events," see *Richmond Sentinel*, Mar. 6, 1865, in Durden, *The Gray and the Black, 248.*

89. S. Cooper to the Secretary of War, Nov. 11, 1862, and Thos. M. Jones to S. Cooper, Apr. 12, 1862, both LRCSW, roll 97.

90. *Jackson Mississippian* reprinted in Durden, *The Gray and the Black*, 29–32, quotations at 30.

8. THE FALL

1. Robin Blackburn, *The Overthrow of Colonial Slavery, 1776–1848* (London, 1988), 58 and throughout.

2. *Richmond Sentinel*, Mar. 6, 1865, *Raleigh Confederate*, Nov. 23, 1864, *Charles-*

ton Mercury, Jan. 13, 1865, in Robert F. Durden, *The Gray and the Black: The Confederate Debate on Emancipation* (Baton Rouge, 1972), 248, 253, 233.

3. The major exception is the British colonies. For an overview of most cases, see Blackburn, *Overthrow of Colonial Slavery.* On the American Revolution, see Benjamin Quarles, *The Negro in the American Revolution* (Chapel Hill, 1961); Phillip D. Morgan and Andrew Jackson O'Shaughnessy, "Arming Slaves in the American Revolution," in *Arming Slaves from Classical Times to the Modern Age,* ed. Christopher Leslie Brown and Philip D. Morgan (New Haven, 2006). On Haiti, see C. L. R. James, *The Black Jacobins: Toussaint L'Ouverture and the San Domingo Revolution* (1938; New York, 1963); Carolyn Fick, *The Making of Haiti: The Saint Domingue Revolution from Below* (Knoxville, 1990). On Cuba, see Rebecca Scott, *Slave Emancipation in Cuba: The Transition to Free Labor, 1860–1899* (Princeton, 1985); Ada Ferrer, *Insurgent Cuba: Race, Nation and Revolution, 1868–1898* (Chapel Hill, 1999). On Brazil, see Hendrik Kraay, "Slavery, Citizenship and Military Service in Brazil's Mobilization for the Paraguayan War," *Slavery and Abolition* 18, no. 3 (Dec. 1997): 228–256.
4. Robin Blackburn references the context of war without identifying it as a causal factor. See Blackburn, *Overthrow of Colonial Slavery,* 58; *Richmond Whig,* Feb. 17, 1865, in Durden, *The Gray and the Black,* 236–239, quotation at 237.
5. For an introduction, see Brown and Morgan, *Arming Slaves.*
6. Jefferson Davis, "Address to the Senate and House of Representatives of the Confederate States of America," Nov. 7, 1864, *O.R.,* ser. 4, 3:790–800, quotation at 799. With rare exception the literature on arming the slaves in the Confederacy assesses the development in light of its meaning for Confederate nationalism. For the major contributions, see the following: N. W. Stephenson, "The Question of Arming the Slaves," *AHR* 18 (Jan. 1913): 295–308; Benjamin Quarles, *The Negro in the Civil War* (1953; New York, 1989); Emory M. Thomas, *The Confederacy as a Revolutionary Experience* (1971; Columbia, S.C., 1991); Durden, *The Gray and the Black;* Paul Escott, *After Secession: Jefferson Davis and the Failure of Confederate Nationalism* (Baton Rouge, 1979); Emory M. Thomas, *The Confederate Nation: 1861–1865* (New York, 1979); Philip D. Dillard, "Independence or Slavery: The Confederate Debate over Arming the Slaves" (Ph.D. diss., Rice University, 1999). For one exception, see Bruce Levine, *Confederate Emancipation: Southern Plans to Free and Arm the Slaves during the Civil War* (New York, 2006).
7. James, *Black Jacobins;* and more recently Fick, *The Making of Haiti;* Blackburn, *Overthrow of Colonial Slavery;* David Geggus, *Slavery, War, and Revolution* (New York, 1982); Geggus, *Haitian Revolutionary Studies* (Bloomington, 2002); Laurent Dubois, *Avengers of the New World: The Story of the Haitian Revolution* (Cambridge, Mass., 2004); John Garrigus, *Before Haiti: Race and Citizenship in French San-Domingue* (New York, 2006). My own thinking on the subject has been powerfully shaped by Elizabeth Colwill. See her essay "'Fêtes de l'hymen, fêtes de la liberté': Marriage, Manhood, and Emancipation in Revolutionary Saint-Domingue," in *The World of the Haitian Revolution,* ed. David Patrick Geggus and Norman Fiering (Bloomington, 2009), 125–155.

8. Geggus, *Haitian Revolutionary Studies,* 99–118, and Geggus, "The Arming of Slaves in the Haitian Revolution," in Brown and Morgan, *Arming Slaves,* 209–302.
9. Fick, *The Making of Haiti,* 115–116; Blackburn, *Overthrow of Colonial Slavery,* 194. For the numbers, see Geggus, "The Arming of Slaves," 222–223.
10. Blackburn, *Overthrow of Colonial Slavery,* 218; Colwill, "'Fêtes de l'hymen'"; Fick, *The Making of Haiti,* 161.
11. Laurent Dubois and John D. Garrigus, eds., *Slave Revolution in the Caribbean, 1789–1804: A Brief History with Documents* (New York, 2006), 129–132; Blackburn, *Overthrow of Colonial Slavery,* 218.
12. See Fick, *The Making of Haiti;* Colwill, "'Fêtes de l'hymen'"; Geggus, *Slavery, War and Revolution;* Dubois, *Avengers of the New World.*
13. *Emancipation Proclamation,* Jan. 1, 1863, www.yale.edu/lawweb/avalon/emancipa.htm.
14. Ethelbert Barksdale quoted in *Richmond Sentinel,* Mar. 6, 1865; "Policy of Employing Negro Troops, Speech of H. C. Chambers," both in Durden, *The Gray and the Black,* 141, 246.
15. "War is a game that cannot be played without men," Judah P. Benjamin said at a critical juncture. "Where are the men?" See *Richmond Dispatch,* Feb. 10, 1865, in Durden, *The Gray and the Black,* 192–195, quotation at 194; John A. Campbell to Jefferson Davis, Apr. 28, 1861, *PJD,* 7:138; Jefferson Davis, Address to the Congress of the Confederate States, Feb. 25, 1862, *PJD,* 8:59.
16. For the estimates, see George Randolph to President Davis, Oct. 20, 1862, *PJD,* 8:453; Ira Berlin, Joseph Reidy, and Leslie Rowland, eds., *Freedom: A Documentary History of Emancipation, 1861–1867,* ser. 2: *The Black Military Experience* (Cambridge, UK, 1982), table 1, 12. F. W. Pickens to Milledge Luke Bonham, Jan. 11, 1862, Pickens-Bonham Papers, box 4, folder 120, LC; Jefferson Davis, Speech at Jackson, Dec. 26, 1862, *PJD,* 8:567. Davis's analysis is oft-repeated. See Gary Gallagher, *The Confederate War: How Popular Will, Nationalism, and Military Strategy Could Not Stave Off Defeat* (New York, 1997). On the comparative size of Northern and Southern military populations, see Herman Hattaway and Archer Jones, *How the North Won: A Military History of the Civil War* (Urbana, 1983), 114.
17. Randolph to Davis, Oct. 20, 1862, *PJD,* 8:453, and Albert Burton Moore, *Conscription and Conflict in the Confederacy* (1924; Columbia, S.C., 1996), 13, 140, 308. J. E. Leigh et al. to Governor John Pettus, Apr. 1862, Pettus Papers, roll 6, MDAH; *Richmond Dispatch,* Feb. 10, 1865, in Durden, *The Gray and the Black,* 194.
18. James M. McPherson, *Battle Cry of Freedom: The Civil War Era* (New York, 1988), 424, 844, 855; Drew Gilpin Faust, *This Republic of Suffering: Death and the American Civil War* (New York, 2008), xi.
19. Excerpts from Testimony of Captain C. B. Wilder before the American Freedmen's Inquiry Commission, May 9, 1863, in Ira Berlin et al., eds., *Freedom: A Documentary History of Emancipation, 1861–1867,* ser. 1, vol. 1: *The Destruction of Slavery* (Cambridge, UK, 1985), 90, 813–818.

20. *Emancipation Proclamation;* Abraham Lincoln, interview of Aug. 19, 1864, in Durden, *The Gray and the Black,* 23–24. On the need to move away from a history of emancipation focused too narrowly on the great document, see Ira Berlin et al., *Slaves No More: Three Essays on Emancipation and the Civil War* (Cambridge, UK, 1992), 5–6.
21. Brig. Genl J. W. Phelps to Capt. R. S. Davis, July 30, 1862, in Berlin et al., *Black Military Experience,* 62–63; Preliminary Emancipation Proclamation, Sept. 22, 1862, in *U.S. Statutes at Large, Treaties, and Proclamations of the United States of America* (Boston, 1863), 12:1267–68; Jefferson Davis to the Senate and House of Representatives of the Confederate States, Jan. 12, 1863, in *O.R.,* ser. 4, 2:336–350, quotation at 345.
22. Berlin et al., *Black Military Experience,* table 1, 12, 113, 87–88. The Second Confiscation Act, July 17, 1862, and the Militia Act, July 17, 1862, in *U.S. Statutes at Large,* 12:589–592, 597–600.
23. General in Chief H. W. Halleck to Major General Grant, Mar. 31, 1863, and Major George L. Stearns to Hon Edwin Stanton, Aug. 17, 1863, both in Berlin et al., *Black Military Experience,* 143–144, 98–101; Adj. Gen. L. Thomas to Hon. Edwin Stanton, Aug. 23, 1863, and 1st Lt. Hiram W. Allen to Col. A. G. Draper, Nov. 17, 1863, both in Berlin et al., *Destruction of Slavery,* 308–310, 92–93.
24. General Orders No. 46, Dec. 5, 1863, in Berlin et al., *Black Military Experience* 135–138, Lt. Gen. E. Kirby Smith to Maj. Genl. Price, Sept. 4, 1863, and Lorenzo Thomas, all in Berlin et al., *Destruction of Slavery,* 772–773, 309. On marriage and gender in the Union's military emancipation policies, see Stephanie McCurry, "War, Gender and Emancipation in the Civil War South," in *Lincoln's Proclamation: Emancipation Reconsidered,* ed. William A. Blair and Karen Fisher Younger (Chapel Hill, 2009).
25. Robert E. Lee to Jefferson Davis, July 8, 1863, *PJD,* 9:266–268, quotation at 266; Jefferson Davis to Robert E. Lee, July 28, 1863, *PJD,* 9:307–311, quotation at 308; McPherson, *Battle Cry of Freedom,* 635–665.
26. W. C. Bibb to Hon. James A. Seddon, July 23, 1863, in Berlin et al., *Destruction of Slavery,* 704–706.
27. The Davis administration pursued new impressment legislation, although it took until Feb. 1864 to get it. See Chapter 7.
28. Samuel W. Melton to Hon. James A. Seddon, Nov. 11, 1863, *O.R.,* ser. 4, 2:944–952, quotation at 946.
29. James A. Seddon to His Excellency Jefferson Davis, Nov. 26, 1863, *O.R.*, ser. 4, 2:990–1018, quotations at 995, 999, 1018.
30. Moore, *Conscription and Conflict;* on enlistment rates, see Gallagher, *The Confederate War,* 28–29.
31. Philip Dillard confirmed the pattern of greater support for arming slaves in states that bore the brunt of battle. Dillard, "Independence or Slavery."
32. John B. Jones, *A Rebel War Clerk's Diary* (Philadelphia, 1866), 1:391; Benjamin Bolling to Jefferson Davis, July 24, 1863, and Leonidas Walthall to Davis, Aug. 11, 1863, *PJD,* 9:304, 339–341; Levine, *Confederate Emancipation,* 24–25.
33. *Montgomery Weekly Mail,* Sept. 2, 1863, in Durden, *The Gray and the Black,*

32–34, quotation at 32; Senate and House of Representatives, Alabama, Joint Resolutions in Relation to the Increase of the Army of the Confederate States, Approved Aug. 29, 1863, *O.R.,* ser. 4, 2:767.

34. *Montgomery Weekly Mail,* Sept. 2, 1863, in Durden, *The Gray and the Black,* 32–34.
35. It is usually seen as preamble to a story that gets serious only in fall 1864.
36. *Richmond Whig,* Feb. 17, 1865, in Durden, *The Gray and the Black,* 236–239.
37. *Jackson Mississippian* reprinted in *Montgomery Weekly Mail,* Sept. 9, 1863, in Durden, *The Gray and the Black,* 29–32.
38. Major General Patrick R. Cleburne et al. to Commanding General, the Corps, Division, Brigade and Regimental Commanders of the Army of Tennessee, Jan. 2, 1864, *O.R.*, ser. 1, vol. 52, pt. 2, 586–592. On Cleburne, see Durden, *The Gray and the Black,* 53–55, 273, and Levine, *Confederate Emancipation,* 26–29. The literature has not put much, if any, emphasis on the way that policy was forced on officials by slaves themselves. See Dillard, "Independence or Slavery," and Levine, *Confederate Emancipation.* The debate over "who freed the slaves" has been conducted wholly in relation to Union policy. For an introduction, see James McPherson, "Who Freed the Slaves?" in *Drawn with the Sword: Reflections on the American Civil War* (New York, 1996), 192–207; and Ira Berlin, "Emancipation and Its Meaning in American Life," *Reconstruction* 2, no. 3 (1994): 35–44. The editors of the Freedmen and Southern Society Project cast the Confederate decision to arm slaves as a desperate last gamble with no discernible meaning for the comparative history of slavery and emancipation. See Berlin et al., *Destruction of Slavery,* 682.
39. Cleburne to Commanding General et al., Jan. 2, 1864, 586–587, *O.R.,* ser. 1, vol. 52, pt. 2, 587; Levine, *Confederate Emancipation,* 25–27. Hindman also advocated only for more aggressive use of slaves as military laborers. See T. C. Hindman to Jefferson Davis, Dalton, Georgia, Jan. 16, 1864, HU.
40. Cleburne to Commanding General et al., Jan. 2, 1864, *O.R.,* ser. 1, vol. 52, pt. 2, 588, 590.
41. Ibid., 590.
42. Ibid., 591; for the comparative case, see McCurry, "War, Gender and Emancipation."
43. Cleburne to Commanding General et al., Jan. 2, 1864, *O.R.,* ser. 1, vol. 52, pt. 2, 591.
44. Ibid., 590.
45. Brigadier General Patton Anderson to Lieutenant General Leonidas Polk, Jan. 14, 1864, in Durden, *The Gray and the Black,* 63–65, quotation on 64; W. H. T. Walker to President Davis, Jan. 12, 1864, and President Davis to W. H. T. Walker, Jan. 23, 1864, *PJD,* 10:170, 197–198; J. E. Johnston, General, Circular, Lieutenant General Hardee etc., Jan. 31, 1864 [with postscript to Major General Cleburne], *O.R.,* ser. 1, vol. 52, pt. 2, 608; J. E. Johnston, General to Hon. James A. Seddon, Secretary of War, Feb. 2, 1864, *O.R.,* ser. 1, vol. 52, pt. 2, 608–609. About 1890 a copy was found in the effects of Calhoun Benham, a deceased member of Major General Cleburne's staff. See *PJD,* 10:177–179. Cle-

burne was passed over for promotion three times before his death. See Levine, *Confederate Emancipation,* 27–29.

46. Susan M. Robinson, Nancy Powers and Margaret Merryman to President Davis, Oct. 19, 1864, and F. Kendall to Mr. President, Sept. 16, 1864, *PJD,* 11:112–113, 45–46.
47. *Macon Daily Telegraph,* Sept. 24, 1864, *PJD,* 11:60–63; Levine, *Confederate Emancipation,* 30; James Seddon to the President of the Confederate States, Nov. 3, 1864, *O.R.,* ser. 4, 3:756–771, quotation at 761.
48. Governor Henry W. Allen to Honorable James A. Seddon, Sept. 26, 1864, in Berlin et al., *Black Military Experience,* 287–288; Levine, *Confederate Emancipation,* 31–32; *Vicksburg Daily Herald,* Oct. 22, 1864.
49. *Richmond Enquirer,* Oct. 6, 1864, *Lynchburg Virginian,* Oct. 8, 20, 1864, *Mobile Register,* Nov. 3, 1864, *New Orleans Picayune,* Nov. 3, 1864, all in Durden, *The Gray and the Black,* 74–75, 76–77, 77–79, 79–80, 80–81.
50. *Mobile Tribune,* Nov. 4, 1864, *Macon Telegraph and Confederate,* Nov. 19, 1864, both in Durden, *The Gray and the Black,* 81–83, 124–125.
51. Historians differ on whether Confederates passed the test, but few refuse the framework. Durden (overturning Thomas) famously insisted they failed; Philip Dillard recently has insisted they passed, even as his own evidence undercuts that conclusion. Bruce Levine has tried to shift the discussion to one about the motives in endorsing emancipation. The emphasis in the debate has been too much on emancipation and too little on enlistment, which was always the primary objective. This is most clear in the oldest treatment, Stephenson, "Question of Arming the Slaves."
52. *Lynchburg Republican,* Nov. 2, 1864, in Durden, *The Gray and the Black,* 92–95.
53. Allen Caperton to My Dear Sir, Oct., 1864, Allen Caperton to My Dear Sir, Oct. 18, 1864, Allen Caperton Letters, Grigsby Family Papers, VHS.
54. Caperton to My Dear Sir, Oct. 1864.
55. William Porcher Miles to General Robert E. Lee, Oct. 24, 1864, in Durden, *The Gray and the Black,* 135–136. One treasury clerk relayed a conversation with Confederate senator Semmes from early November in which the senator expressed his intention to oppose "putting negroes in the army." See John Johnson to Dear Albert, Nov. 3, 1864, Albert A. Batchelor Papers, box 1, folder 8, LSU.
56. James Seddon to Jefferson Davis, Oct. 27, 1864, HU.
57. James Seddon to the President of the Confederate States, Nov. 3, 1864, *O.R.*, ser. 4, 3:756–771, quotations at 761, 762.
58. Jefferson Davis, "Address to the Senate and House of Representatives of the Confederate States of America," Nov. 7, 1864, *O.R.,* ser. 4, 3:790–800.
59. Ibid., 798, 799.
60. The political implications of arming slaves in a republic—even more than the labor implications of emancipating them—were the toughest stumbling block for Davis. Thus Bruce Levine's emphasis on emancipation as a way to control the terms of labor in a post-emancipation South, though interesting, was the

preoccupation of a very few men, notably Stringfellow most obviously. See Levine, *Confederate Emancipation,* 89–109.

61. *Charleston Mercury,* Nov. 12, 1864.
62. Ibid., Nov. 12, 3, 1864, Jan. 13, 31, 1865; *Richmond Daily Examiner,* Nov. 8, 1864.
63. *Richmond Enquirer,* Nov. 11, 1864, Feb. 11, 1865.
64. *North Carolina Standard,* Nov. 4, 1864, Jan. 17, 1865. For papers that proposed no change in slave soldiers' status, see *Richmond Sentinel,* Nov. 8, 1864, *Richmond Whig,* Nov. 9, 1864, *Macon Telegraph,* Nov. 14, 1864.
65. Davis's role has been a matter of some disagreement since Stephenson's 1913 article cast Benjamin and Lee as the prime movers and Davis as a belated partner. This representation was vigorously disputed by Robert Durden in 1972, and Davis's role was further confirmed by Bruce Levine in his recent treatment of the subject. The issue was understandably more touchy in 1913. For his rebuke of the senators, see *National Intelligencer,* Mar. 25, 1865. On Hampton Roads, see McPherson, *Battle Cry of Freedom,* 821–825. On the Kenner mission, see *PJD,* 11:269–272, 277–278; McPherson, *Battle Cry of Freedom,* 837–838. Rumors of secret negotiations circulated in Europe prior to that. See *London Index,* Feb. 2, 1865, 77. On the message to Congress, see Message of the President, Richmond, Virginia, Feb. 21, 1865, Rare Book Room, LVA.
66. J. P. Benjamin to Frederick A. Porcher, Dec. 21, 1864, *O.R.,* ser. 4, 3:959–960; William Porcher Miles to General Robert E. Lee, Oct. 21, 1864, and Miles to Lee, Nov. 3, 1864, in Durden, *The Gray and the Black,* 135–136, 136–137.
67. James A. Seddon to Major General Howell Cobb, Dec. 30, 1864, and Howell Cobb to Hon. James A. Seddon, Jan. 8, 1865, *O.R.,* ser. 4, 3:981, 1009–10. For evidence of the constant demands for reinforcements, see Howell Cobb to Jefferson Davis, Nov. 17, 1864, Jan. 6, 1865, *PJD,* 11:169, 283.
68. Andrew Hunter to General R. E. Lee, Jan. 7, 1865, and Lee to Hunter, Jan. 11, 1865, *O.R.,* ser. 4, 3:1006–08, 1012–13. On Hunter's enduring opposition, see Frank E. Vandiver, ed., *Proceedings of the Second Confederate Congress, December 15, 1864–March 18, 1865,* vol. 52 of *Southern Historical Society Papers* (Richmond, 1959), 455.
69. R. E. Lee, General to Hon. Andrew Hunter, Jan. 11, 1865, *O.R.,* ser. 4, 3:1012–13.
70. Ibid.
71. Judging by the terms of the Preliminary Emancipation Proclamation.
72. *Richmond Dispatch,* Feb. 10, 1865, and *Macon Telegraph,* Feb. 12, 1865.
73. J. H. Stringfellow to President Davis, Feb. 8, 1865, *O.R.,* ser. 4, 3:1067–70; *Richmond Daily Examiner,* Feb. 25, 1865, in Durden, *The Gray and the Black,* 225–228, quotations on 227, 228. Stringfellow exemplifies Levine's argument that emancipation was an attempt to control the terms of labor in a post-emancipation society. See Levine, *Confederate Emancipation,* 99–102.
74. *Richmond Whig,* Feb. 17, 1865, in Durden, *The Gray and the Black,* 236–239; *Richmond Whig,* Mar. 9, 1865.
75. Governor William Smith, *Message to Gentlemen of the Senate and House of Delegates,* Dec. 7, 1864, Governor William Smith Papers, box 4, folder 8, LVA; for

the Virginia law, see Durden, *The Gray and the Black,* 249–250, and *O.R.,* ser. 1, vol. 46, pt. 3, 1315. On developments in the Virginia legislature, see Stephenson, "Question of Arming the Slaves."

76. All of these developments can be followed in Davis's correspondence. See *PJD,* vol. 11, and McPherson, *Battle Cry of Freedom,* 807–852.
77. Stephenson, "Question of Arming the Slaves," 298.
78. William A. Graham to David Swain, Feb. 22, 1865 in Durden, *The Gray and the Black,* 240–241; Vandiver, *Proceedings,* 325, 456.
79. Vandiver, *Proceedings,* 329–330.
80. Ibid., 329–331, 330, 324, 330–331.
81. *Speech of Hon. Thos. S. Gholson of Virginia on the Policy of Employing Negro Troops, and the Duty of All Classes to Aid in the Prosecution of the War* (Richmond, 1865), Special Collections, LVA.
82. Recent work has made it clear that black men's right to bear arms, the idea of black militias, and the rearming of white militias were central to the violent political contestation of power in the postwar and post-emancipation South. See Eric Foner, *Reconstruction: America's Unfinished Revolution, 1863–1877* (New York, 1998), and Steven Hahn, *A Nation under Our Feet: Black Political Struggles in the Rural South from Slavery to the Great Migration* (Cambridge, Mass., 2003).
83. Vandiver, *Proceedings,* 345; *Minority Report on the Bill to Increase the Military Force of the Confederate States,* Special Collections, LVA. The signers were William Porcher Miles, Thomas S. Gholson, W. N. H. Smith, Julian Hartridge, and Stephen H. Darden.
84. *Minority Report.*
85. *Richmond Dispatch,* Feb. 10, 1865, and *Macon Telegraph,* Feb. 12, 1865; J. P. Benjamin to General in Chief R. E. Lee, Feb. 11, 1865, *O.R.,* ser. 1, vol. 46, pt. 2, 1229; O. Latrobe to Maj. Gen. J. B. Kershaw, Feb. 16, 1865, *O.R.,* ser. 1, vol. 46, pt. 2, 1236. For examples of soldiers' resolutions, see Berlin et al., *Black Military Experience,* 297, and Durden, *The Gray and the Black,* 216–217, 210–220, 223; Vandiver, *Proceedings,* 354; as evidence of a "die-hard rebel" mentality, see Jason Phillips, *Diehard Rebels: The Confederate Culture of Invincibility* (Athens, Ga., 2007), 157–164.
86. *Richmond Sentinel,* Mar. 6, 1865; R. E. Lee to Ethelbert Barksdale, Feb. 18, 1865, in Durden, *The Gray and the Black,* 206–207.
87. Vandiver, *Proceedings,* 454–455; *Richmond Whig,* Mar. 9, 1865; Allen Caperton to My Dear Sir, Feb. 23, 1865, Allen Caperton Letters, Hugh Blair Grigsby Papers. For the vote in the house, see Stephenson, "Question of Arming the Slaves," 301.
88. General Order No. 14, *O.R.,* ser. 4, 3:1161–62.
89. For Dillard, the debate over enlisting and emancipating slave men posed a simple binary test of Confederate nationalism, "slavery or independence," that Southerners passed with flying colors, proving that "they would sacrifice everything, even slavery, to achieve their independence." Here he attempts to

overturn Robert Durden, who famously insisted that white Southerners "yet lacked . . . the moral courage . . . to voluntarily abandon the peculiar institution." See Dillard, "Independence or Slavery," 282; Durden, *The Gray and the Black,* xii.

90. General Order No. 14, *O.R.,* ser. 4, 3:1161–62, quotation on 1161.

91. The Confederate decision to arm slaves was "a final and desperate gamble to forestall defeat," the editors' insight thus rendering it a nonevent in the comparative history of the destruction of slavery they otherwise document so richly. See Berlin et al., *Destruction of Slavery,* 682. Rebecca Scott thus compares all sides in the Cuban War to the Union side in the American Civil War, seemingly unaware that the Confederacy offers a better match for the actions of anti-insurgent Spanish forces, who, like the Confederates, had been forced into a grudging and contingent emancipation to get slave soldiers. See Scott, *Slave Emancipation in Cuba,* 77. Hendrik Kraay describes a relationship between the state and a slaveholding ruling class in Brazil very like that of the Confederate state and ruling class, but he appears unaware of the similarity. See Hendrik Kraay, "Slavery, Citizenship, and Military Service in Brazil's Mobilization for the Paraguayan War," *Slavery and Abolition* 18, no. 3 (Dec. 1997): 228–256; Kraay, "Arming Slaves in Brazil from the Seventeenth Century to the Nineteenth Century," in Brown and Morgan, *Arming Slaves,* 146–179.

92. Richard Launcelot Maury Diary, Feb. 20, 1865, VHS; Howell Cobb to Hon. James A. Seddon, Jan. 8, 1865, *O.R.,* ser. 4, 3:1009–10.

93. *PJD,* 11:430, 462–464, 429–430, 438, 439–441; J. J. Jackson to Jonathan Worth, Mar. 4, 1865, in *The Correspondence of Jonathan Worth,* ed. J. G. de Roulhac Hamilton (Raleigh, 1909), 1:362–363; Robert E. Lee to Mr. President, Mar. 21, 1865, *PJD,* 11:450–452.

94. *Richmond Dispatch,* Mar. 21, 25, 1865, in Durden, *The Gray and the Black,* 271–273, 275; William Smith to General R. E. Lee, Mar. 25, 1865, and William Smith, Mar. 3, 1865 [Note on petition for pardon of Peter a Slave], William Smith Executive Papers, Mfm reel 5024, 5025, LVA; William Smith to President Davis, Mar. 27, 1865, in Durden, *The Gray and the Black,* 278–279; Requisition of the Governor, William Smith, Broadside, Dec. 1864, UVA; William Smith, Printed Circular, Executive Department, Richmond, Mar. 14, 1865, William Smith Papers, box 5, folder 7, LVA; *Richmond Whig,* Mar. 31, 1865, in Durden, *The Gray and the Black,* 276.

95. For the law and General Order No. 14, see *O.R.,* ser. 4, 3:1161–62. For the Virginia law, see *O.R.,* ser. 1, vol. 46, pt. 3, 1315. Robert E. Lee to Jefferson Davis, Mar. 10, 1865, in Durden, *The Gray and the Black,* 276–277, and Robert E. Lee to Jefferson Davis, Mar. 24, 1865, *O.R.,* ser. 1, vol. 46, pt. 3, 1339.

96. *Richmond Dispatch,* Mar. 21, 23, 1865; Maury Diary, Feb. 21, Mar. 23, 1865; *Richmond Whig,* Mar. 31, 1865, in Durden, *The Gray and the Black,* 276.

97. Jefferson Davis to William Smith, Mar. 25, 30, 1865, *O.R.,* ser. 1, vol. 46, pt. 3, 1348–49, 1366–67; Jefferson Davis to General R. E. Lee, Apr. 1, 1865, *O.R.,* ser. 1, vol. 46, pt. 3, 1370. Governor Smith promised to try to secure a manumission

provision from the Virginia legislature. See Governor William Smith to President Davis, Mar. 27, 1865, in Durden, *The Gray and the Black,* 278–279.

98. On the recruitment of slave soldiers from Winder Hospital, see *Richmond Dispatch,* Mar. 23, 1865, and Durden, *The Gray and the Black,* 270. For examples of two historians, see Durden, *The Gray and the Black,* 270, and Clarence L. Mohr, *On the Threshold of Freedom: Masters and Slaves in Civil War Georgia* (Athens, Ga., 1986), 274–285.
99. William Smith, Mar. 3, 1865; *Two Diaries from Middle St. John's Berkeley, South Carolina, February–May 1865* (St. John's Hunting Club, 1921), SCL, 17. The hanging of Harry was Mar. 22, 1865.
100. Leon Litwack, "Many Thousands Gone: Black Southerners and the Confederacy," in *The Old South in the Crucible of War,* ed. Harry P. Owens and James J. Cooke (Jackson, 1983), 60.
101. On the last days, see McPherson, *Battle Cry of Freedom,* 831–852.

Acknowledgments

This book will be forever associated in my mind with my children, who grew up in the years it took to write it. When I began, one was a toddler and the other an infant, and now they are teenagers full of life and purpose, starting down their own paths. The richness of that experience—of intellectual life and motherhood combined—was more than I had ever hoped for. That few generations of women before me had that privilege makes it all the more treasured. Still, the work takes resources, and it gives me great pleasure to finally thank the people and institutions who helped me do mine.

For fellowships and sabbaticals that provided critical time for research and writing I would like to thank the John Simon Guggenheim Memorial Foundation and the Deans of the Colleges of Arts and Sciences at Northwestern University and the University of Pennsylvania. At Northwestern, Eric Sundquist provided a one-year leave from teaching that jumpstarted research for the book; at Penn, Rebecca Bushnell provided another that allowed me to finish the writing. Amy Gutmann, President of the University of Pennsylvania, made her support clear at a critical moment in my career and for that I thank her too.

The research for this project required some creative strategies, including photocopying of documents in state archives across the South. In that task I had the assistance of many graduate students, most of them Ph.D. students involved in exciting projects of their own. For that research assistance and for the intellectual companionship I thank Margaret Storey, V. Elaine Thompson, and my own students Aaron Astor, Joanna Cohen, Gregory Downs, Rene Hayden, Matthew Karp, Erik Mathisen, and Eric Taylor.

Numbers of people extended invitations to share work over the years it took to write this book. Those were invariably important occasions for me in trying out arguments and sounding their limits. But most important of all was the experience I had repeatedly of meeting people who seemed to join me in the project, thinking through the issues with me and lending their knowledge to it. An early invitation from Larry Powell to visit Tulane was one such occasion, as was the history department seminar at the University of Illinois at Chicago, and the invitation by Drew Faust to give the presidential address at the Southern Association of Women Historians. Other invitations—from Nancy Cott to join a conference at the Radcliffe Institute, William Blair to come to Penn State, Bill Link to present to the Milbauer Seminar at University of Florida, Frances Clarke to present at the University of Sydney, and John Rodrigue to give a lecture at Stonehill College—offered similar opportunities to share work and I thank all those in attendance for their searching questions, critical engagement, and personal support. In addition I would like to thank Gary Gallagher and Joan Waugh for the invitation to participate in a conference on the Civil War at the Huntington Library and for the community of scholars who welcomed me when I arrived. A few ideas in this book were initially developed in chapters published in *Wars within a War: Controversy and Conflict over the American Civil War,* edited by Gary W. Gallagher and Joan Waugh, and *Lincoln's Proclamation: Emancipation Reconsidered,* edited by William A. Blair and Karen Fisher Younger, both published by the University of North Carolina Press.

For the past twenty years I have had the privilege of living in a community of scholars, some of whom have become like family. Not all of them read this book as I was writing it, but their love and support of me and my children, and their confidence in the endeavor made it possible. For that I thank Larry and Diana Powell, Ira and Martha Berlin, Drew Faust, and Sheldon and Lucy Hackney. Bryant Simon's friendship is one of the best things about living in Philadelphia. His warm spirit and steadiness has sustained me in the last few years. Sally Gordon kept me going at the end and brought a lot of wisdom and humor to the task. Brigitte Cooperman's interest in the vagaries of book writing and history departments is a delight, as is her cooking and company. Elizabeth Colwill and I have been best friends since graduate school. In all those years she has supported me in every endeavor, intellectual and personal. I thank her for all of it and especially for the year in Princeton, the conversations about Saint-Domingue, and the chance once again to share work and life.

A number of people read this book in its entirety and I am deeply grateful to them all. Two readers for Harvard University Press—Amy Dru Stanley and one who remained anonymous—offered critical advice and formulations of the argument so sharp and precise I borrowed them wholesale. At the late manuscript moment, when spirits flag and doubt creeps in, their readings carried me over the finish line. Bill Blair read the whole manuscript carefully and saved me from mistakes, but he also answered innumerable emails over the years asking for information and advice. He is the very model of generous collegiality, and I am a grateful beneficiary. Christine Stansell read every line of this book. When I arrived at Penn in 2003 she invited me to become her writing partner. A highly unequal relationship, it went on for six years as we swapped chapters, fixed sentences, found titles, hashed out problems, and kept each other going. We finished at the same time. Amazing. For the whole experience I offer heartfelt thanks. Finally I would like to thank my colleague Bruce Kuklick, who, as everyone knows, always tells you exactly what he thinks. So when he read my manuscript and told me that a few arguments were stupid but that the rest was pretty good, I knew I was in the clear.

Joyce Seltzer, my editor at Harvard University Press, has been with this project a long time. Her commitment to the process, to authors, and to book publishing is especially valuable in these times and I count myself lucky to have had her in my corner.

As this long project draws to a close I would like, once again, to express my love and thanks to my family: my mother and father, Margaret and Sylvester McCurry, my sisters and brother, and my nieces and nephews. None of them are academics and most will never read this book. But that is not what matters. They say, "Auntie Steph—is your book finished yet?" or "What is it about?" But mostly they just make me and their cousins happy, drawing us into their lives and holding us close. I would also like to acknowledge my teacher, Craig Simpson, of the University of Western Ontario. Neither time nor distance diminishes his importance in my eyes.

Steven Hahn has been in my life much longer than this book. Over twenty-five years we have shared life and work and his love and support have taken every possible form. Steve knows what it takes to write a book and he certainly knows what it took to write this one. I could not have done it without him. But amidst it all, I have been sustained most by his example, by the boundless curiosity and vitality he brings to intellectual life, his constant readiness to ask new questions, take up new problems, rethink old ones, learn new things. It is a priceless gift in a life full of others he has given me. With much love, I thank him for all of it.

This book is for my children, Declan and Saoirse, whose presence lent such special meaning to the writing of it. For the joy they brought to everyday life, for the humor, wit, and enthusiasm they bring to the table, for the way they make us a family, and, especially, for they way they light up the path ahead. With love and pride, this book is for them.

Index